T3-BSD-844

Into the Temple Courts

SOCIETY OF BIBLICAL LITERATURE

DISSERTATION SERIES
Michael V. Fox, Old Testament Editor
Mark Allan Powell, New Testament Editor

Number 169

INTO THE TEMPLE COURTS

The Place of the Synagogues in the Second Temple Period

by

Donald D. Binder

Donald D. Binder

INTO THE TEMPLE COURTS
The Place of the Synagogues in the Second Temple Period

Society of Biblical Literature
Atlanta, Georgia

Into the Temple Courts
The Place of the Synagogues in the Second Temple Period

by

Donald D. Binder
Ph. D., Southern Methodist University, 1997
Victor P. Furnish, Advisor

Library of Congress Cataloging-in-Publication Data

Binder, Donald D.
Into the temple courts : the place of the synagogues in the Second Temple period / Donald D. Binder.
p. cm. — (Dissertation series ; no. 169)
Includes bibliographical references.
ISBN 0-88414-008-3 (cloth : alk. paper)
1. Synagogues—History—To 1500. 2. Judaism—History—Post-exilic period, 586 B.C.–210 A.D. I. Title. II. Series: Dissertation series (Society of Biblical Literature) ; no. 169.
BM653.B56 1999
296.6'5'09014—dc21 99-44123
CIP

08 07 06 05 04 03 02 01 00 99 5 4 3 2 1

Printed in the United States of America
on acid-free paper

Dedication

For Chris, Christopher and Peter
in thanksgiving

Table of Contents

List of Illustrations

LIST OF TABLES

PREFACE

Fortunately for scholars in the field of Biblical studies, the archaeologist's spade continues to unearth new discoveries, providing them with a steady stream of new data from which to theorize. This boon is sometimes also a bane, however, when it comes to the publication of earlier research.

With respect to the present study, after the completion of this manuscript in August of 1997, archaeologist Ehud Netzer announced on March 29, 1998, the discovery of what he claimed to be the hitherto oldest synagogue unearthed in Palestine. Uncovered beneath the ruins of a Herodian palace in Wadi Kelt near ancient Jericho, the structure was part of a Hasmonean palace complex destroyed in 31 B.C.E. by an earthquake. The proposed synagogue was built sometime between 75–50 B.C.E. and is reported to be similar in design to the synagogue at Gamla, replete with a ritual bath and a triclinium possibly used for ritual meals.[*]

While additional data on the structure are needed before a more definitive determination can be made, if Netzer's identification is upheld, the find has obvious implications for the view presented in the current study—that there was a close affiliation between the Temple and the synagogues—since the Hasmoneans were, of course, the high priestly keepers of the Temple cult.

Although the publication process has prevented this study from discussing Netzer's find, modern technology has provided a partial solution to the problems posed by such discoveries—namely, the Internet. Accordingly, even prior to the publication of this printed study, I launched a companion web site to this volume, containing information on recent developments pertaining to the investigation of synagogues from

[*]See Abraham Rabinovich, "World's Oldest Synagogue Unearthed Near Jericho," *Jerusalem Post*, 30 March 1998, 1; "Oldest Synagogue Found in Israel," *The Associated Press*, 29 March 1998; Ehud Netzer, "Le scoperte sotto il palazzo di Erode,"*Archeo*, Anno XIV, no. 7 (July 1998): 32–37.

the Second Temple period. Not intended to replace the detail of information and argumentation presented in this book, the site is designed as a more general introduction to the subfield. Housed on the computer system at Southern Methodist University, the pages can currently be accessed at: www.smu.edu/~dbinder. If, owing to the vicissitudes of cyberspace, the reader at some future point is unable to reach the site at this address, simply search for it with one of the many search-engines, using the keywords "ancient" and "synagogue" or some variation thereof. I shall endeavor to maintain the site for many years to come.

Adhering to the recent and welcome trend of making academic publications accessible not only to the scholar, but also to the public at large, I have sought to tailor the text of this study to serve the interests of both populations. Thus I have provided English translations of all ancient materials and have transliterated Greek, Hebrew and Aramaic words within the main body of the text (except in quotations of modern works, where the original rendering is maintained), while preserving the original letter-forms in the notes, in indented quotations of inscriptions, and in parentheses or brackets. I have also included more definitions and background material than most scholars would normally need; I appeal to their role as educators and ask their indulgence of these asides in the interest of the general reader.

Finally, in offering this study, I realize that as a "Son of Adam" (and Eve), I approach the topic of ancient synagogues as an outsider. I am also aware that the history of Christian scholarship within Judaic studies has, to put it kindly, been checkered.

I have therefore sought within this volume to present all the relevant evidence so that the reader can make his or her critical judgments on my interpretations. I have been and expect to be challenged on various conclusions. That, after all, is what scholarly engagement is about. Nevertheless, I believe that the views expressed in this study provide to persons of all creeds a reasonable, coherent, and meaningful portrait of the early synagogues—and I respectfully submit them for the reader's consideration.

Though this study bears the name of a single author, numerous individuals and institutions have been involved in its production. It is their contributions I would here like to acknowledge. First and foremost, I would like to thank my dissertation supervisor, Dr. Victor P. Furnish, not only for his scholarly guidance and keen editorial eye, but also for his encouragement and support throughout this project's development. Likewise, this study has been enhanced through the incisive comments and suggestions of two other members of my dissertation committee, Dr. Jouette M. Bassler and Dr. C. Clifton Black II. My gratitude similarly goes to the fourth member of the committee, Dr. G. Peter Richardson, both for his own scholarly contributions within the field of Ancient Synagogue studies and for his willingness to evaluate this study in its final form. I also thank Dr. Joseph B. Tyson for his suggestions on the use of Luke-Acts as a historical source, and for his review and critique of several portions of this manuscript.

This study would not have been possible without the archaeological insights of Dr. James F. Strange, whose architectural analyses of the Galilean-type synagogue serendipitously coincided with the thesis emerging from the literary and epigraphic evidence I was beginning to explore. His comments on numerous archaeological details have been incorporated throughout this study. Along similar lines, I appreciate the advice of Dr. Roger Bagnall with respect to the epigraphic issues arising at various points. I am likewise grateful for the comments of Dr. Paul Trebilco on the Mindus Faustus inscription, dealt with in chapter four, and for the willingness of Dr. John H. Kroll to provide access to some as yet unpublished inscriptions from the synagogue at Sardis that are of relevance to the interpretation of this dedication.

I am indebted to Dr. Lee I. Levine for his relaying of information about the recently discovered structure at Kiryat Sefer, which may yet prove to be a Second Temple synagogue. I regret that, because we were simultaneously involved in parallel projects, I was not able to incorporate into this study the insights of his forthcoming book, *The Ancient Synagogue*, which promises to set a new standard for synagogue research. Thanks also to Dr. J. Andrew Overman for relaying to me information on the recently discovered synagogue at Chersonesus, though as it turns out, the structure has not been securely dated to the first century. His comments on the Bosporus manumission inscriptions were similarly thought-provoking.

I owe a debt of gratitude to Dr. Ramsay MacMullen for our helpful discussion of the role of emotions in religion and for his encouragement of my pursuit of this type of research within New Testament studies. Similarly insightful were the comments of Dr. Leander Keck on the relationship between the synagogue and the *ekklēsia*. Thanks also to Dr.

Richard Oster for his bibliographic suggestions and to Paul Gavrilyuk for his help in translating some of the secondary literature written in Russian.

Among the institutions assisting in this research, Southern Methodist University has, of course, been foremost. I am particularly grateful to the university for the bestowal of a John Hick's fellowship which allowed me to visit or re-visit many of the sites discussed in this study. I appreciate also the assistance of the staff at the Bridwell Library, particularly that of James Powell, who labored tirelessly to fulfill my innumerable book and journal requests. The staff of the Graduate Program of Religious Studies at SMU has been equally supportive, especially Lucy Cobbe, the Administrative Assistant of the program. Faculty and fellow students within the program provided much-needed moral support, as did family, friends and parishioners from St. John's and St. James' Episcopal churches in Dallas, and Trinity Episcopal Cathedral in Miami.

For permission to reproduce various figures and photos, I would like to gratefully acknowledge the Israel Exploration Society, Soprintendenza Archeologica di Ostia, Franciscan Printing Press, Hestia Press, Oxford University Press, E. de Boccard Press and Danny Syon.

Last, but not least, I would like to thank my wife, Chris, and my sons, Christopher and Peter, for all their love and care throughout this process. It is on their behalf that this book is dedicated.

Dallas, Texas
Friday, July 16, 1999

Donald D. Binder

List of Abbreviations

ABD	D. N. Freedman, ed., *Anchor Bible Dictionary*
AJA	*American Journal of Archaeology*
AJC	Y. Meshorer, *Ancient Jewish Coinage*
ANET	J. B. Pritchard, ed., *Ancient Near Eastern Texts*
ANRW	W. Haase, ed., *Aufstieg und Niedergang der römischen Welt: Geschichte und Kultur Roms im Spiegel der neueren Forschung*
ASR	Lee I. Levine, ed., *Ancient Synagogues Revealed*
ATLA	American Theological Library Association
AusBR	*Australian Biblical Review*
AUSS	*Andrews University Seminary Studies*
AvP	*Die Altertümer von Pergamon*
BA	*Biblical Archaeologist*
BAR	*Biblical Archaeology Review*
BASOR	*Bulletin of the American Schools of Oriental Research*
BCH	*Bulletin de Correspondance Hellénique*
BDF	F. Blass, A. Debrunner, and R. W. Funk, *A Greek Grammar of the NT*
Bib	*Biblica*
BJRL	*Bulletin of the John Rylands University Library of Manchester*
BK	*Bibel und Kirke*
BTB	*Biblical Theology Bulletin*
BZ	*Biblische Zeitschrift*
CBQ	*Catholic Biblical Quarterly*
CH	*Church History*
CIJ	Jean Baptiste Frey, ed., *Corpus Inscriptionum Judaicarum* (vol. 1, rev. ed.)
CIL	*Corpus Inscriptionum Latinanum*
CIRB	I. Struve, ed., *Corpus Inscriptionum Regni Bosporani*
CJZC	Gert Lüderitz, and Joyce Maire Reynolds, eds., *Corpus jüdischer Zeugnisse aus der Cyrenaika*

CPJ Avigdor Tcherikover, Alexander Fuks, and Menahem Stern, eds., *Corpus Papyrorum Judaicarum*
DF Baruch Lifshitz, *Donateurs et fondateurs dans les synagogues juives*
EAEHL Michael Avi-Yonah and Ephriam Stern, eds., *Encyclopedia of Archaeological Excavations in the Holy Land*
Ebib *Estudios Biblicos*
ESI *Excavations and Surveys in Israel*
EvQ *Evangelical Quarterly*
FD *Fouilles de Delphes*
GD Philippe Bruneau and Jean Ducat, *Guide de Delos*
GLAJJ Menahem Stern, ed., *Greek and Latin Authors on Jews and Judaism*
HAR *Hebrew Annual Review*
HBT *Horizons in Biblical Theology*
HJP Emil Schürer, Geza Vermes, and Fergus Millar, *A History of the Jewish People in the Time of Jesus Christ*, Revised English ed.
HTR *Harvard Theological Review*
HUCA *Hebrew Union College Annual*
ID *Inscriptions de Délos*
IDB George Arthur Buttrick, ed., *The Interpreter's Dictionary of the Bible*
IDBSup Supplementary volume to IDB
IEJ *Israel Exploration Journal*
IG *Inscriptiones Graecae*
Int *Interpretation*
IvEph *Die Inschriften von Ephesos*
JBL *Journal of Biblical Literature*
JIE William Horbury, and David Noy, eds., *Jewish Inscriptions of Graeco-Roman Egypt*
JIWE David Noy, ed., *Jewish Inscriptions of Western Europe*
JJS *Journal of Jewish Studies*
JQR *Jewish Quarterly Review*
JRS *Journal of Roman Studies*
JSJ *Journal for the Study of Judaism in the Persian, Hellenistic and Roman Period*
JSNT *Journal for the Study of the New Testament*
JTS *Journal of Theological Studies*
LCL Loeb Classical Library

LSJ	Liddell-Scott-Jones, *Greek-English Lexicon*
JSGRP	Erwin R. Goodenough, *Jewish Symbols in the Greco-Roman Period*
NDIEC	G. H. R. Horsley (vol. 1–5), S. R. Llewelyn (vol. 6–7), ed., *New Documents Illustrating Early Christianity*
NedTTs	*Nederlands Theologisch Tijdschrift*
NEAEHL	Ephraim Stern, ed., *The New Encyclopedia of Archaeological Excavations in the Holy Land*
NovT	*Novum Testamentum*
NRSV	New Revised Standard Version
NTS	*New Testament Studies*
OEA	E. M. Meyers, ed., *The Oxford Encyclopedia of Archaeology in the Near East*
OGIS	Wilhelmus Dittenberger, ed., *Orientis Graeci inscriptiones selectae*
OTP	J. H. Charlesworth, ed., *The Old Testament Pseudepigrapha*
PEQ	*Palestine Exploration Quarterly*
PW	Pauly-Wissowa, *Real-Encyclopädie der classischen Altertumswissenschaft*
PWSup	Supplement to PW
RB	*Revue biblique*
REJ	*Revue des études juives*
RelSRev	*Religious Studies Review*
RevExp	*Review and Expositor*
RevQ	*Revue de Qumran*
RevScRel	*Revue des sciences religieuses*
RHPR	*Revue d'Histoire et de Philosophie Religieuses*
RSR	*Recherches de Science Religieuses*
SB	*Sammelbuch griechischer Urkunden aus Ägypten*
ScEs	*Science et esprit*
SEG	*Supplementum Epigraphicum Graecum*
SJT	*Scottish Journal of Theology*
SR	*Studies in Religion/Sciences religieuses*
ST	*Studia Theologica*
TDNT	G. Kittel and G. Friedrich, eds., *Theological Dictionary of the New Testament*
TynBul	*Tyndale Bulletin*
TZ	*Theologische Zeitschrift*
ZNW	*Zeitschrift für die Neutestamentliche Wissenschaft und die Kunde der Alteren Kirche*

INTRODUCTION

If one were to walk into any modern university library and type the keywords "ancient" and "synagogue" into the library's computer catalogue, he or she would observe anywhere from two to five dozen citations scroll across the screen, depending upon the quality of the library's collection in that particular area. A similar query made to the ATLA CD-ROM database would yield nearly two hundred entries. The ambitious reader who took the time to tally-up the number of references in the (select) bibliography at the end of this volume would soon reach the conclusion that the quantity of items called out of the computer catalogue and the CD-ROM constitutes only the tip of the iceberg with regard to research on ancient synagogues.[1]

With so much ink having been spilt on this topic, the question naturally arises: Why another book on ancient synagogues? In response to this reasonable query, let me begin by making two observations. First, as is obvious from the subtitle of this volume, this investigation will specifically confine itself to Second-Temple-period synagogues, that is, synagogues that existed during the period between Zerubbabel's reconstruction of the Jerusalem Temple in the late sixth century B.C.E. and the Temple's final destruction in 70 C.E. by Titus. This period was chosen for several reasons. To begin with, it is during this time that our first solid evidence for the existence of synagogues emerges—in Egypt during the third century B.C.E. On the other end of this time-span, the year 70 C.E. serves as a pivotal year for this investigation since it marks not only the cessation of the Temple cult, but also the abrupt termination of a high

---

[1]Here and throughout this study the term *synagogue* will be used to refer to both a congregational institution and the building within which the institution was located. In a subsequent chapter, we will see that this usage reflects the usage of the word *synagōgē* in the Second Temple period: a *synagōgē* (congregation) met within a *synagōgē* (building). Occasionally, in order to emphasize one particular aspect of the term, phrases such as "synagogue structure" or "synagogue congregation" will be used. Otherwise, so as to avoid such cumbersome locutions, the context should make clear whether a building, a congregation or both are indicated.

priestly hegemony that, except for a few brief periods, had administered affairs in Palestine since the end of the Babylonian exile. These two shifts—the loss of the high priesthood and the loss of the temple cult—are important to this investigation because they signal both a major change in Jewish leadership in Palestine and an equally significant change in the nature and focus of Jewish worship and community life throughout the empire.

With regard to the leadership issue, it is important to note that the war with Rome ended with the execution or enslavement of both the priestly aristocracy and the Zealot leadership of the revolt. The Pharisees, who before the war had been positioned in a secondary political tier, survived in sufficient numbers to fill this sudden power vacuum and become the leading political force in Palestine, with the Essenes, Christians, priests and Levites being among the lesser players.[2] While the Pharisaic/Rabbinic dominance of the region does not appear to have solidified until at least after the suppression of the Bar Kokhba revolt in 135 C.E., the heightened polemic against the Pharisees in Matthew's Gospel (c. 85 C.E.) suggests that the Pharisees nevertheless wielded considerable power in Syro-Palestine even during the earlier period.[3] The implication of this sudden change in power for the present study is that an investigation confined to the Second Temple period could potentially reveal different patterns of leadership within Palestinian synagogues than might be found in the period following the Temple's destruction.

The second major shift alluded to above—the shift in the nature and focus of Jewish worship and community life—is equally important to this study. In the eyes of most Jews, sacrifices could only be offered at the

---

[2]On the view that the Pharisees constituted a "retainer class" prior to the Jewish War, see Anthony J. Saldarini, *Pharisees, Scribes and Sadducees in Palestinian Society: A Sociological Approach* (Wilmington, DE: M. Glazier, 1988). In his book, *From Politics to Piety* (Englewood Cliffs, N.J.: Prentice-Hall, 1973), Jacob Neusner takes the position that, beginning with Hillel (c. 50 B.C.E.–10 C.E.), the Pharisees abandoned political activism for more quietistic ways. This view, however, discounts the evidence presented by Josephus depicting the Pharisees as being involved in various political intrigues from the time of Herod the Great up through the Jewish War (e.g., Josephus, *Ant.* 17.41–43, 18.4, 23; *Vita* 20–23, 189–198). For a critique of Neusner's view, see E. P. Sanders, *Judaism: Practice and Belief, 63 BCE–66 CE* (London: Trinity Press International, 1992), 380–412.

[3]E.g., Matt 23. See Anthony J. Saldarini, *Matthew's Christian-Jewish Community* (Chicago: The University of Chicago Press, 1994), 44–52 for a helpful commentary on this chapter, though one which nevertheless understates the degree of separation between the Pharisees and the Matthean community.

centralized cultic site in Jerusalem. Consequently, Titus' destruction of the Temple meant that the various daily, weekly and monthly sacrifices as well as the annual festivals could no longer take place. This negative aspect of the post-70 period reached well beyond the confines of Palestine. Unlike the issue of Jewish leadership in Palestine, an issue which probably had minimal effect on the Jewish diaspora, the loss of the Temple cult itself had a greater impact on these distant Jews: pilgrimages from abroad could no longer be made to the Temple to render sacrifices, nor could votive offerings from individuals or communities outside of Palestine be presented in Jerusalem.[4] Even the diaspora's participation in the collection of the half-shekel Temple tax was curtailed in the aftermath of the war, as Emperor Vespasian transformed this offering into a new imperial tax to be levied upon Jews empire-wide in punishment for the revolt.[5] The import of the cult's demise for this study is that, for the period after 70 C.E., we are no longer able to observe the living relationship between the synagogues and the Temple; we can no longer examine what connections between the two institutions existed, if any. We are left only with images of the various strands of Judaism attempting to reconstruct themselves in the aftermath of a tremendous loss.

This leads us to the second observation: aside from the present volume, no book-length treatment of Second Temple synagogues currently exists. The great bulk of the published literature has typically examined synagogues dating from the Late Roman and Byzantine periods, often without distinguishing these structures and their functions from the buildings of the earlier period (more on this below). This is not to say that the topic of Second Temple synagogues has never been broached in the scholarly literature. On the contrary, scores of articles and essays have been written on the subject, with the topic of synagogue origins being particularly popular. Nevertheless, these treatments have frequently suffered from methodological shortcomings that have rendered their conclusions suspect. While we will be noting these throughout the body of this study, in the following section of this chapter we will make

---

[4]For literary attestation of sacrifices being made by pilgrims from the diaspora, see Josephus, *Ant.* 18.312–313, 20.49; Philo, *Legat.* 155–158, 311, 315, 356. For the discovery of a votive offering to the temple by a Jew from the island of Rhodes, see Benjamin Isaac, "A Donation for Herod's Temple in Jerusalem," *IEJ* 33 (1983): 86–92.

[5]On widespread payment of the Temple tax by diaspora Jews, see Josephus, *Ant.* 16.27–28, 162–167, 169–173; Philo, *Spec.* 1.77–78; Cicero, *Pro Flacc.* 66–69. On Vespasian's transformation of this tax, see Josephus, *BJ* 7.218; *JIWE* 2.603.

an initial inquiry into the major problems inherent in much of the older literature. At the same time we will look at some of the steps that recent researchers have begun to take in order to remedy these problems. After an examination of current trends in the literature, I will present a statement of the particular approach to be adopted in this study.

Methodological Problems in Synagogue Research

As briefly mentioned above, there has been a tendency in some of the literature to combine the synagogal evidence from many different periods to create a more or less static picture of a "typical" ancient synagogue. The downside of this practice for the examination of pre-70 synagogues is that it can result in a distorted picture of the earlier institution. Moreover, treatments that conflate sources in this manner effectively manufacture a monolithic entity out of an institution that exhibited a great deal of heterogeneity even in the earlier period.

In further addressing this tendency, it will be helpful to distinguish between *architectural anachronism* and *literary anachronism*, keeping in mind that these are frequently both present within the literature under discussion.

The first of these problems, architectural anachronism, is the error of displaying and discussing the archaeological remains of synagogues from a period later than the one under consideration. Now, in almost any examination of ancient architecture, one notes a certain continuity in the overall form of a particular type of edifice. For example, one can usually recognize an ancient theater by virtue of its semi-circular auditorium (cavea), its orchestra pit, and its stage-building (skene). After one has studied a particular type of ancient structure as it developed over time, however, one is frequently able to date the structure to a particular period. To extend our example, the earlier Greek style of theater, which was dominant up to the turn of the era, typically had a circular orchestra and a relatively small stage-building that was physically separated from the auditorium. In the earliest theaters, the drama took place in the orchestra, with the stage-building serving as a back-drop. By way of contrast, the later Roman style of theater had a semi-circular orchestra, which was used for the seating of dignitaries. The auditorium was physically connected to the stage-building, which itself was transformed into a massive structure several stories tall and was adorned with statues of the imperial family. The action took place on an elevated platform (proskene) situated between the orchestra and the face of the stage-building.[6]

Now, it might be asked, besides being useful in the dating of a theater, do these differences in style mean anything to the historian? I would submit that they do. For example, one might argue that the heightening of the stage-building and the addition of the imperial statues in the Roman period were architectural manifestations of a widening campaign of imperial propaganda. Similarly, one might make a case that the seating of dignitaries in an orchestra removed from the main body of the people in the auditorium points to a drift towards elitism in the emerging Roman empire. Of course, wide-reaching conclusions such as these should never be drawn solely from the evolution of a single type of architecture, but only after an analysis of various other pieces (and types) of evidence.

This brief outline of the ancient theater's development is illuminating to our discussion of scholarly treatments of ancient synagogues, for clearly, if one were reading about theaters of the Hellenistic period, one would expect the examination to focus on the earlier Greek theaters and not on the Roman theaters from the later period. The Roman theater might be mentioned as a footnote to the study, or it might perhaps be employed as a foil within the examination to accentuate the peculiar aspects of the earlier kind of theater. But it would not dominate the discussion. Similarly, if one were to read about Second Temple synagogues, one would expect the discussion to concentrate upon synagogues built in that particular era, not ones constructed two to five centuries later. Yet when one turns to books and articles on synagogues from the "biblical period," it is not uncommon to find pictures and discussions of the limestone synagogue at Capernaum (IV–V C.E.), the frescoes from the synagogue at Dura-Europos (III C.E.), or the zodiac mosaic from the Beth Alpha synagogue (VI C.E.), among other late examples.[7] Even if we recognize that the New Testament period reaches past 70 C.E. to as late as 150 C.E. in the case of 2 Peter, none of these comparisons comes close to being contemporaneous with the biblical literature.[8] In any case, all of the New

---

[6]See D.S. Robertson, *Greek and Roman Architecture*, 2nd ed. (Cambridge: Cambridge University Press, 1969), 164–169, 271–283.

[7]E.g., Isaiah Sonne, "Synagogue" in *IDB* 4.476–491; Howard Clark Kee, *Understanding the New Testament*, 4th ed. (Englewood Cliffs, N.J.: Prentice-Hall, 1983), 104; Joseph B. Tyson, *The New Testament and Early Christianity* (New York: Macmillan, 1984), 93–94.

[8]The date given for 2 Peter constitutes the upper terminus. Many scholars would opt for an earlier date. For a survey of the critical issues, see Andrew Chester and

Testament sources mentioning synagogues should probably be dated to no later than the end of the first century and, with the exception of Revelation, all of the citations invariably refer to synagogues in a pre-70 C.E. setting.[9]

In defense of the older literature it should be stated that, prior to the 1960s, with the exception of the Delos synagogue (I B.C.E.), no synagogue remains had been dated to the Second Temple period. The same cannot be said of more recent treatments since we now have several examples of synagogues dated by a majority of archaeologists to the period before 70 C.E. Despite this fact, the tendency to focus the discussion on the later materials persists. For example, in his article on synagogues in the *Anchor Bible Dictionary* (1992),[10] Eric Meyers devotes a single paragraph to the description of the synagogues at Gamla, Masada and Herodium, each typically dated to the Second Temple period. Yet there are no plans or pictures and no extended analysis of these structures and their features. The bulk of the architectural discussion (covering five pages) is devoted to the synagogues at Beth She'arim, Gush Ḥalav, Nabratein and Khirbet Shema', all buildings dating to the third century C.E.[11] Indeed, three-dimensional plans of the Gush Ḥalav and the Khirbet Shema' synagogues are depicted as well as an artist's reconstruction of the torah shrine at Nabratein—this last despite the fact that such fixed structures are not attested in the period covered by the Bible, much less the Second Temple period. Of course, Meyers knows this and mentions this fact in passing. However, because so much of the discussion is directed toward the third-century structures, the overall impression left upon the reader is that synagogues from the biblical period correspond closely to the synagogues from the later era. A similar impression is made in Helmut Koester's widely used text, *Introduction to the New Testament* (revised in 1995), where, in a section entitled "Judaism in the Hellenistic Period," he inserts a picture of the Sardis synagogue as it existed in the

---

Ralph P. Martin, *The Theology of the Letter of James, Peter and Jude* (Cambridge: Cambridge University Press, 1994), 137–151.

[9]On the problem of literary anachronism within the latest of these sources (Matthew and Luke-Acts), see below.

[10]Eric M. Meyers, "Synagogue" in *ABD* 4.251–260.

[11]An earlier phase of the Nabratein synagogue may date to some time during the second century C.E., so there is possibly some overlap between this structure and the later documents of the New Testament (Jude, 2 Peter), although these were written in the diaspora, not in Palestine, and they never make reference to synagogues.

fifth century C.E.[12] The accompanying caption calls special attention to the synagogue's fixed torah shrine and to images of eagles carved on its monumental table, all features unattested in synagogues of the Hellenistic era. Since Koester is discussing a period six centuries earlier than the building depicted in the photograph, one wonders why he did not instead include a picture of the Delos synagogue, a structure dating to the era being treated in his text.

I present these two examples not to single out these two researchers. I cite them merely to illustrate the fact that, even in this day and age, researchers can remain fixated upon later synagogal structures despite the fact that their circumscribed period of study is centuries earlier. While the later edifices are indeed interesting and more numerous than those dating to before 70 C.E., one must take care to distinguish them from the earlier examples. To practice conflation of periods is to risk papering over important differences between structures from different times. In order to guard against this, discussions of synagogue architecture must be stratified chronologically, with pre-70 synagogues used to speak of that era, Late Roman synagogues used in discussions of that period, and so on. This principle is especially important when one recalls the shifts occurring after the Temple's destruction. With changes in both leadership and patterns of worship, later architects and builders may have felt freer to introduce new elements into the designs of their synagogues. Some continuity may have existed across the centuries, but this may have been overshadowed by significant differences. In the case of the synagogue, features such as fixed torah shrines, mosaics or frescoes depicting living creatures, even inscriptions of menorahs, while prominent in later structures, are all features unattested in our period. It is the historian's task to note these discrepancies and to take them into account when creating an overall interpretive scheme for understanding the nature of an institution in its different phases.

Fortunately, the unearthing of several Second Temple synagogues over the last thirty-five years has made researchers more alert to the danger of projecting back later stylistic features onto the earlier structures. The more recent archaeological literature typically has been careful to give special consideration to the pre-70 buildings. For example, Lee Levine's collection of essays, *Ancient Synagogues Revealed* (1982), devotes a separate section to synagogue remains of the Second Temple

---

[12]Helmut Koester, *Introduction to the New Testament*, 2nd ed. (New York: Fortress Press, 1995), 1.207.

period.[13] Other authors and editors have followed suit.[14] This practice of chronological stratification has even reached the level of more general treatments with the appearance in 1992 of E. P. Sanders' *Judaism: Practice and Belief, 63 BCE–66 CE*, wherein the author discusses only those synagogue remains dating to the period prior to the destruction of the Temple.[15] One hopes that future revisions of other texts on "Second Temple Period Judaism" or "The New Testament Period" will soon join in this more critical approach.

The second of the methodological problems mentioned above, that of literary anachronism, is the practice of relying upon literary sources from a much later period than the one under consideration. As with architectural anachronism, the danger in this procedure is that the later sources may reflect the customs and practices of that day and not of the earlier era. With regard to the study of synagogues, until recently, the commonplace practice of scholars has been to base their portrait of the early synagogues upon tractates from the rabbinic literature. There are several difficulties with this procedure. The first of these is the problem of bias, a problem that is intertwined with the issue of anachronism. While the rabbinic literature almost certainly contains some historical remembrances, the rabbinic schools did not set out to chronicle history. Rather, the compilers of the various documents in this vast corpus each sought to express a worldview not necessarily of how things were, but of how things *should have been*. Hence the literature is more often prescriptive than descriptive. Here it might be pointed out that even ancient historians wrote with some measure of prescriptive bias. As we shall see in our examination of Josephus' writings, this first-century historian had his own set of biases, which not infrequently led to key omissions or embellishments in his account. Yet these can be identified and ameliorated. Moreover, certain conventions in the historiological genre limited the degree to which one could distort commonly known facts or events. Stepping over the boundaries of these conventions would threaten a loss of credibility with one's audience—a result which was the

---

[13] *ASR* 19–41.

[14] E.g., Dan Urman, and Paul Virgil McCracken Flesher, eds., *Ancient Synagogues: Historical Analysis and Archaeological Discovery* (New York: E.J. Brill, 1995), 1.3–50 is entitled, "The Origins of Ancient Synagogues"; three of the four articles in this section are devoted strictly to the examination of the pre-70 C.E. evidence.

[15] Op. cit., 200–202. Sanders in some cases, however, may be guilty of literary anachronism. See Jacob Neusner, review of *Judaism: Practice and Belief, 63 BCE–67 CE*, by E. P. Sanders, *JSJ* 24, no. 2 (1994): 317–323.

last thing the ancient historian desired.[16] With regard to the rabbinic compilers, while there was certainly a desire to have a particular saying taken seriously or authoritatively, because sayings were transmitted orally, verification of the original utterance (and its authority) by the early audiences would have been extremely difficult. Consequently there was little to inhibit the introduction of individual biases and embellishments at each stage of the transmission process.

When modern historians try to link some of these sayings to the pre-70 period, they are faced with a second and perhaps even greater problem than the difficulty of prescriptive bias: the earliest of the rabbinic compilations, the Mishnah, dates to the beginning of the third century C.E., nearly a century-and-a-half after the destruction of the Temple. Other works such as the Tosefta (c. 250 C.E.), the Jerusalem Talmud (IV C.E.) and the Babylonia Talmud (VI C.E.) date considerably later. Sidestepping for a moment the problem of whether a particular saying is prescriptive or descriptive, how are researchers to know whether or not the saying was transmitted reliably? If a talmudic saying is attributed to a sage from the first century, the centuries that separated the actual writing down of the saying from its reputed utterance make its verification extremely problematic. The potential exists that the saying may have actually been spoken by a later rabbi whose viewpoint was projected back upon the earlier period. Or, more simply, the final reporter of the saying may have embellished it to correspond with the viewpoints of his own day. If this viewpoint happens to agree with the actual practices of the day, (i.e., it is descriptive rather than prescriptive), we face the same problem of anachronism that we saw above in the case of later architecture being seen as representative of the earlier style. In any case, it is not uncommon for various rabbinic sayings to contradict each other. In the arena of our topic, for example, various numbers of synagogues are stated to have existed in Jerusalem before the fall of the Temple: 394 (*b. Ketub.* 105a), 460 (*y. Ketub.* 35c [61–64]) and 480 (*y. Ketub.* 73d [32–35]). Which of these numbers is correct, if any? Or are we to take the figures merely as "ballpark guesses" and conclude that Jerusalem contained synagogues numbering in the hundreds? If so, how can we be sure that the later rabbis making these sayings were not merely assuming that hundreds of synagogues existed in Jerusalem in the first century because such numbers of synagogues existed in some large cities of the fourth through

[16]For example, observe Josephus' expressed concern over the credibility of his account in *BJ* 1.13–16.

sixth centuries C.E.? Or (to shift into a hypothetically prescriptive mode), perhaps *no* synagogues existed in first-century Jerusalem, but for some reason the rabbis believed that hundreds of them *ought to have* existed—perhaps as a way of underscoring the prominence of the early sages and their houses.

As noted above, up until very recently it was a widely held practice for synagogue researchers to cite talmudic sayings without considering the very real danger of anachronism. Hence, it was commonly believed, for example, that the early synagogues subscribed to fixed lectionaries,[17] or that the Pharisees exercised supreme leadership over the services held inside.[18] Yet these practices and leadership patterns reflect those existing in the Byzantine period rather than the Second Temple period. Little or no evidence for these practices comes from the first century. This kind of literary anachronism leaves us with a distorted picture of the pre-70 synagogal institution. Despite the fact that such literary anachronism has come under severe critique (as we shall see), conclusions fostered by this uncritical methodology remain highly influential because they are contained in many of the standard biblical reference works.[19]

The landscape of synagogal studies (and Jewish studies in general) began to shift dramatically in the 1970s, largely as the result of the scholarship of Jacob Neusner. In 1971, with the appearance of his work, *The Rabbinic Sayings about the Pharisees before 70*, Neusner launched an opening salvo against what he perceived to be a serious misappropriation of rabbinic literature in the study of history. In the introduction of this three-volume study, Neusner stated the matter rather sharply:

> New Testament scholars customarily give careful attention to critical considerations when using New Testament materials for historic purposes. But they quote Talmudic stories as contemporary, first-hand, accurate historical accounts. They would not think, when discussing a story about Jesus, of neglecting its internal signs of development or of ignoring several

---

[17]E.g., George Foot Moore, *Judaism in the First Centuries of the Christian Era: The Age of the Tannaim* (Cambridge: Harvard University Press, 1927), 298–300.

[18]E.g., Louis Finkelstein, *The Pharisees*, 3rd ed. (Philadelphia: Jewish Publication Society of America, 1962), 568–569.

[19]E.g., Sonne, "Synagogue," in *IDB* 4.476–491; Wolfgang Schrage, "Συναγωγή" in TDNT 8.798–852; Emil Schürer, Geza Vermes, and Fergus Millar, *A History of the Jewish People in the Time of Jesus Christ*, Revised English ed. 3 vols. (Edinburgh: T. & T. Clark, 1973–86); Samuel Krauss, *Synagogale Altertümer* (Berlin: Hildesheim, 1922).

> versions of the same story in their attempt to discover what, if anything, can be said about actual events. Yet they cite rabbinic stories of what rabbis said and did as if critical considerations important in New Testament studies simply do not apply. In this they are abetted by Jewish historians who in a pseudorthodox spirit maintain the pretense that wherever or whenever a story was finally written down, whether in third-century Babylonia or tenth-century Italy, said story accurately and reliably relates the exact details of what really happened in the time of which it speaks. From the moment a Pharisaic master or rabbinic sage said or did something, it is supposed, a process automatically was set in motion orally to record, then orally to transmit, an exact detailed historical account of the saying or the event. The relationship between the event and the story that purports to preserve it is never investigated; it is simply supposed to be perfect correspondence.[20]

As a positive contribution towards bringing order out of what had been methodological chaos, Neusner went on in this study to compile and analyze only those rabbinic sayings or stories attributed to figures (or their houses) known to have lived during the Second Temple period. While this method could not assure the historicity of the pericopae, it did present a useful first step towards the identification of a more reliable stratum of earlier material. Later, Neusner advanced this methodology even further by focusing strictly on material from the oldest rabbinic compilation, the Mishnah, and checking to see whether the logical progression of a debate corresponded to the historical order of the characters. Thus, for example, if a rabbi from the Yavneh period (70–130 C.E.) was said to have stated the *premise* of a particular dispute, but a *corollary* within that same dispute was attributed to a rabbi from the Second Temple period, then doubt was cast upon the pre-70 attribution. However, if the situation were reversed—the earlier authority's statement embodied the premise and a later authority's contained the corollary—then the early attribution was deemed plausible, if not altogether verified. Neusner's application of this methodology was painstakingly worked out over the course of forty-three volumes,[21] whose

---

[20]Jacob Neusner, *The Rabbinic Traditions about the Pharisees before 70*, (Leiden: E. J. Brill, 1971), 1.1–2.

[21]Jacob Neusner, *A History of the Mishnaic Law of Purities*, 22 vols. (Leiden: Brill, 1974–77); idem, *A History of the Mishnaic Law of Holy Things*, 6 vols. (Leiden: Brill, 1978); idem, *A History of the Mishnaic Law of Women* 5 vols. (Leiden: Brill, 1979–80); idem, *A History of the Mishnaic Law of Appointed Times*, 5 vols. (Leiden: Brill, 1981–82); idem, *A History of the Mishnaic Law of Damages*, 5 vols. (Leiden: Brill, 1982). Additional volumes on the tractates of the Division of Agriculture were published by several of Neusner's students.

conclusions were summarized in his book, *Judaism, the Evidence of the Mishnah.*[22]

With regard to research on pre-70 synagogues, Neusner's work has had enormous implications, for even when utilizing the first of the above methods—accepting *any* early attributions, a practice which yields a greater amount of data—Neusner noted a puzzling silence on the part of the early authorities:

> They supply no rules about synagogue life, all the more so about reading the Torah and preaching in synagogues. It would be difficult to maintain that the [Pharisee] sect claimed to exercise influence in the life of synagogues not controlled by its own members or widely preached in synagogues.[23]

From this summary we may conclude *not* that the Pharisees did not participate in the synagogues, but simply that what probably constitutes the earliest and most reliable stratum of evidence from the rabbinic writings yields us no useful information about pre-70 synagogues.[24]

As a consequence of Neusner's results, over roughly the last fifteen years most researchers of Second Temple synagogues have limited their examinations to literary materials contemporaneous with the era under examination.[25] This development is to be commended. We have already examined the various dangers inherent in using the later rabbinic material to speak about the earlier period. Neusner's industrious program of identifying early pericopae has given historians a new set of tools with which to conduct their research in a more methodologically sound

---

[22]Jacob Neusner, *Judaism, the Evidence of the Mishnah* (Chicago: University of Chicago Press, 1981).

[23]Neusner, *Rabbinic Traditions*, 3.289–290.

[24]E. P. Sanders, who in general accepts Neusner's method, has criticized him for not applying it consistently. See E. P. Sanders, *Jewish Law from Jesus to the Mishnah* (Philadelphia: Trinity Press International, 1990), 152–254. Despite this, Sanders accepts Neusner's conclusions regarding the early material's silence on the synagogues (*Judaism*, 398).

[25]For Neusner's criticism of researchers who uncritically continue to rely on later rabbinic material when speaking of the Second Temple period see Jacob Neusner, *The Documentary Foundation of Rabbinic Culture: Mopping up after Debates With Gerald L. Bruns, S.J.D. Cohen, Arnold Maria Goldberg, Susan Handelman, Christine Hayes, James Kugel, Peter Schaefer, Eliezer Segal, E.P. Sanders, and Lawrence H. Schiffman* (Atlanta, Ga.: Scholars Press, 1995), 179–207; idem, *Ancient Judaism: Debates and Disputes* (Atlanta, Ga.: Scholars Press, 1996), 245–252; idem, *Uppsala Addresses: And Other Recent Essays and Reviews on Judaism Then and Now* (Atlanta, Ga.: Scholars Press, 1996), 87–112.

fashion. For our more specific enterprise, however, we are left with no relevant rabbinic material and must therefore resort to the use of other sources of historical information.

Recent Trends in the Research

The conclusions reached in the foregoing discussion lead us now to consider the most recent research on Second Temple synagogues. As indicated, the silence of the early rabbinic material on this institution has led researchers to focus upon other sources of evidence contemporaneous with the subject matter. This is not such a sorry state of affairs as it might at first seem, for the relevant sources are both numerous and diverse. There are (1) *literary sources*, including the various writings of the Bible (the Hebrew scriptures, LXX and New Testament) and the Pseudepigrapha, the works of Philo and Josephus, the Dead Sea scrolls, and the documents from the Egyptian papyri, (2) *inscriptions*, including those found in Egypt, Cyrenaica, Palestine, Asia Minor, Italy, the Bosporus, and the Aegean, and (3) *site remains*, such as those excavated at Gamla, Masada, Herodium, Capernaum, Qumran, Delos and Ostia. In later chapters we will consider in detail questions regarding the dating, identification and interpretation of these sources. For the moment, however, it will be sufficient to indicate some of the most recent conclusions that researchers have drawn about pre-70 synagogues from an examination of this narrower body of evidence.

In characterizing the most recent studies, it is fair to state that a good portion of them have challenged many ideas traditionally held about synagogues in the pre-70 era. To begin with, a number of scholars have taken issue with the notion that there were synagogue buildings in pre-70 Palestine. One of these, Howard Clark Kee, has argued that the synagogue existed as a formal institution (with a building) only outside of Palestine in the earlier era and, that when the canonical Gospels use the word *synagōgē* they are speaking of an informal religious gathering held probably inside a private house.[26] The only exception he allows is Luke

---

[26]Howard Clark Kee, "The Transformation of the Synagogue after 70 CE: Its Import for Early Christianity," *NTS* 36 (1990): 1–24; idem, "Early Christianity in the Galilee: Reassessing the Evidence from the Gospels" in *The Galilee in Late Antiquity*, edited by Lee I. Levine (New York: The Jewish Theological Seminary of America, 1992), 3–22; idem, "New Finds That Illuminate the World and Text of the Bible: The Greco-Roman Era" in *The Bible in the Twenty-First Century*, edited by Howard Clark Kee (Philadelphia: Trinity Press International, 1993), 89–108; idem, "The Changing

7:5, a verse from the account of the healing of the centurion's slave in Capernaum. In this passage, Jewish elders appeal to Jesus to heed the centurion's plea, stating, "he loves our people, and it is he who built our synagogue for us [ἀγαπᾷ γὰρ τὸ ἔθνος ἡμῶν καὶ τὴν συναγωγὴν αὐτὸς ᾠκοδόμησεν ἡμῖν]."[27] Kee attributes the singularity of this usage to the Hellenistic provenance of Luke-Acts:

> The very fact that "synagogue" here alone in the gospel tradition points unequivocally to a building, rather than to a gathering, serves to confirm the impression that Luke-Acts is a document from a Hellenistic centre, where . . . Jews in the Diaspora had begun to modify houses or public structures in order to serve more effectively the needs of the local Jewish community.[28]

And what of the several structures in Palestine that archaeologists have identified as synagogues of the Second Temple period? Regarding these, Kee writes,

> There is no evidence that [the structures at Masada and Herodium] were structures designed for religious purposes, much less that the routines attested for second-century and later synagogues were practiced there. Other sites that were at first identified as synagogues—at Magdala and Gamala—turn out to be nothing more than private homes in which the pious gathered for prayer . . . Thus there is simply no evidence to speak of synagogues in Palestine as architecturally distinguishable edifices prior to 200 C.E.[29]

In holding the view that Palestinian synagogues did not exist until after the Jewish War, Kee is by no means alone. Richard Horsley, in his recent book on first-century Galilee (1995), following a brief examination of some passages from Josephus and the Gospels, reaches almost identical conclusions:

> It is thus clear from the synoptic Gospel tradition as our principal evidence that the *synagōgai* in Galilee were not buildings, but assemblies or congregations of people . . . In a few passages in Luke-Acts and in Josephus's reports we are evidently seeing a transition usage in which, at least in Hellenistic situations, buildings in which the assemblies met are beginning

---

Meaning of Synagogue: A Response to Richard Oster," *NTS* 40 (1994): 281–283; idem, "Defining the First-Century CE Synagogue," *NTS* 41 (1995): 481–500.

[27]The translation, as with all other biblical translations in this study (unless otherwise indicated), is from the NRSV.

[28]Kee, *Transformation*, 17.

[29]Ibid., 8–9.

> to be referred to as *synagōgai* by association. But *synagōgē* and *knesset* both referred to the local village or town assembly in first- and second-century Galilee.[30]

With regard to the proposed pre-70 synagogue structures, after devoting a single paragraph to an analysis of the evidence, Horsley rejects all of the identifications and concludes that there is "no archaeological or literary evidence for synagogue buildings in Judean or Galilean towns and villages until the third century or later."[31]

Other scholars, while not altogether discounting the archaeological remains of synagogues in Palestine, nevertheless argue that synagogues were not as prominent there in the pre-70 period as was once believed. Thus Paul Flesher posits an antithetical relationship between the Temple and the early diaspora synagogues.[32] In his view, when synagogues first appeared in Galilee in the late first-century B.C.E., their introduction was met with stiff resistence from the priestly leaders of the Temple cult, who perceived them as unwelcome competitors. These leaders, who exercised more power in Judea than in Galilee, prohibited the local population in Judea from constructing and worshiping in them. After an examination of relevant literary and archaeological sources, Flesher concludes that, with the exception of two synagogues in Jerusalem built for diaspora Jews (known from an excavated inscription and from Acts 6:9), "there were no synagogues in Judea prior to the Temple's destruction."[33]

Another intermediate position is that of Eric Meyers, who, upon pondering the discrepancy between the large number of literary references

---

[30]Richard A. Horsley, *Galilee* (Valley Forge, Pa: Trinity Press International, 1995), 226. Horsley's analysis of the relevant sources is on pp. 223–225.

[31]Ibid., 225. The discussion of the excavated remains takes place in the first full paragraph of p. 224. See also idem, *Archaeology History and Society in Galilee* (Valley Forge, Pa: Trinity Press International, 1996), 133.

[32]Paul Virgil McCracken Flesher, "Palestinian Synagogues before 70 C.E.: A Review of the Evidence" in *Ancient Synagogues: Historical Analysis and Archaeological Discovery*, edited by Dan Urman and Paul Virgil McCracken Flesher (New York: E.J. Brill, 1995), 1.27–39. This essay is a slightly modified version of an earlier paper: idem, "Palestinian Synagogues Before 70 CE: A Review of the Evidence" in *Studies in the Ethnology and Literature of Judaism*, edited by J. Neusner and Ernest S. Frerichs (Atlanta: Scholars Press, 1989), 67–81. Flesher's introductory comments in the volumes he co-edited are found in op.cit., 1.xxiv–xxv.

[33]Flesher, "Palestinian Synagogues," 39. The inscription is the famous Theodotus inscription, which will be discussed at length in subsequent chapters. The reference in Acts 6:9 is to the so-called "synagogue of the Freedmen."

to Second Temple synagogues and the present dearth of excavated remains in Palestine, proposes that private homes frequently served as centers for congregational worship:

> In the first centuries, large private houses were used as places of worship alongside other buildings that came to be utilized for worship and other matters requiring public assembly. In Palestine, it would seem, it was about a hundred years after the destruction of the Temple that the synagogue *as a building* began to emerge as a central feature of Jewish communal life.[34]

Meyers' ambivalence about the early evidence helps us understand why he chose to focus his *Anchor Bible Dictionary* article on the third-century structures, as we observed above: in his view, pre-70 synagogue buildings in Palestine were still in an embryonic stage of development and could not yet be categorized according to a coherent architectural form. Ironically, his extended treatment of the later synagogue structures in his article fosters an impression opposite the one contained in the above quotation.

Already at several points in our review of the literature we have encountered the position that synagogue buildings evolved out of prayer meetings in private homes. As we have seen, Kee and Horsley argue for an early third-century C.E. date for this transition in Palestine, while Meyers opts for a somewhat earlier date. In setting forth this developmental scheme, these researchers are drawing parallels with the meeting patterns of early Christians. The reasoning is that, since early Christian congregations met in private homes, Jewish congregations commonly did the same thing. Kee, for instance, surveying the various references to synagogues in Mark's Gospel, comments,

> The fact that in two of these passages ([Mark] 1:23; 1:39) the pronomial adjective is added, "in *their* synagogue" already implies that the followers of Jesus have their assemblies as well, which they see as outwardly similar to, but substantively in tension with the assemblies of the Pharisees.[35]

The last part of this sentence contains the crux of the matter. While no researcher would deny that a similarity existed between the early Christian *ekklēsia* and the Jewish synagogal communities, the question remains open as to how far one should push this analogy. Were the

---

[34]Meyers, "Synagogue," 225. Emphasis in original.

[35]Kee, "Transformations," 13.

Christians to some degree innovators, or were they simply mimicking the standard meeting practices of the Jewish milieu from which they emerged? As is amply clear, Kee maintains the latter.

In defending the legitimacy of this position, Kee draws heavily on the work of L. Michael White, who, in his recent book, *Building God's House* (1990),[36] argues that the transformation of the Christian house-churches into the public buildings of the fourth century finds its reflection in a parallel development in the Jewish synagogue buildings. Unlike the bulk of Kee's treatments, however, White's analysis focuses upon diaspora synagogues, specifically, those at Delos (I B.C.E.), Ostia (I C.E.), Priene (II C.E.), Sardis (II–III C.E.), Dura-Europos (II–III C.E.), and Stobi (III C.E.).[37] From his examination of the site plans of these six excavated structures, White states, "of these six, five were renovated from private domestic edifices, and in each case they had been houses typical of domestic architecture in that locale."[38] Combining this statement with an analysis of various literary citations and inscriptions, White draws the following conclusion:

> Certainly prior to 70, but continuing through the second century as well, the establishment of synagogue communities throughout the Diaspora must have generally followed the same steps as those followed at Delos, Priene, and Stobi. Private household gatherings gradually gave rise to formal establishments through a process of architectural adaptation sponsored in large measure by private benefactions.[39]

---

[36]L. Michael White, *Building God's House in the Roman World: Architectural Adaptation among Pagans, Jews, and Christians* (Baltimore, Md.: Johns Hopkins University Press, 1990).

[37]It is worth noting, however, that in his brief discussion of Palestinian synagogues, White takes a position similar to that of Kee: "Long-standing assumptions concerning the institution in Roman Palestine during the first century C.E. may have no historical grounding. While references to synagogues are known from late first-century sources, it does not appear that there was a formally ordered rabbinical institution as such prior to the second century C.E. Moreover, there is no archaeological evidence for exclusively synagogue buildings in the Homeland dating to the first century" (*Building God's House*, 61).

[38]White, *Building God's House*, 62.

[39]Ibid., 92. For another statement of this viewpoint, see Eric M. Meyers and L. Michael White, "Jews and Christians in a Roman World," *Archaeology* 42, no. 2 (1989): 31–33.

White's conclusions have been accepted by so many recent researchers that it would not be unfair to say that his position presently constitutes the majority position.[40]

While White, Kee, et al. argue for a basic continuity between the meeting facilities of Jews and early Christians, another researcher, Heather McKay, proposes a fundamental difference in meeting *purposes* between the two groups. According to McKay, while it is clear that early Christians met regularly for corporate prayer (e.g., 1 Cor 12–14, Acts 2), the notion that Jews gathered in synagogues on the Sabbath for communal worship is baseless. The volume incorporating her defense of this hypothesis (1994) forms an exception to the general rule that most recent studies on Second Temple synagogues have been brief: the laborious process of having to prove a negative has led McKay to spend over 250 pages examining various literary and epigraphic references to the Sabbath dating from pre-exilic times all the way up to 200 C.E.[41] Following this lengthy treatment, on the last page of her study, McKay concludes, "there is no unequivocal evidence that the sabbath was a day of worship for non-priestly Jews certainly as far as the end of the second century of the Common Era."[42] In her view, Sabbath gatherings in synagogues (private homes in the case of Palestine) were strictly for the reading and exposition of Torah, not for prayer.

---

[40]To Kee, Meyers and Horsley's acceptance of White's conclusions, add the following: Saldarini, *Matthew's Christian-Jewish Community*, 100; Bradley Blue, "Acts and the House Church" in *The Book of Acts in Its First Century Setting*, edited by David W. Gill and Conrad Gempf (Grand Rapids, Michigan: Wm. B. Eerdmans, 1994), 136; John McRay, *Archaeology and the New Testament* (Grand Rapids, Mich.: Baker Book House, 1991), 72.

[41]Heather A. McKay, *Sabbath and Synagogue: The Question of Sabbath Worship in Ancient Judaism* (Leiden; New York: E.J. Brill, 1994). This volume grew out of an article published three years earlier: idem, "New Moon or Sabbath?" in *The Sabbath in Jewish and Christian Traditions*, edited by Tamara C. Eskenazi, Daniel J. Harrington and William H. Shea (New York: The Crossroads Publishing Company, 1991), 12–27. Beyond the defense of her overall hypothesis, it is also noteworthy that McKay agrees with Kee and Horsley's verdict on the existence (or rather, non-existence) of synagogue structures in pre-70 Palestine: "There is no archaeological or epigraphic evidence that points unequivocally to the existence of synagogue buildings in first-century Palestine . . . First-century 'synagogues' are—on the whole—groups of male Jews. Any architectural remains of synagogue buildings in Palestine belong to a time later than the first century CE" (*Sabbath and Synagogue*, 250).

[42]McKay, *Sabbath and Synagogue*, 251.

A somewhat related position on this matter is taken by Lee Levine, who maintains that synagogues served as worship centers only outside of Palestine:

> There is no reference in Palestinian sources to the existence of organized communal prayer at that time [the Second Temple period], with the possible exception of the Qumran community, many of whose ideas and practices were different from those of the rest of society. (In contrast, the Diaspora synagogue, called *proseuche*—in Greek, "place of prayer"—presumably featured the element of prayer, although the reading of the Torah appears to have been central there as well.) Only after the destruction of the Second Temple did the synagogue in Palestine develop and expand as a place of worship.[43]

A final traditional belief about synagogues challenged recently is the phenomenon of the so-called "God-fearers" (φοβούμενοι/σεβομένοι τὸν θεόν), pagan sympathizers of Judaism who have not fully converted to the religion. References to God-fearers turn up quite frequently in the book of Acts, the best known of these being Cornelius, the Roman centurion, whom Luke presents as the first Gentile convert to Christianity (Acts 10:2, 22, 35). Others are depicted as being members of synagogue congregations in Luke's portrayals of Paul's various missionary activities, with many of them also going on to become Christians (Acts 13:16, 26, 43, 50; 16:14; 17:4, 17; 18:7). Citing a lack of corroborating inscriptionary evidence from synagogues in the diaspora, Thomas Kraabel has argued that God-fearers are a Lucan literary invention:

> The God-fearers are a symbol to help Luke show how Christianity had become a Gentile religion legitimately and without losing its Old Testament roots. The Jewish mission to Gentiles recalled in the God-fearers is ample precedent for the far more extensive mission to Gentiles which Christianity had in fact undertaken with such success. Once that point has been made, Luke can let the God-fearers disappear from his story. That is just what they do, and that is why there is no further reference to them in the New

---

[43]Lee I. Levine, "Synagogues," in *NEAEHL* 4.1421. Cf. idem, "The Second Temple Synagogue: The Formative Years" in *The Synagogue in Late Antiquity*, edited by Lee I. Levine (Philadelphia: American Schools of Oriental Research, 1987), 19–20. Similarly, Steven Fine and Eric Meyers state, "Communal prayer is not presented as a function of synagogues before 70 CE" (Steven Fine and Eric M. Meyers, "Synagogues" in *OEA* 5.118).

> Testament and no clear independent record of them in the material evidence from the classical world.[44]

Kraabel concludes his examination with a plea for historians to stop using the figure of the God-fearer as the quintessential example of the "inadequacy of Judaism" in the Greco-Roman world. "The New Testament," he writes, "provides no evidence of such a failure, if the God-fearer texts are properly understood."[45]

The foregoing exposition of some of the most recent literature about early synagogues attests to a trend that is at variance with much of the earlier research. While the older studies uniformly held that the synagogue was a highly formalized institution in the first century, replete with its own specialized architecture and open to Gentiles, the newer research, as we have seen, has frequently portrayed "synagogues" as being informal gatherings of Jews in private homes for Torah study. The full-blown synagogal institutions depicted in the older viewpoint are presented as being more a phenomenon of the third century C.E. in Palestine and somewhat earlier in the diaspora.

This portrait has not been without its challengers. Kraabel's article, for instance, met with a flurry of responses, mostly in the aftermath of the publication of an inscription from Aphrodisias (Asia Minor) where Jews, proselytes and God-fearers (*theosebeis* in the inscription) are clearly delineated as separate groups.[46] The inscription, however, dates to the

---

[44]A. Thomas Kraabel, "The Disappearance of the 'God-Fearers'," *Numen* 28 (1981): 120–121. For a similar set of arguments, see Robert S. MacLennan and A. Thomas Kraabel, "The God-Fearers—A Literary and Theological Invention," *BAR* 12, no. 5 (1986): 46–53.

[45]Kraabel, "The Disappearance of the 'God-Fearers'," 122.

[46]Louis H. Feldman, "The Omnipresence of the God-Fearers," *BAR* 12, no. 5 (1986): 58–63; Robert F. Tannenbaum, "Jews and God-Fearers in the Holy City of Aphrodite," *BAR* 12, no. 5 (1986): 44–57; John G. Gager, "Jews, Gentiles, and Synagogues in the Book of Acts," *HTR* 79, no. 1–3 (1986): 91–99; Joyce Maire Reynolds and Robert Tannenbaum, *Jews and God-Fearers at Aphrodisias: Greek Inscriptions with Commentary: Texts from the Excavations at Aphrodisias Conducted by Kenan T. Erim* vol. 12 (Cambridge: Cambridge Philological Society, 1987); Irina A. Levinskaya, "The Inscription from Aphrodisias and the Problem of God-Fearers," *TynBul* 41 (1990): 312–318; Paul R. Trebilco, *Jewish Communities in Asia Minor* (Cambridge England; New York: Cambridge University Press, 1991), 145–166; J. Andrew Overman, "The God-Fearers: Some Neglected Features" in *Diaspora Jews and Judaism: Essays in Honor of, and in Dialogue with, A. Thomas Kraabel*, edited by J. Overman and R. MacLennan (Atlanta: Scholars Press, 1992), 145–152. Kraabel responds to these criticisms in A. Thomas Kraabel, "Afterward" in *Diaspora Jews and*

third century C.E., and so the question needs to be re-examined for the pre-70 period.

Kee's conclusions have been met with responses by Richard Oster, Rainer Riesner and, in passing, Lee Levine and James Strange.[47] These authors argue that Kee's reconstruction either ignores or discounts pertinent evidence. For his part, Kee and those sharing similar views remain unconvinced.[48] Other recent writers have pushed back the transitional period in Palestine to the first century B.C.E. and have pointed to evidence suggesting that Palestinian synagogue structures existed in this period as *public* architecture which served a variety of functions.[49] Still other authors have highlighted the Egyptian origins of the synagogue or have sought to place early synagogue architecture within a larger Greco-Roman context.[50] All of these treatments, however, have been quite

---

Judaism, 347–357.

[47]Richard E. Oster, "Supposed Anachronism in Luke-Acts' Use of ΣΥΝΑΓΩΓΗ: A Rejoinder to H C Kee," *NTS* 39 (1993): 178–208; Rainer Riesner, "Synagogues in Jerusalem" in *The Book of Acts in Its Palestinian Setting*, edited by Richard Bauckham (Grand Rapids, Mich.: William B. Eerdmans Pub. Co., 1995), 179–211; Lee I. Levine, "The Nature and Origin of the Palestinian Synagogue Reconsidered," *JBL* 115 (1996): 428, n. 4; James F. Strange, "The Art and Archaeology of Ancient Judaism" in *Judaism in Late Antiquity*, edited by Jacob Neusner (Leiden; New York: E.J. Brill, 1995), 73. For a more recent rebuttal, see Kenneth Atkinson, "On Further Defining the First Century CE Synagogue: Fact or Fiction? A Rejoinder to H. C. Kee," *NTS* 43 (1997): 491–502.

[48]See especially Kee, "The Changing Meaning of Synagogue: A Response to Richard Oster," 281–283. Kee has not yet responded to Riesner or Levine in print. Horsley is similarly dismissive of Oster's work in Richard A. Horsley, *Archaeology History and Society in Galilee*, 223, n. 38. Flesher has not yet responded to Riesner's arguments. Likewise, McKay's work apparently was completed before any of the above critiques were offered.

[49]See Lester L. Grabbe, "Synagogues in Pre-70 Palestine: A Re-assessment" in *Ancient Synagogues: Historical Analysis and Archaeological Discovery*, edited by Dan Urman and Paul Virgil McCracken Flesher (New York: E.J. Brill, 1995), 1.17–26; Levine, "Nature and Origin of the Palestinian Synagogues," pass.

[50]E.g., J. Gwyn Griffiths, "Egypt and the Rise of the Synagogue" in *Ancient Synagogues: Historical Analysis and Archaeological Discovery*, edited by Dan Urman and Paul Virgil McCracken Flesher (New York: E.J. Brill, 1995), 1.3–16; Aryeh Kasher, "Synagogues as 'Houses of Prayer' and 'Holy Places' in the Jewish Communities of Hellenistic and Roman Egypt" in *Ancient Synagogues: Historical Analysis and Archaeological Discovery*, edited by Dan Urman and Paul Virgil McCracken Flesher (New York: E.J. Brill, 1995), 1.205–220; Paul E. Dion, "Synagogues et temples dans l'Egypte hellénistique," *ScEs* 29 (1977): 45–75; Gideon Foerster, "Architectural Models of the Greco-Roman Period and the Origin of The

limited in their scope. None of them has pulled together all of the pre-70 evidence in order to present it comprehensively and systematically. That, of course, is the circumscribed task of the present study. It is to a fuller exposition of this task that we now turn.

CONCLUDING OBSERVATIONS AND PROPOSAL

Our consideration of recent trends in the literature leads us to return to the question posed at the beginning of this chapter: Why another book on ancient synagogues? Given the recent dramatic shifts in methodology and the present turbulent state of the literature, the time seems ripe for an in-depth treatment and analysis of the relevant primary sources in an attempt to adjudicate the views articulated in the most recent studies and to present an overarching interpretation of the evidence that is nonetheless sensitive to the critical concerns noted above. In the previous section we observed several positive developments within recent studies of Second Temple synagogues. Most researchers are now taking greater care to stratify the literary and architectural sources, thus mitigating the danger of anachronism. Moreover, they are also now becoming more critical in their readings of the early literary evidence. Ancient sources are rarely taken at face value, but are submitted to sophisticated analyses that attempt to identify and control any biases which might distort our portrait of the early synagogues.

Despite these advances, the question remains open as to how successful recent researchers have been in presenting their historical reconstructions. Have they done justice to the full extent of the data? Have their treatments of the relevant sources been cogently argued? Have they considered evidence that might conflict with their final position? Of course, answers to questions such as these can only be formulated after

---

'Galilean' Synagogue" in *ASR* 45–48; Zvi 'Uri Ma'oz, "The Synagogue in the Second Temple Period—Architectural and Social Interpretation" in *Eretz-Israel*, edited by J. Aviram (Jerusalem: Israel Exploration Society, 1992), 23.224–228 [Hebrew]; Ehud Netzer, "The Herodian Triclinia: A Prototype for the 'Galilean-Type' Synagogue" in *ASR* 49–51; Ernest Marie Laperrousaz, "A propos des deux plus anciennes synagogues actuellement connues de Palestine, et dernières nouvelles archéologiques de Jèrusalem," *REJ* 144, no. 1–3 (1985): 297–304; Beat Brenk, "Zu den Grundriestypen der fruehsten Synagogen Palaestinas" in *Atti Del IX Congresso Internazionale Di Archeologia Cristiana: Roma, 21–27 Settembre 1975*, edited by Cristiana Congresso internazionale di archeologia (Citta del Vaticano, Roma: Pontificio istituto di archeologia cristiana, 1978), 539–550.

analyzing individual arguments in light of the evidence. Nevertheless, at this stage of the investigation some preliminary comments are in order. To begin with, a close reading of the arguments presented by recent authors leads me to believe that, in their treatments of the early synagogues, many of these researchers have paradoxically gone both "too far" and "not far enough." Where they have gone too far is in their treatment of the literary sources. While a "hermeneutics of suspicion" now constitutes part of the stock-in-trade of modern historians, when this hermeneutic is pressed to the point where it appears unwarranted, one starts to become suspicious of the conclusions drawn by the researcher. In *any* field of research, it is not uncommon for a hypothesis to take on a life of its own, with the evidence being consciously or unconsciously tailored to conform to a Procrustean bed. In the field of ancient history, the danger is especially great because the data are usually very fragmentary and the authors of the sources are no longer present for questioning. When these conditions are combined with critical readings of ancient documents, arguments based on silence can emerge. However, the silence may only be apparent. The researcher may have discounted important pieces of evidence, attributing them to authorial biases or anachronism. Here the problem is one of deciding whether or not a particular interpretation is appropriately critical. Such judgments, of course, can only be made on a case-by-case basis. Yet, as I shall argue, some of the recent synagogue researchers appear to have gone too far in their criticisms because they have not gone far enough in their consideration of relevant data. In some cases, they appear to be unaware of the existence of conflicting data. In other instances, they seem cognizant of evidence at odds with their own conclusions, but discount or minimize the implications of this evidence.

As might be expected, our consideration of these lacunae will suggest a portrait at odds with those offered by many of the recent researchers. First, it seems clear that synagogues existed in Palestine as formal institutions with their own buildings and functionaries as early as the first century B.C.E. In the diaspora, they appeared even earlier, being well-attested in Egypt in the third century B.C.E. Within two centuries they were flourishing in Jewish centers around the Mediterranean. Second, no solid evidence from our period presently exists to indicate that synagogues emerged from meetings in private homes. On the other hand, the data uniformly support the view that synagogue buildings constituted public, monumental architecture as opposed to private, domestic dwellings. Third, evidence exists attesting to the presence of both public and private prayer within the synagogues of Palestine and the diaspora. Finally, the existence of the God-fearers receives confirmation from evidence outside of the treatment accorded them in Acts.

A central task of this study will be to lay before the reader in an orderly manner the existing data along with a critical analysis and interpretation of that data so that the reader can make his or her own judgments on each of these propositions. In accordance with the methodological concerns noted in the previous sections, the data will be limited to only those literary, epigraphic and archaeological sources contemporaneous with the period of the Second Temple. Among these sources will be documents written within a generation of the Temple's demise yet making reference back to the pre-70 period. While these will be counted as evidence, they will also be scrutinized for any hint of anachronism or bias. Moreover, the rhetorical tendencies of all documents mentioning Second Temple synagogues will be considered and taken into account before drawing historical conclusions from their witness. Beyond this, consideration will also be given to the provenance of the sources, with care being taken to address possible patterns of local variation among the synagogues. Particular attention will be given to evidence suggesting differences between diaspora and Palestinian synagogues, while at the same time any points of similarity will also be noted. Finally, special treatment will be given to what we might imprecisely label "sectarian synagogues," those synagogues belonging to the Essenes, the Therapeutae and the Samaritans, groups that were at some degree of variance with the larger Jewish society. Christians might also have been included within this treatment, yet the emergence and development of the Christian *ekklēsia* deserves an examination beyond what can be given in this study. I will, however, reserve space at its conclusion to suggest some potential implications of this study for enhancing our understanding of the formation and evolution of the *ekklēsia* as well as for the continuing evolution of the synagogues in the Rabbinic period.

A second major task of this study will be to present a proposal that addresses yet another way in which I believe recent researchers have not gone far enough in their analyses. The basis of this assertion is best introduced through a brief look at one of the leading assumptions that has been present within much of the research on the pre-70 synagogues.

As we noted above, much of the older literature set forth the view that the early synagogues served as rivals to the Temple cult—a sort of protest movement against a moribund institution whose priests were corrupt and whose sacrifices were no longer seen as efficacious.[51] In his now classic study, *Hellenistic Civilization and the Jews* (1959), Avigdor Tcherikover stated this proposition rather succinctly:

> The urban population sought other intellectual leaders who lived and thought in a manner more akin to themselves. Hence rose the class of scribes, the flesh and bone of the broad city populace, which took upon itself the task of interpreting the Torah neglected by the priests . . . Possibly the new scribal interpretations were delivered in the synagogues which had now for the first time risen and spread in Judea, and thus was created the important opposition between the Temple and the Synagogue.[52]

This position was by no means confined to the older literature. As late as 1981, in an essay included in his compendium, *Ancient Synagogues: The State of the Research*, Joseph Gutmann was able to present a reconstruction of the early synagogues that is strikingly similar to Tcherikover's:

> The goal of the new Pharisaic religion was to assure the individual's salvation after death and his bodily resurrection in the messianic age. All this was to be achieved by each individual without sacrifice or priests but through the observance of the laws (the *halakhot*), systematically set forth in the divinely revealed two-fold Law. The synagogue, one of the unique Pharisaic institutions, became an important meeting place where through prayers and ceremonial practices the individual Jew could affirm his loyalty to the two-fold Pharisaic law, with the guarantee that its observance would bring about salvation of his soul and resurrection. Thus a major historical event in second-century B.C.E. Judea ushered in the Pharisees and their new institution—the synagogue—whose existence is not historically demonstratable prior to the Hasmonean revolt.[53]

---

[51]This is not meant to imply that *all* earlier studies viewed the synagogue and the Temple as rivals (e.g., Schrage, "Συναγωγή," 822–824). However, most of these based their conclusions at least partially upon the belief that a synagogue existed within the Temple complex, a thesis itself founded upon a faulty interpretation of later rabbinic material (e.g., *m. Meg* 1.3, *b. Ber.* 6a, 7b). See Sidney B. Hoenig, "Supposititious Temple-Synagogue," *JQR* 54 (1963): 115–131; Solomon Zeitlin, "There Was No Synagogue in the Temple," *JQR* 53 (1962): 168–169.

[52]Avigdor Tcherikover, *Hellenistic Civilization and the Jews* (Philadelphia: Jewish Publication Society of America, 1959), 124–125.

[53]Joseph Gutmann, "Synagogue Origins: Theories and Facts" in *Ancient Synagogues: The State of the Research*, edited by Joseph Gutmann (Chico, California: Scholars Press, 1981), 4.

More recent research has submitted these reconstructions to a partial critique. Lester Grabbe, for example, has argued that the common assumption that the Pharisees founded or dominated the pre-70 synagogues is not to be found in any of the first-century material. We have already seen evidence to this effect in our review above of Neusner's analysis of the early rabbinic attestations. Grabbe, while briefly alluding to Neusner's conclusions, limits his own examination to the canonical Gospels and the works of Josephus. Aside from John 12:42,[54] which he argues reflects the internecine strife arising *after* the Temple's destruction, Grabbe finds in this material no reference to the Pharisees as leaders in the early synagogues.[55] In a similar vein, other researchers have pointed out that Josephus numbers the Pharisees at only 6,000 during the time of Herod the Great, with the great bulk of these being located in Jerusalem. In view of this fact, the scholars argue, any portrait of Pharisaic dominance of synagogues outside of Judea seems unlikely.[56] This argument is confirmed when one notes that the rise of the Pharisees can be dated to no earlier than the Maccabean revolt in the mid-second-century B.C.E. Yet epigraphic evidence attests to the presence of synagogues in Egypt nearly a century earlier. It follows that any connection between the early Egyptian synagogues and the Pharisees is extremely problematic.[57]

While synagogue researchers have been inclined to accept these conclusions, they have not been as quick to notice the deeper flaw in Tcherikover and Gutmann's reconstructions: neither the Pharisees nor any other identifiable Jewish group in the pre-70 period can with certainty be identified as being "anti-Temple."[58] On the contrary, the overwhelming bulk of evidence suggests that Jews everywhere hallowed and supported this institution. Just a few passages will suffice to demonstrate the depth and breadth of this sentiment.

---

[54]John 12:42: "Nevertheless many, even of the authorities, believed in [Jesus]. But because of the Pharisees they did not confess it, for fear that they would be put out of the synagogue [ἀποσυνάγωγοι]."

[55]Grabbe, "Synagogues in Pre-70 Palestine," 23–24. In a subsequent chapter, we will explore other passages which Grabbe missed in his examination.

[56]E. P. Sanders, *Judaism*, 398.

[57]Flesher, "Palestinian Synagogues before 70 C.E.," 27–28.

[58]This point has recently been made by E. P. Sanders (*Judaism*, 77–82). See also S. J. D Cohen, *From the Maccabees to the Mishnah* (Philadelphia: Westminster Press, 1987), 62–69.

We begin with an assertion by Josephus, who, in describing the towers overlooking the Temple, makes the following comments:

> Whoever is master of these [the fortresses guarding the Temple] had the whole nation in his power, for sacrifices could not be made without (controlling) these places, and it was impossible for any of the Jews to forgo offering these, for they would rather give up their lives than the worship which they are accustomed to offer God (*Ant.* 15.248).[59]

Since Josephus was himself a priest (as well as a Pharisee!) one might expect him to express a pro-Temple sentiment.[60] Yet his characterization is borne out by other writers. Philo, for example, who had been in Rome in 40 C.E. to petition Gaius over some grievances of the Alexandrian Jews, relates the poignant story of how he came to hear the news of Gaius' proclamation about erecting a statue of Zeus in the midst of the Jerusalem Temple:

> While we were anxiously considering the statement of our case, since we were always expecting to be summoned, there came to us one with a troubled look in his bloodshot eyes and gasping convulsively. He drew us a little way apart since there were some people standing near and said, "Have you heard the new tidings?" and when he was going to report it he was brought up short, as a flood of tears streamed from his eyes. He began again and the second time stopped short and so too a third time. When we saw this we were all in a flutter and bade him tell us the matter which he said had brought him there . . . He managed with difficulty while sobbing and breathing spasmodically to say, "Our temple is lost, Gaius has ordered a colossal statue to be set up within the inner sanctuary dedicated to himself under the name of Zeus." As we marvelled at his words and, petrified by consternation, could not get any further, since we stood there speechless and powerless in a state of collapse with our hearts turned to water (*Legat.* 186–189).

Philo goes on to recount that when the Legate of Syria, Petronius, marched into Palestine to execute this appointed task, "the inhabitants of the holy city and the rest of the country" streamed out to meet him, baring their throats and asking to be slaughtered rather than have their Temple defiled (*Legat.* 225–243). Even given the likely embellishments of this account, Philo's portrait can hardly be viewed as depicting an anti-Temple sentiment among the Jews. Nor should the Gaius incident be

---

[59]The translation, as with those of all other Greco-Roman texts quoted in this study (unless otherwise indicated), is from the LCL.

[60]On Josephus' account of his Pharisaism see *Vita* 12.

viewed exclusively as a kind of "rallying around the flag" phenomenon—at least not from Philo's point of view: while reflecting upon one of his own pilgrimages to the Temple, Philo attests to widespread participation in the Temple cult:

> Countless multitudes from countless cities come, some over land, others over sea, from east and west and north and south at every feast . . . Friendships are formed between those who hitherto knew not each other, and the sacrifices and libations are the occasion of reciprocity of feeling and constitute the surest pledge that all are of one mind (*Spec.* 1.70; cf. Acts 2:5–11).

Other documents similarly attest to the importance of the Temple cult among Jews. The so-called *Letter of Aristeas* (II B.C.E.), for example, goes to great lengths to praise the work of the priests and the beauty of the Temple edifice (*Ep. Arist.* 41–120). 3 Maccabees (I B.C.E.) narrates a tale about how God miraculously saved the Temple and thousands of worshipers from the wrath of Ptolemy IV. Ben Sirach (II B.C.E.) elevates the role of Aaron and his high priestly progeny above that of Moses (Sir 45:1–22, 50:1–21) and advises his readers to "fear the Lord, and honor his priests" (Sir 7:29).[61] The flow of the Temple tax and the contribution of votive offerings to the Temple from all over the diaspora are so well-documented that they constitute one of the few things we can say with certainty about Jewish practices in the Second Temple period.[62]

Beyond this widespread support of the cult during its existence, in the aftermath of the Temple's destruction, as best as we can tell, great shock and sorrow erupted among Palestinian Jews. 4 Ezra (c. 100 C.E.) and 2 Baruch (II C.E.) serve as moving statements of this deep despair.[63] Yet

---

[61]See Ellis Rivkin, "Ben Sira and the Non Existence of the Synagogue: A Study in Historical Method" in *In the Time of Harvest, Essays in Honor of Abba Hillel Silver on the Occasion of his 70th Birthday*, edited by Daniel Jeremy Silver (New York: Macmillan, 1963), 320–354.

[62]See citations in nn. 4 and 5, above.

[63]The fourth *Sibylline Oracle*, written probably in the 80s (C.E.), constitutes the only clear rejection of the Temple in the Jewish literature (especially vv. 24–25). Yet this view may have been fostered from theological reflection upon the Temple's demise: the author may have interpreted the destruction as proof of God's judgment upon the cult. Some of the Christian literature reflects a similar view. Werner Kelber, for instance, argues that Mark's Gospel was written in part as a polemic against the Jerusalem church's messianic hopes which were centered on the Temple (Mark 13). See Werner H. Kelber, *The Kingdom in Mark: A New Place and a New Time* (Philadelphia: Fortress Press, 1974), 109–147; idem, *Mark's Story of Jesus* (Philadelphia: Fortress Press, 1979), 57–70.

even then the cult was not abandoned: during the Bar Kokhba revolt, hopes were rekindled that the Temple would be rebuilt, as is attested by various coins from this period depicting the Temple façade.[64] Similar ambitions reemerged more than two centuries later during the brief reign of Julian the Apostate (361–363 C.E.).[65]

The few dissenting voices such as the Essenes and the author of the Psalms of Solomon were opposed not to the Temple cult itself, but rather to what they perceived to be a corrupt priesthood. The Essenes, while holding the Hasmonean priesthood in contempt, nevertheless hoped to supplant the existing dynasties and inaugurate their own new Temple in Jerusalem.[66] Similarly, the composer of the Psalms of Solomon (I B.C.E.), writing in the aftermath of Pompey's desecration of the Temple in 63 B.C.E., lays blame for this catastrophe on the Hasmonean priesthood, stating, "with pomp they set up a monarchy because of their arrogance; and they did not glorify your honorable name" (*Pss. Sol.* 17:6). Despite these criticisms—inspired because the author hallowed the sanctity of the Temple—the psalmist goes on to predict that Jerusalem will be purged and made holy again (*Pss. Sol.* 17:30).[67]

The Samaritans, of course, serve as somewhat of an exceptional case, since they disdained the Jerusalem cult in favor of their own worship center on Mt. Gerizim.[68] Yet this was not a rejection of a sacrificial mode of worship, only a dispute over the location of the cult. The same can also

---

[64]*AJC* 2.272, no. 51–53; Dan Barag, "The Table of the Showbread and the Facade of the Temple on Coins of the Bar-Kokhba Revolt" in *Ancient Jerusalem Revealed*, edited by Hillel Geva (Jerusalem: Israel Exploration Society, 1994), 272–276.

[65]E. Mary Smallwood, *The Jews under Roman Rule: From Pompey to Diocletian* (Leiden: Brill, 1976), 544.

[66]For criticism of the Hasmoneans (probably Jonathan Maccabaeus, the "Wicked Priest") see 1QpHab 8.4–13, 9.7–12, 11.2–9. The *Temple Scroll* (11QT) presents the Essene's reconstruction of the Jerusalem Temple and cult. See Yigael Yadin, *The Temple Scroll: The Hidden Law of the Dead Sea Sect* (London: Weidenfeld and Nicolson, 1985), 112–169.

[67]Along these lines it is worth noting that Luke had no difficulty in portraying Paul as being involved in sacrifice (Acts 21:26). Whether or not this account is accurate is another matter (note, however, 1 Cor 9:20). In the pre-70 period, Christians had to wrestle with the continuing significance of the cult, a task that was made much easier after the Temple's destruction. An important point is that the cult was not totally discarded, but reinterpreted with Christ absorbing the place of the Temple (John 2:21), the high priesthood (Heb 5:5–6), the feasts (John 7:37–38) and the sacrificial victim (Rom 3:24–25; Rev 13:8).

[68]See Josephus, *Ant.* 11:87, 12.10, 13.74–79, 254–256; John 4:20.

be said of the Temple of Onias in Leontopolis, which, as best as we can tell, had only a very limited following.[69]

In view of the overwhelming evidence demonstrating the centrality of the Temple to Jews both in Palestine and in the diaspora, it is difficult to conceive of the early synagogues being in opposition to the Temple cult. The fact that first-century Jews such as Philo and Josephus could hold both institutions in high esteem strongly suggests that such a perceived oppositional relationship is illusory.

Why then the persistence of this view in proposals such as the one recently proffered by Paul Flesher? Why then do other recent reconstructions tend to play down possible connections between the Temple and the synagogue and present the early synagogues instead as privatized, domestic gatherings of the pious? Is it possible that what we have behind these proposals is a rationalistic bias which views the destruction of the Temple cult as a step already destined within the evolution of religions? Or perhaps it may be something related to this. In his celebrated book, *Paul and Palestinian Judaism*, E. P. Sanders, noting a prominent Law/Grace dichotomy in earlier reconstructions of ancient Jewish and Christian theologies, suggested that these were largely "the retrojection of the Protestant-Catholic debate into ancient history, with Judaism taking the role of Catholicism and Christianity the role of Lutheranism."[70] Is it possible that this Protestant-Catholic debate may have been rejoined on another level, this time with the Temple cult assuming the role of Catholicism and "the common-folk inhabiting the synagogues" bearing the standard of Protestantism? If so, then instead of the debate centering around the issues of law and grace, in this instance the chief antipodes are sacramentalism and pietism. It is not my intention to explore this possibility at any length, except to observe that a number of both the old and the more recent historical reconstructions of the Second Temple synagogues bear a striking resemblance to seventeenth-century pietistic movements. This, of course, does not mean that the reconstructions are necessarily wrong; the observation only serves as a possible explanation for why the well-attested prominence of the sacrificial cult in the first century is frequently ignored in the work of many scholars of this period.

---

[69]See Robert Hayward, "The Jewish Temple at Leontopolis: A Reconsideration," *JJS* 33 (1982): 429–443.

[70]E. P. Sanders, *Paul and Palestinian Judaism: A Comparison of Patterns of Religion* (Philadelphia: Fortress Press, 1977), 57.

If we endeavor to set such potential biases aside and examine the evidence more evenhandedly, it should come as no surprise that sacrificial worship was central to first-century Judaism. In subscribing to a sacrificial cult, Jews of the first century were little different from the rest of the peoples encompassing the Mediterranean. Greeks and Romans, Egyptians and Nabateans, Scythians and Parthians—all these and many others participated in sacrifice.[71] Indeed, up to the start of the Jewish War, Gentiles from around the Greco-Roman world presented sacrifices in the Jerusalem Temple.[72] Additionally, the Temple priests offered sacrifices daily on behalf of the Roman emperor. In return, the imperial family donated golden vials, libation bowls and "a multitude of other sumptuous offerings" to the cult.[73]

Thus there was a great deal of commonality between the Jewish cult and the cults of the surrounding nations. Of course Judaism's spurning of idolatry and the adherence to monotheism kept the exchange rather one-sided: while Gentiles could and did worship in the Jewish Temple, most Jews would adamantly refuse to sacrifice at any cultic site except their own. Nevertheless, any first-century Gentile entering the outer court of the Temple in Jerusalem would not have considered the mode of worship exercised within the Temple's inner courts totally foreign to his or her own experience. The Jerusalem Temple would merely have been perceived as one among many of the sacrificial centers found throughout the Roman Empire.

The foregoing observations now lead us finally to a proposal. Given the evidence for the widespread practice of sacrifice in antiquity and the sweeping support of Jews for the centralized cult, the hypothesis naturally

---

[71]See Walter Burkert, *Greek Religion* (Cambridge, Mass.: Harvard University Press, 1985), 54–118; John E. Stambaugh, "The Functions of Roman Temples" in *ANRW* II.16.1.554–608.

[72]Josephus, *Ant.* 11.336, 12.406, 13.55, 13.243, 16.14, 18.122; *Ap.* 2.48; cf. 3 Macc 1:9, *Ep. Arist.* 45, Philo, *Legat.* 232. According to Josephus, the final spark to ignite the revolt was the refusal of Eleazar, son of the high priest Ananias, to accept gifts or sacrifices from foreigners. Josephus states that the high priests and the Pharisees were brought in to convince him and his followers that the law permitted such sacrifices. The appeal, however, was to no avail (*BJ* 2.409–421).

[73]Philo, *Legat.* 319. On the offerings for the emperor: Josephus, *BJ* 2.197; Philo, *Legat.* 291.

emerges that the synagogues should not be viewed as being in opposition to the Temple, but rather as extensions of it. Specifically, I will argue that the synagogues in both Palestine and the diaspora served as subsidiary sacred precincts that extended spatially the sacrality of the Temple shrine and allowed Jews everywhere participation within the central cult. This hypothesis should not be construed as suggesting that all synagogue congregations held identical religious beliefs or were under the tight control of the centralized high priesthood. Such a position obviously could not be maintained in light of the multiplicity of viewpoints found within the various Jewish documents from the pre-70 period. Nevertheless, the evidence surveyed above suggests the Temple with its cult served as a unifying institution for Jews in both Palestine and the diaspora.

In developing this thesis, the concept of the sacred must be recognized as all-important, for the ancients divided their world into zones of the sacred (*hieros*) and the profane (*bebelos*). Regarding this conceptualization, Walter Burkert writes:

> *Hieros* was without doubt the decisive concept for demarcating the sphere of the religious from Mycenaean times. In fact this word does have a delimiting, defining function, but it is thereby almost exclusively a predicate of things: the sacred as such is the sacrifice, especially the sacrificial animal, and the sanctuary with temple and altar. Sacred, too, are the votive gifts in the sanctuary; the money that is donated to the god; the land which cannot be cultivated; further, everything which has to do with the sanctuary, from the sacred way to Eleusis to the sacred war for Delphi . . . . *Hieros* would accordingly have to be defined as that which belongs to a god or sanctuary in an irrevocable way. The opposite is *bebelos*, profane. Man consecrates something, some possession, in that he takes it away from his own disposal and surrenders it to the god.[74]

Consonant with this worldview, as a way of extending the sacrality of a temple shrine (*naos*), the ancients would dedicate the surrounding sacred precincts (*hieros periboloi/temenē/hieron*) or other, more distant sacred places (*hieroi topoi/hiera*) to the god or goddess believed to be resident within the central shrine. In the minds of the ancients, the holiness and the power of these divine beings flowed out from the central shrines and into the sacred areas, blessing the activities transpiring therein.[75] This was

---

[74]Burkert, *Greek Religion*, 269.

[75]On the temple as the vortex between heaven and earth, see Mircea Eliade, *The Sacred and the Profane*, 1st American ed. (New York: Harcourt, 1959), 8–65; idem,

powerful medicine that evoked a measure of reverence within those entering these sacred places. Or at least that was the general expectation—one that could be violated by unscrupulous persons of poor upbringing. Hence Philo was able to complain that the debaucheries of pagans took to new heights when they spilled over from private abodes into sacred areas:

> So long as they [the Gentiles] confine their unseemly doings to houses or unconsecrated places [οἰκίαις ἢ χωρίοις βεβήλοις], their sin seems less to me. But when their wickedness like a rushing torrent spreads over every place and invades and violates the most sacred temples [ἱερῶν τοῖς ἁγιωτάτοις], it straightway overturns all that is venerable in them, and as a result come sacrifices unholy, offerings unmeet, vows unfulfilled, their rites and mysteries a mockery, their piety but a bastard growth, their holiness debased, their purity impure, their truth falsehood, their worship a sacrilege (*Cher*. 94).

The problem with the pagans, in Philo's view, was not merely their behavior, but their violation of sacred space. And here it mattered not that it was pagan sacred space being dishonored: however misguided the Gentile worship of idols might have been, the larger point was that these areas were still consecrated to a deity and must therefore be treated with reverence. To the ancient mind, failure to honor the sanctity of a sacred place threatened to provoke the wrath of the possessor deity against the entire populace.[76] In Philo's case, while he may not have been worried about baiting the anger of Zeus—who in his mind did not exist—simply the semantic association between pagan "gods" (*theoi*) and the Jewish "Most High God" (*Theos Hypsistos*) was enough to give him pause. Hence he warned his readers: "We must refrain from speaking insultingly of these [pagan gods], lest any of Moses' disciples get into the habit of treating lightly the name 'god' in general, for it is a title worthy of the highest respect and love" (*Mos*. 2.205).[77]

With regard to city or community planning, the essential difference between the Jewish situation and that of the Gentiles was the deuteronomic prohibition against erecting other shrines (*naoi*) or altars (*thysiastēria*) apart from the one in Jerusalem (e.g., Deut 12:13–14,

---

"Sacred Architecture and Symbolism" in *Symbolism, the Sacred, and the Arts*, edited by Mircea Eliade and Diane Apostolos-Cappadona (New York: Crossroad, 1985), 105–129.

[76]Thus Josephus blames the destruction of Palestine during the Jewish War on the desecration of the Jerusalem Temple by the Zealots (*BJ* 5.5–20).

[77]Cf. the similar beliefs of Josephus as expressed in *Ap*. 2.237–38.

16:5–6).[78] This left Jews removed from the Temple in a quandary, since they certainly desired all the benefits that accrued from having a temple nearby.[79] Even Jews living in the various suburbs of Jerusalem, unlike their Gentile counterparts, could not build subsidiary shrines or altars to consecrate the civic activities of their borough. Their solution, as will be argued throughout this study, was to erect synagogues. Like the courts surrounding the Temple shrine in Jerusalem, these structures were also dedicated to the Jewish God. Taken out of the realm of human possession (*bebelos*), they passed into the hands of the deity (*hieros*) and became sacred edifices. Effectively, they served as distant Temple courts—sacred precincts in miniature where worshipers could gather and look to the center, to the shrine of the Holy One in Jerusalem.[80]

In presenting this hypothesis, it should be noted that even among researchers who accept the existence of early synagogue buildings, there is a reluctance to appreciate the sacred nature of these structures. Joan Branham, for example, while correctly noting the centrality of the Jerusalem Temple for ancient Jews, maintains that the emergence of the synagogues as sacred edifices was a *post*-70 development: "The Temple's unique association with the Divine Presence and its sacrificial means of communicating with God are deferred *after* its destruction—spatially, temporally, and formally—to the liturgy and space of the synagogue."[81] Despite this conclusion, it is noteworthy that in making her case for the sacred nature of the Late Antique synagogues, Branham refers to sources not only from the Talmudic age, but also from the period *predating* the Temple's destruction.[82] This suggests that the association of which

[78]These verses, of course, do not mention Jerusalem, but during the Second Temple period were understood as references to the Holy City. See Josephus, *Ant.* 4.200, 13.54.

[79]Numerous references to "high places" (במות) in the Hebrew scriptures are certainly testimonies to this (e.g., Lev 26:30, Num 33:52, 1Kgs 3:2ff).

[80]Or in the case of the Samaritans, to Mt. Gerizim.

[81]Joan R. Branham, "Vicarious Sacrality: Temple Space in Ancient Synagogues" in *Ancient Synagogues: Historical Analysis and Archaeological Discovery*, edited by Dan Urman and Paul Virgil McCracken Flesher (New York: E.J. Brill, 1995), 2.345. Emphasis added.

[82]Ibid., 334, n. 59: "One inscription from the time of the Ptolemies [*JIE* 9] mentions 'sacred precincts' ἱερὸν περίβολον." Despite this acknowledgment, Branham elsewhere states that "the synagogue is not marked off by boundary indicators comparable to the *temenos* of the Temple" (ibid., 330). In another place (ibid., 334, n. 53), Branham alludes to various Roman decrees protecting the sanctity of the synagogues but does not mention that these decrees were issued *prior* to the Temple's

Branham writes was one that originated during the Second Temple period, becoming more overtly manifested during the era with which her essay is concerned.

In a similar vein, Peter Richardson, who has recently compared Second Temple synagogues to *collegia* or "voluntary societies," also arrives at a negative verdict both with respect to the structures' sacrality and their connection to the Jerusalem Temple:

> None of the synagogues was decorated with symbols reminiscent of the Temple in Jerusalem. Such symbols—found profusely in later synagogues in mosaic floors, capitals, lintels, and other architectural features—were completely absent in pre-70 buildings . . . No elements in pre-70 synagogues directed attention to the Temple in Jerusalem, not even orientation, for the synagogue had not yet replaced the centre of worship in Jerusalem, and none of its features needed to call the Temple to mind. Quite the contrary, synagogues had an architectural character radically different from the Temple. They provided spaces intended for multiple community functions, not for functions modeled on the Temple's highly articulated functions and notions of holiness.[83]

Several points need to be made in response to this conclusion. To begin with, during the Late Roman and Byzantine periods, there was clearly a more liberal interpretation of the Second Commandment than during the period of the Second Temple: as Richardson rightly notes, whereas iconic symbolism abounds in the later synagogues, it is absent in the earlier structures. Yet this was true not only in the synagogues, but also in the Temple, where excavators have uncovered architectural fragments bearing only geometric and floral motifs.[84] As Rachel Hachlili observes, the subdued use of symbolism during this period was "a defense

---

destruction.

[83]Peter Richardson, "Early Synagogues as Collegia in the Diaspora and Palestine" in *Voluntary Associations*, edited by John S. Kloppenborg and Steven G. Wilson (London: Routledge, 1996), 102, 103.

[84]See B. Mazar, "The Archaeological Excavations near the Temple Mount" in *Jerusalem Revealed: Archaeology in the Holy City, 1968–1974*, edited by Yigael Yadin (Jerusalem: Israel Exploration Society, 1975), 28–29; Meir Ben-Dov, *In the Shadow of the Temple*, trans. Ina Friedman (New York: Harper & Row, 1985), 138–139. Richardson himself makes the point that "the rebuilding of the Temple in Jerusalem [by Herod] contained, with one important exception, no figures" (Peter Richardson, "Law and Piety in Herod's Architecture," *SR* 15, no. 3 [1986]: 350). The exception is an eagle placed over the main gate by Herod. Near the end of Herod's reign, two zealous Jews tore down the offending image (Josephus, *Ant.* 15.267–291).

against the Hellenistic assault on [Jewish] religion and culture at a time when the Hellenistic rulers were attempting to force Jews into idolatry."[85] Consequently, synagogue researchers of the earlier period must recalibrate their criteria of sacred iconography, adjusting it to the more conservative attitudes of the times. As we shall see in subsequent chapters, symbols found within the ruins of Second Temple synagogues or with excavated inscriptions closely match those found in the excavations of Temple area. Furthermore, we will discover that these same symbols are alluded to within the Hebrew scriptures and clearly carry a cultic significance.[86]

A second, related point is that, while we will find some diversity among early synagogue architecture—particularly in the diaspora—we will also note the recent proposal of archaeologist James Strange, who argues that the early Galilean-type synagogue found in Palestine was modeled upon the Temple courts.[87] In addition, we will observe that the early evidence regarding synagogue orientation, while fragmentary, suggests an adherence to two separate traditions, both related to the placement of the Jerusalem Temple.[88]

Thirdly, by contrasting the synagogues' "multiple community functions" with the Temple's "highly articulated" ones, Richardson apparently adopts a minimalist view of the Temple's role within Jewish society.[89] As we will see, however, the Jerusalem Temple, like all Near Eastern temples, served a variety of community functions. Moreover,

---

[85]Rachel Hachlili, *Ancient Jewish Art and Archaeology in the Land of Israel* (New York: E.J. Brill, 1988), 235.

[86]See the treatment of the Theodotus inscription in chapter two, the Gamla synagogue in chapter three, and the Delos synagogue in chapter four.

[87]See chapter three, below. It should also be mentioned that, although Richardson correctly recognizes the importance of *mikvaoth* in identifying the Second Temple synagogues of Palestine ("Early Synagogues as Collegia," 92), he does not take the next step and ask why these ritual baths were commonly built near such structures. Nor does he notice the parallel between this arrangement and that found in Jerusalem, where ritual baths surrounded the Temple complex.

[88]See chapters three and four, below.

[89]The same can be said of Shaye Cohen's examination of the Temple cult, which dwells on the sacrificial role of the sanctuary to the exclusion of all other functions. See Shaye J. D. Cohen, "The Temple and the Synagogue" in *The Temple in Antiquity: Ancient Records and Modern Perspectives*, edited by T. Madsen (Provo, Utah: Religious Studies Center, Brigham Young University, 1984), 151–174. Like Branham, Cohen deals primarily with the emergence of the Late Antique synagogue after the Temple's destruction.

these closely match those attested within the early synagogues—with, of course, the important exception of animal sacrifice. As for this last, our study will discover that the early synagogues commonly served as collection places for monies to be used for offering sacrifices at the central sanctuary on behalf of the local congregations.[90]

Finally, while this study would tend to agree with Richardson's conclusion that "[Second Temple] synagogues functioned as—and were perceived as—collegia"[91] (at least in certain parts of the diaspora),[92] it would also point out that the examples of collegia (*scholae*) which Richardson cites are all cultic structures dedicated to a pagan deity.[93] These too served as "miniature temples," often replete with idols, altars and votive offerings. Consequently, if such pagan structures served as the architectural models for certain diaspora synagogues, it is likely that the builders sought to adhere to the local conventions of what constituted a sacred edifice, while at the same time adapting them to cohere with Jewish (or Samaritan) beliefs regarding the erection of idols and altars. Indeed, the absence of the latter in itself suggests an allegiance to a central cult.[94]

In addition to James Strange, one synagogue researcher who recently *has* subscribed to the view that the early synagogues were sacred places

---

[90]See chapters three, four and six, below.

[91]Richardson, "Early Synagogues as Collegia," 90.

[92]As Simeon Guterman has pointed out, only the synagogues in the western half of the empire were constituted as *collegia licita*; those in the eastern half were authorized either as a result of treaty (Palestine) or as a reconfirmation of an earlier status under the Hellenistic rulers (Simeon L. Guterman, *Religious Toleration and Persecution in Ancient Rome* [London: Aiglon, 1951], 75–158). Generally, this meant that the synagogues in the east—at least those in cities with a long-established Jewish presence—served a larger set of functions (e.g., law courts, places of refuge) than those in Italy. See chapters four and six, below.

[93]In addition to Mithraea, Richardson mentions the Bakcheion in Athens which "was a large hall with a decorated altar built for the worship of Dionysos" ("Early Synagogues as Collegia," 97). For a consideration of another cultic hall, see the treatment of the House of the Poseidoniasts in chapter four, below.

[94]On this point, see B. Hudson McLean, "The Place of Cult in Voluntary Associations and Christian Churches on Delos" in *Voluntary Associations*, edited by John S. Kloppenborg and Steven G. Wilson (London: Routledge, 1996), 195. While McLean rightly recognizes the relationship between the Delos synagogue and a central cultic site, his definition of "cultic" (viz., the offering of animal sacrifices or adoration of an idol only) is too narrow. See the treatment of the Delos synagogue in chapter four, below.

modeled after the Jerusalem Temple is Israeli scholar Areyah Kasher. Following a survey of the early Egyptian evidence, Kasher concludes:

> The Jewish synagogues in ancient Egypt were erected on the basis of similarity to the Temple in Jerusalem as a place of prayer and gathering together in festive convocations on Sabbaths and festivals. Since all the communal institutions clustered around them . . . they stood at the center of the daily Jewish communal life.[95]

While we will draw upon Kasher's analysis in our treatment of the Egyptian synagogues, the present study may be construed as an expansion of his hypothesis: that Second Temple synagogues not only in Egypt, but also in Palestine and the rest of the diaspora, while removed from the centralized cult geographically, nevertheless served as spatial vortices, allowing Jews everywhere to be connected with the Temple. In support of this conceptualization, we will consider evidence showing that the synagogues shared with the Temple courts common functions and functionaries, common terminology, and in some cases, even common architecture. Along the way we will note how circumstances may have led to the adoption of supplementary functions. Nevertheless, in no case do these functions appear to be at odds with the sacrificial worship of the centralized Temple cult.

The examination will proceed in the following manner. In chapter one, we will explore the nature of the various sources relevant for our inquiry of Second Temple synagogues, particularly noting the issues of dating, identification and interpretation. Chapter two will involve a detailed study of the many ancient terms for the synagogues in an effort to gain an initial understanding of the variety of functions of these buildings. Chapters three and four will constitute an exploration of the synagogues' origins and development in Palestine and the diaspora, respectively. In these chapters we will examine at length the early site remains which have been identified as synagogues by archaeologists and assess the claims made about these structures. The various synagogue functionaries and functions will be considered in detail in chapters five and six. These in turn will be compared with those of the Temple courts in order to see what degree of correlation existed. In chapter seven, we will treat the evidence for the synagogues of the Essenes, Therapeutae and Samaritans, paying close attention to the peculiarities of these groups.

---

[95]Kasher, "Synagogues as 'Houses of Prayer' and 'Holy Places' in the Jewish Communities of Hellenistic and Roman Egypt," 218.

A concluding chapter will sum up the results of the study and explore briefly its implications for research on both the evolution of the synagogues in the Rabbinic period and the formation and evolution of the Christian *ekklēsia.*

CHAPTER 1
SOURCES

In this chapter we turn to an initial treatment of the primary sources of our study. As outlined in the introduction, these sources are of three types: literary, inscriptionary and architectural. At this point, our purpose is not to launch an in-depth exploration of specific pieces of evidence dealing with synagogues, but to lay the groundwork for such an investigation. Thus in this chapter we will not go through each source citation by citation. Instead we will be content to highlight potential pitfalls of a more general nature that will later guide our more specific discussion. Within the present investigation, we will be concerned with the three crucial issues of *dating*, *identification*, and *interpretation*.

We have already addressed the importance of the first of these issues in the preceding chapter. There we saw that 70 C.E. served as a pivotal year in Jewish history since both the centralized cult and the high priestly leadership ceased to exist in the aftermath of Titus' conquest of Jerusalem. Because the events of 70 C.E. may have had wide-reaching implications for the evolution of the synagogues, this year was set as the upper terminus for this study. The materials we will consider within subsequent chapters must therefore be securely dated to this period. In some instances, such as with the writings of Philo, this is easily established. Other cases are more problematic. Undated inscriptions, for example, pose somewhat of a problem since the science of paleography does not provide researchers with as narrow a range of dates as they would like. Similarly, ancient texts are often assigned to dates covering a fairly wide swath. Fortunately, the dating of most of the literary documents pertinent to our study is not under wide dispute. Where controversies exist, we will naturally focus greater attention on this issue.

Documents written after 70 C.E. will merit special consideration. As stated in the previous chapter, only those compositions written within a generation of the Temple's destruction (c. 100 C.E.) will be counted as evidence. Moreover, in order to meet our criteria, these sources must also refer back to the pre-70 era. Consequently, references to synagogues made in the book of Revelation will not be taken up in this study, for although the document was written within our given parameters (probably during the 90s), it nevertheless refers to synagogues as they existed in Asia Minor *after* 70 C.E.[1] In the case of later documents that *do* make reference back to the earlier period, we will explore ways in which these writings might potentially have projected back onto the pre-70 period developments from the later era.

The second of the above issues, that of identification, is particularly prominent in connection with discussions of archaeological remains. Many of the disputes outlined in the preceding chapter revolve around whether or not an excavated structure should be identified as a synagogue building. What sort of criteria do archaeologists employ when making such identifications? Are the given criteria sufficient for securing these claims? Have other possibilities been given due consideration? We will take up questions such as these in this chapter's treatment of archaeological remains.

The issue of identification is not confined to the consideration of ancient architecture. Referents of inscriptions are sometimes difficult to identify. So are some of those found in literary sources. In the next chapter we will deal more specifically with terms used by the ancient authors when making reference to synagogues. Here we will merely raise some of the difficulties surrounding the identification of these terms.

The final issue, that of interpretation, is related to those of dating and identification, since these latter provide the foundation for the former. Nevertheless, interpretation also involves other factors. With regard to ancient literature, of primary concern is the literary character of a document and the biases that might have influenced an ancient writer to present a description in a certain way. Does the genre of the document suggest that the descriptions presented by the author correspond to an objective reality? If so, is there good reason to believe that the author presented a skewed description? For example, was the writer hostile toward the leaders and members of the synagogues? Or was he trying to

---

[1]The dating of Revelation to late in the reign of Domitian (c. 95 C.E.) constitutes the majority position. See Adela Yarbro Collins, "Revelation, Book of" in *ABD* 5.694–708; Elisabeth Schüssler Fiorenza, *The Book of Revelation: Justice and Judgment* (Philadelphia: Fortress Press, 1985); Leonard Thompson, *The Book of Revelation: Apocalypse and Empire* (New York: Oxford University Press, 1990); Charles H. Talbert, *The Apocalypse* (Louisville, Kentucky: Westminster John Knox Press, 1994), 8–9. For a dating prior to 70 C.E., see J. Massyngberde Ford, *Revelation* (New York: Doubleday, 1975), 50–56.

curry favor? In short, did the author have any vested interest in tailoring a description in a certain way?

Inscriptions come with their own set of interpretive problems not unrelated to those of literary documents. With these, one might ask: does the inscription contain formulaic language important to our understanding of the monument? Does it make exaggerated claims or understate certain aspects which might be of relevance? Similarly with architectural remains: Were the builders of a structure under certain constraints? How might matters such as geography, availability of material, and function have played a part in a design?

Finding the answers to questions such as these helps the interpreter to compensate for certain circumstances and biases connected with a particular piece of evidence. The results of such analyses might not always be conclusive, but they nevertheless might shift the probabilities in favor of a particular view. At the very least, posing such questions raises the possibility of other interpretations that might not emerge from a less critical reading of the data.

Our consideration of the foregoing questions and issues will commence with an examination of the various literary sources containing probable references to synagogues. We will then turn to problems connected with the use of synagogue inscriptions. Finally, we will examine the issues surrounding early synagogue remains.

Literary Sources

3 Maccabees[2]

As many as four synagogue references may be found in 3 Maccabees. The book was composed by a Jewish author in a flowery style of Greek suggestive of an Alexandrian provenance, a hypothesis confirmed by the narrative itself, which focuses much of its attention on events represented as taking place in Alexandria and its environs. On the basis of vocabulary and literary style, the work is typically dated to early in the first century B.C.E.[3]

---

[2]For general discussions see, e.g., H. Anderson, "3 Maccabees" in *OTP* 2.509–529; *HJP* 3.537–542; and M. Hadas, *The Third and Fourth Book of Maccabees* (New York: Harper, 1953), 1–27.

[3]All attempts to link the production of 3 Maccabees to a specific historical event (e.g., Gaius' attempt to set up an image in the Temple in 40 C.E.) have failed on the lack of clear historical referents. The first-century B.C.E. date is assigned on the basis

The narrative begins with Ptolemy IV Philopater's defeat of Antiochus III at Raphia (217 B.C.E.). Afterwards, Philopater visits the Jerusalem Temple, offers sacrifices and then demands to enter the sanctuary. When he meets with resistance from the priests and the people, he threatens the residents of Jerusalem with death. Following a long prayer offered by the high priest, God strikes Philopater with a temporary paralysis so that he is unable to carry out his threats. Returning to Egypt, he vents his wrath on the Jews there by denying them access to their "sanctuaries" (ἱερά) unless they offer sacrifice to Dionysus. When most of the Jews refuse and continue to frequent their "places" (τόποι), Philopater plots to have elephants trample them to death in the Schedian hippodrome. Eleazar, a respected local priest, then prays a long prayer on behalf of his people. Again God intervenes by sending two angels who turn back the elephants and transform the king's wrath to pity. He repents of his plans and becomes a benefactor of the Jews. Seven days of feasting ensues, all at Philopater's expense. He then gives the Jews permission to slaughter those among them who had apostatized themselves by offering sacrifices to the pagan deity. Some three hundred are put to death, and a second seven-day festival is inaugurated to mark their deliverance. At the conclusion of the festival, a "place of prayer" (προσευχή) is dedicated at the festival site in Ptolemais, and the Jews return to their homes.

While on the surface 3 Maccabees appears to recount historical events, it should nevertheless be understood as one of the historical romances that flourished during the Hellenistic and later periods. These romantic works typically embellished events in the lives of historical characters by weaving together a plot wherein a conflict develops only to be relieved in the climax by the intervention of the gods. The Jewish book *Joseph and Aseneth*, which takes up the problem of Joseph's marriage to the daughter of an Egyptian priest (Gen 41:45), is another example of this genre. Non-Jewish examples include Chariton's *Chaereas and Calirrhoe*, Xenophon's *Ephesiaca*, and Achilles Tatius' *Cleitophron and Leucippe*. Although most of the "events" of these romances were understood by both reader and author as being fictitious, the setting of the works nevertheless incorporated elements assumed to be understood by the audience. As Christine Thomas writes, "Part of the pleasure of reading [romances] is recognizing what one already knows; the authors played on

of certain similarities of vocabulary and grammatical structure found in writings of the same period. See Anderson, "3 Maccabees," 510–512.

preexisting assumptions to create audience appeal."[4] Consequently, much of the "furniture" of 3 Maccabees would have been familiar to the early readers because such trappings actually existed in their external world. This observation is important to our investigation since 3 Maccabees employs three terms for the early synagogues attested in other early sources.[5] In its use of these terms, 3 Maccabees thus draws on the experiences of the intended audience in order to lend the narrative movement and plausibility.

Beyond functioning as an entertainment piece, the more specific purpose of 3 Maccabees has been a matter of some debate. On the one side, H. Anderson has maintained that the book had a twofold function:

> [it was written], on the one hand, to edify and encourage the faithful within the fold of his own people, and, on the other hand, to commend them to outsiders as a "special people" and to defend and justify their mode and quality of life, their religious sensitivities, and their continuing religious observances.[6]

David Williams has recently challenged both of these conclusions.[7] He points out that 3 Maccabees can hardly be seen as catering to a non-Jewish audience, since it contains much material that would have been offensive to Gentiles (e.g., 4:1; 6:9, 11, 12). As for serving the resident Alexandrian Jewish audience, Williams argues that there are no clear indicators that the work was written to bolster the faith of Jews facing a specific crisis situation. His own view is that 3 Maccabees functioned as an apologetic work which sought to counteract Palestinian suspicions that the Alexandrian Jews had fallen prey to religious syncretism. Hence Alexandrian Jews, like their Palestinian counterparts, are portrayed as being faithful even in the face of persecution. Moreover, just as Philopater threatened the sanctity of the Jerusalem Temple, he is also portrayed as threatening the Alexandrian synagogues. Despite these threats, most of the Alexandrian Jews remained faithful and continued to frequent their synagogues. Those few Jews who apostatized themselves

---

[4]Christine M. Thomas, "At Home in the City of Artemis" in *Ephesos: Metropolis of Asia*, edited by Helmut Koester (Valley Forge, Pennsylvania: Trinity Press International, 1995), 84.

[5]3 Macc 7:20 (προσευχή), 2:28 (ἱερόν), 3:29, 4:18 (τόπος). Other sources using these terms will be discussed in depth in the next chapter.

[6]Anderson, "3 Maccabees," 513.

[7]David S. Williams, *3 Maccabees:* A Defense of Diaspora Judaism?" *Journal for the Study of the Pseudepigrapha* 13 (1995): 17–29.

are put to death at the end of the narrative. On top of this, the Alexandrian Jews are depicted as keeping the *kashrut* laws (3:4), praying (5:7–9), offering thanks to God (6:29) and erecting a synagogue in God's honor (7:20). Because of their faithfulness, they too are delivered from the wrath of Philopater, just as were their Palestinian counterparts. Williams concludes by suggesting that:

> the author of [3 Maccabees] appears to provide an apologetic designed to convey the message that Palestinian Jewry and Diaspora Jewry constitute a corporate entity, and to show that God approves of both sectors. Thus, the book closes by stating: "Blessed be the Deliverer of *Israel* through all times!" (7:23).[8]

This attractive interpretation has the benefit of explaining why the action begins in Palestine and then shifts to Egypt. If we accept this view, then 3 Maccabees should be seen as an attempt to cement the relationship between Egyptian and Palestinian Jews. From this one document, we cannot say for certain how widespread this interest was among Egyptian Jews. In fact, if 3 Maccabees functioned as an apology, then the situation in Egypt was certainly not as rosy as the narrative suggests. Nevertheless, even a historical romance had to have some semblance of plausibility. Otherwise, it would cease to be a romance and instead be classified as a satire—and there are hardly indicators of that in 3 Maccabees. Thus it would appear that some identifiable segment of Alexandrian Jewry in this period was deeply committed to the Torah and viewed itself in solidarity with the priestly leadership in Jerusalem. Moreover, in the view of the author of 3 Maccabees, the Egyptian synagogues functioned for the faithful as centers of piety and monuments of God's benevolence—just as the Temple functioned in this manner for the Jews living in Jerusalem.

The Writings of Philo[9]

Philo is one of our most important sources of information about Second Temple synagogues: his writings contain more than two dozen

---

[8]Williams, "*3 Maccabees*," 29. Emphasis in original.

[9]For general discussions see, e.g., P. Borgen, "Philo of Alexandria" in *Jewish Writings of the Second Temple Period*, edited by Michael E. Stone (Philadelphia: Fortress Press, 1984), 233–282; and Jenny Morris, "The Jewish Philosopher Philo" in *HJP* 3.809–889. Also, *ANRW* II.21.1 contains thirteen substantial essays devoted to the writings of Philo.

references to them. Additionally, he is our sole source of information about the Therapeutae, and he has some valuable things to say about the Essenes as well. Finally, the form of many of Philo's works may correspond to that of homilies preached in the Alexandrian synagogues.

Unfortunately, not much is known about Philo's personal life. He was born in Alexandria to a prominent Jewish family in the second half of the first century B.C.E. Josephus states that Philo's brother, Alexander, was an alabarch (customs official) who was wealthy enough to lend King Agrippa I 200,000 drachmae.[10] According to Josephus, this same Alexander had the Temple gates decorated with gold and silver.[11] Alexander's son, Tiberius Julius Alexander, turned apostate in order to advance his career within the imperial ranks. He went on to become one of the procurators of Judea and later prefect of Egypt. Josephus writes that he suppressed a Jewish uprising in Alexandria just prior to the Jewish War. Later, Alexander became one of Titus' advisors during the siege of Jerusalem.[12]

As for Philo himself, when he was advanced in years he was deemed worthy to lead the Jewish delegation to Gaius (40 C.E.), as we saw in the last chapter.[13] Despite his great knowledge of both Greek philosophy and Jewish law, Philo does not appear to have been from a priestly family. Jerome's statement to the contrary has absolutely no support from early sources.[14] Moreover, Philo's own writings about the activities of the Temple seem quite "bookish" and do not always square with those of Josephus (who was a priest). Consequently, there is little to substantiate Jerome's late assertion.[15]

---

[10]Josephus, *Ant.* 18.159–160.

[11]Josephus, *BJ* 5.205.

[12]Josephus, *BJ* 2.220, 223, 309, 492–493; 4.616–618; 5.45, 205, 510; 6.237, 242; *Ant.* 20.100–103. See also Philo's dialogue about a dissertation written by the younger Alexander over the rationality of animals in *De animalibus. De Providentia* represents a dialogue between Philo and Alexander over the presence of providence in the world.

[13]Recounted in Philo's *Legatio ad Gaium.* See also Josephus, *Ant.* 18.259.

[14]Jerome, *De vir. ill.* 11.

[15]*Contra* the attempt made to resurrect the credibility of Jerome's claim in Daniel R. Schwartz, "Philo's Priestly Descent" in *Nourished with Peace: Studies in Hellenistic Judaism in Memory of Samuel Sandmel*, edited by Burton L. Mack et al. (Chico, Calif.: Scholars Press, 1984), 155–171. Schwartz argues that Jerome's use of "priestly family" (*genere sacerdotum*) would not have underscored Philo's importance as a source (157–160). Then, however, he turns around and argues that priests were among the leading notables in Alexandria, thus contradicting his earlier argument (160–162). On Philo's lack of knowledge of the Jerusalem Temple and its cult, see I. Heinemann, "Philo von Alexandrien" in PWSup 20.1, col. 3.

Philo wrote exclusively in Greek and probably had little knowledge of Aramaic or Hebrew—at least his extant writings do not betray that he was fluent in either language.[16] His Bible was not the Hebrew text, but the Septuagint, which he believed was a divinely inspired translation of the original.[17] Despite the language barrier and the influence of Stoic and Platonic thought on his writings, Philo nevertheless remained socially and spiritually connected to Palestine. As we saw in the previous chapter, he made pilgrimages to Jerusalem, perhaps annually.[18] He revered the Temple and its cult and commended its leaders to his audience.

Because Philo died sometime in the 40s, we do not have to worry about anachronism (except, of course, when he comments on the early biblical period). However, in his writings we may encounter provincialism: the tendency to express the affairs of other regions in the categories of one's own province. Moreover, we cannot generalize that Philo's allegorical methods of interpretation held wide currency in Palestine or, for that matter, in Alexandria itself. Nevertheless, they were representative of at least one segment of Alexandrian Jewry and may have been influential elsewhere.

The extant Philonic corpus is voluminous, numbering thirty-six works, some of which have been only partially preserved. A few texts exist only in Latin or Armenian translations. The bulk of Philo's compositions are allegorical commentaries on the Pentateuch. These have been classified according to three types:[19] (1) works which present a question-and-answer format (e.g., *Quaestiones et Solutiones*), (2) works which provide a verse-by-verse commentary on a segment of scripture (e.g., *De migratione Abrahami* on Gen 12:1–6), and (3) works attempting to systematize the Mosaic laws (e.g., *De specialibus legibus*). Included under this last category are writings which deal with the laws indirectly through an exploration of the virtues of one of the biblical patriarchs such as Abraham (*De Abrahamo*) or Moses (*De vita Mosis*). Generically, these are classified as Greco-Roman biographies, works which focus on the lives of famous heroes. Non-Jewish examples include Isocrates' *Evangoras* (IV B.C.E.) and Xenophon's *Agesilaus* (IV B.C.E.). Although all of the Pentateuchal commentaries are heavily steeped in allegorical interpretations, occasionally Philo breaks out of this mode and provides

---

[16]See Borgen, "Philo of Alexandria," 257, n. 131.

[17]Philo, *Mos.* 2.26–44.

[18]Philo, *Prov.* 2.64.

[19]Morris, "The Jewish Philosopher Philo," 825–856.

illustrations from personal experiences. It is from passages such as these that we find occasional references to synagogues.

Of greater importance to our enterprise are the non-allegorical works, some of which provide descriptions of situations from Philo's own time. Chief among these are the accounts of the clashes between the Alexandrian Jews and Greeks in 38 C.E. (*In Flaccum*) and the subsequent embassy to Rome, which we have already encountered (*Legatio ad Gaium*). While these works are clearly apologetic, they nevertheless provide an important perspective with regard to the synagogues, since these were the focus of the Greek attacks. Because Philo was personally involved with the events described in these two books, they constitute valuable historical sources for our understanding of the synagogues in Egypt, Rome and elsewhere.

Three other thematic works furnish important information about two Jewish sectarian groups. In *De vita contemplativa*, Philo presents the Therapeutae as illustrative of the contemplative life *par excellence*. Consequently, his description is idealized, overplaying the single-hearted devotedness of the group. The same can be said of the brief treatments given the Essenes in *Quod omnis probus liber* and *Hypothetica*, the second of which is preserved only as a fragment in Eusebius' *Praeparatio Evangelica*.[20] Despite their brevity, when these two treatments are combined with the material remains from the Qumran excavations and with passages from Josephus and the Dead Sea scrolls, we obtain a considerable amount of data about the Essenes. Moreover, the sources can be compared with one another critically. Unfortunately, the same cannot be said in the case of the Therapeutae, although Geza Vermes has argued that this sect bore a close affinity to the Essenes and might be considered a sub-group.[21]

Pseudo-Philo's *Biblical Antiquities*[22]

This document, also known as *Liber Antiquitatum Biblicarum*, currently exists only in Latin translation. The original was most likely

---

[20]Though a few scholars previously questioned the Philonic authorship of *Hypothetica*, it is now generally accepted. See *HJP* 3.866–868; Borgen, "Philo of Alexandria," 247.

[21]G. Vermes, "Essene and Therapeutai," *RevQ* 3 (1962): 494–504.

[22]Discussions include: *HJP* 3.1.325–331; D. J. Harrington, "Pseudo-Philo" in *OTP*, 297–377; Howard Jacobson, *A Commentary of Pseudo-Philo's Liber Antiquitatum Biblicarum*, 2 vols. (Leiden; New York: E.J. Brill, 1996).

written in Hebrew and then translated into Greek before being rendered into Latin. The use of Hebrew in the original text and the familiarity of the work with the geography of Palestine has led to the assignment of a Palestinian origin. The book constitutes a retelling of the history of Israel, from the creation of Adam up to the reign of David. While incorporating biblical texts, it nevertheless expands and contracts different parts of the biblical narrative. In this respect, it resembles *Jubilees*, 4 Ezra and 2 Baruch, although none of the apocalyptic features of these three works appear in *Biblical Antiquities*. Nor can the book be linked with certainty to any sectarian group. Unlike *1 Enoch* and *Jubilees*, it has not been recovered in one of the Qumran caves. Rather, it appears to be a compendium of various popular legends woven into the framework of a continuous biblical narrative. Thus D. Harrington characterizes the composition "as a witness to the understanding of the Bible in the Palestinian synagogues prior to A.D. 70 and as a link to the material later gathered in the traditional midrashic compilations."[23] Although there is no sure connection between *Biblical Antiquities* and the synagogues of Palestine, this seems a reasonable hypothesis. Given the tenuousness of this proposition, however, this study will refer only to a single passage in *Biblical Antiquities*—one that attests to the importance of communal prayer on the Sabbath in the Second Temple period.

The nature of the preceding claim requires that a pre-70 dating of the book be established. We have already seen that Harrington assigns a date before the fall of the Temple. Vermes shares this opinion.[24] Recently, however, Howard Jacobson has argued for a second century C.E. date for this document.[25] He has two main arguments for this position. First, he notes that in *Biblical Antiquities* 19:7, God is portrayed as saying to Moses:

> I will show you the place where [Israel] will serve me for 740 years. And after this it will be turned over into the hands of their enemies, and they will destroy it, and foreigners will encircle it. And it will be on that day as it was on the day I smashed the tablets of the covenant that I drew up for you on Horeb; and when they sinned, what was written on them flew away. Now that day was the seventeenth day of the fourth month [Tammuz 17].[26]

---

[23]Harrington, "Pseudo-Philo," 302.

[24]*HJP* 3.1.329.

[25]See Jacobson, *A Commentary of Pseudo-Philo's Liber Antiquitatum Biblicarum*, 1.199–210.

[26]Harrington's translation. Jacobson emends the text to read "440 years."

Jacobson takes this to be a reference to the destruction of the Temple in 70 C.E. since the biblical text states that Nebuchadrezzar breached the walls of Jerusalem on the *ninth* day of the fourth month (Tammuz 9; Jer 39:2, 52:6–7) rather than the seventeenth (Tammuz 17). This claim is based on the fact that Josephus and some later Rabbinic sources give Tammuz 17 as a day *connected* to the fall of Jerusalem in 70 C.E.[27] Yet if we actually turn to Josephus, we see that Tammuz 17 was neither the day that the Temple was destroyed nor the city walls breached, events implied in the above quotation; rather, it was the day that the foundations of the Antionia fortress were razed and the daily sacrifices ceased. The Temple itself was not destroyed until the tenth of the following month (Ab 10)—a day corresponding to Nebuchadrezzar's burning of the first Temple, a coincidence noted by Josephus (*BJ* 6.249–251; cf. Jer 52:12).[28] A second point is that, in the earliest of the Rabbinic traditions cited as evidence by Jacobson, *m. Ta'anith* 4.6, there are strong indications that Tammuz 17 was associated with the capture of Jerusalem not by Titus, but by Nebuchadrezzar:

> Five things befell our fathers on the 17th of Tammuz and five on the 9th of Ab. On the 17th of Tammuz the Tables [of the Ten Commandments] were broken, and the Daily Whole-offering ceased, and the City was breached, and Apostomus burnt the [Scrolls of the] Law, and an idol was set up in the Sanctuary. On the 9th of Ab it was decreed against our fathers that they should not enter into the Land [of Israel], and the Temple was destroyed the first and the second time, and Beth-Tor was captured and the City was plowed up.[29]

Here we should note that both lists of five are clearly given in chronological order.[30] The reference to the ceasing of the daily offering

---

[27]Josephus, *BJ* 6.93–94; *m. Ta'anit* 4.6, *Seder Olam Rabbah* 6.

[28]We also see a certain looseness with regard to specific dates. For example, 2 Kings 25:8 gives the date of Nebuchadrezzar's destruction of the first Temple as Ab 7. The date assigned in the rabbinic literature for both destructions is Ab 9 (see the following quotation of *m. Ta'anit* 4.6).

[29]Translation, Herbert Danby, trans., *The Mishnah*, (Oxford: Clarendon Press, 1933).

[30]First group of five: (1) the smashing of the tablets by Moses (Ex 32:19), (2) the ceasing of the daily sacrifice under Nebuchadrezzar (Jer 52:6), (3) the breaching of the walls of Jerusalem by Nebuchadrezzar (Jer 52:7), (4) Some otherwise unknown incident involving the burning of sacred scrolls by Apostomus, one of Antiochus IV's generals (1 Mac 1:56?), (5) the placement of the idol in the Temple by Antiochus IV (1 Macc 1:54). Second group: (1) the Israelites prohibited from entering the promised

in the first list is probably an inference drawn from Jer 52:6, “On the ninth day of the fourth month the famine [during Nebuchadrezzar’s siege] became so severe in the city that there was no food for the people of the land.” The very next verse in Jeremiah states that “a breach was made in the city wall”—language identical to that found in the above passage from the Mishnah.[31] Since the subsequent references in the first of the above lists refer to events from the Maccabean period, the earlier reference to the breaching of the walls cannot have meant the destruction of Jerusalem by the Romans—otherwise it would have been placed last in the list. While we cannot secure a pre-70 date for the above saying,[32] the fact remains that a tradition connecting Tammuz 17 with Nebuchadrezzar’s breach of Jerusalem’s walls was in circulation in Palestine at least as early as the second century C.E., while there is an absence of an early association between this date and either Jerusalem’s capture or the Temple’s destruction in 70 C.E. Consequently, there is no compelling reason to read *Biblical Antiquities* 19:7 as a reference to the Second Temple’s destruction. This is particularly the case when one notices nothing else in 19:7 suggesting two destructions. Moreover, the figure of 740 years given in the verse seems to be a reference to the number of years that the Israelites were in Palestine up until the Babylonian exile.[33]

Jacobson’s second argument runs as follows:

---

land (Num 14:29ff), (2) the destruction of the Temple by Nebuchadrezzar (Jer 52:10), (3) the destruction of the Temple by Titus, (4) the defeat of Bar Kochba at Bittir, (5) Hadrian’s transformation of Jerusalem into Aelia Capitolina.

[31]*m. Ta’anith* 4.6: והוּבְקְעָה הָעִיר “and the city was breached”; Jer 52:7: הָעִיר וַתִּבָּקַע “and the city was breached.”

[32]Neusner assigns the saying to the Ushan period (140–170 C.E.), a natural inference given the reference in the passage to the Bar Kokhba revolt (*A History of the Mishnaic Law of Appointed Times*, 5.172). The segments connecting Tammuz 17 with Nebuchadrezzar’s capture of Jerusalem may date earlier.

[33]Josephus gives figures of 1062 years (*Ant.* 10.147) and 1082 years (*Ant.* 20.230, *Ap.* 2.19) between the Exodus and the Babylonian destruction of Jerusalem. Most commentators assume the 740 years begins with the building of the Temple in the time of Solomon. Yet the verse seems better understood as a reference to the period between Joshua’s conquest and the exile: sacrificial worship in Israel (suggested by the Latin *in quo mihi servient* in 19:7) did not begin with the building of the Temple, but commenced as soon as Joshua’s conquest had been completed. *Biblical Antiquities* may have compressed the number of years that the Judges ruled over Israel to arrive at a figure lower than those offered by Josephus. An example of such compression is the figure of 850 years given in *Seder Olam Rabbah* 11.

> At [*Bib. Ant.*] 26.13 God tells Cenez that when the Temple (i.e. Solomon's Temple, as is clear from 26.12) will fall, both the miraculous new stones and the old ones (i.e. those of the priestly breastplate) will be removed by God and not be restored till eschatological times. But if [*Biblical Antiquities*] were writing while the second Temple was still standing, it is unlikely that he would declare that the priestly stones were taken by God at the destruction of the first Temple, not to be returned till eschatological times. For he (and his audience) would have been aware that the priestly stones were in fact intact and in place during the second Temple period, though they no longer functioned as of old.[34]

The problem with this argument is that there were stories floating around pre-70 Palestine that the original vessels and appointments of the first Temple were being kept by God. For example, 2 Maccabees 2:5–8 states:

> Jeremiah came and found a cave-dwelling, and he brought there the tent and the ark and the altar of incense; then he sealed up the entrance. Some of those who followed him came up intending to mark the way, but could not find it. When Jeremiah learned of it, he rebuked them and declared: "The place shall remain unknown until God gathers his people together again and shows his mercy. Then the Lord will disclose these things, and the glory of the Lord and the cloud will appear, as they were shown in the case of Moses, and as Solomon asked that the place should be specially consecrated."

Similarly, Josephus records that during the governorship of Pilate a certain Samaritan led a group to Mt. Gerizim, promising that upon their arrival at the top "he would show them the sacred vessels which were buried there, where Moses had deposited them" (*Ant.* 18.85). Given the presence of legends such as these, it is therefore *not* very strange that *Biblical Antiquities* would hold that the priestly stones of the first Temple were hidden by God, even though other stones were being employed in an existing (second) Temple.[35]

On the positive side of the argument for a pre-70 dating, it should be noted that every substantive Jewish document from the post-70 period makes clear reference to the destruction of the Temple by the Romans

---

[34] Jacobson, *A Commentary of Pseudo-Philo's Liber Antiquitatum Biblicarum*, 1.206.

[35] It should be noted that just because Josephus may have believed that the priestly stones were the originals does not mean that everyone shared this view (*Ant.* 3.216–218). His statement that the stones had ceased to shine two-hundred years prior to his writing of *Antiquities* may even hint at the existence of other explanations as to why the stones did not shine like the ones of old (*Ant.* 3.218).

(e.g., 4 Ezra, 2 Baruch, the Mishnah). Yet this is not the case in *Biblical Antiquities.* As Vermes observes: "It might well be asked whether a Palestinian Jewish book written during the last decades of the first century A.D. would not reveal some more obvious traces of the impact of the great national catastrophe."[36] The absence of any such indicators, combined with an attitude within the text that the cult still functioned (e.g., 22:8), makes it probable that *Biblical Antiquities* was produced prior to the Temple's destruction in 70 C.E.

The Writings of Josephus[37]

Josephus is yet another important source for this study, as his writings contain over two dozen synagogue references. Particularly valuable are his preservation of a number of imperial decrees regarding the status of synagogues located in various cities in Asia Minor. Equally important are his references to synagogues in Syria, Egypt, Galilee and Judea. Finally, he gives useful descriptions of the activities of the Essenes.

From his own writings we know a great deal about Josephus' life, though the self-descriptions are typically romanticized, as one might expect. Josephus was born in Jerusalem in either 37 or 38 C.E. to an aristocratic priestly family (*Vita* 2, 5). Rather bombastically, Josephus writes that by age fourteen, "the chief priests and the leading men of the city used constantly to come to me for precise information on some particular in our ordinances" (*Vita* 9). According to his account, when he was sixteen he undertook a personal investigation of the philosophies of the Pharisees, Sadducees, and Essenes. He also claims to have spent three years in the wilderness with a certain Bannus, an ascetic hermit (*Vita* 11). At age nineteen, he finally decided to govern his life according to the rule of the Pharisees, "a sect having points of resemblance to that which the Greeks call the Stoic school" (*Vita* 12). He visited Rome in his twenty-sixth year (64 C.E.) in order to plead before Nero the case of some fellow priests who had been imprisoned "on a slight and trifling charge" (*Vita*

---

[36]*HJP* 3.1.329.

[37]For general treatments, see *HJP* 1.43–63; H.W. Attridge, "Josephus and His Works" in *Jewish Writings of the Second Temple Period*, edited by Michael E. Stone (Philadelphia: Fortress Press, 1984), 185–232; Tessa Rajak, *Josephus* (Philadelphia: Fortress Press, 1983); S. J. D. Cohen, *Josephus in Galilee and Rome: His Vita and Development as a Historian* (Leiden: Brill, 1979); Per Bilde, *Flavius Josephus between Jerusalem and Rome* (Sheffield, England: JSOT Press, 1988). See also the essays in *ANRW* II.21.2.

13). Only two years later at the outbreak of the war with Rome (66 C.E.) he was given command of the defensive forces in Galilee (*Vita* 28–29, *BJ* 2.568ff). After enduring a series of Roman victories, Josephus was finally captured following the fall of Jotapata in 67. Vespasian spared his life because of Josephus' prophecy that the general was destined to become the Roman emperor. Thereafter, Josephus served as a guide and translator for the Romans up until the fall of Jerusalem. For his services, Vespasian, who had indeed gone on to become emperor, rewarded Josephus with plots of land around Jerusalem and an apartment in Rome, where he lived for the remainder of his life.

Turning his focus toward literary activities, Josephus first produced *War* (*Bellum Judaicum*), a detailed account of the Jewish War in seven books. Later, he wrote a twenty-volume work, *Antiquities* (*Antiquitates Judaicae*), which presents a history of the Jewish people from the creation of Adam up until the war with Rome. Josephus attached to this work his auto-biography, *Life* (*Vita*), which served as an apology against attacks made against him by Justus of Tiberias, a Jew who had challenged Josephus' authority during the war. The last of Josephus' compositions, *Against Apion* (*Contra Apion*), was written to counter a number of anti-Semitic ideas promulgated by several Greek and Egyptian authors. All of these works were composed in Greek, *War* with the help of assistants (*Ap*. 1.50). The audience for all of these works was primarily Gentile, though certainly with an awareness that Jews might also read his works. Josephus died around the year 100 C.E.

Although it was common earlier in the century to disparage the accuracy of Josephus' accounts, recent archaeological work in Israel has vindicated many of the historian's descriptions, though they are by no means flawless.[38] In *War* and *Antiquities*, Josephus wrote self-consciously as a Greco-Roman historian, intending to correct what he saw to be the erroneous accounts of Greek historians and pundits, all the while promising his readers that he would present a factual account of the events, based upon either his own participation in the events or his careful research of ancient and recent sources. Both of these intents are explicitly stated in the prologue of *War*, where Josephus writes:

---

[38]See Magen Broshi, "The Credibility of Josephus," *JJS* 33 (1982): 379–384. For a chronicle of the movement towards a more positive evaluation of Josephus, see Bilde, *Flavius Josephus*, 123–171.

> The industrious writer is not one who merely remodels the scheme and arrangement of another's work, but one who uses fresh materials and makes the framework of the history his own. For myself, at a vast expenditure of money and pains, I, a foreigner, present to Greeks and Romans this memorial of great achievements [i.e., *War*]. As for the native Greeks, where personal profit or lawsuit is concerned, their mouths are at once agape and their tongues loosed; but in the matter of history, where veracity and laborious collection of the facts are essential, they are mute, leaving to inferior and ill-informed writers the task of describing the exploits of their rulers. Let us at least hold historical truth in honour, since by the Greeks it is disregarded (*BJ* 15–16).

Of course, such locutions were almost formulaic in the introductions of Greco-Roman histories (cf. Luke 1:1–4), where they served to underscore both the accuracy of the ensuing account and the credentials of the author. Despite this fact, Josephus nonetheless appears to have approached his task diligently and thoughtfully. In *War* he relied not only on his own personal experiences in the conflict, but also on imperial commentaries (*Vita* 342, 358), which recorded various events, figures and geographical descriptions. He also made extensive use of sources in *Antiquities*, where he draws on both the Septuagint and the Hebrew text for the early parts of his narrative, and upon the writings of Jewish historians such as Nicolaus of Damascus (one of Herod the Great's courtiers) and Cleodemus Malchus (*Ant.* 1.240) for later details. In his use of such sources, Josephus sometimes displays a degree of sophistication that seems almost modern. For example, commenting on one of Nicolaus' accounts, Josephus writes:

> For since [Nicolaus] lived in Herod's realm and was one of his associates, he wrote to please him and to be of service to him, dwelling only on those things that redounded to his glory, and transforming his obviously unjust acts into the opposite or concealing them with the greatest care (*Ant.* 16.184–85).

Along these same lines he elsewhere states:

> We have said nothing more than what is true, and have not, by inserting into the history various plausible and seductive passages meant to deceive and entertain, attempted to evade critical inquiry, asking to be instantly believed; nor should we be indulgently held blameless if we depart from what is proper to a historical narrative; on the contrary, we ask that no hearing be given us unless we are able to establish the truth with demonstrations and convincing evidence (*Ant.* 8.56).

From these passages we see that Josephus was not unaware of the problem of individual bias and that he possessed an understanding of the ways one might arbitrate between conflicting reports. He also had some sense as to how customs can change over time, as can be observed from one of his explanatory notes about the time of David: "in ancient times virgins wore long-sleeved tunics reaching to the ankle, in order not to be exposed" (*Ant.* 7.171).

Of course, his awareness of the dangers of bias and anachronism did not exempt Josephus from falling prey to them. This is most easily seen when comparing Josephus' narrative of biblical history with the biblical texts themselves. For example, in his account of the giving of the law at Mt. Sinai Josephus omits the story of the golden calf—probably out of fear of giving his Greek opponents ammunition for their belief that Moses was an apostate Egyptian priest (*Ant.* 3.99).

Most notable in Josephus' writings are apologetic tendencies that run in several different directions. In *War* and *Life*, Josephus is clearly concerned to justify both his competence as a general and his decision to throw his support over to the Romans. Consequently, in *War* he transforms his own efforts in Galilee into heroic deeds and attributes his change of heart regarding the Romans to a visionary experience (*BJ* 3.351). *Life* takes a different tack, with Josephus there portraying himself as a responsible aristocrat attempting to mitigate the effects of a disastrous war brought on by his villainous Jewish opponents. A second apologetic tendency is identical to the one which Josephus identified in the writings of Nicolaus of Damascus: the glorification of one's patrons. Here, because *War* was written for the Flavians, Josephus goes to great lengths to lionize the deeds of Vespasian and Titus, while at the same time mitigating their responsibilities for Roman atrocities committed during the war. The tendencies of *Antiquities* and *Against Apion* run in yet a third direction, for in these works he tries to justify the antiquity of the Jewish nation and the nobility of the Jewish way of life. As a result, he often tries to shine the best possible light on Jewish history and traditions.

To maintain that Josephus always sorted his accounts to conform with the tendencies just noted is, however, too simplistic a position. Despite the presence of a certain amount of rationalization in his work, Josephus nevertheless frequently reports incidents that are embarrassing to both Romans and Jews. For example, Josephus attributes the outbreak of the Jewish war in part to the incompetence of the Roman procurators, not hesitating to point out their many vices (*BJ* 2:223–278). He also does not hold back from criticizing the behavior of both the Jewish aristocracy (*Vita* 189–194) and the various factions involved in the war (*BJ* 4.147–154). Consequently, his promise in *Antiquities* 1.7 neither to add nor omit important pieces of information from his account is partially borne out in his historical writings (cf. *BJ* 1.24, 26). *Against Apion*, on the other hand, invites greater scrutiny, since it is unabashedly apologetic.

Unfortunately, Josephus apparently was never able to write a projected composition devoted specifically to explaining Jewish customs in a systematic way (*Ant.* 1.25, 4.198). As a consequence, because Josephus was most often involved in recording historical events, references to synagogues in his works typically arise either incidentally or when certain episodes involve the synagogues. While we might dispute Josephus' interpretation of the events taking place in the synagogues, his accompanying descriptions of the synagogues themselves are less prone to criticism. Unlike the modern researcher, Josephus was not interested in demonstrating the existence (or non-existence) of synagogues in a certain locale; he merely mentions them as part of the backdrop of particular incidents, assuming that his readers would understand his references. As we have suggested, the one place where greater scrutiny is in order is in *Against Apion*, where in a few cases Josephus attempts to counter certain slanders about activities that supposedly went on in the synagogues.

What of the problem of anachronism in Josephus' references to the synagogues? Josephus always refers to synagogues as they existed prior to 70 C.E. Most often these references are to incidents that took place during Josephus' lifetime and consequently reflect his own experience of the synagogues. Beyond this, there was very little time for dramatic shifts to have taken place in the case of *War*, which had to have been composed no later than Vespasian's death in 79, since Josephus states that he presented a copy of the work to the Emperor himself (*Vita* 359–361).[39] Moreover, Josephus mentions that his Greek edition of *War* was based on

---

[39]On the suggestion that our present edition of *War* was a later revision, see Attridge, "Josephus," 192–193. Generally, it is maintained that books one through six of our present edition of *War* were written no later than the reign of Titus (d. 81 C.E.). Some have argued that book seven was written—or at least revamped—under the subsequent reign of Domitian since certain passages in this book glorify Domitian (e.g., *BJ* 7.85–88). Such a conclusion is hardly inevitable, however, since Josephus goes out of his way in *War* to curry favor with the other two Flavians. In book seven, with the action switching to Rome, he has an opportunity to do so also with Domitian, who had not been involved in the war in Palestine.

an Aramaic original, which had to have been written even earlier (*BJ* 1.3, 6). *Antiquities*, *Life* and *Against Apion* are dated to the middle 90s and so might potentially be prone to anachronism or even provincialism, since by then Josephus had lived in Rome for over two decades. However, the bulk of the synagogue references from *Antiquities* and *Against Apion* come from either quotations of earlier imperial decrees or the writings of earlier authors. On the basis of form analysis, the authenticity of these quotations has generally been upheld by researchers.[40] *Life* has been taken by many researchers to be a reworking of memoirs written shortly after the war. It contains one section pertinent to our study and might possibly be tainted with anachronism or provincialism, at least to some degree. The greatest danger of anachronism in Josephus' writings, however, is when he attributes customs of his own time to that of Moses or some other ancient period. Fortunately, since we have the biblical texts as a control, we can observe Josephus' redactional tendencies at work and draw appropriate conclusions from a comparative analysis of the texts.

The Dead Sea Scrolls[41]

The discovery of the Dead Sea Scrolls ranks as one of the most prominent archaeological events of the twentieth century. Because of their unearthing, we now know more about the Essenes than any other Jewish group of the Second Temple period. Consequently, the scrolls are of great relevance to this study's treatment of the Essene synagogues.[42]

---

[40]See Bilde, *Flavius Josephus*, 198–199; Tessa Rajak, "Was there a Roman Charter for the Jews?" *JRS* 74 (1984): 107–123. Rajak argues for the general authenticity of the decrees in *Ant.* 14 and 16, but suggests that Josephus may have emended one of the decrees to exaggerate the citizenry claims of the Jews in Alexandria.

[41]Standard references and introductions include: *HJP* 3.380–469; Florentino Garcia Martinez, *The Dead Sea Scrolls Translated* (Leiden: Brill, 1994); James H. Charlesworth, *The Dead Sea Scrolls: Hebrew, Aramaic, and Greek Texts with English Translations*, 10 vols. (Tübingen: J.C.B. Mohr [P. Siebeck]; Louisville: Westminster/John Knox Press, 1994–); James C. VanderKam, *The Dead Sea Scrolls Today* (Grand Rapids, Mich.: Eerdmans, 1994); Lawrence H. Schiffman, *Reclaiming the Dead Sea Scrolls: The History of Judaism, the Background Of Christianity, the Lost Library of Qumran* (Philadelphia: Jewish Publication Society, 1994).

[42]The scrolls have been dated through the use of both paleography and carbon-14 dating. The range of dates extends from III B.C.E. to I C.E., with the earliest materials being non-sectarian. In most cases the paleographic results overlap with those determined by radiocarbon dating. In one case, that of the Testament of Kohath, there

Bedouin shepherds discovered the first seven scrolls in 1947. Since that time, over 700 manuscripts have been found in eleven caves surrounding Khirbet Qumran (Caves I–XI), the site of an abandoned community located on the northwestern corner of the Dead Sea.[43] Also, in 1963, Yigael Yadin's excavations at the Herodian fortress Masada unearthed fragments of the work, *Songs of the Sabbath Sacrifices*, a sectarian composition previously found in Cave IV, just opposite the Qumran ruins.[44]

The archaeological case for connecting the scrolls with the community at Qumran was originally made by Roland de Vaux, the initial excavator of Khirbet Qumran. His conclusions have since been accepted by most researchers. De Vaux upheld the linkage by observing that the pottery in the caves can be dated to the same period as the abandoned site (I C.E.), and, moreover, that inscriptions on ostraca (potsherds) found at Qumran match the style of writing found in the scrolls.[45]

The link between the scrolls and the Essenes has been ascertained through a comparison of the sectarian writings with descriptions of the Essenes found in the writings of Philo and Josephus. Although discrepancies exist between the accounts, the similarities are striking and have convinced most researchers that the Dead Sea sect and the Essenes are one and the same. A description of the Dead Sea area by ancient geographer Pliny the Elder (d. 79 C.E.) has provided additional support for this identification:

---

is a wide discrepancy, with the C-14 method dating the document to IV B.C.E. and paleography to I B.C.E. In this case, the scroll material may have simply been unused for three centuries. See F. M. Cross, "The Development of the Jewish Scripts" in *The Bible and the Ancient Near East: Essays in Honor of W. F. Albright*, edited by G. E. Wright (Garden City, N.Y.: Doubleday, 1961), 133–202; G. Bonani et al., "Radiocarbon Dating of the Dead Sea Scrolls," *Atiqot* 20 (1991): 27–32. For a summary of the results of paleographical analyses, see Schiffman, *Reclaiming the Dead Sea Scrolls*, 32–33.

[43]For a complete catalogue of the scrolls, see Vermes, *The Dead Sea Scrolls in English*, xxxvi–lvi.

[44]See C. A. Newsom and Y. Yadin, "The Masada Fragment of the Qumran *Songs of the Sabbath Sacrifice*," *IEJ* 34 (1984): 77–88.

[45]See Roland de Vaux, *Archaeology and the Dead Sea Scrolls* (Oxford: Oxford University Press, 1973), 102–109. On paleographic grounds, however, de Vaux disputes the connection between the Copper Scroll (3Q15) and the Qumran community (ibid., 108–109).

> On the west side of the Dead Sea, but out of range of the noxious exhalations of the coast, is the solitary tribe of the Essenes, which is remarkable beyond all the other tribes in the whole world, as it has no women and has renounced all sexual desire, has no money, and has only palm-trees for company. Day by day the throng of refugees is recruited to an equal number by numerous accessions of persons tired of life and driven thither by the waves of fortune to adopt their manners (*NH* 5.73).

Although Pliny's last comment about the recruitment of war refugees conflicts with archaeological evidence dating the destruction of Khirbet Qumran to 68 C.E., most scholars believe that Pliny was referring to the community located at Qumran.[46]

Researchers typically classify the non-biblical scrolls among four categories of which only the first three are relevant to the current study: (1) community rules, (2) biblical interpretation, (3) hymns and liturgical texts, and (4) miscellaneous compositions.[47] The first of the categories, community rules, contains five documents. Two of these—the *Community Rule* (1QS) and the *Damascus Document* (CD)—appear to describe rules actually maintained by the sect, while the other three—the *War Rule* (1QM), the *Temple Scroll* (11QT) and the fragmentary *Messianic Rule* (1QSa)—project rules that the sect hoped to enact after regaining control of the Jerusalem Temple. While the *Community Rule* was among the first of the scrolls to be discovered by the Bedouin, copies of the *Damascus Document* had actually been found in the genizah (sacred depository) of the Ben Ezra Synagogue in Cairo by Solomon Schechter in 1896. Although Schechter had tried to link this composition to the Essenes, his

---

[46]On the discrepancies between Pliny's description and the excavated Qumran remains, see VanderKam, *The Dead Sea Scrolls Today*, 71–75. Schiffman is reluctant to accept the identification between the Essenes and the Dead Sea sect. While he notes some discrepancies between the accounts of Josephus, Philo and Pliny, on the one hand, and the Dead Sea sect, on the other, he is unable to overcome the striking similarities between the pictures presented in the two sets of witnesses. See Schiffman, *Reclaiming the Dead Sea Scrolls*, 97–112, 127–143.

[47]The miscellanea from Qumran include horoscopes (4Q186), calendars (4QMishmaroth, 6Q17), and the enigmatic Copper Scroll (3Q15), a document containing directions to sixty-four underground hiding places where treasure hoards—totaling sixty-five tons of silver and twenty-six tons of gold—are reputed to have been buried. Unfortunately, none of the descriptions refer to synagogue buildings. Moreover, on paleographic grounds, J. T. Milik has dated this scroll to 100 C.E., thus placing it beyond the confines of our investigation (M. Baillet, J. T. Milik, and Roland de Vaux, *Les "Petites Grottes" de Qumran* [Oxford: Clarendon Press, 1962], 199–302).

suggestion was not taken seriously until fragments of the document appeared among the Dead Sea scrolls.

As we will explore in more detail in the chapter devoted to sectarian synagogues, the *Community Rule* and the *Damascus Document* conflict at various points and may provide evidence for variations of practice among different groups of Essenes. Although there are only three possible reference in these rules to synagogue *buildings* (CD 11.21–23; 20.10, 13), these documents nevertheless contain directives suggesting the standard practices of the community during congregational gatherings that were likely held in such structures. The remaining three rules are useful for discerning the sect's commitment to sacrificial worship in a restored (earthly) Temple and for their preservation of a liturgical calendar (in 1QT) at odds with the one actually employed in Jerusalem. Also, 1QM possibly contains a reference to a synagogue building (1QM 3.4).

While all of the rules are prescriptive in content, they nevertheless may closely reflect the actual practices of the sect—much less so, of course, in the case of 1QM, 11QT and 1QSa, which project rules into the future. Fortunately, we have some control over the prescriptive nature of these writings since we can compare them to the descriptive accounts of Philo, Josephus and Pliny. Evidence from the archaeological remains of Khirbet Qumran can likewise serve as an important control. Yet because the descriptions in the texts just mentioned might either be idealized or simply mistaken, caution must be used when rendering judgment on the degree of the sect's adherence to its own rules on the basis of a correlation between these sets of texts. While comparison of specific community rules with the archaeological evidence is less susceptible to this problem, other difficulties persist, such as whether a particular rule was to be the norm for the Qumran community or for Essene communities located elsewhere.

Among the examples of biblical interpretation most important to our endeavor are the *Pesharim* (singular, *Pesher*), sectarian commentaries on the Bible. Most often these provide continuous, verse-by-verse interpretation on an entire (usually prophetic) book of scripture: 4Q161–4 (Isaiah), 4Q166–7 (Hosea), 1Q14 (Micah), 4Q169 (Nahum), 1QpHab (Habakkuk), and 4Q171 (Psalms). Other *Pesharim* are arranged topically (11Q13, 4Q174). Unfortunately, all of the *Pesharim* are preserved in a very fragmentary state. Nevertheless, they give us important glimpses of a type of biblical interpretation that probably went on within the congregational gatherings of the Essenes. Moreover, references in these *Pesharim* to events surrounding the formation of the sect have helped scholars to reconstruct the sect's history. The same can be said about the recently released document, the Halakhic Letter (4QMMT), an apology sent by the early Essenes to the high priestly leadership, outlining the differences in the interpretation of biblical purity laws.

Although usually grouped with the biblical materials, the Aramaic Targums (4Q156–157, 11Q10) and the Greek Septuagint fragments (7Q1–5) found in the Qumran caves comprise another, more subtle type of biblical interpretation. While it is difficult to determine in what manner the sectarians made use of these scripture translations, their very presence at Qumran suggests that Aramaic and Greek may have functioned in some capacity in *non*-sectarian synagogues in Palestine.

The hymns and liturgical texts are useful to our project for the light that they shed on the worship practices of the Essenes. Most often, these correspond to prayers or original hymns to be said or sung during festivals or holy days associated with Temple ritual (e.g., 4Q507–509, Prayers for the Festivals). Certain passages in the scrolls (e.g., 1QS 9.1–5) indicate that these prayers and hymns were not being preserved for future use in an Essene-controlled Temple, but were employed in the regular worship of the sectarian community. Of special interest here are the *Songs of the Sabbath Sacrifice* (4Q400–407, 11Q5–6), which we have already mentioned in connection with Yadin's excavations at Masada. Because of the strong link between the synagogues and Sabbath gatherings, these provide us with evidence for weekly corporate worship for at least this one sectarian group.[48] Along these lines, special mention must also be made of the *Psalms Scroll* (11Q5), which is usually classified with the biblical material. However, because this scroll presents the psalms in a rearranged order and includes other, non-biblical hymns, some scholars have argued that the sectarians used this scroll as a hymnal. If this hypothesis is accepted, then the *Psalms Scroll* gives us an important glimpse into the worship patterns of the Essenes.

---

[48]Even McKay, who believes there was no corporate Sabbath worship before 200 C.E., concedes this point. However, she characterizes the Essenes as constituting a priestly caste. Thus the scroll evidence fails to meet her definition of corporate Sabbath worship, since this definition requires that *non-priestly* Jews be involved in regular weekly worship. See McKay, *Sabbath and Synagogue*, 55–56. We shall investigate her claims on this matter more closely in chapter seven.

The Writings of Paul

The undisputed Pauline letters (1 Thess, Gal, 1 and 2 Cor, Rom, Phil, Philem), all dated before 64 C.E., are not major sources of evidence for this investigation.[49] Nevertheless, these materials provide information that will be useful in the conclusion of this study, where we will briefly treat the relationship between the synagogues and the emerging Christian *ekklēsiai*. Moreover, the corpus functions as an important control upon Acts' account of Paul's missionary activities in the synagogues.

The fact that so few references to the synagogues appear in the Pauline writings should not come as a surprise to us: Paul wrote his epistles to congregations he either founded or hoped to visit (Romans) primarily to address internal disputes. Allusions to his involvement with Jewish groups were incidental to this function. While recent synagogue scholars have noted that Paul never uses the word *synagōgē*, we should not take this as evidence that Luke invented the apostle's interaction with the synagogues. In fact, there are several indicators in the Pauline writings upholding the accounts of Acts that depict Paul as beginning his missionary work in the synagogues. Chief among these is 2 Cor 11:24 where Paul, cataloguing his missionary trials, states, "Five times I have received from the Jews the forty lashes minus one." Two verses later (11:26) Paul alludes to being in danger from people of his own nation (κινδύνοις ἐκ γένους). Similarly, in 1 Cor 9:20 Paul writes, "To the Jews I became as a Jew, in order to win Jews. To those under the law I became as one under the law (though I myself am not under the law) so that I might win those under the law." While none of these comments demands the conclusion that Paul entered the synagogues to recruit his converts, this view seems most likely. Further corroboration of Acts' placement of Paul in the synagogues is seen in the apostle's naming of Crispus and Sosthenes as converts or associates (1 Cor 1:1, 14). In Acts, these men are listed as being *archisynagōgoi*, "rulers of the synagogue," in Corinth

---

[49]The following are the usual dates for the Pauline epistles: 1 Thess, 50–51; Gal, 48–55; 1 Cor, 54–55; 2 Cor, 55–56; Rom, 56–57; Phil 56, or 62; Philem, 56 or 62. The alternate dates for the last two epistles arise from whether one accepts as the occasion for their writing an Ephesian (c. 56) or a Roman (c. 62) imprisonment of the apostle. 2 Cor consists of anywhere from three to six fragments, one of which (6:14–7:1) is probably a later interpolation. Similarly, Phil probably consists of three letter fragments. See Koester, *Introduction to the New Testament*, 2.103–104; Werner George Kümmel, *Introduction to the New Testament*, trans. Kee, Howard Clark, revised ed. (Nashville: Abingdon Press, 1975), 210–335 .

(Acts 18:8, 17). Admittedly, Paul never uses this title, but his mention of the names serves as at least a partial confirmation of Acts' account.[50]

Elsewhere, Paul possibly refers to the reading of Torah in the synagogues when he writes, "Right up to the present day the same veil remains at the public reading of the old covenant . . . indeed, to the present, whenever Moses is read a veil lies over their hearts" (2 Cor 3:14–15).[51] If we accept this identification, the negative outlook of this passage suggests that, by the time this segment was written (c. 55 C.E.), Paul either chose not to frequent or was prohibited from frequenting the synagogues. Correspondingly, the last time Acts depicts Paul inside a synagogue is in 19:8, where the apostle is said to have frequented the synagogue in Ephesus for three months at the start of his ministry in that city. Thereafter, Acts states that Paul broke his ties with the synagogue and moved into the hall of Tyrannus (19:9). This depiction correlates well with the attitude expressed in the passage cited from 2 Corinthians, since this document was written toward the end of Paul's residence in Ephesus.

James[52]

Only one passage in James (2:1–4) uses the term *synagōgē*, and this apparently in reference to a Christian synagogue or assembly. As such, it may constitute evidence that certain groups of early Christians adopted for their assemblies or meeting places the term *synagōgē*.[53] Unfortunately,

---

[50]Opinions are divided, of course, over whether the Sosthenes in Acts is the same as the one mentioned in 1 Corinthians.

[51]ἄχρι γὰρ τῆς σήμερον ἡμέρας τὸ αὐτὸ κάλυμμα ἐπὶ τῇ ἀναγνώσει τῆς παλαιᾶς διαθήκης μένει . . . ἀλλ' ἕως σήμερον ἡνίκα ἂν ἀναγινώσκηται Μωϋσῆς, κάλυμμα ἐπὶ τὴν καρδίαν αὐτῶν κεῖται. Translation from Victor Paul Furnish, *II Corinthians* (Garden City, N.Y.: Doubleday, 1984), 202. See Furnish's interpretive comments on pp. 208, 233–234.

[52]Representative discussions include: Luke Timothy Johnson, *The Letter of James* (New York: Doubleday, 1995); M. Dibelius and H. Greeven, *A Commentary on the Epistle of James*, revised ed. (Philadelphia: Fortress Press, 1976); Peter H. Davids, *The Epistle of James* (Grand Rapids, Mich.: Eerdmans, 1982); Andrew Chester and Ralph P. Martin, *The Theology of the Letter of James, Peter and Jude* (Cambridge: Cambridge University Press, 1994), 3–62.

[53]On this usage, Schrage writes, "Jm. 2:2 offers the only NT example to show that συναγωγή could also be used in the Christian sense. The only debatable point is whether the word refers to the place of meeting or the meeting; one thing that can be ruled out is that συναγωγή here means the Christian community itself, cf. [James] 5:14" ("Συναγωγή," 834–835). This last reference is to the use of *ekklēsia* by James to denote the Christian community. Cf. Rainer, "Synagogues in Jerusalem," 207–208.

the dating of James is extremely problematic, with the majority of scholars holding that it was written near the end of the first century in response to an extreme form of Paulinism that disregarded good works. In defense of this position, these scholars point to James 2:14 ("What good is it, my brothers and sisters, if you say you have faith but do not have works? Can faith save you?") which is antithetical to Paul's statement in Romans 3:28 ("For we hold that a person is justified by faith apart from works prescribed by the law"). Moreover, they note that James 2:23 contains a key Pauline text from Genesis 15:6, "Abraham believed God, and it was reckoned to him as righteousness," quoted by Paul in both Galatians 3:6 and Romans 4:3. Yet, unlike Paul, James interprets the text along the lines of the position seen above in James 2:14.

The problem with these arguments is that they can be turned on their head: it may have been Paul who reinterpreted the Genesis passage to combat an earlier interpretation originating from the Palestinian churches. On the other side of the discussion, those who support an earlier dating for James point to the absence of any references to the Temple's destruction in the letter and to the frequent attention the epistle pays to the needs of poorer Christians (2:2–6, 15–16)—a situation that matches the plight of the early Palestinian churches (e.g., Gal 2:10). Complicating this debate even further is the fact that the so-called "letter" of James in fact consists of a series of logia dressed up in epistolary garb. Hence, an anonymous editor may have been drawing on earlier, traditional material to deal with events from his own time. The excellent Greek of this document recommends this last proposal, since when we remember that even Josephus needed help in translating his first work, it seems unlikely that James the brother of Jesus (d. 62), the purported author of the letter, could have written in such elegant Greek.[54] Yet nothing is certain. Consequently, we will only make reference to this passage in the conclusion of this study, when we deal with the development of the early *ekklēsia*. Even then, from this passage we will make no specific claims regarding the chronology of the Christian use of *synagōgē*.

Another alternative is that the passage refers to Christians who continued to attend Jewish synagogues.

[54]Martin Hengel argues that James might have had a secretary versed in Greek rhetoric. See Martin Hengel, "Der Jakobusbrief als antipaulinische Polemik" in *Tradition and Interpretation in the New Testament*, edited by G. F. Hawthorn and O. Betz (Grand Rapids: Wm. B. Eerdmans, 1987), 251. Davids upholds a Syro-Palestinian provenance for James, noting that references to the "early" and "late" rains in 5:7 only make sense for this region of the Mediterranean. See Davids, *The Epistle of James*, 183–184.

The Synoptic Gospels[55]

The Synoptic Gospels contain over three dozen references to synagogues or synagogue officials and hence constitute an important body of evidence for this study. Because of the literary connections between these three Gospels, we will consider them together.

As is well known, there has been a standing debate in New Testament scholarship over the relationship between the Synoptics, with the majority of researchers adhering to some form of a two-source theory, which holds that Mark and the hypothetical document "Q" served as primary sources for Matthew and Luke. According to this view, these latter two documents each had a pool of other source materials usually dubbed "Special Matthew" and "Special Luke."[56] The present study will adopt this majority position.[57]

The dating of the three Gospels is also a matter of some debate, even among adherents of the two-source theory. Nevertheless, Mark is typically dated to just before or after 70 C.E. on the basis of the so-called "Little Apocalypse" (Mark 13), whose preoccupation with the Temple's destruction suggests that this event either had just happened or was imminent when the Gospel was written. The provenance of Mark is held to be either Rome or Syro-Palestine, with the latter view currently receiving strong support. Q is dated even earlier than Mark, usually to the 50s, with nearly all researchers maintaining that this collection of logia and miracle accounts originated in Syro-Palestine. The date of Matthew is usually set in the late 80s. As with Q, most researchers hold that it was composed in Syro-Palestine. Luke is dated to around the same period and

---

[55]Treatments of the two-source theory and the genre of the Synoptics can be found in: Helmut Koester, *Ancient Christian Gospels: Their History and Development* (London: SCM Press; Philadelphia: Trinity Press International, 1990); David E. Aune, *The New Testament in Its Literary Environment* (Philadelphia: Westminster Press, 1987), 1–157; Richard A. Burridge, *What are the Gospels?* (Cambridge: Cambridge University Press, 1992); Adela Yarbro Collins, *The Beginning of the Gospel* (Minneapolis: Fortress Press, 1992).

[56]Frequently, materials which can with some confidence be regarded as Lucan and Matthean compositions are also labeled "Special Luke" and "Special Matthew," even though these are not source materials.

[57]The minority position holds that Matthew served as the primary source for Luke and Mark. See William F. Farmer, *The Synoptic problem, A Critical Analysis* (New York: Macmillan, 1964). Scholars holding this position will therefore find this study's treatment of the Synoptics unsatisfactory. Nevertheless, most of what is found in the Synoptics about the synagogues is reiterated in other sources. Consequently, the conclusions of this study should still merit the attention of scholars holding the minority view.

was written outside of Palestine, most likely somewhere in Asia Minor or Greece.

If we accept these dates, then we need only be concerned with anachronism in the cases of Matthew and Luke.[58] Yet this concern is mitigated by the fact that both of these documents take the bulk of their references from Mark or Q, as can be seen in Table 1:

Table 1[59]
Sources of Synagogue References in Matthew and Luke

		Sources			**Total Occurrences**
Number of References to Synagogues		Mark	Q	Sp. M/Sp. L	
	Matthew	5–6	1–2	2	9
	Luke	12–14	1–3	2–3	17

In the cases where Mark is the source, we can easily see where Matthew and Luke made changes to Mark's composition. The changed material may or may not reflect anachronistic tendencies: conclusions about these must be made on a case-by-case basis. The situation is more complicated when Q is the source, for then we must decide whether Matthew or Luke is more faithful to the original account. This is best done through arguments which first note the general biases of the authors and then bring these to bear on the passage in question. The materials from both Special Matthew and Special Luke are most suspect, though these need not automatically be taken as being anachronistic.

The question of the genre of the Synoptics has recently evoked a great deal of discussion. Whereas in the not-too-distant past scholars held Mark to be *sui generis* and a generic model for the other two Synoptics, current thought has been more inclined to locate the Gospels within the larger context of Greco-Roman literature.[60] This shift resulted from researchers'

---

[58]That is to say, Mark probably is not tainted by anachronism for the pre-70 period. Whether or not the account accurately reflects the milieu of the historical Jesus is another question.

[59]Ranges of occurrences are presented in some of the cells because in certain cases the source of particular passages in Matthew or Luke is uncertain.

[60]The former view is seen most recently in the writings of Norman Perrin, who is clearly influenced by the Bultmannian school. See Norman Perrin and Dennis C. Duling, *The New Testament: An Introduction*, 2nd ed. (New York: Harcourt Brace Jovanovich, 1982), 233. For examples of the latter view, see below.

growing awareness of certain difficulties with the once dominant theory that the written Gospels were literary adaptations of early Christian preaching or kerygma. Evidence for the shape of such oral kerygma had been reconstructed from combining various elements in Paul's letters (e.g., Rom 1:1–4, 1 Cor 15:3–8) with the sermonic speeches in Acts (e.g., 2:14–39, 3:12–26). This reconstruction held that the paradigmatic sermon emphasized the crucifixion and resurrection of Jesus and his subsequent glorification to the right hand of God. References to scriptures from the Old Testament were included, as well as a call to repentance and belief in the risen Christ. Among the optional materials in the early sermon were allusions to Jesus' earthly ministry and to the preaching of John the Baptist. As stated, this view held that the written Gospels evolved from this kerygmatic form. Hence we have Martin Kähler's famous dictum that the Gospels were "Passion narratives with extended introductions."[61]

While more recent researchers have pointed out the difficulties of reconstructing an *oral* form from such a hodgepodge of *literary* material, the real deathblow to the kerygmatic theory came with the disclosure of serious discrepancies between the written Gospels and the reconstructed oral kerygma. David Aune, for example, has argued that the form, content and function of the kerygma differ substantially from those of the Gospels.[62] Regarding the first of these, the kerygmata in Acts are embedded in speeches addressed to an audience in the first person. The Gospels, on the other hand, were written primarily with a third person narration. The Gospels differ from the content of the reconstructed kerygma in that the bulk of the former are concerned with the *earthly* ministry of Jesus, whereas the latter focuses on Christ's exalted state and on making a *direct appeal* to the listeners to repentance and faith—elements not readily apparent in the Synoptics. Finally, Aune argues that the function of the Gospels was not evangelistic but served to provide "*historical legitimation* of the saving significance of Jesus."[63] Aune intimates that both the reconstructed kerygma and the Expanded Gospel theory were partially the consequence of the dialectical and existential theologies of Karl Barth and Rudolf Bultmann, which sought to insulate the historical Jesus from the kerygmatic Christ.[64]

---

[61]Martin Kähler, *The So-called Historical Jesus and the Historic, Biblical Christ* (Philadelphia: Fortress Press, 1964), 80, n. 2. Cf. C. H. Dodd, *The Apostolic Preaching and Its Developments* (Chicago: Willett, Clark & Company, 1937), pass.

[62]Aune, *The New Testament in Its Literary Environment*, 19–25.

[63]Ibid., 25. Emphasis in original.

[64]Ibid., 21.

As a counterproposal to the expanded Gospel theory, researchers have held up the genre of the ancient Greco-Roman biography (βίος), which we have already encountered in our discussion of Philo and Josephus' writings. Earlier studies had dismissed this comparison because researchers sought an exact match between the form of the Gospels and an idealized form of the ancient biography. More recent scholarship, however, has noted a certain fluidity in the biographic genre, with ancient authors incorporating into their work elements from other genres, such as legends and philosophical discourses.

To date, Richard Burridge has presented the most systematic comparison of the Gospels with the ancient biographies. He begins by developing a list of biographical features from such works as Satyrus' *Euripides* (III B.C.E.), Nepos' *Atticus* (I B.C.E.) and Philo's *De vita Mosis* (I C.E.). These encompass (1) opening features (e.g., title, opening words), (2) subject (i.e., proportion of attention paid to a protagonist), (3) external features (e.g., length, use of sources), and (4) internal features (e.g., style, tone). At the end of his study, Burridge presents the following summary of his analysis:

> (i) The gospels lack any title which might indicate βίοι, but Luke begins with a formal Preface, while Mark and Matthew commence with the subject's name—both of which are common opening features in βίοι.
>
> (ii) Manual analysis has shown the same pattern of dominance of verb subjects was found in Graeco-Roman βίοι: Jesus is the subject of a large number of the verbs, with a further portion occurring in his parables and teaching. All three synoptic gospels devote a large amount of their text to his Passion and death; however, such an uneven allocation of space to the subject's important period is common among βίοι.
>
> (iii) As regards external features, the synoptic gospels have a similar mode of representation, size, structure and scale to those found in βίοι; further, they use a similar range of literary units, selected from oral and written sources to provide characterization indirectly by word and deed, as is the case in ancient βίοι.
>
> (iv) Among internal features, the settings, topics, atmosphere, quality of characterization and range of purposes are roughly comparable; the style and social setting are probably further down the social scale than our βίοι, but it is likely that other βίοι were available at these levels which have not survived.[65]

---

[65]Burridge, *What are the Gospels?* 218. See below for Aune's view that Luke constituted the first volume of a two-volume Greco-Roman historiography.

Burridge concludes by noting the high degree of correlation between the Synoptics and Greco-Roman biographies and by stating that the Gospels "exhibit more of the features than are shown by works at the edges of the genre."[66]

What are the implications of these conclusions for our study? In short, they serve to undergird the notion that the Gospel writers sought to refer to actual places and events. Whether or not one accepts the historicity of an event or the actuality of a place, however, depends on an analysis of individual cases. As Aune writes:

> To claim that the Evangelists wrote biography with historical intentions, then, does not guarantee that they preserved a single historical fact. It does suggest that they restricted the scope of invention to that appropriate to the biographical task as popularly understood.[67]

From the last part of this quotation it follows that in the places where synagogue references in the Synoptics appear incidental to a particular narrative episode, there is little reason to be unduly skeptical about the existence of attested synagogues—though the historian would naturally welcome independent attestation. Greater scrutiny is needed, however, when one attempts to draw from the Synoptics conclusions about synagogue leadership, since the early Christians appear to have been caught in a power struggle with this leadership. Hence the descriptions in the Synoptics might be skewed. In order to identify such potential distortions, we must turn our attention to the biases of the individual Gospels.

We have already noted the preoccupation that Mark has with the Temple's destruction. This has led some researchers to suggest that Mark was written as a reaction against certain messianic ideas which were linked to the Temple.[68] These are attested in Josephus (*BJ* 6.285–287) and may have held sway among the members of the Jerusalem church. Jesus' harsh criticism of his own family (3:21, 31–35) and of Peter, James and John (8:32–33, 10:35–41)—all leaders of the early Jerusalem church—suggests that the Second Evangelist arranged his material to castigate the mother church for its failure to embrace the Gentile mission and the servanthood role of the apostolate. In fact, at various points, Matthew and Luke soften or omit these criticisms, throwing them even

---

[66]Ibid.

[67]Aune, *The New Testament in Its Literary Environment*, 65.

[68]See, for example, Kelber, *The Kingdom in Mark*, 109–147.

more into relief when the accounts are read side by side (e.g., Matt 16:17–19, 20:20).

If Mark's criticism of the disciples seems rather focused, the attacks against the ruling authorities are less so. No one Jewish group stands out as the opponent of Jesus *par excellence*. Jesus levels criticism proportionately at a number of Jewish groups including the Pharisees (7:5–15, 8:15), the scribes (2:6–12) and the Herodians (3:6). These same groups along with the Chief Priests and the Sadducees are represented as being Jesus' opponents (3:6, 12:13, 18, 14:1). Despite this generally negative treatment, in certain places Mark presents Jesus being more cordial with the Jewish leaders, as when he responds to the plea of Jairus, an *archisynagōgos* (5:22, 36, 38), or when he states that a certain scribe is "not far from the kingdom of God" (12:34).

In contrast to Mark's scattershot critique of the Jewish authorities, Matthew's attacks against the Jewish leadership are much more concentrated on the scribes and Pharisees. As Stephen Wilson notes:

> There are many more references to Pharisees in Matthew than in Mark, though Luke has approximately the same number. Scribes alone or scribes and Pharisees together, however, are Matthean favorites. They are involved (21:45; 22:15; 27:62) in Jesus' death, but unlike the chief priests and elders who are largely confined to Jerusalem, they turn up at all stages of Jesus' public career. The relentlessly negative portrait of them strikes an unpleasant tone, but even so the ferocious attack in Matthew 23 comes as something of a surprise. The level of animosity, unprecedented in Matthew, let alone the other Gospels, strongly suggests that the scribes and Pharisees stand for contemporaries with whom the author is in conflict.[69]

Even more important for our enterprise is that the scribes and Pharisees are depicted as constituting the leadership of the synagogues in Matthew's Gospel, as can be seen in 23:2–6, where they are portrayed as sitting on "Moses' seat" and as desiring "the best seats in the synagogues." Moses' seat is usually interpreted as being a type of judgment seat in the synagogues. From such a position of power, the scribes and Pharisees are depicted in Matthew as waging a relentless campaign against the Christians: "I send you prophets, sages, and scribes, some of whom you will kill and crucify, and some you will flog in your synagogues and pursue from town to town" (23:34). Whatever the truth

---

[69]S. G. Wilson, *Related Strangers: Jews and Christians, 70–170* C.E. (Minneapolis, MN: Fortress Press, 1995), 51.

of such claims—and no doubt they are exaggerated—they speak of the situation surrounding Matthew's community c. 85 C.E., and not the pre-70 period.[70] While persecution of Christians in the synagogues is attested prior to the Temple's destruction (Mark 13:9; cf. 2 Cor 11:24), with some of it being instigated by Pharisees (Phil 3:5–6, Gal 1:13), we have no clear evidence that the scribes and Pharisees had either the means or the desire to enact such a wide-spread campaign against Christians prior to 70 C.E. Hence, in passages where Matthew speaks of the synagogue leadership, we must take care not to project Matthew's perception of the situation in his time back onto the earlier period.

In contrast to Matthew's unrelenting criticism of the scribes and Pharisees is the somewhat more congenial picture presented by Luke. While Jesus can certainly be critical of the scribes and Pharisees in Luke (11:39–44, 12:1, 18:10–14), elsewhere in Luke Jesus actually feasts with them (7:36, 11:37, 14:1). In another place, a Pharisee warns Jesus of danger from Herod (13:31). Still elsewhere, Luke omits from his sources Pharisaic involvement in the plots against Jesus during the last week in Jerusalem (though the scribes remain, 19:47, 20:1). Later, in Acts, certain Pharisees—including Paul—become Christians (Acts 15:5, 23:6), while others defend the right of the Christians to worship freely (Acts 5:34–40, 23:9). Although there may be some truth in all of this, Luke appears to be either currying favor with Pharisaic elements in his day or (more likely) trying to cast Jewish-Christian tensions as a series of internecine squabbles. Since the Romans were typically tolerant of such matters, Luke may have hoped to deflect suspicions of sedition away from the fledgling sect. In any case, unlike Matthew, Luke does not attribute to the scribes and Pharisees the leadership of the synagogues, though they are portrayed as frequenting them (6:7) and of seeking the best seats inside them (12:46). Yet these passages are taken over from Mark with little revision.

The two passages connected to the synagogue where Luke apparently feels free to improvise are in Jesus' inaugural sermon at Nazareth (4:16–30) and in a healing incident where an *archisynagōgos* (*not* a scribe or Pharisee) takes issue with Jesus about healing on the Sabbath (13:10–20). The first of these is clearly a Lucan expansion of Mark 6:2, which briefly mentions Jesus' return home after his baptism: the passage

---

[70]On the exaggerations, notice that crucifixion is a Roman form of execution, requiring Roman approval. Hence Matthew seems to lay the guilt of Roman brutalities at the feet of the scribes and Pharisees (Matt 27:24–25).

is filled with Lucan motifs including concern for the poor (4:18) and sensitivity to Gentiles (4:25–27).[71] Yet while one might dispute the historicity of this episode, there is good reason for believing that Luke here and elsewhere sought to portray pre-70 synagogue scenes with some degree of accuracy. To explain why, we note that William Kurz has argued cogently that Luke's writings reflect the author's familiarity with Greco-Roman rhetoric:

> Rhetorical schoolboy *progymnasmata* (exercises which often were practices in prosopopoeia [speech-writing]) were standard in first-century Hellenistic schools and trained young boys to create speeches that fit the character of historical or mythical figures. It is probable that such exercises formed part of the early training of the author of Luke-Acts. That Luke at least employed the technique with ease is demonstrated by the distinctive coloration he gives to speeches delivered to different audiences: to the Jerusalem Jews in Acts 2 and 3, to the diaspora Jews in Acts 13, and to the pagans in the Acts 17 Areopagus speech.[72]

One of the exercises in the *progymnasmata* that actually came before the composition of speeches was the creation of narratives (*narratio*). Stanley Bonner notes that in this exercise, students were encouraged to write plausibly "by envisaging the events from the point of view of the persons, the occasion, and the place concerned, and describing the actions or reactions according to what seemed most *likely* to have happened."[73] Thus while the scene in 4:16–30 is paradigmic in Luke's account, the author, relying on his rhetorical training, would have instinctively sought to portray the trappings of the synagogue story as plausibly as possible.[74]

---

[71]See Philip Francis Esler, *Community and Gospel in Luke-Acts* (Cambridge: Cambridge University Press, 1987), 166–167.

[72]William S. Kurz, "Hellenistic Rhetoric in the Christological Proof of Luke-Acts," *CBQ* 42 (1980): 186. Kurz extensively documents Luke's use of other Greco-Roman rhetorical forms and figures.

[73]Stanley F. Bonner, *Education in Ancient Rome* (Berkeley: University of California Press, 1977), 262–263. Emphasis in original. See also Theon, *Per. Pros.* 84.5ff.

[74]Here we might also note Nils Lund's observation that Luke typically spurned chiastic patterns, which, as he documents, were more common among Jewish writings. Yet Lund does identify one such structure in Luke 4:16–21, Jesus' inaugural sermon in Nazareth. Lund accounts for its presence by noting the distinctively Jewish setting of the scene: "Luke, with true artistic feeling for the scene he describes, permits the quotation to retain the form he knew was prevalent in the synagogue" (Nils Lund, *Chiasmus in the New Testament* [Chapel Hill: The University of North Carolina Press,

This, of course, does not mean we should refrain from scrutinizing the description for hints of anachronism, provincialism or bias. The argument merely suggests that the descriptive accuracy of this synagogue scene—and others we encounter in Luke-Acts—should not be dismissed out of hand.

While we might uphold Luke's intent to portray details accurately, we must note that his knowledge of Galilee does not appear to be as extensive as that of the Roman provinces in the northern part of the Mediterranean, or even of Jerusalem and Caesarea.[75] For example, commentators have long noted deficiencies in Luke's understanding of Galilean geography (4:44, 17:11).[76] In other places Luke appears to adjust his sources to make Galilean village life more intelligible to the Greco-Roman urbanite.[77] Consequently, Luke's portrayal of the Galilean synagogues is most likely drawn from his understanding of synagogues in the diaspora or in Syro-Palestinian cities.

John[78]

The Gospel of John contains five references to synagogues. Unfortunately, the bulk of these seem to be tainted by anachronism, as we shall see.

1942], 238). While Lund held that Luke inherited the structure from Q, alternatively, Luke may have composed this chiastic structure himself for the same reason given in the quotation.

[75]Luke-Acts' knowledge of Jerusalem and the coastal areas of Palestine is generally very good. See Martin Hengel, "The Geography of Palestine in Acts" in *The Book of Acts in Its Palestinian Setting*, edited by Richard Bauckham (Grand Rapids, Mich.: William B. Eerdmans Pub. Co., 1995), 27–78.

[76]See Joseph A. Fitzmyer, *The Gospel According to Luke* (Garden City, N.Y.: Doubleday, 1981), 1.15.

[77]Note especially Luke 5:19, where Luke changes his source (Mark 2:4) which has the paralytic's being lowered through the thatched roof characteristic of houses in Galilean villages. Luke instead depicts a tiled roof characteristic of homes in Syro-Palestinian cities. Ibid., 1.582.

[78]Treatments of critical questions pertaining to the compositional history of John include: Raymond E. Brown, *The Gospel According to John*, 2 vols. (Garden City, N.Y.: Doubleday, 1966); idem, *The Community of the Beloved Disciple* (New York: Paulist Press, 1979); J. Louis Martyn, *History and Theology in the Fourth Gospel*, revised ed. (Nashville: Abingdon, 1979); Martinus C. de Boer, *Johannine Perspectives on the Death of Jesus* (Kampen, The Netherlands: Kok Pharos, 1996), 19–82.

Most scholars agree that the final redaction of John occurred sometime during the 90s. The composition history of the document is complicated and still a subject of debate. Raymond Brown's influential commentary on John maintains that our present Gospel is actually a third edition. In this view the first edition was composed by "a dominant or master preacher and theologian who gave shape to the main body of surviving Johannine material."[79] Later, this writer, dubbed "the Evangelist" by Brown, published a second edition incorporating passages left out of the first edition. Brown detects these secondary insertions from a number of disruptions in the text. The final form of the Gospel was brought about by a later redactor who extensively edited and expanded the second edition in response to various crises faced by the Johannine community.[80]

More recent composition theories are even more complex, as can be seen in the writings of Martinus de Boer, who argues for *four* separate editions of the Gospel.[81] The end result of these theories for the historian is that John paradoxically contains some very early traditions as well as material that reflects the situation of the later Johannine community.

Of primary importance for this study is that one of the major crises taken up by the final redactor of John is the expulsion of the Johannine community from the synagogues. This can be seen in several passages which speak of Jews fearing expulsion from the synagogue if they confessed belief in Jesus. For example, in 12:42 we find the statement, "many, even of the authorities [ἀρχόντων], believed in [Jesus]. But because of the Pharisees they did not confess it, for fear that they would be put out of the synagogue [ἀποσυνάγωγοι γένωνται]" (cf. 9:22, 16:2). Clearly this statement is anachronistic, reflecting not the lifetime of Jesus, but of the later emerging Church.

Various attempts have been made to date this break between the Johannine community and the synagogues. For example, J. Louis Martyn has proposed a date corresponding to the reformulation of one of the benedictions used in the synagogue liturgy.[82] The reformulation changes the twelfth of the Eighteen Benedictions into a curse against "the heretics" (*Birkath ha-Minim*), presumably Christians. Pointing to a passage from the Babylonian Talmud, Martyn argues that the shift took

---

[79]Raymond Brown, *The Gospel According to John*, 1.xxxv.

[80]The additions include 1:1–18; 3:31–36; 6:51–58; 11–12; 15–17; 21.

[81]See de Boer, *Johannine Perspectives on the Death of Jesus*, 73–77.

[82]J. Louis Martyn, *History and Theology in the Fourth Gospel*, 50–62.

place at the rabbinic discussions at Jamnia (Yavneh) under Gamaliel II (80–115 C.E.): "Rabban Gamaliel said to the Sages: Is there one among you who can word a benediction relating to the Minim [heretics]? Samuel the Small arose and composed it."[83] Since its first presentation, however, Martyn's proposal has been criticized on several grounds. First, the connection between the passages in John and the composition of the *Birkath ha-Minim* is tenuous at best.[84] Second, and more importantly, Neusner and others have observed that we lack any early attestation for the shift of the Twelfth Benediction. Consequently, the 80–90 C.E. date Martyn assigns to the reformulation may be based on an anachronism.[85]

If Martyn's proposal is too speculative, it seems safe to say that the threat of excommunication alluded to in John took place *after* 70 C.E. since the Pharisees are portrayed as being behind the expulsions. As we saw in our treatment of Matthew's Gospel, the Pharisees did not come to power until after the fall of the Jerusalem. Thus while some Christians left or were expelled from the synagogues prior to 70 C.E., the references in John suggest that a more widespread pattern of expulsion took place in Syro-Palestine near the end of the first century.

Because of the complex composition history of the Fourth Gospel, Johannine scholars have been less inclined then their Synoptic counterparts to classify John as biography. Nevertheless, scholars such as Burridge and Aune have made persuasive arguments to this effect.[86] For example, Aune, responding to the apparent problem that the "two-level drama" theory (i.e., that John addresses the issues of two periods, 30 C.E. and 95 C.E.) creates for a biographic classification of John, writes:

---

[83]*B. Berakoth* 28b. Translation from J. Louis Martyn, *History and Theology in the Fourth Gospel*, 54.

[84]For a summary of this criticism, see de Boer, *Johannine Perspectives on the Death of Jesus*, 69. In the revised edition of *History and Theology*, Martyn (in a footnote) attenuated his claims regarding the connection between the Fourth Gospel and the *Birkath ha-Minim*. See op. cit., 54, n. 69.

[85]Neusner has made this point repeatedly, most recently in Neusner, *Uppsala Addresses*, 83. See also Anthony Saldarini, *Matthew's Christian-Jewish Community*, 220–221, n. 53.

[86]See Burridge, *What are the Gospels?* 220–239; Aune, *The New Testament in Its Literary Environment*, 61–63. Recently, some Johannine scholars appear to be leaning in the direction of classifying John as a biography—though more from a rejection of the Expanded Gospel theory than from a consideration of generic features. See de Boer, *Johannine Perspectives on the Death of Jesus*, 19–30.

> Ancient Hellenistic biographers and historians also wrote on two levels, combining ideas from their own time with events from the past. This can be explained in two complementary ways: (1) They lacked the historical imagination to mentally reenact the different experience of those whose actions they were describing, and projected their own cultural experience into the past. (2) Most historians and biographers of the Hellenistic period regarded the past as normative for present conduct, i.e., it provided moral guidance for the present and future . . . Hellenistic history and biography, no less than the Gospels, tended to *merge* the past with the present. If the Gospels and Acts deserve the (exaggerated) designation "theology in narrative form," then Greco-Roman history and biography fully merit the label "ideology in narrative form." Functionally the differences are minimal.[87]

The implications of Aune's statement for our interpretation of John is that where ideology appears to be lacking in the narrative, we have more secure grounds for considering a description to be of historical value. Of course, this does not exempt us from examining other considerations such as source analysis and independent attestation. Unfortunately, the synagogue references in John untainted by ideology and anachronism are so few that this Gospel leaves us with little helpful information about synagogues from the Second Temple period. Occasionally, however, John can be used as secondary corroboration of other sources.

Acts of the Apostles[88]

Acts contains nearly two dozen synagogue references, making it an important source for this study. This is especially the case because most of these references occur in narratives describing events in Syria, Asia Minor and Greece.

Since Acts is the companion volume of the Gospel of Luke, much of what was written above on Luke's Gospel applies to our discussion of Acts. There, we saw that most scholars date Luke to the 80s. Because

---

[87]Aune, *The New Testament in Its Literary Environment*, 62.

[88]For general discussions, see Hans Conzelmann, *Acts of the Apostles: A Commentary on the Acts of the Apostles* (Philadelphia: Fortress Press, 1987); Ernst Haenchen, *The Book of Acts: A Commentary* (Philadelphia: Westminister, 1971); Colin J. Hemer, and Conrad H. Gempf, *The Book of Acts in the Setting of Hellenistic History* (Tübingen: J.C.B. Mohr, 1989); Luke Timothy Johnson, *The Acts of the Apostles* (Collegeville, Minn.: Liturgical Press, 1992). See also the volumes in the recent series on Acts: Bruce W. Winter, ed. *The Book of Acts in Its First Century Setting*, 6 vols. (Grand Rapids, Mich.: William B. Eerdmans Pub. Co., 1993–). To date, five of the projected six volumes have appeared.

Acts was written after Luke (Acts 1:1), it is usually dated to sometime in the 90s. As with Luke, Acts was also written outside of Palestine, most likely in Asia Minor or Greece since the author seems particularly familiar with these regions.

While the Third Gospel has been classified by some recent scholars as biography, Acts is now beginning to be viewed as an example of Greco-Roman historiography. To be sure, there is a great deal of overlap between these two genres. Indeed, whereas Burridge classifies Luke as biography and Acts as historiography, Aune views Luke as the first book in a two-volume historiography.[89] We need not arbitrate between these two positions since writers of Greco-Roman biography and historiography both sought to make their works plausible to their audiences.

In connection with this intention, Colin Hemer has compiled an impressive list of passages in Acts where Luke's descriptions are substantiated by other ancient sources. Summarizing his analysis, Hemer writes:

> We discovered a wealth of material suggesting an author or sources familiar with the particular locations and at the times in question. Many of these connections have only recently come to light with the publication of new collections of papyri and inscriptions. We considered these details from various, often overlapping, perspectives, risking repetitiveness, since our interest was not primarily in the details themselves, but rather in the way that they supported and confirmed different ways of reading the text—various levels in the relationship of the narrative with the history it purports to

---

[89]See Aune, *The New Testament in Its Literary Environment*, 77–157; Burridge, *What are the Gospels?* 243–247. Aune classifies Luke-Acts as historiography on the basis of a favorable comparison between these volumes and other Greco-Roman historiographies. Among the points of contact are: (1) historical preface (Luke 1:1–4), (2) genealogy (Luke 3:23–38), (3) symposia (Luke 7:36–50, 11:37–54), (4) speeches (e.g., Acts 7:2–53, 20:18–35, 24:10–21), (5) letters (Acts 15:23–29, 23:26–30), (6) dramatic episodes (e.g., Acts 10:1–11:18, 25:13–26:32), (7) digressions (Acts 17:21, 18:24–25, 21:29, 23:8), (8) summaries (Luke 4:14, 37, 7:17; Acts 1:14, 8:1b-4, 9:31, 11:19–21, 19:11–12, 28:30–31) and (9) travel narratives (e.g., Luke 9:51–19:44; Acts 12:25–21:16, 27:1–28:16). In connection with the last of these, we should note Aune's remarks on the so-called "we passages" in Acts. Aune finds parallels to them in the writings of Polybius. From an analysis of these, he concludes, "the occurrence of the 'we' passages in Acts constitutes an implicit claim that the author is not an armchair historian, but one who had personally visited the regions he describes . . . In fact the 'we' passages suggest that the author either personally experienced the events narrated (cf. Luke 1:2–3) or at least intended to foster that impression" (124).

> describe. By and large, these perspectives all converged to support the general reliability of the narrative, through the details so intricately yet often unintentionally woven into that narrative.[90]

This evaluation does not mean that we should render a favorable verdict on the historicity of all the events presented in Acts. On the contrary, most of the specific incidents depicted in Acts are unverifiable. Nor should we interpret Hemer's conclusions as signifying that Acts is free from theological biases, since we have already seen that *all* Greco-Roman writings incorporated some amount of ideology. Hemer's study does indicate, however, that Luke's portrayal of local color in Acts is frequently correct. This is of importance to our investigation, since we are not concerned with specific incidents, but with general patterns and features. Like the Gospels, Acts must not be dismissed as a work of "mere theology" that is of no historical value.[91]

Nevertheless, are there areas in which Luke's theology or ideology might have distorted his depiction of the synagogues? There are indeed. To begin, many commentators have noted a repeating pattern in Acts' presentation of Paul's missionary efforts (9:20–25, 13:14–49, 14:1–3, 17:1–9, 10–14, 18:1–8, 19:8–10). Typically, Paul and his associates first enter a synagogue upon their arrival in a city or town. Their preaching in the synagogue initially meets with some acceptance, especially from among the Gentile God-fearers. Soon, however, the tide turns against them, and they leave the synagogue in order to focus their efforts among the Gentiles.

This pattern appears to correspond to a linear progression running from Jew to God-fearer to Gentile. It also follows Acts' account of Christianity's geographical expansion which begins in Jerusalem, makes stops in Samaria and in several Greco-Roman cities, and ends in Rome (cf. 1:18). Aside from this "procession of the Gospel," Luke's portrayal of Paul and his entourage as victims of theological intransigence on the

---

[90]Hemer, *The Book of Acts in the Setting of Hellenistic History*, 412. Hemer's comparative analysis is found on pp. 101–220.

[91]This is the earlier view of Ernst Haenchen, who writes, "Luke was no professional historian and was not interested in writing a history of early Christianity, aside from the fact that in his time the concepts *history and early Christianity* were still nonexistent" ("The Book of Acts as Source Material for the History of Early Christianity" in *Studies in Luke-Acts*, edited by Leander E. Keck and J. Louis Martyn [Nashville: Abingdon Press, 1966], 258).

part of the Jews serves his purpose of legitimating the Christian movement.

Given these tendencies, Kraabel was justified in being suspicious of the place of the God-fearers in Acts' narrative.[92] Yet his verdict that the God-fearers are a literary creation is not the only possible alternative. Ancient historians frequently created paradigms from certain outstanding incidents in order to reinforce their interpretations of certain outcomes. Moreover, the persuasiveness of their presentations drew from the presence of recognizable characters in their accounts. Josephus, for instance, stereotypically depicted the Zealots and Sicarii as villains responsible for the destruction of Jerusalem (e.g., *BJ* 2.256–57; *Ant.* 18.4–10, 23–25; 20.160–166, 185–188). While we should realize that the actual case was much more complex, we should not conclude that Josephus created these two groups to further his own agenda. Nor should we dismiss as fiction all of the incidents where Josephus presents the Zealots and Sicarii in a bad light—though we certainly need to question the accuracy and representativeness of these accounts. Similarly with Acts, we might question the recurrence of the synagogue incidents in every city Paul visited. On the other hand, we should consider the possibility that Luke's pattern may well be a generalization based on one or more actual incidents—a possibility that takes on greater weight when we factor in the supporting evidence we have seen from Paul's own writings. The same can be said regarding the God-fearers. While we should question whether Paul's appeal to them may have been as successful as Acts portrays, we should not hastily conclude that Luke created the God-fearers to serve his theological purposes. In fact, such invention would have risked contradicting the experiences of Luke's readers and of losing rather than gaining credibility with them. Of course, we need to look at whether or not outside evidence exists to support the view that the God-fearers existed in the Second Temple period. That task remains for a future chapter.

---

[92]For an exposition of Kraabel's position, see the introduction, above, and excursus two in chapter five, below.

Papyri[93]

Unfortunately, from our period we only possess three papyri which mention synagogues (*proseuchai*), all from Egypt. Despite the lack of quantity, these documents are important witnesses to the antiquity of the synagogues in Egypt, as they all date to before the turn of the era. Indeed, one of them dates to the third century B.C.E. These documents can be found in volume one of Victor Tcherikover's standard three-volume collection of Jewish papyri, *Corpus Papyrorum Judaicarum*.[94]

The papyri, all written in Greek, are dated through paleography, which is more refined for this medium than for inscriptions. The earliest document, a letter to Ptolemy Philopater, can be fixed precisely to 218 B.C.E. because it contains a date. The other two documents consist of a land survey and the minutes of a burial association held inside a synagogue. Unfortunately, the latter is very fragmentary and difficult to interpret. The various sigla used in the transcription of papyri match those used in inscriptions. These and problems of identification will be discussed in the following section.

INSCRIPTIONS[95]

We presently possess about three dozen synagogue inscriptions of a dating earlier than 70 C.E. Having been discovered throughout the Mediterranean world, these monuments underscore the importance of the synagogue in both Palestine and the diaspora.

For years, the standard compendium of Jewish inscriptions has been Jean-Baptist Frey's two-volume *Corpus Inscriptionum Judaicarum* (*CIJ*).[96] This set includes transcriptions, photographs and French

---

[93]For a useful introduction to papyrology, see Italo Gallo, *Greek and Latin Papyrology* (London: Institute of Classical Studies, 1986).

[94]Avigdor Tcherikover, Alexander Fuks, and Menahem Stern, *Corpus Papyrorum Judaicarum*, 3 vols. (Cambridge, Mass.: Harvard University Press, 1957–64).

[95]General treatises on epigraphy include: A. G. Woodhead, *The Study of Greek Inscriptions*, 2nd ed. (Cambridge; New York: Cambridge University Press, 1981); Arthur Ernest Gordon, *Illustrated Introduction to Latin Epigraphy* (Berkeley: University of California Press, 1983); Fergus Millar, "Epigraphy" in *Ancient Greece and Rome: The Sources of History*, edited by Michael Crawford (Cambridge: Cambridge University Press, 1983), 80–136; Laurence H. Kant, "Jewish Inscriptions in Greek and Latin" in *ANRW* II.20.2.671–713.

[96]Jean Baptiste Frey, *Corpus Inscriptionum Iudaicarum*, 2 vols. (Rome: Poniticio Instituto di Archeologia Christiana, 1936–52).

translations of Jewish inscriptions dating from the third century B.C.E. to the seventh century C.E. Despite the comprehensiveness of Frey's collection, even at the time of its publication, errors of various sort were noted.[97] These were partly corrected in Baruch Lifshitz's revision of volume one of *CIJ* (1975).[98] With the wealth of recent archaeological discoveries, despite Lifshitz's revision, *CIJ* has been badly in need of updating. This need has been partially met by a recent series of volumes produced by the Jewish Inscriptions Project at the University of Cambridge. Currently this project has produced three volumes covering inscriptions from Egypt and Italy.[99] Each inscription includes a transcription, English translation, bibliography and extensive commentary. Letter-form summaries also accompany each inscription, and photographs are included for many of the monuments. When the series is complete, it will represent the new standard in Jewish epigraphy for the Hellenistic through Byzantine periods. In the meantime, various excavation reports and other sources must be consulted in order to supplement the regions covered in *CIJ* that have not yet been superseded by the volumes of the Jewish Inscriptions Project.[100]

As indicated in the introduction of this chapter, there are a number of difficulties that accompany the use of inscriptions as historical evidence. Chief among these is dating. While paleographers have developed a chronology of letter forms, these can usually date an inscription only to

---

[97]E.g., L. Robert, "Un corpus des inscription juives," *REJ* 101 (1937): 73–86.

[98]Jean Baptiste Frey, *Corpus of Jewish Inscriptions: Jewish Inscriptions from the Third Century B.C. to the Seventh Century A.D.* (New York: Ktav Pub. House, 1975). Lifshitz's prolegomenon updates and corrects Frey's original volume. Occasional English translations are provided.

[99]William Horbury and David Noy, *Jewish Inscriptions of Graeco-Roman Egypt: With an Index of the Jewish Inscriptions of Egypt and Cyrenaica* (Cambridge: Cambridge University Press, 1992); David Noy, *Jewish Inscriptions of Western Europe*, 2 vols. (Cambridge; New York: Cambridge University Press, 1993–95). Note comments and corrections in: Greg H. R. Horsley, "Towards a New *Corpus Inscriptionum Iudaicarum*?" *Jewish Studies Quarterly* 2 (1995): 77–101.

[100]Chief among these are the annual volumes of *Supplementum Epigraphicum Graecum* (*SEG*). Other important collections include: Gert Lüderitz, and Joyce Maire Reynolds, *Corpus jüdischer Zeugnisse aus der Cyrenaika* (Wiesbaden: Ludwig Reichert, 1983); J. M. Reynolds, "Inscriptions" in *Excavations at Sidi Khrebish Benghazi (Berenice)*, edited by J. A. Lloyd (Hertford: Stephen Austin and Sons, 1977), 233–254; B. Lifshitz, *Donateurs et fondateurs dans les synagogues Juives* (Paris: J. Gabalda et Cie, 1967). See Pieter Willem Van der Horst, *Ancient Jewish Epitaphs* (Kampen, The Netherlands: Kok Pharos Publishing House, 1991), 11–16 for a list of other sources.

within a century or two. Hence the epigraphist frequently relies on considerations such as decoration, terminology, and archaeological context. Best of all is when the inscription mentions the name of an identifiable ruler or other political official. In these cases, the inscription can often be dated to a specific year. Fortuitously, many of the inscriptions used in this study contain such allusions and allow us to assign some fairly precise dates. In other instances we will need to rely on the other considerations just noted.

Another problem facing the epigraphist of Jewish inscriptions is that of identification. In other words, how is one to know if an inscription is Jewish? The criteria for making such a determination usually include the mention of Jewish names, the use of Jewish iconography and references to Jewish functionaries and institutions. Obviously this last consideration is essential for this study, since we are interested in a specific Jewish institution. As stated earlier, however, we will postpone our discussion of synagogue terminology until the next chapter.

The presence of Hebrew in inscriptions is also another of the criteria used in identifying an inscription as Jewish. However, we currently possess no Hebrew synagogue inscriptions from the pre-70 period.[101] With two exceptions (which are in Latin), all of the inscriptions dating to our period are in Greek.

Many of the inscriptions we will encounter in this study are fragmentary. Letters and words are frequently illegible or missing all together, and sometimes the words that can be read contain obvious errors. When possible, the epigraphist must attempt to reconstruct such lacunae in the inscription. Sometimes this reconstruction is aided by recourse to a standardized formula known from other inscriptions. Other times it is mere speculation. Standard transcriptions place reconstructions in square brackets [ ], with the more speculative of them containing question marks. Double square brackets [[ ]] indicate intentional erasures. New inscriptions over erasures or remnants of erased letters are included inside the double square brackets. Editorial reconstructions of erasures are placed in yet a third pair of square brackets [[[ ]]]. Dots inside square brackets [. . .] represent the estimated number of missing spaces. Dashes so enclosed [- - -] signify that the number cannot be determined. Unsure readings of letters contain a dot subscript, ω̣. Corrections of an engraver's omission are placed in angular brackets <>,

[101]Two ostraca with Hebrew writing, however, were discovered inside the structure at Masada identified as a synagogue.

while braces { } surround existing letters that were probably engraved erroneously. Expansions of abbreviations are set inside round brackets ( ). The word *vacat* indicates that an area of the inscription was intentionally left vacant.

There are a number of genres of Jewish inscriptions. The ones pertinent to this study are dedications, honorific inscriptions, decrees, legal instruments and epitaphs.[102] *Dedications* comprise the largest number of inscriptions we will see in this study. These concern the construction or renovation of a synagogue or one of its appointments. Usually named are: (1) the person or group financing the project, (2) the person or persons on whose behalf the dedication is being offered (if any), and (3) the divinity to whom the dedication is given (often implicit). Sometimes the dedication makes reference to a vow that the donor has fulfilled through the contribution of the dedicated structure or object.

Honorific inscriptions are somewhat related to dedications. Whereas the latter comprise a sort of self-monument, the former officially praise a patron or benefactor separate from the body erecting the stele. In some cases these inscriptions also refer to regular ceremonies during which the patron will be perpetually honored. Inscriptions of this genre sometimes overlap with the genre of *decrees*. What causes the latter to stand out is the recording on the monument of an official resolution. Typically this is signified by the presence of the verb "have resolved" (ἔδοξεν) and by the recording of the governing body's vote.

Legal instruments formally register the execution of a legal transaction. In this study, they pertain to a number of manumission inscriptions unearthed in the Crimea. The language is formulaic and in two cases incorporates the names of pagan divinities.

Examples of the final genre, that of *epitaphs*, typically mention the name of the deceased, along with any office held, occupation, length of life, and notable virtues.[103] Occasionally the name of the spouse or relative who composed the epitaph is listed also. Although we possess many epitaphs of synagogue functionaries from Jewish catacombs in Rome, Beth She'arim (Galilee) and elsewhere, most of these date to well after our period. Nevertheless, we do have a few relevant examples of this genre that fit within our dating parameters.

---

[102]For a fuller discussion of these, see Kant, *Jewish Inscriptions*, 675–681.

[103]For a more detailed discussion, see Van der Horst, *Ancient Jewish Epitaphs*, pass.

While the inscriptions we will examine in this study are tantalizingly brief, they do, however, provide illuminating encounters with the early synagogues and their congregations. Their value arises not only from the literary evidence they provide, but also from their very character as public monuments. This last point is especially noteworthy since one of the objectives of this study is to determine the degree of institutionalization that existed within the early synagogues. Our consideration of these monuments in subsequent chapters will clearly aid our investigation of this issue.

ARCHITECTURAL REMAINS[104]

There are presently nearly a dozen structures that excavators have identified as the remains of Second Temple synagogues. As we saw in the literature review of the previous chapter, the identification of these structures has been hotly contested by some recent scholars. Yet since few of these researchers have explicated the reasons why archaeologists have made these identifications, it is essential that we here delineate the criteria excavators employ when determining whether or not a structure might possibly be a synagogue.[105]

We begin with the issue of dating. Typically, the various phases of a building are dated through stratigraphic methods that feature analyses of pottery, coins and artifacts. Of these, coins provide the most precise

---

[104]Standard treatments include: Rachel Hachlili, *Ancient Jewish Art and Archaeology in the Land of Israel* (New York: E.J. Brill, 1988); Marilyn Joyce Segal Chiat, *Handbook of Synagogue Architecture* (Chico, Calif.: Scholars Press, 1982); Frowald Hüttenmeister and Gottfried Reeg, *Die antiken Synagogen in Israel*, 2 vols. (Wiesbaden: Reichert, 1977); Sylvester J. Saller, *Second Revised Catalogue of the Ancient Synagogues of the Holy Land* (Jerusalem: Franciscan Printing Press, 1972).

[105]Many recent researchers have based their claims regarding these structures on an essay by Marilyn Chiat wherein she pointed out some methodological problems with the identification of pre-70 synagogues (Marilyn J. Chiat, "First-Century Synagogue Architecture: Methodological Problems" in *Ancient Synagogues: The State of Research*, edited by Joseph Gutmann [Chico, California: Scholars Press, 1981], 49–60.). Here it must be noted that Chiat by no means refuted the validity of all of the identifications; rather, she pointed out the inconsistent application of some of these criteria and called into question others. One of these latter is the use of the orientation of the structure (e.g., towards Jerusalem). Because even later synagogues did not uniformly face towards Jerusalem, in this study we will not make use of this criterion. However, once a structure has been identified as a synagogue on the basis of other criteria, I will reserve the right to comment on the orientation of the synagogue.

dating, since they usually bear dates or the image of a public official whose years in office are known. The analysis of ceramics has also greatly advanced in recent years, though pottery still does not supply as precise a date as do coins. Nevertheless, potsherds abounded in antiquity and are consequently the most abundant source of evidence for the dating of occupational levels. In addition to coins and pottery, certain artifacts such as lamps can also provide a relatively narrow range of dates.

Aside from these methods, a building can sometimes be dated by observing the style of its construction. Less frequently, an accompanying dedicatory inscription establishes the date of a structure's foundation. In still other cases, historical sources can supply a precise date of a building's destruction, since ancient historians frequently recorded the years when battles took place or various natural disasters occurred.

Hand in hand with the dating of a structure's foundation and occupational levels is the process of identification. In the case of later synagogues, identification is relatively easy because most Late Roman and Byzantine synagogue remains contain obvious examples of Jewish sacred iconography and many dedicatory inscriptions. The process is more difficult for earlier structures, since the period prior to 70 C.E. was apparently more conservative with regard to the use of sacred iconography, as we noted in the previous chapter.[106] Judgments on the sacrality of a particular symbol must therefore be inferred from the presence of that symbol among the *contemporary* ruins of a structure known to have been sacred (e.g., the Temple) and/or from the symbol's ascription of cultic distinction within early Jewish writings.[107] As we shall see in chapters three and four, two symbols found within early synagogues—the rosette and the palm—likely held a cultic significance, as they were recovered among the remains of Herod's Temple and figure prominently among the early Jewish writings which deal with the Temple cult. On the other hand, while many dedicatory inscriptions exist and were obviously employed in our period, few of these have been discovered inside an excavated structure. Consequently, archaeologists have had to rely on additional criteria.

---

[106]E.g., Josephus, *BJ* 2.195ff., *Ant.* 18.55–59, 121–122, 263–64; *Vita* 65; Philo, *Legat*. 299–305.

[107]On this point, see Colin Renfrew, "The Archaeology of Religion" in *The Ancient Mind: Elements of Cognitive Archaeology*, edited by Colin Renfrew and Ezra B. W. Zubrow (Cambridge: Cambridge University Press, 1994), 53–54.

The first of these is the correspondence of a structure to later synagogue typology. The assumption here is that earlier synagogues retained the general architectural form of the synagogues from a later period. One of these forms is known as the Galilean-type synagogue, which consists of a rectangular hall with benches along the inside walls on two or more sides and rows of supporting columns running between the benches and the center of the hall. The well-known limestone synagogue at Capernaum (IV–V C.E.) is an example of this type of structure.[108] While it is dangerous to extrapolate backwards, in this case the move is justified by the fact that a hall at Delos (I B.C.E.) that conforms to this typology fairly closely was also connected to a dedicatory inscription identifying the structure as a synagogue (*proseuchē*). While this criterion is useful in identifying earlier synagogal structures, its shortcoming is that it might lead the archaeologist to miss the presence of other synagogue types not attested in the later period.

Another manner in which earlier synagogues are identified is through excavating the lower strata of later synagogues. In some cases, the remains from the lower occupational phase suggest that the structure functioned in the same manner as the later edifice. Thus even though a lower stratum might not contain any dedicatory inscriptions or iconography useful in making an identification, the identification can be argued on the basis of architectural continuity.

A final criterion used in the identification of early synagogues is the presence of features known from early inscriptions and literary evidence. One of these features is the ritual bath or *mikveh* (plural: *mikvaoth*).[109]

---

[108]On the classification of the pre-70 Palestinian synagogues as Galilean-type synagogues, see e.g., N. Avigad, “The ‘Galilean’ Synagogue and its Predecessors” in *ASR* 42–44; Gideon Foerster, “Architectural Models of the Greco-Roman Period and the Origin of The ‘Galilean’ Synagogue” in *ASR* 45–48; Ehud Netzer, “The Herodian Triclinia: A Prototype for the ‘Galilean-Type’ Synagogue” in *ASR* 49–51; Asher Ovadiah, and Talila Michaeli, “Observations on the Origin of the Architectural Plan of Ancient Synagogues,” *JJS* 38 (1987): 234–241. Cf. Z. Ma‘oz, “The Synagogue of Gamla and the Typology of Second-Temple Synagogues” in *ASR* 41, n. 1. The focus of this study upon the Galilean-type synagogues does not mean that other architectural types of these structures were not extant in the pre-70 period (or in the later period, for that matter). As we will see, it is likely that one of the rooms at Qumran, not conforming to this type, might also be classified as a synagogue on the basis of other criteria. However, most of the pre-70 synagogue candidates excavated in Palestine thus far *do* conform to the typology of the Galilean synagogue.

[109]Baths near synagogues are attested in *CIJ* 2.1404; Josephus, *BJ* 2.128. See also Ronny Reich, “The Synagogue and the *Miqweh* in Eretz-Israel in the Second -Temple,

The existence of a *mikveh* near a structure conforming to the typology of the Galilean synagogue can thus serve as supporting evidence for the identification of an early structure as a synagogue. So can the presence of an adjoining dining room or living quarters, which are also attested in the early evidence.[110] Finally, the unearthing of scriptures in such an edifice also constitutes supporting evidence, since the early sources attest that scripture readings took place inside synagogues.[111]

Typically archaeologists use a combination of these criteria to make the case that a certain edifice is indeed a synagogue. As we can see from the discussion, the identification of early synagogues partially depends on the use of literary and inscriptionary evidence. Additional use of such evidence includes the mention of a synagogue in a particular place at a particular time. For example, Josephus mentions that a synagogue (*proseuchē*) existed in Tiberias during the Jewish War (*Vita* 276–303). Although this structure has never been found, if in the future excavators were to uncover in that city a large public building with benches along the walls, and if this building were to date to the first century C.E. and contain an inscription mentioning an *archōn* named Jesus, Josephus' allusion to the Tiberian synagogue and its *archōn* would aid archaeologists in securing the identification of the structure. The process of identification is thus the convergence of the literary, epigraphic and architectural lines of evidence.

CONCLUSION

The foregoing examination has identified the critical issues surrounding the various sources that will be used in the subsequent chapters of this investigation. By keeping these firmly in mind, we should be able to avoid the pitfalls of anachronism, provincialism and bias that have tainted earlier studies. On the other hand, our examination has suggested that some researchers have been too dismissive of the historical value of several of our literary sources—particularly the materials from the New Testament. However, when used in concert with other sources of historical data, these materials can significantly advance our

---

Mishnaic, and Talmudic Periods" in *Ancient Synagogues: Historical Analysis and Archaeological Discovery*, edited by Dan Urman and Paul Virgil McCracken Flesher (New York: E.J. Brill, 1995), 1.289–297.

[110] *CIJ* 2.1404; Josephus, *BJ* 2.128, *Ant.* 16.162–165; Philo, *Contempl.* 64–89.

[111] *CIJ* 2.1404, Josephus, *BJ* 2.285–292, *Ant.* 16.162–165; Philo, *Somn.* 2.123-129; Acts 17:10–14.

understanding of the pre-70 synagogues. In general, the presence of multiple attestations of specific synagogal phenomena serve to solidify claims made about these phenomena. Particularly welcome are multiple attestations across different media of evidence. When multiple attestations are lacking, the evidence should be understood as being only suggestive. Conversely, when evidence from different sources begins to mount, continued adherence to theories at variance with this evidence should be viewed as sheer dogmatism. In this latter instance, standard historical practice requires that the aberrant theory be either modified or discarded.

Having completed our survey of the early sources, we are ready to begin a more in-depth examination of the evidence. It is thus to the important topic of synagogue terminology that we now turn.

CHAPTER 2
TERMINOLOGY

Throughout the past two chapters the term *synagogue* has been used to refer to both a Jewish congregation and the building wherein this congregation met. It is now time to justify this usage for the pre-70 period.

As we observed in the introductory chapter, some recent researchers (Kee, R. Horsley, McKay) have disputed the existence of synagogue buildings in Palestine prior to the Second Temple period. In their view, while synagogue buildings in the diaspora known as *proseuchai* were beginning to emerge from religious gatherings in private homes, within Palestine no such buildings existed until well after the fall of Jerusalem. Intermediary positions maintain that these buildings were largely confined to areas outside Judea (Flesher) or were not specialized structures (White, Meyers). Thus, in the more extreme of these formulations, when the Gospels or other first-century documents use the Greek word *synagōgē*, the root of our English *synagogue*, either they refer to an informal religious gathering, or they inaccurately project onto the homeland an institution (with a building) that existed in Palestine only after 70 C.E.

These proposals underscore the need for a study of the disputed terms to determine whether translators are being anachronistic when they render the words *synagōgē* or *proseuchē* into the English word *synagogue*. To what did these words refer? How did their usage evolve over time? In what ways did context affect their meanings? In this chapter we will address questions such as these.

Although the words *synagōgē* and *proseuchē* have dominated recent discussions about Second Temple synagogues, researchers have long recognized that the ancients used several other terms alongside these two appellations.[1] Unfortunately, scholars have usually just listed these other terms without exploring them in any depth. As a remedy to this situation,

---

[1]Krauss, *Synagogale Altertümer*, 15–17; Schrage, "Συναγωγή," 808; *HJP* 2.440–441; Levine, "The Second Temple Synagogue: The Formative Years," 13; Oster, "Supposed Anachronism in Luke-Acts' Use of ΣΥΝΑΓΩΓΗ," 186.

we will also submit each of these words to a linguistic analysis in order to gain a better understanding of their basic meanings and how the ancients employed them vis-à-vis the Second Temple synagogues.

In order to prevent this chapter from encompassing the entire study, we will not here examine every possible citation, but only a representative sample. Other references will be reserved for examination in future chapters.

SYNAGŌGĒ

The basic sense of the word *synagōgē* can be seen from its constituent parts, *syn* + *agō*, "bring together." As a verbal noun it thus means "a bringing together," or less awkwardly, "a gathering." In its earliest uses it meant this quite literally. For example, in the Septuagint's rendering of Gen 1:9 we have: "And God said, 'Let the waters under the sky be gathered together into one gathering [συναγωγήν].'" This gathering could be of things, as in the Genesis passage, of ideas ("conclusions," Aristotle, *Rh.* 1400b.26), or of persons. This last sense is attested most often, especially in Jewish writings.

While Gentile authors could use this term to speak of various types of gatherings, such as birthday celebrations or religious assemblies,[2] in early Jewish writings, *synagōgē* above all meant the assembled congregation of Israel. This is especially seen in the Septuagint, which routinely renders two Hebrew words, *'ēdāh* and *qāhāl* into *synagōgē.* Both Hebrew terms frequently occur in the Pentateuch, where they signify the cultic and legal community of Israel. For instance, in Lev 8:3, Moses is commanded to "assemble the whole congregation [כל־הָעֵדָה/πᾶσαν τὴν συναγωγήν] at the entrance of the tent of meeting." Similarly, in Deut 5:22, Moses recalls to the people that God had gathered "all of your congregation [כָּל־קְהַלְכֶם/πᾶσαν συναγωγὴν ὑμῶν]" before Mount Sinai to present them with the Torah.

In some later writings of the Apocrypha and Pseudepigrapha, the congregation of Israel is viewed as being divided into many congregations. For example, *Pss. Sol.* 10:7 (I B.C.E.) states that the "congregations of Israel [συναγωγαὶ 'Ισραήλ] will glorify the name of the Lord" (cf. *Pss. Sol.* 17:43). Likewise, Sir 24:23 (II B.C.E.) also uses the plural when it declares that the "congregations of Jacob [συναγωγαῖς 'Ιακώβ]" were the inheritors of the Pentatuech.[3]

---

[2]See citations in Schrage, "Συναγωγή," 800–801.

[3]See also Sus 41, 60 (II B.C.E.) which refer to a local congregation (*synagōgē*).

Despite the fact that *synagōgē* occurs over 200 times in the LXX, in no clear case is it used for a *place* of assembly.[4] Nor is there any instance in the Pseudepigrapha where *synagōgē* is so used.[5] This would seem to give credence to the claim that during the period of the Second Temple, *synagōgē* had not yet undergone the process of metonymy, whereby the *gathering place* took on the name of the *gathered congregation*. But there is still other evidence to be considered.

We begin with the Synoptics. It will be recalled that of all the synagogue references in the Synoptics, Kee accepts only Luke 7:5—the story of the centurion who built the Capernaum synagogue—as containing a usage of *synagōgē* that unequivocally refers to a building. He writes:

> The fact that this detail about a synagogue constructed in Capernaum is found only in Luke's version of this incident and is missing from the Q equivalent in Matthew 8:5–13, coupled with the dating of Luke to the turn of the second

---

[4]The one possible exception is the OG text of Sus 28 which John Collins translates, "But the lawless men turned away, murmuring threats among themselves and plotting to put her [Susanna] to death. They came to the synagogue of the city where they sojourned, and all the Israelites who were there assembled [Οἱ δὲ παράνομαι ἄνδρες ἀπέστερεψαν ἀπειλοῦντες ἐν ἑαυτοῖς καὶ ἐνεδρεύοντεσς ἵνα θανατώσουσιν αὐτήν· καὶ ἐλθούτες ἐπὶ τὴν συναγωγὴν τῆς πόλεως, οὗ παρῳκοῦσαν, καὶ συνήδρευσαν οἱ ὄντες ἐκεῖ πάντες οἱ υἱοὶ ᾽Ισραηλ]" (John J. Collins, *Daniel: A Commentary on the Book of Daniel* [Minneapolis: Fortress Press, 1993], 420). The translation appears correct since rendering *synagōgē* as "congregation" would make the second half of the sentence—which states that the people in the city gathered—redundant. The Theodotion version has Susanna's trial taking place at Joakim's house. This discrepancy should not be taken as evidence for the hypothesis that synagogues emerged from homes. First of all, the OG version of Susanna not only predates that of Theodotus, but the latter is dependent upon the former (ibid., 426). Secondly, as Collins points out, the shift in venue of Susanna's trial in the Theodotion version is explained by the fact that it helps Daniel's examination of the false witnesses since the evidence (the trees in question) is visible from the house (ibid., 431). Because the OG of Susanna dates to c. 100 B.C.E. (ibid., 437), if we were to accept Collins' translation, then we have here the earliest use of *synagōgē* for a building. Because the OG is probably based on a Hebrew original, a Palestinian provenance seems most likely (ibid., 438). See also Schrage, "Συναγωγή," 805; Levine, "The Nature and Origin of the Palestinian Synagogue Reconsidered," 441. Cf. Kee, "Defining the First-Century CE Synagogue," 485, n. 13. Kee apparently examines only the Theodotion version of Susanna 28.

[5]*Synagōgē* is found in the following passages of the Pseudepigrapha: *T. Levi* 11:5; *T. Benj.* 11:2, 3; *Pss. Sol.* 10:7; 17:16, 43, 44.

> century . . . point to Luke's having read the post-70 developments back into the first half of the first century C.E.[6]

We need not quibble here with Kee's dating of Luke, though it is on the upper extreme of scholarly opinion. Of more interest is his claim that Matthew's version of the story better preserves the tradition found in Q. This requires argumentation and cannot be assumed. Here are the two versions side by side, with the major discrepancies placed in bold type:[7]

> Matt 8:5 When he entered Capernaum, a centurion came to him, appealing to him 6 and saying, "Lord, my servant is lying at home paralyzed, in terrible distress." 7 And he said to him, "I will come and cure him." 8 The centurion answered, "Lord, I am not worthy to have you come under my roof; but only speak the word, and my servant will be healed. 9 For I also am a man under authority, with soldiers under me; and I say to one, 'Go,' and he goes, and to another, 'Come,' and he comes, and to my slave, 'Do this,' and the slave does it." 10 When Jesus heard him, he was amazed and said to those who followed him, "Truly I tell you, in no one in Israel have I found such faith. 11 **I tell you, many will come from east and west and will eat with Abraham and Isaac and Jacob in the kingdom of heaven,** 12 **while the heirs of the kingdom will be thrown into the outer darkness, where there will be weeping and gnashing of teeth."** 13 And to the centurion

> Luke 7:1 After Jesus had finished all his sayings in the hearing of the people, he entered Capernaum. 2 A centurion there had a slave whom he valued highly, and who was ill and close to death. 3 When he heard about Jesus, **he sent some Jewish elders to him, asking him to come and heal his slave.** 4 **When they came to Jesus, they appealed to him earnestly, saying, "He is worthy of having you do this for him,** 5 **for he loves our people, and it is he who built our synagogue for us."** [ἀγαπᾷ γὰρ τὸ ἔθνος ἡμῶν καὶ τὴν συναγωγὴν αὐτὸς ᾠκοδόμησεν ἡμῖν.] 6 **And Jesus went with them, but when he was not far from the house, the centurion sent friends to say to him,** "Lord, do not trouble yourself, for I am not worthy to have you come under my roof; 7 **therefore I did not presume to come to you.** But only speak the word, and let my servant be healed. 8 For I also am a man set under authority, with soldiers under me; and I say to one, "Go,"

[6]Kee, *Early Christianity in the Galilee*, 10.

[7]Scholars are divided over the question of whether Luke 7:3–5 should be included in Q. See John S. Kloppenborg, *Q Parallels: Synopsis, Critical Notes, and Concordance* (Sonoma, Calif.: Polebridge Press, 1988), 50. To my knowledge, no scholar has previously proposed the set of arguments presented below.

Jesus said, "Go; let it be done for you according to your faith." And the servant was healed in that hour.	and he goes, and to another, "Come," and he comes, and to my slave, "Do this," and the slave does it." 9 When Jesus heard this he was amazed at him, and turning to the crowd that followed him, he said, "I tell you, not even in Israel have I found such faith." 10 When those who had been sent returned to the house, they found the slave in good health.

At first glance, it appears easy to decide that Matthew contains the more accurate rendering of Q since, aside from the insertion of other Q material in vv. 11–12 (cf. Luke 13:28–29), Matthew's version appears to be the more primitive of the two stories. Moreover, Matthew's rendering has affinities with the Johannine account about an official (βασιλικός) coming directly to Jesus to ask him to cure his son (John 4:46–53). As Fitzmyer writes, "If the double delegation sent to Jesus were part of 'Q,' its omission by Matthew would be more difficult to explain than to regard it as a Lucan compositional addition to the 'Q' form."[8]

While the second delegation (6b) is awkward and probably constitutes a Lucan redaction, there are good reasons for maintaining that the first delegation was originally a part of the Q material. To begin with, we should note that the passage containing the first delegation forms a parallel with the remainder of the story. Thus the Jewish leaders state the credentials of the centurion by saying, "He is *worthy* of having you do this for him ["Αξιός ἐστιν ᾧ παρέξῃ τοῦτο]" (4b). This pronouncement stands in marked contrast to the centurion's own words, "I am *not worthy* to have you come under my roof [οὐ γὰρ ἱκανός εἰμι ἵνα ὑπὸ τὴν στέγην μου εἰσέλθῃς]" (6d). When placed side by side, the twin statements not only underscore the humility of the centurion, but also highlight Jesus' final utterance, "I tell you, not even in Israel have I found such faith" (9c || Matt 8:10c). Given the coherence of this theme across both segments, it seems more likely that this parallel was already contained in Q rather than it being the result of a Lucan redaction.[9]

---

[8]Fitzmyer, *The Gospel According to Luke*, 1.649.

[9]Note also that Luke's reference to the *presbyteroi* of the synagogue in v. 3 coheres with the use of this term in the Theodotus inscription (*CIJ* 2.1404, ll. 9–10) which dates to this period (see below).

If Q did contain the segment, why then would Matthew omit it? Here we must remember from the previous chapter Matthew's relentless hostility toward both the synagogue and any officials connected with it. Consequently, the verses mentioning the synagogue elders constitute just the type of material we would expect Matthew to omit. That Matthew made such omissions can be established from his treatment of Mark's account of the healing of Jairus' daughter (Mark 5:22–43 || Matt 9:18–30 || Luke 8:41–56). In Mark's rendering (which Luke follows), Jairus is called an *archisynagōgos*, a "leader of the synagogue" (Mark 5:22, 35, 36, 38; cf. Luke 8:41, 8:49). That Jesus could so aid an official of the synagogue was apparently more than Matthew could stomach: he omits Jairus' name altogether and refers to him with the more generic term *archōn*, "leader" (Matt 9:18, 23).[10] It is therefore likely that Matthew follows this same pattern in the centurion passage, omitting from Q a reference connecting Jesus to the synagogue in a positive way. This conclusion is further indicated when we observe that Matthew stands alone among the four Gospel writers in failing to mention the existence of a synagogue in Capernaum:[11] elsewhere he inexplicably fails to recount from his Marcan source the story of Jesus' healing of the man with the unclean spirit in the Capernaum synagogue (Mark 1:21–29 || Luke 4:13–38). Thus it would appear that for some unknown reason Matthew systematically sought to repress information linking Jesus to the synagogue at Capernaum.

Taking all this together, in all probability, Luke better preserves the Q tradition in the above passage, as he generally does throughout his Gospel.[12] In this case, Kee's charge that Luke was being anachronistic in this passage is without foundation since Q dates to well before the destruction of the Temple (c. 50–60 C.E.).

Kee's claim that there are no other Synoptic uses of *synagōgē* for a building also merits attention. While Kee is correct in noting the ambiguity in the majority of Synoptic uses, that ambiguity cuts both ways. One need not conclude that *synagōgē* predominately refers to a gathering. In fact there are several indications within the Synoptics and Acts that suggest the opposite.

---

[10]Note that the NRSV's translation of Matt 9:18 inaccurately renders *archōn* as "leader of the synagogue," thus missing the crucial distinction between the term used in this verse and that used in its parallel in Mark 5:22.

[11]The references in the Gospels are: Mark 1:21–29; Luke 4:13–38, 7:1–10; John 6:59.

[12]See Koester, *Ancient Christian Gospels*, 133–134.

Beginning our examination with Mark, the Gospel least likely to be judged as referring to the post-70 period, we notice that in three passages Jesus or the Pharisees are portrayed as "entering" (εἰσῆλθεν εἰς) or "leaving" (ἐξελθόντες ἐκ) a synagogue (1:29, 3:1, 6). The locative function of the Greek word-pairs just cited remains constant throughout Mark. Whenever they are used, they signify an entry into or an exit out of a place or structure with a definite boundary, such as a house (7:17) or a boat (5:2, 6:54).[13] In contrast, the Greek word-pairs just mentioned are absent whenever Mark refers to Jesus' movement in relationship to a crowd (ὄχλος)—a term similar in meaning to "gathering." In the two places that do express movement from a crowd, the preposition *apo*, "from," is used. Thus we have Jesus "entering a house from the crowd [εἰσῆλθεν εἰς οἶκον ἀπὸ τοῦ ὄχλου]" (7:17) or Jesus taking a deaf and dumb man away "from the crowd [ἀπὸ τοῦ ὄχλου]" (7:33). Mark's consistent usage of the two word-pairs just examined suggests that, in the three passages cited (1:29; 3:1, 6), *synagōgē* refers to a building and not a gathering.[14]

Elsewhere, both Luke and Matthew portray Jesus as criticizing the scribes and/or Pharisees because "they love to have the place of honor at banquets and the best seats in the synagogues [φιλοῦσιν δὲ τὴν

---

[13]The other uses of these word-pairs in Mark are in connection with the Tent of Meeting (2:26), bodies of swine or humans (spirits or powers entering or exiting; 1:25; 5:8, 13, 30; 9:25), the region of Tyre (7:31) and the Temple (11:11).

[14]A similar analysis holds for Luke-Acts and Matthew. The former represents entry into a synagogue in two places: "And [Jesus], according to his custom on the Sabbath, entered the synagogue [καὶ εἰσῆλθεν κατὰ τὸ εἰωθὸς αὐτῷ ἐν τῇ ἡμέρᾳ τῶν σαββάτων εἰς τὴν συναγωγήν]" (Luke 4:16); "And entering the synagogue . . . [καὶ [εἰς]ελθόντες εἰς τὴν συναγωγὴν]" (Acts 13:14). Like Mark, Luke-Acts only uses εἰσῆλθεν εἰς when referring to an entry into a bounded place (Luke 1:40 [house], 4:38 [house], 6:4 [Tent of Meeting], 7:1 [Capernaum], 7:44 [house], 8:30 [possessed man], 8:33 [swine], 9:52 [village], 10:38 [village], 17:27 [ark], 22:3 [Satan into Judas]; Acts 1:13 [city], 3:8 [Temple], 5:21 [Temple], 9:17 [house], 10:24 [Caesarea], 11:8 [a mouth], 11:12 [house], 14:20 [city], 18:7 [house], 28:16 [Rome]). Luke never portrays anyone as entering a crowd. Matthew, on the other hand, uses only ἦλθεν εἰς when referring to an entry into a bounded place (Matt 2:11 [house], 2:23 [Nazareth], 4:13 [Capernaum], 8:14 [house], 8:28 [country of Gadarenes], 9:23 [house], 9:28 [house], 13:54 [town], 16:5 [shore], 16:13 [district of Caesarea Philippi], 17:24 [Capernaum], 17:25 [house], 21:23 [Temple], 27:33 [Golgotha], 28:11 [city]). In one place (Matt 12:9), Matthew uses this construction with respect to movement into a synagogue: "[Jesus] left that place and entered their synagogue [Καὶ μεταβὰς ἐκεῖθεν ἦλθεν εἰς τὴν συναγωγὴν αὐτῶν]." Matthew never portrays anyone as entering a crowd.

πρωτοκλισίαν ἐν τοῖς δείπνοις καὶ τὰς πρωτοκαθεδρίας ἐν ταῖς συναγωγαῖς]" (Matt 23:6 || Luke 20:46, 11:43). One might argue that the passages are anachronistic, except that they are derived from Q.[15] Moreover, Mark 12:38–39 contains an almost identical saying:

> Beware of the scribes, who like to walk around in long robes, and to be greeted with respect in the marketplaces, and to have the best seats in the synagogues and places of honor at banquets! [Βλέπετε ἀπὸ τῶν γραμματέων τῶν θελόντων ἐν στολαῖς περιπατεῖν καὶ ἀσπασμοὺς ἐν ταῖς ἀγοραῖς καὶ πρωτοκαθεδρίας ἐν ταῖς συναγωγαῖς καὶ πρωτοκλισίας ἐν τοῖς δείπνοις].

Here, Kee denies that the term *prōtokathedra* ("best seat") refers to a physical seat: "it can mean only the most visible location in the gathering taking place in a home or public meeting hall."[16] Yet this interpretation strains the usual meaning of the root *kathedra*, which is a physical chair or seat.[17] Moreover, Kee's statement that such a gathering took place in a home or meeting hall begs the question of why *synagōgē* could refer *only* to the gathering and not to the structure housing the gathering. Kee leaves this question unanswered.

Although Kee considers the Lucan writings anachronistic, it is worth noting that in Acts 18:7 we find another instance where *synagōgē* clearly refers to a building rather than a congregation. The passage depicts Paul leaving a synagogue in Corinth and moving into the house of Titius Justus, whose "house was next door to the synagogue [ἡ οἰκία ἦν συνομοροῦσα τῇ συναγωγῇ]."[18]

On the other side of the argument, Kee can only produce from the New Testament one reference where *synagōgē* unambiguously refers to

---

[15]See Fitzmyer, *The Gospel According to Luke*, 2.1316, 942–946. In one article, Kee presumed the lateness of the Matthean passage: "Possible hints of formalization are offered in what I regard as a late tradition in Mt 23.6, where there is condemnation of those who 'love the first seats in the synagogue'" ("New Finds That Illuminate the World and Text of the Bible," 105). Later, he apparently realized the problem with this position and argued as outlined in the above text ("Defining the First-Century CE Synagogue," 489).

[16]Kee, "Defining the First-Century CE Synagogue," 489.

[17]LSJ, BAGD s.v. καθέδρα. For typical usages, see Matt 21:12 and Mark 11:15, the passages referring to Jesus' overturning of the money changers' chairs in the Temple. See also the LXX of 1 Sam 20:25; 1 Kgs 10:19; 2 Chr 9:18.

[18]Kee mentions this passage, but argues that the synagogue must have been a house, since it is located next door to a residence. See Kee, *Transformation*, 18; idem, "Defining the First-Century CE Synagogue," 491.

a congregation. Ironically, it is a passage from Acts, which refers to a "congregation breaking up [λυθείσης δὲ τῆς συναγωγῆς]" in Pisidian Antioch (13:43).[19] Yet this usage must be viewed in light of Acts' statement that Paul and Barnabbas had previously "entered into the synagogue [[εἰσ]ελθόντες εἰς τὴν συναγωγήν]" in that city (Acts 13:14).[20] Thus we have a congregation meeting in a synagogue.

Yet another difficulty with Kee's theory that "synagogues" were meetings in private homes emerges from the observation that nowhere in the Gospels (or Acts) does the term *synagōgē* appear in connection with a gathering inside a house. For example, Mark 2:1–12 presents a scene in which Jesus teaches inside Peter's home at Capernaum. Although the scribes have gathered to listen (v. 6), the assembled group is not referred to as a *synagōgē*, but simply as a "crowd" (ὄχλος; v. 4,)—the operative term used throughout the Gospels for informal gatherings in homes, on hillsides, and elsewhere.[21] If prior to 70 C.E. "synagogues" were primarily informal gatherings in private homes, why then do the Gospels nowhere openly state this? The natural inference is that, when speaking of a group of people, the Gospel writers restricted their use of the term *synagōgē* to descriptions of congregations meeting inside a specialized structure also known as a *synagōgē*.

The foregoing discussion suggests that even if we had the Synoptics and Acts alone as witnesses, we would have evidence to indicate that the term *synagōgē* had undergone the process of metonymy by at least the end of the Second Temple period. However, there is yet more evidence to substantiate this claim.

We begin with the writings of Josephus, which contain several citations where *synagōgē* is clearly used to speak of a building.[22] The

---

[19]Kee, "Defining the First-Century CE Synagogue," 491.

[20]See the above analysis of Mark, Matthew, and Luke-Acts.

[21]Mark 3:20 provides yet another example of a "crowd" gathering in a home. For other examples, see Matt 9:23–25 and Luke 5:29. Nowhere in the New Testament is there a use of *synagōgē* comparable to the formula "the church [ἐκκλησία] in so-and-so's house [οἶκος]," used in reference to Christian assemblies (Rom 16:5, 1 Cor 16:19, Col 4:15, Philem 1:2).

[22]Aside from the passages quoted below from Kee's writings, additional treatments of the Josephus and Philo passages can be found in Oster, "Supposed Anachronism in Luke-Acts' Use of ΣΥΝΑΓΩΓΗ," 188–191; Frowald G. Hüttenmeister, "'Synagoge' und 'Proseuche' bei Josephus und in anderen antiken Quellen" in *Begegnungen zwischen Christentum und Judentum in Antike und Mittelalter: Festschrift fur Heinz Schreckenberg*, edited by Dietrich-Alex Koch and Hermann Lichtenberger (Gottingen: Vandenhoeck & Ruprecht, 1993), 175–178;

earliest of these is a passage from a letter issued by Petronius, the Legate of Syria, to the residents of Dora (located on the coast of Palestine) sometime in the early 40s (C.E.). The form of the letter corresponds to the official Roman letters of the period. Because Josephus had access to the imperial archives, its authenticity is highly probable. Moreover, even if Josephus had tampered with the letter (for instance, to place the Jews in a more favorable light), it is unlikely that he would have substituted *synagōgē* for another word such as *proseuchē* since this would have undermined the authenticity of the letter.

The occasion of the letter arose from an incident where some residents of Dora placed a statue of Caesar inside a *synagōgē*. The relevant section runs as follows:

> Publius Petronius, legate of Tiberius Claudius Caesar Augustus Germanicus, to the leading men of Dora speaks: Inasmuch as certain of you have had such mad audacity, notwithstanding the issuance of an edict of Claudius Caesar Augustus Germanicus pertaining to the permission granted the Jews to observe the customs of their fathers, not to obey this edict, but to do the very reverse, in that you have prevented the Jews from having a synagogue [συναγωγὴν Ἰουδαίων κωλύοντας εἶναι] by transferring to it [διὰ τὸ μεταθεῖναι ἐν αὐτῇ] an image of Caesar, you have thereby sinned not only against the law of the Jews, but also against the emperor, whose image was better placed in his own shrine [ἐν τῷ ἰδιῳ ναῷ] than in that of another [ἢ ἐν ἀλλοτρίῳ], especially in the synagogue [ταῦτα ἐν τῷ τῆς συναγωγῆς τόπῳ]; for by natural law each must be lord over his own place [ἰδίων τόπων], in accordance with Caesar's decree (*Ant.* 19.303–305).

In the first usage, *synagōgē* clearly signifies a place, as can be seen from the reference to the transferring of Caesar's image into it (ἐν αὐτῇ).[23] Moreover, we see that, far from being depicted as a home where Jews met for an informal gathering, the synagogue is likened by Petronius to a

---

Martin Hengel, "Proseuche und Synagoge: jüdische Gemeinde, Gotteshaus und Gottesdienst in der Diaspora und in Palästina" in *Tradition und Glaube: Das fruehe Christentum in seiner Umwelt*, edited by Gert Jeremias et al. (Gottingen: Vandenhoeck & Ruprecht, 1971), 157–184; Riesner, "Synagogues in Jerusalem," 179–184.

[23]Kee argues that "Petronius declared that these desecrators had prevented the Jews from *being* (εἶναι) a synagogue by their action of transferring this object into that Jewish place of gathering (ἐν τῷ τῆς συναγωγῆς τόπῳ), where the group had a right to be in charge of their own place" ("Defining the First-Century CE Synagogue," 487). This interpretation overlooks the fact that συναγωγήν is the antecedent of ἐν αὐτῇ. See Hüttenmeister, "'Synagoge' und 'Proseuche' bei Josephus und in anderen antiken Quellen," 177.

Temple shrine (ναός). That this view is not merely a misconception on Petronius' part is borne out by the fact that the offending Dorans thought the edifice appropriate enough to place Caesar's image inside. The second usage of *synagōgē* is less clear, as it might either be translated "the place of the synagogue" or "the place of the congregation."[24] Yet even if it is the latter, we see the metonymic process going on right before our eyes.

Josephus' preface to Petronius' letter contains an additional use of *synagōgē* that corresponds to the first of the above usages:

> A very short time after this, certain young men of Dora, who set a higher value on audacity than on holiness and were by nature recklessly bold, brought an image of Caesar into the synagogue of the Jews [εἰς τήν τῶν Ἰουδαίων συναγωγήν] and set it up. This provoked Agrippa exceedingly, for it was tantamount to an overthrow of the laws of his fathers. Without delay he went to see Publius Petronius, the governor of Syria, and denounced the people of Dora (*Ant.* 19.300–301).

Another place in Josephus' writings where *synagōgē* refers to a building is in the account of an incident transpiring in Caesarea Maritima just prior to the outbreak of the Jewish War. The scene is much like the one just depicted, except in this case, the perpetrators violate the synagogue's space from the outside:

> The Jews in Caesarea had a synagogue adjoining a plot of ground [οἱ γὰρ ἐν Καισαρείᾳ Ἰουδαῖοι, συναγωγὴν ἔχοντες παρὰ χωρίον] owned by a Greek of that city; this site they had frequently endeavoured to purchase, offering a price far exceeding its true value. The proprietor, disdaining their solicitations, by way of insult further proceeded to build upon the site and erect workshops, leaving the Jews only a narrow and extremely awkward passage . . . On the following day, which was a sabbath, when the Jews assembled at the synagogue [τῶν Ἰουδαίων εἰς τήν συναγωγὴν συναθροισθέντων], they found that one of the Caesarean mischief-makers had placed beside the entrance a pot, turned bottom upwards, upon which he was sacrificing birds. This spectacle of what they considered an outrage upon their laws and a desecration of the spot enraged the Jews beyond endurance. The steady-going and peaceable members of the congregation were in favour of immediate recourse to the authorities; but the factious folk and the passionate youth were burning for a fight. The Caesarean party, on their side, stood prepared for action, for they had, by a concerted plan, sent the man on to the mock sacrifice; and so they soon came to blows. Jucundus, the calvary commander commissioned to intervene, came up, removed the pot and

[24]On the use of *topos* as a technical term for a temple or sacred place, see below.

> endeavoured to quell the riot, but was unable to cope with the violence of the Caesareans. The Jews, thereupon, snatched up their copy of the Law and withdrew to Narbata, a Jewish district sixty furlongs distant from Caesarea (*BJ* 2.285–305).

In commenting on this passage, Kee offers a rare concession:

> Here the phrase εἰς τὴν συναγωγήν almost certainly means 'into the meeting', but it cannot be completely excluded that, following the destruction of the temple in 70 CE, the term συναγωγή, which earlier had been used with reference to the Jewish group meetings, began to be used to refer as well to the structure where they met.[25]

By stating that the shift in usage comes *after* 70 C.E., Kee maintains that Josephus was being anachronistic in this passage. Yet because *War* was written in the 70s, this seems highly unlikely.[26]

We will briefly mention a final relevant passage from Josephus' writings, as it will be given further consideration in a subsequent section of this chapter. The passage concerns a synagogue in Antioch in Syria. Josephus states that this structure had been the beneficiary of many votive offerings taken by Antiochus Epiphanes (d. 164 B.C.E.) from the Temple. Antiochus' successors were said to have "restored to the Jews of Antioch all such votive offerings as were made of brass, to be laid up in their synagogue [εἰς τὴν συναγωγήν]" (*BJ* 7.43). As with the previous citation from *War*, Kee maintains that Josephus' usage is anachronistic—in this

---

[25]Kee, "Defining the First-Century CE Synagogue," 488.

[26]In order to lend more credence to this position, in a footnote (ibid., n. 19), Kee cites Robert Eisler's theory (as summarized by H. Thackeray) that our current version of *War* is a revised edition written after Vespasian's death (79 C.E.). Yet when we turn to the citation, we find that Eisler only argued that the introduction and the conclusion of *War* were later additions: "[Dr. Eisler] acutely suggests that Josephus strove to complete his work by the day of the triumph and to present a copy to the two emperors on that memorable occasion. The sequel, including the penultimate chapter about the destruction of the other Jewish temple, that of Onias in Egypt, in A.D. 73 (B. vii. 420–436), was, in Dr. Eisler's opinion, added after that event, the opportunity being taken at the same time to prefix to the whole work a corresponding chapter about its foundation (B. i. 33) and contemporary Hasmonaean history" (H. St. J. Thackeray, *Josephus* [Cambridge, MA: Harvard University Press, 1957], 2.xii). Thackeray otherwise dates *War* to between 75 and 79 C.E.

case for both the second century B.C.E. and the entire Second Temple period.[27]

The charge of anachronism is more difficult to level against Philo's writings, since the author died about twenty-five years before the Temple's destruction. However, because Philo lived in Alexandria where *proseuchē* was the standard term for the synagogue building (as we shall see), the word *synagōgē* rarely appears in his writings. Of five references, four are simply quotations from Numbers 27:16–17 (LXX).[28] In the fifth case, however, Philo uses the term in reference to the Essenes in Palestine. He states that on the Sabbath "they abstain from all other work and proceed to sacred spots which they call synagogues [εἰς ἱεροὺς ἀφικόμενοι τόπους, οἵ καλοῦνται συναγωγαί]" (*Prob.* 81). Here *synagōgai* clearly refers to places (τόπους) and not to the persons gathered in the places. Moreover, since Philo uses *synagōgai* when speaking of a Palestinian locale, it is likely that he understood this usage to be peculiar to that region.[29]

Kee's two-sentence assessment of this passage is puzzling. Immediately after quoting the Philo segment he writes:

> In the Community Rule from Qumran (1QS 6.8–9) the rule is that when the congregation assembles, "each man shall sit in his place: the priests shall sit first, and the elders second, and all the rest of the people according to their rank." There is here no indication of special architectural features, but simply of seating order in a room or an assembly hall.[30]

This locution side-steps the main issue: in his description of the Essenes, Philo calls their places of worship *synagōgai*. The fact that architectural details are not mentioned by him or the Community Rule is beside the point.[31]

---

[27]Kee, "Early Christianity in the Galilee: Reassessing the Evidence from the Gospels," 9.

[28]Philo, *Agr.* 44 (2x), *Post.* 67 (2x).

[29]This point is made in Riesner, "Synagogues in Jerusalem," 182. It is possible that the phrase בית מועד, "house of the assembly" in 1QM 3.4 is equivalent to *synagōgē*. See Schrage, "Συναγωγή," 810 as well as the discussion of the Essenes in chapter seven, below.

[30]Kee, "Defining the First-Century CE Synagogue," 488.

[31]Riesner calls attention to another puzzling remark made elsewhere by Kee on the Philo passage. Kee comments: "The process of change of terminology for places of Jewish study and worship has begun" ("The Changing Meaning of Synagogue," 282). Riesner observes: "This remark somewhat obscures the fact that a Diaspora author

Turning now to the epigraphic evidence, clearly the most important inscription for the understanding of the Palestinian usage of *synagōgē* is the well-known Theodotus inscription (*CIJ* 2.1404), discovered in Jerusalem by the French excavator R. Weill in 1913:[32]

> Θ[ε]όδοτος Οὐεττήνου, ἱερεὺς καὶ
> ἀ[ρ]χισυνάγωγος, υἱὸς ἀρχισυν[αγώ]-
> γ[ο]υ, υἱωνὸς ἀρχισυν[α]γώγου, ᾠκο-
> δόμησε τὴν συναγωγὴν εἰς ἀν[άγν]ω-
> σ[ιν] νόμου καὶ εἰς [δ]ιδαχ[ὴ]ν ἐντολῶν, καὶ
> τ[ὸ]ν ξενῶνα, κα[ὶ τὰ] δώματα καὶ τὰ χρη-
> σ[τ]ήρια τῶν ὑδάτων εἰς κατάλυμα τοῖ-
> ς [χ]ρῄζουσιν ἀπὸ τῆς ξέ[ν]ης, ἣν ἐθεμε-
> λ[ίω]σαν οἱ πατέρες [α]ὐτοῦ καί οἱ πρε-
> σ[β]ύτεροι καὶ Σιμων[ί]δης
>
> Theodotus, (son) of Vettenus, priest and
> *archisynagōgos*, son of an *archisynagōgos*,
> grandson of an *archisynagōgos*, built
> the *synagōgē* for the reading of the law and
> the teaching of the commandments, and
> the guest-chamber and the rooms and the
> water installations for lodging for those needing them
> from abroad, which his fathers, the elders
> and Simonides founded[33]

In line four, we clearly see that the term *synagōgē* refers to the structure that Theodotus had built. Moreover, some of functions listed for the building correspond to those features commonly associated with synagogues in the New Testament and elsewhere (assuming, of course, we render *synagōgē* as "synagogue" in these sources).

Understandably, the issue of dating is crucial in determining whether this usage reflects the pre-70 period. Until recently, there was virtual unanimity among scholars that this inscription should be dated to before the destruction of the Jerusalem Temple. Kee, however, has challenged this consensus, arguing that the inscription dates much later, specifically,

---

writing around AD 40 can use συναγωγή for a synagogue building" ("Synagogues in Jerusalem," 182).

[32]The excavation notes, site plans and photos are found in Raymond Weill, *La cité de David. Compte rendu des fouilles executeés à Jérusalem, sur le site de la ville primitive, campagne de 1913–1914* (Paris: P. Geuthner, 1920).

[33]Author's translation. Cf. Riesner, *Synagogues in Jerusalem*, 193–194; Meyers, "Synagogue," 252.

to the “mid- to late third century.”[34] In defending this position, Kee implies that earlier scholars had dated the inscription arbitrarily and without recourse to paleography or archaeological analysis. Yet his own examination of the inscription’s paleography consists of the following sentence: “Estimates of the date of the inscription by a number of distinguished epigraphers whom I consulted formally converged on the period from the mid-second to the late third century CE.”[35] Nowhere does Kee name these epigraphers or state the reasons for their conclusions.

In fact, extensive paleographic analyses of the Theodotus inscription have existed in publication for quite some time. In a recent essay, Rainer Riesner summarizes the conclusions of these studies:

> The famous epigrapher C. Clermont-Ganneau compared the Theodotus inscription with the inscription prohibiting pagans from entering the inner part of the Herodian Temple (*CIJ* II, no. 1400) which he had found in 1871. Clermont-Ganneau judged both inscriptions contemporary, the Theodotus inscription even slightly earlier, in any case before AD 70. L. H. Vincent compared two other inscriptions from the early 2nd century AD and thought one should not be too dogmatic on the palaeographical dating, although he accepted on general considerations a date prior to AD 70. In a special study of inscriptions of the early Imperial age M. Holleau subscribed to Clermont-Ganneau’s date . . . This judgment was accepted in the edition of the inscription in the *Supplementum Epigraphicum Graecum* (VIII, 1937, 25) and by J. B. Frey in the *Corpus Inscriptionum Judaicarum* (II, 1952, 333). It seems that no author assigned it to a time later than the early 2nd century AD on palaeographical arguments.[36]

---

[34]Kee, “Defining the First-Century CE Synagogue,” 499. This most recent assessment (1995) clashes with Kee’s earlier published remarks. In one study he dates the Theodotus inscription to “no earlier than the fourth century” (“The Changing Meaning of Synagogue” [1994], 283). In another he assigns “a second century date to the building erected by Theodotus in Jerusalem” (“Early Christianity in the Galilee” [1992], 6).

[35]Elsewhere Kee writes, “A recent survey by epigraphers of the Classical period, however, shows them to be in agreement that this inscription could be as late as the third century” (“Early Christianity in the Galilee,” 5).

[36]Riesner, “Synagogues in Jerusalem,” 194–195. The references cited are: C. Clermont-Gannaeu, “Découverte à Jérusalem d’une synagogue de l’époque Hérodienne” in *Syria* (Paris, 1920), 190–197; L. H. Vincent, “Dècouverte de la «synagogue des affranchis» a Jérusalem,” *RB* 30 (1921): 247–277; M. Holleau, “Une inscription trouvée à Broussé,” *BCH* 48 (1924): 1–57. Hüttenmeister’s extensive bibliography on the Theodotus inscription presents the same conclusion. See Hüttenmeister and Reeg, *Die antiken Synagogen in Israel*, 1.192–195.

Riesner goes on to mention the recent discovery of another inscription in Jerusalem that dates to the twentieth year of the reign of Herod the Great (18/17 B.C.E.). The letters of this private dedicatory inscription match the Theodotus inscription even more closely than the official warning inscription (*CIJ* 2.1400) that Clermont-Ganneau used as the basis of his comparison.[37]

On the other hand, when one places the Theodotus inscription next to inscriptions dating from the period to which Kee assigns this monument (III C.E.), one sees marked differences in the letter forms. Particularly striking are differences in the appearance of the sigmas. In the Theodotus inscription these are of the branched variety (Σ). In the middle of the second century C.E., this style was being superseded by the lunate form of the sigma (C), which had been popular in Egyptian inscriptions even in the Second Temple period.[38] One searches in vain through *CIJ* or the Beth She‘arim inscriptions for a monument from the third century or later bearing a branched sigma.[39]

If paleography can only assign a definite *terminus ad quem* of the early second century, then why does the scholarly consensus date the inscription prior to the Temple's destruction? The answer to this is found in an analysis of the archaeological context of the inscription's discovery. Weill discovered the inscription amid some rubble inside a cistern on the southern part of the old City of David in Jerusalem. Although the excavation predated the use of stratigraphic methods, it is noteworthy that the artifacts which Weill discovered in his excavation all date to the Second Temple period.[40] Riesner surveys the City of David excavations in the areas adjoining Weill's expedition and discovers that archaeologists have found nothing there later than the Second Temple period. He quotes H. Geva as stating: "A summary of the finds indicates that for most of the Roman period [after AD 70] the City of David remained largely outside the built-up municipal area of Aelia Capitolina, serving mainly as a

[37]Ibid., 195. The inscription can be found in Isaac, "A Donation for Herod's Temple in Jerusalem," 86–92.

[38]E.g., *JIE* 116 (=*CIJ* 2.1532). On the shift of the sigma from the branched to the lunate form beginning in III B.C.E. Egypt, see Shimon Applebaum, *Jews and Greeks in Ancient Cyrene*, (Leiden: E. J. Brill, 1979), 147.

[39]Note particularly the discussion of the paleographic criteria used for the dating of a III C.E. inscription from Beth She‘arim in Moshe Schwabe and Baruch Lifshitz, *Beth She'arim II* (Jerusalem: Massada Press, 1974), 106–107.

[40]See Weill, *La cité de David*, plate XXV.

source for building stones."[41] Weill himself had discovered evidence of this quarrying, which dates to the foundation of Aelia Capitolina in 135 C.E. (see fig. 1).[42] Some of the quarrying extended into a bath complex which must be dated even earlier. As Riesner points out, these baths can now more accurately be identified as *mikvaoth* or ritual baths.[43] Because the Theodotus inscription mentions a bath establishment adjoining the synagogue, it is possible that the excavated *mikvaoth* constitute the remnants of this complex. Although the quarrying stripped out the area around the cistern and the baths, Weill did find several layers of dressed limestone blocks and stone paving which he believed to be the remains of the synagogue. Additional stones containing geometric motifs attested in the Second Temple period (e.g., the rosette) were found in the cistern with the inscription.[44]

In addition to the archaeological evidence, the historical circumstances surrounding the Jewish occupation of Jerusalem reinforce the early dating of the Theodotus inscription. After the suppression of the Bar Kokhba revolt in 135 C.E., Jews were forbidden to live in the city for at least a century.[45] Prior to that, following the Jewish defeat in 70 C.E.,

---

[41]Quoted in Riesner, "Synagogues in Jerusalem," 196–197 from H. Geva, "Jerusalem: The Roman Period" in *NEAEHL* 2.766.

[42]Kathleen M. Kenyon, *Digging Up Jerusalem* (New York: Praeger, 1974), 31–32, 263–264.

[43]Riesner, "Synagogues in Jerusalem," 197. The baths can be seen on figure 1, marked P1–P6. P1 and P2 appear to be a divided *mikveh* interrupted by quarry Q3, while P4 is likely an *otsar* or storage pool for the *mikvaoth*. P5 and P6 are poorly preserved because of quarrying. According to Weill's plan, the depths of the pools whose tops and bottoms are still intact are: P1/P2, 2.44 m.; P3, 2.54 m.; P4, 0.76 m. Kee refers to these pools as "Roman baths" and argues that they should be dated to the construction of Aelia Capitolina in 135 C.E. ("Defining the First-Century CE Synagogue," 483). The fact that the quarrying took place during the construction of Aelia Capitolina rules out this possibility. Moreover, Roman baths are quite different in configuration than the pools uncovered by Weill. See Reich, "The Synagogue and the *Miqweh* in Eretz-Israel in the Second-Temple, Mishnaic, and Talmudic Periods," 289–297. Reich's treatment of the *mikvaoth* near the cistern that contained the Theodotus inscription is found on pp. 291–292. He notes that, with the exception of Sepphoris, the presence of *mikvaoth* declined precipitously after the Second Temple period (pp. 296–297).

[44]Riesner, "Synagogues in Jerusalem," 197–198. See Weill, *La cité de David*, 98–100, plate XXV. On the significance of the rosette, see the discussion of the Gamla synagogue in the next chapter.

[45]See Smallwood, *The Jews under Roman Rule*, 428–506, 526–538. At several places Kee argues that Jews were allowed back into the city as early as the late second

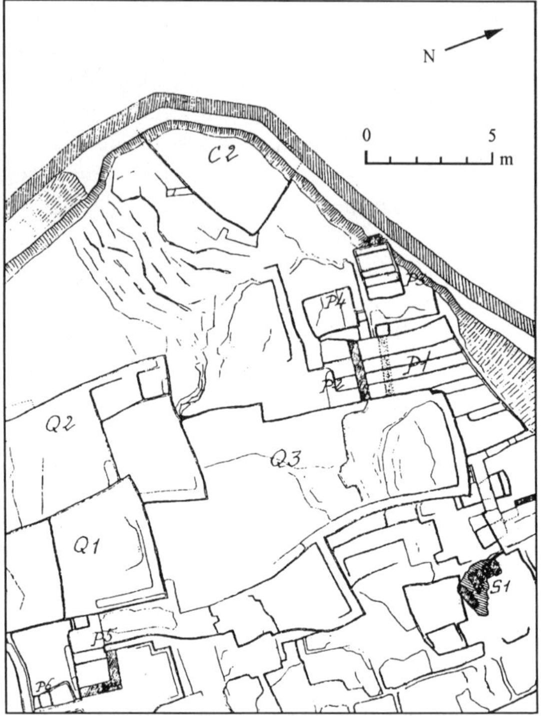

Figure 1. Plan of the area where the Theodotus inscription was discovered. C2 is the cistern in which the inscription was found. P1–P6 represent the *mikvaoth* and storage pools. S1 indicates the well-dressed stones found *in situ*. Q1–Q3 signify three of the quarries dug during the erection of Aelia Capitolina. (After Weill, *La cité de David*, planche III.)

the bulk of the Jewish population in Jerusalem was either killed or enslaved. Consequently, the intervening period in Jerusalem was one marked by a struggle for survival, with few resources being available for the building of synagogues with hostels for pilgrims. Taking all the

century. See Kee, "Defining the First-Century CE Synagogue," 497–499; idem, "Early Christianity in the Galilee," 6. Whatever the merits of these arguments, the earlier dating obtained from the paleographic and archaeological evidence makes these discussions superfluous.

evidence together, the case for dating the Theodotus inscription prior to 70 C.E. is thus very strong.

With this established, we see the inscription's use of *synagōgē* for a building supports the conclusions drawn from our earlier examination of the literary evidence. Additionally, the inscription attests to the presence of monumental synagogal architecture in Judea during the Second Temple period. Finally, the inscription indicates that the synagogue serviced a formalized institution, replete with officials and regularized functions. This picture forms a striking contrast to the one presented by Kee and other recent researchers.

If the word *synagōgē* could be used to refer to a building in Palestine during the Second Temple period, can we infer that this was the case also in the diaspora? The evidence here is mixed. While Josephus and Philo could use this term to refer to structures in Syria and Palestine, we have only the evidence of Acts for this usage in the northern half of the Mediterranean. Acts may be anachronistic on this point, or it might simply be continuing the usage of *synagōgē* found in the Gospel of Luke. In one place, however, Acts twice uses the term *proseuchē* in reference to a structure in Philippi (16:13–16). Since this segment is found in the so-called "we passages," the usage might reflect that of an earlier source which Luke retains.[46] If so, Luke's use of *synagōgē* elsewhere in Acts may reflect the growing use of this term in the diaspora near the end of the first century. This thesis is supported by several pre-70 inscriptions from the Bosporus Kingdom (Crimea) that distinguish between the synagogue congregation, which is called a *synagōgē*, and the synagogue building, which is called a *proseuchē*.[47]

On the other hand, there is one inscription from Berenice (Benghazi) in Cyrenaica (*CJZC* 72), which suggests that, near the end of the Second Temple period, the term *synagōgē* began to be more widely used in the diaspora in reference to a building. The relevant section of the inscription reads:

---

[46]For a recent linguistic analysis of the "we" passages in Acts, see Stanley E. Porter, "The 'We' Passages" in *The Book of Acts in Graeco-Roman Setting,* edited by David W. J. Gill and Conrad Gempf (Grand Rapids, Mich.: William B. Eerdmans Pub. Co., 1994), 545–574. Porter concludes that the 'we' passages were an earlier written source. Conzelmann is not as certain (*Acts of the Apostles*, xxxviii–xl).

[47]E.g., *CIJ* 1.683, 683a, 684, all dating to the first century C.E. These will be examined below and more extensively in chapters four and six.

("Ετει) β' Νέρωνος Κλαυδίου Καίσαρος Δρούσου
Γεργμανικοῦ Αὐτοκράτορος χόϊαχ ις'
ἐφάην τῇ συναγωγῇ τῶν ἐν Βερνεικίδι
Ἰουδαίων τοὺς ἐπιδιδοντες εἰς ἐπισκευ-
ὴν τῆς συναγωγῆς ἀναγράψαι αὐτοὺς εἰστή-
λην λίθου Παρίου

In the second year of the emperor Nero Claudius Caesar Drusus
Germanicus, on the 6th of Choarch.
It was resolved by the congregation
of the Jews in Berenice and its vicinity that (the names of)
those who donated to the repairs of the synagogue be inscribed
on a stele of Parian marble.[48]

The second year of Nero's reign was 55/56 C.E. Aside from its location in the diaspora, what is significant about this inscription is that it uses *synagōgē* in two different ways: while the usage in line three signifies the Jewish congregation, in line five, *synagōgē* refers to an architectural structure. Thus we see a dual usage here much like Acts' use of *synagōgē* to refer to both the synagogue congregation and the synagogue building at Pisidian Antioch (13:43, 14; see above). Because the inscription refers to the repair of a pre-existing synagogue, the use of *synagōgē* for a building dates even earlier, though how much earlier cannot be determined.[49]

To sum up: in this examination we have seen how, within a Jewish context, *synagōgē* came first to signify the larger congregation of Israel, then individual congregations, and, last of all, the buildings wherein the congregations met. Exactly when *synagōgē* was undergoing the metonymic process is unclear. Given the numerous uses of this word for a building in the first century C.E., a dating of about a century earlier seems most likely for Syro-Palestine.[50] Outside of that region, *synagōgē*

---

[48]Author's translation. Cf. Oster, "Supposed Anachronism in Luke-Acts' Use of ΣΥΝΑΓΩΓΗ," 187; Applebaum, *Jews and Greeks in Ancient Cyrene*, 162, n. 149; Hengel, "Proseuche und Synagoge," 182–183. To date, Kee has not discussed this inscription.

[49]If this synagogue corresponds to the Jewish *amphitheatron* attested in Berenice (see below), then the structure existed in the first century B.C.E. but was not called a *synagōgē* until sometime after 25 C.E.

[50]While it is generally assumed that the Aramaic counterpart of *synagōgē* was בית כנשתא (Hebrew: בית הכנסת), we currently possess neither epigraphic nor literary evidence from our period making clear use of this phrase. (See, however, chapter three for a discussion of an ostracon from Elath dating to VI B.C.E. that

appears to refer to a building only beginning in the first half of the first century C.E., though an earlier date cannot be ruled out. Additionally, the evidence we have examined so far indicates that the *synagōgai* were monumental structures enclosing sacred space capable of being violated by pagan idols and rituals. They served a variety of functions and were governed by functionaries bearing various titles. In short, they served as centers for formalized institutions.

PROSEUCHĒ

The basic meaning of *proseuchē* is "prayer." The verb from which it is derived, *proseuchomai*, typically refers to the act of making petitionary prayer, often associated with a vow (*euchē*). *Proseuchē* thus represents the embodiment of that action.[51] Hence the LXX of 2 Chr 6:19 can speak of "the prayer that your servant [Solomon] prays to you [τῆς προσευχῆς ἧς ὁ παῖς σου προσεύχεται ἐναντίον σου]." While rarely used outside of Jewish writings (where *euchē* is preferred), the LXX routinely uses the word *proseuchē* to translate the Hebrew word *tᵉfillāh*, which also means "prayer."[52] In a few places in the LXX, *proseuchē* is used in reference to a particular "place of prayer." For example, the Temple is referred to as a "house of prayer" (οἶκος προσευχῆς) in three passages (Isa 56:7, 60:7;

---

purportedly uses this phrase, though the reading is far from certain.) For later uses, see Schrage, "Συναγωγή," 808–809; Krauss, *Synagogale Altertümer*, 17–24; *HJP* 2.439–440. See also chapter seven for possible Hebrew terms used of the synagogues by the Essenes.

[51]See H. Greeven, "Προσεύχομαι, Προσευχή" in *TDNT* 2.807–808.

[52]Some authors have thought that a fourth century B.C.E. inscription from Epidaurus (*IG* 4 *editio minor* no. 106, l. 27) makes reference to a pagan *proseuchē* since it contains the Doric form of the word (ποτευχας) and is connected with an altar. Irina Levinskaya, however, rightly points out that the inscription is so fragmentary that it cannot be determined whether *poteuchas* refers to a structure or simply to "prayers" (Irina A. Levinskaya, "A Jewish or Gentile Prayer House? The Meaning of *Proseuche*," *TynBul* 41 [1990]: 154–159). No other early inscription coming from a pagan milieu uses *proseuchē* in reference to a building. Most epigraphers take the presence of the term with this usage as being diagnostic for an inscription's Jewishness. That *proseuchē* was a Jewish term can possibly be inferred from a place in Philo's writings where he mentions that in the persecution of Alexandrian Jews, the prefect, Flaccus, made an "attack against our laws by seizing the *proseuchai* without even leaving them their name [μηδὲ τοὔνομα ὑπολιπομένῳ]" (*Flacc.* 53). See Hüttenmeister, "'Synagoge' und 'Proseuche' bei Josephus und in anderen antiken Quellen," 170.

1 Macc 7:37; cf. Matt 21:13; Mark 11:17; Luke 19:46).[53] Elsewhere, 1 Macc 3:46 states that a "place of prayer [τόπος προσευχῆς]" had formerly been in Mitzpah—probably a reference to an ancient sacrificial site once visited by Samuel (1 Sam 7:5–10).[54] The final instance is one we noted in the previous chapter in our discussion of 3 Maccabees. Within the plot of that novella, after the Egyptian Jews had slaughtered the apostates from among their ranks, they celebrated a festival in Ptolemais. The text then reads: "after inscribing [the festival days] as holy on a pillar and dedicating a *proseuchē* at the site of the festival, they departed unharmed, free, and overjoyed [ἃς καὶ ἀνιερώσαντες ἐν στήλῃ κατὰ τὸν τῆς συμποσίας τόπον προσευχῆς καθιδρύσαντες ἀνέλυσαν ἀσινεῖς ἐλεύθεροι ὑπερχαρεῖς]" (7:20).

Proseuchē also refers to a building in a number of inscriptions and papyri from Egypt. One of the earliest of the inscriptions (*JIE* 117 = *CPJ* 3.1532a) reads:[55]

ὑπὲρ βασιλέως	On behalf of King
Πτολεμαίου τοῦ	Ptolemy, son of
Πτολεμα̣ί̣ο̣υ̣ καὶ	Ptolemy, and
βασιλίσσης	Queen
Βερενίκης τῆς	Berenice his
γυναικὸς καὶ	wife and
ἀδελφῆς καὶ τῶν	sister and their
τέκνων οἱ ἐν Κροκ[ο]-	children, the Jews in
δίλων πόλει Ἰου[δαῖ]-	Crocodilopolis (dedicated)
οι τὴν προ̣[σ]ε̣[υχ]ή̣[ν]	the *proseuchē*
κ[αὶ - - -]	and . . .

The Ptolemy referred to in the inscription is Ptolemy III Euergetes, who married Berenice in 246 B.C.E. The reference to their children in line eight

---

[53]Because the LXX uses *oikos* and *topos* interchangeably when referring to the Temple (e.g., 2 Chr 6:20, 7:12; Ps 25:8, LXX), a *proseuchē* (or a *topos*) as a "place of prayer" may have derived from the passages mentioning the Temple as a "house of prayer." Note also that in 1Kgs 8:42, the MT refers to a foreigner who "prays towards this house" (וְהִתְפַּלֵּל אֶל־הַבַּיִת הַזֶּה), i.e., towards the Temple. The LXX reads "they will pray towards this *place*" (προσεύξονται εἰς τὸν τόπον τοῦτον). On this point, see Kasher, "Synagogues as 'Houses of Prayer' and 'Holy Places'," 208–210.

[54]See Hüttenmeister, "'Synagoge' und 'Proseuche' bei Josephus und in anderen antiken Quellen," 165.

[55]Translation is from *JIE*. The above transcription takes into account slight corrections noted in Horsley, "Towards a New *Corpus Inscriptionum Iudaicarum*?" 94.

indicates that the inscription dates to sometime after this but before Euergetes' death in 221 B.C.E. Inscriptions similar to this one have been found in the Egyptian cities of Alexandria (*JIE* 9, 13), Schedia (*JIE* 22), Nitriai (*JIE* 25), Athribis (*JIE* 27, 28) and Xenephyris (*JIE* 24). These all date to the Hellenistic or Early Roman periods and use the term *proseuchē* in reference to a building. In some of the inscriptions, actual architectural features are mentioned, such as a *pylon* (*JIE* 24), a monumental gateway, or an *exedra* (ἐξέδραν, *JIE* 28), an annex to a main hall. In another instance, unspecified appurtenances (συνκύροντα) are referred to in the dedication (*JIE* 25). One inscription mentions the names of two *prostatēs* or presiding officers (*JIE* 24), while a land survey in one of the papyri indicates that the congregation of a *proseuchē* leased out a consecrated garden (ἱερὰς παραδείσος) to a tenant (*CPJ* 1.134).

While we will examine these inscriptions and papyri more closely in chapter four, here it is worth noting that the evidence reviewed so far suggests that the Egyptian *proseuchai* were monumental buildings dedicated to the Jewish Deity. Moreover, the mention in the inscriptions of official Jewish representatives and the use of dedicatory formulas honoring the ruling monarchs both presuppose formalized institutions, not ad hoc gatherings in domestic residences. Finally, the metonymic process whereby the term *proseuchē* went from meaning "prayer" to signifying "a place of prayer" suggests that a primary function of the buildings was to provide a venue for the offering of prayers. This last point seems obvious, but it is one that Heather McKay misses when she excludes prayer as a Sabbath activity for Jews up until the third century C.E.[56]

From these observations the question naturally arises whether the structures referred to in these inscriptions and papyri can be viewed as counterparts to the *synagōgai* attested somewhat later. A number years ago, Ellis Rivkin attempted to argue that the *proseuchai* shared none of the defining functions adduced for the *synagōgai*. Noting that the early epigraphic evidence from Egypt consisted mainly of dedications offered in honor of the Ptolemaic rulers, Rivkin proposed that these *proseuchai* constituted loyalty shrines:

> The *proseuche* . . . was not a prayer-house in general, but a shrine for prayers to be offered for the reigning family. The *proseuche* represented for the Jews

---

[56]The main thesis of McKay's book, *Sabbath and Synagogue*. For a more complete statement of this thesis, see the introduction, above.

> the solution of a delicate problem: how loyalty to a pagan regime that deified its emperors could be made compatible with the belief in a single God.[57]

While it is admittedly difficult to discern all the functions for the earliest of the *proseuchai*, owing to the sparsity of the evidence, it is worth noting that one inscription from Egypt dating to the second century B.C.E. simply dedicates the *proseuchē* to "God Most High" (θεῶι ὑψίστωι) without mentioning the rulers.[58] It must also be recognized that the dedications themselves are formulaic and closely parallel inscriptions from pagan temples.[59] To infer from these that the *proseuchai* served as places where prayers were offered *only* for the ruler would be like inferring that the petitioners inside an Egyptian Serapeum never prayed for healing.

In any case, by the first century C.E. we do have literary sources which better expand our understanding of the types of activities that went on inside the *proseuchai*. Referring to the *proseuchai* of the Jews in Rome, for example, Philo writes: "[Augustus] knew therefore that they have *proseuchai* and meet together in them, particularly on the sacred sabbaths when they receive as a body a training in their ancestral philosophy" (*Legat*. 155). The functions Philo here describes for the *proseuchai* are much like those outlined for the *synagōgē* in the Theodotus inscription.[60]

Rivkin tried to account for this passage by arguing that Philo mistakenly called the structures in Rome *proseuchai* when they were in fact *synagōgai* founded by Palestinian Jews.[61] A difficulty with this

---

[57]Ellis Rivkin, "Ben Sira and the Non Existence of the Synagogue: A Study in Historical Method" in *In the Time of Harvest, Essays in Honor of Abba Hillel Silver on the Occasion of his 70th Birthday*, edited by Daniel Jeremy Silver (New York: Macmillan, 1963), 352.

[58]*JIE* 9. The inscription is fragmentary, but there does not appear to be room in the missing lines for mention of the ruler.

[59]See Paul M. Fraser, *Ptolemaic Alexandria* (Oxford: Clarendon Press, 1972), 1.282–283 and chapter four, below.

[60]Cf. the following passage wherein Philo uses the variant *proseuktērion* (a *hapax legomenon*): "Even now this practice is retained, and the Jews every seventh day occupy themselves with the philosophy of their fathers, dedicating that time to the acquiring of knowledge and the study of the truths of nature. For what are our *proseuktēria* throughout the cities but schools of prudence and courage and temperance and justice and also of piety, holiness and every virtue by which duties to God and men are discerned and rightly performed?" (*Mos*. 2.216). For commentary on this passage, see the treatment of *didaskaleion* below.

[61]Rivkin, "Ben Sira and the Non Existence of the Synagogue," 351–354. In defense of his position, Rivkin points to Philo's quotation of a letter by Agrippa I where the latter uses the term *synagōgion* in reference to the structures in Asia Minor

argument is that there exists a first-century pagan epitaph from Rome which uses the term *proseucha*, the Latin cognate of the Greek *proseuchē* (*JIWE* 2.602):[62]

Dis M(anibus).	To the Di Manes.
P(ublio) Corfido	For P. Corfidius
Signino	Signinus,
pomario	fruiterer
de agger	from the rampart
a proseucha	by the *proseucha*
Q(uintus) Sallustius	Q. Sallustius
Hermes	Hermes
amico benemerenti	for his well-deserving friend.
et numerum	Also a number
ollarum decem.	of urns: 10

Conversely, we currently possess no inscriptions from pre-70 Rome that use *synagōgē* (Latin, *synagoga*) for a building.[63] Consequently, it seems most likely that *proseuchē*/*proseucha* was the common term for synagogue buildings in Rome and that Philo's usage in the cited passage is not tainted by provincialism. That Philo understood *proseuchai* to be present not only in Egypt and Rome, but throughout the entire Jewish

---

(*Legat.* 312). This argument fails on two counts. First, the letter was most likely written by Philo as it carries his literary style (see below). Secondly, Rivkin fails to notice that Philo elsewhere uses the term *synagōgion* to refer to structures in *Alexandria* (*Somn.* 2.123–129). The only inference to be drawn here is that the terms *synagōgion* and *proseuchē* were interchangeable for Philo.

[62]Translation from *JIWE*. The term *proseucha* has been retained in the above translation for *JIWE*'s "synagogue." From slightly after our period (c. 105 C.E.), Juvenal, writing satirically about the trials of living in Rome, uses the same form of the word. In this case the term is used insultingly by a bully who confronts the satirist in the streets of Rome: "'Where are you from?' shouts he; 'whose swipes, whose beans have blown you out? With what cobbler have you been munching cut leeks and boiled sheep's head?—What, sirrah, no answer? Speak out, or take that upon your shins! Where is your stand? In what *proseucha* shall I find you?'" (*Sat.* 3.292–296). That Juvenal should use this term is remarkable since he writes after the conclusion of the Jewish War when there would have been a massive influx of Jewish slaves from Palestine. Presumably they would have used the preferred Palestinian word *synagōgē*. Thus the term *proseucha* must have been entrenched earlier.

[63]The Jewish epitaphs from Rome bearing the terms *synagōgē* or *synagoga* date to centuries after our period. Moreover, it cannot be determined with certainty whether these usages refer to a congregation or to a synagogue building (or both), though Leon believes the former to be the case (Harry J. Leon and Carolyn Osiek, *The Jews of Ancient Rome*, updated ed. [Peabody, Mass.: Hendrickson Publishers, 1995], 139).

diaspora can be seen from a passage written in the aftermath of the desecration of several *proseuchai* in Alexandria (38 C.E.):

> It was perfectly clear that the rumour of the overthrowing of the *proseuchai* beginning at Alexandria would spread at once to the nomes of Egypt and speed from Egypt to the East and the nations of the East and from the Hypotaenia and Marea, which are the outskirts of Libya, to the West and the nations of the West. For so populous are the Jews that no one country can hold them, and therefore they settle in very many of the most prosperous countries in Europe and Asia both in the islands and on the mainland, and while they hold the Holy City where stands the sacred Temple of the most high God to be their mother city, yet those which are their by inheritance from their fathers, grandfathers, and ancestors even farther back, are in each case accounted by them to be their fatherland in which they were born and reared, while to some of them they have come at the time of their foundation as immigrants to the satisfaction of the founders. And it was to be feared that people everywhere might take their cue from Alexandria, and outrage their Jewish fellow-citizens by rioting against their *proseuchai* and ancestral customs (*Flacc.* 45–47).

Philo's use of *proseuchē* to refer to synagogue buildings throughout the diaspora agrees not only with epigraphic evidence from Egypt and Rome, but also with inscriptions from Delos (e.g., *CIJ* 1.726) and several sites in the Crimea (e.g., *CIJ* 1.683a, 690, 691). Moreover, Josephus records a decree from the first century B.C.E. giving the Jews of Halicarnassus (Asia Minor) permission to build *proseuchai* (*Ant.* 14.256–258).

If there was a distinction between the *proseuchai* and *synagōgai*, it was not one of different function (at least not in the radical way that Rivkin proposed) but of geographical usage: while Jews in the diaspora commonly referred to their synagogue buildings as *proseuchai*, those in Syro-Palestine preferred the term *synagōgē*. Martin Hengel argued this position a number of years ago in a well-known essay wherein he suggested that the Jews in Palestine refrained from using *proseuchē* for their synagogues out of deference to the passage in Isaiah 56:7 which calls the Temple "a house of prayer," as we have seen.[64] Whether or not this was the reason for the different usages, we have already noted evidence that by the middle of the first century C.E. the terms were beginning to be used interchangeably in at least some parts of the diaspora. Thus we have the use of *synagōgē* for a building in the inscription from Berenice (*CJZC* 72; 55 C.E.) and Acts' use of both

[64] Hengel, "Proseuche und Synagoge," 177–178.

synagōgē(e.g., 18:7) and *proseuchē*(16:13, 16) in reference to synagogue buildings in the diaspora.

Conversely, Josephus is able to refer to a structure in Palestine (viz., Tiberias) with the term *proseuchē*. Calling the *proseuchē* "a huge building, capable of accommodating a large crowd [μέγιστον οἴκημα καὶ πολὺν ὄχλον ἐπιδέξασθαι δυνάμενον]" (*Vita* 277), the historian goes on to relate his activities within this edifice during the second year of the Jewish revolt (67 C.E.). Froward Hüttenmeister has argued that this building was known as a *proseuchē* because it resembled a large structure in Alexandria which the Tosefta describes in similar terms (*t. Sulk.* 4.6).[65] Aside from Hüttenmeister's uncritical use of a third-century source, his solution is too speculative. A more satisfactory interpretation arises from the observation that the usage of *proseuchē* comes within *Life*, one of Josephus' last compositions. In his first two works, *War* and *Antiquities*, Josephus uses *proseuchē* only once in reference to a building—and this is contained in the quotation of a decree from Asia (*Ant.* 14.256–258). Otherwise, his standard term for synagogue buildings is *synagōgē*, as we saw in the previous section. However, this usage never returns in his last two works, *Life* and *Against Apion*, which were written in the nineties.[66] It is therefore likely that, when calling the Tiberian structure a *proseuchē*, Josephus was taking over the common usage of his adopted home—Rome. In all likelihood then, the Tiberians themselves would normally have called their structure a *synagōgē* (or the Aramaic and Hebrew equivalents). If we accept this solution, then we have additional evidence that the terms *synagōgē* and *proseuchē* were becoming interchangeable in the first century C.E.

In summary, *proseuchē* initially meant "prayer," a usage that continued especially in Jewish and Christian writings (e.g., 3 Macc 6:16, Jdt 13:3, Matt 6:6, Rom 12:12). Beginning in Egypt in the third century B.C.E., however, it took on the additional meaning, "a place of prayer." By the first century B.C.E. (and possibly earlier), *proseuchē* became the common term for synagogue buildings throughout the diaspora, with the possible exceptions of Syria and Cyrenaica. In contrast, within Palestine *synagōgē* emerged as the standard term for a synagogue building.

---

[65]Hüttenmeister, "'Synagoge' und 'Proseuche' bei Josephus und in anderen antiken Quellen," 179–180.

[66]In *Ap.* 2.10–11, Josephus quotes Apion (c. 50 C.E.) using the term *proseuchē* in reference to structures in Jerusalem.

Despite this geographic preference, when referring to a building, the two terms can be viewed as being nearly synonymous. Thus while an inscription from Berenice (*CJZC* 72) can speak of a *synagōgē* (congregation) donating money for the repairs of a *synagōgē* (building), inscriptions from the Crimea (e.g., *CIJ* 1.683, 683a) can analogously refer to a *synagōgē* (congregation) meeting inside a *proseuchē*. Further indication of congruence comes from the fact that some first-century authors appear to use *synagōgē* and *proseuchē* interchangeably. Finally, sources from this same period represent the buildings signified by the two terms as having similar functions. Chief among these was to serve as established meeting centers for the study of the scriptures on the Sabbath. While we will explore other functions in a later chapter, here we note that, given the overlap in terminology, these functions are better collated according to geographical location than by the specific label used of the synagogue building. At the same time, certain functions can be inferred from the labels themselves. Thus the very term *proseuchē* suggests the activity of prayer, just as *synagōgē* implies the act of gathering.

A final point is that in the material surveyed in this section, we found no hint that the term *proseuchē*, when used of a building, refers to anything other than a consecrated Jewish edifice that served as an assembly place for an institutionalized community. This same observation was made in the previous section; it is one that will be made repeatedly in the course of this study.

SYNAGŌGION

Because *synagōgion* is in the same word family as *synagōgē*, most synagogue researchers have treated the former term as a variant of the latter. Despite this scholarly practice, *synagōgion* deserves its own treatment since its meaning is more specific than that of *synagōgē*. Moreover, unlike the latter word, which was predominant in Palestinian usage, *synagōgion* appears as a term for the synagogues only in the writings of Philo.

Synagōgion is rarely found in ancient writings. When it is present, it has the meaning of "a picnic" or "a place of picnicking."[67] Because Philo uses the term in reference to the *proseuchai*, we might be tempted to conclude that the structures to which he was referring housed dining

---

[67]See Schrage, "Συναγωγή," 800–801; LSJ s.v. συναγώγιον.

facilities. Yet this conclusion is difficult to infer from Philo's two uses of *synagōgion*, which suggest a less gastronomic function.

The first citation comes from a treatise on the interpretation of dreams. In order to exemplify the vice of vainglory, Philo relates the following story:

> Not long ago I knew one of the ruling class [ἡγεμονικῶν] who when he had Egypt in his charge and under his authority purposed to disturb our ancestral customs and especially to do away with the law of the Seventh Day which we regard with most reverence and awe. He tried to compel men to do service to him on it and perform other actions which contravene our established custom, thinking that if he could destroy the ancestral rule of the Sabbath it would lead the way to irregularity in all other matters, and a general backsliding. And when he saw that those on whom he was exercising pressure were not submitting to his orders, and that the rest of the population instead of taking the matter calmly were intensely indignant and shewed themselves as mournful and disconsolate as they would were their native city being sacked and razed, and its citizens being sold into captivity, he thought good to try to argue them into breaking the law. "Suppose," he said, "there was a sudden inroad of the enemy or an inundation caused by the river rising and breaking through the dam, or a blazing conflagration or a thunderbolt or famine, or plague or earthquake, or any other trouble either of human or divine agency, will you stay at home perfectly quiet? Or will you appear in public in your usual guise, with your right hand tucked inside the left held close to the flank under the cloak lest you should even unconsciously do anything that might help to save you? And will you sit in your *synagōgia* and assemble your regular company [καὶ καθεδεῖσθε ἐν τοῖς συναγωγίοις ὑμων, τὸν εἰωθοὐτα θίασον ἀγείροντεσς] and read in security your holy books [ἱερὰς βίβλους], expounding any obscure point and in leisurely comfort discussing at length your ancestral philosophy? No, you will throw all these off and gird yourselves up for the assistance of yourselves, your parents and your children, and the other persons who are nearest and dearest to you, and indeed also your chattels and wealth to save them too from annihilation" (*Somn.* 2.123–128).

It is unclear if the ruler referred to is Flaccus, who instigated a persecution of the Alexandrian Jews in 38 C.E., or an earlier prefect of Egypt. Also uncertain is whether *synagōgia* means "congregations" or "places where the congregations met." In all probability, the latter is signified since the "gathering of the regular company" implies that the companies were gathered in the *synagōgia*.[68] We need to note, however,

[68]So Kee, "The Changing Meaning of Synagogue," 282. Schrage is not as certain ("Συναγωγή," 808, n. 51). Cf. *HJP* 2.440.

that the activities mentioned—the gathering on the Sabbath for the reading and discussion of Torah—correspond to those outlined in Philo's discussion of the *proseuchai* (*Legat.* 155). Of interest here is that *synagōgia* is not Philo's term, but one he places in the mouth of the ruler. Thus Philo may have recorded the ruler's actual term or used a word he believed to be reflective of Roman usage. This seems likely, as the word *thiason* (plural: *thiasoi*; translated "company" above) typically represented religious cults or clubs of other sorts. While these *thiasoi* were common throughout the empire, in Rome the emperors viewed the cults as seedbeds of sedition and frequently outlawed them in the capital and elsewhere.[69] Hence it is probable that the Alexandrian ruler perceived an analogous situation with the Jews in Egypt and sought to implement legislation mimicking edicts issued for the capital city. The ruler thus lumped the Jewish *proseuchai* together with the pagan *synagōgia*, which elsewhere served as centers for Bacchic feasts and the like.[70]

This hypothesis receives confirmation from the second passage employing the word *synagōgion*, which comes from a letter purported to have been written by King Agrippa I to Gaius in 40 C.E. The letter sought to dissuade the emperor from erecting a statue of Zeus in the Jerusalem Temple. In order to show Gaius how this action would be breaking with previous traditions, Agrippa cites the special treatment given the Jews living in Asia Minor under Augustus:

> While I have a great abundance of evidence to show the wishes of your great-grandfather Augustus I will content myself with two examples. The first is a letter which he sent to the governors of the provinces in Asia, as he had learnt that the sacred first-fruits were treated with disrespect. He ordered that the Jews alone should be permitted by them to assemble in *synagōgia* [ἐπιτρέπωσι τοῖς Ἰουδαίοις μόνοις εἰς τὰ συναγώγια συνέρχεσθαι]. These gatherings [συνόδους], he said, were not based on drunkenness and carousing to promote conspiracy and so to do grave injury to the cause of peace, but were schools [διδασκαλεῖα] of temperance and justice where men while

---

[69]See Walter Burkert, *Ancient Mystery Cults* (Cambridge, Mass.: Harvard University Press, 1987), 32–53; Wendy Cotter, "The Collegia and Roman Law: State Restrictions on Voluntary Associations, 64 BCE–200 CE" in *Voluntary Associations*, edited by John S. Kloppenborg and Steven G. Wilson (London: Routledge, 1996), 74–89; Richardson, "Early Synagogues as Collegia," 93.

[70]On Philo's negative view of pagan *thiasoi*, see *Flacc.* 136–138; Torrey Seland, "Philo and the Clubs and Associations of Alexandria" in *Voluntary Associations*, edited by John S. Kloppenborg and Steven G. Wilson (London: Routledge, 1996), 110–127.

> practising virtue subscribed the annual first-fruits to pay for the sacrifices which they offer and commissioned sacred envoys to take them to the temple in Jerusalem. Then he commanded that no one should hinder the Jews from meeting or subscribing or sending envoys to Jerusalem according to their ancestral practice. For these were certainly the substance if not the actual words of his instructions (*Legat.* 311–313).

As we shall see, the word *didaskaleion*, "school," is one of Philo's favorite terms in connection with the synagogues. Consequently, it is likely that the letter is Philo's own free composition. However, since Philo was the leader of an Alexandrian delegation in Rome at the time, it is also possible that Philo helped Agrippa compose the letter. In either case, we should observe how "Agrippa" attempts to distinguish the Jewish *synagōgia* from pagan examples: the latter he characterizes as buildings set aside for orgiastic feasts, while the former are "schools of temperance and justice." Thus, in the eyes of Agrippa/Philo, the analogy between the *proseuchai* and the pagan *synagōgia* was rather superficial. Another point is that while the word *synodos*, "gathering," could refer to a festival assembly, it frequently meant a meeting for deliberation over legal matters.[71] Consequently, it had a more positive connotation than *thiasos*. So did *didaskaleion*, which referred to the school building itself.

From the foregoing it appears we should *not* view *synagōgion* as a Jewish term for their meeting places, but one used of their facilities by outsiders. Thus Agrippa (or Philo) heavily qualifies the application of this term to the synagogues, nearly redefining the meaning of *synagōgion* in the process. On the other hand, because Agrippa's letter is an apology, there likely was some analogy between the Gentile *synagōgia* and the Jewish synagogues. However, beyond the observation that the pagan *synagōgia*, like the Jewish *proseuchai*, housed the activities of cultic groups, it is difficult to discern from the above passages how far to push the analogy. What is clear from the second citation is that the groups meeting inside the Jewish *synagōgia* were formalized organizations that could legally collect money and send official envoys to the mother city. Moreover, the fact that the envoys are represented as offering sacrifices on behalf of their congregations belies the notion that the synagogues in Asia Minor were anti-Temple.

---

[71]E.g., Pausanias 10.3.3; Demosthenes, 54.9. See LSJ s.v. συνόδος, θίασος.

Hieron

The noun *hieron* is related to the adjective *hieros*, "sacred" or "dedicated to the gods."[72] *Hieron* could thus refer to "a sacrifice" or "a cultic object." More often it meant "a temple," a place dedicated to the gods. A *hieron* was distinguished from the shrine of the temple complex, the *naos*, which typically housed the cultic image, if any. In this usage, *hieron* signified a sacred area attached to a *naos*.

Because *hieron* was so often used of pagan temples, the Alexandrian translators of the LXX reserved this term for such cultic sites (e.g., Ezek 27:6) and refrained from using it for the Jerusalem Temple. Thus while the LXX normally calls the Temple shrine a "house" (οἶκος/בַּיִת; Ps 64:5) or a *naos* (ναός/הֵיכָל; 1 Kgs 6:17), it refers to the surrounding area with the term "court(s)" (αὐλή/חָצֵר; Ezek 40:17).

Somewhat later, the authors of 1–4 Maccabees and 1 Esdras dropped the earlier Jewish aversion toward *hieron* and made it the standard term for the Jerusalem Temple. This usage was followed by Philo, Josephus and the various authors of the New Testament writings. When referring to the Jerusalem Temple, these authors can use *hieron* to refer to the Court of Priests (Josephus, *Ant.* 8:95), the Court of Women (Josephus, *Ant.* 8:97; Luke 2:24), the Court of Israel (Josephus, *Ant.* 8:96; Acts 21:26), the Court of the Gentiles (*BJ* 6.244; Matt 21:12), or the entire Temple complex (Josephus, *BJ* 5.184; Philo, *Legat.* 157; Mark 13:3). *Naos* remained the standard designation for the Temple shrine.

In addition to these usages, *hieron* was also employed as a term for the synagogues, a fact long recognized by researchers.[73] However, because *hieron* could also refer not only to the Jerusalem Temple, but to the temples at Leontopolis, Mt. Gerizim and to pagan temples anywhere, our criteria for determining such a usage must be carefully spelled out.[74] First of all, the usage must be set within a Jewish and not a pagan context.

---

[72]See Gottlob Schrenk, "Ἱερός, Ἱερόν" in *TDNT* 3.221–247; LSJ s.v. ἱερός.

[73]E.g., Krauss, *Synagogale Altertümer*, 86–87; Schrage, "Συναγωγή," 808; Hengel, "Proseuche und Synagoge," 168; Dion, "Synagogues et temples dans l'Égypte hellénistique," 52; Levine, "The Second Temple Synagogue," 13.

[74]Schrage's erroneous listing of several uses of *hieron* for a synagogue by Philo (*Legat.* 188, 194, 198, 232, 238, 265) results from a failure to apply carefully these criteria: in each instance, *hieron* refers to the Jerusalem Temple. See Schrage, "Συναγωγή," 808, n. 50. The error is repeated in Kurt Hruby, *Die Synagoge. Geschichtliche Entwicklung einer Institution* (Zürich: Theologisher Verlag, 1971), 72, n. 262.

Secondly, it cannot refer to the rival temples in Leontopolis and Samaria. Thirdly, it must not refer to the Jerusalem Temple itself. Finally, if the usage generally refers to Jerusalem, *hieron* must be in the plural (*hiera*).

We begin our examination with the writings of Josephus. Our first passage demonstrates Josephus' clearest use of *hieron* for a synagogue. It refers to a synagogue in Antioch, which, according to Josephus, existed in the time of Antiochus Epiphanes (d. 164 B.C.E.):

> For, although Antiochus surnamed Epiphanes sacked Jerusalem and plundered the temple [τὸν νεὼν ἐσύλησεν], his successors on the throne restored to the Jews of Antioch all such votive offerings [ἀναθημάτων] as were made of brass, to be laid up in their synagogue [εἰς τὴν συναγωγὴν αὐτῶν ἀναθέντες], and, moreover, granted them citizen rights on an equality with the Greeks. Continuing to receive similar treatment from later monarchs [τὸν αὐτὸν δὲ τρόπον καὶ τῶν μετὰ ταῦτα βασιλέων αὐτοῖς προσφερομένων], the Jewish colony grew in numbers, and their richly designed and costly offerings formed a splendid ornament to the *hieron* [τῶν ἀναθημάτων τὸ ἱερὸν ἐξελάμπρυναν] (*BJ* 7.44–45).

Here, we see *synagōgē* and *hieron* used in reference to the same structure: the Jerusalem Temple cannot be meant in the second half of the passage, for the focus clearly shifts from the plundering of the Temple (*naos*) to the growth of the Jewish colony in Antioch.[75] What is remarkable here is that not only did Antiochus' successors deem the synagogue in Antioch worthy of housing votive offerings from the sacked Temple, but they also contributed additional gifts to the synagogue. Josephus' use of the term *hieron* in this passage indicates that the Antiochian synagogue was a consecrated edifice; it, like the votive offerings housed inside, was considered the sacred property of the Divine.

A second passage from Josephus is a description of the triumph in Rome following the Jewish War. Consisting of parades combined with various public spectacles, Roman triumphs were designed to herald the victorious military leaders while simultaneously heaping shame upon the defeated nation. To this end, the Romans would spare a certain number of captives in order to display them on floats depicting scenes from the war. On one such float in the triumph following the Jewish War, Josephus states that there appeared an image of *hiera* set on fire:

---

[75]See Schrage, "Συναγωγή," 808, n. 50; Dion, "Synagogues et temples dans l'Égypte hellénistique," 52; Hengel, "Proseuche und Synagoge," 168; Krauss, *Synagogale Altertümer*, 86–87; Levine, "The Second Temple Synagogue," 13.

> But nothing in the procession excited so much astonishment as the structure of the moving stages; indeed, their massiveness afforded ground for alarm and misgiving as to their stability, many of them being three or four stories high, while the magnificence of the fabric was a source at once of delight and amazement. For many were enveloped in tapestries interwoven with gold, and all had a framework of gold and wrought ivory. The war was shown by numerous representations, in separate sections, affording a very vivid picture of its episodes. Here was to be seen a prosperous country devastated, there whole battalions of the enemy slaughtered; here a party in flight, there others led into captivity; walls of surpassing compass demolished by engines, strong fortresses overpowered, cities with well-manned defenses completely mastered and an army pouring within the ramparts, an area all deluged with blood, the hands of those incapable of resistance raised in supplication, *hiera* set on fire [πῦρ τε ἐνιέμενον ἱεροῖς], houses pulled down over their owners' heads, and, after general desolation and woe, rivers flowing, not over a cultivated land, nor supplying drink to man and beast, but across a country still on every side in flames. For to such sufferings were the Jews destined when they plunged into the war; and the art and magnificent workmanship of these structures now portrayed the incidents to those who had not witnessed them, as though they were happening before their eyes. On each of the stages was stationed the general of one of the captured cities in the attitude in which he was taken. A number of ships also followed. The spoils in general were borne in promiscuous heaps; but conspicuous above all stood out those captured in the temple at Jerusalem ['Ιεροσολυμοις ἱερῷ]. These consisted of a golden table, many talents in weight, and a lampstand, likewise made of gold, but constructed on a different pattern from those which we use in ordinary life. Affixed to a pedestal was a central shaft, from which there extended slender branches, arranged trident-fashion, a wrought lamp being attached to the extremity of each branch; of these there were seven, indicated the honour paid to that number among the Jews. After these, and last of all the spoils, was carried a copy of the Jewish Law. Then followed a large party carrying images of victory, all made of ivory and gold. Behind them drove Vespasian, followed by Titus; while Domitian rode beside them, in magnificent apparel and mounted on a steed that was itself a sight (*BJ* 7.139–152).

The *hiera* are clearly synagogues, for the term is in the plural and used in a Jewish context. Moreover, the *hiera* are differentiated from the Temple, as that structure's spoils are depicted later in the procession.[76] The parade itself appears to be arranged chronologically, according to the events of the war. The mention of the ships is probably a reference to the battle on

---

[76]See Schrage, "Συναγωγή," 808, n. 50; Dion, "Synagogues et temples dans l'Égypte hellénistique," 53; Levine, "The Palestinian Synagogue Reconsidered," 430, n. 14.

the Sea of Galilee (67 C.E.; *BJ* 3.522–531). Prior to that operation, according to Josephus, Vespasian had set fire to the city of Gabara (Galilee) and its surrounding villages (*BJ* 3.132–134). Possibly the burning of the *hiera* can be situated there, though this is mere speculation. In general, the passage appears to refer to structures in Galilee, the theater of the first part of the war. Note also that *hiera* are differentiated from houses (*oikoi*) in the above description.

Yet another passage from Josephus refers to *hiera* in Palestine. Taken from Josephus' description of the early years of the Jewish War (c. 67–68 C.E.), this scene portrays marauding bands of brigands devastating the Judean countryside:

> Throughout the other parts of Judaea, moreover, the predatory bands, hitherto quiescent, now began to bestir themselves. And as in the body when inflammation attacks the principal member all the members catch the infection, so the sedition and disorder in the capital gave the scoundrels in the country free license to plunder; and each gang after pillaging their own village made off into the wilderness. Then joining forces and swearing mutual allegiance, they would proceed by companies—smaller than an army but larger than a mere band of robbers—to fall upon *hiera* and cities [προσέπιπτον ἱεροῖς καὶ πόλεσιν]. The unfortunate victims of their attacks suffered the miseries of captives of war, but were deprived of the chance of retaliation, because their foes in robber fashion at once decamped with their prey. There was, in fact, no portion of Judaea which did not share in the ruin of the capital (*BJ* 4.406–409).

As with the previous quotation, *hiera* is in the plural and used in a Jewish context. Clearly, synagogues are meant.[77]

It is well known that Josephus blamed the Zealots and Sicarii for the disastrous Jewish losses during the Jewish War. Just prior to the quoted passage, the historian relates a story of how the Sicarii from Masada had attacked the town of En-gedi during the Feast of the Unleavened Bread (*BJ* 4.300–405). Because the above passage immediately follows that account, Josephus appears to link the Sicarii with common bandits who irreverently sacked their country's own synagogues. Indeed, one might even say that his mention of the sacrilegious treatment of the *hiera* by the bandits introduces in microcosm his later account of the Zealots' desecration of the Temple (*BJ* 5.5–20). In any case, the above passage undermines Paul Flesher's notion of an antithetical relationship between

---

[77]See Dion, "Synagogues et temples dans l'Égypte hellénistique," 53; Levine, "The Palestinian Synagogue Reconsidered," 430, n. 14.

the Temple and the synagogues: Josephus not only assumes that synagogues existed in Judea, but he also depicts their looting as an impious act, different only in degree from the treatment later accorded the Temple.[78]

In addition to the above passages, Josephus quotes two earlier authors who use *hieron* in reference to synagogues (*Ant.* 13.65–68; *Ap.* 1.209–212). We will reserve our examination of these citations for future chapters.[79]

Before turning to other sources, however, we will examine two other places where Josephus might possibly use *hieron* to refer to a synagogue. The two citations, neither of which is found in any of the standard synagogue reference lists, are parallel accounts from *War* and *Antiquities* that describe Herod the Great's flight from Judea in 40 B.C.E. Retreating from his rival Antigonus, nephew of the High Priest Hyrcanus II, Herod passed south through Idumea and entered Nabatea, hoping to find support from Malchus, the Arabian king. Josephus goes on to report Herod's actions immediately after being turned away by the Nabateans:

> Herod, finding the Arabs hostile to him for the very reasons which had made him look for their warm friendship, gave the messengers the reply which his feelings dictated and turned back toward Egypt. The first evening he encamped in one of the *hieron* of the country [τῶν ἐπιχωρίων ἱερον], where he picked up those of his men who had been left in the rear. The next day he advanced to Rhinocorura, where he received news of his brother's death (*BJ* 1.277–278).

> Then, on deciding to retire, [Herod] very prudently took the road to Egypt. And on that occasion he lodged in a certain *hieron* where he had left many of his followers [ἔν τινι ἱερῷ κατάγεται καταλελοίπει γὰρ αὐτόθι πολλοὺς τῶν ἐπομένων]. The next day he came to Rhinocoroua, where he heard of his brother's fate (*Ant.* 14.374).

Of crucial importance for our interpretation is whether the *hieron* was located in Idumea or Nabatea. The former possibility seems more likely since Herod undoubtedly would have left his supporters in his own country (he was half-Idumean). Moreover, Idumea was just to the north of Rhinocoroua (Egypt), where Herod is stated to have arrived the day after visiting the *hieron* in question. Ralph Marcus, the translator of the Loeb edition of *Antiquities*, concurs with this assessment, writing, "the

---

[78]Flesher, "Palestinian Synagogues before 70 C.E.," pass.

[79]See chapters three, four and six, below.

temple was probably Idumaean."[80] Marcus, however, misses the point that the Idumeans had been forcibly proselytized during the earlier reign of John Hyrcanus (c. 125 B.C.E.). Of their conversion, Josephus writes:

> [Hyrcanus] permitted them to remain in their country so long as they had themselves circumcised and were willing to observe the laws of the Jews. And so, out of attachment to the land of their fathers, they submitted to circumcision and to making their manner of life conform in all other respects to that of the Jews. And from that time on they have continued to be Jews (*Ant.* 13.257–258).

While the Jews do not appear to have accorded the Idumeans the highest regard (Antigonus calls Herod a "half-Jew" [ἡμιιουδίος], *Ant.* 14.403), nowhere does Josephus indicate that the Idumeans were openly syncretistic.[81] Indeed, in his account of the Zealots' initial refusal to allow the Idumeans entrance into Jerusalem during the Jewish War, Josephus mentions no charge of syncretism being leveled against them (*BJ* 4.238–269). On the contrary, the Idumeans are portrayed as taking great offense at being kept from their "national sacred rites [πατρίων ἱερῶν εἴργετε]" in the Temple (*BJ* 4.279). When they did finally gain entry into the city, according to Josephus, they joined one of the Zealot factions and subsequently committed a number of atrocities (*BJ* 4.300). Thus the historian can hardly be viewed as currying favor with the Idumeans. In fact he goes on to record that during the course of the war, the Romans punished the Idumeans by devastating their cities and villages, along with the rest of Palestine (*BJ* 4.447–448).

From all this it follows that to exclude Idumea from under the Jewish umbrella would be comparable to excluding Galilee. Indeed, the latter region was fully incorporated into Judaism nearly a quarter of a century *after* Idumea—hence Nathaniel's famous question, "Can anything good come out of Nazareth?" (John 1:46).[82] Therefore, if the *hieron* in question

---

[80]Ralph Marcus, trans. *Josephus* (Cambridge Mass.: Harvard University Press, 1958), 7.645, n. d.

[81]Josephus does mention a certain Costobarus, whose ancestors were priests of the Idumean god Koze (Qozach). He was one of Herod's governors (of Idumea) and was also husband of Salome, Herod's sister. According to Josephus, Costobarus was resentful over the forced conversions of the previous century. In an attempt to turn back the clock, he tried to turn Cleopatra against Herod. The plot, however, did not succeed, and Herod eventually had him executed (*Ant.* 15.255–258).

[82]Josephus, *Ant.* 13.318–319; *BJ* 1.76. See Smallwood, *The Jews under Roman Rule*, 14.

was located in Idumea—which on balance seems likely—then we have in the two cited passages references to an Idumean synagogue, perhaps even one converted from an earlier temple.

Although we should be cautious and place question marks next to the last two citations, if we include them in our count, *hieron* occurs most often among terms for the synagogue in Josephus' writings (*hieron* 7x, *synagōgē* 6x, *proseuchē* 5x). How are we to account for this surprising fact? Aside from noting that two of these uses of *hieron* are contained within quotations of other authors, Josephus' own frequent use of this word as a term for the synagogue is probably best explained by the fact that he wrote primarily for a non-Jewish audience. Thus while it is unlikely that *hieron* was a common Jewish word for synagogues—it is unattested in inscriptions—*hieron* was apparently a very apt term for Jews to use when speaking to outsiders about their synagogues. If the non-Jew was unfamiliar with Jewish nomenclature, then the use of *hieron* would evoke the image of an analogous Gentile structure—with important differences, of course (e.g., no cultic image).[83]

If this hypothesis is correct, then we would expect *hieron* to be used by non-Jews for the synagogues. This in fact is the case in two instances from our period. The first is from a preserved fragment written by the Greek historian Agatharchides of Cnidus (II B.C.E.), which we shall examine in a subsequent chapter (Josephus, *Ap.* 1.209–212).[84] The other is found in 3 Maccabees, which represents a Gentile ruler, Ptolemy Philopater, issuing the following decree against the Jews of Alexandria:

---

[83]In the two quotations in Josephus' writings where *hieron* is used for a synagogue, one is by a pagan author (*Ap.* 1.209–212), and the other is by a Jew writing to a pagan (*Ant.* 13.65–68).

[84]See chapters three and six, below. It is worth mentioning that just after our period (c. 109 C.E.), the Roman historian Tacitus, providing background about the Jewish War, employs the Latin term *templum* in reference to the synagogues: "The Jews conceive of one god only, and that with the mind only: they regard as impious those who make from perishable materials representations of gods in man's image; that supreme and eternal being is to them incapable of representation and without end. Therefore they set up no statues in their cities, still less in their temples [*nulla simulacra urbibus suis, nedum templis sistunt*]; this flattery is not paid their kings, nor this honour given to the Caesars" (*Hist.* 5.5.4). The Jerusalem Temple cannot be meant since earlier Tacitus mentions that inside the central shrine was placed "a statue of that creature whose guidance enabled [the Israelites] to put an end to their wandering and thirst" (*Hist.* 5.4.2). For commentary, see *GLAJJ* 2.43.

"None of those who do not sacrifice shall enter their *heira* [μηδένα τῶν μὴ θυόντων εἰς τὰ ἱερὰ αὐτῶν εἰσιέναι], and all Jews shall be subjected to a registration involving poll tax and to the status of slaves. Those who object to this are to be taken by force and put to death; those who are registered are also to be branded on their bodies by fire with the ivy-leaf symbol of Dionysus, and they shall also be reduced to their former limited status." In order that he might not appear to be an enemy of all, he inscribed below: "But if any of them prefer to join those who have been initiated into the mysteries, they shall have equal citizenship with the Alexandrians" (3 Macc 2:28–30).

In crafting the decree, the author of 3 Maccabees apparently tried to reflect the language used of the Alexandrian synagogues by Gentiles.[85] Nowhere else in the document is *hieron* used in this way.

If Jews could use *hieron* with Gentiles to refer to their synagogues, there are two passages within Philo's writings that suggest that Jews might have used this word even among themselves. We will consider one of these passages here and preserve the other (*Deus*. 7–8) for a future chapter.[86] The segment to be considered here, one unnoted in any of the standard lists of synagogue references, comes from a passage in one of Philo's writings about the proper place of women in society:

A woman, then, should not be a busybody, meddling with matters outside her household concerns, but should seek a life of seclusion. She should not shew herself off like a vagrant in the streets before the eyes of other men, except when she has to go to the *hieron* [πλὴν εἰς ἱερον ὁπότε δέοι βαδίζειν], and even then she should take pains to go, not when the market is full, but when most people have gone home, and so like a free-born lady worthy of the name, with everything quiet around her, make her oblations and offer her prayers [θυσίας ἐπιτελοῦσα καὶ εὐχας] to avert the evil and gain the good (*Spec.* 3.171–172).

Philo's audience for *Special Laws* was Jewish or primarily Jewish.[87] Moreover, he clearly was referring not to the Jerusalem Temple, but to a structure in Alexandria. Regarding the usage, F. H. Colson, the translator of the Loeb edition, writes: "Philo may mean the synagogue . . . [but] it seems to me more probable that he is giving advice to the female

---

[85]See Dion, "Synagogues et temples dans l'Égypte hellénistique," 48–49; Levine, "The Palestinian Synagogue Reconsidered," 430, n. 14; idem, "The Second Temple Synagogue," 13.

[86]See chapter six, below.

[87]In *Spec.* 1.51–52, Philo speaks of proselytes, but elsewhere assumes that his readers are Jews by birth (e.g., *Spec.* 1.54–57).

population in general and does not feel any necessity to speak disrespectfully of their religious observances."[88] Despite this judgment, Colson's first suggestion is probably correct: it is unlikely that Philo, who earlier in his treatise railed against idolatry (*Spec.* 1.21–27), would have recommended that a woman—even a Gentile woman—should enter an idol temple to offer prayers and oblations. Nor should we take "oblations" (θυσία) too literally, as this word could mean not only sacrifices, but any type of religious ritual.[89] Hence, the quoted passage provides us with an example of a Jew using *hieron* when addressing a Jewish audience.

In summary, while Philo can employ *hieron* as a term for the synagogue with Jewish audiences (*Deus.* 7–8, *Spec.* 3.171–172), the word appears to be used by Jews primarily when speaking to Gentiles about their synagogues. Unlike the preserved uses of *synagōgion*, however, *hieron* is used without qualifications: there are no denials that cultic images were housed within Jewish *hiera* or that sacrifices were offered inside. Presumably this is because these facts were well known, even among Gentiles. Conversely, the use of *hieron* by Jews to represent their synagogues to Gentiles suggests similarities in appearance and function between the pagan temples and the Jewish structures. That Gentiles could refer to the synagogues with this same term (Agatharchides ap. Josephus, *Ap.* 1.209–212) indicates that both groups perceived these similarities. We should finally note that because the basic meaning of *hieron* is "a place dedicated to God," the use of this word as term for the synagogue was not inappropriate, particularly in view of the numerous inscriptions which explicitly or implicitly dedicate the synagogue and or its appurtenances to the Jewish Deity (e.g., *JIE* 9, 13, 22, 25, 27, 28, 24, 117).

---

[88]F. H. Colson, trans. *Philo* (Cambridge Mass.: Harvard University Press, 1937), 7.582, n. a. Colson further writes, "Possibly τὸ ἵερον may have become in the διασπορά a conventional name for the synagogue as the best possible substitute for the temple, particularly in Alexandria where the synagogue is said to have been especially magnificent and famous . . . and so too with the common collocation εὐχὰς καὶ θυσίας for the due performance of all religious rites possible" (ibid., 640).

[89]E.g., Plutarch *Thes.* 20. Note also that "sacrifice" (θυσία) and "prayer" (προσευχή) form a parallel in Ps 141:2 (LXX). See the discussion of prayer in chapter six, below.

HIEROS PERIBOLOS

Hieros Peribolos, "sacred precinct," is virtually synonymous with *hieron*. Often the designation is used in connection with the asylum rights of pagan temples. Within Jewish writings, the expression almost always refers to the precincts of the Jerusalem Temple. For example, 2 Macc 6:4 speaks of the *hieroi periboloi* of the Jerusalem Temple being profaned by prostitutes during the persecution of Antiochus Epiphanes. Likewise, Sir 50:2 mentions that the high priest Simon II (d. 196 B.C.E.) fortified the Temple and "laid the foundations for the high double walls, the high retaining walls for the *hieros peribolos* [ὑπ’ αὐτοῦ ἐθεμελιώθη ὕψος διπλῆς ἀνάλημμα ὑψηλὸν περιβόλου ἱεροῦ]"—a reference to the Court of the Gentiles. The writings of Josephus and Philo contain similar usages (*BJ* 2.400; *Spec.* 1.261).

Hieros Peribolos can also be used of synagogues. Our first example of this usage comes from an inscription found in Alexandria dating to sometime in the second century B.C.E. (*JIE* 9 = *CIJ* 2.1433):[90]

[- - -]	
[- - θε]ῶι ὑψίστωι	. . . to God, the Highest
[- - τ]ὸ̣ ἱερὸν	. . . the sacred
[περίβολον καὶ] τὴν προσ-	precinct and the *proseuchē*
[ευχὴν καὶ τὰ συγ]κύροντα	and its appurtenances

The Jewish provenance of the inscription is established from the phrase "God, the Highest" (θεος ὑψίστος), a common expression for God by Jews in the diaspora (used frequently in the LXX for עליון), and from the partially reconstructed word *proseuchē*. While *hieros peribolos* is also a partial reconstruction, the editorial supplement is strongly supported by similar formulas found in dedicatory inscriptions from pagan temples. For example, Paul-Eugène Dion cites an Egyptian inscription from a temple of Hermupoli Magna that concludes, "and the precinct and all its appurtenances [[κ]αὶ τὸν περιβολον καὶ τὰ συν|κύροντα πάντα]."[91]

The above inscription provides us with clear evidence that Jews in Egypt used *hieros peribolos* not merely as an expression of convenience, but as a term associated with their *proseuchai*. The fact that the former is

---

[90]Translation from *JIE*.

[91]*OGIS* 182. See Dion, "Synagogues et temples dans l'Egypte hellénistique," 60. Dion also mentions *OGIS* 52, 65, 92 and *SB* 4206 as forming close parallels.

distinguished from the latter with the conjunction "and" (καί) suggests that the *proseuchē* proper was set inside a larger sacred area, perhaps delineated by a wall.[92]

Our second and final example of this usage comes from Philo's writings. Referring to the desecration of *proseuchai* in Alexandria during the governorship of Flaccus, Philo writes:

> Now the Jews though naturally well-disposed for peace could not be expected to remain quiet whatever happened, not only because with all men the determination to fight for their institutions outweighs even the danger to life, but also because they are the only people under the sun who by losing their *proseuchai* were losing also what they would have valued as worth dying many thousand deaths, namely, their means of showing reverence to their benefactors, since they no longer had the *hieroi periboloi* where they could set forth their thankfulness [οὐκ ἔχοντες ἱεροὺς περιβόλους, οἷς ἐνδιαθήσονται τὸ εὐχάριστον] (*Flacc.* 48).

Again, we have the linkage of the *hieroi periboloi* with the *proseuchai*, only in this case we have a function attached to them: they served as places where various dedicatory inscriptions could be set up honoring the rulers. *Hieroi periboloi* may refer either to the *proseuchai* themselves or (more likely) to courts surrounding the *proseuchai*, since these would be more visible to the public. In either case, it is striking to see the same language used of the Jerusalem Temple applied to the *proseuchai*.

To sum up: *hieros peribolos* appears to be a term used by Jews in Egypt in connection with their *proseuchai*, probably indicative of precincts surrounding a centralized synagogue building. These precincts contained dedicatory inscriptions honoring rulers and other patrons of the synagogue congregation. Whether the term *hieros peribolos* was used of synagogues by Jews outside of Egypt is not known, though Philo does apply it in a blanket reference to synagogues throughout the empire.[93]

---

[92]See Kasher, "Synagogues as 'Houses of Prayer' and 'Holy Places'," 215–216.

[93]Just prior to the quoted usage of *hieros peribolos* by Philo, he writes, "It was to be feared that people everywhere might take their cue from Alexandria, and outrage their Jewish fellow-citizens by rioting against their *proseuchai* and ancestral customs" (*Flacc.* 47). People from "everywhere" refers to places where Jews lived throughout the empire, which Philo lists as "from Egypt to the East and the nations of the East and from the Hypotaenia and Marea, which are the outskirts of Libya, to the West and the nations of the West" (*Flacc.* 45).

DIDASKALEION

Didaskaleion, which is related to the noun *didaskalia* ("teaching"), refers to an edifice wherein regular instruction took place, i.e., a school.[94] The term thus designates a physical structure rather than a class, which was known as a *scholē* or "school gathering" (though this latter term could also mean a building).[95] Hence the Athenian orator Aeschines (IV B.C.E.) could write of teachers being forbidden to open up their *didaskaleia* before sunrise (καὶ τοὺς διδασκάλους τὰ διδασκαλεῖα . . . ἀνοῖγειν μὲν ἀπαγορεύει μὴ πρότερον πρὶν ἂν ἥλιος ἀνίσχῃ; *Tim.* 10).

Although the term does not appear in the LXX or the New Testament, *didaskalia* and *didaskō* ("to teach") occur with great frequency, often in connection with the Temple (1 Esdr 9:49; Mark 14:49) or the synagogues (Matt 4:23, Luke 13:10; cf. *CIJ* 2.1404). Of our early sources, only Philo refers to the synagogues as *didaskaleia*. We have already seen one example of this usage in our study of the term *synagōgion* (*Legat.* 311–313). Philo uses *didaskaleion* in this manner in four additional places, including the following two passages:

> Further, when [Moses] forbids bodily labour on the seventh day, He permits the exercise of the higher activities, namely, those employed in the study of the principles of virtue's lore. For the law bids us take the time for studying philosophy and thereby improve the soul and the dominant mind. So each seventh day there stand wide open in every city thousands of *didaskaleia* [μυρία κατὰ πᾶσαν πόλιν διδασκαλεῖα] of good sense, temperance, courage, justice and other virtues in which the scholars sit in order quietly with ears alert and with full attention, so much do they thirst for the draught which the teacher's words supply, while one of special experience rises and sets forth what is best and sure to be profitable and will make the whole of life grow to something better (*Spec.* 2.61–62).

> For it was customary on every day when opportunity offered and pre-eminently on the seventh day, as I have explained above, to pursue the study of wisdom with the ruler expounding and instructing the people what they should say and do, while they received edification and betterment in moral principles and conduct. Even now this practice is retained, and the Jews every seventh day occupy themselves with the philosophy of their fathers, dedicating that time to the acquiring of knowledge and the study of the truths of nature. For what are our *proseukteria* throughout the cities but *didaskaleia* [τὰ γὰρ κατὰ πόλεις προσευκτήρια τί ἕτερόν ἐστιν ἢ

[94]See LSJ s.v. διδασκαλεῖα.

[95]See LSJ s.v. σχολή. Cf. "the *scholē* of Tyrannus" in Acts 19:9.

> διδασκαλεῖα] of prudence and courage and temperance and justice and also of piety, holiness and every virtue by which duties to God and men are discerned and rightly performed? (*Mos.* 2.214–216).[96]

These similarly worded passages show that Philo is trying to draw a comparison between the synagogues (*proseuktērion* being another form of *proseuchē*) and the common Greco-Roman schoolhouses. The analogy is based upon a similarity in function between the two types of buildings: both served as places of instruction. Since education in the Greco-Roman world incorporated the teaching of traditional (largely Stoic) virtues, Philo is clearly trying to present the synagogues as Jewish centers for promoting this same type of education. Consequently, *didaskaleion* was probably not a common term for the synagogues, but Philo's own extension of one of the synagogue's purposes.

We should also note that in the first passage, Philo presents the synagogues as being present in every city of the empire and as numbering in the "thousands." While this is hyperbole, Philo's statement nevertheless presumes that the synagogue was a widespread phenomenon in the first century. A similar comment applies to the claim made in the second passage that Moses established the synagogues: the utterance demonstrates the philosopher's belief that the institutionalization of the synagogues was an ancient phenomenon.

In summary, while *didaskaleion* appears to be Philo's own term for the synagogue, the word does accurately represent one of the functions of the synagogues—that of disseminating knowledge—as can be seen from other sources, including the New Testament, Josephus' writings, and the Theodotus inscription. Because of Philo's obvious interest in scholarship,

---

[96]Philo's two other uses of this term, while somewhat oblique, nevertheless are best understood as references to synagogues. Thus in *Dec.* 40, Philo, commenting on the Ten Commandments, writes that "[Moses] wills that no king or despot swollen with arrogance and contempt should despise an insignificant private person but should study in the school of the divine laws [τὰ τῶν ἱερῶν νόμων διδασκαλεῖα] and abate his supercilious airs." Likewise in *Praem.* 66 he states that "from this household [i.e., Jacob's household], increased in the course of time to a great multitude, were founded flourishing and orderly cities, schools of wisdom, justice and religion [διδασκαλεῖα φρονήσεως καὶ δικαιοσύνης καὶ ὁσιότητος], where also the rest of virtue and how to acquire it is the sublime subject of their research." Note that these two references imply that synagogues were present in Palestine as well as in the diaspora.

however, we should not over-interpret his usage of this term and conclude that the synagogues *only* functioned as places where study took place.[97]

TOPOS

Topos is a common term in Greco-Roman writings, where its basic meaning is "a place" or "a defined area." It could signify a town, a dwelling place or a general region.[98] Additionally, *topos* could take on the more specific meaning of "sanctuary."[99] While less frequent in pagan literature, among Jewish writings this latter usage seems to have risen from the Septuagint's translation of *māqōm* (מָקוֹם), "place," which in some cases was used as a technical term for cultic sites such as those at Bethel (Gen 28:11) and Shechem (Gen 12:6). Later, the Temple itself was called the "Holy Place" (ἁγίος τόπος/מְקוֹם קֹדֶשׁ; Ps. 24:3) or simply "the place" (ὁ τόπος/הַמָּקוֹם; 1 Kings 8:35). The use of *topos* by itself to refer to the Temple continues in some of the books of the Apocrypha and New Testament (2 Macc 2:8, 3:2; 3 Macc 1:29; Acts 6:13, 21:28). Philo uses *hieros topos* for the Temple in one passage (*Legat.* 318).

We have already seen instances where *topos*, used in this narrower sense, can be combined with other words to signify a synagogue. Hence a letter of P. Petronius, quoted in a previous section of this chapter, refers

---

[97]E.g., Steve Mason, while noting that outsiders could treat diaspora Judaism as a cult, nevertheless states, "the cultic aspects of Judaism—temple, sacrifice, priesthood—were visible only in Jerusalem and only before 70; what the rest of the world saw was the synagogue/*proseuchē*, which served as a place for study, discussion of sacred texts, and moral exhortation" (Steve N. Mason, "*Philosophiai:* Graeco-Roman, Judean and Christian" in *Voluntary Associations*, edited by John S. Kloppenborg and Steven G. Wilson [London: Routledge, 1996], 42; cf. Arthur Darby Nock, *Conversion: The Old and the New in Religion from Alexander the Great to Augustine* [London: Oxford University Press, 1933], 62). Unless one adheres to a very narrow definition of *cult* (animal sacrifice only), this position claims too much, particularly in view of the common synagogue term, *proseuchē*, which implies the exercise of prayer, a cultic activity. For a fuller treatment of the "cultic" functions of synagogues, see chapter six, below. On the artificiality of the cult-school dichotomy, see Michel Despland, *The Education of Desire* (Toronto: University of Toronto Press, 1985), 85–105; Loveday Alexander, "Paul and the Hellenistic Schools: The Evidence of Galen" in *Paul in His Hellenistic Context*, edited by Troels Engberg-Pedersen (Minneapolis: Fortress Press, 1995), 60–83.

[98]See Helmut Köster, "Τόπος" in *TDNT* 8.187–189.

[99]Ibid., 189–190, 195–199, 204–205; Arthur Darby Nock, "The Gild of Zeus Hypsisto," *HTR* 29 (1936): 46.

to the synagogue at Dora with the expression *topos synagōgēs* (*Ant.* 19.304). Elsewhere, we saw that Philo calls the synagogues of the Essenes *hieroi topoi* (*Prob.* 81). In addition to these instances, synagogue researchers have noted other places where *topos* by itself refers to synagogue buildings.

The first of these is found in 3 Maccabees, one of the above-mentioned documents that frequently uses *topos* to refer to the Jerusalem Temple. Indeed, in 3 Maccabees 1:9–2:24, where the narrative action takes place in Jerusalem, *topos* refers exclusively to the Temple, seven times by itself (1:9, 23, 29; 2:9, 10, 16) and once in the expression *hagios topos*, "holy place" (2:14). However, when the action shifts from Jerusalem to Alexandria, and Philopater begins to vent his wrath upon the Jews there, the ruler is depicted as issuing the following order:

> 27 Those who shelter any of the Jews, whether old people or children or even infants, will be tortured to death with the most hateful torments, together with their families. 28 Any who are willing to give information will receive the property of those who incur the punishment, and also two thousand drachmas from the royal treasury, and will be awarded their freedom. 29 Every *topos* [πᾶς δὲ τόπος] detected sheltering a Jew is to be made unapproachable and burned with fire, and shall become useless for all time to any mortal creature (3 Macc 3:27–29).

Here, *topos* refers not to domestic residences, but to sanctuaries of some sort, since vv. 27–28 deal with the treatment of owners of private property. Moreover, the reference to the burning of the *topoi* parallels a similar threat made to the Jerusalem Temple in 3 Macc 5:43.

But can we say that *topos* refers to synagogues? In general, Philopater's order appears to be a special revocation of a temple's right of asylum.[100] From an inscription we will examine in chapter six (*JIE* 125), we know that at least some of the synagogues in Egypt were granted the right of asylum under Ptolemy Euergetes II (145–116 B.C.E.). The author of 3 Maccabees, writing in the first century B.C.E., apparently assumed that this right existed for the synagogues even during the earlier reign of Philopater (which may have in fact been true). Thus, the above usage of *topos* appears to be a blanket statement aimed not just at the

---

[100]For an example of *topos* used in reference to asylum rights, see *CIG* 2737, a *senatus consultum* from the first century B.C.E. (*CIG* 2737) which refers to the temple of Aphrodite at Aphrodisias as ὁ τόπος ἄσυλος (l. B. 13). For additional uses of this phrase in Ptolemaic Egypt, see Köster, "Τόπος," 190.

Jewish synagogues but at all sacred places. The same verdict can be rendered for the following passage, which recounts how Philopater's orders were not being carried out successfully:[101]

> 17 But after the previously mentioned interval of time the scribes declared to the king that they were no longer able to take the census of the Jews because of their immense number, 18 though most of them were still in the country, some still residing in their homes, and some at a *topos* [τῶν δὲ καὶ κατὰ τόπον]; the task was impossible for all the generals in Egypt (3 Macc 4:17–18).

Although there are different textual readings of 18c, the above variant has the best witness.[102] We need not depart from this reading, as some commentators do, since taking *topos* in the technical sense of "sanctuary" as in 3:29 makes the meaning of the text perfectly clear: the author wants to show how God went about thwarting Philopator's designs on the Egyptian Jews.[103] Consequently, the scribes were unable to register them, even though most of the Jews had not fled the country. They faithfully awaited God's deliverance, with some remaining patiently in their homes and others taking refuge in temples or synagogues that defied Philopator's orders.

If in the above passages, *topos* refers generally to all sanctuaries (including synagogues), in two decrees of Sardis (Asia Minor) preserved by Josephus in *Antiquities*, the term is aimed more specifically at the sacred buildings belonging to the Jewish population:

> The following decree was passed by the council and people on the motion of the magistrates. Whereas the Jewish citizens living in our city have continually received many great privileges from the people and have now come before the council and the people and have pleaded that as their laws and freedom have been restored to them by the Roman Senate and people,

---

[101]This passage, incidentally, is not found in any of the standard lists of synagogue references.

[102]The above text is from Codex Alexandrinus (V C.E.), which is usually the most reliable of the texts. The Lucianic recension has "on the journey" (κατὰ τόν πόρον), while Codex Venetus (IX C.E.) has "according to custom" (κατὰ τρόπον). These variants can probably be attributed to the scribes' failure to recognize the technical sense in which *topos* is being used in the passage.

[103]H. Anderson prefers the reading by the Lucianic rescension, calling that of Codex Alexandrinus nonsensical. See H. Anderson, "3 Maccabees" in *OTP*, 2.523, n. e. Note also that 4:21 shows the author's interpretation of the events: "But this was an act of the invincible providence of him who was aiding the Jews from heaven."

> they may, in accordance with their accepted customs, come together and have a communal life and adjudicate suits among themselves, and that a *topos* be given them [δοθῇ τε καὶ τόπος αὐτοῖς] in which they may gather together with their wives and children and offer their ancestral prayers and sacrifices to God [τὰς πατρίους εὐχὰς καὶ θυσίας τῷ θεῷ], it has therefore been decreed by the council and people that permission shall be given them to come together on stated days to do those things which are in accordance with their laws, and also that a *topos* shall be set apart by the magistrates for them to build and inhabit [καὶ τόπον ὑπὸ τῶν στρτηςῶν εἰς οἰκοδομίαν καὶ οἴκησιν αὐτῶν], such as they may consider suitable for this purpose, and that the market-officials of the city shall be charged with the duty of having suitable food for them brought in (*Ant.* 14.259–261).

> Lucius Antionius, son of Marcus, proquaestor and propraetor, to the magistrates, council and people of Sardis, greeting. Jewish citizens of ours have come to me and pointed out that from the earliest times they have had an association of their own [σύνοδον ἔχειν ἰδίαν] in accordance with their native laws and a *topos* of their own [τόπον ἴδιον], in which they decide their own affairs and controversies with one another; and upon their request that it be permitted them to do these things, I decided that they might be maintained, and permitted them so to do (*Ant.* 14.235).

Scholars have had difficulty establishing the relationship between these two decrees. The latter is dated to 49 B.C.E., and the former usually to sometime afterward, simply because it appears later in Josephus' collection of decrees. However, Josephus did not always arrange these decrees chronologically.[104] Moreover, the latter decree presumes that the Jews of Sardis already had a *topos* wherein they settled their disputes—it

---

[104]E.g., Josephus reproduces a set of decrees from Julius Caesar (c. 48–46 B.C.E.; *Ant.* 14.190–216) prior to quoting a decree from the time of Hyrcanus I (d. 104 B.C.E.; *Ant.* 14.247–255). An analysis of *Ant.* 14.190–264 reveals that Josephus arranged his decrees not chronologically, but according to the level of authority possessed by the author(s): *Ant.* 14.190–216 are decrees from Julius Caesar; 14.217–222 is a decree from the Roman Senate; 14.223–246 are by various governors or consuls (with replies from two cities); 14.247–264 are decrees from Asian cities. On these passages, see A. Thomas Kraabel, "Paganism and Judaism: The Sardis Evidence" in *Paganisme, Judaïsme, Christianisme: Influences et affrontements dans le monde antique*, edited by André Benoit, Marc Philonenko and Cyrille Vogel (Paris: Éditions E. De Boccard, 1978), 16–18; Oster, "Supposed Anachronism in Luke-Acts' Use of ΣΥΝΑΓΩΓΗ," 186; Shaye J. D. Cohen, "Pagan and Christian Evidence on the Ancient Synagogue" in *The Synagogue in Late Antiquity*, edited by Lee I. Levine (Philadelphia: American Schools of Oriental Research, 1987), 165–166; Paul R. Trebilco, *Jewish Communities in Asia Minor* (Cambridge England; New York: Cambridge University Press, 1991), 38–39.

merely recertifies their right to continue their "synods" within their *topos*. The former decree actually established the right for this *topos* to be built and for the synods to meet: the first half ("whereas") contains the petition, and the second half ("therefore") resolves that the petition be granted. It is likely, therefore, that the former decree was issued first, perhaps during the time of Hyrcanus I (d. 104 B.C.E.) since Josephus records a decree from the nearby city of Pergamum dating to the same period and also written in response to a senatorial decree.[105] The functions outlined for the *topos* are consistent with the functions we have seen for Jewish synagogues: it was used for gatherings on the Sabbath ("appointed days"), for prayers, and for the settling of internal disputes. We previously encountered this last function in the letter of Agrippa I, quoted in Philo's writings. There, all the Jews of Asia were mentioned as having "synods" (σύνοδοι) in their *synagōgia* (*Legat.* 311). The Sardis decrees clarify that this term should be understood in the technical sense of "legal gatherings." Hence the Jewish community in Sardis was allowed not only to meet and study Torah, but also to enforce some of its edicts among its membership.

The phrase "ancestral prayers and sacrifices to God" in the first decree argues that *topos* is used in both decrees not generically, but in the technical sense of "sanctuary." The same can be said with respect to the previously mentioned letter of Petronius to the Dorans, which states that "each must be lord over his own *topos* [ἰδίων τόπων], in accordance with Caesar's decree" (*Ant.* 19.305). *Topos* there referred both to Caesar's own shrine (*naos*) and to the Jewish synagogue. The terminology in the Sardian decrees is identical to Petronius' usage.

In summary, *topos* refers to synagogues in several passages, the context in each case suggesting it carries the technical sense of "sanctuary" or "sacred place"—a usage seen elsewhere in Jewish and

---

[105] *Ant.* 14.247–255. The decree from Pergamum reads in part: "Whereupon the [Roman] Senate passed a decree concerning the matters on which [representatives of the Jewish nation] spoke, to the effect that King Antiochus, son of Antiochus, shall do no injury to the Jews, the allies of the Romans; and that the fortresses, harbours, territory and whatever else he may have taken from them shall be restored to them . . . [we] passed a decree that we on our part, being allies of the Romans, would do everything possible on behalf of the Jews in accordance with the decree of the Senate" (*Ant.* 14.249–250, 253). This decree is followed by one from Halicarnassus (*Ant.* 14.256–258; date omitted) and then by the above decree from the people of Sardis. Finally, a decree from the people of Ephesus is quoted. This last dates to either 74 or 42 B.C.E.

Greco-Roman literature. When it appears as a term for the synagogue, *topos* is sometimes linked with other words such as *hieros* (Philo, *Prob.* 81) and *synagōgē* (Josephus, *Ant.* 19.304). Both Jewish and pagan writers can use *topos* to refer to synagogue buildings, the latter typically in official documents.

AMPHITHEATRON

Amphitheatron literally means, "having seats for spectators all round."[106] Like its English cognate, "amphitheater," the term normally refers to an elliptical structure in which an audience sits in seats along the outer perimeter facing inward towards an open, central area.[107] Amphitheaters were designed by Roman architects primarily to house gladiatorial contests. The earliest surviving example of a stone amphitheater is at Pompeii, dating to 80 B.C.E., although this was known as a *spectacula* (*CIL* 10.852). Rome did not have a permanent amphitheater until 30 B.C.E. Prior to that time, gladiatorial contests were held in wooden amphitheaters set up in the Forum Romana and the Circus Maximus.[108] In the east, Herod the Great, hoping to further Romanize his subjects, introduced amphitheaters to Palestine, building them at Jericho (Josephus, *Ant.* 17.194), Jerusalem (*Ant.* 15.268–271) and Caesarea Maritima (*Ant.* 15.331–341). The earliest use of the word in a literary source is in Strabo's *Geographica* (14.1.43), written c. 20 C.E., where the term refers to a structure at Nysa in Asia Minor.

While the amphitheaters housed various public spectacles, they also served as places for public gatherings. The amphitheater in Jericho, for example, was used for a public trial (Josephus, *Ant.* 17.161) and for the official announcement of Herod's death (Josephus, *BJ* 1.666–667).

In two inscriptions from Berenice in Cyrenaica, the term *amphitheatron* likely refers to a synagogue building. One of these (*CJCZ* 71), which we shall consider in a later chapter, is a decree from the "politeuma of the Jews" honoring a certain Marcus Tittius, a Gentile public official. The other (*CJCZ* 70), produced below, is a similar decree, this time recognizing the contributions of a fellow Jew toward the

---

[106]LSJ s.v. ἀμφιθέατρος.

[107]See Robertson, *Greek and Roman Architecture*, 283–289.

[108]See John E. Stambaugh, *The Ancient Roman City* (Baltimore, Md.: The Johns Hopkins University Press, 1988), 233–237.

renovation of the *ampitheatron.* The decree probably dates to 6–8 B.C.E.:[109]

Λ[.]γ΄ Φ[αμ]ενῶθ ϵ΄ ἐπὶ ἀρχόντων Ἀ̣ρίμμα τοῦ
[.......]ος Δωρίωνος τοῦ Πτολεμαίου
Ζ̣ε̣λα̣ι̣ου τοῦ [Γ]ναίου Ἀρίστωνος τοῦ Ἀραξα-
[..]ν̣τ̣ο̣ς Σαρα[πί]ω̣νος τοῦ Ἀνδρομάχου Νικία
τ[οῦ ....]Α̣[.]ΣΑ̣[....] τ̣ο̣ῦ̣ Σίμωνος ἐπεὶ
[Δέκ]μος Ο[ὐαλέριος Γ]αΐο[υ Διον]ύσιος Π̣Ρ̣Η̣Π̣ΟΤΗΣ
[.........]Ω̣ΓΗ̣Σ̣ ἀνὴρ καλὸς καὶ ἀγαθὸς ὢν δια-
τελε[ῖ λόγῳ καὶ ἔργῳ καὶ αἱρ]έσε̣ι̣ καὶ ποιῶν ἀγαθὸν
[ὅτι] ἂ̣[ν] δ[ύνηται καὶ κοι]ν̣ᾶι καὶ ἰδίαι ἑκάστωι τῶν
π̣[ο]λ̣ί̣τ̣[ων] καὶ δ[ὴ καὶ] ἐκονίασεν τοῦ ἀνφιθεάτρου
τ[ὸ ἔδ]α̣φος καὶ το̣ὺ̣[ς] τ̣οίχους ἐζωγράφησεν
ἔ[δοξε τοῖς ἄ]ρχουσι καὶ τῶι πολιτεύματι
τ̣[ῶν] ἐ̣ν̣ Β̣ε̣ρ̣ν̣ι̣κ̣ί̣δ̣ι̣ Ἰ̣ο̣υδαίων καταγράψαι αὐτὸν εἰς
τὸ τ̣ῶ̣ν̣ τ[......]ΕΥΕΙ̣Σ̣Υ̣Δ̣Ι̣Ο̣Υ̣ κ̣α̣ὶ εἶεν ἀλειτούρ-
γητο[ν πά]σης [λε]ιτουρ[γί]ας [ὁ]μ̣οίως δὲ καὶ στε-
φα[νοῦν α]ὐτὸν καθ᾽ ἑκάστην σύνοδον καὶ νουμ̣η̣-
νία̣ν̣ σ̣τ̣ε̣[φ]άνωι [ἐλ]αίνωι καὶ λημνίσκωι ὀνομαστί
τὸ [δ]ὲ ψήφισμα τόδε ἀναγράψαντες οἱ ἄρχον[τες]
[εἰ]ς στήλην λίθου Παρίου θετωσαν εἰς τὸν ἐ[πι]-
[σημ]ό̣τατον [τόπ]ον τοῦ ἀμφιθεάτρου
vacat λευκαὶ πᾶσαι *vacat*
vacat
Δέκμος Οὐαλέριος Γαΐου Διονύσιος
τὸ ἔ̣[δ]α̣[φ]ος ἐκονίασεν καὶ τὸ ἀμφι-
θέατρον καὶ ἐζωγράφησεν τοῖς
ἰδίοις δαπανήμασιν ἐπίδομα
vacat τῶι πολιτεύματι *vacat*

In the year 3, on the 5th Phamenoth, in the archonship of Arimmas son of . . ., Dorion son of Ptolemaios, Zelaios son of Gnius, Ariston son of Araxa . . ., Serapion son of Andromachos, Nikias | son of . . ., N. son of Simon. Whereas Dec(i)mus Valerius Dionysios son of Gaius . . . remains an honourable and good man in word and deed and by inclination, doing whatever good he can, both in a public capacity and as a private individual to each one of the | citizens, and in particular plastered the floor of the amphitheatre and painted its walls, the *archontēs* and the politeuma of the Jews at Berenike resolved to register him in the . . . of the . . . and (resolved) that he be exempted from liturgies | of every kind; and likewise (they resolved) to crown him with an olive crown and a woollen fillet, naming him at each synod and at the new moon. After engraving this resolution on a stele

[109]See Applebaum, *Jews and Greeks in Ancient Cyrene*, 148–151.

> of Parian marble the *archontēs* are to set it in the most visible | place in the amphitheater. (Votes:) all white. Dec(i)mus Valerius Dionysios son of Gaius plastered the floor and the amphitheatre and painted (it) at his | own expense as a contribution to the politeuma.[110]

The meaning of *politeuma* in this inscription and in *CJCZ* 71 has been much debated. While most scholars have held that the term refers to the entire Jewish population in Berenice, Gert Lüderitz has recently argued that *politeuma* here refers to a council of Jewish officials. His primary argument is that the use of stones for voting (white stones for "yes," black stones for "no") is found within other such councils (βουλή) in the Greco-Roman world. In contrast, plenary gatherings of the people (δῆμος) typically voted by a show of hands.[111]

This argument, however, is far from decisive. First of all, elsewhere the term *politeuma* can refer to an entire ethnic group living in a foreign land, as Lüderitz himself points out.[112] Secondly, Strabo states that the Jews of Cyrene were legally classified as a separate entity, distinguished from other resident aliens.[113] *Politeuma* in the Berenice inscription likely refers to this legal classification. Thirdly, in the inscription to Marcus Tittius (*CJCZ* 71), the official is honored for his benefactions "to the Jews of our politeuma, both collectively and individually [τοῖς ἐκ τοῦ πολιτεύματος ἡμῶν Ἰουδαίοις καὶ κοινῆ καὶ κατ᾽ ἰδίαν]" (ll. 18–19). If the politeuma consisted only of an inner council of the Jews of Berenice, this would be a strange locution indeed: surely the entire Jewish population is meant.[114] Finally, a later inscription from Berenice, while

---

[110]Translation is from *NDIEC* 4.203.

[111]See Gert Lüderitz, "What is the Politeuma?" in *Studies in Early Jewish Epigraphy*, edited by Jan Willem Van Henten and Pieter Willem Van der Horst (New York: E. J. Brill, 1994), 215–219. For the position that the politeuma consisted of all of the Jews in Berenice, see: Applebaum, *Jews and Greeks in Ancient Cyrene*, 160; Smallwood, *The Jews under Roman Rule*, 141.

[112]Ibid., 196–204. Examples cited include *SEG* 8.573 (III–II B.C.E., Cilicians in Egypt), 2.871 (II B.C.E., Boeotians in Egypt), *PTeb.* 1.32 (II B.C.E., Cretans in Egypt), *CIG* 2.5866c (I B.C.E., Phrygians in Pompeii).

[113]Quoted in Josephus, *Ant.* 14.115–188.

[114]Lüderitz himself has noted this difficulty with his interpretation, but writes, "perhaps one should not overinterpret the *politeuma*'s use of formulas of speech, and perhaps M. Tittius had only been dealing with members of the politeuma . . . if one thinks that all the Jews of Berenice were members of this politeuma, it would follow that the Jewish population of Berenice was either quite insignificant or that a large politeuma had a ridiculously complicated voting system for decrees" ("What is Politeuma?" 220, n. 97).

retaining the term *archontēs*, drops the word *politeuma* altogether in favor of *synagōgē* as a term for the resident Jewish congregation (*CJZC* 72).[115] When we add in the possibility that the Jewish population of Berenice may well have been small enough to vote with stones rather than hands, Lüderitz's argument loses a great deal of force. On balance, it therefore seems more likely that *politeuma* referred to the entire Jewish population of Berenice.

Returning to the above inscription, we see that line 16 refers to "synods" meeting inside the *amphitheatron*—language identical to that used of gatherings inside the *synagōgia* in Asia (Philo, *Legat.* 311–313) and the *topos* in Sardis (Josephus, *Ant.* 14.235). Although unstated, the gatherings were probably weekly, with additional assemblies coming at the New Moon and on other sacred days (the other inscription from Berenice mentions a gathering on the Feast of the Tabernacles [*CJZC* 70, ll. 1–2]).

Lüderitz has also argued that *amphitheatron* in the Berenice inscriptions does not refer to a Roman amphitheater, but to a Greek council hall or bouleterion. The reasoning here is that gladiatorial amphitheaters did not have plastered floors, as this structure appears to have had (ll. 10–11). Additionally, the term *amphitheatron* was still in a state of flux at this time: at the turn of the era it could have referred to any type of building with seating all around. Thus Lüderitz concludes:

> The assumption that this "amphitheatron" in Berenice, where the Jewish decrees were set up, was a Jewish building with seats along the walls modeled after the type of a town hall is not too far fetched. It seems to have been a building for meetings, probably the one where the politeuma and the archons met regularly.[116]

While Lüderitz's position makes for a reasonable hypothesis, we must again demur from his narrow definition of *politeuma*: the examples of council halls that we have from the Greco-Roman world typically seated from 700–1500 people—clearly more than would have constituted the

---

[115]See the section on *synagōgē*, above.

[116]Lüderitz, "What is the Politeuma?" 213–214. For a similar conclusion, see Applebaum, *Jews and Greeks in Ancient Cyrene*, 164–166. Cf. Reynolds, "Inscriptions," 247; *JSGRP* 2.143–144, 12.52 n. 11. See also the discussion of Berenice in chapter four.

posited inner council of the Jews in Berenice.[117] Moreover, these structures were used not only for council meetings, but also for popular assemblies.[118]

Can we speak of the Berenice *amphitheatron* as a synagogue? While the two inscriptions fail to mention some of the common functions normally associated with the synagogues, such as the study of Torah, the presence of others seems to be indicated. As already argued, the gatherings held inside the structure were probably weekly and incorporated the entire Jewish population. Similarly, the assemblies on the New Moon and at the Feast of the Tabernacles corresponded to festival days or days of special observance in the Jerusalem Temple. Additionally, like the *topos* in Sardis, the *amphitheatron* in Berenice housed a body invested with a measure of autonomy. Finally, like the *proseuchai* of Egypt, the *amphitheatron* in Berenice contained inscriptions honoring certain members of the ruling establishment. When we add in the fact that the excavated remains of pre-70 synagogues have "seating all around," it is reasonable to conclude that *amphitheatron* in the Berenice inscriptions refers to a synagogue building.[119]

While we cannot positively connect the *synagōgē* of *CJZC* 72 with the *amphitheatron* of *CJZC* 70–71, a possible scenario is that when the term *amphitheatron* became more and more identified with structures housing gladiatorial shows in the first century C.E., the Jews of Berenice dropped this word in favor of *synagōgē*. Why this term was chosen over *proseuchē* is unknown. Perhaps *synagōgē* was gaining more currency in the diaspora at this time. Or perhaps the Jews of Berenice wished to associate their structure more closely with structures in the homeland. Whatever the case, the *amphitheatron* clearly housed a formal Jewish institution, replete with defined leadership and regularized voting procedures. Because the meetings corresponded to Temple festivals or

---

[117]The Jewish ruling council of Alexandria, a city far bigger than Berenice, probably consisted of seventy-one members. See Smallwood, *The Jews under Roman Rule*, 226–227. The total Jewish population of Berenice in the first century B.C.E. is unknown, although estimates for the entire population of Berenice range from 25,000–35,000 (Applebaum, *The Jews of Ancient Cyrenaica*, 193–194).

[118]See Robertson, *Greek and Roman Architecture*, 169–182, especially 176, n. 2.

[119]*Amphitheatron* is listed as a term for the synagogue in: Levine, "The Palestinian Synagogue Reconsidered," 430, n.19; idem, "The Second Temple Synagogue," 13; Oster, "Supposed Anachronism in Luke-Acts' Use of ΣΥΝΑΓΩΓΗ," 186. On the seating in the excavated remains of pre-70 synagogues, see chapters three and four, below.

days of special observance, they probably incorporated ritual elements, though what these may have constituted is unspecified.

OIKOS, OIKĒMA

The basic meaning of the synonymous words *oikos* and *oikēma* is "dwelling place." The terms most often refer to a domestic residence (or rooms), but can also be used of public buildings such as temples or treasuries.[120] In the LXX, *oikos* (used 1545 times) usually refers to a house (e.g., Lev 14:44) or a household (e.g., Gen 12:17). However, it is also a frequent locution for the Jerusalem Temple, which is called "a house of God" (e.g., Isa 2:2, οἶκος τοῦ θεου/בֵּית־יְהוָה), "a house of the Lord" (e.g., 1 Kgs 7:40, οἶκος κυρίου/בֵּית יְהוָה) or simply "a house" (e.g., 1 Kgs 3:2). As mentioned earlier, the Temple can also be called "a house of prayer" (Isa 56:7, 1 Macc 7:37, οἶκος προσευχῆς/בֵּית־תְּפִלָּה). *Oikēma*, which is used only three times in the LXX, never refers to the Temple.[121]

We have already encountered one use of *oikēma* in Josephus' description of the *proseuchē* in Tiberias, which is called "a huge building, capable of accommodating a large crowd [μέγιστον οἴκημα καὶ πολὺν ὄχλον ἐπιδέξασθαι δυνάμενον]" (*Vita* 277). Because only public functions are mentioned for this building, *oikēma* is used here in the general sense of "edifice" or "hall" rather than "private house"—an interpretation furthered supported by Josephus' statement that the entire Tiberian council, which numbered 600 persons (*BJ* 2.641), met inside. Two additional usages by Josephus and Philo refer to rooms inside the synagogues of the Essenes and Therapeutae (*BJ* 2.128; *Contempl.* 33).

Oikos appears once in reference to a synagogue in an inscription found at Acmonia in Phrygia (*DF* 33):[122]

> Τὸν κατασκευασθέ[ν]τα ο[ἶ]κον ὑπὸ Ἰουλίας Σεουήρας Π. Τυρρώνιος Κλάδος, ὁ διὰ βίου ἀρχισυνάγωγος καὶ Λούκιος Λουκίου ἀρχισυνάγωγος καὶ Ποπίλιος Ζωτικὸς ἄρχων ἐπεσκεύασαν ἐκ τε τῶν ἰδίων καὶ τῶν συν-

[120]See Otto Michel, "οἶκος" in *TDNT* 5.119–120.

[121]In Tobit 2:4 it signifies a room in a private home, in Wis 13:15 a niche in a wall, and in Ezek 16:24 a stage in a public square.

[122]Author's translation. Cf. Trebilco, *Jewish Communities in Asia Minor*, 58–59.The transcription is taken from *DF* 33 rather than *CIJ* 2.766 as the latter is riddled with errors. Some critical apparatus has been added following *HJP* 3.1.31.

καταθεμένων καὶ ἔγραψαν τοὺς τοί-
χους καὶ τὴν ὀροφὴν καὶ ἐποίησαν
τὴν τῶν θυρίδων ἀσφάλειαν καὶ τὸν
[λυ]πὸν πάντα κόσμον οὕστινας κα[ὶ]
ἡ συναγωγὴ ἐτείμησεν ὅπλω ἐπιχρύ-
σῳ διά τε τὴν ἐνάρετον αὐτῶν δ[ι]άθ[ε]-
σιν καὶ τὴν πρὸς τὴν συναγωγὴν εὔνοιάν
τε καὶ σ[που]δήν

This building was erected by Julia Severa; P(ublius) Tyrronios Clados, *archisynagōgos* for life, and Lucius, son of Lucius, *archisynagōgos*, and Popilios Zoticos, *archōn*, restored it with their own funds and with money which had been deposited, and they donated the (painted) murals for the walls and the ceiling, and they secured the windows and made all the rest of the ornamentation, and the congregation honored them with a gilded shield on account of their virtuous disposition, goodwill and zeal for the congregation.

This inscription is typically dated to 60–70 C.E. because Julia Severa is known from several inscriptions and coins as being a high priestess of the imperial cult in Acmonia during the reign of Nero.[123] Since she functioned in this capacity, it seems improbable that she was a proselyte or God-fearer. It is more likely that she served as a Gentile patron of the Jews in Acmonia, just as Marcus Tittius did for the Jews in Berenice or the Roman centurion did for the Jews in Capernaum (if we judge Luke's account historical).

The exact meaning of *oikos* in the inscription is difficult to determine. Did Julia Severa donate to the Jews a domestic residence that their leaders then renovated into a synagogue? This type of renovation is seen at the synagogue at Dura-Europos, but that transformation dates to the late second and early third centuries C.E. and may have been influenced by Christian practices. Because the inscription does not mention the structure functioning as a residence, but as a public edifice, *oikos* is most likely being used in the general sense of "building." This is the solution adopted in most translations, including the one above.[124] Yet since the Hebrew terms *bēt hakᵉneset*, "house of the congregation" (בית הכנסת), and *bēt*

---

[123]See William M. Ramsay, *Cities and Bishoprics of Phrygia* (Oxford: Clarendon Press, 1897), 2.638–640, 647–651; Trebilco, *Jewish Communities in Asia Minor*, 58–60.

[124]For further discussion of interpretive issues, see L. Michael White, *Domus Ecclesiae Domus Dei: Adaptation and Development in the Setting For Early Christian Assembly* (Ann Arbor, Mich.: University Microfilms International, 1990), 270–272; *HJP* 2.440; Krauss, *Synagogale Altertümer*, 25.

t^e^fillāh, "house of prayer" were later used of the synagogues, it is also possible that *oikos* is here used in a technical sense.[125] Since *proseuchē* is well-attested for synagogue buildings in the diaspora during this period, *oikos* might draw also on the LXX of Isaiah 56:7, which calls the Jerusalem Temple a "house of prayer," as we have already seen. While this interpretation cannot be ruled out, it would be more compelling if *oikos proseuchēs* actually appeared on the inscription or was attested elsewhere during the Second Temple period. Given this uncertainty, the more prudent course is to follow the majority of interpreters and translate *oikos* simply as "building."

In summary, *oikos* and *oikēma* appear occasionally as terms for the synagogue. When they do occur, their usage is in the general sense of "building" or "chamber" rather than "domestic residence." In the case of the Acmonia inscription, two other interpretations are possible: (1) Julia Severa donated some sort of structure that the Acmonian Jews then converted into a synagogue, or (2) *oikos* is used as a shortened version of *oikos proseuchēs* or even *oikos synagōgēs*.

SABBATEION

Sabbateion is derived from *sabbaton*, the Greek transliteration of the Hebrew *shabbāt*, "seventh day."[126] While the latter Greek term occurs frequently in Jewish writings, *sabbateion*, "a place of the sabbath," appears only once, in a decree of Augustus to the people of Asia. Preserved in the writings of Josephus, the document dates to 2–3 C.E.:

> Caesar Augustus, Pontifex Maximus with tribunician power, decrees as follows. Since the Jewish nation has been found well disposed to the Roman people not only at the present time but also in the time past, and especially in the time of my father the emperor Caesar, as has their high priest Hyrcanus, it has been decided by me and my council under oath, with the consent of the Roman people, that the Jews may follow their own customs in accordance with the law of their fathers, just as they followed them in the time of Hyrcanus, high priest of the Most High God, and that their sacred monies

[125]See Krauss, *Synagogale Altertümer*, 2–11. While these phrases are not attested for our period, note that the expressions בית מועד, "house of assembly" (1QM 3.4), בית השתחות, "house of prostration" (CD 11.22) and בית התורה, "house of Torah" (CD 20.10, 13) may be used in the Essene literature to refer to their synagogues. For further discussion, see chapter seven, below. For the use of *oikos* by itself in reference to the later synagogue unearthed at Sardis, see *DF* 20, 21.

[126]See Eduard Lohse, "Σάββατον, Σαββατισμός, Παρασκευή" in *TDNT* 7.1–34.

> shall be inviolable and may be sent up to Jerusalem and delivered to the treasurers in Jerusalem, and that they need not give bond (to appear in court) on the Sabbath or on the day of preparation for it (Sabbath Eve) after the ninth hour. And if anyone is caught stealing their sacred books or their sacred monies from a *sabbateion* or an ark (of the Law) [or a banquet hall; ἐὰν δέ τις φωραθῇ κλέπτων τὰς ἱερὰς βίβλους αὐτων ἢ τᾶ ἱερα χρήματα ἔκ τε σαββατείου ἔκ τε ἀαρῶνος/ἀνδρῶνος], he shall be regarded as sacrilegious [εἶναι αὐτὸν ἱερόσυλον], and his property shall be confiscated to the public treasury of the Romans (*Ant.* 16.162–165).

Sabbateion clearly refers to synagogue buildings, as we see the same functions ascribed to the term as to the terms *proseuchē* and *synagōgē*: the *sabbateion* served as a repository of sacred writings and of funds collected for the Jerusalem Temple (cf. Josephus, *BJ* 2.285–292; Philo, *Legat.* 155–158). Moreover, the use of *sabbateion* in itself denotes that such structures served as the meeting places for Jews on the Sabbath (cf. Josephus, *Ant.* 14.256–258, *BJ* 2.285–292; Philo, *Mos.* 2.214–216). Because this word is unattested elsewhere, it may well be a neologism. The possibility remains, however, that the term had some currency beyond this single document.

Of interest is the mention of either an "ark" or a "banquet hall" associated with the *sabbateia*. If we read the former, then we have the first evidence for a Torah shrine that also stored sacred offerings. Because fixed Torah shrines have not been found in synagogues from the pre-70 period, such arks would probably have been moveable structures. More likely, however, a banquet hall is meant. This reading would account for the two uses of *synagōgion* ("place of picnicking") in Philo's writings. Such feasting facilities are attested in the Theodotus inscription (*CIJ* 2.1404) and in the remains of the synagogue at Ostia.[127]

Because *sabbateion* is a *hapax legomenon*, we cannot infer much about its currency beyond the quoted document.[128] Nevertheless, the usage clearly refers to structures existing in Asia during the reign of Augustus. The *sabbateia* housed both "sacred scriptures" and "sacred funds"; moreover, they served as meeting places for Jews on the Sabbath. Because the edict goes on to mention a formal resolution offered by the Asian Jews on behalf of Augustus, the Jews in this province apparently

---

[127]See chapter four, below.

[128]The term σαμβαθεῖον appears in a second century C.E. epitaph from Thyatira (*CIJ* 2.752), which some scholars take as a reference to a synagogue. It may also, however, refer to a shrine of the god Sambethe. See *HJP* 3.1.624–626; Krauss, *Synagogale Altertümer*, 25–27.

had some sort of regional organization. While the exact nature of this organization is unknown, its very existence argues against the view that the meetings held inside the *sabbateia* were informal gatherings: not only do the congregations within the Asian *sabbateia* appear to be formally constituted, but they are also part of a larger regional organization, capable of conducting business with the emperor. Also, the fact that the *sabbateia* are represented as collecting funds for the Jerusalem Temple undermines the notion that there was any sort of oppositional relationship between the institutions associated with the respective structures.

SEMNEION

Semneion is not included in any of the standard lists of synagogue terms. Nevertheless, the word appears in Philo's writings in association with the meeting place of the *Therapeutae*. Because *semneion* is unattested elsewhere, it is likely that either (1) Philo coined the word or (2) it originated with the Therapeutae themselves. Because Philo identified his own views closely with those of the Therapeutae, it is difficult to decide between the alternatives. In either case, it is curious that the word never reappears in ancient writings.[129]

Semneion is derived from *semnos*, "noble," or "honorable." The LXX uses it very rarely, once to translate the Hebrew *nāgīd* ("princely," Prov 8:6) and in another, *nōʿam* ("delightfulness," Prov 15:26). 2 Macc 3:12 employs a related word, *semnotēs*, to speak of "the sanctity and inviolability of the [Jerusalem] temple that is honored throughout the whole world [κόσμον ἱεροῦ σεμνότητι καὶ ἀσυλίᾳ παντελῶς ἀμήχανον εἶναι]." Along similar lines Philo speaks of Gaius wishing to ruin "the sanctity of [the Jerusalem] temple [τήν τοῦ ἱεροῦ σεμνότητα]" through the introduction of an idol (*Legat.* 198). These latter usages preserve the earliest sense of this family of words: *semnos* was a property attributed to the Greek gods—they were held to be "lofty" and "august." Hence Philo can speak of God's name and his laws in identical terms (*Spec.* 2.253, 4.179).[130]

Philo uses *semneion* three times in his description of the Therapeutae. In the first and third usages, *semneion* refers to a private cell (μοναστήριον) located in each house inhabited by the Therapeutae.

---

[129]The word may appear in PCair, Mas 1.67096, l. 18, which dates to 573 C.E. and refers to the Kellia.

[130]See Werner Foerster, "Σεμνός, Σεμνοτή," in *TDNT* 7.191–196.

Individual members of the community remained in solitude in these cells for most of the day, praying, studying and composing hymns (*Comtempl.* 29–30). On the Sabbath, however, they emerged and gathered in a "common *semneion*," described by Philo as in the following terms:

> This common *semneion* [τὸ δὲ κοινὸν τοῦτο σεμνεῖον] in which they meet every seventh day is a double enclosure [διπλοῦς ἐστι περίβολος], one portion set apart for the use of the men, the other for the women. For women too regularly make part of the audience with the same ardour and the same sense of their calling. The wall between the two chambers [ὁ δὲ μεταξὺ τῶν οἴκων τοῖχος] rises up from the ground to three or four cubits [five to six feet] built in the form of a breast work, while the space above up to the roof is left open. This arrangement serves two purposes; the modesty becoming to the female sex is preserved, while the women sitting within ear-shot can easily follow what is said since there is nothing to obstruct the voice of the speaker (*Contempl.* 32–33).

During the Sabbath gathering, the senior member among them (πρεσβύτατος) instructed the rest of the congregation in the finer points of their doctrines, presumably derived from the scriptures. Afterwards, members of the community returned to their individual homes to repeat the process. Every fifty days, they met in a central dining area, apparently connected to the common *semneion*. There they ate a modest meal and engaged in discussions of the sacred writings and joined in dancing and the singing of hymns (*Contempl.* 64–89).[131]

While we will examine the practices of the Therapeutae more carefully in chapter seven, here we note that the common *semneion* appears to be the sect's version of a synagogue: its functions correspond to those adduced for structures elsewhere called *synagōgai* and *proseuchai*. These functions extended somewhat into the private cells that were also called *semneia*. Yet we cannot really refer to these as "mini-synagogues," since there was no gathering in them, only private contemplation. Hence on the Sabbath, the community did not break into small groups and meet in the residences of its members; rather, a separate communal building was constructed for this purpose. The use of the same term to designate the two different kinds of structures thus refers to the godliness of the pursuits followed inside the structures rather than any

---

[131]For a reconstruction of the arrangement of the Therapuetae community, see G. Peter Richardson, "Philo and Eusebius on Monasteries and Monasticism: The Therapeutae and Kellia" in *Origins and Method*, edited by Bradley H McLean (Sheffield: JSOT Press, 1993), 345–353.

similarity in architecture. This observation is in accord with Philo's purpose in writing *De vita contempletiva*, which was to exemplify through the Therapeutae how pious practices could extend into every quarter of one's life (*Contempl.* 1).

As was the case with the word *sabbateion*, it remains a mystery as to how much currency *semneion* had outside of the community of the Therapeutae. For that matter, since only Philo uses this term, we cannot be sure that the Therapeutae even used *semneion* to refer to either of the structures he describes. Nevertheless, this remains a distinct possibility. Whatever the truth may be, Philo's description of the customs observed within the common *semneion* provides us with a valuable record of the synagogal practices of one Jewish group during the Second Temple period.

CONCLUSION

We began this chapter by recalling the positions of some recent researchers who maintain that, during the Second Temple period, "synagogues" were primarily informal gatherings in Jewish homes. The ensuing analysis of the various synagogue terms has demonstrated that not only is this view unsubstantiated by the literary and inscriptionary record, but is actually at odds with it (see summary in Table 2).[132] As we have seen, inscriptionary and papyrological sources attest to the existence of *proseuchai* in Egypt as early as the third century B.C.E. (e.g., *JIE* 9, 13, 22, 27, 28, 117; *CPJ* 1.134). This same evidence suggested that these structures were not private homes but monumental structures that bore an affinity to pagan temples and cultic sites. That Jews in Egypt viewed these buildings as enclosing sacred space can be seen from the use of the term *hieros peribolos* in an inscription from Egypt (*JIE* 9) and in Philo's writings (*Flacc.* 48). Philo's use of *hieron* in reference to the Alexandrian

---

[132]The total given for the use of *synagōgē* in the New Testament excludes the usages of James (1x) and Revelation (2x) and that of *aposynagōgē* in John (3x). The specific usages of *synagōgē* have been tabulated according to the discussion earlier in the chapter. Those usages of *synagōgē* in the New Testament which are classified as uncertain most likely also refer to synagogue buildings, though this cannot be determined beyond a reasonable doubt. The distinction is somewhat academic since all sources uniformly place a *synagōgē* (congregation) inside a structure designated by one of the terms in the list. Additional uses of *proseuchē* (2x) and *synagōgē* (congregation, 1x) not included in the tabulation are found in an inscription from Panticapaeum (*CIJ* 1.683) that dates to slightly after our period (81 C.E.).

Table 2
Greek and Latin Terms Used of the Second Temple Synagogues

Term	Source	Occurrences
Synagōgē	Inscriptions	2 (building), 7 (congregation), 1 (uncertain)
	Papyri	1 (congregation)
	Josephus	5 (building), 1 (uncertain)
	Philo	1 (building)
	New Testament	19 (building), 1 (congregation), 33 (uncertain)
Proseuchē, Proseucha	Inscriptions	20
	Papyri	5
	3 Macc	1
	Josephus	5
	Philo	19
	New Testament	2
Proseuktērion	Philo	1
Synagōgion	Philo	2
Hieron	3 Macc	1
	Josephus	7 (2 uncertain)
	Philo	3
Hieros Peribolos	Inscriptions	1
	Philo	1
Didaskaleion	Philo	5
Topos	3 Macc	2
	Josephus	5
	Philo	1
Amphitheatron	Inscriptions	4
Oikos	Inscriptions	1
	Philo	1
Oikēma	Josephus	2
Sabbateion	Josephus	1
Semneion	Philo	1

synagogues further underscores this point (*Spec*. 3.171–172; *Deus*. 7–8). By the end of the Second Temple period, the synagogues flourished throughout the diaspora, as can be seen in Philo's writings (e.g., *Spec.* 2.61–62, *Mos.* 2.214–216), in the decrees quoted by Josephus in *Antiquities* (e.g., *Ant.* 16.162–165), in Acts (e.g., Acts 9:2; 13:5, 14; 17:1) and in inscriptions from Rome (*JIWE* 2.602), Delos (e.g., *CIJ* 1.726), Berenice (*CJCZ* 70–72), Asia (*DF* 33) and the Bosporus Kingdom (e.g., *CIJ* 1.683a, 690, 691). Most often these diaspora structures were known as *proseuchai*, though inscriptions also attest the terms *amphitheatron* (*CJCZ* 70–71), *oikos* (*DF* 33) and *synagōgē* (*CJCZ* 72). The first of these is used only in Berenice, and probably refers to the seating arrangement in a public hall rather than a gladiatorial amphitheater. The second term, attested at Acmonia, appears to refer more generally to a building, possibly one that had undergone extensive renovation in order to make it acceptable for use as a synagogue. *Oikos* may also be shorthand for "house of prayer" or "house of the congregation," both of which were used as terms for the synagogue in the Rabbinic period (in Hebrew). The final term, *synagōgē*, is attested in only one inscription for a synagogue building in the diaspora, though several inscriptions from the diaspora use this word to denote the congregation assembled in the synagogue building. Acts also uses this word for synagogue buildings in the diaspora, as does Josephus for the synagogues in Antioch (*BJ* 7.43) and Dora (*Ant.* 19.300–305). Thus it would appear that this usage of *synagōgē* was gaining currency in the diaspora sometime in the first century C.E.

In contrast to the diaspora usage of *proseuchē*, *synagōgē* became the standard term for synagogue buildings in Palestine by at least the turn of the era, as is demonstrated by the Theodotus inscription (*CIJ* 2.1404) and by the writings of Josephus (*BJ* 2.285–305), Philo (*Prob.* 81) and the New Testament (e.g., Mark 1:29, 3:1, 6; Luke 7:5; Matt 23:6). That these were typically monumental structures can be inferred not only from the Theodotus inscription, but also from Josephus' use of *hieron* to describe both the burning synagogues in the triumphal procession in Rome (*BJ* 7.139–152) and the synagogues in Judea looted by bandits during early years of the Jewish War (*BJ* 4.406–409). Josephus may also refer to an Idumean synagogue with the same term (*BJ* 1.277–278; *Ant.* 14.374). The high incidence of *hieron* as a synagogue term in the writings of Josephus can be best accounted for by the fact that Josephus' audience was primarily Gentile and *hieron* served as a convenient word with which to refer to the Jewish structures. Outside of Josephus' writings and a pagan decree depicted in 3 Maccabees (2:28), only Philo uses *hieron* in reference to the synagogue (*Spec*. 3.171–172; *Deus*. 7–8). The apparent reluctance of Jews to use this term for their synagogues among themselves may be because *hieron* was used both of pagan structures and of the Jerusalem Temple. Such deference toward the Jerusalem Temple, however, should not be interpreted as indicating an oppositional relationship between Temple and synagogue. On the contrary, in the diaspora the synagogues served as repositories for offerings to the Temple (e.g., Philo, *Legat.* 311; Josephus, *Ant.* 16.162–165)—hardly a sign of antipathy between the two institutions. Similarly in Judea, Theodotus was both priest and *archisynagōgos*—as were his father and grandfather (*CIJ* 2.1404). Moreover, Josephus, himself a priest, not only frequented synagogues but expressed outrage when they were violated in any way (e.g., *Ant.* 19.300–301; *BJ* 2.285–305; *Vita* 277ff.). Such an attitude suggests that the synagogues, like the Temple itself, were sacred edifices.

That Gentiles also perceived them in this way can be seen from the fact that whenever they sought to offend the Jews, they typically attacked the sanctity of the synagogues (e.g., Josephus, *BJ* 2.285–305, *Ant.* 19.300–305; Philo, *Flacc.* 47). Gentile use of the terms *hieron* (e.g., Agatharchides ap. Josephus, *Ap.* 1.209–212), *synagōgion* (Philo, *Somn.* 2.123–128) and even *topos* (this last in a technical sense; e.g., Josephus, *Ant.* 19.305) for the synagogues also undergirds the position that outsiders viewed these buildings as sacred structures since the words can refer either to sanctuaries (*hieron*, *topos*) or dining facilities used by mystery cults (*synagōgion*). Though feasting may have been one of the activities connected with the synagogues, a more common function of these structures appears to have been the reading and study of Torah on the Sabbath, as is suggested by the terms *didaskaleion* (Philo, *Legat.* 311–313; *Spec*. 2.61–62; *Mos* 2.214–216; *Praem*. 66; *Dec.* 40) and *sabbateion* (Josephus, *Ant.* 16.162–165). In some cases, the synagogues also appear to have been centers for the administration of the law and for the honoring of patrons, both Jewish and Gentile. The activity of prayer in the synagogues is also suggested by the term *proseuchē*, which was used to refer to synagogues both in the diaspora and in Palestine.

CHAPTER 3
PALESTINIAN SYNAGOGUES

In the previous chapter's examination of synagogue terminology, we encountered literary and epigraphic evidence attesting to the presence of synagogue buildings in Palestine by at least the turn of the era. We begin this chapter with a brief review of that evidence. Following this review, we will turn to an examination of architectural remains of structures in Palestine identified by excavators as synagogues. After rendering verdicts on the cogency of the various proposals for pre-70 synagogue remains, we will close this chapter with a discussion of how the emergence of the synagogues in Palestine might best be explained in light of the relevant evidence.

LITERARY AND EPIGRAPHIC EVIDENCE

Beginning our review with the evidence for synagogues in Galilee, we recall that Josephus makes several references to his activities within a *proseuchē* in Tiberias at the beginning of the Jewish War (*Vita* 276–303). Here we should note that the synagogue at Tiberias must have been quite large since Josephus states that the entire *boulē* of the city and a crowd of the populace (βουλὴν πᾶσαν . . . καὶ τὸν δημοτικὸν ὄχλον) met inside (*Vita* 284). As we observed in the last chapter, the *boulē* of Tiberias alone had 600 members (*BJ* 2.641). Elsewhere Josephus alludes to representations of burning synagogues (*hiera*) being paraded in the triumph in Rome following Titus' victory in that war (*BJ* 7.139–152). As was suggested in the previous chapter, these too were likely located in Galilee. Finally, if we take *synagōgē* in the Gospels as referring either to synagogue buildings or to the congregations meeting inside such buildings—a usage uniformly attested in Jewish writings and inscriptions of the first century C.E. (as we have seen)—then we have attestations of synagogues in Capernaum, (Mark 1:21; Luke 4:33; 7:1–4, 8:41; John 6:59), Nazareth (Mark 6:1; Luke 4:16; Matt 13:54), and in unspecified locations elsewhere in Galilee (Mark 1:39, 3:1, 5:22, 35–41; Matt 4:23,

9:23, 12:9; Luke 4:44, 13:10, 14:15).[1] The fact that Mark is a source in each set of attestations secures a *terminus ad quem* of 70 C.E. for the New Testament evidence alluding to these structures. Recalling our prior discussion of the Gospels being classified generically as biographies, it seems more likely that Mark and the other Gospel writers did not invent the existence of these synagogues but preserved them as biographical facts which in turn served as trappings for their narratives. Hence, the probability that the synagogues in Nazareth and Capernaum actually existed is fairly high—particularly in the latter instance since John and probably Q independently attest its existence.[2] Similarly, the Gospels' depiction of synagogues scattered about Galilee receives at least partial confirmation from Josephus' two allusions.

Moving on to a consideration of Judea, Samaria and Idumea, Josephus specifically refers to a synagogue existing in Caesarea Maritima just prior to the Jewish War (*BJ* 2.285–292). In the last chapter, we observed that this synagogue was said to have adjoined a plot of land owned by a Greek. In order to convince the Roman procurator, Florus, to prevent the Greek from building so close to the Jewish structure, the "notables" (*dynatoi*) of the synagogue were said to have offered him a bribe of eight talents—equivalent in today's currency rates to US $1,920,000.[3] Even if this figure is exaggerated, it is likely that the Caesarea synagogue was not a private house (or a meeting inside such a structure), but a monumental building that could not easily be rebuilt elsewhere. The remainder of the account, which states that open conflict broke out between the Jewish congregation and the Greeks when some of the latter sacrificed birds near the synagogue entrance, implies that the Greeks were committing sacrilege on or near Jewish sacred space.

In another place Josephus mentions bandits sacking various synagogues (*hiera*) in unspecified Judean villages (*BJ* 4.406–409). Also, if we accept that Josephus' two references to a *hieron* visited by Herod

---

[1]Luke 4:44 actually refers to "synagogues of Judea." Yet Flesher rightly points out that this is a general reference to northern Palestine. See Flesher, "Palestinian Synagogues before 70 C.E.," 31; Fitzmyer, *The Gospel According to Luke*, 1.530–534.

[2]While John 6:25c–58 reflects Johannine language and motifs, the mention of a synagogue at Capernaum in the concluding coda (v. 59) is likely an earlier tradition used to frame Jesus' discourse in the preceding verses. See Brown, *The Gospel According to John*, 1.284. For the inclusion of Luke 7:5 in Q, see the arguments presented in the previous chapter.

[3]Based on the calculation 8 talents = 48,000 denarii x US $40 (a modern daily wage for a laborer; Matt 20:2).

allude to a structure in Idumea rather than Nabatea (*BJ* 1.277; *Ant.* 14.374), then we also have evidence for the existence of a synagogue in the former of these regions in 40 B.C.E.

Within Jerusalem, the Theodotus inscription (*CIJ* 2.1404) attests to the presence of a synagogue in the City of David during the Second Temple period.[4] Also, Philo's mention of the Essene *synagōgai* (plural) probably refers to structures in Jerusalem rather than at Qumran since Philo likely obtained knowledge of this group from his pilgrimages to the former place (*Prob.* 81; *Prov.* 64). Moreover, several passages from the writings of Josephus suggest that one or more Essene communities were located in or near the holy city (*BJ* 1.78–80, 5.145; *Ant.* 13.311, 15.371–379).[5] Weaker attestation comes from the Synoptics, which depict Jesus referring to synagogues during his ministry in Jerusalem (Mark 12:38–40; Matt 23:6 || Luke 20:47 = Q). While no specific synagogues are mentioned in these pericopae, given the setting of these utterances, presumably the Gospel writers believed the sayings applied to structures existing in Jerusalem as well as in other parts of Palestine.[6]

The presence of synagogues in Jerusalem is made explicit in several references in Acts. The first of these mentions "the synagogue of the Freedmen (as it was called), Cyrenians, Alexandrians, and others of those from Cilicia and Asia [τῆς συναγωγῆς τῆς λεγομένης Λιβερτίνων καὶ Κυρηναίων καὶ 'Αλεξανδρέων καὶ τῶν ἀπὸ Κιλικίας καὶ 'Ασίας]" (Acts 6:9). This passage may allude to as many as five separate synagogues, one for each group. On another reading, the passage could refer to a single synagogue consisting of freed Jewish slaves (and their descendants) from

---

[4]For the dating of this inscription to before 70 C.E., see the discussion in the previous chapter. It is noteworthy that even Flesher accepts the pre-70 dating of this inscription. See Flesher, "Palestinian Synagogues before 70 C.E.," 33–34. R. Horsley does not mention the Theodotus inscription in either of his two recent books on Galilee (1995, 1996).

[5]See Riesner, "Synagogues in Jerusalem," 190–193; idem, "Das jerusalemer Essenerviertel—Antwort auf einige Einwände" in *Intertestamental Essays*, edited by Zdzislaw J. Kapera (Krackow: The Enigma Press, 1992), 179–186. For further discussion of the location of Essene synagogues, see chapter seven.

[6]Similarly, in Acts 15:21, James, the brother of Jesus, is depicted as saying, "in every city, for generations past, Moses has had those who proclaim him, for he has been read aloud every sabbath in the synagogues [Μωϋσῆς γὰρ ἐκ γενεῶν ἀρχαίων κατὰ πόλιν τοὺς κηρύσσοντας αὐτὸν ἔχει ἐν ταῖς συναγωγαῖς κατὰ πᾶν σάββατον ἀναγινωσκόμενος]." Presumably Jerusalem was included among the cities alluded to in this passage. On the reliability of the local color in the speeches of Acts, see below.

the four cities or regions mentioned.[7] The specificity of the reference suggests that Luke had access to knowledge (either first-hand or through a source) of the particular synagogue(s) mentioned.[8] Whatever the origin of this knowledge, there is nothing to suggest that Luke invented the existence of the synagogue(s).

Two other allusions from Acts are found within a pair of speeches made by Paul before Felix and Agrippa II:

> It is not more than twelve days since I went up to worship in Jerusalem. They did not find me disputing with anyone in the temple or stirring up a crowd either in the synagogues or throughout the city [οὐ πλείους εἰσίν μοι ἡμέραι δώδεκα ἀφ᾽ ἧς ἀνέβην προσκυνήσων εἰς Ἰερουσαλήμ, καὶ οὔτε ἐν τῷ ἱερῷ εὗρόν με πρός τινα διαλεγόμενον ἢ ἐπίστασιν ποιοῦντα ὄχλου οὔτε ἐν ταῖς συναγωγαῖς οὔτε κατὰ τὴν πόλιν] (Acts 24:11b–12).[9]

> I myself was convinced that I ought to do many things against the name of Jesus of Nazareth. And that is what I did in Jerusalem; with authority received from the chief priests, I not only locked up many of the saints in prison, but I also cast my vote against them when they were being condemned to death. By punishing them often in all the synagogues I tried to force them to blaspheme; and since I was so furiously enraged at them, I pursued them even to foreign cities [καὶ κατὰ πάσας τὰς συναγωγὰς πολλάκις τιμωρῶν αὐτοὺς ἠνάγκαζον βλασφημεῖν περισσῶς τε ἐμμαινόμενος αὐτοῖς ἐδίωκον ἕως καὶ εἰς τὰς ἔξω πόλεις] (Acts 26:9–11).

These are, of course, Lucan compositions. As William Kurz has demonstrated, the speeches are examples of forensic oratory and probably

---

[7]So Conzelmann (*Acts of the Apostles*, 47).This is the one passage from the New Testament that Flesher accepts as evidence for synagogues in Jerusalem. See Flesher, "Palestinian Synagogues before 70 C.E.," 32–33. Many scholars have sought to identify this synagogue with that of the Theodotus inscription. While not impossible, this suggestion is too speculative. See Gustav Adolf Deissmann, *Light from the Ancient East: The New Testament Illustrated by Recently Discovered Texts of the Graeco-Roman World*, 4th ed. (New York: George H. Doran, 1927), 439–441; Riesner, "Synagogues in Jerusalem," 204–206.

[8]Martin Hengel maintains that the passage presupposes a written source. See Hengel, "The Geography of Palestine in Acts," 47; Porter, "The 'We' Passages," 545–574.

[9]Although we did not devote space to this passage in the previous chapter, here we should note that this is another instance where *synagōgai* should be translated as "synagogue buildings," since it would be awkward to refer to a crowd "in the gatherings."

reflect Luke's training in the rhetorical schools.[10] Recalling our discussion in chapter one that the authors of such speeches always strove to present background allusions as plausibly as possible (in order to be persuasive), at the very least we can say that Luke *believed* that synagogues existed in Jerusalem during the time of Paul. However, because Luke was generally well-informed about the topography of antebellum Jerusalem, in all probability the allusions in these two passages reflect not just a misguided belief, but an accurate depiction of the pre-70 period.[11] Certainly his allusions cohere with the evidence of the Theodotus inscription and with Philo's mention of the Essene synagogues (if these latter were indeed in or near Jerusalem, as seems likely).

Additional literary evidence for the existence of synagogues in pre-70 Jerusalem comes from the writings of two pagan authors who were briefly mentioned in the previous chapter. Both references are found in fragments preserved by Josephus in *Against Apion*. The first of these, which we will consider more fully in a later chapter, is by the Greek historian Agatharchides of Cnidus (II B.C.E.), who refers to *hiera* (plural) existing in Jerusalem during the time of Ptolemy I Soter (d. 301 B.C.E.; *Ap.* 1.209–212)—a likely reference to synagogues.[12] While the reference may reflect anachronism or provincialism on the part of Agatharchides, Josephus himself assessed this passage as one of the few places where a Gentile actually depicted the practices and customs of the Jews accurately (*Ap.* 1.212). Of course, in this belief Josephus might also have been anachronistic—though probably only for the fourth century B.C.E. and *not* for the end of the Second Temple period.[13]

---

[10]Kurz, "Hellenistic Rhetoric in the Christological Proof of Luke-Acts," 185. Flesher discounts these passages (as well as Acts 22:19), stating that they "reflect a post-70 diaspora situation" ("Palestinian Synagogues before 70 C.E.," 32). Yet this is too quick a dismissal, particularly in view of the fact that Flesher accepts the historicity of the synagogues mentioned in Acts 6:9. If Luke had knowledge of synagogues in Jerusalem before 70 C.E. (as Flesher maintains for Acts 6:9), then it is more likely that Luke, following standard rhetorical practices, would have relied on this knowledge to color his speeches rather than invent the existence of such synagogues. See Riesner, "Synagogues in Jerusalem," 204.

[11]See Hengel, "The Geography of Palestine in Acts," 27–51.

[12]For commentary on this passage and a discussion of Agatharchides, see *GLAJJ* 1.104–109; Molly Whittaker, *Jews and Christians: Graeco-Roman Views* (Cambridge: Cambridge University Press, 1984), 67–68.

[13]Shaye Cohen reaches a similar conclusion, even holding out the possibility that Agatharchides was correct in making this attribution for the fourth century B.C.E. See Cohen, "Pagan and Christian Evidence on the Ancient Synagogue," 162–163. It is

The other passage is one Josephus quotes from Apion's lost work, *History of Egypt* (before 50 C.E.):[14]

> Moses, as I have heard from old people in Egypt, was a native of Heliopolis, who, being pledged to the customs of his country, erected *proseuchai*, open to the air, in the various precincts of the city, all facing eastwards; such being the orientation also of Heliopolis. In place of obelisks he set up pillars, beneath which was a model of a boat; and the shadow cast on this basin by the statue described a circle corresponding to the course of the sun in the heavens (Apion ap. Josephus, *Ap.* 2.10–11).

The city referred to in the above passage is Jerusalem. Curiously, Josephus, focusing on the allusions to Moses and to the temple of Onias in Heliopolis, offers his rebuttal of Apion's statement by referring not to the *proseuchai*, but to the tabernacle and Solomon's Temple:

> Such is the grammarian's amazing statement. Its mendacious character needs no comment; it is exposed by the facts. When Moses built the first tabernacle for God, he neither placed in it himself, nor instructed his successors to make, any graven imagery of this kind. When Solomon, later on, built the temple at Jerusalem [τὸν ναὸν τὸν ἐν Ἱεροσολύμοις], he too refrained from any curiosities of art such as Apion has conceived (*Ap.* 2.12).

Here it appears that Josephus so closely identified the synagogues with the Temple that he focuses on the latter to present an *a maiore ad minorem* argument so that by disproving the alleged practices vis-à-vis the tabernacle and the Temple, he disproves them with regard to the synagogues. In any case, he does not contradict Apion's allusion to the presence of *proseuchai* in Jerusalem. While Apion's statement is partially tainted by provincialism (i.e., his use of the term *proseuchai* rather than *synagōgai*), he may have had reliable information about the existence of synagogues in Jerusalem and used this information as an entree for making his slur.[15]

---

more likely that Agatharchides was correct for the second century B.C.E.—especially if we render *synagōgē* as "synagogue" in the OG of Susanna 28 (see chapter two).

[14]For commentary on this passage and a discussion of Apion, see *GLAJJ* 1.389–390, 392–395; Whittaker, *Jews and Christians*, 54.

[15]Cohen's analysis agrees with this assessment. See Cohen, "Pagan and Christian Evidence on the Ancient Synagogue," 162–163.

ARCHITECTURAL EVIDENCE

The foregoing review of the literary and epigraphic data strongly suggests that synagogues were present throughout Palestine during the Second Temple period, both within cities (Jerusalem, Tiberias, Caesarea Maritima) and villages (Capernaum, Nazareth, others unspecified). Moreover, the evidence implies that several synagogues existed within Jerusalem itself, though how many cannot be exactly determined. Finally, to reiterate a point from the previous chapter, the sources present the synagogues as public, consecrated structures that served as the meeting places for Sabbath assemblies and other gatherings. In one case (the synagogue of Theodotus), the data also indicate the presence of public baths and guest rooms.

How does this evidence square with discoveries of Second Temple synagogue remains? Since the early 1960s, archaeologists have uncovered in Palestine a total of seven structures that have been proposed as candidates for pre-70 synagogues—those at Gamla, Masada, Herodium, Capernaum, Magdala, Shuafat, and Kiryat Sefer. In addition to these finds, archaeologists have suggested that structures associated with the Theodotus inscription and several rooms in the Qumran remains should also be identified as synagogues. Finally, earlier in this century a report was issued describing an early synagogue, no longer visible, at Chorazin.

Since we have already discussed the structures associated with the Theodotus inscription in the previous chapter, we will not replicate those findings here. Also, we will delay a discussion of the Qumran excavations until chapter seven. The bulk of this section, then, will be devoted to an examination of the evidence underlying the other proposals. Verdicts regarding these identifications will be rendered in view of the criteria set forth in chapter one. Those criteria are: (1) the presence of an identifying inscription in or near the excavated remains, (2) the conformity of the structure to the architectural typology of later synagogues (e.g., a rectangular building with benches along three or four sides and supporting columns), (3) the apparent continuity of function for an earlier stratum of a later synagogue, and (4) the presence of scriptures, religious art, ritual baths and dining rooms in or near the structure. In addition, literary sources attesting to the presence of a synagogue in a specific location at a specific time may serve as supporting evidence.

As we will see, none of the structures we will examine satisfy all the criteria. Thus we can only speak in terms of probabilities rather than certainty. Moreover, because not all of the final excavation reports have yet been published, in some instances our verdict must remain tentative until their release. This is particularly the case with the structures at Shuafat and Kiryat Sefer, since only brief reports of these sites are currently available. On the other hand, final reports do exist for the excavations at Masada, Herodium, Magdala and Capernaum. While we lack such a report for the Gamla structure, its excavations have been well-documented. Despite these caveats, we should nevertheless be able to reach reasonable conclusions in most of the cases.

Gamla[16]

The ancient city of Gamla (also known as Gamala) is located in the lower Golan, on a steep ridge that rises to a height of 330 meters above the surrounding terrain. Josephus presents the following description of the city:

> From a lofty mountain there descends a rugged spur rising in the middle to a hump, the declivity from the summit of which is of the same length before as behind, so that in form the ridge resembles a camel [καμήλῳ]; whence it derives its name, the natives pronouncing the sharp sound of that word inaccurately. Its sides and face are cleft all round by inaccessible ravines, but at the tail end, where it hangs on to the mountain, it is somewhat easier of approach; but this quarter also the inhabitants, by cutting a trench across it, had rendered difficult of access. The houses were built against the steep mountain flank and astonishingly huddled together, one on top of the other,

---

[16]The following sources have been used as the basis for the descriptions of the Gamla structure: Shmarya Gutman and Yoel Rapel, *Gamla—A City in Rebellion* (Israel: The Ministry of Defense, 1994; in Hebrew), 99–108; Shmarya Gutman, *Gamla: The First Eight Seasons of Excavations* (Tel Aviv: Kibbutz Meuhad, 1981; in Hebrew); idem, *Gamla: Historical Setting: The First Season of Excavations* (Tel Aviv, 1977; in Hebrew); idem, "The Synagogue at Gamla" in *ASR* 30–34; idem, "Gamala" in *NEAEHL* 2.459–463; idem, "Gamla-1983," *ESI* 3 (1984): 26–27; S. Gutman, and D. Wagner, "Gamla-1984/1985/1986," *ESI* 5 (1986): 38–41; S. Gutman, et al., "Gamla-1987/1988," *ESI* 9 (1989–1990): 9–15; Z. Ma'oz, "The Synagogue of Gamla and the Typology of Second-Temple Synagogues" in *ASR* 35–41. See also Marilyn Joyce Segal Chiat, *Handbook of Synagogue Architecture* (Chico, Calif.: Scholars Press, 1982), 282–284; Hachlili, *Ancient Jewish Art and Archaeology in the Land of Israel* (New York: E.J. Brill, 1988), 84–88; Hershel Shanks, "Gamla: The Masada of the North," *BAR* 5, no. 1 (1979): 12–19; Danny Syon, "Gamla: Portrait of a Rebellion," *BAR* 18, no. 1 (1992): 21–37.

> and this perpendicular site gave the city the appearance of being suspended in air and falling headlong upon itself (*BJ* 4.5–6).

The earliest mention of Gamla is in connection with Alexander Jannaeus' three-year campaign to conquer the cities of the Golan and Gilead—an effort that proved successful (c. 83–80 B.C.E.; *BJ* 1.105, *Ant.* 13.394). Later, during the census of Quirinius (6 C.E.), "Judas the Galilean," a native of Gamla, incited a revolt that was quickly crushed by the Romans (*BJ* 2.118, *Ant.* 18.4–10; cf. Acts 5:37). Josephus names Judas, a disciple of a Pharisee named Saddok (Zadok), as the founder of the Zealot movement, whose adherents the historian characterizes as "[agreeing] in all other respects with the opinions of the Pharisees, except that they have a passion for liberty that is almost unconquerable, since they are convinced that God alone is their leader and master" (*Ant.* 18.23).

Sadly, Gamla is most remembered for the catastrophic defeat it suffered at the hands of Titus and Vespasian, since Josephus—who witnessed the campaign as a captive of the Romans—describes the battle for the city in vivid detail (*BJ* 4.1–83). Initially throwing in its lot with the Romans (*Vita*, 11, 61), Gamla quickly joined the rebel cause and was among the cities fortified by Josephus in 66 C.E. (*BJ* 2.568–574; *Vita* 177–185). In 67, Roman forces besieged the city for seven months before finally breaching the walls. According to Josephus, all the inhabitants and refugees (numbering 9,000) were killed except for two women who had hid themselves during the ensuing slaughter (*BJ* 4.81–82).

Despite Gamla's infamy, the site was not excavated until 1976, owing to the fact that earlier archaeologists had mistakenly identified Gamla as Jamlieh, which is located some nine miles southeast of the current site. Shmaryah Gutman, the director of the ongoing excavations at Gamla, made the present identification of the city on the basis of a correspondence between the excavated remains and Josephus' description. The presence of the camel-back ridge, a citadel, a breached wall, and thousands of Roman arrowheads and ballista stones (used in catapults) makes the identification certain.

The area of the site covers some forty-five acres, of which only two small sections—one on the east and one on the west—have currently been excavated. Evidence uncovered so far suggests that the city was abandoned following the Roman victory, since the latest coins found on the site date to 67 C.E.

The building identified by Gutman as a synagogue was unearthed in the first season of the excavation (see figs. 2 and 3). Abutting the northeast wall of the city, the rectangular structure measures 25.5 x 17

Figure 2. View of the Gamla synagogue from the north corner, looking toward the entrance. Among the distinctive features of the building are tiers of benches arranged along the perimeter and rows of columns intervening between the seating and the center of the hall. Note also the pile of ballista stones in the right background of the photo. (Photo: Danny Syon, Gamla Excavations.)

meters on the exterior and is aligned lengthwise on a northeast to southwest axis. The interior of the building (20 x 16 m) is lined with two to four rows of stone benches (each c. 35 cm high) on all four sides and along the main entryway on the southwest. At the top of these benches are platforms (2.1 m wide on the southwest, 2.4 m wide elsewhere), which run into the walls on all sides of the building, interrupted only by the main entrance. A shorter bench is centered along the northeast wall just above the platform on that side. The benches enclose an unpaved hall (loc. 1001, 1002; 13.4 x 9.3 m) surrounded by sixteen columns (the corner ones heart-shaped), supported by flagstones on the periphery of the central area. While the sixteen columns clearly supported the roof of the structure, a strip of stone paving near the center of the hall may have served as a base for two columns used to support a stone table.

The building has three entrances: two in the southwest wall and one in the eastern corner of the southeast wall. The larger of the two entrances on the southwest (loc. 1003; 1.5 m wide) has a small exedra adjoining it on the exterior (loc. 1020; 7.8 x 2.5 m). This entrance opens into the center of the hall, creating an interruption in the rows of benches, while

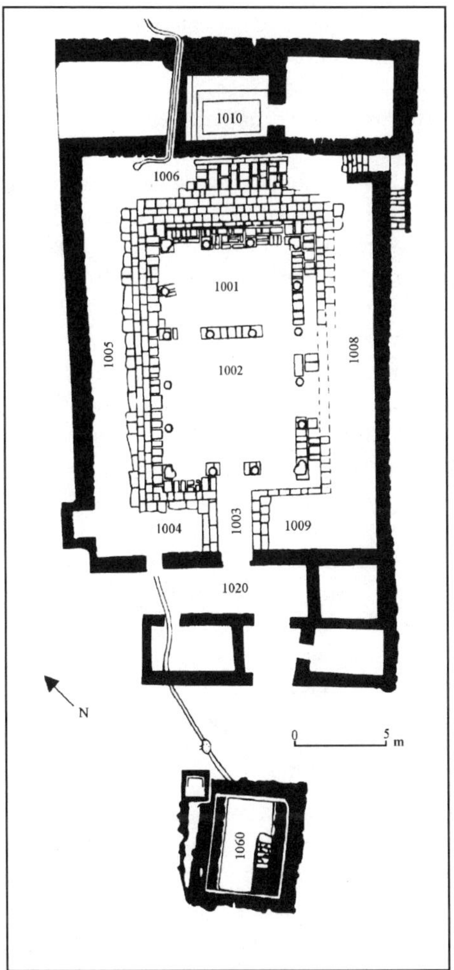

Figure 3. Plan of Gamla complex. The main structure consists of a central, unpaved area (loc. 1001, 1002), surrounded by benches with platforms at the top (loc. 1004, 1005, 1006, 1008, 1009). Ancillary features include a "study room" (loc. 1010), exedra (loc. 1020), and *mikveh* (loc. 1060). (After plan by Hagit Tahan, Gamla Excavations.)

the smaller entrance (0.9 m wide), located to the northwest of the main entrance, leads onto the platform above the benches (loc. 1004). The entry in the southeast wall (1 m wide) incorporates stairs leading three meters down to a narrow street that runs parallel to the southeast wall of the building.

Near the west corner of the northwest wall is a niche apparently used for storage. The south corner of the hall consists of a recess about 3 m deep. Two small rooms of unknown purpose lie adjacent to the exedra, one being entered from the northwest, the other from the northeast off the exedra.

The northeast wall of the building forms the first section of the city wall. Three small rooms were uncovered here. The center room (loc. 1010) is encircled by rows of benches, three of them on the northwest side, two on the northeast side, and one each on the southeast and southwest sides. Entered by a door connecting it with the room to the southeast, the chamber with the benches has a window cut through the center of its southwestern wall into the main hall of the structure. A water channel from an aqueduct outside the wall also penetrates the city wall and ends in a small basin near the northern corner of the structure's interior. In Gutman's opinion, this basin was used for the washing of hands.[17] Inside the building was also found a broken lintel bearing an inscribed figure of a six-petalled rosette flanked by date palms.

About ten meters to the southwest of the structure lies a *mikveh* (loc. 1060; 4 x 4.5 m), so identified by the six steps which descend into the pool from the entrance on the southern corner. The surviving walls of the bath are 3.15 m deep on the northwest and 2.02 m on the southeast. All the walls are covered with several layers of waterproof plaster. The water apparently rose to a height of 1.55 m since 0.4-meter-wide shelves exist across the southeast and northwest walls of the bath at this level. Water entered the southeastern wall of the *mikveh* through a plastered channel that collected water drained from the roof of the proposed synagogue. It is also possible that at some point this channel was connected to the channel that supplied water to the basin inside the hall.[18] An *otsar*, or storage tank, measuring 70 cm square and about 60 cm deep, is located near the northern corner of the *mikveh*.

---

[17]S. Gutman, "Gamala," 70.

[18]See Reich, "The Synagogue and the *Miqweh* in Eretz-Israel in the Second-Temple, Mishnaic, and Talmudic Periods," 290.

While the building was originally dated to the reign of Alexander Jannaeus (d. 76 B.C.E.), soundings from two meters under the floor of the structure uncovered a Herodian lamp fragment and a coin from the reign of Herod the Great.[19] These suggest a founding in the second half of the first century B.C.E. The structure was clearly demolished during the battle with the Romans, since many ballista stones and arrowheads were found in the northeastern side of the structure and near the main entrance. Also, evidence of burning was found inside the structure along with iron nails scattered about the interior—most likely remains from the collapse of the building's wooden roof.

In an early article on the structure at Gamla, Gutman presented the following rationale for his identification of this building as a synagogue:

> The interior layout of this building clearly indicates that it was intended for public assembly. The benches and the surrounding floors obviously served some public function. The arrangement of the benches, especially the ones on the [north]east, together with the layout of the main entrance is noteworthy in this respect. Another notable feature in the plan of the hall is the several entrances—relating to the separate floors—and the main doorway onto the central floor of the hall. This would seem to have a direct bearing on the nature of the function of the building. At present, we can note that there are no pagan motifs or traces of pagan cult within the building; such remains are usually evident even in secular "council houses" . . . Certain architectural features also typify the style of synagogues, even in later periods: the heart-sectioned corner columns (three were found *in situ*); the carvings on the broken lintel found near the main doorway, and the large niche at the western corner of the building.[20]

Here we observe that Gutman's statement regarding the public nature of this building stands in marked contrast to Kee's characterization of this structure as one of the "private homes in which the pious gathered for prayer."[21] Currently, the proposed synagogue is the largest building excavated at Gamla. To my knowledge, no archaeologist has ever argued that this structure is a house.[22]

---

[19]S. Gutman, "Gamla-1983," 26. Curiously, in a later article (1993), Gutman retains the earlier dating of the structure ("Gamala," 460).

[20]S. Gutman, "The Synagogue at Gamla," 34.

[21]Kee, "The Transformation of the Synagogue after 70 CE," 8–9. See the introductory chapter of this volume for a further discussion.

[22]Cf. Similar assessments in Oster, "Supposed Anachronism in Luke-Acts' Use of ΣΥΝΑΓΩΓΗ" 194; Riesner, "Synagogues in Jerusalem," 184–187; Atkinson, "The First-Century CE Synagogue," 495–498.

Returning to Gutman's other comments, we should note that because heart-shaped columns and niches are found in other types of buildings, his mention of these is not so decisive for his identification. However, Gutman might have added that the arrangement of the hall's interior—where benches run along the sides of the building and rows of columns line the central area—finds its closest architectural parallel in the so-called Galilean synagogues of the third century C.E. and later. Moreover, he might have mentioned that the presence of the nearby *mikveh* suggests a religious purpose for the building, as does the hand-basin, which may have been used by readers before handling sacred writings.

In connection with Gutman's allusion to the two motifs incised on the lintel of the building—the rosette and the date palm—Z. Ma'oz notes:

> The rosette is a common motif in Jewish art of the Second Temple period. It appears on reliefs found in the Jerusalem Temple area, on the façades of rock-hewn tombs, on sarcophagi, as well as on stone tables and jewelry boxes . . . The date palm is less prevalent in Jewish art, though it occurs on Hasmonaean and Herodian coins, as well as on the Judaea Capta coin series struck by the Romans to commemorate their victory over Judaea. This motif apparently symbolized Judaea and the Jewish people in general.[23]

---

[23]Ma'oz, "The Synagogue of Gamla and the Typology of Second-Temple Synagogues," 39. Rachel Hachlili similarly states that "the rosette is the most prominent motif in Jewish art and could be said to exemplify it" (*Ancient Jewish Art and Archaeology in the Land of Israel*, 80; cf *JSGRP* 4.132). The frequent appearance of the rosette on Jewish funerary art of this period further suggests the sacred character of this symbol (on this point, see Bernard Goldman, *The Sacred Portal: A Primary Symbol in Judaic Art* [Lanham, Md: University Press of America, Inc., 1986], 107–112; Renfrew, "The Archaeology of Religion," 52). For photos of the rosettes uncovered in the Temple Mount excavations, see B. Mazar, "The Archaeological Excavations near the Temple Mount" 28–29; Ben-Dov, *In the Shadow of the Temple*, 138–139. In one architectural fragment pictured, a rosette is flanked by palmettes. Flesher, while at one point agreeing that these artistic motifs are Jewish ("Palestinian Synagogues before 70 C.E.," 38), earlier in his essay writes, "none of these structures [those at Gamla, Masada and Herodium] have any features that would identify them as specifically Jewish, let alone as synagogues" (ibid., 38). Flesher nonetheless accepts the identification of the Gamla structure (ibid., 38–39). Richardson incorrectly states that the Gamla synagogue had "no symbolic decoration" (Richardson, "Early Synagogues as Collegia," 102; cf. idem, "Religion, Architecture and Ethics," 31: "[the Gamla synagogue] is not marked by religious symbols or iconography of any kind").

The appearance of these two motifs on the lintel suggests that this public building housed the "assembled congregation of Israel" in Gamla—a view that fits well with the meaning of *synagōgē* in Jewish writings of the Second Temple period, as we observed in the previous chapter. We should add that Ezek 40:31 states that there were "palm trees" (φοίνικες/תִּמֹרִים) inscribed on the posts of the inner court of the Temple and at other places around the court (Ezek 40:16, 22, 26, 34, 37; 41:18, 19, 20, 25, 26). Likewise, Solomon was said to have carved this motif on the walls, doors and door posts of the Temple shrine along with a pattern of "open flowers" (פְּטֻרֵי צִצִּים, 1 Kgs 6:29, 32, 35). Here, the underlying Hebrew can be translated literally as "opened fins" (the LXX renders this as διαπεπετασμένα πέταλα, "petals spread out on all sides")—clearly a reference to the rosette. As Ma'oz pointed out in the above quotation, the rosette was the most prominent of the motifs found among the excavated remains of Herod's Temple. In one architectural fragment uncovered, a rosette is seen flanked by palmettes. The use of these same two symbols on the lintel of the Gamla structure can hardly have been accidental.[24]

In summary, when judged by the criteria set forth for identifying a building as a synagogue, the Gamla structure fares rather well. While no inscriptions have been found, the architectural typology of the building conforms to that of the later Galilean synagogues. Additionally, there is the presence of a *mikveh* adjoining the structure. Finally, the building incorporates Jewish artistic motifs that almost certainly had religious significance. Taking this evidence together, it is therefore likely that the building is a synagogue.

If we accept this conclusion, as have the majority of archaeologists, then we can move on and make some additional observations. First of all, we note that the orientation of the building's façade is toward Jerusalem, as has been pointed out by many researchers. This suggests the custom attested in the Hebrew Scriptures and Apocrypha of praying while facing in the direction of the holy city (1 Kgs 8:30, 44, 48; 2 Chr 6:34, 38; Dan

[24]On the presence of the palmette among the excavated remains of the Temple mount, see the previous note. Josephus states that bronze palms buds were fastened onto the so-called pillars of Jachin and Boaz (*Ant.* 8.77–78; cf. 1 Kgs 7:13–22). Elsewhere, he follows his source and notes that palm trees decorated the lavers used in Court of the Priests (*Ant.* 8:84–85; cf. 1 Kgs 7:36). The palm tree (or other sort of tree) may also be the precursor of the menorah. See *JSGRP* 4.72–74; Th. A. Busnick, *Der Tempel von Jerusalem* (Leiden: E. J. Brill, 1970), 1.272–274.

6:10; 1 Esdr 4:58).[25] Many later synagogue builders not only adopted the practice of orienting the façades of their houses of worship toward Jerusalem, but also placed Torah shrines at that end of the interior of the buildings. Hence, the worshipers, while entering the synagogue with their backs toward Jerusalem, later turned around and faced the holy city when offering their prayers.[26] While the Torah shrine is absent from the Gamla synagogue (though possibly the niche near the western corner of the building might have housed the scrolls), given the orientation of the building, it is possible that the later synagogal custom of praying in the direction of Jerusalem was already being practiced in the Gamla synagogue. Even if this interpretation seems too speculative, the fact that the façade faces toward Jerusalem can hardly be accidental: the builders of the synagogue apparently wanted to establish a connection between the synagogue and the holy city.[27]

A second observation has to do with the placement of the strip of stones in the center of the hall. Here, we recall that the central area of the hall is unpaved. Ma'oz has suggested that fine carpets adorned the unpaved area around the strip of stones that probably served as the base for a stone table. He writes, "during the services, the Torah scroll may have been brought into the center of the hall from its storage space."[28] If this was indeed the case, then the focal point of that part of the service would have been the hall's center.

While the uniformity of the rows of benches around the hall implies a relative equality among those seated there, it should be recalled that a

---

[25]See Samuel Safrai, "The Synagogue and Its Worship" in *Society and Religion in the Second Temple Period*, edited by Michael Avi-Yonah and Zvi Baras (Jerusalem: Jewish History Publications Ltd., 1977), 94.

[26]See Gideon Foerster, "The Ancient Synagogues of the Galilee" in *The Galilee in Late Antiquity*, edited by Lee Levine (New York: Jewish Theological Seminary of America, 1992), 289–319; Hachlili, *Ancient Jewish Art and Archaeology in the Land of Israel*, 167.

[27]The position that the placement of the façade was "accidental since the location [of the building] would hardly admit of any other arrangement" (Richardson, "Early Synagogues as Collegia," 101) needs to be evaluated in view of the likelihood that the architects chose the building site for precisely this reason. As we will see, the façade of the synagogue at Ostia (phase I) and possibly that of the earlier synagogue at Capernaum were also oriented toward Jerusalem. In view of this, as well as of the early literary evidence and the later building practices (see above), the arrangement of the Gamla synagogue must not be so quickly dismissed as accidental.

[28]Ma'oz, "The Synagogue of Gamla and the Typology of Second-Temple Synagogues," 38.

separate bench was placed against the northeastern wall near the water-basin. The prominence of this location, which overlooks the rest of the hall, suggests that the leaders of the assembly sat there.[29] These persons also may have used the nearby water-basin before handling the sacred scrolls (this interpretation, of course, does not preclude the possibility that others *not* seated on the upper bench also made use of the water-basin). Finally, if this bench was reserved for the use of the leaders, then they would have had ready access to the entrance near the eastern corner of the synagogue, should they have wanted to make an entry or exit separate from the larger body of the congregation.

The function of the rooms within the city wall has been a matter of some discussion, with most scholars maintaining that the room with the benches served as a semi-private study room (the others for storage?).[30] Ma'oz, however, noting the segregation of men and women within the Sabbath gatherings of the Therapeutae (Philo, *Contempl.* 30–33), has suggested that women sat in this room, separate from the male congregation. In support of this theory, he points to the separate entryway posted near the door of the adjoining room as well as to the room's window overlooking the main hall, which would have allowed the persons inside the small room to overhear the service in the hall.[31] While we will deal more fully with the place of women in the synagogues in chapter five, here we note that a shortcoming of Ma'oz's proposal is the size differential between the room and the main hall. Assuming a general

---

[29]Richardson, who concludes that the arrangement of the benches within the Palestinian synagogues evince a social entity that was "democratic" and analogous to "the 'puritan' and left-wing streams of reformed Christianity" ("Early Synagogues as Collegia," 102), does not mention the upper bench in his description of the Gamla synagogue. The presence of this bench, as well as the existence of various synagogal offices (see chapter five), suggests that the Palestinian synagogues may not have been as democratic as Richardson conjectures (see also chapter four's consideration of the Delos synagogue, wherein excavators recovered the remains of an elaborate marble throne).

[30]E.g., S. Gutman, "Gamala," 461–462; Syon, "Gamla: Portrait of a Rebellion," 32.

[31]Ma'oz, "The Synagogue in the Second Temple Period—Architectural and Social Interpretation," 341. Ma'oz's statement regarding the significance of the entryway clashes with his earlier opinion that "there is no connection between the position of the entrances or the landings and the isolation of the women into a special gallery. The view that synagogues of [the Second Temple] period did not contain a women's gallery is supported by the synagogue at Gamla where no traces of any separation are found" ("The Synagogue of Gamla and the Typology of Second-Temple Synagogues," 39).

equality between the number of Jewish males and females in Gamla, Ma'oz's suggestion implies that only a few Jewish women attended the Sabbath services. While this is not impossible, it seems rather unlikely. Hence the interpretation that the room served as a study room is to be preferred.

The extent of the usage of the *mikveh* adjoining the synagogue is also a matter we shall take up more fully in a later chapter. Here we propose, however, that the *mikveh* served as a "public ritual bath" in which Jews could purify themselves sometime prior to their entry into the synagogue. The public nature of this facility is suggested not only by its proximity to a public structure, but also by the Theodotus inscription, which mentions the erection of baths (*mikvaoth*?) for the use of pilgrims to the holy city.

Masada[32]

The ancient fortress of Masada is located near the western shore of the Dead Sea about ten miles south of the town of En-gedi. Situated on top of a cliff rising over 1,200 feet above the surrounding desert, the fortress was originally constructed during the reign of Alexander Jannaeus (103–76 B.C.E.) and later extensively expanded under Herod the Great (37–4 B.C.E.), who added two luxurious palaces, a Roman bathhouse, twelve huge cisterns, and a number of other structures. According to Josephus, near the beginning of the Jewish War, a large band of Sicarii somehow managed to take possession of Masada from the attending Roman garrison (*BJ* 2.408). Josephus goes on to describe in detail the campaign undertaken against the Sicarii in 73 C.E. by Roman legions under the command of Flavius Silva. The lengthy siege of the fortress ended with the Romans breaking through the defensive walls only to discover that all but a few hidden women and children had committed suicide (*BJ* 7.252–406).

Masada was first systematically excavated between 1963 and 1965 by a team under the direction of Yigael Yadin. The excavations uncovered

---

[32]The description of the Masada structure is based on the following sources: Ehud Netzer, *Masada III: The Yigael Yadin Excavations, 1963–1965: Final Reports* (Jerusalem: Israel Exploration Society: Hebrew University of Jerusalem, 1989), 3.402–413; Yigael Yadin, *Masada* (New York: Random House, 1966), 181–191; idem, "The Excavation of Masada 1963/64: Preliminary Report," *IEJ* 15 (1965): 74–79; idem, "The Synagogue at Masada" in *ASR* 19–23; idem, "Masada" in *EAEHL* 3.793–816. Although the structure does not lie exactly on an east-west axis, we will maintain this convention, since it is used consistently in the excavation reports.

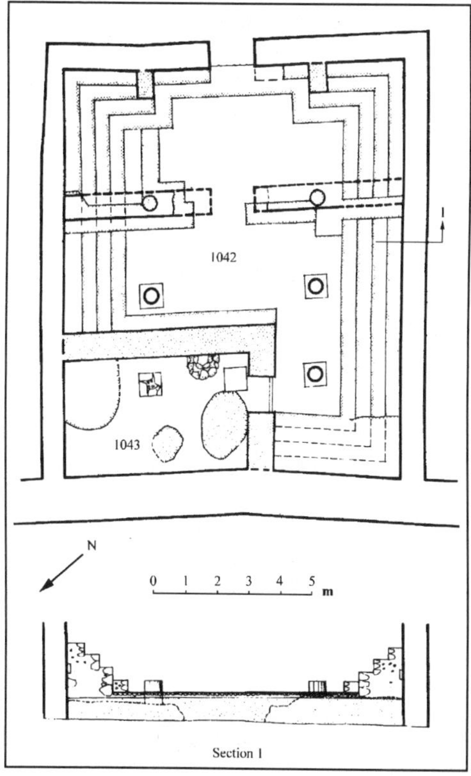

Figure 4. Plan of the Masada synagogue. In its final phase, the structure consisted of an assembly hall with rows of benches lining the walls (locus 1042) and a chamber that served as the residence of an attendant, possibly a priest alluded to in an inscription recovered nearby (locus 1043). Fragments of Deuteronomy and Ezekiel were found buried in pits in the latter room. According to Netzer, the hall can seat as many as 250 persons. (Plan: Israel Exploration Society, Jerusalem.)

evidence of occupation from the time of Jannaeus through the Byzantine era, including a period of habitation by the Jewish rebels. During the first season of excavation, a structure that Yadin subsequently identified as a synagogue was uncovered in the northwestern section of the upper plateau of the fortress (see figs. 4 and 5). Built into the casemate wall that circles the plateau, the rectangular building measures 15 x 12 meters and was constructed in two distinct phases.

In the first phase, dated to the period of Herod, a wall divided the structure into two rooms: an antechamber (10.5 x 3.6 m) on the east and a small hall (10.5 x 8 m) to the west. Entry into the structure was from the east, through a threshold (1.35 m wide) in the middle of the eastern wall of the antechamber. A second opening similarly placed in the partition wall allowed entry into the inner room. Five columns (40–45 cm in diameter) were arranged in the inner room in a U-shaped configuration that opened to the west. The western wall of this room also served as the outer wall of the casemate. The floor of the entire structure was originally covered with white lime plaster, layered on top of a thick gravel fill placed over the bedrock.

The second phase of the building dates to the period of occupation by the rebels, during which extensive renovations were undertaken. The partition wall of the original structure was demolished, and a small, rectangular room (locus 1043; 5.7 x 3.5 m) was erected on the northwestern corner of the building. This room was entered through an opening in its southern wall. A niche is found on the eastern part of this wall, just outside the entrance to the room. The two columns from the earlier phase were removed from loc. 1043 while two others were added in the main area of the structure (locus 1042) on top of the foundation of the dismantled partition wall. Thus two rows of columns were created—two on the north and three on the south. Two pilasters (55 cm wide, extending inward 85 cm), each aligned with a row of columns, were also added to the interior of the eastern wall to give extra support to the roof, which was also reconstructed during this period. Four tiers of benches (each c. 35 cm high, 45 cm wide) were built along the outer walls of the main hall (two tiers between the pilasters and the main entry), with one bench also placed against the western wall that formed the length of the smaller room. One of the tiers on the eastern wall continues across the main entryway, creating a step into the center of the hall. The benches were made out of dolomite fieldstones, sandstone and reused architectural fragments, and were coated with a layer of earth plaster, as were the walls of the hall during this phase. The floor of the main hall at this stage consisted of ash lime plaster laid over a bedding of stones and potsherds. The floor of the small room was made of beaten earth.

During the second season, soundings taken beneath the floor of the corner room revealed two pits which had been dug during the second phase of occupation. These were then refilled with a mixture of gravel,

Figure 5. Overhead view of the Masada synagogue. Note the structure's position in the western casemate wall of the fortress. (Photo: Israel Exploration Society, Jerusalem.)

organic material and potsherds. The first pit, 80 cm in diameter, was dug to a depth of 70 cm. At the bottom of the pit excavators discovered parchment fragments of the book of Deuteronomy. The second pit, dug to a similar depth, was oval in shape (2 x 1.4 m). It contained fragments of a scroll of Ezekiel. On the surface of the floor were the remains of an oven and evidence of a conflagration. Among the burnt items were chalices, portions of a bronze bowl and a large quartz hand-bowl. Just outside the corner room, two ostraca were found, one with the words "priest's tithe" (מעשר כהן) and the other with the name "Hezekiah" (חזקיה).[33]

Fifteen meters to the north of the structure, excavators uncovered a *mikveh* (locus 1301), apparently built by the rebels. Measuring 3.4 x 2.6 m, seven stairs (75 cm wide) descend into the pool, which reaches a depth of two meters. It was fed by a channel from the northeast that collected rainwater from a nearby room.[34]

---

[33]See Yigael Yadin, and Joseph Naveh, "The Aramaic and Hebrew Ostraca and Jar Inscriptions" in *Masada: The Yigael Yadin Excavations, 1963–1965: Final Reports*, edited by Ehud Netzer (Jerusalem: Israel Exploration Society: Hebrew University of Jerusalem, 1989), 1.32.

[34]While Netzer merely describes the installation as a "pool," (*Masada III*, 398), Reich, comparing this pool with others from Jerusalem and Jericho, identifies it as a *mikveh* ("The Synagogue and the *Miqweh* in Eretz-Israel," 290). Note also that one meter to the north of the synagogue, excavators uncovered a stepped pool (locus 1048),

In the final report of the Masada excavations, Ehud Netzer offered the following assessment of the purpose of the structure in its second phase:

> The identification of this building as a Zealot synagogue seems to be incontrovertible. This is based on two significant points: (1) the internal structure of the hall with its benches, typical of a place of assembly; (2) the scroll fragments found beneath the floor of Room 1043, most probably a *genizah* (repository for worn and disused sacred scripts).[35]

During the excavations, Yadin himself had reached this same conclusion, even suggesting that the first phase of the building may have been used as a synagogue.[36] However, this latter proposal was based on the assumption that Herod would have included a synagogue inside the fortress for members of his court. This assumption has since been rendered suspect by more recent excavations at several of Herod's palaces that have failed to find such structures.[37] Netzer argues that the earlier structure served as a stable, pointing to a layer of organic material on top of the original floor (interpreted as animal dung) and to the arrangement of the columns which may have served as tethering posts.[38] While this

---

apparently built by the rebels since it interrupted a passageway that led into two sections of the casemate wall (loci 1045 and 1046). Enclosed by walls on all four sides, the pool (2.0 x 0.9–1.3 m) reaches to a depth of four meters and was apparently accessed by a ladder hung from the roofs of the adjoining wall segments. The pool was lined with successive layers of ash lime plaster. Although Netzer simply calls this an "unusual pool" (op. cit. 401) its function could hardly have been for the additional storage of water, since a large cistern (cistern 1901) lies nearby. Given the stepped configuration of the pool, it is possible that it served as a private *mikveh* for the person or persons dwelling in locus 1043. Yadin himself believed this pool was somehow connected with the synagogue ("Masada," 810).

[35]Netzer, *Masada III*, 410. Flesher complains that "the final reports for the synagogues at both Masada and Herodium took nearly three decades to appear. Thus most discussion of their identification and character has been on the basis of brief preliminary remarks, rather than on complete presentation of the data" ("Synagogues Before 70 CE," 35). Despite the fact that he elsewhere cites the final report of Masada in his essay, Flesher nowhere presents to the reader Netzer's conclusions regarding the identification of the renovated structure.

[36]See Yadin, *Masada*, 185.

[37]This point is made by Netzer, who excavated Herod's winter palace at Jericho. See Netzer, *Masada III*, 411.

[38]Flesher is troubled by the fact that Jews could construct a synagogue on top of a layer of animal dung ("Palestinian Synagogues before 70 C.E.," 36). Yet it should be pointed out that someone (apparently a Jew) had no difficulty depositing sacred writings within such material (the fact that *two* pits were dug argues against the theory

hypothesis is not without its problems (stable floors were not typically plastered), whatever the building may have been in its earlier phase, there is nothing in its original configuration to suggest continuity of function with the renovated structure.

Returning our discussion to the identification of the second phase of the building, we find that several of our criteria are met in the Masada structure. First, the renovated hall consists of rows of benches on four sides with columns intervening between the benches and the center of the hall. Secondly, scriptures were found deposited within the room adjoining the main hall. Finally, a *mikveh* is located near the structure. Taking all this together, it seems highly likely that the building served as a synagogue for the rebels.

Having established the probability of this identification, we turn to some further observations. Beginning with a discussion of the corner room (locus 1043), we recall Netzer's identification of this room as a genizah. While this is certainly one of the functions served by the room, it must be noted that the presence of an oven suggests that the area served as someone's domicile—a point originally made by Yadin.[39] Calling attention to the ostracon bearing the words "priest's tithe" found near this room, Yadin further proposed that "the back room appears to have served as the dwelling of a priest."[40] This hypothesis finds support in Yadin's discovery of other ostraca attesting to the presence of priests at Masada during the revolt.[41]

Regarding the placement of the room in the synagogue, elsewhere in the various sections of the casemate wall excavators uncovered stoves and personal items, all pointing to the conclusion that many of the rebels had used these areas as dwelling places.[42] Because the synagogue was fashioned out of a structure that was part of the casemate wall, the

---

that the deposits were made out of desperation). Also, when one notes that animal dung was a common component of ancient plasters, one realizes that our sensibilities differ from those of the ancients.

[39]Yadin, "The Excavation of Masada 1963/64: Preliminary Report," 78.

[40]Ibid.

[41]See Yadin et al. "The Aramaic and Hebrew Ostraca and Jar Inscriptions," 32–39. One ostracon (no. 1237-878/1) mentions a certain Aqavia, a hitherto unknown son of the High Priest Ananias (the latter, incidentally, was murdered during the early part of the Jewish War). It reads, "A[nani]as the High Priest, Aqavia his son [עקביה בריה ח[נני]ה כהנא רבא]" (op. cit: 37). Other ostraca come from smashed vessels that had been classified according to their purity status—a duty assigned to priests.

[42]See Yadin, *Masada*, 140–163.

construction of the corner room for the dwelling of an attendant would likely have been viewed as appropriate. It should be noted that if we consider as a serious possibility Yadin's hypothesis that a priest resided in this room, then we once again find a difficulty with the proposal that an incompatibility existed between the Temple and the synagogues.[43] Finally, we should observe that the placement of sleeping quarters in the Masada synagogue parallels the arrangement of the synagogue of Theodotus, which also contained such rooms (albeit for pilgrims).

Turning to the synagogue hall itself, we observe that its size, though smaller than the Gamla synagogue, was still sufficient to hold a significant crowd—by Netzer's estimate, more than 250 persons could have assembled inside.[44] Josephus numbers the rebels at Masada at 967, including women and children (*BJ* 7.400). If this figure is reliable, then only a segment of the community could have met inside the structure at any one time. Assuming that the synagogue served as a Sabbath meeting place (as the literature indicates), perhaps this problem was solved by having different assembly times for different groups or by having the overflow crowd sit outside (or both). Netzer notes that the lower row of benches was added on the north and the south sides after the initial construction of the upper three tiers (*two* rows were added on the east side).[45] It is possible that this modification was due to the arrival of refugees after the initial occupation of the fortress. While the presence of only a single tier along the wall of the corner room might be explained by the proximity of the supporting column, it is also possible that this bench was preserved for the leaders of the assemblies.[46] In any case, the arrangement parallels that seen at Gamla, where a single row of benches also sits against the wall opposite the main entrance.

As was probably the case at Gamla, the *mikveh* near the synagogue at Masada was likely for public use. Yadin himself was quick to point out

---

[43]This observation is also upheld on the alternate hypothesis that a non-priestly attendant dwelling in the room was collecting tithes to be given to the priests.

[44]Netzer, *Masada III*, 412.

[45]Ibid., 407. On the north and south sides, the upper three tiers were founded on the original white plaster floor, while the lowest row was built on top of the upper floor. On the east side, the upper two rows were laid on top of the white plaster floor, and the lower two on the floor above.

[46]The parallel between this bench and the similarly placed tier in the Gamla synagogue has gone unnoted in the scholarly literature. Cf. Yadin's statement that the leaders sat on the eastern benches so that they could face towards Jerusalem ("Masada," 810).

the rebels' concern with ritual purity: elsewhere in the complex the Sicarii built three other ritual baths, two in Building IX (loci 298, 368; 75 m southeast of the synagogue) and one in Building VII (60 m east of the synagogue).[47] Reich argues that these more distant structures were also used in connection with the synagogue, but were placed further away because there was greater potential in these other locations for collecting rainwater.[48] Other pieces of evidence that demonstrate the rebels' concern with ritual purity include a number of ostraca from broken vessels that were classified according to their degree of purity.[49]

The discovery of the Ezekiel scroll in the small room of the synagogue suggests that not only did services include the recitation of Torah, but also readings from the Prophets. In locus 1039, a section of the casemate wall just twelve meters south of the synagogue, a number of additional scrolls were found, all dating to the rebel occupation. All in Hebrew, these included fragments of Genesis (1039-317), Leviticus (1039-270), Psalms (1039-160), and the *Songs of the Sabbath Sacrifice* (1039-200).[50] As was noted in chapter one, the last of these works was also discovered at Qumran. It is possible that it too was used within services held in the synagogue. This same comment applies to the other scrolls found elsewhere at Masada, including fragments of Sirach (in the Hebrew original) and *Jubilees*. That the language of all of these scrolls is Hebrew and not Aramaic argues that written Targums were not used in the synagogue services there, though it is possible that after a passage was read in Hebrew it may have been translated orally for the congregation. However, the extensive use of Hebrew in the ostraca recovered at Masada suggests that most if not all the rebels could readily understand Hebrew as well as Aramaic.

---

[47]See Netzer, *Masada III*, 13–16, 221–222, 227–228. For Yadin's melodramatic account of Rabbi David Muntzberg's certification of one of the *mikvaoth*, see Yadin, *Masada*, 164–167.

[48]Reich, "Synagogue and Ritual Bath During the Second Temple and the Period of the Mishna and Talmud," 290–291.

[49]See note 41 above.

[50]See Yadin, "The Excavation of Masada 1963/64," 81–82. Prior to their deposit in the ground, some of these scrolls may have been stored in the niche located just outside loc. 1043.

Herodium[51]

Herodium (or Herodion) lies about 7.5 miles south of Jerusalem. Built c. 24 B.C.E. by Herod the Great to commemorate an earlier victory over his Hasmonean and Parthian enemies (Josephus, *BJ* 1.265; *Ant.* 14.359–360), the fortress rests on top of a hill rising some 400 feet above the surrounding terrain. Josephus describes it in the following terms:

> This fortress, which is some sixty stades distant from Jerusalem, is naturally strong and very suitable for such a structure, for reasonably near by is a hill, raised to a (greater) height by the hand of man and rounded off in the shape of a breast. At intervals it has round towers, and it has a steep ascent formed of two hundred steps of hewn stone. Within it are costly royal apartments made for security and for ornament at the same time (Ant. 15.324).

While Herod himself was said to have been buried there (*BJ* 1.67–673, *Ant.* 17.196–199), neither his body nor his tomb has ever been found. During the Jewish War the fortress came under control of the Sicarii. Unlike the protracted siege of Masada, however, Herodium was apparently taken with little difficulty following the fall of Jerusalem (*BJ* 7.163). From references in the Bar Kokhba letters found at Murabba'at, we know that Herodium also served as one of Bar Kokhba's command centers during the revolt of 132–135 C.E.[52]

The first excavations of Herodium were conducted between 1962 and 1967 by a team under the direction of Virgilio Corbo. These revealed an occupational history lasting from the fortress's construction by Herod to its habitation by Christian monks during the Byzantine period. Corbo also uncovered evidence attesting to the presence of Jewish rebels during both the First Jewish War and the Bar Kokhba Revolt.

---

[51]The description of the structure at Herodium is based on the following sources: Virgilio C. Corbo, *Herodion: Gli Edifici della Reggia-Fortrezza* vol. 1 (Jerusalem: Franciscan Printing Press, 1989); Gideon Foerster, "The Synagogues at Masada and Herodium" in *ASR* 24–29.

[52]For texts of the relevant letters from Murabba'at, see E. Jerry Vardaman, "History of Herodium" in *The Teacher's Yoke: Studies in Memory of Henry Trantham*, edited by E. Jerry Vardaman and James Leo Garrett, Jr. (Waco, Tx.: Baylor University Press, 1964), 80–81.

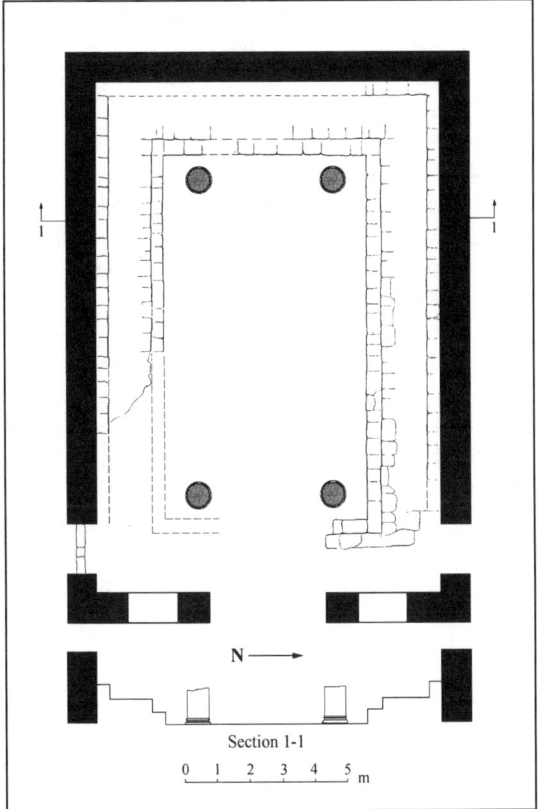

Figure 6. Plan of the Herodium synagogue. This room, previously a triclinium, was adapted through the addition of benches on four sides. A *mikveh* (not shown) was hewn out of the floor a few meters north of the synagogue entrance. (Plan: Israel Exploration Society, Jerusalem.)

Corbo's excavations ended following the Six Day War, when the region fell into Israeli hands. Subsequently, restoration of the excavated remains was undertaken by Gideon Foerster in 1969. Archaeological work resumed in 1970 under Ehud Netzer, whose investigations focused on the installations at the base of Herodium.

The room Corbo identified as a synagogue (Room 15) is rectangular in shape (15.15 x 10.6 m) and adjoins a large peristyle court inside the central area of the fortress (see figs. 6 and 7). Flanked by two small windows (1.48 m wide), the main entrance of the room (3.46 m wide) is in the center of the eastern wall. Smaller entryways are located on the northern and southern walls at the eastern end of the room.

The remains of this room suggest two phases. During the first phase, the room served as Herod's grand triclinium or dining room. The floor was originally laid in *opus sectile* (colored stone tile), though currently only the bedding remains. While as many as six columns may have been arranged in two rows, some reconstructions suggest that only four columns were present.[53]

In the second phase, the two windows and the doors on the north and the south were blocked up with debris, and the main entrance was narrowed to a width of only 1.6 meters. Three rows of benches (each c. 40 cm high) were built around the four walls of the room, interrupted only by the main entrance. These were constructed out of blocks of masonry and architectural fragments taken from other parts of the fortress. The bottom and top rows of benches each have a width of 40 cm, while the width of the center row is more than three times as wide, measuring 1.4 m. This variance allowed easier access to the upper row of benches. Reconstructions locate four columns in the room, placed near the foot of the benches, one at each corner.[54]

Just to the east of the room near the window on the northern side of the eastern wall lies a *mikveh*, measuring 1.5 meters wide by 2 meters long. Entered from the south, four stairs lead downward about two meters to a base just over half a meter long. Just to the south of the *mikveh* lies

---

[53]Corbo's original plan showed four columns ("L'Herodion di Giabal Fuereidis, Relazione preliminare della terza e qaurta campagna di scavi archeologici," plan 1). His final report shows six columns (*Herodion*, plans 1–2). Foerster's plan depicts four columns ("The Synagogues at Masada and Herodium," 28). Corbo's final plan is to be preferred since six columns were probably needed to support the ceiling. See next note.

[54]According to Foerster's plan ("The Synagogues at Masada and Herodium," 28). Curiously, Corbo's final plan shows only *two* columns in the reconstructed synagogue, both on the north side (*Herodion*, plan 3). Since Corbo only found one column (in the northeast corner) *in situ* (ibid., 53), any reconstruction should take into account how many columns it would have taken to support the ceiling. In this regard, even Foerster's reconstruction appears inadequate, as probably six columns would have been needed (cf. the five columns, wall and two pilasters used to support the roof of the similarly dimensioned synagogue at Masada). While Corbo notes that two of the original columns and capitals of the triclinium were incorporated into the benches of the synagogue (ibid.), Foerster points out that other columns were probably taken from the peristyle ("The Synagogues at Masada and Herodium," 24).

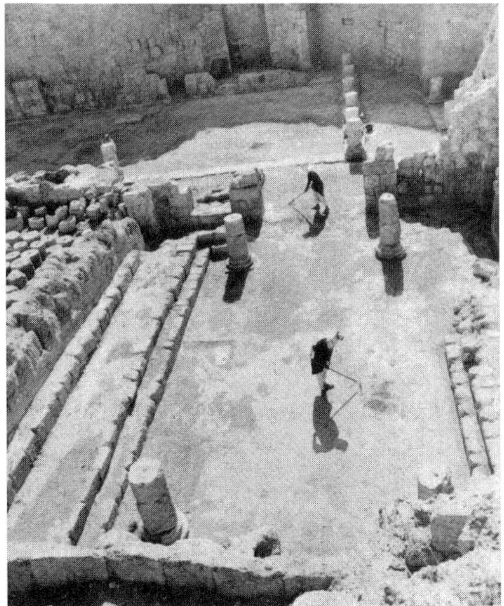

Figure 7. View of the Herodium synagogue from the west. When the room was transformed, both windows were blocked-up and the main entrance was narrowed to a width of 1.6 m. (Photo: Israel Exploration Society, Jerusalem.)

a storage pool (1.2 x 2.0 m) with an adjacent bathtub (1.2 x 0.6 m). All these structures were hewn out of the western side of the Herodian peristyle court by the rebels.

Corbo identified the reconstructed triclinium as a synagogue on the basis of a comparison with the similarly designed structures at Masada and Gamla. The presence of the adjoining *mikveh* was also seen as supporting evidence for the identification of the room as a synagogue.[55] Foerster and Netzer subsequently defended this proposal, and it has been adopted by many other archaeologists.[56] Because the structure meets two

---

[55]See Corbo, *Herodion*, 75.

[56]Foerster, "The Synagogues at Masada and Herodium"; idem, "Herodium" in *NEAEHL* 2.618–621; Ehud Netzer, "The Herodian Triclinia: A Prototype for the 'Galilean-Type' Synagogue" in *ASR* 49–51; idem, "Did the Magdala Springhouse Serve As a Synagogue?" in *Synagogues in Antiquity*, edited by Aryeh Kasher, Aharon Oppenheimer and Uriel Rappaport (Jerusalem: Yad Izhak Ben Zvi, 1987 [Hebrew]), 165–172; Doron Chen, "The Design of the Ancient Synagogues in Judea: Masada and

of our stated criteria—that of architectural typology and the presence of a *mikveh*—this study accepts the proposed identification.

With regard to the chronological parameters of this study, however, one difficulty remains: the issue of dating the reconstructions. Originally, Corbo assigned them simply to "the Jewish Wars," while Foerster dated them to the First Jewish War. However, in his final report, Corbo, noting the difficulty of distinguishing the two rebel occupations, dated nearly all the reconstructions at Herodium—including the synagogue and *mikveh*—to the Bar Kokhba revolt. Unfortunately, nowhere in his report does Corbo defend his new position with arguments from archaeology.

In a review of Corbo's final report, Joseph Patrich argues that the synagogue is better dated to the First Jewish War because of its resemblance to the structures at Masada and Gamla.[57] He also notes that the majority of the coins scattered about the site date from the First Jewish War.[58] While neither of these arguments is decisive, they tend to tip the scale in favor of the earlier dating. This conclusion is further suggested when we recall that the Sicarii at Masada went through significant efforts to build a synagogue and several *mikvaoth*. Because a similar group inhabited Herodium during the First Jewish War, it seems likely that they would have followed suit. Moreover, since the fortress was in the possession of the rebels from about 66 to 71 C.E., they certainly had ample time to make the renovations to the triclinium. In fact, given that the rebels at Herodium were cut off from worship in Jerusalem (or anywhere else, for that matter) during most of those five years, the construction of a synagogue in that period would seem a natural development. Thus, although the dating of the structure is not as firmly established as we would like—a situation that could possibly be remedied by taking soundings in the benches—presently it seems more probable that the synagogue was built during the First Revolt than during the Second.

Some of the same observations made for the synagogues at Gamla and Masada can be adduced for the structure at Herodium. First of all, the hall is sizable and able to accommodate a fairly large crowd. Though none of

---

Herodium," *BASOR* 239 (1980): 37–40; Levine, "Synagogues," 1421–1424; Strange, "The Art and Archaeology of Ancient Judaism," 64–114.

[57]Joseph Patrich, "Corbo's Excavations at Herodium: A Review Article," *IEJ* 42 (1992): 243.

[58]"Of the 102 coins on from the site . . . 47 are of the First Revolt and only 16 of the Second (if we disregard a hoard of approximately 1,000 bronze coins from this period found in the southern exedra)" (ibid.).

Herodium's excavators give a figure, because the room's dimensions closely match those of the synagogue at Masada, we might apply Netzer's estimate of 250 persons for the Masada synagogue to Herodium. Unfortunately, Josephus does not mention the number of rebels occupying Herodium during the revolt, and so we are unable to compare this estimate to the total number of occupants. A second point is that, as with the other two structures, the presence of the *mikveh* so close to the synagogue underscores the concern for ritual purity before entering the place of worship.

Another noteworthy observation is that the rebels blocked up the windows and two of the doorways in the triclinium and narrowed the main entryway. When we recall that the structures at Masada and Gamla also lacked windows (though it is possible that the latter had some in a demolished clerestory level), it appears that the preference was for a darkened room lit by lamps. Alternatively, the center of the rooms may have been open to the air, with roofs extending out only as far as the columns. In this case, the lighting would have been provided by the exposed portion of the ceiling.

A final point is that in the Herodium synagogue, a row of benches sits in a prominent position opposite the entryway. As we have seen, this was also the case at Gamla and Masada, though the layout in these latter structures differs somewhat from the seating configuration at Herodium, where the upper bench continues around the other walls. As was previously suggested, it is possible that the leaders of the synagogue services sat in this tier since it gave them a commanding view of the proceedings. On the other hand, because the benches there are identical with those throughout the rest of the hall, the prominence accorded these spots is not as pronounced as would have been the case if the builders had erected stylized chairs.

Capernaum[59]

Aside from various references to Capernaum in the Gospels, the earliest literary attestation of Capernaum is from Josephus, who refers to the village in connection with a fertile spring (*BJ* 3.519–521). Elsewhere, he briefly mentions spending a night there with a fever during the second year of the Jewish War (*Vita* 403–404). For centuries, Capernaum has traditionally been identified as a site located on the northwestern shore of the Sea of Galilee, about three miles west of the upper Jordan River. In 1838, Edward Robinson correctly identified there the remains of a synagogue that was partly excavated by Charles Wilson between 1865 and 1866. More extensive excavations took place in the early twentieth century, first by Heinrich Kohl and Carl Watzinger (1905) and then by Wendelin von Menden (1906–1915). In 1921, the synagogue was partially restored by Gaudenzio Orfali. In more recent times, Virgilio Corbo and Stanislao Loffreda conducted nineteen seasons at Capernaum between 1968 and 1986, excavating not only the synagogue, but also a nearby church that had long been associated with the house of St. Peter.

As previously mentioned, the Capernaum synagogue is an example of a Galilean synagogue, a type which features benches along the walls with rows of columns between the seating and the center of the hall (see fig. 8). Constructed out of white limestone, the main hall of the synagogue measures 20.4 x 18.6 meters and has three entrances cut through the southern wall, which is oriented towards Jerusalem. A fourth entrance is in the far western side of the northern hall. It leads to a chamber with stairs on the exterior of its eastern and western sides. Though their purpose is still a subject of debate, the stairs may have led to a second-story balcony.

Two rows of benches were constructed on the eastern and western sides of the main hall. The center of the hall is encased by rows of columns built on top of three stylobates (foundation walls), two running from north to south along opposite sides of the hall, and one running from east to west, connecting the first two stylobates at their northernmost

[59]The descriptions given in this section are based upon the following sources: Virgilio C. Corbo, "Resti dell Sinagoga del Primo Secolo a Cafarnao" in *Studia Hierosolymitana III* (1982), 314–357; Stanislao Loffreda, "Ceramica Ellenistico-Romana nel Sottosuolo della Sinagoga di Cafarnao" in *Studia Hierosolymitana III* (1982), 273–313; Stanislao Loffreda, *Recovering Capharnaum* 2nd ed. (Jerusalem: Franciscan Printing Press, 1993); James F. Strange and Hershel Shanks, "Synagogue Where Jesus Preached Found at Capernaum," *BAR* 9, no. 6 (1983): 25–31.

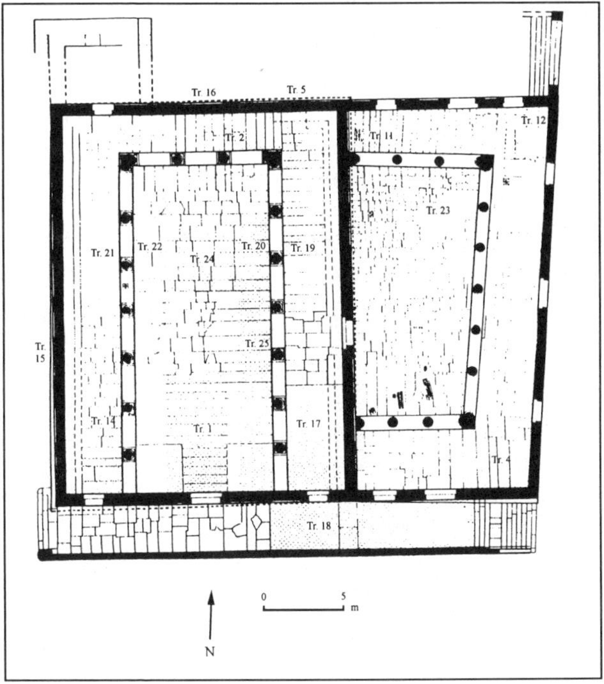

Figure 8. Plan of the IV–V century synagogue at Capernaum. The complex consists of a prayer hall (west), courtyard (east) and porch (south). The structure on the northwest corner of the building *may* be the remains of a stairwell leading to a balcony. (After Corbo, "Resti della sinagoga a Cafarnao," 343.)

ends. A door in the eastern wall leads into a courtyard, which is equal in length to the main hall but measures only 11.25 meters across the front. A narrow porch runs across the width of both of these rooms on the south side. The identification of the building as a synagogue was established not only by the arrangement of the architectural features, but by the presence of various Jewish religious carvings such as a menorah, incense shovel, and ark.

Until recently, archaeologists had dated this synagogue to the second or third century C.E. on the basis of typology. However, the more recent excavations of Corbo and Loffreda have established a late-fourth through mid-fifth century date for the founding. This was determined when the excavators dug a number of trenches in and around the synagogue. In the trench underneath the pavers of the central nave (trench 24) they uncovered several strata: first a 30 cm layer of mortar (stratum C), then an intermittent layer of limestone chips, and then a one-meter layer of fill consisting of basalt stones, dirt, pottery and architectural fragments (stratum B). Beneath this, on top of a floor made of basalt cobblestones (stratum A), they found pottery dating from the first through the fourth centuries C.E. This, of course, fixed the founding of the limestone synagogue to no earlier than fourth century.

Of interest to this study are the other discoveries made in these trenching operations. When Loffreda and Corbo first began their soundings, they thought that the basalt cobblestone floor underneath the fill indicated that the synagogue had been built on top of a residential section dating to the first century C.E. at the latest. (Coins and pottery from the Hellenistic period were found underneath this floor.)[60] However, as they continued to sink additional trenches around the synagogue, they noticed that directly beneath the four walls of the main hall lay another set of walls made of basalt blocks. These walls are 1.2 to 1.3 meters thick (compared to a 0.7 m thickness for the walls of the limestone synagogue) and rest directly on top of the cobblestone floor (see fig. 9). While they form a continuous, rectangular base underneath the walls of the main hall, they do not appear underneath the walls of the eastern courtyard. Further

---

[60]The earlier interpretation that the cobblestone floor was of a residential area is found in S. Loffreda, "The Late Chronology of the Synagogue of Capernaum" in *ASR* 52–56. Kee refers to this report in support of his thesis that the fourth-century synagogue at Capernaum "was built on top of a house" ("Defining the First-Century CE Synagogue," 495). However, Kee neglects to mention Corbo and Loffreda's revised conclusions based upon their subsequent excavations. The excavators did indeed uncover the walls of earlier houses in the eastern (trenches 17 and 18) and western (trenches 14 and 21) aisles of the synagogue, but not in the center (trenches 1, 2, 20, 24 and 25). These walls date to the Late Hellenistic and Early Roman periods (one wall in trench 21 dates to the thirteenth century B.C.E.!). In light of the discovery of the basalt walls and the nearly continuous stone pavement, Corbo has plausibly argued that these structures were leveled in the first century C.E. to make way for the new structure ("Resti della Sinagoga del Primo Secolo a Cafarnao," 339). As an alternate proposal, Loffreda has suggested that the first-century structure only consisted of the area circumscribed by the two inner basalt walls ("Ceramica Ellenistico-Romana nel Sottosuolo della Sinagoga di Cafarnao," 312). However, the absence of wall-remains on the north and south make this view unlikely. Moreover, the fact that no intervening stratum exists between the first-century stone floor and any of the basalt walls argues in favor of Corbo's proposal.

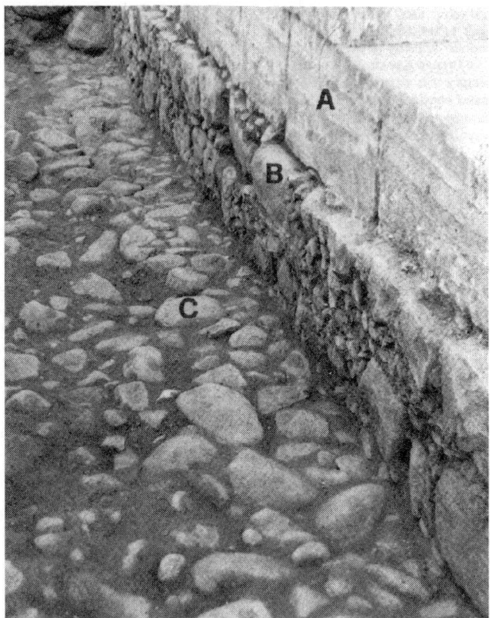

Figure 9. View of Trench 25, looking north: A. East stylobate of the IV–V century synagogue; B. The Basalt Stone Wall (MB 5); C. First-century C.E. stone pavement. (From Loffreda, *Recovering Capharnaum*, 46.)

soundings also revealed that similar walls served as the foundations of the eastern and western stylobates, though not the northern one.

These findings led Loffreda and Corbo to the conclusion that the stone-paved area inside the basalt walls constituted the remains not of private houses, but of a public building. This was a natural inference since the private homes excavated at Capernaum all had unhewn stone walls and most had beaten-earth floors.[61] None had walls of dressed stone

[61]The suggestion that the basalt floor belonged to an earlier synagogue was first proposed by Michael Avi-Yonah in 1973 when he wrote, "This would be a much larger and better paved structure than any other private dwelling in Capernaum. Indeed, would it not be possible to conclude that these were the remnants of a public building (preferably a synagogue) which existed before the present one?" (M. Avi-Yonah, "Editor's Note," *IEJ* 23 [1973]: 43). Corbo and Loffreda initially resisted this interpretation, noting that the courtyards of some insulae were made of basalt stones (S. Loffreda, "A Reply to the Editor," *IEJ*, no. 23 [1973]: 184). It was only with the

(and over a meter thick, at that), and certainly none enclosed an area as large as that contained within the rectangle traced by the basalt walls (see fig. 10). Nor could the excavators conclude that the basalt walls were built in the fourth century as foundations for the later synagogue, as Loffreda himself argues:

> To start with, the foundations of E court were built independently: they simply abut to the "basalt stone wall." Secondly, [the foundations of the E court] are made up of beautiful stone blocks carefully executed and with an excellent refinement of the courses, while the courses of the "basalt stone wall" are inferior both in quality and in finish. Why this striking difference of foundations? Why did the courtyard which was a secondary unit rest upon excellent foundations, while much poorer foundations were found for the prayer hall which was the most important part of the fourth century synagogue? The only answer we can provide is this: the prayer hall simply reused as foundations the walls of a pre-existing building, while the foundation of the E court was built anew much later. This conclusion is strengthened when we analyse the interrelation between the "basalt stone wall" and the courses of the prayer hall resting upon it . . . the "basalt stone wall" is conspicuously discontinuous beneath the stylobates of the prayer hall. What is worse, the N stylobate of the prayer hall rests upon a shaky fill and in that area the "basalt stone wall" is completely missing. Secondly, there is a shift in axiality between the "basalt stone wall" and the outer walls of the prayer hall. Finally, since the "basalt stone wall" sloped from N to S, the builders of the white synagogue had to taper all the stones of the first course in the opposite direction, i.e. from S to N, and, furthermore, they used pebbles to fill the undulant top of the "basalt stone wall." For all these

---

opening of trenches 24 and 25 in 1981 that the excavators revised their opinion in view of the new evidence (Loffreda, "Ceramica Ellenistico-Romana nel Sottosuolo della Sinagoga di Cafarnao," 274, 311–312; Corbo, "Resti della Sinagoga del Primo Secolo a Cafarnao," 337–341). This exchange undermines the recent charge of Jack Sanders, who states that Corbo and Loffreda dug underneath the fourth-century synagogue merely to discover "the synagogue of Jesus." He writes: "One has to confess to a certain frustration with the Franciscan style of archaeology, which seems to belong to the time of Schliemann. They know what they are going to find when they dig, and when they find it they seek no further evidence" (Jack T. Sanders, *Schismatics, Sectarians, Dissidents, Deviants: The First One Hundred Years of Jewish-Christian Relations* [London: SCM Press, 1993], 38). Sanders' theory that the floor was laid in the second or third century C.E. (ibid.) fails in view of the fact that *all* of the coins and pottery recovered underneath the basalt floor date to the Hellenistic period (Loffreda, "Ceramica Ellenistico-Romana nel Sottosuolo della Sinagoga di Cafarnao," 311–12). Generally on domestic architecture, see Yizhar Hirschfeld, *The Palestinian Dwelling in the Roman-Byzantine Period* (Jerusalem: Franciscan Printing Press; Israel Exploration Society, 1995), 21–107.

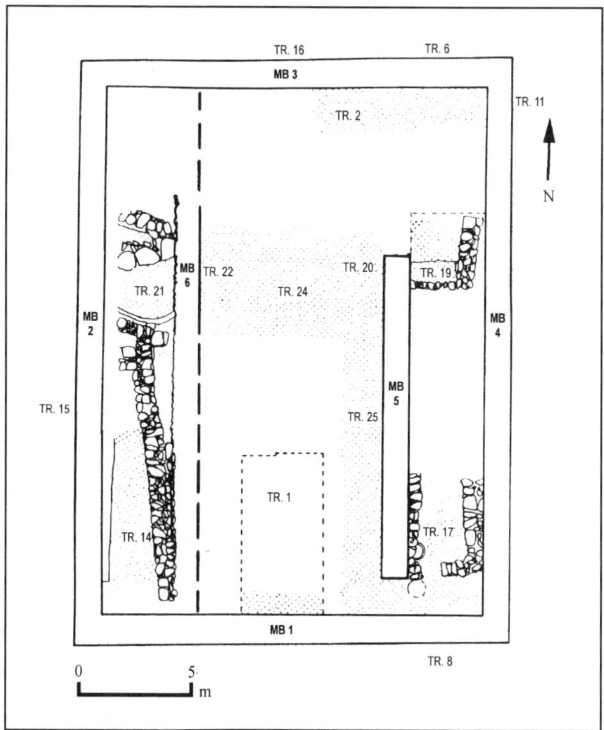

Figure 10. Plan of the first-century C.E. synagogue at Capernaum. The building consists of four outer walls (MB 1–4) and two stylobates (MB 5–6). The inside was paved with a cobblestone floor. (After Corbo, *Resti della sinagoga a Cafarnao*, 345.)

reasons we must conclude that the "basalt stone wall" belongs to a synagogue predating the white synagogue.[62]

If Loffreda's final conclusion seems a bit presumptuous, here we must note several points. First of all, Capernaum was only a small village occupying about fifteen acres and consisting primarily of private insulae.[63] To date, the basalt structure constitutes the only public building uncovered from the first century in the extensive excavations at Capernaum. Second, in the later period, synagogues were frequently

[62]Loffreda, *Recovering Capharnaum*, 48–49.
[63]Ibid., 18.

founded upon the remains of pre-existing synagogues, as the earlier structures were considered sacred.[64] This may have been the case with the fourth-century synagogue, especially in view of the fact its builders decided to erect the structure in the proximity of the church built on top of the house believed to belong to St. Peter.[65] Third, while traces of benches in the earlier structure have not been found (they may have been torn out), the presence of the two basalt stylobates indicates that rows of columns were present in the earlier structure, just as we have seen in the synagogues at Gamla, Masada and Herodium. Corbo points out that several column drums (one in gray granite) were discovered in the fill level beneath the layer of mortar (stratum B). These almost certainly came from the earlier building—if not from there, then from where else in Capernaum?[66] Fourth, the general continuity in the plans of the first- and fourth-century structures suggests that both served the same function. Finally, as noted at the beginning of this chapter, there is strong literary evidence attesting to the presence of a synagogue at Capernaum in the first century.

The combined force of the archaeological evidence and the literary attestation makes it probable that the basalt stone walls and the stone floor constitute the remains of a synagogue constructed in the first century C.E. If this identification is accepted, then the Capernaum synagogue represents the largest synagogue discovered thus far from the Second Temple period. Measuring 24.5 by 18.7 meters on the outside (22 x 16.5 m. on the inside), it is slightly larger than the synagogue at Gamla. While it seems odd that a village like Capernaum should have a synagogue comparable in size to a walled city such as Gamla, it is also possible that other synagogues lie buried in the unexcavated sections of Gamla, their remains waiting to be recovered.[67]

Corbo points out that the entrance to the lower structure has not been found. Noting a slight break in the western basalt wall, he proposes that

---

[64]Examples include the synagogues at Nabratein, En-Gedi, and Beth She'arim. For additional cases, refer to Table 2 in Hachlili, *Ancient Jewish Art and Archeology in the Land of Israel*, 148–149.

[65]This point is made in Loffreda, *Recovering Capharnaum*, 47.

[66]So Corbo, "Resti della Sinagoga del Primo Secolo a Cafarnao," 339.

[67]Syon notes that a second lintel with a rosette flanked by palm trees was discovered on the *western* side of Gamla. This suggests the presence of a second synagogue in the city. See Syon, "Gamla: Portrait of a Rebellion," 35.

this may have been the location of the entrance.[68] However, since the main entrances of the limestone synagogue were constructed on the south side of the main hall, another possibility is that one or more entrances in the earlier structure were also located there and were simply copied by the later builders. The likelihood of this proposal is strengthened by the presence of a street just south of the synagogue. If the main entrance was located on the south side of the building, then the façade of the earlier structure would also have been oriented toward Jerusalem—a situation we encountered in the Gamla synagogue.

A final observation is that, unlike the other three Second Temple synagogues, the Capernaum synagogue does not have a *mikveh* located near it. However, we can easily account for this fact by noting that the village was built on the shores of the Sea of Galilee, whose waters could be used for ritual cleansings. Conversely, the synagogues at Gamla, Masada and Herodium had no such natural bodies of water nearby.

Magdala[69]

Located on the western shore of the Sea of Galilee just a mile north of Tiberias, Magdala is perhaps best known as the hometown of Mary Magdalene (e.g., Matt 27:56). Josephus calls the city Tarichea ("salted fish") and mentions it as the place from which he launched a sham fleet of boats during the first year of the Jewish War in order to convince the residents of Tiberias to submit to his authority (*BJ* 2.632–637; *Vita* 163–164). The following year, Titus easily captured the city (*BJ* 3.492–502), and Vespasian later convened a war tribunal there that resulted in the slaughter of 12,000 refugees and the enslavement of 36,000 more (*BJ* 3.532–542).

Excavations at the site were conducted between 1971 and 1976 under Virgilio Corbo. These revealed that the city, while Jewish, was built on a Roman plan, with the major north-south street (*cardo maximus*) intersecting the major east-west street (*decumanus*) at the center of the city. The building Corbo identified as a "mini-synagogue" lies on the

[68]Corbo, "Resti della Sinagoga del Primo Secolo a Cafarnao," 339. Cf., Strange and Shanks, "Synagogue Where Jesus Preached Found at Capernaum," 30–31.

[69]The description of the structure at Magdala is based on the following sources: P.V.C. Corbo, "Scavi Archaelogici a Magdala," *Liber Annuus* 24 (1974): 5–37; idem, "La Citta romana di Magdala" in *Studia Hierosolymitana in onore del P. Bellarmino Bagatti*, edited by Michele Piccirillo et al. (Jerusalem: Franciscan Print. Press, 1976), 365–368; Netzer, "Did the Magdala Springhouse Serve As a Synagogue?" 165–172.

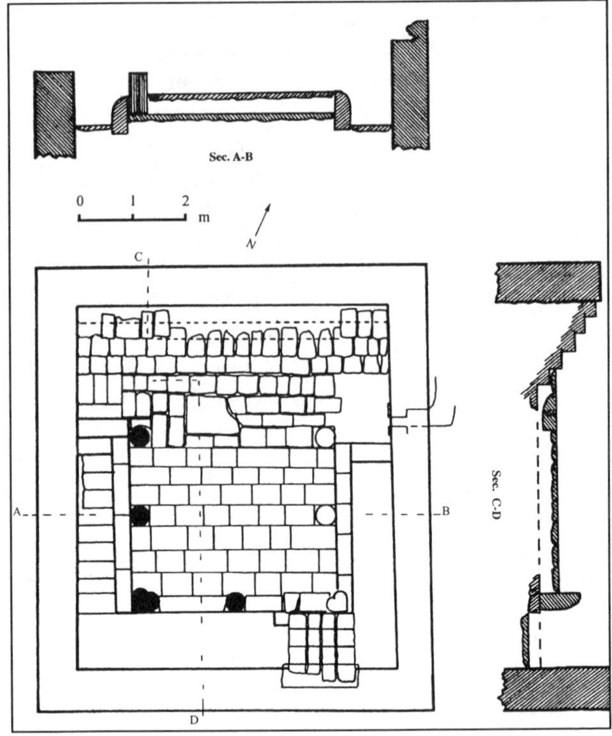

Figure 11. Plan of the structure at Magdala. The building consists of stairs leading down to a room with water channels on three sides. Although Corbo argued that the building was originally a synagogue, it more likely served as a springhouse in both phases. (After Corbo, "Scavi Archeologici a Magdala," 24.)

southeast corner of two roads and is oriented along an almost north-south axis (the building tilts several degrees to the west; see fig. 11). Measuring 7.25 (east-west) x 8.16 (north-south) meters, the structure has five tiers on its northern side (four *in situ*), each about 30 cm wide, but varying in height (25, 24.5, 23 and 19 cm, from bottom to top). Seven Doric columns (two heart-shaped) form a U-shaped configuration that opens to the northern side. Corbo identified two levels of pavements, one dating to the building's construction in the first century B.C.E., and the other to a century later. The floor of the second phase was built over top of the bottom tier.

Corbo states that the synagogue was transformed into a springhouse in the later phase, with channels (56–60 cm deep) being laid along the western, eastern and southern walls. These were fed by a conduit which entered the building through the eastern wall. While no entry to the structure has been found, Corbo surmises that it was positioned along the eastern wall, since that side of the building was later expanded outward by two meters.[70]

Although some archaeologists have accepted Corbo's identification of this building as a synagogue, there are clearly some problems. First of all, the arrangement of the building does not conform to that seen in other Galilean-style synagogues: tiers are found only on one side of the building, and these are not separated from the central area of the structure by intervening columns. Moreover, on closer examination of the tiers, it becomes clear that these are not rows of benches at all. Here, we must recall that the heights of the benches in the other synagogues are 35 cm (Gamla and Masada) and 40 cm (Herodium). In contrast, the heights of the tiers in the Magdala structure, which range from 19 to 25 cm, are clearly too low to have served as benches. On the other hand, these tiers are the perfect height to have functioned as stairs, an identification that Corbo for some reason dismissed as ridiculous ("ridicolo!").[71] Despite this dismissal, since a major road lay immediately to the north of the structure, it is evident that the entrance to the building was from the north—not the east—and that these stairs led from the side of the road down into the structure.

Because of this misidentification and because the structure meets none of our other criteria—there are no inscriptions, no scriptures, no religious art, etc.—Corbo's identification of this building as a synagogue must be rejected.

If not a synagogue, then what was this building in its first phase? Netzer has argued that the building was a springhouse in all phases, with the columns supporting an upper clerestory level which allowed light into the building.[72] The addition of the later floor can probably be attributed to the rising of the ancient water table, a fact that Corbo himself had noted. (During the winters between his excavations, water flooded the building to a height of 1.7 m.)[73] Eventually, this water level became so

---

[70]Corbo, "Scavi Archaelogici a Magdala," 22.
[71]Ibid.
[72]See Netzer, "Did the Magdala Springhouse Serve As a Synagogue?" 165–172.
[73]Corbo, "Scavi Archaelogici a Magdala," 26.

high that the building had to be abandoned during the Middle Roman period. A water tower to the west then served as the main reservoir.[74]

Shuafat[75]

In 1991, archaeologist Alexander Onn uncovered an agricultural settlement near modern Shuafat, an Arab suburb just north of Jerusalem. According to reports, the settlement was founded in the second century B.C.E. and was inhabited until 31 B.C.E. when a catastrophic earthquake inflicted considerable damage to the area. The complex measures about 50 meters square and contains the remains of several *mikvaoth*. In the early first century B.C.E., a subterranean room in this complex was renovated. Benches were erected around the walls of the room, which was divided in half by a low stone wall. A niche was cut into the wall that was oriented toward Jerusalem.

Unfortunately, none of the existing publications on this site gives either the plan or the dimensions of this room. Moreover, while Onn compared the room to the synagogues at Masada and Herodium, fellow excavator Zvi Greenhut called the structure a "prayer room," an expression that is perhaps indicative of a diminutive size.[76] Similarly, Riesner at first referred to the room as "the oldest synagogue hitherto found."[77] In a more recent publication, however, he too speaks of the structure more cautiously as a "prayer room."[78]

Because of the sparsity of the archaeological data, the function of the room is difficult to evaluate at this time. However, if the room's size is as small as seems suggested by Greenhut and Riesner's use of the expression, "prayer room," then to apply the term "synagogue" to the structure may be a misnomer, since the ancient literary and epigraphic sources refer to synagogues as places of *public* gathering. If a religious function for the room can be determined (and here the presence of the

---

[74]Ibid., 28.

[75]The description of the structure at Shuafat is based on the following sources: Abraham Rabinovich, "Oldest Jewish Prayer Room Discovered on Shuafat Ridge," *Jerusalem Post*, 8 April 1991, 1; Riesner, "Synagogues in Jerusalem," 192; idem, "Neue Funde in Israel," *BK* 46 (1991): 183; idem, "Die bisher älteste Synagoge gefunden," *Idea Spekrum*, 28 August 1991, 17.

[76]Rabinovich, "Oldest Jewish Prayer Room Discovered on Shuafat Ridge," 1.

[77]Riesner, "Die bisher älteste Synagoge gefunden," 17; cf. idem, "Neue Funde in Israel," 183.

[78]Riesner, "Synagogues in Jerusalem," 192.

mikvaoth is suggestive), then perhaps we could better refer to the room as a "prayer closet" for private use (cf. Jdt 8:5; Matt 6:6).[79]

Kiryat Sefer

In November 1995, two brief news releases were issued reporting that Israeli excavator Yitzhak Magen had uncovered a synagogue next to the Jewish settlement of Kiryat Sefer near the town of Modi'in in the West Bank (twenty miles northwest of Jerusalem). Comparing the structure to the synagogues found at Masada and Gamla, Magen is quoted as stating, "We imagine that before us is one of the most ancient synagogues built in the days of the Second Temple."[80] In the vicinity of the structure, excavators also discovered a hoard of "hundreds" of gold and silver coins dating to the end of the Bar Kokhba Revolt.[81]

Lee Levine has described the building as measuring about eight meters square, with benches on three sides and four columns resting on top of a stone paved floor. The entrance to the structure is on the northwest side. Coins and pottery date the building to the first century C.E. or possibly slightly later. In Levine's opinion, the structure is "a very convincing candidate for a late Second Temple synagogue."[82] While we must wait for more detailed reports, it is possible that the structure at Kiryat Sefer may be yet another pre-70 synagogue. If so, its dimensions will make it the smallest example yet recovered from this period.

---

[79]Kee's comments about this site are worth quoting: "A recent survey of leading archaeologists in the USA and Israel concerning this alleged find produced two kinds of response: (1) most of those whose major interests includes ancient synagogues had never heard the report, since it did not appear in a scholarly publication; (2) those who heard the claim dismissed it as an unwarranted publicity-seeking act by an inexperienced archaeologist. A leading scholar, Lee Levine of the Seminary of Judaic Studies in Jerusalem said that the claim lacks any 'substantive evidence,' and that his survey of the site led him to see that an 'interesting room' had been found, but with no evidence of any kind that it had ever functioned as a synagogue" ("New Finds That Illuminate the World and Text of the Bible," 94, n. 3). Nevertheless, an intriguing possibility is that this complex serviced an Essene community, since Josephus hints that such a community lived in or near Jerusalem (see chapter seven).

[80]Randall Palmer, "Israelis Find What May Be 2,000-year-old Synagogue," *Reuters*, 20 November 1995.

[81]Evelyn Gordon, "News In Brief," *Jerusalem Post*, 21 November 1995.

[82]Letter to the author dated 23 August 1996.

Chorazin

Chorazin is mentioned for the first time in the New Testament (Matt 11:21 || Lk 10:13 = Q), and from patristic references it has been identified as Khirbat Karazeh, located about two-and-a-half miles north of Capernaum. Occupying an area of about twelve acres, Chorazin has yielded the remains of a third-century Galilean-type synagogue that was excavated first by H. Kohl and C. Watzinger in 1905–07 and later by J. Ory in 1926. Of interest to this study is a report filed by Ory that describes the remains of a structure located about 200 meters west of the third-century synagogue:

> A square colonnaded building of small dimensions, of a disposition similar to the interior arrangement of the synagogue, 7 columns 3 on each side [*sic*], the entrance was afforded through the east wall, were supporting the roof, and the whole space between the colonnade and walls on three sides was occupied with sitting benches in probably 5 courses. The columns and 1–3 courses of the benches are still existing.[83]

In a visit to the site during the 70s, Foerster was unable to locate these remains. However, as anyone who has excavated in Israel knows, the weeds and the brush can quickly cover over previously exposed ruins making them very difficult to find. Since it is unlikely that Ory fabricated the building's existence, this is probably what happened to the remains of the structure he described.[84]

Thus, somewhere amid Chorazin's ruins may lie a second synagogue—perhaps even one dating to the Second Temple period. Ory's description and the presence of the nearby third-century structure suggest that both possibilities may not be too far-fetched. One hopes that future surveys will succeed in finding the lost structure. Until then, Ory's report can only remain a footnote to the study of Second Temple synagogues.

---

[83]Quoted in Gideon Foerster, "The Synagogues at Masada and Herodion," *Journal of Jewish Art* 3–4 (1977): 8. Ory's report is file no. 120 of the Israel Department of Antiquities in the Rockefeller Museum, Jerusalem.

[84]Foerster writes, "About 50 years have passed since this report was written, so it is quite likely that the vestiges of the building Ory describes, exposed at the time of his visit, have since become covered over" (ibid., n. 18).

Summary of Results

The above examination has netted us a total of four structures that we can confidently state are the remains of synagogues built in Palestine during the period of the Second Temple: those at Gamla, Masada, Herodium and Capernaum (stratum A; see Table 3). On the other hand, for reasons already stated, we must reject the identification of the structure at Magdala as a synagogue—as Netzer has argued, the building almost certainly served as a springhouse in all phases. For the present, we must withhold final judgment on the claims made for structures at Shuafat and Kiryat Sefer, pending the publication of more detailed reports. On the face of it, the latter of these structures appears the more promising of the two candidates.

Table 3
Second Temple Synagogues of Palestine

	Probable Foundation Date	**Dimensions (in meters)**	**Number of Rows of Benches**	**Number of Rows of Columns**	**Orientation of Façade**
Gamla	late I B.C.E.	25.5 x 17	4	4	SW (towards Jerusalem)
Masada	c. 66 C.E.	15 x 12	4	2	SE
Herodium	c. 66 C.E.	15.5 x 10.6	3	2	E
Capernaum (Stratum A)	early I C.E.	24.5 x 18.7	?	2	South (towards Jerusalem)?

Our investigation has also suggested that a systematic survey of Chorazin should be undertaken in the future in order to verify the existence of the structure described in Ory's 1926 report. It may well be that this building could also be identified as a synagogue from the Second Temple period. In addition, archaeological probes are indicated for both the Herodium synagogue and the area associated with Weill's discovery of the Theodotus inscription. The objective of the former probe would be to clarify further the date of the synagogue's founding—whether it was during the First or the Second Revolt. This could be accomplished by removing sections of the benches in search of coins or ceramics in the sealed areas underneath. The goal of the latter probe would be to determine the nature of the complex represented by the *mikvaoth*, the paving and the row of dressed stones mentioned in Weill's report. The recovery of additional data might validate (or refute) Weill's hypothesis that these remains represent the ruins of the synagogue mentioned in the Theodotus inscription.

Discussion

The identification of synagogue buildings at Gamla, Masada, Herodium and Capernaum casts further doubt upon the view of some recent scholars that Palestinian "synagogues" in the Second Temple period consisted of informal prayer gatherings in private homes. The classification of these four buildings as synagogues results from the convergence of literary, epigraphic and archaeological lines of data, with all three types of evidence pointing to synagogues as public buildings enclosing sacred space. Regarding this last point, while the sacred nature of these early synagogues is not seen as dramatically as in later structures, it is nonetheless discernible. As we have observed, *mikvaoth* are located near three of the synagogues (Gamla, Masada and Herodium), suggesting that purity requirements were connected with the structures. Likewise, a water basin may have served for the washing of hands before the reading of scripture in the Gamla synagogue.[85] At Masada we have the use of the back room in the synagogue as a genizah. This room apparently functioned as the abode of a priest or someone who collected tithes for the priests. Finally, in the Gamla synagogue we encounter the use of Jewish symbols that clearly had some religious significance: both rosette and palm motifs have been found among the ruins of the Temple mount. Moreover, the former is mentioned as a symbol found in Solomon's Temple (1 Kgs 6:29–35), while several passages in Ezek 40–41 and 1 Kgs 6–7 mention palm trees as being inscribed on the stones of the inner court

---

[85]Notably, among his list of "archaeological indicators of ritual," Colin Renfrew specifies the following criterion: "Concepts of cleanliness and pollution may be reflected in the facilities (e.g. pools or basins of water) and maintenance of the sacred area" ("The Archaeology of Religion," 51). Richardson, while rightly noting the import of the *mikvaoth* for the identification of early synagogues, nevertheless does not take into account their presence when evaluating the sacrality of these structures ("Early Synagogues as Collegia," 92).

of the Temple.[86] That more elaborate religious symbolism is not seen in these structures can be explained, on the one hand, by the strict interpretation of the Second Commandment during this period and, on the other, by the deference accorded the Temple while it was still standing.[87]

The identification of the four pre-70 synagogues also calls into question the practice of those researchers who prefer to call these structures simply "Jewish public places" or "buildings in which Jewish assemblies met."[88] These scholars must explain why they favor such cumbersome locutions over the term "synagogue" in view of the fact that Jews of the Second Temple period employed the word *synagōgē* (among others) to refer to the Jewish public place *par excellence.* While it is laudable that these scholars wish to correct the anachronistic interpretations of an earlier generation of scholarship, their focus on the discontinuity between the earlier and the later structures comes at the expense of important continuities. Along these lines, although there is certainly a measure of architectural discontinuity between these buildings and later synagogues (e.g., no fixed Torah shrine, lack of iconic imagery),

---

[86]Again, among his list of archaeological indicators of ritual, Renfrew includes the following criterion: "The ritualistic symbols will often relate iconographically to the deities worshipped and to their associated myth" ("The Archaeology of Religion," 51). The association of the rosette and the palm with the central cultic site in both the Jewish sacred writings and the actual material remains of that site strongly suggests the sacred character of these symbols. Their presence among the remains of the Gamla synagogue further signals that this structure was part of a "single coherent system" centered at Jerusalem (ibid., 54).

[87]On the deference accorded the Temple in the pre-70 era, see the discussion in the introduction of this study, above. Regarding the strict interpretation of the Second Commandment, Josephus records many instances of civil disturbances resulting from the insensitivities of the Romans and Herod on this count (e.g., *BJ* 2.195ff., *Ant.* 18.55–59, 121–122, 263–64; *Vita* 65; also Philo, *Legat.* 299–305). It is noteworthy that both the Hasmonean and the Herodian rulers of Palestine took care not to use iconic images on their coins. The one exception is a coin issued near the end of Herod the Great's life probably in connection with the king's condemnation of two rabbis for tearing down a golden eagle he had erected over the gate of the Temple (*AJC* 2.238.23; incident in *BJ* 1.648–655). Also, even after Archelaus' removal, the Roman procurators of Judea only issued coins with aniconic art. See David Hendlin, *Guide to Biblical Coins* (New York: Amphora Books, 1987), 39–69, 81–97; Richardson, "Law and Piety in Herod's Architecture," 347–360; Hachlili, *Jewish Art and Archaeology in the Land of Israel*, 234–236.

[88]E.g., "buildings in which the assemblies met" (R. Horsley, *Galilee*, 226); "buildings that came to be utilized for worship and other matters requiring public assembly" (Meyers, "Synagogues," 225).

the general layout of the four synagogues not only conforms to an identifiable architectural type, but also clearly reflects that of synagogues from a later period. As we have seen, it is such architectural parallels that aided archaeologists in identifying these structures as synagogues in the first place. Thus to persist in calling these structures "Jewish public places" because they do not contain fixed Torah shrines is equivalent to calling Greek theaters "semi-circular Greek public places" because they lack the multistoried skene of the Roman theaters. It is both more accurate and more helpful to call the above structures "synagogues," while at the same time pointing out architectural differences between Second Temple synagogues and examples from later periods.

Even among some scholars who accept the above identifications, the notion persists that synagogues were not a common feature of the Palestinian landscape during the Second Temple period. While we will discuss the emergence of the Palestinian synagogues in the next section, here we recall that the literary sources from the end of the Second Temple period consistently assume the existence of such structures throughout Palestine. As we have seen, there is little reason to doubt these sources on this point. If such is the case, then why have only a few structures from this period been hitherto identified as synagogues?

Here it must be remembered that Palestine suffered two devastating wars in the first two centuries of our era. Considerable damage was inflicted upon the infrastructure of the country during these conflicts. Because synagogues were the architectural manifestations of the local Jewish communities, it stands to reason that these structures would have been among the first targets of Roman retribution. In support of this is the fact that Josephus mentions the images of synagogues being paraded in the subsequent triumph in Rome (*BJ* 7.139–152). Thus a reasonable hypothesis is that other demolished synagogues built prior to 70 C.E. continue to rest underneath centuries of accumulated dust and debris, awaiting the archaeologist's spade.[89]

A second, related point is that in many ways archaeology in Israel is still in its infancy. Whole villages remain yet unidentified, as do innumerable structures mentioned in dependable literary sources (e.g., the amphitheaters of Jerusalem and Tiberias). Moreover, sites previously thought unfruitful are currently yielding spectacular finds. To give one example, fifteen years ago surveyors at Sepphoris in Galilee thought there

---

[89]For a similar assessment, see E. P. Sanders, *Jewish Law from Jesus to the Mishnah*, 77.

was little left to recover of that ancient city. Yet presently, the excavations there occupy the labors of no fewer than four separate universities.[90] Other potential sites cannot be explored because they either lie buried under modern buildings or within disputed territory.

To put the matter further in context: few scholars would dispute that synagogues (*proseuchai*) were a common feature of Egyptian Jewry in the Hellenistic and Roman periods. Yet to date *not one* such structure has been identified in all of Egypt. The same can be said of ancient Rome. This all suggests that the next century is likely to be an exciting period for archaeological discoveries in Israel and throughout the Jewish diaspora. As excavations accelerate, there can be little doubt that more architectural evidence for pre-70 synagogues will be recovered. For the present, the remains of the structures at Gamla, Masada, Herodium and Capernaum nevertheless confirm the existence of synagogue buildings in Palestine during the Second Temple period.[91]

Before concluding this section, further attention should be paid to the issue of synagogue orientation. As we have seen, at Gamla and possibly at Capernaum, the façades of the synagogues are oriented toward Jerusalem, suggesting that the congregations in these structures prayed in the direction of the holy city (cf. 1 Kgs 8:30, 44, 48; 2 Chr 6:34, 38; Dan 6:10; 1 Esdr 4:58). On the other hand, the synagogues at Masada and Herodium are oriented toward the east or southeast. In several articles and essays, Foerster has suggested that the façades of these synagogues (and of the lost structure at Chorazin) were following a divergent rabbinic *halakha* from the Tosefta which states that "one should only place the entrance to synagogues in the east, for we find that in the Temple the entrance faced the east" (*t. Megillah* 3.22).[92] Here, Foerster need not have relied on this late document for a witness to this custom, since, as we have observed, Apion mentions that synagogues (*proseuchai*) in

---

[90]See Rebecca Martin Nagy, et al., eds., *Sepphoris in Galilee*. (Winona Lake: Eisenbrauns, 1996), pass.

[91]A final point on this matter is that the builders of the two ad hoc synagogues at Masada and Herodium must have had a model for their structures. While it is possible that the structures at Gamla and Capernaum served as these models, it is unlikely that the synagogues there represented the *only* two examples of this distinctive style of architecture. It is more probable that the rebel builders modeled their synagogues on structures commonly featured throughout the homeland.

[92]Foerster, "The Synagogues at Masada and Herodium," 29. Cf. idem, "The Ancient Synagogues of the Galilee" in *The Galilee in Late Antiquity*, edited by L. Levine (New York: Jewish Theological Seminary of America, 1992), 294–295.

Jerusalem were oriented toward the east (Josephus, *Ap.* 2.10–11). Although Apion is certainly not the most reliable source for ancient Jewish customs, it is quite possible that he is accurate on this point and used his knowledge of the eastern orientation of the synagogues to connect both them and Moses (their supposed founder) to the temple at Leontopolis, which he also believed faced eastward.[93]

If this was a divergent custom of the time, it is possible that the existing structures at Masada and Herodium were chosen for their eastern orientation (though admittedly the former of these buildings is not on a perfect west-east axis—but neither was the Jerusalem Temple).[94] As we will later see in our treatment of the Therapeutae, Philo mentions that this group concluded some of their services "with their faces and whole body turned to the east" in prayer (*Contempl.* 89). This practice of facing eastward in prayer may have been exercised outside of the circle of the Therapeutae among Jews in general (Ezek 8:16?) and could have been a consideration in the design of synagogues in the Second Temple period. If so, such synagogues may have been built to imitate the orientation of the Jerusalem Temple, as the saying from the Tosefta rightly noted.[95]

THE EMERGENCE OF THE PALESTINIAN SYNAGOGUES

The topic of synagogue origins has probably evoked more scholarly discussion than any other single issue in ancient synagogal studies. Proposed dates for the emergence of this institution range from before the period of the First Temple all the way up to the third century C.E. Likewise, some researchers view the synagogue as originating in Palestine, while others see it as an import from the diaspora. While we will not examine each of these theories in any detail—that task has

---

[93]In his report on Masada, Netzer writes, "In the present state of research we still do not know whether the traditions governing the orientation of synagogues or the location of their entrances were already effective, or whether they evolved only after the destruction of the Second Temple" (*Masada III*, 410–411). Apion's statement serves as at least one bit of evidence suggesting that *some* synagogues in the pre-70 period were oriented toward the east.

[94]See the plan in *NEAEHL* 2.718. According to the reconstruction presented there, the Temple façade faced toward the northeast.

[95]Richardson, while noting that the Gamla synagogue faced Jerusalem, nevertheless concludes "in early Palestinian synagogues orientation to Jerusalem was irrelevant; it mattered little to the builders how the building faced" ("Early Synagogues as Collegia," 102). The likely presence of a divergent custom may help explain why not all early synagogues were oriented toward Jerusalem.

already been ably undertaken elsewhere[96]—here we will briefly review some of the major lines of thought in light of the evidence set forth in the previous sections of this chapter. This analysis will lead us, on the one hand, to reject many of these theories as being unsupported by the evidence, and on the other, to accept a modified version of a proposal recently set forth by Lee Levine. Incorporating the architectural insights of James Strange, this refined proposition will suggest a link between the synagogues and the Temple, with the former serving as spatial extensions of the latter.

Synagogue Origin Theories

In reviewing the more widely held theories about synagogue origins, one could essentially progress through the centuries that researchers have proposed for the founding of this institution. If we adopt this course, we see that most suggestions are typically linked with some ancient crisis or noteworthy historical event. Thus one of the earliest of the proposed foundation periods dates to the reforms of King Josiah in the late seventh century B.C.E. Here, several theorists have argued that Josiah's destruction of the *bamoth* or high places (2 Kgs 23:1–20) resulted in a religious void for those living in those Palestinian cities and villages distant from the Temple.[97] Another line of thought—indeed, the dominant one a generation ago—maintains that the synagogue emerged in Babylon in the sixth century B.C.E. following Nebuchadrezzar's destruction of Solomon's Temple.[98] Yet a third set of researchers, noting the Torah-

---

[96]E.g., H. H. Rowley, *Worship in Ancient Israel: Its Forms and Meaning* (London: S. P. C. K., 1967), 213–245; J. Weingreen, "The Origin of the Synagogue," *Hermathena* 98 (1964): 68–84; Sonne, "Synagogue," 478–480; Schrage, "Συναγωγή," 810–813; Krauss, *Synagogale Altertümer*, 52–66; Joseph Gutmann, "The Origin of the Synagogue: The Current State of the Research" in *The Synagogue: Studies in Origins, Archaeology, and Architecture*, edited by Joseph Gutmann (New York: Ktav Pub. House, 1975), 72–76.

[97]Julius Wellhausen, *Israelitische und Jüdische Geschichte* (Berline: Georg Reimer, 1897), 193; Weingreen, "The Origin of the Synagogue," 72, 78; Adolph Lods, *The Prophets and the Rise of Judaism*, trans. S. H. Hooke (London: Kegan Paul, Trench, Trubner & Co., 1937), 154; Julian Morgenstern, *Studi Orientalistici in onore di Giorgio Levi Della Vida* (Rome: Istituto per l'Oriente, 1956), 2.192–198.

[98]Rowley, *Worship in Ancient Israel*, 224–227; George Foot Moore, *Judaism in the First Centuries of the Christian Era: The Age of the Tannaim* (Cambridge: Harvard University Press, 1927), 1.283; Carlo Sigonio, *De republica Hebraeorum Libri VII* (Frankfurt, 1582), 63–64.

reading ceremony of Ezra and Nehemiah (Neh 8:1–10:40), ascribes the synagogue's origin to the return of the exiles in the fifth century B.C.E.[99]

The problem with these suggestions is that they lack supporting evidence. From the literary side, there are no clear references to synagogues as houses of worship in the Hebrew scriptures; those few places where referents are discerned are ambiguous at best.[100] The archaeological record for the pre-exilic and early post-exilic periods is equally scant: it consists of a blurred ostracon from sixth century Elath that some researchers have read as *bēt k^enīshāh Yerushalem* (בית כנשה ירשלם), Aramaic for "the house of the gathering, Jerusalem."[101] The reading, however, is far from certain, and even those researchers who have cited this ostracon as early evidence for Palestinian synagogues have done so very cautiously.[102]

The silence of the early literary and archaeological record has led more recent scholars to propose much later dates for the emergence of the synagogue in Palestine. Since we have already encountered several of these theories and their proponents in earlier discussions, here we but summarize three of the leading proposals: (1) synagogues originated with the Pharisees in the early Maccabean period,[103] (2) synagogues per se did

---

[99]W. Bacher, "Synagogue" in *A Dictionary of the Bible*, edited by James Hastings (Edinburgh: Clark, 1902), 636–637; Louis Finkelstein, *The Pharisees*, 3rd ed. (Philadelphia: Jewish Publication Society of America, 1962), 567.

[100]Psa 74:8b is often cited: "they burned all the meeting places of God in the land [שָׂרְפוּ כָל־מוֹעֲדֵי־אֵל בָּאָרֶץ]." Some translators have rendered מוֹעֲדֵי־אֵל "synagogues of God" (so KJV), yet there is no precedent for this translation. Significantly, both the LXX and the Theodotion translation render this phrase "festivals of God [ἑορτὰς τοῦ θϵοῦ]," indicating that the early translators did not have this understanding of מוֹעֲדֵי־אֵל—though to what it refers is a mystery. See Rowley, *Worship in Ancient Israel*, 218–221. On the other hand, the reference to Nebuchadrezzar's burning of "the house of the people [בֵּית הָעָם]" (Jer 39:8), taken by some to be a reference to the synagogue, should probably be emended to "the houses of the people [בָּתֵּי הָעָם]" (so NRSV) since the parallel account in 2 Kgs 25:9 refers to "the houses of Jerusalem [בָּתֵּי יְרוּשָׁלַםִ]." See Weingreen, "The Origin of the Synagogue," 73.

[101]Charles C. Torrey, "A Synagogue at Elath?" *BASOR* 84 (1941): 4–5. Cf. the quite different reading in Nelson Glueck, "Ostraca from Elath," *BASOR* 82 (1941): 7–11.

[102]Weingreen, "The Origin of the Synagogue," 69–70; Rowley, *Worship in Ancient Israel*, 222.

[103]See, e.g., Martin Hengel, *Judaism and Hellenism: Studies in Their Encounter in Palestine During The Early Hellenistic Period*, 2 vols. (Philadelphia: Fortress Press, 1974), 1.82; Gutmann, "Synagogue Origins," 4; Tcherikover, *Hellenistic Civilization*

not exist at all in Palestine during the Second Temple period,[104] and (3) synagogues were introduced into Palestine by diaspora Jews near the turn of the era.[105]

How do these theories hold up in light of the available evidence? As we saw in the introduction of this study, there is little to recommend the view that the synagogue served as a Pharisaic institution during the Second Temple period: such a position stems from an uncritical reading of the rabbinic literature and the Gospels of Matthew and John (e.g., Matt 23:2; John 9:1–34, 12:42). To be sure, Pharisees frequented synagogues during this time (Mark 3:1–6), but they did not dominate them as they began to do after the fall of Jerusalem.[106] Also untenable is the position that synagogues did not exist in Palestine in the Second Temple period: repeatedly in this study we have encountered literary, epigraphic and architectural evidence that affirms the presence of synagogues in Palestine by at least the turn of the era.[107]

---

and the Jews, 124–125.

[104]See, e.g., Sidney B. Hoenig, "The Ancient City-Square: The Forerunner of the Synagogue" in *ANRW*, II.19.1.448–476; Solomon Zeitlin, "The Origin of the Synagogue" in *The Synagogue: Studies in Origins, Archaeology, and Architecture*, edited by Joseph Gutmann (New York: Ktav Pub. House, 1975), 14–26; Kee, "Defining the First-Century CE Synagogue"; idem, "The Changing Meaning of Synagogue: A Response to Richard Oster"; idem, "The Transformation of the Synagogue after 70 CE: Its Import for Early Christianity"; Horsley, *Galilee*, 224–226; idem, *Archaeology History and Society in Galilee*, 131–135.

[105]Flesher, "Palestinian Synagogues before 70 CE"; Richardson, "Early Synagogues as Collegia."

[106]See the discussions and references in the introduction and in chapter one's treatment of the Synoptics and John.

[107]One of the adherents of this theory, R. Horsley misleadingly claims a consensus for his position: "There now seems to be a critical consensus emerging that 'no synagogue [buildings] have been found in Palestine for the almost two hundred years following the destruction of the Temple.' They begin appearing only the second half of the third century C.E." (*Archaeology History and Society in Galilee*, 133; brackets in original). The embedded quotation is taken from Levine, "Synagogues," 1422. However, Horsley misrepresents Levine's position: the latter *only* refers to an apparent hiatus in synagogue construction in Palestine between 70 C.E. and the third century C.E. In the paragraph immediately preceding the sentence quoted by Horsley, Levine writes, "The earliest evidence for the existence of synagogues in Palestine dates to the first century C.E. in several instances perhaps as early as the late first century B.C.E. Three buildings (at Gamala, Masada, and Herodium) are dated to the first century C.E. (Gamala may date from the late first century B.C.E.) as well as the Theodotos inscription from Jerusalem, which specifically mentions a synagogue and its functions" (op. cit., 1422). The consensus Horsley thinks he has found is thus illusory—at least

If the first two proposals fail to gain support from the evidence, what of the third of the above theories? At first glance, the notion that the synagogue was imported from the diaspora appears attractive since Egypt supplies us with the earliest solid evidence for the existence of the synagogues (*proseuchai*). Moreover, some of the literary references to Palestinian synagogues indicate that their congregants were diaspora Jews (Acts 6:9).[108] Indeed, it is even possible to argue that the synagogue of the Theodotus inscription was built by foreign Jews since the monument is in Greek and refers to servicing the needs of pilgrims from abroad.[109]

While it is apparent that *some* synagogues in Palestine served diaspora congregations, other evidence clearly attests the presence of synagogues whose constituency consisted of Jews native to the homeland. For instance, we have seen that the Essenes frequented synagogues (*Prob.* 81), and this sect can hardly be characterized as a product of the diaspora.[110] The same can be said of the fiercely nationalistic Sicarii who built the synagogues of Masada and Herodium.[111] More broadly, because Josephus and the Gospel writers depict synagogues as scattered about not only the cities but also the villages of Judea and Galilee, it is unlikely that the majority of these structures were founded by communities of diaspora Jews.

---

among archaeologists. Equally inaccurate is Kee's claim (written in 1995) that "recently Levine's understanding of the synagogue in the early Roman period has been significantly altered, and now more nearly resembles the historical view set forth in this essay [i.e., that synagogue buildings didn't emerge until III C.E.]" ("Defining the First-Century CE Synagogue," 481, n. 1). For Levine's latest position on this matter (which is consonant with his earlier views), see below.

[108]Flesher, "Synagogues Before 70 C.E.," 32.

[109]Ibid., 33–34.

[110]That is, unless one takes the mention of "the new covenant in the land of Damascus [הברית החדשה בארץ דמשק]" in CD 6:19 literally. Most scholars, however, take this as a symbolic reference to the sect's exile from the larger community of Israel. See *HJP* 3.1.390 n. 5.

[111]Of the nationalism of the Sicarii, Josephus writes, "The Sicarii clubbed together against those who consented to submit to Rome and in every way treated them as enemies, plundering their property, rounding up their cattle, and setting fire to their habitations; protesting that such persons were no other than aliens, who so ignobly sacrificed the hard-won liberty of the Jews and admitted their preference for the Roman rule" (*BJ* 7.254–255). While the account is likely exaggerated, the Sicarii nevertheless hardly seem the type quick to embrace foreign ideas and institutions—even if these came from other Jews.

If Jews from abroad did not build the majority of synagogues in the homeland, is it possible then that Palestinian Jews simply imitated the synagogues constructed by their diaspora counterparts? While we cannot rule out the possibility of some cross-fertilization between the diaspora and Jewish homeland, two considerations argue against this view. First, there is the difference in synagogue terminology noted in the previous chapter, with Palestinian Jews preferring the term *synagōgē* and diaspora Jews the word *proseuchē*. If Palestinian Jews constructed their synagogues in imitation of the diaspora structures, why then did they not also adopt the diaspora nomenclature?

The second point is that sources from our period depict the synagogal institution as being very ancient. Josephus, for example, writes:

> For ignorance [Moses] left no pretext. He appointed the Law to be the most excellent and necessary form of instruction, ordaining, not that it should be heard once for all or twice or on several occasions, but that every week men should desert their other occupations and assemble to listen to the Law and to obtain a thorough and accurate knowledge of it, a practice which all other legislators seem to have neglected [ἀλλ᾽ ἑκάστης ἑβδομάδος τῶν ἄλλων ἔργων ἀφεμένους ἐπὶ τὴν ἀκρόασιν ἐκέλευσε τοῦ νόμου συλλέγεσθαι καὶ τοῦτον ἀκριβῶς ἐκμανθάνειν· ὃ δὴ πάντες ἐοίκασιν οἱ νομοθέται παραλιπεῖν] (*Ap.* 2.175).

In the historian's mind, the synagogal custom of Sabbath meetings dated all the way back to Moses and was always a part of Israel's heritage. While Josephus lacks historical awareness on this point, his belief nevertheless suggests that the synagogues did not enter Palestine via the diaspora in the first century C.E., but emerged in Palestine's distant past.

Of course, some might argue that because in *Against Apion* Josephus was writing against the view that Judaism was an Egyptian religion, he may have sought to hide the Egyptian origin of the Palestinian synagogues. This criticism might be upheld except for the fact that the belief in a Mosaic origin of the synagogues also appears in Philo's writings as well as in the Book of Acts:

> For it was customary on every day when opportunity offered and pre-eminently on the seventh day, as I have explained above, to pursue the study of wisdom with the ruler [Moses] expounding and instructing the people what they should say and do, while they received edification and betterment in moral principles and conduct. Even now this practice is retained, and the Jews every seventh day occupy themselves with the philosophy of their fathers, dedicating that time to the acquiring of knowledge and the study of the truths of nature. For what are our

> *proseukteria* throughout the cities but *didaskaleia* of prudence and courage and temperance and justice and also of piety, holiness and every virtue by which duties to God and men are discerned and rightly performed? (*Mos.* 2.214–216).

> After [Barnabas and Paul] finished speaking, James replied, "My brothers, listen to me. Simeon has related how God first looked favorably on the Gentiles, to take from among them a people for his name. This agrees with the words of the prophets, as it is written, 'After this I will return, and I will rebuild the dwelling of David, which has fallen; from its ruins I will rebuild it, and I will set it up, so that all other peoples may seek the Lord—even all the Gentiles over whom my name has been called. Thus says the Lord, who has been making these things known from long ago.' Therefore I have reached the decision that we should not trouble those Gentiles who are turning to God, but we should write to them to abstain only from things polluted by idols and from fornication and from whatever has been strangled and from blood. For in every city, for generations past, Moses has had those who proclaim him, for he has been read aloud every sabbath in the synagogues" (Acts 15:13–21).

Philo's commentary and James' speech (a Lucan composition) further demonstrate that the belief in the antiquity of the synagogues was widespread among Jews (and Christians) in the first century C.E. When this belief is coupled with the difference in synagogue terminology, it becomes apparent that there was no simple linear movement of the synagogue from the diaspora into Palestine. Rather, the evidence suggests that the emergence of the synagogues in Palestine and the diaspora were parallel developments.

This leads us to the recent work of Lee Levine, who argues that the appearance of the Palestinian synagogues was part of a gradual process that culminated with the formation of synagogue buildings in the late second or early first century B.C.E.[112] Prior to that time, Levine maintains, synagogue congregations met in the city gates, which during the Late Iron Age and Persian Period served as civic centers. In support of this thesis, Levine points to the Iron Age II gates at Megiddo, Hazor, Dan and Beersheba, among others.[113] In contrast to the earlier gates characteristic

---

[112]Levine, "The Nature and Origin of the Palestinian Synagogue Reconsidered," 425–448; idem, "Synagogues," 1421.

[113]Levine, "The Nature and Origin of the Palestinian Synagogue Reconsidered," 435–436. For an examination of the architectural development of cities in Israel between the Early Bronze Age II and the Iron Age II periods, see Volkmar Fritz, *The City in Ancient Israel* (Sheffield, England: Sheffield Academic Press, 1995), 18–120.

of the Middle Bronze II period, which were primarily defensive structures, Iron Age gates incorporated two to six chambers that were used for public purposes. In some cases, a public square was also located adjacent to the gate. Evidence of religious activities at these gates has also been uncovered, with altars or shrines being found in or near the gates of Meggido V A (c. 950–900 B.C.E.), Beersheba IV (IX B.C.E.) and Tel Dan III (IX B.C.E.).[114] This corresponds with the biblical writings which, in one case, locate *bamoth* at the city gates (2 Kgs 23:8). Moreover, other religious activities, such as the reading of the Torah, are also attested at the city gate (Neh 8:1ff).

While noting these, Levine focuses on the "non-religious" functions of the city gate, which included serving as a place of judgment (Deut 17:5, 21:19, 22:24; 2 Sam 15:2; Ps 69:12; Amos 5:15) and as an area for the handling of public affairs (Ruth 4:1–2). According to Levine's theory, during the Hellenistic period, these functions moved into synagogue buildings since "Hellenistic gates had no accompanying rooms and probably no adjacent open area or square."[115] In further support of this hypothesis, Levine notes that the synagogue at Gamla is located against the city wall and near what may have been a city gate.[116] Yet while continuing to function as a place where the Torah was read, for Levine, the synagogues of the Second Temple period served primarily as public forums: "There is no evidence that the synagogue—even as late as the first century C.E.—was anything more than a community center; it was not endowed with any special sanctity or halakic importance that we know of."[117] It was only later, after the destruction of the Temple, that the synagogues began to be perceived as sacred places.

How are we to evaluate Levine's proposal? When placed in the context of twentieth-century synagogue research, it can be viewed as a synthesis of several earlier propositions that have been significantly

---

[114]On the discovery of a *bamah* at Beersheba, see Yigael Yadin, "Beer-sheba: The High Place Destroyed by King Josiah," *BASOR* 222 (1976): 5–17. For the cultic object found at the gate of Tel Dan, see Avraham Biran, "'To the God who is in Dan'" in *Temples and High Places in Biblical Times*, edited by Avraham Biran, Inna Pommerantz and Hannah Katzenstein (Jerusalem: Nelson Glueck School of Biblical Archaeology of Hebrew Union College-Jewish Institute of Religion, 1981), 142–151; idem, *Biblical Dan* (Jerusalem: Israel Exploration Society, 1994), 238–245.

[115]Levine, "The Nature and Origin of the Palestinian Synagogue Reconsidered," 437.

[116]Ibid., 438.

[117]Ibid., 411.

revised. On the one hand, Levine draws on the thesis of Solomon Zeitlin, who argued that the synagogue originally "was *not religious* but secular" and only later acquired religious functions.[118] While Levine agrees with Zeitlin that the (Palestinian) synagogues became places of worship and prayer only *after* the destruction of the Temple, unlike Zeitlin, Levine does not see the synagogues as Pharisee-dominated institutions that stood in opposition to the Temple cultus.[119] On the other hand, Levine's suggestion of the city gate as the precursor of the synagogue derives from the earlier work of Mendel Silber and Sidney Hoenig, as Levine readily acknowledges.[120] However, in contrast to these earlier researchers, Levine, making a much more sophisticated use of archaeological sources, dates the emergence of Palestinian synagogue buildings to the Hellenistic era rather than the Solomonic (Silber) or the Rabbinic periods (Hoenig).

Although Levine's proposal clearly represents a significant advance, it nevertheless retains some of the shortcomings of the earlier theories. To start with, while Levine would probably be opposed to Zeitlin's use of the term "secular," his own work retains a similar but more subtle dichotomy between the "religious" and the "non-religious" functions of the synagogue and city gate. In this regard, how else are we to explain the fact that, on the one hand, Levine can note the place of Torah reading in the synagogues or the early use of *hieron* as a term for the synagogue,

---

[118]Zeitlin, "The Origin of the Synagogue," 19.

[119]Levine, "The Nature and Origin of the Palestinian Synagogue Reconsidered," 440–441. Zeitlin also maintained that synagogue buildings did not exist until after the destruction of the Temple, a proposition to which Levine does not subscribe. It is noteworthy, however, that Levine retains Zeitlin's theory that the village synagogues emerged from the *ma'ămādôt*, the practice of the laity gathering in the towns and reading the Torah while their priestly course was on duty in the Temple (439–440; cf. Zeitlin, "The Origin of the Synagogue," 22–23). Nevertheless, as Levine himself points out, this custom is not attested until the Mishnah (*m. Ta'an.* 4:2). Despite Levine's certainty that this practice dates to the Second Temple period, it should be noted that Neusner assigns the *ma'ămādôt* passage to the Ushan period (140–170 C.E.; Neusner, *Appointed Times*, 5.171–172, 231).

[120]Levine, "The Nature and Origin of the Palestinian Synagogue Reconsidered," 432, n. 27. See Hoenig, "The Ancient City-Square," 448–476; Mendel Silber, *The Origin of the Synagogue* (New Orleans: Steeg, 1915). Hoenig's thesis is based upon the dubious practice of emending חבר עיר ("city administrators") to read רחב עיר ("city square") in several passages from the rabbinic literature. Ironically, R. Horsley, who chides others for their uncritical use of later sources, bases his own theories on Hoenig's work, which itself is founded upon a problematic reading of late sources (R. Horsley, *Galilee*, 226).

and on the other, state that the pre-70 synagogues were not endowed with any special sanctity?[121] Such ambivalence further leads Levine to downplay the "religious" aspects of the early synagogues at the expense of the "non-religious" elements, as can be seen in the statement that the supposed prominence of the former "had more to do with each [literary] source's own agenda than with historical reality."[122] This is surely overstating the matter, to say the least. To be sure, writers such as Josephus and Philo may have focused upon or idealized the "religious" elements of the synagogues, but this hardly means that such elements did not have a prominent place in the historical reality of synagogal practice. When one looks at the wording of the Theodotus inscription, the placement of *mikvaoth* near several early synagogues, the use of a synagogue room at Masada as a genizah and for the collection of priestly tithes, it becomes apparent that Josephus and Philo were not being deceptive when they wrote of the important place of "religious" matters in the synagogues.

This leads us to the point that, when referring to ancient Jewish practices, it is very difficult to distinguish between "religious" and the "non-religious" dimensions. Here it must be recalled that it was Josephus himself who, in describing the Jewish way of life, coined the word "theocracy" (*Ap.* 2.165). In his view, religious law *was* civil law—or at least that was the ideal:

> The cause of [Moses'] success was that the very nature of his legislation made it far more useful than any other; for he did not make religion a department of virtue, but the various virtues—I mean, justice, temperance, fortitude, and mutual harmony in all things between the members of the community—departments of religion [οὐ γὰρ μέρος ἀρετῆς ἐποίησεν τὴν εὐσέβειαν, ἀλλὰ ταύτης μέρη τἆλλα]. Religion governs all our actions and occupations and speech [ἅπασαι γὰρ αἱ πράξεις καὶ διατριβαὶ καὶ λόγοι πάντες ἐπὶ τὴν πρὸς τὸν θεὸν ἡμῖν εὐσέβειαν ἔχουσι τὴν ἀναφοράν]; none of these things did our lawgiver leave unexamined or indeterminate (*Ap.* 2.170–171).[123]

---

[121]Two of the four uses of *hieron* cited by Levine are in reference to Palestinian synagogues. See Levine, "The Nature and Origin of the Palestinian Synagogues Reconsidered," 430, n. 14.

[122]Levine, "The Nature and Origin of the Palestinian Synagogues Reconsidered," 432.

[123]Note also that Philo expresses nearly the same sentiments as Josephus, when he writes: "For all men guard their own customs, but this is especially true of the Jewish nation. Holding that the laws are oracles vouchsafed by God and having been trained

While the above may represent Josephus' version of Plato's *Republic*, it is difficult to escape the evidence that this ideal met with a modicum of success in Palestine of the Second Temple period. Every available source points to the conclusion that most if not all Jews in this era assiduously adhered to such practices as Sabbath observance, circumcision, ritual bathing and the keeping of the *kashrut* laws, to name but a few.[124] Indeed, certain groups of Jews, such as the Essenes and Pharisees, were quite zealous—one might even say fanatical—about adhering to the dictates of Torah. Therefore, when researchers deal with Judaism of this period, it must be recognized that the lines between the "religious" and the "non-religious" (or "secular") are quite blurred—certainly not as clearly defined as in modern western societies. If a modern analogue is required, it would be best to look to anthropological studies of twentieth-century theocracies for points of comparison.

With regard to the synagogues, functions clearly cannot be so neatly assigned to "religious" or "non-religious" categories. For example, while researchers (including Levine) can note that the *proseuchē* in Tiberias served as a place where political meetings convened, it must be recognized that at least one of those meetings incorporated prayer and fasting (Josephus, *Vita* 295). Moreover, the very war being discussed in the *proseuchē* during those meetings was prompted in part by Roman insensitivities to Jewish laws and customs.

Elsewhere, Levine's assertion that the term *synagōgē* "was bereft of any religious connotation" clearly cannot be sustained.[125] While this might be true in pagan writings, as we observed in the previous chapter, in a Jewish context, *synagōgē*, when not referring to a building, most often signifies the cultic and legal congregation of Israel. In particular, the LXX repeatedly uses *synagōgē* in such a manner (e.g., Exod 12:19, Lev 4:21, Num 8:9, Psa 73:2, *Pss. Sol.* 10:7, Sir 24:23). That authors of this period can employ other terms such as *hieron* and *proseuchē* in reference

---

in this doctrine from their earliest years, they carry the likenesses of the commandments enshrined in their souls" (*Legat.* 210).

[124]On this point, see the discussion in the introduction and also E. P. Sanders, *Judaism*, 47–51. The non-Jewish literature, which generally attests the piety of the Jews throughout the empire, is particularly convincing. See Whittaker, *Jews and Christians*, pass.

[125]Levine, "The Nature and Origin of the Palestinian Synagogues Reconsidered," 430.

to Palestinian synagogues further establishes the "religious" nature of these structures.[126]

If Levine's purpose in focusing on the "non-religious" dimensions of the synagogues was to establish more firmly the link between these structures and the city gates, then the strategy was an unnecessary one. As Levine himself has pointed out, both literary and archaeological sources locate the city gate as the place where cultic activities took place. In fact, the evidence presented by Levine can be greatly expanded to demonstrate the sacred nature of the city gates not only in Israelite cities of the Iron through Persian periods, but also throughout the Near East as early as the Middle Bronze age. William Dever, for example, has uncovered the remains of a Canaanite temple of the Middle Bronze IIC period (1650–1550 B.C.E.) next to the northwest gate of ancient Shechem.[127] Similarly, at thirteenth-century Kition on Cyprus, all five temples were found clustered around one of the city gates.[128]

Elsewhere, at Zincirli, a Hittite city in S. E. Turkey, excavators discovered a series of stone reliefs near one of the gates, depicting the procession of a goddess and other semi-divine figures into the city.[129] Similar scenes were found at Iron Age gates in Carchemish (Iraq) and Karatepe (S. E. Turkey), only these depict the god Baʿal in the procession.[130] The presence of these scenes has led Richard Barnett to suggest that the city gates served as ceremonial sites where the local gods were invited to enter through the gates and take up habitation in the temple. Because the Israelites borrowed a good number of customs from their Hittite and neo-Hittite neighbors, Barnett argues that a similar ceremony took place in Solomon's dedication ceremony (1 Kgs 8) and can be discerned in Ezekiel's vision of the restored Temple when the

---

[126]Levine himself notes these usages, but dismisses their import. See ibid., 430, nn. 14, 21.

[127]William G. Dever, "The MB IIC Stratification in the Northwest Gate Area at Shechem," *BASOR* 216 (1974): 31–52.

[128]Vassos Karageorghis, "The Sacred Area of Kition" in *Temples and High Places in Biblical Times*, edited by Avraham Biran, Inna Pommerantz and Hannah Katzenstein (Jerusalem: Nelson Glueck School of Biblical Archaeology of Hebrew Union College-Jewish Institute of Religion, 1981), 82–90.

[129]See Felix von Luschan, *Ausgrabungen in Sendschirli* (Berlin: W. Spemann, 1902), 2.3.122, 208–299, pls. XXXVI–XLIV.

[130]C. L. Woolley, *Carchemish II* (London: The British Museum, 1921), pls. B:17–24, 30b; C. L. Woolley, and Richard D. Barnett, *Carchemish III* (London: The British Museum, 1952), pl. 43a; Winfried Orthmann, *Untersuchungen zur späthethitischen Kunst* (Bonn: R. Habelt, 1971), 105–110, 488–497.

prophet states, "the glory of the LORD entered the temple by the gate facing east, the spirit lifted me up, and brought me into the inner court; and the glory of the LORD filled the temple" (Ezek 43:4).[131]

In support of Barnett's theory, John Tvedtnes notes the passage, "Lift up your heads, O gates . . . that the King of glory may come in" (Psa 24:7).[132] On this allusion, F. M. Cross further comments:

> It is not by chance that we have the expression to lift up the head. It is used verbatim in the Ugaritic material. The comment is made, first of all, that all the gods sitting in the circle of the council bow their heads to their knees. Ba'al was taken away under the power of the god of Chaos. And then, when the god returns as king, the members of the council lift up their heads in joy and rejoicing—the idiom is a perfectly proper one. You have then, in Psalm 24, the personification of the gates, echoing the old mythological scene of the members of the council. It is interesting that the personification of the gates as members of the council of the gods persists even down into Jewish apocalyptic literature. At all events the idiom is that of confidence and joy as one lifts up one's head in expectation.[133]

This all becomes exceedingly interesting when we recall that in the fifth century B.C.E., Ezra and Nehemiah were said to have celebrated the rededication of the Temple with a Torah-reading ceremony at the Water Gate, which was located south of the Temple mount in an area called the Ophel:[134]

---

[131]Richard D. Barnett, "Bringing God into the Temple" in *Temples and High Places in Biblical Times: Proceedings of the Colloquium in Honor of the Centennial of Hebrew Union College-Jewish Institute of Religion, Jerusalem, 14–16 March 1977*, edited by Avraham Birah, Inna Pommerantz and Hannah Katzenstein (Jerusalem: Nelson Glueck School of Biblical Archaeology of Hebrew Union College-Jewish Institute of Religion, 1981), 17.

[132]Ibid., 19.

[133]Ibid., 20. See also Frank Moore Cross, *Canaanite Myth and Hebrew Epic* (Cambridge: Harvard University Press, 1973), 91–111; *ANET* 129–130.

[134]Eilat Mazar has identified the Water Gate about 80 m south of the southern edge of the present Temple mount. It is a four-chambered gate dating from the 9th century B.C.E., whose plan is similar to the gate of Strata VA-IVB at Megiddo. It led into a plaza that was connected with a royal building. The gate apparently survived into the Persian period. See Eilat Mazar, "The Royal Quarter of Biblical Jerusalem: The Ophel" in *Ancient Jerusalem Revealed*, edited by Hillel Geva (Jerusalem: Israel Exploration Society, 1994), 64–72. Levine calls attention to the Nehemiah passage in: Levine, "The Nature and Origin of the Palestinian Synagogue Reconsidered," 435.

> All the people gathered together into the square before the Water Gate. They told the scribe Ezra to bring the book of the law of Moses, which the LORD had given to Israel. Accordingly, the priest Ezra brought the law before the assembly, both men and women and all who could hear with understanding. This was on the first day of the seventh month. He read from it facing the square before the Water Gate from early morning until midday, in the presence of the men and the women and those who could understand; and the ears of all the people were attentive to the book of the law. The scribe Ezra stood on a wooden platform that had been made for the purpose; and beside him stood Mattithiah, Shema, Anaiah, Uriah, Hilkiah, and Maaseiah on his right hand; and Pedaiah, Mishael, Malchijah, Hashum, Hash-baddanah, Zechariah, and Meshullam on his left hand. And Ezra opened the book in the sight of all the people, for he was standing above all the people; and when he opened it, all the people stood up. Then Ezra blessed the LORD, the great God, and all the people answered, "Amen, Amen," lifting up their hands. Then they bowed their heads and worshiped the LORD with their faces to the ground. Also . . . the Levites, helped the people to understand the law, while the people remained in their places. So they read from the book, from the law of God, with interpretation. They gave the sense, so that the people understood the reading (Neh 8:1–8).

The scene was repeated over seven days as Ezra and Nehemiah revived the Feast of Tabernacles (Neh 8:13–18). On the eighth day came a solemn assembly during which Ezra uttered a long prayer of thanksgiving and pledged the commitment of the people (Neh 9). This commitment was sealed in writing by the priests, Levites and other leaders (Neh 10).

That this series of ceremonies represents another instance of "inviting God into the Temple" can hardly be doubted. More generally, it shows that the city gate served as a place of sacred assembly in Israel into the Persian period. Unfortunately, as Levine points out, our sources for this period are meager. Consequently, outside of the above passage, we do not know the specific ways the city gate continued to play a role in regular public gatherings before Alexander's invasion of Palestine in 332 B.C.E.

Levine is also correct in pointing out that during the Hellenistic period, city architecture in Palestine started to change in style, and the chambered gates of the earlier period began to disappear. Likewise, with the gradual Hellenization of Palestine came a simultaneous shift in the civic centers away from the city gates and into the Greek agoras. One can see this shift illustrated in Hellenistic Marisa (Maresha), a city located on the southern coastal plain of Palestine: adjacent to the Hellenistic gate is an enclosed court (Block I), forty-five meters square, surrounded by various rooms and halls.[135] The area clearly served as an agora, and its placement near the city gate demonstrates the transition from the earlier, oriental model to the Hellenistic style of civic center.[136]

Since Jerusalem underwent this same process of Hellenization, we should expect a similar shift in the architecture of this city during the Hellenistic period. Now, when one tries to identify the civic center in Jerusalem during the later era, architecturally, one is attracted to the Temple mount, where the Temple shrine is surrounded by colonnades and stoas, just like most of the Hellenistic agoras. Here, if we initially resist the identification of the Temple complex as an agora, this is probably because we undervalue the agora's sacred nature; nearly every agora throughout the Hellenistic world had a temple physically attached to it. For example, the so-called State Agora at Ephesus boasted a temple to Augustus in its center, exactly where the *naos* of the Jerusalem Temple stood in relationship to the rest of the complex. Likewise, various shrines and altars dotted the ancient agora at Athens.[137]

---

[135]Michael Avi-Yonah, "Maresha" in *NEAEHL* 3.948–951; idem, "Mareshah" in *EAEHL* 3.782–790. Levine mentions Maresha in: Levine, "The Nature and Origin of the Palestinian Synagogue Reconsidered," 437.

[136]A three-chambered building measuring 9 x 3 m is located in the center of the court. While no cultic objects were found, this may have served as an Idumean temple. Unfortunately, the dating of the structure is unclear, as indeed is the later occupational history of the city. Some archaeologists have held that the Hasmoneans destroyed the city at the end of the second century B.C.E. The fact that few coins from the first century B.C.E. were recovered on the site (none from the reign of Jannaeus, one Herodian) would tend to support the hypothesis that the city was transformed into a military outpost in the early first century B.C.E. See Avi-Yonah, "Mareshah," 786–787. According to Josephus, the Parthians destroyed the city in 40 B.C.E. (*BJ* 1.269).

[137]See Werner Jobst, "Zur Lokalisierung des Sebastion-Augusteum in Ephesos," *Istanbuler Mitteilungen* 30 (1980): 241–260. Peter Scherrer argues that the State Agora was a *temenos* or sacred area. See Peter Scherrer, "The City of Ephesos" in *Ephesos: Metropolis of Asia,* edited by Helmut Koester (Valley Forge, Pennsylvania: Trinity Press International, 1995), 4. In general, larger Greco-Roman cities, following the advice of Aristotle (*Pol.* 1331a), had several agoras, with one serving as the central civic center and others as specialized market areas. This can be seen in Ephesus, where a second agora ("the Tetragonos Agora") co-existed with the State Agora. Also at Marisa two other square areas probably served as agoras along with the civic center near the gate. On these see G. Horowitz, "Town Planning of Hellenistic Marisa: A Reappraisal of the Excavations after Eighty Years," *PEQ* 112 (1980): 93–111. On the Hellenization of Palestine in general, see Asem N. Barghouti, "Urbanization of Palestine and Jordan in Hellenistic and Roman Times" in *Studies in the History and Archaeology of Jordan*, edited by Adnan Hadidi (Amman, Jordan: Department of Antiquities, 1982), 1.209–229. With regard to Jerusalem, Josephus mentions the

Historically, the Greek agora was originally a civic and cultic center that (unlike the early Roman forum) only secondarily attracted commercial buildings.[138] This same development can be seen in the Jerusalem Temple, since it is only during the Hellenistic period that commercial activity begins to take place there—both on the Temple mount itself (apparently only in relationship to the Temple cult) and at the mount's base (where excavations have shown that general commercial activity took place).[139]

The movement of the civic center from the city gate to the Temple complex in Jerusalem is nicely illustrated in 1 Esdras, a document probably written in the late second century B.C.E.[140] Here we discover that in 1 Esdras' retelling of the Torah-reading ceremony of Nehemiah 8, Ezra no longer reads at the Water Gate, but "in the open square before the east gate of the temple" (1 Esdras 9:38). This anachronism probably reflects the historical reality of the Hellenistic period, when the Torah-reading ceremony was conducted in front of the Court of Women every seventh year during the Festival of Tabernacles (Deut 31:10–13). Significantly, Josephus follows 1 Esdras rather then Nehemiah on this point, indicating

---

presence of a "timber agora" in the northern Bezetha part of Jerusalem (*BJ* 2.530), and another agora in the Upper City (*BJ* 5.137). Other examples of civic peristylar agoras exist at Aphrodisias, Herakleia on Latmos, Kremna, Nysa, Palmyra, Side, Smyrna, Kos and Thessalonike. See J. J. Coulton, *The Architectural Development of the Greek Stoa* (Oxford: Clarendon Press, 1976), 174–175 and pass. On the Athenian agora, see Homer A. Thompson, *The Agora of Athens: The History, Shape, and Uses of an Ancient City Center* (Princeton: American School of Classical Studies at Athens, 1972), pass.

[138]See E. J. Owens, *The City in the Greek and Roman World* (London and New York: Routledge, 1991), 153–154.

[139]On the buying and selling in the Court of the Gentiles, see Mark 11:15, Matt 21:12, Luke 19:45, John 2:14. Note also that in his description of the Tabernacle of Moses, Josephus states that next to this structure "was an orderly *agora*, articles of merchandise lay ranged each in its place, and artisans of every craft had their workshops" (*Ant*. 3.289). This is absent from the biblical account (Num 2:1) and therefore probably reflects Josephus' understanding of the Temple area in his own time. Note also that 2 Macc 3:4 reports a dispute between the High Priest and the Temple Captain over the administration of the agora. On the excavations that uncovered shops along the base of the Temple mount on its western side, see B. Mazar, "The Archaeological Excavations near the Temple Mount" in *Jerusalem Revealed: Archaeology in the Holy City, 1968–1974*, edited by Yigael Yadin (Jerusalem: Israel Exploration Society, 1975), 26.

[140]On 1 Esdras' date and purpose, see Jacob M. Myers, *I and II Esdras* (Garden City, N.Y.: Doubleday, 1974), 1–20.

that the septennial reading of the law continued to take place in the Temple courts in the first century C.E. (*Ant.* 11.154–158).[141]

Elsewhere, according to Josephus the Temple courts served as a frequent site for public gatherings. It was there that the public reconciliation of Hyrcanus II and Aristobulus II took place before a gathered multitude (*BJ* 1.122). Likewise, the public acclamation of Archelaus was held on the Temple mount, where he sat before the assembly on a golden throne set on a raised platform (*BJ* 2.1–5; *Ant.* 17.200–201). During the procuratorship of Florus, a crowd gathered in the Temple complex to stage a public protest against the governor's stealing from the Temple treasury, with some of the protesters "carrying round a basket [begging] coppers for him as for an unfortunate destitute" (*BJ* 2.294–295). Later, the chief priests assembled the people in the same location and implored them to avoid a confrontation with the governor (*BJ* 2.320–324). In other places, Josephus mentions that trials took place in the Temple courts (*BJ* 4.336), and that public notifications were posted there (*Ant.* 13.128; cf. 1 Macc 11:37). In short, during the Hellenistic and Roman periods, the Temple courts came to function as the main civic center of Jerusalem, adopting the role that had previously been held by the areas adjoining one or more of the city gates.

This leads us finally to explore the architectural precursors of the Palestinian synagogues. Earlier in the century, H. Kohl and C. Watzinger, in their pioneering study on the synagogues of the Galilee, proposed that the Roman basilica served as the inspiration of the Galilean-type synagogue.[142] This suggestion was based upon the structural similarity between the two types of buildings, which were each rectangular in shape and lined with rows of columns. This proposal quickly gained acceptance and for most of the century represented the consensus view.

---

[141]Elsewhere, in Josephus' rendering of Deut 31:10–13, the historian modifies Moses' speech to state that the *high priest* was the one to read the law before the assembled congregation (Deuteronomy does not mention the speaker)—again, likely reflecting the practice of the first century C.E. (*Ant.* 4.209–210).

[142]Kohl and Watzinger, *Antike Synagogen in Galiläa*, 178–180. See also Avigad, "The 'Galilean' Synagogue and its Predecessors," 42–44; Asher Ovadiah, and Talila Michaeli, "Observations on the Origin of the Architectural Plan of Ancient Synagogues," *JJS* 38 (1987): 234–236. On the basilica in general, see Roberts, *Greek and Roman Architecture*, 267–271; Coulton, *The Architectural Development of the Greek Stoa*, 180–183.

Beginning in the 1970s, however, scholars began to question the aptness of the comparison between the two types of structures. Gideon Foerster, for example, wrote:

> The basilica, which originated in the West, reached Palestine and Syria only in the second century of the Christian era. It is a structure of large dimensions whose principal feature is four rows of columns—occasionally two rows—along the walls. Every basilica had a focal point in the form of a tribunal (platform), which was sometimes situated in the apse. There were not benches along its walls. These are only a few of the difficulties that arise in a comparison between the early buildings at Masada and Herodion, or with the Galilean synagogues of the second and third centuries, with the basilica.[143]

Although Strange's recent classification of a first-century C.E. structure in Sepphoris (Galilee) as a basilica somewhat undermines the objection that the basilica arrived too late in Palestine to serve as a model for the Second Temple synagogues, Foerster's other criticisms still retain their force.[144]

The challenge to the previous consensus opened the door for the submission of several other proposals for the origin of the Galilean model, of which the Second Temple synagogues were seen as early examples. Among these is one offered by Netzer, who, reviving a suggestion previously rejected by Kohl and Watzinger, proposed that the Roman *triclinium* was the prototype for the Galilean synagogue since it also served as an assembly room (albeit for entertainment purposes) and was arranged with rows of columns.[145] The difficulty with this suggestion, as Netzer himself has pointed out, is that the *triclinium* lacks the rows of benches characteristic of the Galilean synagogue. In this respect, it is significant that the rebels at Herodium had to modify the *triclinium* there substantially in order for it to meet their purposes.

Foerster himself presented two proposals, the first of which is that the Galilean synagogues were modeled after the audience halls (*pronaoi*) found in the Temples of Atargatis, Artemis and Tyche at Dura-Europos.[146] These date to the early first century C.E. and were used by worshipers not

---

[143]Foerster, "The Synagogues at Masada and Herodion," 9, n. 23.

[144]See James F. Strange, "The Eastern Basilical Building" in *Sepphoris in Galilee*, edited by Rebecca Martin Nagy et al. (Winona Lake: Eisenbrauns, 1996), 116–121.

[145]Netzer, "The Herodian Triclinia: A Prototype for the 'Galilean-Type' Synagogue," 49–51. Cf. Kohl and Watzinger, *Antike Synagogen in Galiläa*, 176–178.

[146]Foerster, "The Synagogues at Masada and Herodium," 28–29; idem, "The Synagogues at Masada and Herodion," 9–11.

allowed into the sanctuary area. In a manner somewhat comparable to the Galilean synagogues, tiers of benches occupy the two short sides of these narrow, rectangular halls. Despite the general similarity of the two types of structures, this proposal has come under criticism on several counts.[147] First, the *pronaoi* lack the colonnades that are found in the Galilean synagogues. Second, the focus in the rooms at Dura-Europos was not toward the center of the hall, as was the case in the synagogues, but toward the side of the room where the ritual took place. Third, the halls date to after the erection of the synagogue at Gamla and therefore could not have served as models. Finally, some researchers have thought it difficult to believe that the synagogue would have been based upon one of the rooms of a pagan temple. This last objection has also been directed against Foerster's second proposal—that the synagogues were modeled on the forecourts of Nabatean temples, which, unlike the rooms at Dura-Europos, had benches against three walls and colonnades intervening between the central altar and the seated worshipers.[148]

The proposal that seems to be gaining the most currency in recent scholarship is one first offered by Yadin, that the Galilean synagogue was based upon Greek council halls such as the *ecclesiasterion* at Priene (II B.C.E.) or the *bouleterion* at Herakleia.[149] Like the Galilean synagogues, these structures typically have rows of benches arranged along the walls.

Despite the growing acceptance of this proposal, James Strange has recently pointed out a significant difference between the various Greco-Roman assembly halls and the Galilean synagogues:

---

[147]See Ma'oz, "The Synagogue of Gamla and the Typology of Second-Temple Synagogues," 41; Ovadiah and Michaeli, "Observations on the Origin of the Architectural Plan of Ancient Synagogues," 238–240; Chiat, "First-Century Synagogue Architecture: Methodological Problems," 49–60.

[148]Foerster, "Architectural Models of the Greco-Roman Period and the Origin of The 'Galilean' Synagogue," 47–48; Ovadiah and Michaeli, "Observations on the Origin of the Architectural Plan of Ancient Synagogues," 240.

[149]Yadin, "The Synagogue at Masada," 20, n. 1. See also Beat Brenk, "Zu den Grundrisstypen der fruehsten Synagogen Palaestinas" in *Atti Del IX Congresso Internazionale Di Archeologia Cristiana: Roma, 21 -27 Settembre 1975*, edited by cristiana Congresso internazionale di archeologia (Citta del Vaticano, Roma: Pontificio istituto di archeologia cristiana, 1978), 539–550; Ma'oz, "The Synagogue of Gamla and the Typology of Second-Temple Synagogues," 35–41; idem, "The Synagogue in the Second Temple Period—Architectural and Social Interpretation," 224–228. On these structures generally, see Roberts, *Greek and Roman Architecture*, 169–182.

> [The Galilean synagogues] have one architectural feature that seems to be almost a constant; it is the habit of their builders to place a row of columns between the benches against the walls and the central worship place. This is a most peculiar arrangement, given the habit of the Romans to place rows of columns behind the backs of gathered spectators or participants in a bouleuterion or in an ecclesiasterion, or even in a theater.[150]

Strange then goes on to offer his own attractive solution to this enduring puzzle:

> The simplest explanation for why this space was organized in such a unique fashion is that the builders were copying a similar arrangement seen in the Second Temple in Jerusalem. Josephus describes the inner courts of the temple as adorned with colonnades or cloisters. Thus the Court of Women, the Court of Israel, and the Court of the Priests would all present this feature . . . then as one watched the sacred proceedings in the Court of the Priests from the vantage of the Court of Israel, one would be watching between columns.[151]

While Strange observes that Josephus only mentions the presence of colonnades in the *Court of Women* in his main description of the Temple in *War* (*BJ* 5.200–226), it should be noted that elsewhere Josephus also alludes to the presence of colonnaded stoas in the *Court of Israel*. For instance, in describing the rebuilding of the Temple under Zerubbabel, Josephus states that "the Jews built stoas around the *naos* within the inner *hieron* [ᾠκοδομήκεσαν γὰρ ἱο Ἰουδαῖου καὶ τὰς ἐν κύκλῳ τοῦ ναοῦ στοὰς τοῦ ἔνδοθεν ἱερου]" (*Ant.* 11.108). Because neither of Josephus' sources (Ezra 6:18; 1 Esdr 7:9) makes mention of the stoas, the allusion is probably anachronistic and indicative of the construction of the Court of Israel during the first century C.E.[152] Still, the addition of the columns to this court can be dated even earlier, since the LXX of Ezek 40:17–19

---

[150]James F. Strange, "First Century Galilee from Archaeology and from the Texts" in *Archaeology and the Galilee: Texts and Contexts in Graeco-Roman and Byzantine Periods*, edited by Douglas R. Edwards and C. Thomas McCollough (Atlanta: Scholars Press, 1997), 43.

[151]Ibid., 43–44. See also idem, "The Art and Archaeology of Ancient Judaism," 75–76.

[152]In his description of Jotham's renovations, Josephus also mentions that stoas were built around the *naos* (*Ant.* 9.237)—information again missing from his sources (2 Chr 27:3; 2 Kgs 15:35). Note also that the *Temple Scroll* mentions the presence of a stoa (פרור) in the inner court in its description of the idealized Temple (11QT 37.9). See Yadin, *The Temple Scroll*, 1.207–208, 2.159. See below.

describes the inner court as having "peristyles round about the court; thirty chambers within the ranges of columns [περίστυλα κύκλῳ τῆς αὐλῆς τριάκοντα παστοφόρια ἐν τοῖς περιστύλοις]." The allusion to the peristyles is absent in the Hebrew text.[153]

One potential problem with Strange's theory is that, while he has accounted for the columns being between the viewer and the focus of attention, he has not proven that there was a counterpart in the Temple to the benches being along the walls, since Josephus is silent on this point. Yet here we should recall Foerster's mention of several Near Eastern temples of this period which *do* have such benches. These include the temple of Baal Shamin in southern Syria and the Nabatean temples at Sûr, Sahur and Petra.[154] Because these temples are all architecturally similar to the Jerusalem Temple, it is likely that the inner courts of the latter also had benches along the wall. Significantly, the idealized Temple of the *Temple Scroll* contains seating along the outer walls of the inner court:

> And [in]side the cou[rt] you shall m[a]ke s[i]tting pl[a]ces for the priests [וע[שׂ]יתמה בח[צר פ]נימה ב[י]ת מושבות לכוהנימ], and tables in front of the sitting places [לפני המושבות], in the inner stoa by the outer wall of the court, places made for the priests, for their sacri[f]ices and for the first fruits and for the tithes" (11QT 37.8–10).[155]

In the actual Temple, the colonnaded area was reserved primarily for the sacrificers to watch their sacrifices being offered (Josephus, *BJ* 5.226).[156]

---

[153]The LXX of Ezek 42:3 similarly mentions the presence of stoas in the inner courts.

[154]Foerster, "Architectural Models of the Greco-Roman Period and the Origin of The 'Galilean' Synagogue," 47–48. Richardson argues that Herod had a hand in building the temple of Baal Shamim as well as the Temple in Jerusalem ("Law and Piety in Herod's Architecture," 351).

[155]Translation, Yadin, *The Temple Scroll*, 2.159. Yadin notes that the reference to the tables for the sacrifices given to the priests is taken from Ezek 40:39–43. Because there is no mention of seating in Ezekiel, it is likely that such seating actually existed in the Temple when the *Temple Scroll* was composed (c. 100 B.C.E.). See ibid., 1.206, 209.

[156]Note, however, Philo's description of the so-called Festival of the Baskets (Deut 26:1–11): "Every person who possesses farms or landed estates takes some of every kind of fruit and fills receptacles which, as I have said, are called baskets, and brings them with joy as a sample offering of his rich fruit-harvest, to the temple, and there standing opposite the altar, gives them to the priest. Meanwhile he recites this beautiful and admirable canticle, or if he does not remember it, he listens with all attention while the priest repeats it" (*Spec.* 2.216).

Despite this difference in function, the notion from the *Temple Scroll* that there was seating along the outer walls of the court may have had a basis in reality.

Alternatively, the roofs of the stoas might have extended out over rows of stairs leading down into the Court of Priests. In this case, the supporting columns would have been at the foot of the stairs, with the latter being used by worshipers for seats. In either case, the presence of benches in temples was likely functional, providing seating for the lengthy wait that was probably entailed during sacrificial proceedings (Luke 1:21).[157]

If Strange has finally solved the riddle of the Galilean synagogue—and it appears that he has—then the movement of the public assemblies from the city gate into the synagogue in Palestine was not a movement into just any type of Hellenistic assembly hall, but into structures modeled after the Temple courts. This proposal would account for the use of the term *synagōgē* in Palestine, since the LXX frequently uses this word when referring to the assembly gathered before the tabernacle. It also explains why Josephus did not hesitate to employ the term *hieron* for the synagogues, as this same word is commonly used of the Temple courts. The possible presence of a priest's dwelling in the Masada synagogue may also find a parallel in the Temple courts, since several passages in the Hebrew scriptures, the Apocrypha and the *Temple Scroll* mention such rooms being located there for use by the attending priests and Levites during their periods of service.[158] Indeed, one passage states that tithes should be brought "to the priest, to the chambers of the house of our God" (Neh 10:37; cf. 1 Esdr 8:59)—which seems to have been the practice at the chamber in the Masada synagogue. As we have also seen, the rosette and the palm trees were important motifs in the Temple courts. It cannot be a coincidence that these also appear on the lintel of the Gamla synagogue. Finally, recalling the strip of stones in the Gamla synagogue that possibly supported a table for the reading of scriptures, we note that the very space where the Torah was being read in

---

[157]Note also that Josephus mentions that a certain Essene named Judas was in the Temple courts and "a considerable number of his disciples were seated beside him [ἦσαν δ' οὐκ ὀλίγοι παρεδρεύοντες αὐτῷ τῶν μανθανόντων]" (*BJ* 1.78)—implying that there was seating somewhere in the courts. Jesus also was said to have sat teaching in the Temple (Matt 26:55; John 8:2; cf. Luke 2:46).

[158]1 Chr 28:12–13; Ezra 8:29; Neh 10:37–38, 12:44, 13:4; Ezek 40:17–42:13, 44:19, 46:19; 1 Macc 4:38, 57, 12:3; 1 Esdr 8:59; 11QT 41.17–42.10, 44.3–45.2, 49.3–7. See also Yadin, *The Temple Scroll*, 1.256–271.

this synagogue corresponds to the space where the Temple priests presented the offerings of the people at the altar. The person reading Torah in the midst of the synagogue could thus be viewed as offering a "sacrifice of the lips" (cf. Hos 14:2). Furthermore, the position of the people seated in the synagogue corresponds to the place where the sacrificers in the Temple watched the priests present their offerings on the altar, as Strange himself observed.

CONCLUSION

In this chapter we have examined literary, epigraphic and architectural evidence attesting to the presence of synagogue buildings in the cities and villages of Palestine by at least the beginning of the Common Era. These buildings served as sacred places of public assembly on the Sabbath when scripture was read and other liturgical activities took place. That the synagogues functioned more generally as civic centers should not be overlooked, but care should be taken not to divorce the "religious" dimensions of the synagogues from the "non-religious" aspects as the two are inextricably intertwined. With this caveat, Levine's proposal that the precursor of the Palestinian synagogue was the city gate is to be accepted since the activities of the latter setting are nearly identical to those adduced for the former. The transition from the city gate to the synagogues took place sometime during the Hellenistic era, probably early in the first century B.C.E. This transformation is seen in the movement of Jerusalem's civic center from the gates to the Temple courts. The architecture of the Second Temple synagogues excavated thus far in Palestine was likely modeled after these courts. In this way, the architecture reinforced the connection between the synagogues and the Temple, allowing worshipers, in a sense, to be transported to the central cultic site. This connection may have been further cemented by the orienting of the synagogue façades either toward Jerusalem (Gamla, Capernaum?) or toward the east (Herodium, Masada), the latter orientation in imitation of the inner courts of the Temple, whose main gates faced eastward. Likewise, the synagogues may, in some cases, have been open to the air—and here Apion's mention of *proseuchai* "open to the air" is suggestive (Josephus, *Ap.* 2.10). If so, most were probably soon covered over for practical reasons. Unlike the sacrifices offered at the Temple, the sacrifice of the lips rendered in the synagogues did not require an open setting.

CHAPTER 4
DIASPORA SYNAGOGUES

Earlier in this study we encountered a passage wherein Philo characterized the Jews in the early Roman Empire as being spread "from Egypt to the East and the nations of the East and from the Hypotaenia and Marea, which are the outskirts of Libya, to the West and the nations of the West" (*Flacc.* 45). Other quotations revealed the philosopher's belief that Jews living in these scattered regions customarily built *proseuchai*, which in turn served as their meeting centers "particularly on the sacred sabbaths when they receive as a body a training in their ancestral philosophy" (*Legat.* 155; cf. *Flacc.* 47, *Leg.* 2.61–62, *Mos.* 2.214–216).

Although we might take issue with Philo's use of Platonic language in reference to these synagogues, other evidence we have previously examined largely supports Philo's overall portrait: synagogues existed throughout the Jewish diaspora in the first century C.E., and they shared many of the same functions with their Palestinian counterparts. It is the task of the present chapter to assemble in an orderly fashion the evidence associated with diaspora synagogues in order to gain a more nuanced understanding of the variety of manifestations of this institution. However, because this evidence is quite voluminous and covers many different geographical locations, we will not adopt the course of the previous chapter and consider literary and epigraphic evidence separately from architectural data. Instead, we will survey all the media of evidence together and investigate diaspora communities region by region.

Unfortunately, since we will only be examining those locations for which synagogues are attested, several environs known to have been inhabited by Jews will be absent from our discussion. Most regrettable in this respect is the omission of the Babylonian diaspora, for although sizable Jewish communities clearly resided in Mesopotamia during the Second Temple period (e.g., Josephus, *Ant.* 18.312–313), there are neither any contemporaneous literary allusions to pre-70 C.E. synagogues there (outside of sweeping statements by Philo and others) nor any bits of archaeological evidence pointing to the existence of synagogues there prior to 70 C.E.

Another unavoidable aspect of our survey is that the quality and quantity of the relevant data vary from region to region. In this regard, we are best informed about the synagogues of Egypt, thanks not only to Philo's writings and other literary sources, but also to an abundance of inscriptions and papyri. On the other hand, we have only the testimony of Acts for synagogues in Macedonia and the entire mainland of Greece. Elsewhere, the evidence for the Bosporus Kingdom in the Crimea presents the interpreter with a different set of challenges: it consists entirely of manumission inscriptions uncovered at several sites there over the past hundred years. While these are quite fascinating, they nevertheless present tantalizingly brief glimpses of the synagogues existing in that region just after the turn of the era.

With respect to architectural remains in the diaspora, we find ourselves in a situation opposite that encountered in the previous chapter. There, we faced a small geographical area and a relatively sizable number of candidates for pre-70 synagogue remains. In this chapter, however, despite the vast range of territories to be surveyed, we will find that there are only two sites that have been identified by excavators as Second Temple synagogues—those at Delos and at Ostia—and the cogency of even these two identifications has not gone unquestioned. When we encounter these structures within our survey, we will retain the same criteria used in the previous chapter for evaluating the claims made about these architectural remains.

Before launching into our investigation, two sets of preliminary comments need to be made. The first of these regard the recent writings of Michael White, who maintains that diaspora synagogues emerged out of private household gatherings, a practice that he believes is reflected in the use of renovated houses for synagogue buildings.[1] As was noted in the introduction, White bases his conclusions primarily on an analysis of the remains of six diaspora synagogues—five of which he argues were previously domestic dwellings. Unfortunately, three of this latter group

---

[1]White consistently makes this claim in the following works: L. Michael White, "The Delos Synagogue Revisited: Recent Fieldwork in the Graeco-Roman Diaspora," *HTR* 80 (1987): 133–160; idem, *Domus Ecclesiae Domus Dei: Adaptation and Development in the Setting For Early Christian Assembly* (Ann Arbor, Mich.: University Microfilms International, 1990); idem, *Building God's House in the Roman World* (later republished as idem, *The Social Origins of Christian Architecture*, vol. 1 [Valley Forge, Pa.: Trinity Press International, 1996]); idem, *The Social Origins of Christian Architecture*, vol. 2 (Valley Forge, Pa.: Trinity Press International, 1997); Eric M. Meyers and L. Michael White, "Jews and Christians in a Roman World," *Archaeology* 42, no. 2 (1989): 26–33.

(at Priene, Dura-Europos and Stobi) date to periods beyond the parameters of this study, and so we will not be able to scrutinize White's claims regarding them.[2] However, from our investigation of the two structures that *do* fall within the purview of this study (Delos and Ostia), we will find cause to question seriously White's overall hypothesis. With respect to the structure at Delos, while we will agree with some (though not all) of his architectural analyses, we will find that these analyses invite a different interpretation than the one White offers. On the other hand, we will discover that White's claim that the lower stratum of the synagogue at Ostia was a house finds no support from the data.

Aside from these problems, it should be noted that White's study does not discuss the early evidence from Egypt, where references to such architectural features as pylons (*JIE* 24), exedras (*JIE* 28) and sacred precincts (*JIE* 9; Philo, *Flacc.* 48) stand at odds with his characterization of diaspora synagogues as renovated houses. Moreover, White does not mention the various uses of *hieron* and *hieros peribolos* in reference to the diaspora synagogues (e.g., 3 Macc 2:28; Josephus, *BJ* 7.44–45, *Ant.* 13.65–68; Philo, *Spec.* 3.171–172, *Flacc.* 48; *JIE* 9), usages which indicate that diaspora synagogues were consecrated buildings, not houses that remained in private use.

The second set of preliminary comments concerns what I believe to be a more tenable position, that of Peter Richardson. As was noted in the introduction of this study, Richardson has recently proposed that synagogues emerged in the diaspora as *collegia* or voluntary religious

---

[2]With regard to the later synagogue architecture, it should also be noted that White does not discuss the remains of several diaspora synagogues whose designs must also be taken into account. These include the synagogues at Aegina (Greece), Apamea (Syria), Naro (Tunisa), Gerasa (Jordan) and Elche (Spain). More recently, synagogue finds at Bova Marina (Italy), Plovdiv (Italy) and Chersonesus (Crimea) may make White's hypothesis difficult to sustain, even for the post-70 C.E. period (e.g., the synagogue at Chersonesus is a basilica). Moreover, it should be noted that in no case—even with the synagogue at Dura-Europos—has White demonstrated that Jews used a private house as a synagogue prior to its architectural transformation into a public building. Indeed, the transformation of such buildings suggests that their previous state was judged inadequate for use as synagogues. (On this point, see Oster, "Supposed Anachronism in Luke-Acts' Use of ΣΥΝΑΓΩΓΗ," 192–193.) For a recent, more comprehensive survey of diaspora synagogues, see Leonard Victor Rutgers, "Diaspora Synagogues: Synagogue Archaeology in the Greco-Roman World" in *Sacred Realm: The Emergence of the Synagogue in the Ancient World*, edited by Steven Fine (New York: Oxford University Press and Yeshiva University Museum, 1996), 67–95. For the synagogue at Chersonesus, see Robert S. MacLennan, "In Search of the Jewish Diaspora," *BAR* 22, no. 2 (1996): 44–51.

societies. Hence, after surveying the relevant synagogue evidence and comparing it with various aspects of the *collegia*, Richardson concludes, "the development of synagogue buildings before 70 CE cohered with [the *collegia*'s] social character and legal definition in the same period. Early synagogues . . . were collegia."[3]

While this study would tend to support Richardson's view, it would also suggest that it is in need of some refinement. We begin with his treatment of the legal definition of the synagogues—a matter that is intertwined with their social character. In dealing with this issue, Richardson draws upon the earlier work of Simeon Guterman and Mary Smallwood, who both addressed the question of the legal status of the diaspora synagogues under the Roman Republic and early Empire. Thus Richardson quotes Guterman as stating, "on the basis of Josephus's specific evidence and the general similarity in the organization of synagogues and the collegia we may feel justified in regarding the Jewish communities as *collegia licita.*"[4] What is not explicated, however, is that Guterman was referring *only* to the legal status of the synagogues in Rome and the western provinces. With respect to their legal definition, Guterman himself drew a sharp distinction between the synagogues in the western half of the empire and those in the east:

> Judaism was a *religio licita*, or authorized religion, and its synagogues *collegia licita*, or authorized associations, in the western parts of the Roman Empire, such as Italy, Spain, and Gaul, where Jews enjoyed Roman citizenship in large numbers . . . Judaism was a national cult in Palestine and a quasi-national cult in the Hellenistic cities of the East. Its position in Palestine was based on the old *faedus* or treaty with Rome and its position in the eastern Greek cities was based on the dispositions of the Hellenistic rulers, subsequently confirmed by Rome.[5]

---

[3]Richardson, "Early Synagogues as Collegia," 104.

[4]Ibid., 90, from Guterman, *Religious Toleration and Persecution in Rome*, 150. Immediately following the quote, Richardson writes, "More recently, Mary Smallwood has affirmed [Guterman's] view" (op. cit., 90).

[5]Guterman, *Religious Toleration and Persecution in Rome*, 158; transposed at ellipsis. Guterman notes that Roman law did not recognize the possession of multiple citizenships by its own citizenry. It therefore could not sanction the practice of foreign *national* rites among conclaves of Roman citizens, which would have included the Jews in Rome, who obtained citizenship in great numbers through manumission. The synagogues' classification as *collegia licita* provided a legal means whereby these Jews could retain their Roman citizenry yet still practice their *religio.* Conversely, Jewish communities in the eastern provinces were allowed to retain more of their national character and to exercise civil and criminal jurisdiction among their

If Guterman could thus distinguish between the legal status of the synagogues in the eastern and western provinces, Smallwood argues that the classification of the synagogues as *collegia* was rather artificial:

> [*Collegia*] was a convenient label, but though the synagogues resembled *collegia* superficially in holding meetings open to members only and in possessing funds, they differed radically from them in other respects: their functions were wider than those of *collegia*, since they were responsible for the organization and administration of all aspects of the life of the community and not for a single aspect, religious worship, alone; the various synagogues in a city, though separate autonomous entities, were not isolated units but jointly formed the Jewish community of that city, which was in turn part of the worldwide Jewish nation and subject to some degree, if only morally and spiritually, to the central religious authority of Jerusalem; membership was automatic for a Jew by right of birth, without question of admission or enrolment; on the other hand, membership was exclusive to Jews and proselytes, while other *collegia* were corporations with voluntary, open membership. The classification of the synagogues as *collegia* meant that their case needed special consideration when action was taken against the *collegia*.[6]

Richardson himself notes these "special considerations" of which Smallwood writes, compiling the following list of special privileges enjoyed by the diaspora synagogues, but not by other *collegia*:

> Even though a collegium was not a legal person, Jewish communities could collect the half-shekel Temple tax and send it to Jerusalem; they could also send larger voluntary gifts (an arrangement that was resented, resulting in delegations being attacked); they could collect and transmit produce as fulfillment of the requirements for tithing first-fruits . . . Other rights could be exercised individually: exemption from military service, freedom to observe the Sabbath, opportunity to adjudicate their own civil suits. Local communities of the Diaspora were able to preserve their way of life against

---

membership (ibid., 75–78, 134–135). For additional considerations of the legal question, see Jean Juster, *Les Jeufs dans l'Empire Romain: leur condition juridique, économique et sociale* (Paris: Paul Geuthner, 1914), 1.338–390, 409–485; G. La Piana, "Foreign Groups in Rome During the First Centuries of the Empire," *HTR* 20 (1927): 341–351; Alfredo Mordechai Rabello, "The Legal Condition of the Jews in the Roman Empire" in *ANRW* II.13.662–762; Wendy Cotter, "The Collegia and Roman Law: State Restrictions on Voluntary Associations, 64 BCE–200 CE" in *Voluntary Associations*, edited by John S. Kloppenborg and Steven G. Wilson (London: Routledge, 1996), 74–89.

[6]Smallwood, *The Jews under Roman Rule*, 133–134.

> the weight of opinion in many of the cities in which they settled, and they had official sanction for this preservation.[7]

In view of these extensive differences, Richardson concedes at various points in his study that "[the synagogues'] status was special," that "they were both like and unlike other *thiasoi* and collegia," and that their "privileges [went] beyond what other collegia could claim."[8] Given these repeated qualifications, as well as the above analyses and conclusions of Guterman and Smallwood, Richardson's view that the early synagogues were *collegia* appears to fit best with the situation in the western half of the empire—and even there the designation "quasi-national cult" is perhaps more appropriate.

From the vantage of this study, a second area in which Richardson's proposal needs refinement concerns a point of comparison between the *collegia* and the synagogue that is perhaps the most apt—the cultic element. Here, Richardson's analysis seems to downplay this aspect of the synagogues, even though it is one that is strongly suggested by his own comparison. Thus when it comes to citing examples of pagan *collegia* (*scholae*), he can refer to Mithraea and to the Athenian Bakcheion with its "decorated altar built for the worship of Dionysos."[9] The early synagogues, on the other hand, are characterized as "unsophisticated" liturgically, where "no feature . . . was modeled on the Jerusalem Temple, its character, divisions, or motifs."[10] Since collegial halls themselves formed "miniature temples," either containing shrines or being otherwise connected to the shrine of a patron god, a comparison between them and the synagogues might have suggested that the latter were closely associated with the shrine of the Jewish Deity in Jerusalem.[11]

Consonant with this view, whether we classify them as "*collegia* with special status" (western provinces) or "quasi-national cults" (eastern provinces), this chapter's investigation will suggest that diaspora synagogues, no less than their Palestinian counterparts, served as distant

---

[7]Richardson, "Early Synagogues as Voluntary Associations," 96.

[8]Ibid., 93, 96, 103.

[9]Ibid., 97.

[10]Ibid., 103.

[11]See Stambaugh, "The Functions of Roman Temples," 588–591; McLean, "The Place of Cult in Voluntary Associations and Christian Churches on Delos," 195. See also the treatment of the House of the Poseidoniasts in the section dealing with Delos, below. In one inscription, this entire cultic hall is referred to as a *temenos* (*ID* 1520, ll. 11–12); in another, the hall is dedicated to the patron deity (*ID* 1774).

sacred precincts, allowing worshipers to be connected to the central shrine in Jerusalem. In addition, our examination will lead to the proposal that synagogue buildings in the diaspora arose from gatherings held either outside (or on the periphery of) the cities in which they were built—or, paradoxically, near public squares. Whether these synagogues were newly built structures or structures renovated from earlier buildings, they uniformly served as public edifices rather than private dwellings. These synagogues, moreover, are routinely portrayed as buildings enclosing sacred space that could be violated by sacrilegious behavior.

Our survey will begin in the east with Egypt and Cyrenaica and then proceed northward around the rim of the Mediterranean—making one detour to the Crimea—before ending in Italy. The chapter will conclude with some final observations and conclusions on the findings uncovered in the investigation.

EGYPT

That Jews and Egyptians have had dealings with each other since the second millennium B.C.E. is well-known. In the post-exilic period, however, the earliest evidence for a Jewish settlement in Egypt comes from seven fifth-century Aramaic papyri from Elephantine, an island fortress located in the Nile River on Egypt's southern frontier (Upper Egypt).[12] The Jewish colony there may have originated as part of a military force used by Psammetichus II (594–589 B.C.E.) in his campaigns against Ethiopia.[13] Probably as a result of Nebuchadrezzar's destruction of the Jerusalem Temple in 586 B.C.E., the Jews at Elephantine erected a temple to "Yaho" wherein their coterie of priests offered not only incense, meal-offerings and drink-offerings but also animal sacrifices. A letter dated 407 B.C.E. describes the destruction of the Elephantine temple three years earlier by a force of Egyptians. The temple was never rebuilt, and the colony was probably dissolved in the early fourth century B.C.E.[14]

Although Jewish refugees probably fled to Egypt after the Babylonian conquest of Palestine (Jer 42:14–22), the first great influx of Jews to this country does not appear to have occurred until the wars of Ptolemy I against the rival Diadochi (320–301 B.C.E.). Invading Palestine four times in those wars, Ptolemy I is said to have "removed from the land of the

---

[12] See *ANET* 491–492. Four ostraca also exist from this site.

[13] So *Ep. Arist.* 13.

[14] Smallwood, *The Jews under Roman Rule*, 220.

Jews into Egypt up to one hundred thousand people, from whom he armed about thirty thousand chosen men and settled them through the land in the forts" (*Ep. Arist.* 12–13). While Aristeas' numbers are likely exaggerated, various papyri, inscriptions and ostraca from the third century B.C.E. nonetheless testify to the presence of substantial Jewish populations in all parts of Egypt.[15]

In the following century, with the Seleucid kings of Syria in control of Palestine, Jews continued to emigrate to Egypt, particularly during the persecutions of Antiochus IV. One of the more prominent of the emigrants was Onias IV, whose father, Onias III, had been deposed from the high priesthood in Jerusalem by his brother Jason I in 174 B.C.E. (2 Macc 4:7).[16] Josephus states that, upon his arrival in Egypt, Onias wrote the following letter to the Ptolemy VI (185–145 B.C.E.), requesting to build a new temple in the nome of Heliopolis:[17]

> Many and great are the services which I have rendered you in the course of the war, with the help of God, when I was in Coele-Syria and Phoenicia, and when I came with the Jews to Leontopolis in the nome of Heliopolis and to other places where our nation is settled; and I found that most of them have *hiera*, contrary to what is proper, and that for this reason they are ill-disposed toward one another, as is also the case with the Egyptians because of the multitude of their *hiera* and their varying opinions about the forms of worship; and I have found a most suitable place [τόπου] in the fortress called after Bubastis-of-the-Fields, which abounds in various kinds of trees and is full of sacred animals, wherefore I beg you to permit me to cleanse this *hieron*, which belongs to no one and is in ruins, and to build a *naos* to the Most High God in the likeness of that at Jerusalem and with the same dimensions, on behalf of you and your wife and children, in order that the Jewish inhabitants of Egypt may be able to come together there in mutual harmony and serve your interests. For this indeed is what the prophet Isaiah foretold, "There shall be an altar in Egypt to the Lord God," and many other such things did he prophesy concerning this place (*Ant.* 13.65–68).

While the letter itself was probably not written by Onias, but by a Jew devoted to the Temple of Leontopolis, it is nevertheless instructive for

---

[15]Avigdor Tcherikover, "Prolegomena" in *CPJ* 1.2–4.

[16]In *BJ* 7.423, Josephus attributes the building of the temple at Leontopolis to Onias III. However, it was probably Onias IV who erected this temple. See *HJP* 3.1.145, n. 33.

[17]For a general discussion of the temple of Onias, see Hayward, "The Jewish Temple at Leontopolis," 429–443; M. Delcor, "Le Temple d'Onias en Égypte," *RB* 75 (1968): 188–203.

contrasting Onias' temple with the Egyptian synagogues.[18] As we see, the text alludes to Jewish *hiera* scattered about the area of Heliopolis—almost certainly a reference to the Jewish *proseuchai* in this region attested by inscriptions and papyri (see below).[19] "Onias" objects to these *hiera*, not so much for their existence but because their congregations, like those of Egyptian temples, followed different forms of worship. Hoping to impose some uniformity on this situation, he petitions the ruler to cleanse a ruined pagan temple (*hieron*) and to build a temple shrine (*naos*) on the site. It is not clear whether the author of the above letter wished the new temple to displace the other *hiera* or simply to serve as the central sanctuary for them. In either case, that the envisioned temple at Leontopolis differed from the earlier Jewish *hiera* can be seen not only in the petition to build a *naos* like the one in Jerusalem, but also in the reference to the Isaiah passage (Isa 19:19) which alludes to the future erection of an altar (θυσιαστήριον/מִזְבֵּחַ) in Egypt. Despite these differences, the use of the term *hieron* in referring to both types of structures is nonetheless striking and suggests that the synagogues were essentially sacred precincts without shrines or altars.

Josephus goes on to quote a second letter, purportedly written by the king and queen, granting permission for the temple's construction, which was accomplished shortly thereafter (*Ant.* 13.70–71). Although Onias' temple existed until 74 C.E., when it was demolished by the Romans (*BJ* 7.436), it apparently did not gain the following that the author of the above letter had hoped for: not one mention of it is made in the writings of Philo or of any other Egyptian Jew.[20] On the contrary, these authors uniformly express their unflagging devotion to the Temple in Jerusalem. In view of this, Tcherikover was able to write: "We may consider the building of the temple of Onias not as a demonstration by Egyptian Jewry of feelings inimical to Jerusalem but as an act of an adventurer."[21]

---

[18]So Dion, "Synagogues et temples dans l'Égypte hellénistique," 50. See also Delcor, "Le Temple d'Onias en Égypte," 192–195.

[19]So also Dion, "Synagogues et temples dans l'Égypte hellénistique," 50–51; Hengel, "Proseuche und Synagoge," 158–159; Krauss, *Synagogale Altertümer*, 24.

[20]Gideon Bohak's recent argument that *Joseph and Aseneth* was written as an apology for Onias' temple, while interesting, fails to convince. See Gideon Bohak, *Joseph and Aseneth and the Jewish Temple in Heliopolis* (Atlanta: Scholars Press, 1996).

[21]Tcherikover, "Prolegomena," 45–46. See also Smallwood, *The Jews under Roman Rule*," 367–368; *HJP* 3.1.145–147. Cf. Peter Richardson and Valerie Heuchan, "Jewish Voluntary Associations in Egypt and the Roles of Women" in *Voluntary*

Although the origin of "Onias' letter" is obscure, its representation of synagogues as being in existence in Egypt prior to the construction of the temple at Leontopolis (c. 164 B.C.E.) is confirmed by epigraphic and papyrological sources. In the following sections we will survey this evidence, which is currently available only for Middle and Lower Egypt.

Middle Egypt

In chapter two we noted early synagogal evidence for Middle Egypt in a third-century dedicatory inscription from Arsinoë-Crocodilopolis (*JIE* 117), the metropolis of the Fayum district in the northwestern part of this region.[22] The same *proseuchē* mentioned in that inscription might also be referred to in the following land survey that dates to early in the first century B.C.E. (*CPJ* 1.134):

Col. II

[Βο(ρρᾶ) ἐχο(μένης) Ἑρμι]όνηι Ἀπολλωνίδου ἱερᾶς πραρ(δείσου),
(ὧν) ὑποδο(χείου) (τέταρτον), περιστε(ρῶν), περιστε(ρῶνος) ἐρή(μου) λʹ βʹ,
χέ(ρσου) εή. γεί(τονες) νό(του) Δημητρίου Θρα̣(κός) χέ(ρσος), Βο(ρρᾶ)
προσευ(χή), λι(βός) περίστασις πό(εως), ἀπη(λιώτου) ʼαργα(ίτιδος) διῶρυ(ξ).
Βο(ρρᾶ) [ἐ]χ[ο(μένης)] προσευχῆς Ἰουδαίων διὰ Π̣ε̣ρτ̣όλλου
διὰ μι(σθωτοῦ) Πετεσούχου τοῦ Μαρρήους
ἱερᾶς παρα(δείσου) γ (ἥμισυ) (τέταρτον) ιʹ ςʹ, [σ]τεφά(νοις) καὶ λαχά(νοις) α (ἥμισυ)
γεί(τονες νό(του) Ἑρμιόνης τῆς ʼαπολλωνίδου, Βο(ρρᾶ) καὶ λι(βος)
περίστασις τῆς πό(λεως), ἀπη(λιώτου) ʼαργα(ίτιδος) διῶρυ(ξ).
Βο(ρρᾶ) ἐχο(μένη) [ε]ἰσβαί(νουσα) λι(βός) παρὰ τὴν πό(λιν) σχοι(νίου) δ
(ἥμισυ)
Σαραπίων ὁ παρὰ τῆς βα(σιλίσσης) Ἱερὰ α, (ὧν) οἰκιῶν

Associations, edited by John S. Kloppenborg and Steven G. Wilson (London: Routledge, 1996), 226–239. Flinders Petrie claimed to have discovered the foundations of Onias' temple. A review of his findings and arguments suggests to me that researchers should not be so dismissive of his claims. See W. M. Flinders Petrie, *Hyksos and Israelite Cities* (London: School of Archaeology, 1906), 19–27, pls. XXII–XXVII; idem, *Egypt and Israel* (London: Society for Promoting Christian Knowledge, 1911), 97–110.

[22]For more a more detailed survey of the Jewish presence in Arsinoë-Crocodilopolis, see Aryeh Kasher, *The Jews in Hellenistic and Roman Egypt: The Struggle for Equal Rights*, rev. English ed. (Tübingen: J.C.B. Mohr, 1985), 138–144.

ἐρή(μων) (ἥμισυ) ἐρή(μου) (ἥμισυ). [[. . . . .]]
ιη.

Col. III

β . . . [. . .] . α . [- - -]
γεί(τονες) νό(του) προσευχῆς Ἰουδαίων, βο(ρρᾶ) [καὶ λι(βὸς) περίστα(σις)] πόλεως,
ἀπη(λιώτου) ’αργαίτιδος διῶρυ(ξ).
ἕως περιστάσεως πό(λεως) βο(ρρᾶ).

Col. II

Situated to the north, a consecrated garden the property of Hermione daughter of Apollonides (5 13/32 arourai). Of these a quarter (of an aroura) occupied by a storehouse, 1/32 by an empty dovecote, and 5⅛ are waste land. Neighbours: to the south, waste land belonging to Demetrios the Thracian; to the north, a *proseuchē*; to the west the city boundary; to the east the canal of Argaitis. Situated to the north, a Jewish *proseuchē* represented by Pertollos, and a consecrated garden cultivated by a tenant, Petesouchos son of Marres, of 3 13/16 arourai and 1½ arourai planted with flowers and vegetables. Neighbors: to the south Hermione daughter of Apollonides; to the north and west the city boundary; to the east the canal of Argaitis. Situated to the north, and narrowing the west outside the city for 4½ schoinia, Sarapion, who holds from the Queen 1 aroura of sacred land, of which half is occupied by empty houses, and half is unoccupied.

Col. III

. . . Neighbors: to the south the Jewish *proseuchē*; to the north and west the city boundary; to the east the canal of Argaitis. Northwards as far as the city boundary . . .[23]

From the above survey we know that the *proseuchē* was located on the outskirts of Arsinoë, just east and south of the city boundaries and west of the canal of Argaitis (l. 17). The members of the *proseuchē*, represented by a certain Pertollos, leased out a consecrated garden (l. 20, ἱερᾶς παραδείσου) to a tenant, Petesouchos, who may or may not have been a Jew. The plots to the north (the land of Sarapion) and to the south (the land of Hermione) were also classified as sacred lands. The fact that the site was located next to a canal suggests that it was chosen because of

[23]Translation from *CPJ*. The term *proseuchē* has been substituted for "synagogue."

the access it provided to a body of water appropriate for ritual cleansings.[24]

The property occupied by the *proseuchē* was quite capacious: its area, given as 3 13/16 arourai, is equal to about 10,427 square meters or just over two-and-a-half acres. Similarly, the sacred garden leased by the members of the *proseuchē*, recorded as 1½ arourai, is about 4,102 square meters or a little over an acre of land. The size of these properties and the monumental nature of the inscription attached to the *proseuchē* (if it is indeed the same as the one mentioned in *JIE* 117) make it difficult to speak of this structure as a renovated house.[25]

The only other synagogue for which we have early evidence in Middle Egypt is located in the village of Alexandrou-Nesos, also in the Fayum district. The evidence consists of a petition (*CPJ* 1.129), dated 218 B.C.E. and addressed to Ptolemy IV (221–204 B.C.E.):

> [Βασιλεῖ Πτολεμαίωι χαίρειν τῶ]ν ἐν τῆι Ἀλεξάνδρου νήσωι. ἀδικοῦμαι ὑπὸ
> [Δωροθέου Ἰουδαίου κατοικοῦντος τὴν [[α]ὐτὴν]] κώμην. τοῦ γάρ ϵ (ἔτους), ὡς αἱ πρόσοδοι, Φαμενὼ[θ]
> [ὁ Δωρόθεος μου σὺν] τῆι συνερίθωι μου, προσνοήσας ἱμάτιόν μου
> [ἄξιον (δραχμὰς)] αὐτὸ ὤιχετο ἔχων. αἰσθομένης δέ μου κατε[- - -]
> [- - - τὸ ἱμ]άτιον ἐν τῆι προσευχῆι τῶν Ἰουδαίων ἐπιλα-
> [- - -]ωπους. ἐπιπαραγίνετα[ι] δὲ Λήζελμις (ἑκατοντάρουρος)
> [- - - τὸ ἱμά]ιον Νικομάχωι τῶι νακόρωι ἕως κρίσεως
> [- - -] δέομαι οὖν σου, βασιλεῦ, προστάξαι Διοφάνει
> [τῶι στρατηγῶι γράψαι τῶι ἐπι]στάτει ἀποστεῖλαι τὸν Δωρόθεον καὶ Νι-
> [κόμαχον - - - ἱμ]άτιον ἐπ᾽ αὐτὸν καί, ἐὰν ἦι ἅ γράφω ἀληθῆ,
> [ἐπαναγκάσαι αὐτὸν ἀποδοῦναι μοι τὸ ἱμ]άτιον ἢ τὴν τιμήν, περὶ δὲ τῆς ῥαιδιουργίας

---

[24]Although it is beyond the confines of this study, it is worth noting a papyrus dating from 113 C.E. (*CPJ* 2.432) that mentions two synagogues at Arsinoë-Crocodilopolis, one called a *proseuchē* and the other a *eucheion*. Each building is taxed nearly twice as much for monthly water consumption than a nearby bath establishment.

[25]For the sake of comparison, we note that ll. 25–26 state that immediately to the north of the *proseuchē* was an estate measuring one aroura (about two-thirds of an acre), of which half was empty and half was filled with vacant houses (plural). Thus the plot occupied by the *proseuchē* took up a space more than seven times larger than that filled by these houses. While the *proseuchē* proper may not have taken up the entire two-and-a-half acres, because the surveyor was meticulous about noting ancillary buildings (as with the dovecote in l. 15) and waste land (e.g., ll. 15, 16), we can be fairly certain that only the *proseuchē* was located on this land, and that its complex filled the entire area mentioned in the survey.

[- - - τούτου γὰρ γενομένου, ἔσομα[ι] διὰ σέ, βασιλε[ῦ],
[τοῦ δικαίου τετευχυῖα]. εὐτ[ύ]χει

To King Ptolemy, greeting from . . . who lives in Alexandrou Nesos. I have been wronged by Dorotheos, (a Jew who lives in the) same village. In the 5th year, according to the financial calendar, on Phamenoth . . . (as I was talking to) my workmate, my cloak (which is worth . . . drachmai) caught Dorotheos' eye, and he made off with it. When I saw him (he fled) to the Jewish *proseuchē* (holding) the cloak, (while I called for help). Lezelmis, a holder of 100 arourai, came up to help (and gave) the cloak to Nikomachos the (*proseuchē*) verger to keep till the case was tried. Therefore I beg you, my king, to command Diophanes the strategos (to write to the) epistates telling him to order Dorotheos and Nikomachos to hand over the cloak to him, and, if what I write is true (to make him give me the) cloak or its value; as for the injury . . . If this happens, I shall have received justice through you, my king. Farewell.[26]

In the incident described above, an unnamed woman had her cloak stolen by a certain Dorotheos. When Dorotheos was caught in the act, he made off to the *proseuchē*, with the woman in hot pursuit. Following the intervention of Lezelmis, the cloak was deposited with Nikomachos, the attendant of the *proseuchē*, until the matter could be officially resolved.

Several things are of interest in this papyrus, not the least of which that a synagogue could exist in an Egyptian *village* at such an early date. Beyond this is the mention of the synagogue *nakoros* (l. 7, Doric for *neōkoros*), translated "verger" above. While we will have more to say about the office signified by this word in the next chapter, here we note that, in the Greek world, this term normally meant the "warden of a temple"—whether used of a person, or beginning in the Early Roman period, of a city. Indeed, whenever this word appears in the writings of Josephus and Philo, it is used exclusively in reference to the guardians of the Jerusalem Temple (e.g., *BJ* 1.153; *Legat*. 1.156, 2.120, *Mos*. 2.276). That this same title could be used for one of the officers of an Egyptian *proseuchē* further suggests the "temple-like" qualities of this institution in Egypt.[27]

A final, related point is that, upon being caught in an illegal act, Dorotheos immediately fled to the *proseuchē*. This implies that the *proseuchē* was invested with the right of asylum. In chapter six, we will

---

[26]The translation from *CPJ* has been modified by replacing "synagogue" with "*proseuchē*."

[27]See Kasher, *The Jews in Hellenistic and Roman Egypt*, 147; Dion, "Synagogues et temples dans l'Égypte hellénistique," 65–74.

examine more closely an inscription from the first century B.C.E. (*JIE* 125) that further demonstrates that this right was granted to the synagogues in Egypt. Because the right of asylum was given only to temples, it would seem that in Egypt, the synagogues were essentially recognized by the Ptolemaic rulers as "Jewish temples."[28]

Lower Egypt Excluding Alexandria

Moving northward into Lower Egypt, our survey leads us to note the presence of synagogue inscriptions recovered from several scattered cities. The oldest of these monuments (*JIE* 22 = *CIJ* 2.1440) is from Schedia, a city located about twelve miles east of Alexandria on the Canopic Branch of the Nile:[29]

ὑπὲρ βασιλέως	On behalf of king
Πτολεμαίου καὶ	Ptolemy and
βασιλίσσης	queen Berenice his sister
Βερενίκης ἀδελ-	and wife and
φῆς καὶ γυναικὸς καὶ	their children,
τῶν τέκνων	the Jews (dedicated)
τὴν προσευχὴν	the *proseuchē*
οἱ Ἰουδαῖοι	

This inscription, like the nearly identical one from Arsinoë-Crocodilopolis (*JIE* 117), dedicates the founding of a synagogue on behalf of Ptolemy III Euergetes, who married Berenice II in 246 B.C.E. The mention of the children in line 6 indicates that the building was constructed sometime after this but before Euergetes' death in 221 B.C.E. Although the inscription does not provide us with specific information about the Jewish community in Schedia, beyond the fact that it was large enough in the third century to erect a public structure, attention should be called to the practice of dedicating the synagogues on behalf of the ruling monarchs, seen in this and many of the other inscriptions we shall encounter in this chapter. Here, Paul Fraser observes the close correspondence between these inscriptions and those of pagan temples: "in most instances the dedication is indistinguishable from a pagan equivalent save for the substitution of the term 'synagogue' for 'the

---

[28]See Kasher, "Synagogues as 'Houses of Prayer' and 'Holy Places' in the Jewish Communities of Hellenistic and Roman Egypt," 215–216.

[29]This translation, as with all other translations of Egyptian synagogue inscriptions in this chapter, is taken from *JIE*.

shrine' or 'the temple,' and by the name or names of the dedicating party."[30] This should not be taken to mean that the synagogues were in any way syncretistic. As Fraser also points out, the opening formula "on behalf of" (ὑπέρ), used in both Jewish and pagan inscriptions, avoided assignment of divinity to the rulers, while at the same time associating them with the worship taking place inside the sanctuary. It was this same principle that allowed Jews to offer sacrifices "on behalf of" the various Hellenistic and Roman sovereigns in the Temple at Jerusalem (e.g., Josephus, *BJ* 2.197; Philo, *Legat.* 356; 2 Macc 3:31–34). Along these lines, during the period when Gaius was demanding to be worshiped as a god, when informed by Philo and his embassy that the Alexandrian Jews had thrice offered sacrifice in Jerusalem on his behalf, Gaius replied, "All right . . . it is true, you have sacrificed, but to another, even if it was for me; what good is it then? For you have not sacrificed to me" (*Legat.* 357). It was this distinction, so adroitly recognized by Gaius, that allowed Jews to retain their monotheistic practices while at the same time honoring the ruling monarchs. That the Jews in Egypt walked this fine line is further seen in some comments by Philo, who, on the one hand, writes of the presence of "shields and gilded crowns and the slabs and inscriptions" for the emperors in the *proseuchai* (*Legat.* 133), but on the other, states:

> In three hundred years there was a succession of some ten or more [kings of Egypt], and none of them had any images or statues set up for them in our *proseuchai* by the Alexandrians, although they were of the same race and kin as the people and were acknowledged, written and spoken of by them as gods. It was only natural that they who at any rate were men should be so regarded by those who deified dogs and wolves and lions and crocodiles and many other wild animals on the land, in the water and the air, for whom altars and temples and shrines and sacred precincts have been established through the whole of Egypt (*Legat.* 138–139).

Although written apologetically, the above statement is probably for the most part true—at least evidence has not been found to the contrary. Thus while Jews in Egypt were willing—indeed, quite eager—to heap honors upon the rulers inside their synagogues, they expressed outrage when, for

---

[30]Fraser, *Ptolemaic Alexandria*, 1.283. Cf., e.g., *OGIS* 64, 65, 91, 92; *SB* 429, 1436, 1567, 1570, 4206. See Dion, "Synagogues et temples dans l'Égypte hellénistique," 55–57.

example, statues of these same rulers were introduced into their sanctuaries by Greek mobs (*Legat.* 134–137).

Another early inscription from Egypt comes from the city of Xenephyris, located upstream from Schedia on the Canopic Branch of the Nile, about thirty-five miles southeast of Alexandria:[31]

ὑπὲρ βασιλέως Πτολεμαίου καὶ βασιλίσσης Κλεοπάτρας τῆς ἀδελφῆς καὶ βασιλίσσης Κλε-οπάτρας τῆς γυναικός, οἱ ἀπὸ Ξενεφύρεος Ἰουδαῖοι τὸν πυλῶνα τῆς προσευχῆς, προστάντων Θεοδώρου καὶ Ἀχιλλίωνος	On behalf of king Ptolemy and queen Cleopatra the sister and queen Cleopatra the wife, the Jews of Xenephyris (dedicated) the gateway of the *proseuchē* when Theodore and Achillion were presiding (*JIE* 24 = *CIJ* 2.1441)

The inscription dates to the later reign of Ptolemy VIII Euergetes II, who married his niece, Cleopatra III, in c. 140 B.C.E., and his brother's widow, Cleopatra II, in c. 124. He died in 116 B.C.E., leaving behind both wives. While the inscription is thus later than the one from Schedia, it supplies us with more information than the previous example. As we see, the dedication is not of the *proseuchē* itself, but of the pylon attached to the *proseuchē*. Fraser comments that this term, when used in an Egyptian context, "invariably refers to the pylon of an Egyptian-style temple."[32] Such structures were essentially gate-houses built at the entryways of sacred precincts that were enclosed by a surrounding wall, often made out of stone.[33] Thus the Jewish compound at Xenephyris likely consisted of

---

[31]For a more detailed examination of the Jewish community at Xenephyris, see Kasher, *The Jews in Hellenistic and Roman Egypt*, 111–114.

[32]Fraser, *Ptolemaic Alexandria*, 2.443, n. 773. For an example of a dedication of a pylon to a temple of Sarapion and Isis, see *OGIS* 677. See also Dion, "Synagogues et temples dans l'Égypte hellénistique," 61–62. Of Josephus' fifteen uses of this word, nine refer to one of the gates of the Temple (*BJ* 1.617, 4.191, 4.205, 5.202, 6.150; *Ant.* 10.225, 11.108, 15.418, 17.151, 18.29), three to the gates of the Tabernacle (*Ant.* 3.111–112), two to the "sacred" gates of Babylon (*Ant.* 10.225; *Ap.* 1.140) and one to the gates of Herod's court (*BJ* 1.617). The LXX similarly uses πυλών most often when referring to the gates of the Temple (e.g., 1 Kgs 6:33; 1 Chr 9:23, 26; 2 Chr 3:7; Ezek 40:9, 11, 18; 1 Esdr 7:9).

[33]See Kasher, "Synagogues as 'Houses of Prayer' and 'Holy Places' in the Jewish Communities of Hellenistic and Roman Egypt," 216; Griffiths, "Egypt and the Synagogue," 11–12.

such a sacred precinct marked off by a perimeter wall and approached through a pylon.[34] The *proseuchē* proper would have been a building located somewhere in the midst of this precinct.

Mention above is made of two *prostatai* or presiding officers of the synagogue. While we will further explore the meaning of this term in the next chapter, here we note that the use of this word further indicates a high degree of institutionalization in the Egyptian synagogues. Given the monumental nature of the synagogue buildings attested throughout Egypt, this level of formalization should come as little surprise.

Continuing in our survey, earlier in this century, two inscriptions were discovered at Athribis, the metropolis of the Athribic nome, located on the Damietta Branch of the Nile about thirty miles north of modern Cairo. Both inscriptions date to the late second or early first century B.C.E.:

ὑπὲρ βασιλέως Πτολεμαίου καὶ βασιλίσσης Κλεοπάτρας, Πτολεμαῖος Ἐπικύδου, ὁ ἐπιστάτης τῶν πυλακιτῶν, καὶ οἱ ἐν Ἀθρίβει Ἰουδαῖοι, τὴν προσευχὴν θεῶι ὑψίστωι	On behalf of king Ptolemy and queen Cleopatra, Ptolemy son of Epikydes, chief of police, and the Jews in Athribis (dedicated) the *proseuchē* to the Most High God (*JIE* 27 = *CIJ* 2.1443)

ὑπὲρ βασιλέως Πτολεμαίου καὶ βασιλίσσης Κλεοπάτρας καὶ τῶν τέκνων Ἑρμίας καὶ Φιλοτέρα ἡ γυνὴ καὶ τὰ παιδία τήνδε ἐξέδραν τῆι προσευχῆ<ι>	On behalf of king Ptolemy and queen Cleopatra and their children, Hermias and his wife Philotera and their children (gave) this exedra to the *proseuchē* (*JIE* 28 = *CIJ* 2.1444)

The first of the inscriptions is the dedication of the actual *proseuchē*, which is offered to the "Most High God," a common designation for God among diaspora Jews (e.g., Philo, *Legat.* 278; 3 Macc 7:9). There has been some debate over the ethnicity of Ptolemy the police chief (*epistatēs*), with earlier researchers arguing that he was a Gentile.[35] This conclusion was based on the fact that an *epistatēs* was second only to the *stratēgos* in police matters for an entire nome—a position thought to be

---

[34]Cf. Philo's use of *hieros peribolos* in connection with the synagogues (*Flacc.* 51), an expression also seen in an inscription examined in chapter two, above (*JIE* 9).

[35]Tcherikover, *Prolegomena*, 17; *HJP* 3.1.49.

too high ranking to be occupied by a Jew. Kasher, however, has rightly observed that there is no reason to dismiss this latter possibility, particularly in view of other evidence attesting to a Jewish military settlement in the vicinity.[36] On the other hand, it is also possible that Ptolemy was a Gentile patron of the Jews or even a God-fearer. The question must therefore continue to hang in the balance.

The second inscription is a private dedication, naming a particular family who contributed an exedra to the *proseuchē*. While the term *exedra* covered a wide range of meanings, when associated with a public building, it frequently meant an annex set aside for philosophical debate and the discussion of communal matters. Alternatively, it could signify a chamber used by sacristans in temples, as was the case with the Serapeum in Alexandria.[37] Along these lines, in the LXX, this term appears exclusively in the rendering of Ezekiel's description of various priestly chambers (לִשְׁכָּה) in the Temple courts (Ezek 40:44, 45, 46; 42:1, 7, 10, 13; 44:19; 46:19, 23). Some of these chambers served as places where the priests stored their garments (Ezek 44:19), while others were dining rooms where they ate the sacrificial offerings (Ezek 42:13).[38] Although it is unlikely that the exedra in the *proseuchē* of Athribis served only a priestly population, the similarity in terminology may not be coincidental. Some parallel in function might therefore be inferred, with the exedra at Athribis functioning as a dining facility or a place where a *neōkoros* kept the sacred articles of the *proseuchē*. However, in view of Philo's emphasis on the educational aspect of the Egyptian *proseuchai* (e.g., *Legat.* 156), it is perhaps more likely that the exedra served as an ancillary study chamber.

Outside of Alexandria, the remaining place for which we have epigraphic evidence for the presence of a *proseuchē* is Nitriai, which is probably to be equated with el-Barnugi on the southern side of Lake

---

[36] Kasher, *The Jews in Hellenistic and Roman Egypt*, 118–119.

[37] On the range of meanings for *exedra*, see *JIE* pp. 49–50; Kasher, *The Jews in Hellenistic and Roman Egypt*, 116–117.

[38] Of Josephus' seven uses of ἐξέδρα (none of which are taken from Ezekiel), five are in reference to chambers in the Temple courts (*BJ* 5.38, 5.203, 6.150, 6.220, *Ant.* 20.191), one refers to Solomon's judgment hall (*Ant.* 8.134; cf. 1 Kgs 7:2) and one is used to describe "halls" Herod gave as gifts to foreign cities (*BJ* 1.422).

Mareotis.[39] The synagogue inscription (*JIE* 25 = *CIJ* 2.1442), similar in form to the ones previously considered, runs as follows:

ὑπὲρ βασιλέως Πτολεμαίου	On behalf of king Ptolemy
καὶ βασιλίσσης Κλεοπάτρας	and queen Cleopatra
τῆς ἀδελφῆς καὶ βασιλίσσης	the sister and queen
Κλεοπάτρας τῆς γυναικὸς	Cleopatra the wife,
Εὐεργετῶν, οἱ ἐν Νιτρίαις	Benefactors, the Jews in Nitriai
Ἰουδαῖοι τὴν προσευχὴν	(dedicated) the *proseuchē*
καὶ τὰ συνκύροντα	and its appurtenances

For the same reasons as those given for the Xenephyris inscription (*JIE* 24), the above monument dates to the later reign of Ptolemy VIII Euergetes II (d. 116 B.C.E.). The term "benefactor" (l. 5, Εὐεργετῶν) is, of course, an honorific rather than a reference to a specific benefaction. Significantly, however, the above inscription does not follow the pattern of similar monuments from pagan temples which use the phrase "divine benefactor" (θεῶν Εὐεργετῶν; e.g., *OGIS* 64, 65). On the other hand, the non-Jewish inscriptions in which the word "appurtenances" appears (l. 7, συνκύροντα) are uniformly dedications of pagan temples. One monument, for example, mentions "the temple shrine, the sacred area, the attached storage chambers and all the appurtenances [τὸν ναὸν καὶ τὸ ἱερὸν καὶ τα προσόντα αὐτῷ ταμεῖα καὶ τὰ συνκύροντα πάντα]" (*OGIS* 92; cf. 52, 182). The same word also appears in the inscription from Alexandria that mentions the "sacred precincts" of a *proseuchē* dedicated to the Most High God (*JIE* 9), presented in chapter two. Typically, the term refers to structures such as exedras and pylons, encountered in some of the previously quoted synagogue monuments. It may also indicate pieces of furniture or sacred vessels.

Before turning our attention to Alexandria, mention should be made of 3 Maccabees' allusion to a synagogue (*proseuchē*) supposedly erected in Ptolemais, located in the Arsinoite nome (3 Macc 7:20). From the narrative of 3 Maccabees, we recall that after their deliverance from Ptolemy IV Philopater's wrath, the Jews in Egypt executed the apostates

[39]So *JIE* (p. 43). Kasher prefers the identification of Wadi Natrun on the northeast edge of the Great Libyan Desert, roughly seventy-five miles southeast of Alexandria (*The Jews in Hellenistic and Roman Egypt*, 114–116). Another inscription of uncertain reading may point to the existence of a *proseuchē* at Leontopolis: ". . . the *proseuchē* (?) . . . to God the Highest . . . [[- - -][- - τὴν] π̣ροσε̣[υχὴν - -][- - θε]ῶι ὑψίσ[τωι - -]]" (*JIE* 105). On the other hand, *proseuchē* may here refer to "prayer."

among them. Following this, a number of the Jews sailed to Ptolemais whereupon:

> they celebrated their deliverance, for the king had generously provided all things to them for their journey until all of them arrived at their own houses. And when they had all landed in peace with appropriate thanksgiving, there too in like manner they decided to observe these days as a joyous festival during the time of their stay. Then, after inscribing them as holy on a pillar and dedicating a *proseuchē* at the site of the festival, they departed unharmed, free, and overjoyed, since at the king's command they had all of them been brought safely by land and sea and river to their own homes (3 Macc 7:18–20).

Despite the above attestation, not much historical value should be attached to the narrative's reference to the erection of a particular synagogue during the third century B.C.E. As it stands, none of the specific "events" mentioned in this document have any basis in reality. Nevertheless, the document's association of merry-making with a synagogue's erection may be characteristic of an actual pattern of activity in Ptolemaic Egypt—just as the mention of dedicatory pillars at synagogues clearly reflects the customs of that period and provenance.[40] If so, it is striking that such festival activities are customarily associated with the founding of pagan temples or other sacred areas (e.g., Plutarch, *Praec. Rei Publ. Ger.* 816C; Cicero, *Ad Fam.* 7.1).

Alexandria

We now turn in our survey to Alexandria, the most populous and important city in Egypt. Traditionally held to have been founded in 331 B.C.E. by Alexander the Great, Alexandria was the capital of Ptolemaic Egypt and went on to become one of the largest cities in the Roman Empire, with an estimated population of 300,000–800,000 in the first century C.E.[41] The Jewish presence in this city was considerable from

---

[40]Regarding the use of *proseuchē* as a term for the synagogue in this passage, see Hengel, "Proseuche and Synagoge," 163–164; Krauss, *Synagogale Altertümer*, 16; Greeven, "Προσευχή," 808. Note that the Greek word καθεδρύω, which underlies the translation, "dedicating," also carries the sense of "establish" or "found" (LSJ, s.v.). Cf. 2 Macc 4:12 where the term refers to the erection/dedication of a gymnasium in Jerusalem.

[41]See Fraser, *Ptolemaic Alexandria*, 90–92. Polybius presents a figure of 300,000 free persons in Alexandria in 60 B.C.E. Fraser suspects that the total population may

nearly the time of its founding. Indeed, by the first century B.C.E., Jews occupied most of the district known as the Delta, which was located in the northeast section of the city, adjacent to the Mediterranean coastline (Strabo, 794; Josephus, *Ap.* 2.33–35). In the following century, Philo mentions that the Jews inhabited the bulk of yet a second district, with still other Jews living in the remaining three sectors of Alexandria (*Flacc.* 55).[42]

At some point during the Ptolemaic period (c. II B.C.E.), Jews in Alexandria were allowed to form a politeuma, essentially an independent "city within a city" (*Ep. Arist.* 310; Josephus, *Ant.* 12.108). The politeuma was initially led by council of elders usually referred to as a *gerousia.* Somewhat later, a single official known as an ethnarch ("ruler of a people") took control of the community affairs (Strabo ap. Josephus, *Ant.* 14.117). In 10 C.E., however, Augustus dissolved this office and reconstituted the *gerousia*, which probably at this time numbered seventy or seventy-one persons (cf. Philo, *Flacc.* 74). The Alexandrian Jews had their own constitution, archives and popular assembly, and were able to administer legal affairs within their community as they saw fit (Josephus, *BJ* 7.412; *CPJ* 2.153). Some of the privileges of the politeuma included the right to refrain from worshiping the gods of the city, the right not to appear in court on the Sabbath or on other sacred days, and the right to send donations to the Temple in Jerusalem. As we shall see, these rights prevailed throughout most of the diaspora as early as the first century B.C.E.—owing largely to the liberal policy of the Romans in such matters and to the influence of the Herodians. What separated a formalized politeuma from Jewish communities not possessing such a charter is the high degree of internal autonomy enjoyed by the former. For example, if a civil or even criminal case involved only parties who were Jewish, it usually did not have to be brought before the royal or provincial courts, but could be settled within the legal system of the politeuma.[43]

It is unknown in what ways the synagogues served as administrative buildings for the Jewish politeuma in Alexandria. However, because the synagogues are the only public buildings in the city mentioned as the targets of later anti-Jewish attacks (see below), it is reasonable to infer

---

have approached one million, making Alexandria the rival of Rome.

[42]For more detailed treatments of the Jewish presence in Alexandria, see Fraser, *Ptolemaic Alexandria*, 1.54–58; Smallwood, *The Jews under Roman Rule*, 224–255; Kasher, *The Jews in Hellenistic and Roman Egypt*, 168–357.

[43]See Smallwood, *The Jews under Roman Rule*, 224–230.

that these structures served as centers not only for religious activities, but also for community affairs in general. This hypothesis gains further credence when we recall the discussion from the previous chapter about the interconnectedness of religion and politics in ancient Judaism. Philo's mention of a synagogue in Alexandria that was larger and more imposing than the rest (*Legat.* 134) also suggests that this synagogue may have served as the seat of the *gerousia*. Even if this was the case, however, the exact nature of the relationships maintained between the synagogues in Alexandria—and vis-à-vis those in the other Egyptian cities—remains obscure.

The early epigraphic record from Alexandria consists of two inscriptions, one of which we encountered in chapter two (*JIE* 9, II B.C.E.) and have mentioned several times in this chapter in our discussion of sacred precincts. The other monument (*JIE* 13 = *CIJ* 2.1432) constitutes our only example of an Egyptian synagogue erected by an individual. The inscription was discovered in the Gabbary section of Alexandria, located in the western suburbs of the city; it probably dates to the reigns of Cleopatra VII and Ptolemy XIV:[44]

[ὑπὲρ] βα̣σ̣[ιλίσ]-
[ση]ς καὶ β[ασι-
[λ]έως θεῶ̣[ιμε]-
γάλωι ἐ[πηκό]-
ωι (?), Ἄλυπ[ος τὴν]
προσε[υχὴν]
ἐπόει [? *vacat*]
(ἔτους) ιε´ Με[χείρ . .]
vacat

On behalf of the queen and
king, for the great God
who listens to prayer, Alypus
made the *proseuchē* in the
15th year, Mecheir . . .

As we can see, the wording is slightly different in this monument than in previously encountered inscriptions, though the general outline is still recognizable. That the synagogue was financed by an individual need not indicate that the building was diminutive, since a segment of the Jewish

[44]The transcription takes into account some minor corrections noted in Horsley, "Towards a New *Corpus Inscriptionum Iudaicarum*?" 98. An inscription bearing the word *synagōgē* is sometimes cited as another example of a synagogue in Alexandria ("Artemon son of Nikon, *prostatēs* for the 11th year, to the synagogue ['Αρτέμων | Νίκωνος πρ(οστάτης) | τὸ ια´ (ἔτος) τῇ | συναγωγῇ | [. .]υτηκηι]"; *JIE* 20 = *CIJ* 2.1447). However, this probably belongs to a pagan association, since the monument is the base of a statue. Moreover, *proseuchē*, which is the usual term for synagogues in Egypt, is not found on the inscription.

population in Alexandria was aristocratic (Josephus, *Ant.* 18.159–160). If Alypus belonged to this upper echelon, he could easily have afforded to pay for a handsome structure.

When the presence of the above two inscriptions is combined with allusions in 3 Maccabees to various synagogues in and around Alexandria (3 Macc 2:28, 3:29, 4:18), it becomes apparent that several of these structures existed in the capital during the Ptolemaic period, as was clearly the case in Philo's day (see below). Despite their number, evidence suggests that during most of this era, the relationships between Jews, Greeks and Egyptians and their respective houses of worship were not hostile, but in many ways quite amiable.

Unfortunately, this all changed after 30 B.C.E. when Egypt became a Roman province, a move that had the support of the Alexandrian Jews. After being proclaimed "Augustus" in 27 B.C.E., Octavian instituted a taxation policy in Egypt that would have lasting consequences for Jewish and Greek relationships there. According to his decree, all males between the ages of fourteen and sixty-two were required to pay a capitation tax. However, the Greek citizens residing in Alexandria were exempted from the tax, while those citizens living in the leading provincial cities paid at a reduced rate. With respect to the Jewish population, Augustus, though allowing the politeuma in Alexandria to remain intact, classified Jews not with the Greeks, but with the native Egyptians, thus forcing them to pay the new levy.

This edict evidently irked many of the Jewish elite in Alexandria, who resented not only the burden of the tax, but also the reduction of social status that resulted from their being placed in the same class with the Egyptians. As a consequence, some Jews apparently tried to obtain Greek citizenship for their children by enrolling them in the gymnasium. For their part, the Greeks resented these attempts as well as the Jews' earlier support for Rome, recalling especially Antipater's rescue of Julius Caesar in Alexandria in 48 B.C.E. (Josephus, *Ant.* 14.131). Exacerbating this feeling of resentment was the fact that, while the Greeks in Egypt were left kingless under the new order, the Jews had Herod as a king in Palestine.

Hostilities were bound to erupt sooner or later, and during the fourth decade of the present era, several powerful personalities came together to bring about the explosion. In 32 C.E. Tiberius appointed A. Avillius Flaccus as prefect of Egypt. Five years later when Tiberius died and Gaius assumed the throne, Flaccus grew extremely anxious because he had previously supported the exile of Agrippina, the new emperor's mother. At this moment of uncertainty, Isidorus, an ex-gymnasiarch of Alexandria who had earlier left the city after provoking a demonstration against Flaccus, returned to Alexandria and promised the prefect Greek support if Gaius moved against him. In exchange, he asked that poor treatment be accorded the Jews. Flaccus consented to this agreement and bestowed upon Isidorus civic honors. The prefect then began consistently to decide against Jews in the provincial courts. Moreover, he purposefully suppressed a congratulatory letter from the Jewish *gerousia* to the new emperor (Philo, *Flacc.* 9–16, 87–103, 158).

In 38, Agrippa I visited Alexandria, hoping to keep a low profile, no doubt because he owed a large sum of money to Philo's wealthy brother Alexander, the alabarch (Josephus, *Ant.* 18.159–160). The Jews, however, learned that he was in the city and convinced him to send a copy of their original letter to Gaius along with a cover letter explaining why the first letter was late in arriving. They also appear to have persuaded Agrippa to parade through the streets of Alexandria with his bodyguard, as a way to restore Jewish prestige in the city (*Flacc.* 25–31, 103; *Legat.* 178–179).

This display provoked outrage among the kingless Greeks, who, seizing a local idiot named Carabas ("Cabbage"), decked him with royal accouterments and marched him through Alexandria and into the gymnasium shouting in Aramaic, "*Marin*" ("Our King!"). At this point, Agrippa apparently made an unceremonious exit (*Flacc.* 32–40). But the damage was done. Rioting broke out in the city, most of it focusing on the *proseuchai*, as Philo himself describes:

> They collected great bodies of men to attack the *proseuchai*, of which there are many in each section of the city. Some they ravaged, others they demolished with the foundations as well, others they set fire to and burnt regardless in their frenzy and insane fury of the fate of the neighbouring houses, for nothing runs faster than fire when it gets hold of something to feed it. I say nothing of the tributes to the emperors which were pulled down or burnt at the same time, the shields and gilded crowns and the slabs and inscriptions, consideration for which should have made them spare the rest . . . the *proseuchai* which they could not raze or burn out of existence, because so many Jews live massed together in the neighbourhood, they outraged in another way, thereby overthrowing our laws and customs. For they set up images of Gaius in them all and in the largest and most notable a bronze statue of a man mounted on a chariot and four . . . no doubt they had extravagant hopes of getting praise and reaping greater and more splendid benefits for turning our *proseuchai* into new and additional precincts [τεμένη] consecrated to him, though their motive was not to honour him but to take their fill in every way of the miseries of our nation (*Legat.* 132–137).

Flaccus, for his part, not only ignored this behavior, but at the instigation of Isidorus, revoked the Jewish politeuma, essentially making the Jews illegal aliens, subject to deportation. The Delta sector was transformed into the first recorded example of a Jewish ghetto, as Flaccus forced all the Jews of the city to move into this area amid continuing murderous behavior. Flaccus then had 38 members of the lapsed *gerousia* arrested and taken into the theater and scourged. Others were hanged and women were forced to eat pork on pain of death (*Flacc.* 53–72, 86–96; *Legat.* 121–131).

Some weeks later, a dispatch of soldiers finally arrived with warrants for Flaccus' arrest. A new prefect was installed and order was restored to the city (*Flacc.* 104–124). Subsequently, both Greek and Jewish delegations were sent to Gaius, with Philo leading the Jewish contingency. While there, the delegation learned of Gaius' decision to erect a statue to Zeus in the Jerusalem Temple, as we saw in a previous chapter. Philo records that, in addition to this threat, Gaius at this time also moved against Jewish *proseuchai* throughout the empire:

> Having conceived a violent enmity to them he took possession of the *proseuchai* in the other cities after beginning with those of Alexandria, by filling them with images and statues of himself in bodily form. For by permitting others to install them he virtually did it himself. The temple in the Holy City, which alone was left untouched being judged to have all rights of sanctuary, he proceeded to convert and transmogrify into a temple of his own to bear the name of Gaius, "the new Zeus made manifest" (*Legat.* 346).

Although Gaius later halted his plan to erect the statue, his assassination in 41 C.E. interrupted further action on the Alexandrian situation until after the accession of a new emperor. When Claudius assumed the throne, he eventually ruled in favor of the earlier status quo: Jews were allowed to retain their politeuma and to practice their national customs without hindrance, but were not permitted to seek Greek citizenship through attendance in the gymnasium (*CPJ* 2.153). Thus a temporary peace was reestablished, though tensions were to remain strained for years to come.

This series of incidents is quite illuminating to our understanding of the Alexandrian synagogues. First of all, we should note Philo's comment that many *proseuchai* were located in each section of the city. This should come as no surprise, since by the first century C.E., the Jewish population in Alexandria numbered in the tens of thousands. Thus even if each synagogue were able to accommodate several hundred persons, dozens would have been required to service the resident Jewish community. Secondly, Philo mentions that the synagogues housed shields, gilded crowns and monuments to the rulers, though no statues. Again, this is no new revelation, as we have already encountered examples of dedicatory monuments. However, the reference to the shields and the gilded crowns belies the notion that no artistry was permitted in the Alexandrian synagogues; the prohibition was not against artwork per se, but against the erection of graven images. This observation leads to a third point, that it took merely the addition of such graven images to transform the synagogues into sacred precincts (τεμένη) to Gaius. Yet because elsewhere Philo states that the Alexandrian synagogues were "*hieroi periboloi* where [the Jews] could set forth their thankfulness" for their rulers (*Flacc.* 48), the key distinction is again between offering prayers "on behalf of" a monarch and praying "to" an idol. The sacred, temple-like nature of the synagogues remained constant; only the divinity being worshiped changed. A final, related point is that the same treatment accorded the synagogues—and not just the ones in Egypt, but those around the diaspora (*Legat.* 346)—was contemplated for the Temple in Jerusalem. Indeed, Philo understood the fates of both the Temple and the synagogues as intertwined. Thus upon learning of Gaius' plans for the Temple, Philo despaired of even bringing his complaints about the *proseuchai* before the emperor:

> Shall we be allowed to come near him and open our mouths in defense of the *proseuchai* to the destroyer of the all-holy place [πανιέρου]? For clearly to houses less conspicuous and held in lower esteem no regard would be paid by one who insults that most notable and illustrious shrine [νεών] whose beams like the sun's reach every whither, beheld with awe both by east and west (*Legat.* 191).[45]

Here we see that, in Philo's view, while the synagogues could be compared to the Temple, they were subordinate to it, being sanctuaries of lesser esteem. Of even greater interest is that he portrays the Temple shrine as beaming out like the sun in every direction—an appropriate image not only for expressing the shrine's glory, but also for portraying its relationship to the synagogues scattered throughout the diaspora. For Philo, the Temple shrine formed the shining center towards which the lesser sanctuaries directed their gaze.

---

[45]The word "houses" in l. 2 has no counterpart in the Greek text (which simply refers back implicitly to *proseuchai* in l. 1).

Summary

The evidence surveyed in the preceding sections strongly suggests that the synagogues in Egypt were officially sanctioned public buildings that bore great affinities to temples. Inscriptions indicate the presence of such architectural features as exedras, pylons, sacred gardens and sacred precincts that are typically associated with pagan temples as well as with the Temple of Jerusalem. Papyrological evidence indicates that a functionary normally associated with temples—the *neōkoros*—also served in at least one of the Egyptian synagogues. Finally, several of the functions adduced for the synagogues correspond to those commonly associated with temples. These include their serving as repositories for the display of public dedicatory monuments, as places of asylum, and as centers for worship and the public reading and study of sacred writings—although these latter are more characteristically Jewish activities. Where the Jewish *proseuchai* differed from their pagan counterparts was in their lack of a shrine and altar. These were supplied by the main sanctuary in Jerusalem, where envoys from Alexandria went to sacrifice on behalf of the emperor and for other purposes.

The similarities between the Egyptian *proseuchai* and temples have not been lost on earlier researchers. Paul Dion, for example, has suggested that the early temple at Elephantine served as the inspiration for the later *proseuchai.*[46] More persuasive is the position of Areyah Kasher, already mentioned in the introduction of this study. Kasher argues that the Septuagint passage in which the Temple in Jerusalem is called a "house of prayer" (οἶκος προσευχῆς, Isa 56:7) led Egyptian Jews to form their *proseuchai* because of the close association between prayer and sacrifice (e.g., Isa 1:11–16; 1 Kgs 8:27–28). Since prayer could be offered anywhere, the deuteronomic prohibitions against sacrifice outside of Jerusalem could be observed while at the same time a connection to the central cult could be maintained. On this interpretation then, the *proseuchai* emerged as centers for communal prayer, particularly on the Sabbaths and other sacred days when special sacrifices were being offered in Jerusalem.[47] The reading of scripture in the *proseuchai* on these

---

[46]Dion, "Synagogues et temples dans l'Égypte hellénistique," 74–75.

[47]Kasher, "Synagogues as 'Houses of Prayer' and 'Holy Places' in the Jewish Communities of Hellenistic and Roman Egypt," 209–210. For Philo's allusion to the celebration of the Feast of Tabernacles in Alexandria, see *Flacc.* 116–118. More will be said about this celebration and about prayer in general as a function of the synagogues in chapter six.

days also originated from similar activities in the Temple (1 Esdr 9:41).[48] Other functions emerged out of the civic needs of the community.

Because Kasher's hypothesis best fits the evidence for the synagogues in Egypt, it is accepted by this study. As will become apparent throughout the remainder of this chapter, the other diaspora communities followed a similar pattern, establishing synagogues as places for public worship and the settling of communal affairs, all the while holding them subordinate to the central cultic shrine in Jerusalem.

CYRENAICA

Located directly to the west of Egypt, Cyrenaica was colonized by Dorian Greeks in the late seventh century B.C.E. Falling to Alexander the Great in 331 B.C.E., the country subsequently came under the rule of Ptolemy I, who is said to have settled Jews in the region (Josephus, *Ap.* 2.44; *Ant.* 12.7–8). The country became a Roman province in 74 B.C.E., and by that time the Jewish population had expanded so greatly that Strabo documents that the Jews living in the city of Cyrene were assigned their own special classification:

> There were four classes in the state of Cyrene; the first consisted of citizens, the second of farmers, the third of resident aliens (metics), and the fourth of Jews. This people has already made its way into every city, and it is not easy to find any place in the habitable world which has not received this nation and in which it has not made its power felt. And it has come about that Cyrene, which had the same rulers as Egypt, has imitated it in many respects, particularly in notably encouraging and aiding the expansion of the organized groups of Jews [συντάγματα τῶν Ἰουαίων], which observe the national Jewish laws [τοῖς πατρίοις τῶν Ἰουδαίων νόμοις] (Strabo ap. Josephus, *Ant.* 14.115–116).

From Strabo's statement, it is clear that the Jewish organizational scheme in Cyrene resembled that of the Jewish politeuma in Alexandria, though on a smaller scale, since Josephus mentions a Jewish population of only 5,000 in this city in the first century C.E. compared to a resident Jewish population in Alexandria numbering in the tens of thousands.[49] Strabo's comments also imply that more than one Jewish politeuma was established in Cyrenaica, and indeed the discovery of two inscriptions

---

[48]Kasher, "Synagogues as 'Houses of Prayer' and 'Holy Places' in the Jewish Communities of Hellenistic and Roman Egypt," 210–213.

[49]*BJ* 7.438, 445. See Applebaum, *Jews and Greeks in Ancient Cyrene*, 175, 190.

from Berenice mentioning a "politeuma of the Jews" confirms this hypothesis (see below). Presumably the Jews in the three other major cities of Cyrenaica (Teucheira, Ptolemais and Apollonia) also had similar constitutions. While the details of these organizational schemes remain elusive, each community probably had a degree of civic autonomy and similar privileges as those enjoyed by the Jews in Egypt: the right to assemble on the Sabbath, the right to collect money to send to the Temple, and so forth. The existence of one of these privileges is seen in a letter written by M. Agrippa to Cyrene, dated c. 13 B.C.E.:

> Marcus Agrippa to the magistrates, council and people of Cyrene, greeting. The Jews in Cyrene, on whose behalf Augustus has already written to the former praetor of Libya, Flavius, and to the other officials of the province to the effect that the sacred monies may be sent up to Jerusalem without interference, as is their ancestral custom, now complain to me that they are being threatened by certain informers and prevented (from sending these monies) on the pretext of their owing taxes, which are in fact not owed. I therefore order that these monies be restored to the Jews, who are in no way to be molested, and if sacred monies have been taken away from any cities, the persons in charge of these matters shall see that amends are made to the Jews there (*Ant.* 16.169–170).

Agrippa's reference to *cities* (plural) further confirms the existence of organized communities of Jews outside of Cyrene itself. Moreover, his mention of the custom of sending "sacred monies" (ἱερὰ χρήματα) to Jerusalem—an allusion to the half-shekel Temple tax—suggests that these Jewish communities had a measure of solidarity with the Temple and its cult. Indeed, the fact that the Cyrenean Jews protested the confiscation of these monies to the highest echelons of the Roman imperial government underscores the depth of their commitment to fulfilling this obligation. A final point is that, because elsewhere such monies are said to have been collected in the synagogues (e.g., Josephus, *Ant.* 16.162–164), it is likely that this also was the custom in the Cyrenean cities. However, it remains for us to review the epigraphic evidence attesting to the existence of such structures—evidence that is currently available only for Cyrene and Berenice.[50]

---

[50]Procopius' mention of an ancient Jewish *naos* in Boreium (*de Aedific* 6.2.21–23) need not detain us: the attestation is late (VI C.E.) and the claim that the "temple" was established in the time of King Solomon is fanciful.

Cyrene

Cyrene, located near the north-central coast of Cyrenaica, served as the capital of the country. Epigraphic evidence uncovered from the site supports the literary attestations of a significant Jewish presence in the city from Hellenistic times.[51] Jews appear to have comprised a cross-section of the socio-economic spectrum, with some serving as soldiers, others as farmers and still others craftsmen. Although population figures for antiquity are notoriously unreliable, one estimate gives the total population of the city as 135,000 of which Jews comprised about 5,000.[52]

Unfortunately, we currently possess only one inscription from Cyrene hinting at the existence of a synagogue, and its identification is tenuous. The inscription is a fragment from the upper right-hand side of a stele, the top of which was inscribed with a plant-tendril and a leaf. It dates to the end of the first century B.C.E.:[53]

[- - -]ου καὶ Δέκμος Σα-	. . . and Dekmos Sa-
[- - -]ου Σωσ[ά]νδ̣ρου	. . . Sosandros
[- - -]ου τοῦ Τ̇ειμάρχο[υ]	. . . Teimarchos
[- - -]ς καὶ Λεωνίδης· Τι-	. . . and Leonides, Ti-
[- - - τ]η̣ν συναγω-	. . . [the] synago-
[γήν - - -]	[gue] . . .

Because none of the above names are characteristically Jewish and because the word *synagōgē* was sometimes used in Gentile inscriptions, we cannot be certain of a Jewish provenance for this monument. However, Applebaum observes that the form of the stele resembles that of two Jewish inscriptions from Berenice and argues that this favors a Jewish identification.[54] If this argument is accepted, then it remains unclear whether *synagōgē* refers to a Jewish congregation or to a building. As we saw in chapter two, an inscription from Berenice dated

---

[51]E.g., 1 Macc 15:23. See Applebaum, *Jews and Greeks in Ancient Cyrene*, 175–200.

[52]See Applebaum, *Jews and Greeks in Ancient Cyrene*, 102–104, 175.

[53]Scuola archeologica italiana di Atene, *Annuario della Scuola archeologica di Atene e delle missioni italiane in Oriente* vol. 39–40 (Rome: Istituto poligrafico dello stato, 1961–62), no. 116. Author's translation.

[54]Applebaum, *Jews and Greeks in Ancient Cyrene*, 193–194. That the names in the inscription are not characteristically Jewish cannot be used as an argument against a Jewish provenance, since, as Applebaum notes, Jews in Cyrenaica commonly adopted Greek and Roman names.

to 55 C.E. uses this word in both senses. It is therefore possible that the above inscription may use *synagōgē* in reference to a building, though without further context this is impossible to establish.

If uncertainty must remain over the identification of the above inscription, Philo's passing allusion to the existence of synagogues in Cyrenaica (*Flacc.* 45) and Agrippa's mention of sacred monies being collected in Cyrene (*Ant.* 16.169–170) nevertheless argue for the existence of synagogues in this city by the first century B.C.E., possibly earlier. Strabo's allusion to the special classification of Jews of this city (*Ant.* 14.115–116) and archaeological evidence attesting the presence of Jews in Cyrene further support this hypothesis.[55]

Berenice

Located on the coast of western Cyrenaica, just north of the Gulf of Syrtis, Berenice (modern Benghazi) was founded at its present site as a port city in the third century B.C.E. Population estimates for the ancient city suggest a figure of 25,000–35,000.[56] Jewish presence in Berenice is attested in three inscriptions, two of which were quoted and discussed at some length in chapter two (*CJCZ* 70, 72). The first of the inscriptions (*CJCZ* 70), dating to 8–6 B.C.E., is a resolution by the Jewish *archontes* and politeuma expressing gratitude to a certain Decimus Valerius Dionysius for plastering the floors and painting the walls of the amphitheater (ἀμφιθεάτρον) in which the politeuma met. As previously discussed (see chapter two), the word *amphitheatron* here probably refers not to the elliptical structures used in public, gladiatorial displays (whose floors were unplastered), but to a building with seating along the sides, possibly resembling a Greek bouleterion or, for that matter, the early synagogues excavated in Palestine. The reference to the painting of the

---

[55]Fraser's suggestion (which Applebaum seems to accept) that a first-century B.C.E. inscription from Cyrene (*SEG* 18.738) belongs to a synagogue has little merit. It is based on the use of the term συνκύροντα (all but the first two letters are restored in the transcription), a word found in two synagogue inscriptions from Egypt (*JIE* 9, 25). However, non-Jewish inscriptions also used this term (e.g., *OGIS* 52, 182, 92). Moreover, the inscription's reference to Ptolemy VII as a "divine Benefactor" (θεοῦ Εὐεργέτου, l. 2) is unattested elsewhere in Jewish monuments (cf. *JIE* 25). See Applebaum, *Jews and Greeks in Ancient Cyrene*, 194.

[56]This is based on Applebaum's figure of 100,000–150,000 for the four major cities outside Cyrene. See Applebaum, *Jews and Greeks in Ancient Cyrene*, 103, n. 179.

walls indicates artistic ornamentation of some sort in the hall, though the nature of this ornamentation is unspecified.[57]

Decimus was clearly Jewish, since part of the resolution freed him from future liturgies (public works), and the Jewish politeuma could have imposed such obligations only on its own membership. On the other hand, Decimus was also a Roman citizen, as the use of the *tria nomina* indicates. This fact, coupled with his generous benefaction, clearly places him among the elite of the Jewish community, although he is not named as one of the *archontes* of the politeuma. These latter, as best as can be determined from the condition of the inscription, are seven in number, all male. They, along with the politeuma, met at regularly held synods and also on the New Moon. The regular synods very likely met on the Sabbath, which, like the New Moon, corresponded to a sacred day in the Jewish liturgical calendar. At each of these assemblies, Decimus was to be named as a benefactor. In addition, the assembly voted to give Decimus a crown of olive leaves, and the stele containing the resolution was to be placed in the amphitheater.

The second inscription (*CJCZ* 71), which also refers to a politeuma of the Jews, is dated to 24/25 C.E.:

> [Ἔ]τους νε´ Φαῶφ κε´ ἐπὶ συλλόγου τῆς σκηνο-
> πηγίας ἐπὶ ἀρχόντων Κλεάνδρου τοῦ
> Στρατονίκου Εὐφράνορος τοῦ Ἀρίστωνος
> Σωσιγένους τοῦ Σωσίππου Ἀνδρομάχου
> τοῦ Ἀνδρομάχου Μάρκου Λαιλίου Ὀνασί-
> ωνος τοῦ Ἀπολλωνίου Φιλωνίδου τοῦ Ἁγή-
> μονος Αὐτοκλέους τοῦ Ζήνωνος Σωνί-
> κου τοῦ Θεοδότου Ἰωσηπου τοῦ Στράτωνος
> ἐπεὶ Μᾶρκος Τίττιος Σέξτου υἱὸς Αἰμιλία
> ἀνὴρ καλὸς καὶ ἀγαθὸς παραγενηθεὶς εἰς
> τὴν ἐπαρχείαν ἐπὶ δημοσίων πραγμάτων τήν
> τε προστασίαν αὐτῶν ἐποιήσατο φιλανθρώ-
> πως καὶ καλῶς ἐν τε τῆι ἀναστροφῆ ἡσύχιον
> ἦθος ἐνδικνύμενος ἀεὶ διατελῶν τυγχάνει
> οὐ μόνον δὲ ἐν τούτοις ἀβαρῆ ἑαυτὸν παρέσ-
> χηται ἀλλὰ καὶ τοῖς κατ᾽ ἰδίαν ἐντυγχάνουσι
> τῶν πολιτῶν ἔτι δὲ καὶ τοῖς ἐκ τοῦ πολιτεύ-
> ματος ἡμῶν Ἰουδαίοις καὶ κοινῆ καὶ κατ᾽ ἰδίαν
> εὔχρηστον προσστασίαν ποιούμενος οὐ δια-

[57]The word ζωγραφέω used in the inscription (l. 11) means "to paint from life" (LSJ, s.v.), suggesting that more than just geometric designs were painted in the amphitheater. On the other hand, this word can also be used more generally in the sense of "adorn."

λείπει τῆς ἰδίας καλοκάγαθίας ἄξια πράσσων ὧν χάριν ἔδοχε τοῖς ἄρχουσι καὶ τῶι πολιτεύματι τῶν ἐν Βερενίκῃ Ἰουδαίων ἐπαινέσαι τε αὐτὸν καὶ στεφανοῦν ὀνομαστὶ καθ' ἑκάστην σύνοδον καὶ νουμηνίαν στεφάνωι ἐλαίνωι καὶ λημνίσκωι τοὺς δὲ ἄρχοντας ἀναγράψαι τὸ ψήφισμα εἰς στήλην λίθου παρίου καὶ θεῖναι εἰς τὸν ἐπισημότατον τόπον τοῦ ἀμφιθεάτρου

Λευ καὶ πᾶ σαι

In the year 55, on the 25th of Phaoph, during the assembly of the Feast of the Tabernacles, in the archonship of Cleandros, (son) of Stratonicos, Euphranor, (son) of Ariston, Sosigenes, (son) of Sosippos, Andromachos, | (son) of Andromachos, Marcus Laelius Onasion, (son) of Apollonios, Philonides, (son) of Hagemon, Autocles, (son) of Zenon, Sonicos, (son) of Theodotos, and Josepos, (son) of Straton. With regard to Marcus Tittius, son of Sextus, (from the tribe of) Aemilia, | a noble and good man: whereas he has assumed the office of prefect over public affairs, he has exercised kind and just leadership and has always displayed a peaceful demeanor in his daily affairs; | whereas he has not been burdensome to the citizens who petition him privately; whereas he has exercised helpful leadership with regard to the Jews of our politeuma, both corporately and individually; and whereas he has not himself | ceased to act worthily with his own noble kindness: therefore, it seemed well to the *archontes* and to the politeuma of the Jews in Berenice both to honor him and to crown him by name at each synod and each new moon with a crown of olive branches and | a woollen fillet, and that the *archontes* should inscribe the vote on a stele of Parian stone and place it in the most prominent place in the amphitheater. All (stones) white.[58]

In this inscription, we see that the number of *archontes* has increased to nine, with none of the names repeating from the earlier inscription, although Euphranor may have been the son, and Andromachos the brother or nephew of previous *archontes* (Ariston [*CJCZ* 70, l. 3] and Serapion [*CJCZ* 70, l. 4], respectively). Another difference is that one of the new *archontes*—M. Laelius Onasion—was a Roman citizen. This alone does not insure that he was wealthy, since he may have received his citizenship as the result of manumission. His position as *archōn*, of course, indicates that he possessed high status within the Jewish community (true of all *archontes*), if not necessarily a high level of wealth.

---

[58]Author's translation. Cf. Lüderitz, "What is Politeuma?" 212.

Significantly, the meeting in which the above resolution was proffered took place on yet another Jewish sacred day, the Feast of Tabernacles. Unfortunately, the inscription does not outline the specific ritual activities that surely transpired at this gathering. However, the very fact that what moderns would label "secular business" could take place on such a holy day further underscores the point that the religious and non-religious dimensions of Jewish practice in this period are difficult to disentangle. That the inscription honors a Gentile official should not now seem so unusual, after having surveyed a number of similar inscriptions from Egypt. Nevertheless, the generous wording of the inscription indicates that M. Tittius had an extraordinarily good relationship with the Jewish community in Berenice. It is not known if such amiable relationships existed between the Jews and the predominately Greek population of the city, however, since the resolution may have resulted from the prefect's curbing of local Greek hostilities. Given the general antipathy that Greeks appear to have held toward the Jews in this period, such a scenario is well within the realm of possibilities.

A portion of the final inscription from Berenice (*CJCZ* 72) was reproduced in chapter two. Dating to 55 C.E., it mentions neither a politeuma nor an amphitheater. Rather, it refers to the repairs of a *synagōgē* made by the congregation (*synagōgē*) of the Jews. The segment previously unquoted simply reproduces the names of the donors. The translation runs as follows:

Column One

Zenion, son of Zoilos, *archōn*, 10 drachmae
Isidoros, son of Dositheos, *archōn*, 10 drachmae
Dositheos, son of Ammonius, *archōn*, 10 drachmae
Pratis, son of Jonathan, *archōn*, 10 drachmae
Carnedas, son of Cornelius, *archōn*, 10 drachmae
Heracleides, son of Heracleides, *archōn*, 10 drachmae
Thaliarchos, son of Dositheos, *archōn*, 10 drachmae
Sosibios, son of Jason, *archōn*, 10 drachmae
Pratomedes, son of Socrates, *archōn*, 10 drachmae
Antigonos, son of Straton, *archōn*, 10 drachmae
Cartisthenes, son of Archias, priest, 10 drachmae
Lysanias, son of Lysanias, 25 drachmae
Zenodoros, son of Theophilos, 28 drachmae
Marion (?), [son of ?], 25 drachmae
[Stone broken]

Column Two

Alexander, son of Euphranor, 5 drachmae
Isidora, daughter of Serapion, 5 drachmae
Zosime, daughter of Terpolius, 5 drachmae
Polon, son of Dositheos, 5 drachmae

As can be seen, a total of eighteen donors are recorded, including ten *archontes*, one priest (not an *archōn*) and two women (also not *archontes*). Because the lower half of the stone was broken, omitting some donors, we do not know the total amount given for the repairs. What is preserved adds up to 208 drachmae, a fairly significant sum (≈ US $8,320). The ordering scheme used in the list is noteworthy. It begins with the ten *archontes*, who each donated ten drachmae, followed by the priest, who donated the same amount. The fact that the priest is given a place of honor with the *archontes* (although he himself was not an *archōn*) further underscores the point that no incompatibility existed between the Temple and the synagogue (cf. *CIJ* 2.1404, the Theodotus inscription). Additionally, the uniformity of these first eleven donations suggests an agreement between the leaders not to outbid the other in terms of the sums contributed.

The remainder of the donors appear to be ordered roughly in relationship to the amount contributed. Thus the next three donors listed before the stone breaks off contributed sums of twenty-five, twenty-eight and twenty-five drachmae. The contributors of the smallest sums, including the two women, are recorded in the second column, which was clearly continuous with the first. The presence of the gifts of Isidora and Zosime is significant, since it demonstrates that women participated in the financial support of the synagogue, if not the leadership. Because the stone is broken, other women donors may have originally been recorded in column one, possibly contributing greater sums.

It is not known for certain whether the *synagōgē* in this inscription is the same building as the *amphitheatron* in the two earlier monuments. Against the hypothesis that *two* synagogues existed in Berenice at the same time, however, is the phrase, "resolved by the congregation of the Jews of Berenice and its vicinity [ἐφάνη τῇ συναγωγῇ τῶν Βερνεικίδι Ἰουδίων]" (*CJCZ* 72, ll. 3–4), suggesting a unified community of Jews encompassing the whole region.[59] As argued in chapter two, if the *synagōgē* and the *amphitheatron* are to be equated, then the change in

[59]So Applebaum, *Jews and Greeks in Ancient Cyrene*, 162, n. 149.

terminology may have been due to the growing use of the latter term in connection with buildings housing gladiatorial contests. As Applebaum notes, the term *amphitheatron* was in flux at the turn of the era, with the two inscriptions from Berenice constituting the earliest extant uses of the word in an inscription.[60] Even the oldest surviving stone gladiatorial amphitheater from Pompeii, built c. 80 B.C.E., was not called an *amphitheatron*, but a *spectacula* (*CIL* 10.852). It is therefore likely that the Jewish community in Berenice used the word descriptively, meaning, "a place with seats all around." When the usage of *amphitheatron* began to solidify around a meaning designating an arena for gladiatorial shows, the Jewish community, hoping to dissociate their structure from such activities, possibly shifted their terminology to bring it in line with that being used in the homeland. Simultaneously, they may have exchanged the term *politeuma* for the word *synagōgē*, also used in Palestine to designate the local synagogue congregation.

Whether or not one accepts this hypothesis, some overlap likely existed between the families associated with both structures. For instance, Antigonos, one of the *archontes* in the *synagōgē* inscription (*CJCZ* 72), may have been the nephew or the brother of Josepos, an *archōn* listed in the *amphitheatron* inscription dating to 25 C.E. (*CJCZ* 71, l. 8), since the names of their fathers are identical (Straton). Similarly, Alexander's father, Euphranor, mentioned in *CJCZ* 72, may have been the *archōn* by that name mentioned in *CJCZ* 71 (l. 3). Finally, Isidora in *CJCZ* 72 may have been either the daughter or the granddaughter of the Serapion listed as an *archōn* in *CJCZ* 70 (l. 4). Of course, this all assumes that there was little replication of names among the Jewish community in Berenice—a somewhat questionable assumption. However, the overlap of the names of several families somewhat mitigates this problem. Moreover, there is some logic to the notion that archonships tended to stay in certain highly respected families. For instance, Isidoros and Thaliarchos, mentioned as *archontes* in *CJCZ* 72, were probably sons of the *archōn* Dositheos listed in the same inscription (Polon, listed as a donor, may be yet a third son).

Summary

Although the evidence for the presence of synagogues in Cyrenaica is not as plentiful as that found in Egypt, it nevertheless seems clear that synagogues existed in Cyrene and Berenice by at least the first century

---

[60]Ibid., 165.

B.C.E. Literary sources suggest that synagogues were more prevalent in the country at this time, but archaeology has yet to confirm their witness. While the inscription from Cyrene provides little information and its identification is somewhat tenuous, the inscriptions from Berenice demonstrate that the Jews there were organized into a politeuma that met regularly to conduct business and engage in ritual proceedings, possibly in a single building that was first called an *amphitheatron* and later a *synagōgē*. The former word probably did not denote an elliptical structure, but a rectangular building with seats around the inner walls, possibly resembling a bouleterion or one of the early Galilean-type synagogues. Among its functions, the structure served as a repository for inscriptions honoring both Jewish and Gentile benefactors. Literary sources suggest that the building may also have served as a collection site for the half-shekel Temple tax that was regularly transported to Jerusalem. That the building may have functioned in this manner, coupled with the fact that a priest was listed in a position of honor with the *archontes* in one of the inscriptions, underscores the point that the synagogue in Berenice functioned in concert with the Temple cult in Jerusalem. This is further seen in the community's days of meeting, which corresponded to days sacred to the cult, such as the New Moon, the Feast of Tabernacles and, almost certainly, the Sabbath.

The Jewish community in Berenice was governed by an all-male archonship which, between 9 B.C.E. and 55 C.E., grew in number from seven to ten members, possibly indicating a growth in the Jewish population in the city. Women, while not sharing in the archonship, nevertheless contributed to the financial upkeep of the synagogue.

SYRIA

It is difficult to speak of Syria geographically, since its political boundaries were constantly shifting throughout the Second Temple period. During the height of Seleucid domination under Antiochus III (II B.C.E.), Syria engulfed all of Palestine, a situation that changed following Judea's independence under Simon Maccabaeus in 141 B.C.E. After Pompey's conquest of the region in 64–63 B.C.E., however, while the Romans kept the division between Syria and Palestine intact, they later apportioned eastern tracts of the Syrian province to various Nabatean and Herodian rulers. Moreover, following the death of Herod in 4 B.C.E., Augustus attached several Greek cities in Palestine to Syria. In the aftermath of the Jewish War, all of Palestine was incorporated into the

Province of Syria, thus returning the political boundaries to those that had existed three centuries earlier.

Keeping in mind these shifting boundaries, we can generally speak of Syria as constituting the strip of land extending from the region north of Antioch to the southern Phoenician coast, which during the first century C.E. reached as far south as Dora in northwestern Samaria. To the east, the territory extended into the Arabian Desert, encompassing Palmyra in the north and Damascus in the south.[61]

With regard to the Jewish presence in Syria, Josephus writes that "the Jewish race . . . is particularly numerous in Syria, where intermingling is due to the proximity of the two countries" (*BJ* 7.43; cf. Philo, *Flacc.* 234). He further states that the early Seleucid kings settled many Palestinian Jews in Syria, (*BJ* 7. 43–45)—a policy similar to the one adopted by the Ptolemies in Egypt.

The evidence for synagogues in Syria is all literary, consisting solely of references from the writings of Josephus and Acts. Moreover, these are confined to three Syrian cities: Antioch, Damascus and Dora.[62] We begin our survey with Antioch, the capital of Syria.

Antioch

Located on the Orontes River about twenty miles from the Mediterranean coast, Antioch was founded by Seleucis I in 300 B.C.E. Serving as the Seleucid capital of Syria and later as the Roman provincial seat, Antioch emerged as one of the largest cities in the Roman Empire, with an estimated population of 150,000.[63] Estimates for the size of the Jewish population range from twenty-two to forty-five thousand in the first century C.E., with the lower figure probably being more reliable.[64]

---

[61]For a more detailed consideration of the topography of Syria, see Robyn Tracey, "Syria" in *The Book of Acts in Its Palestinian Setting*, edited by Richard Bauckham (Grand Rapids, Mich.: William B. Eerdmans Pub. Co., 1994), 223–232, 268–272.

[62]In addition to these cities, Josephus records letters of friendship to the Jews issued by Julius Caesar to Tyre and Sidon (*Ant.* 14.190–195, 196–198). Although the letters do not specifically refer to synagogues in these cities, their existence is nonetheless implied.

[63]Glanville Downey, "The Size of the Population of Antioch," *Transactions of the American Philological Association* 89 (1958): 84–91.

[64]See Irina Levinskaya, *The Book of Acts in Its Diaspora Setting* (Grand Rapids, Mich.: Wm. B. Eerdmans Publishing Company, 1996), 134; Wayne A. Meeks and Robert L. Wilken, *Jews and Christians in Antioch in the First Four Centuries of the Common Era* (Missoula, Mont.: Scholars Press, 1978), 8.

Josephus speaks of the Jews in the city as being governed by an *archōn* (*BJ* 7.47) and elsewhere mentions bronze tablets inscribed with the privileges of the Jews in Antioch (*BJ* 7.110). Although unspecified, these were probably nearly identical to the rights accorded the Jews throughout the empire, such as the right to assemble on the Sabbath and the right to send donations to Jerusalem. Josephus' reference to the Jews in Antioch being apportioned oil supplies separate from the general stock (*Ant.* 12.120) also hints at the keeping of purity laws by the Antiochian Jews.

Although Josephus thrice states that the Jews in Antioch were granted rights as Greek citizens (*Ant.*, 12.119, *Ap.* 2.39, *BJ* 7.44), actual citizenship was probably only accorded to a few elite Jews, with the larger community likely being constituted as a politeuma similar to the ones at Alexandria and Berenice.[65] Whether or not there existed a ruling *gerousia* under the *archōn* is unknown, although given the situation at Alexandria, this is a good possibility.

Jewish and Greek relationships in Antioch appear to have been quite strained, at least during the time of the Jewish War, since Josephus reports that at that time the Jews were accused of plotting to set a fire to the city (*BJ* 7.45–53). At the suggestion of a certain Antiochus, the apostate son of the Jewish *archōn*, the Jews were forced to offer sacrifices to pagan deities. Josephus writes:

> This test being applied by the Antiochenes, a few submitted and the recalcitrants were massacred. Antiochus, having procured the aid of troops from the Roman general, domineered with severity over his Jewish fellow-citizens, not permitting them to repose on the seventh day, but compelling them to do everything exactly as on other days; and so strictly did he enforce obedience that not only at Antioch was the weekly day of rest abolished, but the example having been started there spread for a short time to the other cities as well (*BJ* 7.52–53).

After the Jewish War, Titus was said to have restored the rights of the Jews in the city (*BJ* 7.108–111). Even so, the passage suggests that most Jews in Antioch kept the Sabbath and refrained from pagan rituals, while others were content to adopt Greek customs and religious practices. That

---

[65]See Glanville Downey, *A History of Antioch in Syria* (Princeton, NJ: Princeton University Press, 1961), 107–111. More recently, John Barclay has expressed scepticism regarding the existence of a Jewish politeuma at Antioch (J. M. C. Barclay, *Jews in the Mediterranean Diaspora from Alexander to Trajan* [Edinburgh: T. & T. Clark, 1996], 245, n. 29). See however, Levinskaya, *The Book of Acts in Its Diaspora Setting*, 129–130.

the son of the Jewish *archōn* was among this latter group hints that most of the syncretistic Jews were among the wealthy and ambitious elite, as was the case with Alexander, Philo's apostate nephew.

Exactly how synagogues served as administrative centers for the Jewish population of Antioch is unknown. The one allusion to a synagogue in this city is from Josephus, who states that the structure was in existence in the second century B.C.E. and that it served as a repository for "votive offerings" previously plundered from the Jerusalem Temple by Antiochus IV (*BJ* 7.44). Subsequently, Seleucid rulers were said to have adorned this same synagogue with "richly designed and costly offerings [which] formed a splendid ornament to the *hieron*" (*BJ* 7.45).[66] That Josephus could portray this (main?) synagogue as functioning in such a capacity and, moreover, refer to it as a *hieron*, suggests that it was temple-like in both appearance and function. Also, because Josephus, himself a priest, wrote so affectionately of this synagogue, there surely must have been a harmonious relationship between its congregation and the Temple hierarchy in Jerusalem. Although we lack specific attestation that Jews in Antioch contributed offerings and donations to the Temple, it is inconceivable that the Jews there refrained from practices exercised by Jewish communities throughout the empire.

As for the date of the synagogue, it is not beyond the realm of possibility that one or more synagogues existed in Antioch in the second century B.C.E., particularly in view of the early Egyptian evidence. Unfortunately, because the modern town of Antakya rests on the site of ancient Antioch, excavations in the city have been and will presumably remain quite limited in scope. Consequently, our only knowledge of synagogues in this city will probably continue to derive from Josephus' singular attestation.

Damascus

Situated in eastern Syria on the Arbana River, Damascus is mentioned already in an inscription dating to the sixteenth century B.C.E. and appears many times in the Hebrew scriptures (e.g., Gen 15:15, 15:2; 2 Sam 8:5). Much later, after the city was conquered by Alexander, it was contested by the Seleucid and Ptolemaic kings, finally ending in the possession of the former. In 111 B.C.E., it became the capital of Antiochus IX, who sought to wrench Syria away from his brother, Antiochus VIII (Josephus,

---

[66]For a fuller consideration of this passage, see chapter two's treatment of *hieron*.

Ant. 13.387–392). After capturing Damascus in 63 B.C.E., Pompey reintegrated the city and its surrounding territories into the newly formed province of Syria (*Ant.*14.29, *BJ* 1.127). In the first century C.E., the city appears to have been given to the Nabatean king, Aretas IV, perhaps in exchange for some service to the Romans (2 Cor 11:32).[67]

Josephus mentions Damascus in connection with an outbreak against the Jews in the city at the beginning of the Jewish War. The Jews were herded into a gymnasium and kept there for a time before being slaughtered—18,000 of them according to one figure (*BJ* 7.368), 10,500 according to another (*BJ* 2.561). While the reliability of these numbers is obviously to be questioned, the figures nevertheless indicate that a significant Jewish community resided in Damascus. This lends some plausibility to the two passages which refer to the presence of synagogues in Damascus, both found in Acts. In the first of these, Paul is said to have gone to the High Priest in Jerusalem to ask "for letters to the synagogues at Damascus, so that if he found any who belonged to the Way, men or women, he might bring them bound to Jerusalem [ἐπιστολὰς εἰς Δαμασκὸν πρὸς τὰς συναγωγάς, ὅπως ἐάν τινας εὕρῃ τῆς ὁδοῦ ὄντας, ἄνδρας τε καὶ γυναῖκας, δεδεμένους ἀγάγῃ εἰς Ἰερουσαλήμ]" (Acts 9:2). Of course, on the way, Paul underwent a conversion experience and was soon baptized a Christian in Damascus. According to Acts, Paul then "began to proclaim Jesus in the synagogues [ἐν ταῖς συναγωγαῖς ἐκήρυσσεν τὸν Ἰησοῦν]" (Acts 9:20), but was soon forced to leave the city because of opposition by the resident Jewish population (Acts 9:22–25).[68]

While Josephus' attestation of a sizable Jewish community in Damascus lends some credibility to Acts' depiction of several Jewish synagogues in the city, of perhaps greater interest is Acts' presumption that the High Priest was able to issue letters to the synagogues in Damascus, requesting that apostates be turned over. This indicates that the writer of Acts believed that some legal entity—such as a politeuma—existed in Damascus, enabling the leaders of the synagogues there to seize such apostates. Whether or not this was true for Damascus is unverified by other sources.[69] Nevertheless, no opposition between the synagogues and the Temple hierarchy existed for the writer of

---

[67]For a review of the epigraphic and numismatic evidence for Damascus, see *HJP* 2.127–130.

[68]Cf. Paul's allusions to his sojourn in Damascus in Gal 1:17, 2 Cor 11:32–33.

[69]So Conzelmann, *Acts of the Apostles*, 71. Josephus states that Herod had been empowered to reclaim a fugitive from beyond his jurisdiction (*BJ* 1.474). It is unclear whether this right was extended to his successors.

Acts—indeed, quite the reverse. The leaders of the synagogues—in the diaspora no less—served as subordinates to the Temple rulers with regard to halakhic issues.

Dora

Like Damascus, Dora (or Dor) is mentioned in an early Egyptian inscription, in this case, one dating to the thirteenth century B.C.E.[70] Located a scant nine miles north of Caesarea Maritima on the Mediterranean coast, it was the southernmost city in the Province of Syria during the time of Herod and the later Roman procurators of Palestine. Prior to Roman rule, Dora was for centuries a Sidonian city that later fell briefly into Seleucid and then Jewish hands in the second and first centuries B.C.E. (1 Macc 15:11–37; Josephus, *Ant.* 13.223, 324). By the turn of the era, Dora seems to have been largely inhabited by Greeks, with a significant Jewish minority.

It will be recalled from chapter two that during the governorship of Petronius (c. 41 C.E.), certain youths of Dora "brought an image of Caesar into the synagogue of the Jews and set it up" (*Ant.* 19.300). This act was probably in connection with the earlier riots in Alexandria, since, as we saw earlier, Philo mentions that the desecration of the Alexandrian *proseuchai* sparked similar actions against the synagogues in other cities (*Legat.* 346). That this was the case can be seen from a segment of the letter to the leaders of Dora where Petronius writes:

> It is ridiculous for me to refer to my own decree after making mention of the edict of the emperor [Claudius] which permits Jews to follow their own customs, yet also, be it noted, bids them to live as fellow citizens with the Greeks . . . For both King Agrippa [I], my most honoured friend, and I have no greater interest than that the Jews should not seize any occasion, under the pretext of self-defense, to gather in one place and proceed to desperate measures. And, that you may be better informed of His Imperial Majesty's policy concerning the whole matter, I have appended his edicts which were published at Alexandria. Although they seem to be universally known, my most honoured friend King Agrippa read them before my tribunal at the time when he pleaded that the Jews ought not to be despoiled of the privileges granted by Augustus. For the future, therefore, I charge you to seek no pretext for sedition or disturbance, but to practice severally each his own religion [θρησκεύειν] (*Ant.* 19. 306–311).

---

[70]See Ephriam Stern, "Dor" in *NEAEHL* 1.357–368; Gideon Foerster, "Dor" in *EAEHL* 1.334–337; *HJP* 2.118–121.

Since Claudius' edict to Alexandria was read in Syria, we see that the Roman policy toward the Jews at this time was fairly uniform in the eastern empire: Jews were allowed to practice their ancestral customs without interference. With regard to the synagogues, the Jews were not to be prevented from having their own houses of worship and were not to have these violated by the introduction of statues—even statues of the emperor. Indeed, Petronius argued in his letter that this action was inappropriate, even sacrilegious, stating that Caesar's image "was better placed in his own shrine than in that of another, especially in the synagogue" (*Ant.* 19.305).

Summary

Although we lack archaeological evidence attesting to the presence of synagogues in Syria during the Second Temple period, the literary sources witnessing to the existence of such structures in Antioch, Damascus and Dora are credible and in some instances reinforce each other's testimony. As was the case with the synagogues in Egypt, these buildings appear to be temple-like in character: they can display votive offerings which were previously housed in the Temple of Jerusalem; they can be referred to with the term *hieron*; and they can be transformed into an imperial shrine merely by the addition of the emperor's statue. Beyond this, Josephus' approving attitude toward the synagogues at Dora and Antioch further demonstrates that no oppositional relationship existed between the Temple and the synagogues. This is also seen in Acts' portrayal of the High Priest's dispatch of a letter to the synagogues at Damascus authorizing the retention of Christians in the city. Even if the incident never took place, it is clear that the author of Acts saw no such negative relationship between the two institutions. Finally, it bears repeating that the synagogues in each of these cities were well-established, legally protected public edifices set aside for the exercise of sacred Jewish customs. For the thousands of Jews living in Syria, they functioned as community centers and houses of worship, probably in similar ways as the synagogues in Egypt and Cyrenaica.

CYPRUS

Since there is only one passing reference to synagogues on Cyprus, our consideration of it need not be lengthy. The island, located in the eastern Mediterranean, was noted in antiquity for its copper mines.

Inhabited during the Hellenistic period primarily by Greeks, it became a Roman province in 23 B.C.E. The earliest attestation for a Jewish presence on the island is 1 Macc 15:16–23, which comprises a letter of friendship from the Roman consul, written c. 139 B.C.E., that was said to have been sent to many cities and regions, including Cyprus. We know little about the Jewish community there, although allusions to it by Josephus (*Ant.* 13.284–287) and Philo (*Legat.* 282) suggest that it was sizable.[71]

Acts 13:5 briefly states that, on their first missionary journey (c. 46–48 C.E.), Paul, Barnabas and Mark, upon arriving in Salamis, a major city on the eastern coast of Cyprus, "proclaimed the word of God in the synagogues of the Jews [ἐν ταῖς συναγωγαῖς τῶν Ἰουδαίων]." Soon thereafter they left the city and continued their missionary work in Paphos, the provincial capital of Cyprus, situated on the western side of the island. While we might question Acts' use of the plural in the above reference, given the other attestations to a sizable Jewish population on Cyprus, there seems little reason to doubt that at least *one* synagogue existed in Salamis. Unfortunately, aside from this bit of information, the passage from Acts adds little to our body of knowledge about the Jewish community in Salamis and its synagogue(s).

GALATIA

The province of Galatia was formed by Augustus in 25 B.C.E. Located in central Asia Minor, it encompassed not only the former kingdom of Galatia, but also portions of Phrygia, Pisidia and Isauria. Galatia was twice enlarged near the turn of the era to include sections of Paphlagonia and Pontus to the north.[72] Thus at its territorial apex during the first century C.E., the province was bordered by Bithynia and Pontus on the north, Asia on the west, Cappadocia on the east, and Lycia, Pamphylia and Cilicia Trachea on the south.

Although the region was inhabited by an ethnically diverse population consisting of Greeks, Galatians, Paphlagonians, Phrygians, Pisidians, Lycaonians and Isuarians, the first governor of the new province established Roman colonies out of several existing Greek cities, including

---

[71]See Alanna Nobbs, "Cyprus" in *The Book of Acts in Its Palestinian Setting*, edited by Richard Bauckham (Grand Rapids, Mich.: William B. Eerdmans Pub. Co., 1994), 279–289; Smallwood, *The Jews under Roman Rule*, 412–415.

[72]See G. Walter Hansen, "Galatia" in *The Book of Acts in Its Palestinian Setting*, edited by Richard Bauckham (Grand Rapids, Mich.: William B. Eerdmans Pub. Co., 1994), 380–382

Pisidian Antioch and Lystra in southern Galatia.[73] The resident, largely Hellenized populations of these cities were thus supplemented with a Latin population consisting primarily of retired Roman soldiers. Another Greek city, Iconium, was not colonized until the time of Hadrian.[74]

Pisidian Antioch and Iconium

Acts states that, on their first missionary tour, Paul and Barnabas visited Pisidian Antioch and found there a synagogue that they soon used as a public forum for their message:

> On the sabbath day they went into the synagogue and sat down. After the reading of the law and the prophets, the officials of the synagogue [οἱ ἀρχισυνάγωγοι] sent them a message, saying, "Brothers, if you have any word of exhortation for the people, give it." So Paul stood up and with a gesture began to speak: "You Israelites, and others who fear God [οἱ φοβούμενοι τὸν θεόν], listen . . . " (Acts 13:14–16).

After preaching his homily, the meeting broke up. Upon leaving the synagogue, Paul and Barnabas were asked by "many Jews and devout converts [πολλοὶ τῶν Ἰουδαίων καὶ τῶν σεβομένων προσηλύτων]" to speak again on the following Sabbath (13:43). According to Acts, the next week nearly the whole town showed up to hear their teaching. The Jews, offended at the presence of so many Gentiles, were now less sympathetic to Paul's message (13:45). Paul in turn denounced the Jewish congregation and the two missionaries subsequently focused their efforts on converting the Gentiles in the city (13:46–49). Eventually, both Jewish and Gentile opponents drove them out of Antioch (13:50–52).

In outline, the same set of scenes is portrayed as taking place in Iconium. Upon entering the city, Paul and Barnabas "went into the Jewish synagogue and spoke in such a way that a great number of both Jews and Greeks became believers" (14:1). Soon, they encountered opposition and were forced to leave Iconium for fear of being stoned (14:2–6).

Although there is no outside confirmation of synagogues in either of the Galatian cities mentioned in Acts, Josephus quotes from a letter written by Antiochus III (c. 210 B.C.E.), informing the satrap of Lydia of his plan to relocate Babylonian Jews to the region:

---

[73]See Barbara Levick, *Roman Colonies in Southern Asia Minor* (Oxford: Clarendon Press, 1967), 130–144 (Antioch), 153–156 (Lystra).

[74]Ibid., 165.

> Learning that the people in Lydia and Phrygia are revolting, I have come to consider this as requiring very serious attention on my part, and, on taking counsel with my friends as to what should be done, I determined to transport two thousand Jewish families with their effects from Mesopotamia and Babylonia to the fortresses and most important places. For I am convinced that they will be loyal guardians of our interests because of their piety to God (*Ant.* 12.148–150).

Presumably these Jews would have been placed in the major cities of the area, which included Antioch and Iconium. Thus Acts' portrayal of synagogues in these two cities is plausible, if not verified.

Of greater interest than the concern for the existence of synagogues in these cities is Acts' depiction of the synagogue congregations and their services. That the congregations gathered on the Sabbath is no new revelation. However, we also see that the service at Antioch consisted of readings from both the Torah and the Prophets. Moreover, several *archisynagōgoi* are represented as sending Paul and Barnabas a message to speak before the assembly. While we will say more about this office in the next chapter, in the passage from Acts, the *archisynagōgoi* were clearly more than esteemed members of the congregation: they were active functionaries who appear to have been in charge of the flow of the service.[75] Acts' portrayal of proselytes, God-fearers and "curious Gentiles" in the synagogues is also something we shall comment upon in the next chapter. Here we but note that this is the first instance in Acts of Gentiles being in attendance in a synagogue.

The Bosporus Kingdom

The Bosporus Kingdom encompassed the coastal areas of the eastern Crimea and the Taman Peninsula where the straights of Kerch (the Cimmerian Bosporus) connect the Black Sea to the Sea of Azov. Homer characterized the early Cimmerian inhabitants of this region as living in a country of darkness that was situated on the northern edge of the populated world (*Od.* 11.13–19). Between the eighth and sixth centuries

---

[75]While the office of *archisynagōgos* will be discussed in the next chapter, here we should mention that the office is elsewhere attested in inscriptions from our period (*CIJ* 2.1404, *JIE* 18, *DF* 33). Though the presence of multiple *archisynagōgoi* is not otherwise attested in our period, in three inscriptions from Berenice (*CJCZ* 70–72), several *archontes* are listed (see above). Likewise, an inscription from Egypt mentions two *prostatai* (*JIE* 24). As shall be argued in the next chapter, both of these titles appear to be analogous to *archisynagōgos*.

B.C.E., several Greek cities were founded in the region, apparently with the permission of the Scythians, the successors to the Cimmerians. The largest and most important of these cities was the Milesian colony of Panticapaeum (modern Kerch), located on the eastern tip of the Crimea, on the western side of the straits of Kerch. Among the colonies established on the eastern side of the straits (the Taman Peninsula) were Phanagoria and Gorgippia.

A succession of dynasties ruled the Bosporus region for centuries, beginning with the Greek Archeanactids (480–438 B.C.E.), followed by the half-Thracian Spartocids (438–110 B.C.E.) and then by the kings of Pontus (110–8 B.C.E.). Just before the turn of the era, Augustus recognized yet a fourth dynasty, which served as a vassal to Rome until the Gothic invasions of the third century C.E. The region was noted for its trade in grain, fish and slaves as well as for its production of fine jewelry and pottery.[76]

Panticapaeum, Phanagoria and Gorgippia

Evidence for a Jewish presence in the Bosporus emerges around the turn of the era, though scholars remain unsure of the region from which the Jews migrated. Asia, Pontus and Egypt have all been proposed as places of origin.[77] As mentioned previously, the evidence for synagogues in the Bosporus Kingdom consists of a series of manumission inscriptions, which appear at Panticapaeum, Phanagoria and Gorgippia, the earliest dating to 18 C.E. The manumissions routinely took place in the synagogues (called *proseuchai*), with the released person or persons sometimes being placed under the guardianship of the Jewish congregation (*synagōgē*) and sometimes being required to attend the synagogue. Because we will more fully discuss the process of

---

[76]For a more detailed history of the region during the Roman period, see M. Rostovtzeff, *Iranians and Greeks in South Russia* (New York: Russell and Russel, 1969), 147–180. Also Omeljan Pritsak, "The Role of the Bosporus Kingdom and Late Hellenism as the Basis for the Medieval Cultures of the Territories North of the Black Sea" in *Mutual Effects of the Islamic and Judeo-Christian Worlds: The East European Pattern*, edited by A. Ascher (New York: Columbia University Press, 1979), 3–5. On recent archaeological discoveries in the region, see Michail J. Treister and Yuri G. Vinogradov, "Archaeology on the Northern Coast of the Black Sea," *Archaeology* 97 (1993): 521–563.

[77]Rostovtzeff, *Iranians and Greeks in South Russia*, 150; Pritsak, "The Role of the Bosporus Kingdom," 14.

manumission in chapter six, we will wait until then to cite most of the inscriptions. The inscriptions to follow will present a small sample of this type of monument.

The first inscription comes from Gorgippia and dates to 41 C.E. (*CIJ* 1.690 = *CIRB* 1123):

> Θεῶι ὑψίστωι παντο̣-
> κράτορι εὐλογητῷ, βα-
> σιλεύοντος βασιλέ-
> ως Μ̣ι̣θ̣ρ̣ι̣δ̣α̣τ̣ο̣υ̣ φιλο-
> Γερμακου καὶ φιλοπάτ-
> ριδος ἔτους ηλτ΄, μη-
> νὸς Δείου, Πόθος Στ-
> ράβωνος ἀνέθηκεν
> τῆι [προσ]ευχῆι κατ᾽ εὐχὴ-
> ν θ[ρ]επτὴν ἑαυτοῦ, ἧ ὄνο̣-
> μα Χρύσα, ἐφ᾽ ᾧ ἧ ἀνέπα-
> φος καὶ ἀνεπηρέαστος
> ἀπὸ παντὸς κληρον[όμ]-
> ου ὑπὸ Δία, Γῆν, Ἥλιο̣[ν]

> To God Most High, almighty and blessed, in the reign of King Mithridates, friend of | [the emperor?] and friend of the homeland, in the year 338, in the month of Deios, I, Pothos, son of Strabonos, dedicated in the *proseuchē* according to my vow, | my homebred slave, named Chrysa, so that she will be free from harm and undisturbed by all my heirs, by Zeus, Ge, Helios[78]

While this inscription begins with the now familiar dedication to the Most High God (cf. *JIE* 27), it is somewhat surprising to see it conclude with a formula to Zeus, Ge and Helios. Emil Schürer, the first scholar to recognize the Jewish nature of this and other Bosporan inscriptions, argued that the references to pagan deities indicated the existence in the Bosporus of a peculiar brand of syncretized Judaism.[79] Later, however, Erwin Goodenough, citing papyrological evidence, argued that this was not at all the case:

> We now know that in documents of manumission of slaves the formula "Zeus, Ge, Helios" was so established that it seems legally to have been quite

---

[78]Author's translation. The transcription is based on the reading found in Levinskaya, *The Book of Acts in Its Diaspora Setting*, 239–240.

[79]Emil Schürer, "Die Juden im bosporanischen Reiche und die Genossenschaften der σεβόμενοι θεὸν ὕψιστον ebendaselbst" in *Sitzungsberichte der Königlich Preussischen Akademie der Wissenschaften zu Berlin* (Berlin, 1897), 1.200–225.

> *de rigueur* . . . it carried no implication of the person's belief, but was introduced into this Jewish document to make the manumission legal in pagan eyes, and involved no threat to the monotheism of the Jew who used it.[80]

Goodenough's judgment has been accepted by recent scholarship[81] and is further strengthened by the fact that the only other Jewish inscription to include this formula is also from Gorgippia, suggesting that it was a peculiarity of that city. The monument (*CIJ* 690a = *CIRB* 1126), which dates to 68 C.E., closely resembles the above inscription, except that its center is badly mutilated, obliterating the reference to the *proseuchē* that it almost certainly contained:

> Θεῶι Ὑψίστωι παν{τα}τοκράτορι
> εὐλογητῶι, βασιλεύοντος βασιλέ-
> ως Ῥησκουπόριδος, φιλοκαίσαρος
> καὶ φιλορωμαίου, εὐσεβοῦς, ἔτους
> δξτʹ, μηνὸς Δαεισίου, Νεοκλῆς
> Ἀθηνοδώ[ρου ἀφίημι ἐλευθέρ]ους ὑπὸ
> Δία, Γῆν Ἥλιον [. . . . .]μου τρο-
> φῆς [. . . . .]
> [- - - - - - - συνεπι]-
> νεύσαντος δὲ κα Ἀθ(η)νοδώρο[υ] Ἀθ[ην]α[ίου]
> τοῦ πατρός μου, ἐ[φ'] ὧι ὦσιν ἀνέ[π]αφοι καὶ ἀ-
> νεπηρέαστοι ἀπὸ παντὸς κληρονόμου
> μου· τρ[έ]πεσ[θ]αί τε αὐτοὺς [ὅπ]-
> ου ἂν βούλωνται διὰ τὸ κύριο[ν]
> κελευθ<εωθ>ῆναι ὑπ' ἐμοῦ
>
> To God the Most High, Almighty, Blessed, under the reign of King Rescuporis, loyal to the Emperor and friend of the Romans, pious, in the year | 364, in the month of Daisius, I Neocles son of Athenodoros set in liberty under Zeus, Ge, Helios (the slaves of . . . bred in my house?) . . . with the assent of Athenodoros son of Athenaios, | my father, wherefore they should be unharmed and undisturbed by all my heirs and may go where they want because of my valid order.[82]

---

[80]Erwin R. Goodenough, "The Bosporus Inscriptions to the Most High God," *JQR* 47 (1956): 222–223. The papyrological reference is *SB* 1.5616.

[81]See Levinskaya, *The Book of Acts in Its Diaspora Setting*, 105–116; Trebilco, *Jewish Communities in Asia Minor*, 136; *HJP* 3.1.37. The latter observes that the Elephantine papyri (*ANET* 491–492) provide further examples of Jews who were willing to make use of pagan oath formulas as a legal necessity.

[82]Transcription and translation from *CIJ*.

Aside from displaying a degree of flexibility among the Jews of Gorgippia with regard to the use of pagan oath formulas, the first and probably also the second of these inscriptions, along with other examples we shall later consider, are noteworthy because they name the synagogue as the venue for the manumissions. This fact further led Schürer to conclude that the Bosporan Jews were highly syncretized, since elsewhere pagan temples served as the usual place for manumissions. This is especially seen in more than a thousand manumission inscriptions unearthed at the sacred precinct of Delphi. These typically depict the owner releasing a slave in the precinct, using formulas similar to the ones found in the Bosporus inscriptions. The owner would ceremoniously sell the slave to the deity, usually with the slave or a benefactor contributing the bulk of the purchase price. The priests of Apollo would receive the money, dedicate it to the god, and then turn it over the former owner, who thus received reimbursement for the loss of the slave. In return, the slave would be set at liberty, though in some instances he or she would be under obligation to work for the former master for a period of time.[83]

A nearly identical process is seen in the Bosporus inscriptions: the slave is dedicated to the Jewish deity, "the Most High God," and is contractually released from all claims of ownership. Because the financial transactions accompanying this process go unmentioned in the inscriptions, we cannot be sure of their exact nature. Nevertheless, it is possible that the parties followed the same process of payment, dedication and reimbursement seen at Delphi. Whatever the case, the fact that the manumissions took place in the synagogues strongly suggests that the Jews of the Bosporus perceived them to be analogous to the pagan temples. This, coupled with the official nature of the inscriptions, indicates that the Bosporus synagogues, like those hitherto encountered in our survey, were sacred buildings that served the religious and civic needs of the resident Jewish communities.

ASIA[84]

When Alexander the Great conquered all of Asia Minor in 334 B.C.E., he ended a long period of Persian domination of the region. Upon his death, the territory first fell to Antigonus, one of Alexander's generals,

[83]See William L. Westermann, "Parmone as General Service Contract," *The Journal of Juristic Papyrology* 2 (1947): 9–50; *NDIEC* 5.70–81; *HJP* 2.1.105–106.

[84]For additional background on Asia, see Trebilco, "Asia," 291–302.

and subsequently to the Seleucids, who took control of the entire subcontinent in 281 B.C.E. Thanks to Roman military intervention, the area west of the river Halys in central Anatolia was granted to the Attalid kings of Pergamum following the battle of Magnesia in 190 B.C.E. When the last of the kings of Pergamum, Attalus III, died in 133 B.C.E., he willed his entire kingdom to the Romans, who in turn formed the province of Asia in 129 B.C.E.

From that time until the third century C.E., the province consisted of the bulk of western Anatolia, including the inland regions of Mysia, Lydia, Caria (added in 84 B.C.E.) and portions of Phrygia (added in 116 B.C.E.), as well as the coastal areas of Aeolia, Ionia, the Troad and several of the Aegean islands. The neighboring provinces were Bithynia and Pontus to the north, Lycia to the south, and Galatia to the east.

In the first century B.C.E., Asia served as the battleground for a series of wars between Rome and Mithridates IV of Pontus. These left the region economically devastated, and it was only under the patronage of the early Roman emperors that the major cities of the province, including Ephesus, Pergamum, Smyrna and Sardis, again began to prosper.

Jewish presence in Asia may date to as early as the fifth century B.C.E., since Obadiah 20 possibly refers to Sardis (סְפָרַד) as one of the cities inhabited by Jews following the Babylonian exile. A more massive movement of Jews into the region came as a result of Antiochus III's relocation of two thousand Jewish families into Lydia and Phrygia at the end of the third century B.C.E. (Josephus, *Ant.* 12.149–150), as noted in our earlier discussion of Galatia. Late second-century evidence for Jewish communities in the region consists of a congratulatory letter to Hyrcanus I from Pergamum (*Ant.* 14.247–255) and an edict from Sardis (*Ant.* 14.259–261) which might also date to this time.

As a result of Hyrcanus II and Antipater's support for Caesar in his eastern campaigns, the victorious Roman dictator not only presented honors to the two leaders, but also began to accord special treatment to Jews both in Palestine and the diaspora. While we have encountered some of these decrees and letters from Caesar and his subordinates in our consideration of other parts of the diaspora, the evidence is most voluminous for Asia. These documents outline three specific benefits to be granted to the Jews living in various parts of the province: (1) the right to gather on the Sabbath and practice Jewish sacred rites (ἱερὰ Ἰουδαϊκά; Josephus, *Ant.* 14.225–226, 234, 236–237, 262–264), (2) the right to collect money and other gifts to be sent to the Jerusalem Temple (*Ant.* 14.225–227) and (3) the right of Jews who were Roman citizens to be exempt from military service (*Ant.* 14.225–227, 228–229, 230, 236–237, 237–240). These letters and edicts were issued in a rather ad hoc manner, with most of them applying to particular Asian cities such as Ephesus or Sardis.

Somewhat later (2–3 C.E.), however, Augustus issued a blanket decree, applying to Jews living throughout the province. We twice encountered this decree in chapter two, once in Josephus' quotation of it, and once in Philo's paraphrase. For comparative purposes, we here reproduce the relevant segments side-by-side:

> Caesar Augustus, Pontifex Maximus with tribunician power, decrees as follows. Since the Jewish nation has been found well disposed to the Roman people not only at the present time but also in the time past, and especially in the time of my father the emperor Caesar, as has their high priest Hyrcanus, it has been decided by me and my council under oath, with the consent of the Roman people, that the Jews may follow their own customs in accordance with the law of their fathers, just as they followed them in the time of Hyrcanus, high priest of the Most High God, and that their sacred monies shall be inviolable and may be sent up to Jerusalem and delivered to the treasurers in Jerusalem, and that they need not give bond (to appear in court) on the Sabbath or on the day of preparation for it (Sabbath Eve) after the ninth hour. And if anyone is caught stealing their sacred books or their sacred monies from a *sabbateion* or an ark (of the Law) [or a banquet hall], he shall be regarded as sacrilegious, and his property shall be confiscated to the public treasury of the Romans. As for the resolution which was offered by them in my honour concerning the piety which I show to all men, and on behalf of Gaius Marcus Censorinus, I order that it and the present edict be set up in the most conspicuous (part of the temple) assigned to me by the federation of Asia (Josephus, *Ant.* 16.162–164).

> While I have a great abundance of evidence to show the wishes of your great-grandfather Augustus I will content myself with two examples. The first is a letter which he sent to the governors of the provinces in Asia, as he had learnt that the sacred first-fruits were treated with disrespect. He ordered that the Jews alone should be permitted by them to assemble in *synagogia*. These gatherings, he said, were not based on drunkenness and carousing to promote conspiracy and so to do grave injury to the cause of peace, but were *didaskaleia* of temperance and justice where men while practising virtue subscribed the annual first-fruits to pay for the sacrifices which they offer and commissioned sacred envoys to take them to the temple in Jerusalem. Then he commanded that no one should hinder the Jews from meeting or subscribing or sending envoys to Jerusalem according to their ancestral practice. For these were certainly the substance if not the actual words of his instructions (Philo, *Legat.* 311–313).

The decree itself outlines the right of the Jews to practice their ancestral customs, which Philo interprets as the right to assemble in synagogues. While both segments allude to the permission given to the Asian Jews to collect sacred monies to send to Jerusalem, the actual decree further specifies that these were stored in either a synagogue or an adjoining dining chamber (or ark). The decree stands alone in mentioning that Jews should not be hauled into the courts on the Sabbath or Sabbath eve. As noted in chapter two, the allusion in the actual decree to the Asian Jews' resolution honoring Augustus indicates that the Jews in the various cities of this province had some sort of regional organization, where representatives were empowered by the local communities to address proclamations on their behalf to the highest echelons of the imperial government.

In what cities were the above-mentioned synagogues located? Although we only have specific evidence for synagogues at Ephesus, Sardis, Halicarnassus and Acmonia, given the extensive literary attestation for Jews residing in this region, such structures probably flourished in cities throughout the province. Other likely candidates include Pergamum, Apamea, Adramyttium, Laodicea, Tralles and Miletus—cities specifically mentioned in early sources as major Jewish havens.[85] Confirmation of these literary attestations remains a goal of Anatolian archaeology into the twenty-first century.

Ephesus

During the reign of Augustus, Ephesus became the capital city of the province, a natural choice because of its location at the intersection of two ancient trade routes, its harbor on the Aegean Sea, and its sizable population, estimated to have been more than 180,000 at the turn of the era.[86] The city was renowned as the site of the ancient temple of Artemis,

---

[85]Cicero states that in 62 B.C.E. a hundred pounds of gold (c. 135,000 drachmae ≈ US $5,400,000) was seized from Jewish offerings in Apamea, twenty pounds (c. 27,000 drachmae ≈ US $1,080,000) from Laodicea, and unknown sums from Adramyttium and Pergamum (*pro Flacc.* 68). The generous amounts from Apamea and Laodicea suggest sizable populations in these cities. Additionally, Josephus quotes edicts implying Jewish communities in Pergamum (*Ant.* 14.247–255), Miletus (*Ant.* 14.244–246), Laodicea and Tralles (*Ant.* 14.241–243) in the second through first centuries B.C.E. See Trebilco, *Jewish Communities in Asia Minor*, 5–20.

[86]See L. Michael White, "Urban Development and Social Change in Imperial Ephesos" in *Ephesos: Metropolis of Asia*, edited by Helmut Koester (Valley Forge,

one of the seven wonders of the world, and during the first century C.E. it rapidly became a major center for the imperial cult.[87]

Josephus states that the Jews in Ionia, including those in Ephesus, were granted citizenship in the city by Antiochus II (261–246 B.C.E.; *Ant.* 12.125). This claim, however, like similar claims made by Josephus for the Jewish communities in Alexandria and Antioch, is dubious. Most likely only individual Jews were members of the local citizenry.[88] On the other hand, the number of edicts addressed to Ephesus dealing with Jewish exemptions from military service—because of scruples over marching on the Sabbath and difficulties in obtaining kosher food—indicates that at least some of the Jews there were Roman citizens (*Ant.* 14.225–227, 228–229, 230, 234, 237–240). One of these edicts, issued by P. Cornelius Dolabella, governor of Asia in 43 B.C.E., also permitted the Jews in the city "to follow their native customs and to come together for sacred and holy rites in accordance with their law, and to make offerings for their sacrifices [συγχωρῶ χρῆσθαι τοῖς πατρίοις ἐθισμοῖς, ἱερῶν ἕνεκα καὶ ἁγίων συναγομένοις, καθὼς αὐτοῖς νόμιμον, καὶ τῶν πρὸς τὰς θυσίας ἀφαιρεμάτων]" (*Ant.* 14.227). The mention of sacrifices is an allusion to the practice of meeting together to collect monies to be sent to Jerusalem in order to render sacrifices at the main sanctuary. This custom is more explicitly stated in several additional documents, including one cited by Philo that was issued by G. Norbanus Flaccus, proconsul of Asia between 31 and 27 B.C.E.:

> Gaius Norbanus Flaccus proconsul to the magistrates of the Ephesians, greeting. Caesar has written to me that the Jews, wherever they may be, regularly according to their old peculiar custom, make a rule of meeting together and subscribing money which they send to Jerusalem. ['Ιουδαίους, οὗ ἂν ὦσιν, ἰδίῳ ἀρχαίῳ ἐθισμῷ νομίζειν συναγομένους χρήματα φέρειν, ἃ πέμπουσιν εἰς 'Ιεροσόλυμα]. He does not wish them to be hindered from doing this. I therefore write to you to let you know that this is what he orders to be done (*Legat.* 315; cf. Josephus, *Ant.* 16.167–168, 172–173).

Letters such as this one were necessary because of restrictions occasionally placed on exports of gold and silver by the Roman Senate or individual governors. In his defense of L. Valerius Flaccus, proconsul of

---

Pennsylvania: Trinity Press International, 1995), 40–43

[87]See Trebilco, "Asia," 302–357 for additional points on Ephesian history, topography and culture.

[88]See Trebilco, *Jewish Communities in Asia Minor*, 168–169.

Asia in 62 B.C.E., the famous orator Cicero argued that such a restriction was the reason that Flaccus "confiscated" money from the Jews in his province (*pro Flacc.* 66–69).[89] Subsequently, Hyrcanus II probably intervened to obtain the exemption that later became standard policy throughout the empire.

The two documents cited suggest that the Jews in Ephesus possessed a synagogue, and indeed, in three passages, Acts makes this point explicit. The first of these briefly states that, on a voyage from Corinth to Caesarea (c. 52 C.E.), Paul landed at Ephesus, got off his boat and "went into the synagogue and had a discussion with the Jews [αὐτὸς δὲ εἰσελθὼν εἰς τὴν συναγωγὴν διελέξατο τοῖς Ἰουδαίοις]" (Acts 18:19). According to the account, the congregation asked him to stay longer but Paul declined (18:20). Promising to return later if God willed, he hopped back on his boat and continued his journey (18:21).

Helmut Koester has suggested that this segment was inserted by the author of Acts in order to present Paul as the first Christian preacher in Ephesus.[90] This seems a plausible hypothesis, given Acts' tendency to highlight the apostle's authority over the churches in the Gentile mission. In any case, on the heels of the preceding passage, Acts portrays the missionary efforts of a second Christian preacher, Apollos:

> Now there came to Ephesus a Jew named Apollos, a native of Alexandria. He was an eloquent man, well-versed in the scriptures. He had been instructed in the Way of the Lord; and he spoke with burning enthusiasm and taught accurately the things concerning Jesus, though he knew only the baptism of John. He began to speak boldly in the synagogue [οὗτός τε ἤρξατο παρρησιάζεσθαι ἐν τῇ συναγωγῇ]; but when Priscilla and Aquila heard him, they took him aside and explained the Way of God to him more accurately (Acts 18:24–26).

This segment, like the previous one, reveals the willingness of the synagogue congregations to allow itinerants to speak in their meetings (at least in Luke's eyes). The passage also presents Priscilla as a member of the congregation, indicating that women participated in the Sabbath gatherings, though their degree of participation is left unstated. Christians

---

[89]See Smallwood *The Jews under Roman Rule*; 125–128, Levinskaya, *The Book of Acts in Its Diaspora Setting*, 145–146

[90]Helmut Koester, "Ephesos in Early Christian Literature" in *Ephesos: Metropolis of Asia*, edited by Helmut Koester (Valley Forge, Pennsylvania: Trinity Press International, 1995), 127–128.

are thus portrayed as being participants in the Ephesian synagogue as late as 52 C.E.

This situation changed dramatically upon Paul's return to the city the following year. In its account of this return visit, Acts repeats its familiar pattern, with Paul entering the synagogue, finding initial acceptance of his message, followed by rejection:

> He entered the synagogue and for three months spoke out boldly [Εἰσελθὼν δὲ εἰς τὴν συναγωγὴν ἐπαρρησιάζετο ἐπὶ μῆνας τρεῖς διαλεγόμενος], and argued persuasively about the kingdom of God. When some stubbornly refused to believe and spoke evil of the Way before the congregation [πλήθους], he left them, taking the disciples with him, and argued daily in the lecture hall of Tyrannus (Acts 19:8–9).

The primary difference between this and earlier synagogue passages in Acts is the lengthy period of time Paul is said to have stayed in the synagogue before leaving—three months, compared to a mere week at Pisidian Antioch (13:14–46), three weeks at Thessalonica (17:2) and probably not much longer at Iconium (14:1–6), Philippi (16:2–40) and Corinth (18:4–7).

The consistent reference to "the synagogue" in the above passages implies that there was only one synagogue at Ephesus. If so, then the building must have been quite large, since the other literary sources imply a sizable Jewish population in the city, though its exact number is unknown. Also unclear is whether the Jews in Ephesus formed a politeuma as in Alexandria, Antioch and elsewhere—though a letter written by Marcus Agrippa decreed that those caught stealing the sacred monies of the Ephesian Jews were to be handed over not to the local magistrates, but to the Jews themselves (Josephus, *Ant.* 16.168). This implies that the Jews of this city possessed a corporate entity, legally empowered to exercise judicial powers.[91] Unfortunately, the excavations at Ephesus have so far failed to uncover much evidence for the Jewish community attested in the literary sources.[92] One hopes that this situation will be remedied in future archaeological explorations.

---

[91]On this question generally, see Trebilco, *Jewish Communities in Asia Minor*, 169–172.

[92]See G. H. R. Horsley, "The Inscriptions of Ephesos and the New Testament," *NovT* 2 (1992): 121–127; PWSup, 12.248–364, 1588–1704. One inscription, *IvEph.* 4.1251, mentions *archisynagōgoi* and *presbyteroi*. However, it probably dates a century or two after our period.

Sardis

Sardis is located on the banks of the southern tributary of the Hermus river in southwestern Lydia. Between 281 and 189 B.C.E. it served as the Seleucid capital of northern Asia Minor. Passing to the Pergamene kings (189 B.C.E.) and then to the Romans (133 B.C.E.), Sardis remained an important city into the Imperial era, with an estimated population of 100,000 in the first century C.E.[93]

As already mentioned, Jewish presence in the city may date as early as the sixth century B.C.E. (Obad 20). If so, this population was supplemented by the import of Mesopotamian Jews into Lydia by Antiochus III late in the third century B.C.E. (Josephus, *Ant.* 12.149–150). The favorable terms mentioned in Antiochus' letter ("you shall give each of them a place to build a house and land to cultivate and plant with vines, and shall exempt them from payment of taxes for ten years") suggest that the Sardian Jews were able to establish themselves rapidly as one of the leading Jewish communities in all of Asia.

In chapter two we encountered two edicts mentioning the presence of a synagogue in Sardis. There it was argued that both edicts employ the word *topos* in a technical sense, meaning "sacred place" or "sanctuary." The first of the edicts, dating as early as the late second century B.C.E.,[94] grants that the Sardian Jews may "come together and have a communal life and adjudicate suits among themselves [συνάγωνται καὶ πολιτεύωνται καὶ διαδικάζωνται πρὸς αὐτούς]" (*Ant.* 14.260). The use of the verb *politeuomai* suggests the creation of a politeuma, a notion confirmed by the permission given to the Sardian Jews to settle law-suits among themselves.[95] In addition, the Jews were allowed to build a synagogue wherein they could presumably settle these juridical affairs as well as to "gather together with their wives and children and offer their ancestral prayers and sacrifices to God [συλλεγόμενοι μετὰ γυναικῶν καὶ τέκνων ἐπιτελῶσι τὰς πατρίους εὐχὰς καὶ θυσίας τῷ θεῷ]" (ibid.). One could hardly ask for a stronger statement that prayer formed an essential part of the communal gatherings in the synagogue. Moreover, the specific mention of women and children in the decree indicates that the *entire*

---

[93]See Trebilco, *Jewish Communities in Asia Minor*, 37.

[94]For arguments regarding the date of the Sardian decree, see the discussion of *topos* in chapter two.

[95]See Smallwood, *The Jews under Roman Rule*, 139–140.

Jewish community at Sardis gathered for these ancestral prayers on the Sabbaths, not just the men.

The first decree from Sardis was later reconfirmed in an edict issued by Lucius Antionius in 49 B.C.E. This edict was prompted by Sardian Jews who approached the propraetor to inform him that "from the earliest times they [had] had an association of their own [σύνοδον ἔχειν ἰδίαν] in accordance with their native laws and a place of their own [τόπον ἴδιον], in which they decide[d] their own affairs and controversies with one another" (*Ant.* 14.235). Like most Roman officials, Lucius was inclined to preserve the earlier status quo; he permitted the politeuma (*synodos*) and the synagogue (*topos*) to function as they had in previous generations.

Yet a third edict dealing with the Sardian Jews was later issued by G. Norbanus Flaccus (31–27 B.C.E.). Like the one sent by this official to Ephesus, the edict concerns the movement of monies out of the province to Jerusalem:

> Gaius Norbanus Flaccus, proconsul, to the magistrates and council of Sardis, greeting. Caesar has written to me, ordering that the Jews shall not be prevented from collecting sums of money, however great they may be, in accordance with their ancestral custom, and sending them up to Jerusalem. I have therefore written to you in order that you may know that Caesar and I wish this to be done (*Ant.* 16.171).

Taken together, the three decrees establish that the Sardian Jews faithfully maintained their ties with the Temple in Jerusalem while at the same time possessing a synagogue in which they gathered for prayers on the Sabbaths and administered their own internal affairs as a politeuma. Unfortunately, this earlier synagogue—not to be confused with the later III–IV century C.E. structure—has not yet been discovered.[96] It may have been destroyed in a devastating earthquake that struck the area in 17 C.E. If so, then the Jews were possibly granted yet another place, only centuries later to inherit the mammoth building unearthed in 1962.[97]

---

[96]In the nineteenth century, an inscription was discovered in Sardis on the remains of a fountain. It reads, "the fountain of the synagogue [συναγωγῆ[ς κρήνη]]" (*CIJ* 2.751). Unfortunately, the date of the inscription is uncertain.

[97]For a description of the later synagogue and some musings about its relationship to the earlier structure, see Kraabel, "Paganism and Judaism: The Sardis Evidence," 13–33; idem, "The Diaspora Synagogue: Archaeological and Epigraphic Evidence Since Sukenik" in *ANRW* II.19.1, 483–488.

Halicarnassus

Situated along the Carian coastline in southwestern Asia, Halicarnassus was founded as a Dorian colony that was later destroyed by Alexander in 334 B.C.E. It was quickly reestablished and continued to serve as an important commercial center thanks primarily to its excellent port. In antiquity, Halicarnassus was also noted as the site of the tomb of King Mausolus (377–353 B.C.E.), one of the seven wonders of the world.

The earliest evidence for a Jewish community in Halicarnassus consists of a brief allusion in 1 Macc 15:23 to a letter of friendship sent to the city by the Romans on behalf of the Jews there (c. 139 B.C.E.). Subsequently, Josephus quotes the following decree, which probably dates to the first century B.C.E., although it is also possible that it was drafted a century earlier in reaction to the letter mentioned in 1 Maccabees:[98]

> Decree of the people of Halicarnassus. "In the priesthood of Memnon, son of Aristides and, by adoption, of Euonymus . . . of Anthesterion, the people passed the following decree on the motion of Marcus Alexander. Whereas at all times we have had a deep regard for piety toward the Deity and holiness, and following the example of the people of Rome, who are benefactors of all mankind, and in conformity with what they have written to our city concerning their friendship and alliance with the Jews, to the effect that their sacred services to God and their customary festivals and religious gatherings shall be carried on [συντελῶνται αὑτοῖς αἱ εἰς τόν θεὸν ἱεροπαιίαι καὶ ἑορταὶ αἱ εἰθισμέναι καὶ σύνοδοι δεδόχθαι], we have also decreed that those Jewish men and women who so wish may observe their Sabbaths and perform their sacred rites in accordance with the Jewish laws [καὶ ἡμῖν Ἰουδαίων τοὺς Βουλομένους ἄνδρας τε καὶ γυναῖκας τά τε σάββατα ἄγειν καὶ τὰ ἱερὰ συντελεῖν κατὰ τοὺς Ἰουδαϊκοὺς νόμους], and may build *proseuchai* near the sea, in accordance with their native custom [καὶ τὰς προσευχὰς ποιεῖσθαι πρὸς τῇ θαλάττῃ κατὰ τὸ πάτριον ἔθος]. And if anyone, whether magistrate or private citizen, prevents them, he shall be liable to the following fine and owe it to the city" (*Ant.* 14.256–258).

There are several things of interest in this decree. First of all, it supplies us with the only extant usage of *proseuchē* in reference to an Asian

---

[98]In favor of the latter proposal is the fact that the edict from Halicarnassus comes immediately after a letter from Pergamum (*Ant.* 14.247–255) dating to the time of Hyrcanus I (134–105 B.C.E.) and before a decree from Sardis (*Ant.* 14.259–261) that probably also dates to the second century B.C.E.

synagogue during our period.[99] This should not come as a surprise, since the term appears in synagogue inscriptions from the Bosporus kingdom, Delos, and Rome—all located in the northern half of the Roman empire. A second point is that, according to the edict, the *proseuchai* were to be built close to the sea because of the "native custom" of the Jews. Most scholars have taken this to be an allusion to biblical purity requirements.[100]

A third notable feature is that women are specifically mentioned in the decree, as was the case at Sardis, underscoring the inclusive nature of the synagogues in Asia. Finally, the allusion to "festivals" (ἑορταί) hints that the Jews in Halicarnassus observed not only the Sabbath, but also other holy days such as the Festival of Tabernacles. In connection with this, the term *synodoi* in the same sentence does not seem to be used as a technical term for a politeuma, as was the case in one of the Sardian edicts, but more generally in the sense of "gatherings." Hence when the above edict was issued, the Jewish community does not appear to have been invested with the authority to administer legal matters among themselves, though it is quite possible that the Jews there settled disputes internally even without formal authorization.

Acmonia

Located in eastern Asia, Acmonia was one of the most important cities in Phrygia. Almost nothing is known about the early history of the Jewish community there, though presumably it was established in the late third century B.C.E. as a result of Antiochus III's decision to move Jews into the region, as has been noted in several places above. It is also likely that Acmonia was one of the cities from which Flaccus appropriated Jewish offerings to the Temple during his administration in 62 B.C.E.[101]

---

[99]On the suggestion that τὰς προσευχὰς ποιεῖσθαι πρὸς τῇ θαλάττῃ should be translated "make prayers by the sea," see Hüttenmeister, "'Synagoge' und 'Proseuche' bei Josephus und in anderen antiken Quellen," 178. The quoted rendering in the LCL translation is the more probable. See Hengel, "Proseuche und Synagoge," 175–176.

[100]See Eleazar L. Sukenik, *Ancient Synagogues in Palestine and Greece* (London: Oxford University Press, 1934), 49–50; Greeven, "Προσευχή," 808; Levine, "The Second Temple Synagogue," 13. See the discussion of ritual washings in chapter six, below.

[101]So Trebilco, theorizing that part of the large sum confiscated at Apamea came from nearby Acmonia (*Jewish Communities in Asia Minor*, 84).

Aside from these references, the only other evidence we have from our period is the dedicatory inscription of a synagogue, quoted in chapter two (*DF* 33). The synagogue building (called an *oikos*)[102] was donated by Julia Severa, a high priestess of the imperial cult in Acmonia during the reign of Nero. Her prominence is seen on several imperial coins issued during Nero's reign where her name appears on the reverse along with the name of her husband, Lucius Servenius Capito (generally as ἐπι Σερουηνίου Καπίτωνος καὶ Ἰουλίας Σεουήρας).[103] Additionally, her name is mentioned in a number of inscriptions which record that she and her husband were *archontes* of Acmonia between the years 59 and 63 C.E.[104] Although William Ramsay thought that Julia Severa was Jewish, given her position as high priestess, it is more likely that she was a Gentile benefactor of the Jews, just as M. Tittius apparently served for the Jews in Berenice.[105] Whatever the exact nature of her relationship with the synagogue, it is clear that in the first century the Acmonian Jews were connected to the highest echelons of power in the city.[106]

Although the inscription states that Julia Severa erected the building, it goes on to honor three men—one of whom was a Roman citizen—for their renovation of the structure, which included the addition of "painted murals on the walls and ceiling" and other unspecified ornamentations. For their contribution, the congregation (*synagōgē*) honored the donors with a gilded shield, presumably to be displayed in the building. While the construction history of the synagogue building is uncertain, the most likely possibility is that Julia Severa initially erected a synagogue for the Jewish community, and the three donors embellished it sometime later.[107] Another alternative is that Julia Severa donated an ordinary structure that was transformed into a synagogue through the renovations.[108]

---

[102]For the translation of *oikos* in this inscription, see the discussion of this term in chapter two.

[103]See Ramsay, *Cities and Bishoprics of Phrygia*, 2.638–640, 647–651; *HJP*, 3.1.31.

[104]Ramsay, *Cities and Bishoprics of Phrygia*, 2.650.

[105]So *HJP*, 3.1.31; Trebilco, *Jewish Communities in Asia Minor*, 58–60.

[106]White suggests that two of the Jewish leaders, Lucius and Tyrronios, were former slaves of the Severa family and of Tyrronios Rapio, another *archōn* of Acmonia in the first century. See White, *Domus Ecclesiae Domus Dei*, 272.

[107]The use of the formula τὸν κατασκευασθέ[ν]τα ο[ἶ]κον ὑπὸ Ἰουλίας Σεουήρας ("this structure was erected by Julia Severa") implies that the building was purposely erected as a synagogue. If a previously existing building had been donated, one would have expected the use of δίδωμι rather than κατασκευάζω.

[108]See White, *Domus Ecclesiae Domus Dei*, 272.

It is of additional interest that each of the men mentioned in the inscription held a different title: one was called an *archisynagōgos dia biou*, the second an *archisynagōgos* and the third an *archōn*. While the possible meaning of each of the three titles will be discussed in the next chapter, here it will be observed that their usage indicates a high degree of institutionalization within the Acmonian synagogue.

Summary

Asia was clearly an important center within the Jewish diaspora during the Second Temple period as can be seen in the number of existing decrees regarding the Jews of this province, which is without parallel elsewhere in the empire. Despite the fact that archaeological evidence for synagogues in this region during our period is slender, available sources attest to the existence of synagogues at Ephesus, Sardis, Halicarnassus and Acmonia by no later than the first century C.E., though as early as the second century B.C.E. in the cases of Sardis and Halicarnassus. Synagogues may also have been located at Miletus, Pergamum, Apamea, Adramyttium, Laodicea and Tralles prior to 70 C.E.

The existing evidence indicates that the Asian synagogues were faithful in supporting the Jerusalem Temple cultus, with envoys being sent annually to pay the Temple tax and to offer sacrifices on behalf of their respective communities.[109] At the same time, the synagogues in this region served as places of sacred assembly for men, women and (at least at Sardis) children on the Sabbath and on other holy days. Scripture

---

[109]Recently, Daniel Schwartz has proposed that the Jews in the diaspora sent money not to the Temple, but merely to Jerusalem (to where, he does not specify). Further, he has asserted that imposition of the *fiscus Judaicus* by Vespasian had nothing to do with the earlier custom of sending the Temple tax to Jerusalem, writing: "to my knowledge, there is no Roman text which links the *fiscus Judaicus* to the destruction of the Temple" (Daniel R. Schwartz, "Temple or City: What did Hellenistic Jews See in Jerusalem?" in *The Centrality of Jerusalem*, edited by M. Poorthuis and Chana Safrai [Kampen, the Netherlands: Pharos, 1996], 126). However, Schwartz does not discuss the following passage: "On all Jews, wheresoever resident, [Vespasian] imposed a poll-tax of two drachms, to be paid annually into the Capitol as formerly contributed by them to the temple at Jerusalem" (Josephus, *BJ* 7.218). Note also that Cicero refers to the Jewish custom of sending money to Jerusalem as a "barbaric superstition [*barbarae supersititioni*]" (*pro Flacc.* 67) indicating that he viewed the contributions to be connected with Jewish cultic practices. For other references mentioning that the money from the diaspora went to the Temple, see e.g., Josephus, *Ant.* 14.227; 16.28, 45, 160, 164, 166, 167, 170, 172; Philo, *Legat.* 216, 313.

reading and preaching is attested for the services held in the Ephesian synagogue, while the offering of prayers is mentioned as a function of the synagogue at Sardis. These buildings also served as repositories for the sacred monies and in some cases may have possessed ancillary dining facilities. At Sardis, the synagogue was also the seat of the Jewish politeuma, wherein the internal legal affairs of the community were settled. The synagogues in the other Asian cities may have functioned similarly, though we lack direct evidence attesting to the authorization of politeumata in these places. Nevertheless, all of the attested synagogues appear to be well-established institutions, with direct or indirect connections to the highest echelons of local and imperial power. This is seen especially in Augustus' decree, which refers to a resolution promulgated by the Asian Jews, indicating some sort of regional organization among the Jewish communities in this province.

The existing evidence does not tell us much about the appearance of the synagogue buildings, though if there was indeed only one synagogue at Ephesus, as implied in Acts, it must have been quite sizable in order for it to have served the local Jewish population. Elsewhere, the walls and ceilings of the Acmonia synagogue were said to have been painted, though the style of ornamentation is unknown. This synagogue also housed dedicatory inscriptions, as has also been attested for the synagogues in Egypt, Cyrenaica, Syria and Palestine.

MACEDONIA

Situated on the northern Balkan Peninsula, ancient Macedonia stretched from the Adriatic Sea to the Aegean and bordered Thracia on the east, Illyricum and Moesia on the north, and Achaia on the south. The most famous Macedonian was, of course, Alexander the Great, who launched his conquest of the western world from his homeland in 336 B.C.E. Upon Alexander's death, Macedonia became a battleground in a series of succession struggles, finally resolved in 276 B.C.E. when Antigonus II secured rulership of the region. In 168 B.C.E., however, Perseus, the last of the Antigonids, suffered a defeat at the hands of the Romans. Macedonia remained free, but became a Roman tributary. Following the suppression of a revolt, Macedonia became a Roman province in 148 B.C.E. Between 15 and 44 C.E., it was combined with Achaia and Moesia to form a single province. Geographically, Macedonia served as a convenient land bridge between the Aegean and Adriatic, with the via Egnatia linking Philippi and Thessalonica in the east to Apollonia and Dyrrachium in the west.[110]

Evidence for Jewish communities in Macedonia prior to the turn of the era is currently non-existent.[111] It is not until Philo's writings that we encounter any record of Jewish colonies there, and this only a passing reference (*Legat.* 281). Nevertheless, Acts mentions the presence of synagogues in three cities of this province—Philippi, Beroea and Thessalonica—and so these must be considered, particularly since one of the passages contains Acts' only uses of the term *proseuchē* as a term for the synagogue.

Philippi

Philippi is located in eastern Macedonia, about twelve miles inland from the harbor city of Neapolis (modern Kavala), situated on the Aegean. Although Philippi was originally established in the Classical period, in 42 B.C.E., Marc Antony refounded the city as a Roman colony. It was subsequently enlarged with the addition of Italian settlers in 30 B.C.E.

Acts states that Paul and Silas arrived in the city (c. 49 C.E.) after putting into the harbor at Neapolis. After remaining in Philippi for several days, they are said to have paid a visit to the local synagogue:

> On the sabbath day we went outside the gate by the river, where we supposed there was a *proseuchē* [τῇ τε ἡμέρᾳ τῶν σαββάτων ἐξήλθομεν ἔξω τῆς πύλης παρὰ ποταμὸν οὗ ἐνομίζομεν προσευχὴν εἶναι]; and we sat down and spoke to the women who had gathered there. A certain woman named Lydia, a worshiper of God [σεβομένη τὸν θεόν], was listening to us; she was from the city of Thyatira and a dealer in purple cloth. The Lord opened her heart to listen eagerly to what was said by Paul. When she and her household were baptized, she urged us, saying, "If you have judged me to be faithful to the Lord, come and stay at my home." And she prevailed upon us (Acts 16:13–15).

The area alluded to in the passage is about a mile-and-a-half west of the town center, where the city gate stood not far from the river Gangites.

---

[110]For additional background on Macedonia, see David W.J. Gill, "Macedonia" in *The Book of Acts in Its Palestinian Setting*, edited by Richard Bauckham (Grand Rapids, Mich.: William B. Eerdmans Pub. Co., 1994), 397–417.

[111]For later evidence, see *HJP* 3.1.64–68; Levinskaya, *The Book of Acts in Its Diaspora Setting*, 154–157.

Regarding this passage, Conzelmann writes, "the accuracy of detail and intensity of local coloring are striking."[112] Because this segment also constitutes one of the "we" passages (16:10–17), interpreters have argued that Luke was employing a written source here.[113] Additional weight is given to this hypothesis from the observation that only in this segment is the term *proseuchē* used in reference to the synagogue (2x). Elsewhere, Acts uses *synagōgē* (19x), which appears only in the parts of Acts *not* utilizing the first person plural. Since *proseuchē* was the usual term for diaspora synagogues prior to 70 C.E.,[114] the segment coheres with the earlier diaspora terminology, further suggesting the use of a written source in this segment.

As was the case with the synagogues at Halicarnassus, which were apparently built near the sea, the synagogue at Philippi was also said to have been located near a body of water. Because the text indicates that Paul and his entourage expected to find a synagogue there, such site placement was probably customary for synagogues in the diaspora.

Somewhat puzzling is that, outside of Paul and Silas, only women are mentioned as being present in the synagogue. This has led some commentators to infer that the term *proseuchē* meant a synagogue for women only.[115] Such an interpretation, however, ignores the wider usage of this word, which in no case implies a specialized structure for women. Moreover, the use of *proseuchē* here is better understood as the incorporation of an earlier source, as previously suggested. A more likely interpretation is that the assembly times were segregated, with women coming at one hour, and men at another.[116] Thus the passages presumes that Paul, being new to the city, was not aware of the local customs of this

---

[112]Conzelmann, *Acts of the Apostles*, 129.

[113]E.g., Porter, "The 'We' Passages," 545–574; C. K. Barrett, *Luke the Historian in Recent Study*, New ed. (Philadelphia: Fortress Press, 1970); William Neil, *The Acts of the Apostles* (London: Oliphants, 1973), 24; Kümmel, *Introduction to the New Testatment*, 174–185; Hemer, *The Book of Acts*, 308–334; cf. Haenchen, *The Book of Acts*, 85; Conzelmann, *Acts of the Apostles*, xxxviii–xl.

[114]See chapter two, above.

[115]See BAGD s.v. προσευχή, 2. The most recent interpreter to hold this opinion is Bradley Blue, who maintains that the *proseuchē* was "a house which was used on a regular basis by the women" ("Acts and the House Church," 152–153, n. 127). If, however, the *proseuchē* at Philippi was presumed to have been reserved for women only, we must wonder why Paul is said to have started to return to this structure at a later time (16:16).

[116]Alternatively, the Jewish population at Philippi may have consisted solely of the Jewish wives of Roman soldiers and bureaucrats.

synagogue and then presents him as using the opportunity to preach his message. According to the account, Paul's only convert was Lydia, a God-fearer originally from Thyatira, who was baptized along with her household.

Subsequently, Paul and his group, while on their way back to the *proseuchē* (16:16), were said to have encountered a slave-girl with a "spirit of divination." Casting out the spirit (v. 18), Paul ran afoul of the girl's owners (vv. 19–21). He and Silas were thereupon dragged before the local authorities, beaten with rods (vv. 22–23), and locked up in prison (vv. 23–24). After converting the jailor and his family (vv. 25–34), the two missionaries were forced to leave the city (vv. 39–40).

Although Acts is the only document to mention the existence of the synagogue in Philippi, its possible use of an earlier source lends some weight to the attestation. From Paul's own writings, moreover, we know that he was the founder of the church in Philippi (Phil 1:5–6), though the apostle does not mention a synagogue being located there.

Thessalonica and Beroea

After leaving Philippi, Paul and Silas were said to have followed the via Egnatia westward to Thessalonica, about a hundred miles distant. The city, located on the Thermaic Gulf, was the capital of one of Macedonia's four districts. It also served as the residence of the Roman governor and was a free city. Acts states that Thessalonica contained a "synagogue of the Jews [συναγωγὴ τῶν Ἰουδαίων]" (17:1). According to the narrative, Paul visited the synagogue on three successive Sabbaths and argued from the scriptures (διελέξατο αὐτοῖς ἀπὸ τῶν γραφῶν; 17:2), convincing not only Jews, but also a number of "pious Greeks" (σεβομένων Ἑλλήνων), including "not a few" of the leading women (γυναικῶν τῶν πρώτων οὐκ ὀλίγαι; v. 4). Soon, however, opposition arose from Jews, and Paul's host Jason was dragged before the magistrates. After being accused of housing men who were "turning the world upside down" and "violating the decrees of Caesar," bond was required of him, presumably to ensure that he ushered his guests out of town as soon as possible (vv. 5–9).

Paul and Silas complied, we are told, and left the city that very night. They journeyed about fifty miles southwest to Beroea, a large city that served as the seat of the Macedonian *koinon*. Nearly the same scene portrayed at Thessalonica repeats itself in the ensuing narrative:

> When they arrived, they went to the Jewish synagogue [οἵτινες παραγενόμενοι εἰς τὴν συναγωγὴν τῶν Ἰουδαίων ἀπῄεσαν]. These Jews were more receptive than those in Thessalonica, for they welcomed the message very eagerly and examined the scriptures every day to see whether these things were so. Many of them therefore believed, including not a few Greek women and men of high standing [πολλοὶ μὲν οὖν ἐξ αὐτῶν ἐπίστευσαν καὶ τῶν Ἑλληνίδων γυναικῶν τῶν εὐσχημόνων καὶ ἀνδρῶν οὐκ ὀλίγοι] (Acts 17:10–12).

The account goes on to state that not long afterwards, the Jews from Thessalonica came down and stirred up the city against Paul, who was again forced to depart for Athens, leaving Silas and Timothy behind (17:13–15).[117]

As for the historical value of the twin accounts, they are prone to criticism because they conform to a paradigm that we have seen repeatedly in Acts. One also questions why Paul had to leave Beroea so suddenly if he had converted men and women of such a high standing as the text suggests. Finally, Paul's own letters imply that his converts at Thessalonica were almost exclusively Gentile (1 Thess 2:14), a fact that seems at odds with Acts' portrayal. On the other hand, the general contours of the passages in Acts cohere with Paul's account in 1 Thessalonians, particularly where he writes that Jewish opposition "drove us out [ἡμᾶς ἐκδιωξάντων]" and displeased God by "hindering us from speaking to the Gentiles [κωλυόντων ἡμᾶς τοῖς ἔθνεσιν λαλῆσαι]" (1 Thess 2:15–16; see also 3:1–2).[118] Elsewhere, the Jason mentioned as Paul's compatriot in Rom 16:21 may be the same one alluded to above. Lastly, although Paul never mentions a church at Beroea, in several places he refers to the existence of churches or individual believers living in undisclosed places in Macedonia (2 Cor 8:1, 9:2; 1 Thess 1:7–8, 4:1; Rom 15:26). Acts' later mention of a certain Sopater from Beroea (20:4) may also correspond to the Sosipater named as one of Paul's companions in Rom 16:21. If this is indeed the case, then Paul's designation of him as a fellow countryman (συγγενής) would support Acts' depiction of Jewish converts being made at Beroea.

---

[117]1 Thess 3:1–2 states that Timothy accompanied Paul to Athens from where the Apostle sent him back to Thessalonica to check on the fledgling church.

[118]Trebilco notes that the use of the Aorist participle ἐκδιωξάντων in 1 Thess 2:15 suggests that a definite event was in mind (*Jewish Communities in Asia Minor*, 200, n. 78).

Another factor in favor of the general accuracy of the account is that Luke's knowledge of the local color of this region is excellent. Commentators have been quick to point out, for instance, that his use of the title *politarch* in reference to the magistrates at Thessalonica (17:6, 8) corresponds to inscriptions first unearthed in that city in the nineteenth century. Prior to that time, the word had been unattested outside of Acts.[119] Thus while we might question Acts' portrayal of the ethnicity and the social status of some of Paul's converts in Thessalonica and Beroea, the attestation of the synagogues in these cities appears plausible, though not as firmly as established as in Ephesus, where outside sources provide more specific corroboration.

ACHAIA

When Augustus created the province of Achaia in 27 B.C.E., its territory encompassed not only the Peloponnese, but also Thessaly, Aetolia, Akarnania and many of the Aegean islands, including Delos. Prior to this time, the region had fallen into Roman hands in 146 B.C.E. as a result of its victory over the Achaian League. Achaia subsequently became a Roman tributary, coming under the administration of Macedonia until Augustus' decision to separate it into a new province. Between 15 and 44 C.E., it was briefly combined with Macedonia and Moesia to form one province, as mentioned in the previous section. Thereafter, Achaia again became a separate province, with Corinth serving as its capital.

Early epigraphic evidence for Jews in Achaia consists of several manumission inscriptions from Delphi and Oropus.[120] These date to between the late third and early second centuries B.C.E. Subsequently, Philo mentions the presence of Jewish colonies in this region (*Legat.* 281). We shall consider more specific attestations in the following sections.

---

[119]Four inscriptions containing the term πολιτάρχης were originally discovered at Thessalonica in the nineteenth century (*IG* 30, 50, 109, 848). More recent excavations have raised the total number of inscriptionary attestations of this word at Thessalonica to twenty-eight. See G. H. R. Horsley, "The Politarchs" in *The Book of Acts in Its Palestinian Setting*, edited by Richard Bauckham (Grand Rapids, Mich.: William B. Eerdmans Pub. Co., 1994), 419–431; *NDIEC* 2.34–35

[120]*CIJ* 1.711b (Oropus), 1.709–711 (Delphi). See *HJP* 3.1.65, Levenskya, *The Book of Acts in its Diaspora Setting*, 154.

Athens and Corinth

According to Acts, after leaving Beroea, Paul went to Athens, a fact confirmed by the apostle's own writings (1 Thess 3:1). While there, Paul is said to have "argued in the synagogue [διελέγετο μὲν οὖν ἐν τῇ συναγωγῇ]" with the Jews and God-fearers (Ἰουδαίοις καὶ τοῖς σεβομένοις; 17:17). Nothing else is said about the synagogue, as the narrative goes on to recount Paul's famous address to the Stoics and Epicureans at the Areopagus (17:18–31), which resulted in a handful of conversions (17:34). Little is known about the Jewish community in Athens, although a number of Jewish epitaphs have been recovered from the city, some of them dating as early as the second century B.C.E., but most to around the time Paul visited the city.[121] In addition, Josephus quotes a decree from Athens dated 105–106 B.C.E. honoring Hyrcanus I for his services to the people of Athens (*Ant.* 14.149–155).[122] Although the Jews of Athens are not mentioned in the decree, Hyrcanus' benefactions to the Athenians suggest as much. From these attestations, Acts' mention of a synagogue in the city is at least plausible, though we gain little knowledge from the allusion.

The next stop on Paul's itinerary was Corinth, located on a narrow isthmus separating the Gulf of Corinth on the West from the Gulf of Saronia on the East. Although Corinth had been demolished by the Romans in 146 B.C.E., archaeological evidence suggests that a reduced population nevertheless remained resident in the city over the next hundred years.[123] In 44 B.C.E., Corinth was reestablished as a Roman colony, with a population of freedmen being imported from Italy, some of whom may have been Jewish. Subsequently, Philo specifically mentions Corinth as a city containing a Jewish community (*Legat.* 281).

Acts states that at the start of Paul's Corinthian ministry, "every sabbath he would argue in the synagogue and would try to convince Jews and Greeks [διελέγετο δὲ ἐν τῇ συναγωγῇ κατὰ πᾶν σάββατον, ἔπειθέν τε Ἰουδαίους καὶ Ἕλληνας]" (18:4). He had some success, converting Crispus, who is said to have been an *archisynagōgos* (18:8). This same

---

[121]*CIJ* 1.715a, c, f, g. Others are of uncertain date (*CIJ* 1.712, 713, 714 [?], 715, 715d, e). See *HJP* 3.1.65; Levenskya, *The Book of Acts in its Diaspora Setting*, 158.

[122]Josephus wrongly states that the decree honored Hyrcanus II (Ant. 14.149; see notes in the LCL edition).

[123]James R. Wiseman, "Corinth and Rome I: 228 B.C.–A.D. 267" in *ANRW* II.7.1, 494–496.

Crispus is perhaps mentioned in 1 Cor 1:14, though Paul does not there refer to him with this title. Although noting this conversion, Acts further relates that after an unspecified period, Paul faced stiff Jewish opposition and left the synagogue, taking up residence with a converted God-fearer (σεβομένου τὸν θεόν), Titius Justus, whose "house was next door to the synagogue [οὗ ἡ οἰκία ἦν συνομοροῦσα τῇ συναγωγῇ]" (18:7). Thus we see that a synagogue could be located in a residential section, though this need not require the conclusion that the synagogue was itself a private house, as Howard Kee maintains.[124]

After spending a year-and-a-half in the city, Paul reportedly faced further opposition from the Jews, who are said to have "made a united attack on Paul and brought him before the tribunal" (18:12). The proconsul, Gallio, who is known to have taken up his position in 51 C.E., dismissed their complaint as an internal Jewish squabble. Following Gallio's refusal to hear the case, Sosthenes, yet another *archisynagōgos*, is said to have been beaten, presumably by the non-Jewish populace. This Sosthenes may also have become a convert, since the same name appears in the opening of 1 Corinthians (1:1), implying that he was well-known to the Corinthian church. If so, then after his beating, Sosthenes underwent a major change of heart and later moved with Paul to Ephesus.

Having reviewed Acts' account, we must now ask whether the synagogue references in this section are reliable. On the positive side, clearly the author of Acts had at least a general knowledge of Corinth, as can particularly be seen in his mention of Gallio's proconsulship. Also, his overall account fits well with Paul's own allusions, as has been pointed out above in several places. On the other hand, one piece of evidence, often cited by New Testament scholars, cannot serve as an external witness: the inscription mentioning the "Synagogue of the Hebrews [[Συνα]γωγὴ Ἑβρ[αίων]]" (*CIJ* 1.718) almost certainly dates to a later period.[125] Nor do we dare extrapolate backwards from this inscription, not only on general principle, but also in view of Josephus' statement that Vespasian had six thousand Jews from Magdala shipped off to Corinth during the course of the Jewish War to work as slaves on

---

[124]Kee, *Transformation*, 18; idem, "Defining the First-Century CE Synagogue," 491.

[125]This is particularly suggested by the ω form of the omega in the monument, which tended to be used more often in the second to third centuries C.E., thereafter being employed exclusively. Prior to that time, the Ω form was predominantly used (early uses of the ω form are largely confined to Egypt, e.g., *JIE* 40 = *CIJ* 2.1539, dating to 8 C.E.). See Furnish, *II Corinthians*, 21–22.

Nero's project of constructing a canal across the isthmus—an effort that was soon abandoned (Josephus, *BJ* 3.540). Since the arrival of these Jews surely changed the character of the Jewish community at Corinth both in terms of its size and socio-economic mix, any attempted extrapolation would be especially problematic.[126]

Despite the unsuitability of the synagogue inscription for our purposes, Acts' mention of a synagogue in Corinth seems plausible given Philo's specific reference to a Jewish community there. Acts' allusion to *archisynagōgoi*, moreover, receives at least partial confirmation from references in Paul's writings, as already noted.

Delos

Although it is one of the smallest of the Aegean islands (1.3 square miles), Delos has a long and storied history. Inhabited as early as the third millennium B.C.E., the island was celebrated in antiquity as the legendary birthplace of Apollo and Artemis. Not only did its cult attract throngs of pilgrims throughout the Classical and Hellenistic periods, but its centralized location and sizable port allowed it to dominate maritime commerce until nearly the turn of the era. Soon thereafter, however, changing trade patterns led to Delos' precipitous decline as a commercial center in the early Imperial period. In addition, the island never fully recovered from devastating attacks suffered during the Mithridatic wars (88 B.C.E.) and in a massive pirate raid (69 B.C.E.). Pausanias, writing in the second century C.E., states that in his time, the island was nearly abandoned (Paus. 8.33.2).[127]

With regard to the Jewish presence on the island, 1 Macc 15:23 mentions Delos as one of the locations to which the Romans sent a letter of friendship in 139 B.C.E. on behalf of the Jewish people. Two second-

---

[126]Kee, while noting the late date of *CIJ* 1.718 and the fact that the stone was not found *in situ*, nevertheless goes on to state: "even so, its recovery in a commercial district fits well with the evidence that these meetings, both Jewish and Christian, were taking place over the first and second century largely in the informal gatherings places of homes and shops" ("Transformation," 18, n. 29). It should be noted that even if we were to adopt Kee's problematic line of reasoning, the area in which the discovery was made (the Lechaeum road) hardly supports his contention, since it contained some of Corinth's most distinguished monumental architecture.

[127]For general historical background on Delos, see the introduction to *GD* and also McLean, "The Place of Cult in Voluntary Associations and Christian Churches on Delos," 186–189.

century Jewish epitaphs from Rhenea (*CIJ* 1.725a, b), the burial island of Delos, confirm the existence of Jews on Delos near the time this letter was written.[128]

In the following century, two decrees were issued concerning the Jews inhabiting the island. The first of these, dated to 49 B.C.E., was promulgated by the people of Delos in response to an order by the Roman legate:

> In the archonship of Boeotus, on the twentieth day of the month of Thargelion, response of the magistrates. The legate Marcus Piso, when resident in our city, having been placed in charge of the recruiting of soldiers, summoned us and a considerable number of citizens, and ordered that if there were any Jews who were Roman citizens, no one should bother them about military service, inasmuch as the consul Lucius Cornelius Lentulus had exempted the Jews from military service in consideration of their religious scruples [δεισιδαιμονίας ἕνεκα]. We must therefore obey the magistrate (Josephus, *Ant.* 14.231–232).

The decree resembles other proclamations issued in Asia during the same period and implies that the Jewish community on Delos included at least some Roman citizens. In addition, the reference to "religious scruples" reflects similar language used in the Asian decrees to refer to Sabbath observance and the eating of kosher foods.

The second edict, issued about the same time as the first, was written by Julius Caesar in response to the complaints of the Delian Jews over the treatment they were receiving at the hands of the regional magistrates in Parium. The fact that the decree was promulgated by Caesar himself underscores the political influence of the Delian Jews within the imperial courts, if not the local council chambers:

> Julius Gaius, Praetor, Consul of the Romans, to the magistrates, council and people of Parium, greeting. The Jews in Delos and some of the neighbouring Jews, some of your envoys also being present, have appealed to me and declared that you are preventing them by statute from observing their national customs and sacred rites [πατρίοις ἔθεσι καὶ ἱεροῖς χρῆσθαι]. Now it displeases me that such statutes should be made against our friends and allies and that they should be forbidden to live in accordance with their customs

---

[128] *ID* 2616, col. 2, l. 53 (II B.C.E.) mentions a Πραῦλος Σαμαρεύς, who some scholars have taken to have been a Jew (see Philippe Bruneau, *Recherches sur les cultes de Delos a l'epoque hellenistique et a l'epoque imperiale* [Paris: E. de Boccard, 1970], 486). In view of recently discovered Samaritan inscriptions (see below), it now seems more likely that he was a Samaritan.

> and to contribute money to common meals and sacred rites [χρήματα εἰς σύνδειπνα καὶ τὰ ἱερὰ εἰσφέρειν] . . . if you have made any statutes against our friends and allies, you will do well to revoke them because of their worthy deeds on our behalf and their goodwill toward us (Josephus, *Ant.* 14.213–216).

The combined allusion to "common meals and sacred rites" suggests the existence on Delos of a synagogue with an ancillary banquet hall used to hold feasts on sacred days (cf. *CIJ* 2.1404; Josephus, *Ant.* 16.164).

As fortune would have it, excavators on Delos claim to have found the partial remains of such a structure on the island's eastern shoreline.[129] Discovered in 1912 by a team under the direction of André Plassart, the remnants of the proposed synagogue (*GD* 80; see fig. 12)[130] consist primarily of a long, rectangular building (15.5 m long x 28.15 m wide), whose façade is oriented toward the east. The exterior walls of the structure were constructed out of gneiss, set to a thickness of about 72 cm, though somewhat narrower in places. The floor of the interior is paved with small pieces of marble.

Although the remains of the main building are currently sectioned into three major segments (Rooms A, B and D), analysis of the structure suggests two construction phases. During the first phase, which dates to the second century B.C.E., Rooms A and B constituted one large hall (internal measurements: 16.90 m [N-S] x 14.40 m [W-E]) that was later divided in half by a wall (0.9 m wide) with three portals. Because this wall incorporates elements from the nearby gymnasium which was wrecked in 88 B.C.E. (*GD* 76), the second phase of the building dates to sometime after that, probably in the mid-first century B.C.E. Portions of

---

[129]The description of the synagogue remains is based on the following reports: André Plassart, "La synagogue juive de Délos," *RB* 23 (1914): 523–534 (originally published in *Mélanges Holleaux, recueil de mémoirs concernant l'antiquité grecque* [Paris: Picard, 1913], 201–215); Belle D. Mazur, *Studies on Jewry in Greece* (Athens: Printing Office Hestia, 1935); Bruneau, *Recherches sur les cultes de Delos*, 480–493, plates VII–IX, plans A–H; idem, "«Les Israélites de Délos» et la juiverie délienne," *BCH* 106 (1982): 465–504; L. Michael White, "The Delos Synagogue Revisited: Recent Fieldwork in the Graeco-Roman Diaspora," *HTR* 80 (1987): 133–160; *JSGRP* 2.71–75; Sukenik, *Ancient Synagogues in Palestine and Greece*, 37–40; Kraabel, "The Diaspora Synagogue," 491–494. Bruneau's two works provide the most detailed plans and documentation, though Plassart and Mazur's studies record some important early observations.

[130]The numbering of the various structures at Delos follows that of the official guidebook of the site, *Guide de Délos* (*GD*).

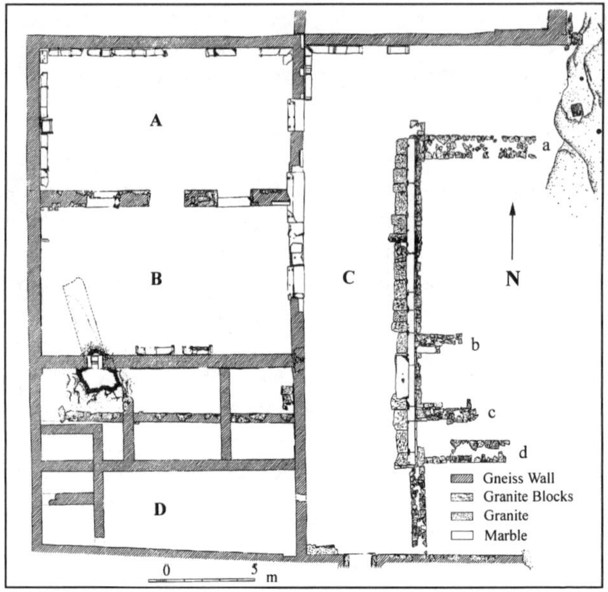

Figure 12. Plan of *GD* 80. Rooms A and B constitute an assembly hall separated by a dividing-wall with three portals. Remains of benches line the outer walls of these rooms on the north, west and south sides. Area C represents the remains of a portico framed in the east by an 18 m long stylobate upon which columns once rested. Two other stylobates (a, d) intersect this stylobate at either end. Between these are probably the remains of stairs leading to the portico (b, c). Room D is a complex of chambers, one of which allowed access to a cistern. (After Bruneau, *Recherches sur les cultes de Delos*, pl. B.)

the east wall were also repaired at this time, with its central portal being walled-up to form an intersection with the dividing wall.[131]

Room A, which also has an entrance in the center of its east wall, contains marble benches (c. 40 cm wide x 40 cm high) along the length of its north and west walls. In the center of the west benches rests a

---

[131]Four monuments from the gymnasium were found reemployed in or near these walls: *IG* 1152 (II B.C.E.) on the south side of the dividing wall; *ID* 1923 *bis* (126/5 B.C.E.) in a repaired portion of the eastern wall; *ID* 1928 (early I B.C.E.) outside the eastern wall near the center of Room A/B; and *IG* 1087 (II B.C.E.) just outside the eastern wall where Room B meets Room D. For discussion of the dating and placement of these inscriptions, see Bruneau, "«Les Israélites de Délos» et la juiverie délienne," 492–493, 495–498.

marble throne with a footrest extending from its base (see fig. 13). An incised palmette once embellished the upper back of the throne; scrollwork, leaf designs, and lion's-feet motifs remain visible on the sides. The centered position of the throne along the back wall of Room A indicates that its placement and the placement of the benches belong to the second phase. It cannot be determined with any degree of certainty if the throne and the benches also belonged to the earlier stage.[132] If so, then they would have been arranged in a different fashion within the unsectioned Room A/B.

Room B, which also has a portal in the center of its east side, contains several benches along its south wall. Benches also appear to have lined the west wall, making Room B nearly a mirror image of Room A.

Room D was also a part of the primary structure, since its east and west walls are bonded with the south wall of Room B. Although several reconstructions of the building have depicted an entrance through the east wall of Room D, the most detailed plans reveal no clear entryway.[133] Inside, Room D is divided into several compartments, some of which may have been later additions. The westernmost of these provided access to a cistern that extends northward beneath Room B (2.00 [W-E] x 6.08 [N-S] x 4.04 m). The top of the cistern is vaulted and, in order to provide a firm support for the wall dividing Room B from Room D, an arch was built into the portion of the wall directly over the cistern. This arch rises 30 cm above the floor and is visible from Room B. The purpose of the other chambers in Room D is difficult to discern since there are no clear entrances into them, nor for that matter, into the room with the cistern. This suggests that they were accessed from the roof or through a second story that is no longer extant. If this was the case, then the chambers may have served as storage compartments.

---

[132]Bruneau posits a first century B.C.E. date for the throne on a comparison with *proedroi* from the same period found in theaters in Athens and Lesbos. Conceivably, however, it could have been installed at some point before the Mithridatic raids. See Bruneau, *Recherches sur les cultes de Delos*, 492.

[133]In Bruneau, *Recherches sur les cultes de Delos*, plan B, there is a c. 35 cm break in the east wall that can hardly be an entrance, particularly when compared to the other entrances which are c. 1.70 m (room B) and c. 1.80 m (room A) wide. For reconstructions including an entry in the east wall of room D, see: White, "The Delos Synagogue Revisited," figs. 2, 5; Mazur, *Studies on Jewry in Greece*, plans 1–2.

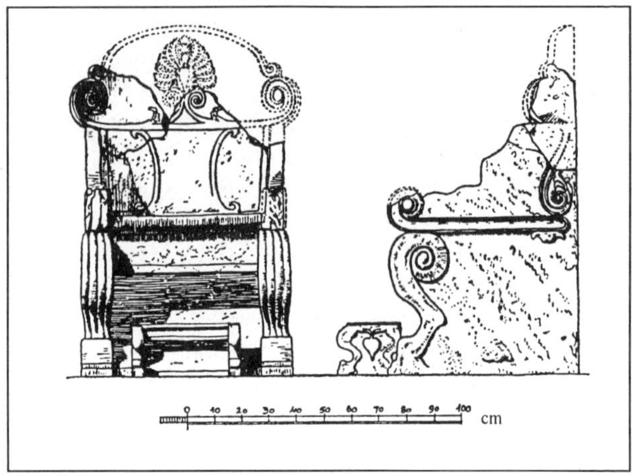

Figure 13. Throne found in the center of the west wall in Room A. The throne is made from marble and has a palmette incised on its back, and scrollwork, leaf and lion's-feet motifs incised on its sides. (From Sukenik, *Ancient Synagogues in Palestine and Greece*, 61.)

Area C on the plan constitutes the remains of a roofed portico where columns were once arranged on an 18-meter-long stylobate (0.725 m wide) that runs parallel to the façade at a distance of about 5 m. Foundation remains of two additional stylobates (labeled a and d) are found perpendicular to the first stylobate at either end.[134] These run eastward c. 5–6 m, thereafter disappearing due to the erosion caused by the intruding sea. Similarly, wall remains currently extend eastward from either side of the building for a distance of 12.6 m on the south and about 15 m on the north before being absorbed by the erosion.[135] Remains of a stairway (labeled b and c) are found intersecting the long stylobate near its southern end.[136] An entryway (c. 1.2 m wide) leads onto the portico through the south wall about two meters east of the façade. Marble benches similar to the ones found inside the building rest on either side

[134]These were first noted by Mazur (*Studies on Jewry in Greece*, 17), who pointed out that they ran equidistant from the north and south walls of the portico (c. 5 m). Bruneau argued that these were later constructions (*Recherches sur les cultes de Delos*, 483), but White subsequently demonstrated that they were integral to the N-S stylobate ("The Delos Synagogue Revisited," 150).

[135]See below, however, for the state of these walls in 1913.

[136]See White, "The Delos Synagogue Revisited, 150–151

of the northwestern corner of the portico. A large, stone water basin sits 3.51 m from this corner between two of the benches on the northern wall.

Plassart identified the building as a synagogue primarily on the strength of several inscriptions found nearby. Four of the five recovered monuments are dedications to "God Most High" (or "the Most High"), an epithet frequently used by diaspora Jews to refer to the Deity, as we have seen. The following is a representative example of this group (*CIJ* 1.729 = *ID* 2328):[137]

Λυσίμαχος
ὑπὲρ ἑαυτου
θεῷ Ὑψίστω
χαριστήριον

Lysimachos
For himself
To God Most High
For a thank-offering

In addition to the inscriptions discovered near the building, Plassart also recovered another monument in an insula adjacent to the nearby stadium (*GD* 79, Habitation IIA; *CIJ* 1.726 = *ID* 2329):

Ἀγαθοκλῆς
καὶ Λυσίμα-
χος ἐπὶ
προσευχῆι

Agathocles
and Lysimachos
for
the *proseuchē*

Because the name Lysimachos is also found in one of the inscriptions recovered in *GD* 80 (quoted above), Plassart argued that this inscription should be linked to the building, thus identifying it as a *proseuchē*.

Plassart's arguments were accepted by many early scholars, including the highly respected archaeologist E. Sukenik.[138] In 1935, however, archaeologist Belle Mazur raised several questions about Plassart's identification. First of all, she argued that the term *proseuchē* in the inscription just quoted should be translated as "prayer" rather than "synagogue" since the definite article did not precede the word, as it had in all previous examples of synagogue inscriptions. Thus in her opinion, the translation should read, "Agathocles and Lysomachos, in fulfillment

---

[137]The other inscriptions are: *CIJ* 1.727 (=*ID* 2331), Ζωσᾶς| Παρίος| Θεῷ| Ὑψίστῳ |εὐχήν ("Zosas of Paros to the God Most High, in offering"); *CIJ* 1.728 (=*ID* 2330), Λαωδίκη Θεῶι|Ὑψιότωι σωθεῖ|σα ταῖς ὑφ' αὑτο|ῦ θαρατήαις|εὐχήν ("Laodice, to God Most High, for healing him of his infirmities, an offering"); *CIJ* 1.730 (=*ID* 2332), Ὑψίσ|τῳ εὐ|χήν Μ|αρκία ("Marcia, an offering to the Most High"); *CIJ* 1.731 (=*ID* 2333), - - - |γενόμενος|ἐλεύθερος (" . . . became free").

[138]Sukenik, *Ancient Synagogues in Palestine and Greece*, 37–40

or pursuance of a prayer."[139] This translation raised the question of whether the prayers being offered were Jewish or pagan, since *proseuchē* in the sense of "prayer" was sometimes used by non-Jews. Mazur opted for the latter alternative, arguing that "God Most High" should be understood as a reference to "Zeus Most High," found in many pagan inscriptions. In support of her position, she observed that the inscriptions constituted the bases of votive offerings. Small cuttings and the remains of lead on the top of two of the bases indicated that metallic figures had previously been soldered onto them. Such figures, she maintained, were indicative of a pagan milieu:

> Our votives are . . . not essentially different from those found in the Zeus Hypsistos sanctuary on the Pnyx on which are represented, mostly in relief, the part of the body, eye, ear, foot, cured by him. A striking proof of the similarity is furnished by the fact that one of our inscriptions actually refers to a healing. This form of votive offering, usual for pagans, is clearly not a Jewish custom.[140]

In further support of her view, Mazur observed that the earliest phase of the putative synagogue had only one architectural parallel on the island—that of a pagan cultic house. While we shall return to her reconstruction shortly in our consideration of the building's original form, here we note that Mazur's arguments were persuasive enough to lead Sukenik to reverse his earlier opinion and to agree that the structure was pagan, not Jewish.[141] However, because Sukenik's original judgment was contained in a widely used text on early synagogues, many scholars remained oblivious to the rising debate.[142]

Somewhat later, Erwin Goodenough blurred the picture even further when he noted from Plassart's report that the putative synagogue contained the remains of lamps with pagan motifs, including figures of

---

[139]Mazur, *Studies on Jewry in Greece*, 21.

[140]Ibid.

[141]E. L. Sukenik, "The Present State of Ancient Synagogue Studies," *Bulletin of the Lewis M. Rabinowitz Fund* 1 (1949): 21–23. For a similar assessment, see also R. Wishchnitzer, *The Architecture of the European Synagogue* (Philadelphia: The Jewish Publication Society of America, 1974), 11.

[142]See Hershel Shanks, *Judaism in Stone: The Archaeology of Ancient Synagogues* (New York: Harper & Row, 1979), 44–44. Shanks lamented that "boatloads of tourists" were still being carted off to see a synagogue that was not in fact a synagogue.

Minerva, Jupiter and Janus.[143] At the same time, however, he also challenged Mazur's judgment with respect to the pagan character of the monuments, observing that these were dedicated not to Zeus Hypsistos, but to *Theos Hypsistos*.[144] After several pages of arguing first for one side and then the other, Goodenough finally arrived at the following conclusion: "While nothing positive indicates that this building was a synagogue, therefore, it might almost certainly, from its inscriptions, its form, its lack of decoration, and its appurtenances, be taken, without any protest, to be probably a synagogue."[145]

Fortunately, we are spared from this ambivalent verdict thanks to a more recent discovery that has helped to clarify the situation somewhat. In 1979–80, two Samaritan stelae were found about 90 m north of *GD* 80 in an unexcavated portion of the shoreline.[146] One of them was a dedicatory inscription of a synagogue that employed the key term *proseuchē* in the same manner as the previously discovered inscription, that is, without the definite article.[147] This gave a local analogy for this usage, suggesting that the inscription discovered by Plassart should be translated "for the *proseuchē*." Moreover, the fact that the inscription is dated to the same time as the construction of *GD* 80 (II B.C.E.) led Thomas Kraabal to propose that the structure was a Samaritan synagogue (more on this possibility below).[148]

---

[143]*JSGRP* 2.72. The initial report of these is found in Plassart, "La synagogue juive de Délos," 531–532. The lamps are catalogued in more detail in Bruneau, *Recherches sur les cultes de Delos*, 484–485.

[144]*JSGRP* 2.73. This argument is repeated in Bruneau, *Recherches sur les cultes de Delos*, 487. Bruneau also notes that the votive bases were not found with parts of the body on them and argues that such votives were different in general form than the ones found in connection with *GD* 80.

[145]*JSGRP* 2.74.

[146]For a report of this discovery and an analysis of the inscriptions, see Bruneau, "«Les Israélites de Délos» et la juiverie délienne," 465–485; A. Thomas Kraabel, "New Evidence of the Samaritan Diaspora has been Found on Delos," *BA* 47 (1984): 44–46. Henceforth, the inscriptions will be identified as Bruneau no. 1 and no. 2. They will be quoted and fully examined in chapter seven.

[147]The key phrase is: κατασκευάσαντα καὶ ἀναθέντα ἐκ τῶν ἰδίων ἐπὶ προσευχῇ θ̣ε̣[οῦ]. Bruneau had originally translated the last three words as "en ex-voto (à Dieu)," "in offering to God." Subsequently, however, White rightly noted that the word κατασκευάσαντα signifies the construction of the *proseuchē*. He therefore translates the above phrase as "for constructing and dedicating to the *proseuchē* of God, out of his own funds." See White, "The Delos Synagogue Revisited," 141–144 (translation on p. 144).

[148]Kraabel, "New Evidence of the Samaritan Diaspora," 45–46.

In any case, evidence now firmly supports the view that at least the second phase of the building functioned as a synagogue.[149] This is indicated first of all by the presence of inscriptions dedicated to "God Most High" near the building and the association with it of another monument that was dedicated "to the *proseuchē*." Secondly, the benches arranged around the outer parts of the walls in Rooms A and B bear a striking resemblance to the arrangement seen in the Galilean-style synagogues from the Second Temple period and later. The major differences are the lack of columniation and the division of the assembly area into two compartments. The former can be attributed to local architectural variation, while the latter implies a segregation of the sexes.[150] Thirdly, the artistic embellishments, though slight, also suggest a Jewish (or Samaritan) provenance. As noted, a palmette graces the back of the throne. Similar depictions of the palmette are seen on three antefixes and a marble lintel recovered from the building's cistern during Philippe Bruneau's re-excavation of the structure in 1962.[151] Also, several rosettes were incised on one of the monuments mentioned above (*CIJ* 1.731). As discussed in the previous chapter, these two symbols were connected with the Temple and are depicted on the lintel of the Gamla synagogue. The presence of the throne also recalls Matthew's mention of the "Seat of Moses" (Matt 23:2).[152] Finally, although there is no proper *mikveh* associated with the building, its location near the ocean parallels the placement of other synagogues near bodies of water (e.g., Halicarnassus, Philippi and Arsinoë). Moreover, the building contains a stone water basin near the main entrance and a large cistern inside, both of which may have been used for ritual cleansings.[153]

---

[149]Some of these arguments have already been offered by Bruneau in his response to Mazur's identification of *GD* 80 as a pagan cultic house. See Bruneau, *Recherches sur les cultes de Delos*, 485–491; idem, "«Les Israélites de Délos» et la juiverie délienne," 489–495.

[150]This was originally Plassart's suggestion ("La synagogue juive de Délos," 531). Later, Goodenough argued that "the women stood in the outer chambers of [Portico] C, or did not attend at all, but not that benches were provided for them in Room B" (*JSGRP* 2.74).

[151]See Bruneau, *Recherches sur les cultes de Delos*, 485 and pl. IX, 3.

[152]Although this passage forms part of a Matthean diatribe against the scribes and Pharisees, it is likely that only the reference to the seat's new occupants is anachronistic since Matthew writes as if this seat had been established for quite some time.

[153]Bruneau comments that, unlike most other cisterns on Delos, which were built as covered reservoirs, the cistern in *GD* 80 allows human access. He suggests that a

If we have succeeded in establishing that the building was a synagogue in its second phase, it remains for us to explore the function of the structure in its initial use. In recent scholarly writings on *GD* 80, the claim has often been repeated that the first stage of this building was a domestic residence. Goodenough, who compared the structure to the later synagogue at Dura-Europos, was the first scholar to present this characterization.[154] Since then, the claim has been repeated by Thomas Kraabal, Eric Myers, Howard Kee and others.[155] The most vigorous proponent of this viewpoint, however, has been Michael White, who has written extensively on *GD* 80, always concluding that "the building was originally a private house near the shore."[156]

Despite the certainty with which White and other scholars proffer this claim, a comparative analysis of the edifice in its first phase with other buildings on Delos will demonstrate that this interpretation is architecturally unsound and can essentially be ruled out. We begin by noting that neither of the excavators of *GD* 80 ever inferred a domestic function for the early phase of the building, and for good reason. First of all, we must recall that Room A/B of the original structure measures 16.90 x 14.40 m on the interior, making it one of the largest "rooms" on the island (Plassart called it "une vaste salle").[157] Indeed, at one quarter the size of the gymnasium courtyard (*GD* 76), it could enclose the whole of the Masada synagogue inside with room to spare. One simply does not find such dimensions within the remains of Delian private homes. Domestic buildings on the island uniformly consist of a central, peristyle courtyard surrounded by small rooms, about 5 x 5 m in size, some slightly larger—none as big as Room A/B in *GD* 80.[158] The large dimensions of Room A/B clearly indicate that it was erected not as part of a private abode, but as a hall within a public building. Thus Bruneau could refer to

---

wooden ladder or stairs may have been used to enter the cistern for ritual ablutions. See Bruneau, *Recherches sur les cultes de Delos*, 490–491.

[154]*JSGRP* 2.73.

[155]Kraabel, "The Diaspora Synagogue," 493; Eric Meyers, "Ancient Synagogues: An Archaeological Introduction" in *Sacred Realm: The Emergence of the Synagogue in the Ancient World*, edited by Steven Fine (New York: Oxford University Press and Yeshiva University Museum, 1996), 13; Rachel Hachlili, "Diaspora Synagogues" in *ABD* 6.261; Kee, "Defining the First-Century CE Synagogue," 495–496; Rutgers, "Diaspora Synagogues, 94. In each instance, the claim is made without argument.

[156]White, *Building God's House*, 64. Cf. idem, "The Delos Synagogue Revisited," 151.

[157]See Plassart, "La synagogue juive de Délos," 523.

[158]See *GD*, pp. 34–36

this room and to the later divided room as "the assembly hall in its two successive phases" ("la salle de réunion dans ses deux états successifs").[159]

Another difference between *GD* 80 and Delian private architecture has to do with the length of the stylobate forming the edge of Portico C. At over 18 m long, this stylobate dwarfs those found inside the courtyards of private homes, which all run less than 10 m in length.[160] Moreover, the width of the stylobate, at 0.725 m, suggests a column-width slightly smaller, no less than 0.65 m.[161] Comparably sized columns found in the island's public architecture soar more than five meters into the sky (see fig. 14).[162] Needless to say, the columns in Delian private homes—even the grandest of them—do not match these dimensions.

---

[159]Bruneau, "«Les Israélites de Délos» et la juiverie délienne," 490. As we shall see, Mazur shares the same opinion.

[160]We should note that White believes that the portico was a later addition, though one added before the second phase when the dividing wall was placed between Room A/B ("The Delos Synagogue Revisited," 151). Against this is the fact that the southern wall of the portico is bonded to the original shell of the building (the northern wall is not, but there was later damage to that end of the building, suggesting repairs at the point where the walls intersected). See Bruneau, *Recherches sur les cultes de Delos*, pl. B and C.

[161]White states that the column widths measured 45–55 cm. in diameter ("The Delos Synagogue Revisited," 150), citing a page (with a photograph) in Plassart's report ("La synagogue juive de Délos," 525). Nothing on this page, however, indicates such a small column width. White may be referring to a column in the foreground of the photograph on that page. If so, then it must be recognized that this was not found *in situ* since it rests on the lower step of the crepidoma, not the stylobate, which is not extant at that point. Since in a later period *GD* 80 contained a kiln used to make lime out of columns, the column was probably located to this step then (or by the excavators themselves). In any case, it should be noted that White's own conjectural drawing of the building ("The Delos Synagogue Revisited," 160, fig. 5) shows the columns nearly as wide as the 72.5 cm stylobate, as was customary in ancient building practices. For example, the House of the Podeisoniasts (*GD* 57, a cultic hall), has a stylobate 69.5 cm wide. Columns found *in situ* measured between 66 cm and 63.5 cm in diameter. See C. Picard, *L'Établissement des Poseidoniastes de Bérytos* (Paris: E. de Boccard, 1921), 89–94; figs. 71–72.

[162]E.g., the House of the Poseidoniasts (*GD* 57), whose stylobate is only 69.5 cm wide has columns rising to a height of 4.96 m. See Picard, *L'Établissement des Poseidoniastes de Bérytos*, pl. IX. For Doric order columns, Vitruvius gives a 7:1 ratio between column height and diameter, though this ratio varied somewhat in different regions. See Vitruvius, *Arch.* 4.3.4; A. W. Lawrence, *Greek Architecture*, 5th ed. (New Haven: Yale University Press, 1996), 103.

Figure 14. The Courtyard of the House of the Poseidoniasts (*GD* 57, a cultic house). Because the stylobate of this structure is slightly narrower than the one in the courtyard of the Delos synagogue (69.5 cm versus 72.5 cm), the columns of the synagogue would have been slightly higher than those shown here (c. 5.2 m). Such dimensions are not found in the private homes of Delos. (From C. Picard, *L'Établissement des Poseidoniastes de Bérytos*, fig. 71.)

In connection with this, it will be recalled that foundation-remains of two stylobates run perpendicular at either end of the stylobate placed parallel to the front of the building. Because these taper off after 5–6 m due to beach erosion, their original length must be reconstructed. White has suggested that these stylobates stopped after about nine meters, forming a truncated tristoa or three-sided portico.[163] Such a plan would in itself allow us to classify the building as a public edifice.[164] Nevertheless, despite the initial attractiveness of this proposal, a difficulty arises when we observe that White's estimate is based upon the more recent plans of Bruneau, which were drawn in the 1960s after decades of erosion had deteriorated the remains of the walls and the stylobates running eastward toward the sea. It follows that on Bruneau's plan, the walls of the portico extend from the face of the building 12.6 m in the south and about 15 m in the north. However, on Plassart's original plan, drafted in 1913, different figures are given for these walls. Unfortunately, because the editors of *Revue biblique* lost the plan Plassart sent them, it was never

---

[163]See White, "The Delos Synagogue Revisited," 149–151, 160, fig. 5. White rightly rejects the earlier proposals of Plassart and Bruneau, the former suggesting that the stylobate extended along the entire eastern façade ("La synagogue juive de Délos," 524–525), and the latter that walls framed the portico to the north and south (*Recherches sur les cultes de Delos*, 483). While noting Bruneau's criticisms of Mazur's proposal of a peristyle court ("The Delos Synagogue Revisited," 149, nn. 67–68), White goes on to rebut these criticisms, allowing him to suggest a tristoa arrangement (ibid., 149–151). White's own rejection of Mazur's proposal of a peristyle arrangement is based on: (1) his observation of "an architectural implantation" on the rock formation near the present termination of the north wall-remains (i.e., an indentation about 60 cm square) and (2) his identification of possible stair-remains leading from the center courtyard onto the portico in front of the façade. The first objection is met by Plassart's plan stating that the north and south wall-remains extended beyond the point of the putative implantation, and also by the fact that there are no architectural parallels on the island for a tristoa (see below). Moreover, the purpose of this indentation is obscure and certainly does not demand the interpretation that it served as a support for a column base, as White maintains. Indeed, the presence of a column at this point would have been unnecessary since the stylobate would have contained the column supporting the roof of the peristyle at the corner in a tristoa. (Here it is instructive that, in his conjectural restoration [ibid., fig. 5], White does not know what to do with this indentation, and so he merely depicts it without any architectural embellishments.) The second point need not be met since the existence of stairs on the stylobate does not dictate that the fourth side of the court was open.

[164]Although White claims that this building was a private house, he does not compare it with examples of other private homes on the island in order to substantiate his claim.

published.[165] Nevertheless, Mazur later obtained it from Plassart in preparation for her analysis of *GD* 80.[166] In her published study of the site, she refers to the plan's measurements of the portico walls, writing, "as the plan of Plassart shows, and as is still to be seen, the north and south walls are preserved for 28 m. and 15 m. respectively beyond the east wall."[167] The measurement given for the north wall suggests that originally the south wall also extended outward 28 m (or more), as it follows a parallel course. Such distances preclude the possibility that the original building was a tristoa, since the northern and southern wings of the portico would have extended outward too far to have remained open.

It should also be pointed out that, even if we did not have Plassart's early figures, there would be reason to question White's proposal as there are no tristoas among the excavated remains at Delos. Hence White's reconstruction lacks a local architectural parallel.

This leads us to consider Mazur's reconstruction of the original building, which, as we have seen, she based on Plassart's original plan and on her own observations made in the 1930s. Mazur argued that the north and south stylobates of the portico originally extended eastward eighteen meters where they were met by a fourth stylobate, forming a square peristyle court (see fig. 15a). Accordingly, the two outer walls of the court extended eastward 28 m—the length of the northern wall-remains in Plassart's plan—where they were both met by a fourth wall, linking the square. Because of the large size of the peristyle (28 x 28 m),

---

[165]See Plassart, "La synagogue juive de Délos," facing page of 523, n. 1. In lieu of the lost plan, the editors inserted a rough drawing of *GD* 80 on this same page. Although this contains little useful information, it does indicate that in 1913 the beach was 26 m distant from the N-S stylobate (or c. 32 m distant from the eastern wall)—considerably further out than when Bruneau drafted his plan (less than 15 m from the stylobate according to Bruneau, *Recherches sur les cultes de Delos*, pl. A).

[166]Mazur, *Studies on Jewry in Greece*, 13.

[167]Ibid., 17. In Plassart's published report he merely states that the north wall extended out "more than 15 m." ("plus de 15 mètres"; "La synagogue juive de Délos," 524) This was apparently written before measurements were taken of this area (which was the last area to be excavated) or before the full extent of the wall-remains were uncovered. Although White cites Mazur at several points in his article on Delos, he nowhere mentions Mazur's figures. This suggests that he did not have access to her study and cites her only through other sources. On the other hand, Bruneau, who clearly had access to Mazur's study, never deals with the question of the wall-remains in his criticism of her (*Recherches sur les cultes de Delos*, 483).

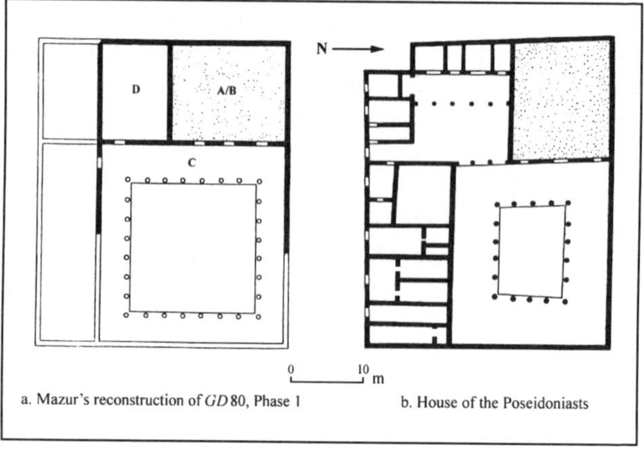

Figure 15. Comparison of *GD* 80 with the House of the Poseidoniasts. Characteristic of both structures are the assembly halls of similar size and placement and the large peristyle courts. (After Mazur, *Studies on Jewry in Greece*, plan 2.)

Mazur hypothesized that additional rooms were connected to the south wall of the building in a (still) unexcavated area.[168]

Although White does not explore Mazur's proposal at any length, he does state that she believed "that the building could not be a 'synagogue' because it was a house."[169] This, however, does not do justice to Mazur's position. The sole reason she disputed the identification was because she judged the monuments associated with the structure to be pagan, as has already been detailed. In fact, Mazur did not understand the original building to be a house at all—at least not in the sense that White uses the word (i.e., a domestic residence). Here, part of the confusion may have risen from the fact that Mazur compared the first phase of *GD* 80 with the so-called House of the Poseidoniasts (*GD* 57; see fig. 15b).[170] While this latter structure may be called a house in common parlance, this is somewhat of a misnomer, since architecturally its size classifies it as a hall (*GD* labels it "L'Établissement des Posidoniastes"). This all becomes

[168]Wall remains along the north wall of *GD* 80 suggest that additional rooms were once extant on this side of the building as well.

[169]White, "The Delos Synagogue Revealed," 140.

[170]Indeed, Goodenough, in first characterizing *GD* 80 as a house, borrows Mazur's language. He, like White, uses the word in a different sense than Mazur. See *JSGRP* 2.73.

clear when we review Mazur's comparison between her reconstruction of *GD* 80 and the House of the Poseidoniasts:

> The ground-plan of the older structure [*GD* 80, phase 1] presents a clear architectural picture. It represents a type familiarly seen in Delos: on a small and simple scale it is the usual Hellenistic house-type; but in this form, however, it bears close resemblance to that of the House of the Poseidoniasts. Characteristic of each is the large court in addition to the peristyle court which obviously satisfied some particular need. Our building thus belongs to a social institution similar to that of the Poseidoniasts. The latter was an association of merchants and shipowners of Beirut whose house served not only as a cult-centre of their God, Poseidon, but also as a business exchange or "bourse" for its members. From the second pre-Christian century, Delos was a commercial centre of great importance and attracted merchants, traders, shipowners, bankers from the countries of the orient. In this heterogeneous foreign population there were, undoubtedly, numerous professional fraternities serving the religious and business ends of related groups. Of these the Poseidoniasts are the only group whose centre is preserved. Our building clearly points, however, to another association, unknown, but not less important than that of the Poseidoniasts.[171]

From Mazur's description we see that both *GD* 80 and the House of the Poseidoniasts were houses not in the sense of "domestic residences," but "guild houses" or "cultic houses." Here, what is puzzling is that White makes a brief but favorable comparison between *GD* 80 and the House of the Poseidoniasts, but—perhaps dwelling on the ambiguous term "house"—he takes this as evidence that *GD* 80 was originally a private home.[172] While the architectural comparison is indeed apt, the similarities between the two structures should have suggested the opposite conclusion in view of the fact that the House of the Poseidoniasts never served as a domestic residence.[173] As Mazur has indicated and as inscriptions and

---

[171]Mazur, *Studies on Jewry in Greece*, 18–19. Mazur also detected the remains of a 2 x 2 m platform in the middle of room A/B, which she believed served as a base for a cultic statue. Subsequently, Bruneau was unable to find these remains (*Recherches sur les cultes de Delos*, 481). These may also have been lost to erosion.

[172]White, "The Delos Synagogue Revisited," 152. White also compares *GD* 80 to the House of the Comedians (*GD* 59), though architecturally, this comparison is not apt since its rooms and court are much smaller than those of *GD* 80.

[173]Immediately after comparing *GD* 80 with the House of the Poseidoniasts, White switches the discussion to a consideration of Sarapeion A, which he claims was adapted from a private home (ibid., 152–153). Whether or not this claim is accepted, it should be noted that *GD* 80 forms no architectural parallel to Sarapeion A. For White's later discussion of Serapeion A, see White, *Building God's House*, 32–37.

artifacts discovered within the building attest, the structure was erected as a public, monumental building that served as a commercial and cultic center for an association of maritime merchants. The cultic element is particularly prominent in this hall, as it contained a main sanctuary with four adjacent chapels housing the idols of various gods. An assembly hall, parallel in size and placement to the assembly hall in *GD* 80, served as the place where cultic and deliberative gatherings met. One recovered inscription dedicates the building to the group's "ancestral gods," while another refers to the entire complex as a *temenos*.[174]

The foregoing analysis of the structure suggests two possible patterns of occupation. In the first scenario, the building was originally constructed as a cultic hall by a pagan association in the second century B.C.E. During the Mithridatic War of 88 B.C.E. and/or the pirate raids of 69 B.C.E., the building was severely damaged and soon abandoned by the members of the association, who moved to more secure areas away from the shore. Subsequently, the vacant building was transformed into a synagogue, serving as such until about the second century C.E. (the date of the latest lamp-types found there). In scenario two, the building was originally built as a synagogue, damaged in the first century B.C.E., and subsequently modified, with a dividing wall being placed in the assembly hall, perhaps as a result of the damage incurred during the raids.

It is difficult to decide in favor of one of these scenarios. In support of the first option is the fact that none of the inscriptions associated with the building date to earlier than the first century B.C.E. Also, if we accept the theory that Room A/B was divided in the second phase in order to segregate the sexes, then it would have to be explained why this division was not incorporated into the original building plan. However, it may be that Room B served not as the seating area for the women, but as an ancillary banquet hall that replaced a similar as yet undiscovered room that was wrecked during the raids. In favor of the second option is the

---

[174]See Bruneau, *Recherches sur les cultes de Delos*, 622–630. The dedicatory inscription of the building (*ID* 1774) reads: "The *koinon* of the Poseidoniasts of Berytos, merchants, shippers, and investors dedicate the building and the stoa and the appurtenances to their ancestral gods [τὸ κοινὸν βηρυτίων Ποσειδωνιαστῶν ἐμπόρων καὶ ναυκλήρων καὶ ἐγδοχέων | τὸν οἶκον καὶ τὴν στοὰν καὶ τα χρηστήρια θεοῖς πατρίοις ἀνέθηκεν]" (Picard, *L'Établissement des Poseidoniastes de Bérytos*, 96). The reference to the hall as a *temenos* is in *ID* 1520, ll. 11–12 (for a recent translation of this lengthy inscription, see McLean, "Voluntary Associations and Churches on Delos," 197–200).

presence of the cistern, which Bruneau calls unusual because, unlike most other cisterns on the island, it allowed human access.

Another factor in this puzzle is the second-century Samaritan inscription mentioning the erection of a *proseuchē* (Bruneau no. 2). If this could somehow be linked to *GD* 80, then it would establish that the building was originally built and maintained as a Samaritan synagogue (scenario two).[175] However, because this inscription and the other were not found in *GD* 80, it is possible that a second synagogue exists on the island, about 90 m north of the present building. Yet even in this instance, a chance remains that the original Samaritan structure was demolished during the first-century raids, leading the Samaritans (rather than the Jews) to move into and renovate *GD* 80 (scenario one). The benefit of this reconstruction is that it would explain the presence of the pagan lamps and the votive bases that were (perhaps) topped with iconic figures, since the Samaritans, while maintaining many Jewish customs, were also said to have been syncretistic (e.g., Josephus, *Ant.* 12.257–261; see chapter seven). The use of these forms is, of course, also possible for a Jewish community, though it would seem a bit uncharacteristic given the conservative manner in which the Second Commandment was being interpreted by Jews during this era.

If all these possibilities seem bewildering, this is all the more reason to hope for renewed excavations in the areas around *GD* 80 and in the portion of the beach where the Samaritan inscriptions were discovered. Until the situation can be further clarified, caution must be exercised in

---

[175]This position has recently been argued in McLean, "Voluntary Associations and Churches on Delos," 191–195. McLean also takes the view that *GD* 80 is an example of a place of assembly "external" to the cult. While we would agree that either the Temple in Jerusalem or on Mt. Gerizim served as a central cultic site for the congregation of *GD* 80, McLean's statement that "the synagogue made no provision for the performance of cultic rites" (ibid., 195) is based upon too narrow a definition of "cult" (i.e., animal sacrifice only). Surely the gathering for public prayer (implied by the term *proseuchē*, *CIJ* 1.726), the setting up of votive offerings (*CIJ* 1.727–730), and the collection of monies for the offering of sacrifices should count as "cultic rites," particularly given the restrictions placed on Jews and Samaritans regarding the erection of shrines or altars. Even Julius Caesar refers to the activities of the Delian Jews (and perhaps the Samaritans) as "sacred rites" (ἱερά; Josephus, *Ant.* 14.214). For a list of archaeological indicators for religious ritual, see Renfrew, "The Archaeology of Religion," 51–52. The criteria include the existence of ritual baths, evidence denoting the practice of prayer, the presence of votive offerings, and the investment of wealth in constructing the cultic building. For a further consideration of other "cultic" functions of the synagogues, see chapter six.

interpreting the remains of *GD* 80 and the artifacts associated with it since we cannot ascertain whether the building in its second phase was Jewish or Samaritan, nor can we decide if the building was originally erected as a synagogue or later transformed into one. At any rate, researchers need to desist from citing *GD* 80 as an example of a private home transformed into a synagogue, as the preceding analysis has demonstrated that this was clearly not the case. In both phases, *GD* 80 existed as a public building of impressive size and design that served the communal needs of one or more cultic associations that were well-organized and, at least initially, well-endowed. In the second phase when the building clearly functioned as a synagogue for either Jews or Samaritans, the high level of institutionalization can be inferred from the presence of the throne, indicating a hierarchical arrangement in which one person served as the leader (the *archisynagōgos*?).[176] It may also be observed that the person sitting on this throne sat opposite the interior façade of the building, as we have seen was possibly the case for the leaders of the synagogues at Gamla, Masada, and Herodium. Moreover, as the plan indicates, the outer façade of the hall faces east. If Jews or Samaritans originally built the hall, the design may intentionally have imitated the arrangement of the inner courts of the Temple at Jerusalem or Gerizim (whose gates faced east),[177] or it may have sought to direct focus in the general direction of the Orient (though Mount Gerizim and Jerusalem actually lie to the southeast). However, since the façades of many temples on the island (as well as the House of the Poseidoniasts) face east, the design may reflect adherence to local cultic practices.

The dividing wall between Rooms A and B presents the first serious architectural evidence suggesting the division of the sexes within the synagogue. While it is also possible that Room B served as a banquet hall (as suggested by the literary evidence), the presence of benches around two sides of the room makes this view somewhat less probable. If Mazur's hunch is correct that additional rooms lie in the unexcavated

---

[176]Richardson, who writes that "the meeting space [of the early synagogues] focused not on some function or office or liturgical feature but on the community itself" ("Early Synagogues as Collegia," 102–103), does not take into account the existence of this *thronos* in his analysis.

[177]Josephus writes that the Samaritan temple, built c. 330 B.C.E. and destroyed by Hyrcanus I in 113 B.C.E., was modeled after the Jerusalem Temple (*Ant.* 13.254–256). Recent excavations of this site, while as yet unpublished, tend to confirm Josephus' report. For further discussion, see chapter seven.

areas south of *GD* 80, then possibly one of these served as a banquet room in one or both phases.

ITALY

Rome

Traditionally held to have been founded in 753 B.C.E., Rome was built on seven hills situated to the east of the Tiber River, about fifteen miles upstream from where it flowed into the Tyrrhenian Sea. During the early Imperial period, Rome's population approached one million and included not only native Romans, but also immigrants from nearly every corner of the empire, many originally brought there as slaves captured in one of Rome's many wars.

It is not known for certain when the first Jews came to live in Rome, although 1 Maccabees refers to several embassies sent to the Roman senate by Judas Maccabaeus (1 Macc 8:17–32) and the later Hasmoneans (1 Macc 12:1–4; 14:24; 15:15–24). Generally, it is held that a substantial number were resident in the capital by the early first century B.C.E., since during his defense of Flaccus in 59 B.C.E., Cicero refers to groups of Jews customarily gathering at the Aurelian Steps in the Roman Forum (*pro Flacc.* 66). Charging the prosecutor with arranging the trial near that site in order to attract a Jewish crowd, Cicero states, "you know how large a group they are, how unanimously they stick together, how influential they are in politics."[178] Cicero goes on to mention how "gold was exported each year in the name of the Jews from Italy and all our provinces to Jerusalem" (*pro Flacc.* 67). This latter allusion indicates that the Jews in Rome, like those scattered throughout the empire, remained in solidarity with the Temple cultus at least to the extent of sending their annual payments of the temple tax to Jerusalem. It is not known whether the Roman Jews had yet erected synagogues, although Cicero's mention of the gatherings at the Aurelian Steps suggests that this site in the corner of the Roman Forum served as a place where at least some of them met for Sabbath observances. It is clear, however, that Cicero was not referring to the thousands of Jewish slaves brought to Rome by Pompey two years

[178]The translation of this and the following quotation is from Leon, *The Jews of Ancient Rome*, 6. For a more detailed treatment of the Jewish presence in Rome, see this volume as well as Smallwood, *The Jews under Roman Rule*, 201–219; Levinskaya, *The Book of Acts in Its Diaspora Setting*, 168–193.

earlier, since these Jews could hardly have been influential in Roman politics.

Whatever the size of the Jewish population in Rome during the early part of the first century B.C.E., Pompey's relocation of Jews to the capital in 61 B.C.E. obviously not only enlarged the resident Jewish population, but also lowered its overall socio-economic status. Apparently this was short-lived, however, since Philo attests that by the time of Augustus most of these Jews had been manumitted. They went on to form a colony in the Transtiverinum, located on the western side of the Tiber, where they also began to erect their synagogues:

> [Augustus] was aware that the great section of Rome on the other side of the Tiber is occupied and inhabited by Jews, most of whom were Roman citizens emancipated. For having been brought as captives to Italy they were liberated by their owners and were not forced to violate any of their native institutions. He knew therefore that they have *proseuchai* and meet together in them, particularly on the sacred sabbaths when they receive as a body a training in their ancestral philosophy. He knew too that they collect money for sacred purposes from their first-fruits and send them to Jerusalem by persons who would offer the sacrifices. Yet nevertheless he neither ejected them from Rome nor deprived them of their Roman citizenship because they were careful to preserve their Jewish citizenship also, nor took any violent measures against the *proseuchai*, nor prevented them from meeting to receive instructions in the laws, nor opposed their offerings of the first-fruits. Indeed so religiously did he respect our interests that supported by wellnigh his whole household he adorned our temple through the costliness of his dedications, and ordered that for all time continuous sacrifices of whole burnt offerings should be carried out every day at his own expense as a tribute to the most high God (*Legat.* 155–157).

Here again, we see that not only did the Jews living in Rome gather in their synagogues on the Sabbath to study Torah, but they also collected sacrificial offerings to be sent to the Temple on the congregations' behalf. The synagogues here as elsewhere in the diaspora appear to have been in solidarity with the Jerusalem Temple.

As noted in the introduction of this chapter, unlike the Jewish communities in Alexandria, Sardis, and elsewhere, the one in Rome does not appear to have been constituted as a politeuma. Instead, it seems to have been segmented into a number of individual congregations that were classified as *collegia* (Greek: *thiasoi*) or "religious societies."[179] This can

---

[179]On the different legal classifications governing the synagogues in the eastern and western halves of the empire, see the introduction of this chapter, above.

be seen in Caesar's letter to the people of Parium (partially quoted in the previous section) where reference is made to governmental treatment of the Jews in Rome:

> Now it displeases me that such statutes should be made against our friends and allies and that they should be forbidden to live in accordance with their customs and to contribute money to common meals and sacred rites, for this they are not forbidden to do even in Rome. For example, Gaius Caesar, our consular praetor, by edict forbade religious societies [θιάσους] to assemble in the city, but these people alone he did not forbid to do so or to collect contributions of money or to hold common meals [μόνους τούτους οὐκ ἐκώλυσεν οὔτε χρήματα συνεισφέρειν οὔτε σύνδειπνα ποιεῖν]. Similarly do I forbid other religious societies [ἄλλους θιάσους] but permit these people alone to assemble and feast in accordance with their native customs and ordinances [τούτοις μόνοις ἐπιτρέπω κατὰ τὰ πάτρια ἔθη καὶ νόμιμα συνάγεσθαί τε καὶ ἑστιᾶσθαι] (Josephus, *Ant.* 14.213–216).

The illicit *thiasoi* alluded to in the edict were similar in constitution to the *koinon* of the Poseidoniasts in Delos. They were typically comprised of individuals sharing a common commercial and/or religious interest. During the periods when the *thiasoi* were legal, members would commonly erect buildings (known as *scholae*) similar to the House of the Posdeidoniasts, containing assembly halls, shrines and dining rooms.[180] The Roman leaders were always suspicious of these *thiasoi*, viewing them as potential political threats. A related fear was that the *thiasoi* would introduce foreign gods, who were often associated with strange rites and bizarre behaviors felt to be harmful to the Roman way of life. Hence in 186 B.C.E., the Senate outlawed all *thiasoi* in Italy associated with Bacchus.[181] Similar concerns must have been behind Caesar's ban on the *thiasoi*, yet it is significant that he allowed the Jews to continue to meet. This was probably as a favor to Hyrcanus II and Antipater, who had supported him in his eastern campaigns. Yet Caesar's decision may also have been made in recognition of the ancient traditions of the Jews, since, in general, Romans tended to respect such traditions—as long as these were not perceived as threats.

---

[180]A number of these have been preserved at Ostia, though they date to somewhat after our period. See Stambaugh, "The Functions of Roman Temples," 588–591; idem, *The Ancient Roman City* (Baltimore, Md.: The Johns Hopkins University Press, 1988), 209–212; Russell Meiggs, *Roman Ostia*, 2nd ed. (Oxford: Clarendon Press, 1973), 311–336.

[181]Livy, 39.9–13. See also Cotter, "The Collegia and Roman Law," 74–89.

As we have seen, Augustus continued to be a patron of the Jews in Rome during his reign, exempting them from a ban on the *thiasoi*, which was applied to all but the most established groups.[182] In addition, Philo states that Augustus allowed the Jews to receive the public dole of money and wheat on an alternate day when the monthly distribution date happened to fall on the Sabbath (*Legat.* 157). By the time of Augustus' rule we can get a clearer picture of the size of the Jewish population in the capital, since Josephus writes that 8,000 of the Jews in Rome showed up in the Temple of Apollo to petition Augustus not to install Archelaus on the throne of Judea (c. 4 B.C.E., *BJ* 2.80–83; *Ant.* 17.300–301). This reference has led to estimates of about 40,000 Jews living in the capital at this time.[183] Such a total indicates that the number of synagogues in the city must have been quite high, although none of our sources ever mentions a figure.

If Augustus served as the patron of the Jews in Rome, their fortune took a different turn under the next several emperors. Expulsions from Rome of at least part of the Jewish population took place under Tiberius (19 C.E.) and Claudius (49 C.E.)—the latter probably because of disputes with the growing number of Christians in the city.[184] The fate of the synagogues as a result of these actions is not known. Most likely, at least some of them were shut down during the period the edicts were in force. In between these expulsions, the Jewish population in Rome had to contend with Gaius (37–41 C.E.), who, as we have seen, was not on the friendliest of terms with the Jews. Nevertheless, he does not appear to have expelled them, though he possibly may have sanctioned the erection of idols within the synagogues in Rome, as Philo hints (*Legat.* 346).

After Claudius' death and Nero's accession in 54 C.E., those Jews who had been expelled were allowed to return. The relationship between Nero and the Jews in Rome seems to have been placid, with the Christians in the city bearing the brunt of the emperor's later excesses. Ironically, one of the only bits of literary evidence we have about Jews living in Rome during his reign comes from the writings of Paul. Near the

---

[182]Philo, *Legat.* 155–157; Suetonius, *Augustus* 32.1.

[183]Leon, *The Jews of Ancient Rome*, 15, 135–136.

[184]Philo, *Legat.* 160; Josephus, *Ant.* 18.81–84; Acts 18:19; Suetonius, *Tiberius*, 36; *Claudius* 25.4; The debate over the nature of these expulsions continues to rage. Most scholars believe that the expulsions were limited to freedmen or to those of recent freedmen stock. See Leon, *The Jews of Ancient Rome*, 16–27; Levinskaya, *The Book of Acts in Its Diaspora Setting*, 171–182.

end of his letter to the Romans, the apostle, referring to disputes between Jewish and Gentile Christians in the city, writes, "Some believe in eating anything, while the weak eat only vegetables . . . Some judge one day to be better than another, while others judge all days to be alike" (Rom 14:2, 5). This implies that some of the Jewish Christians were continuing to eat kosher foods and to keep the Jewish sacred days. Thus we may infer that at the time this letter was written (c. 54 C.E.), it was common for the general Jewish population in Rome to adhere to these same practices.[185] Josephus implies the same in his comments about two priests taken as prisoners to Rome ten years later, for he writes "even in their affliction, they had not forgotten the pious practices of religion, and supported themselves on figs and nuts" (*Vita* 14).

Although it is frequently stated that we know the identity of some eleven or twelve synagogues in Rome during the Second Temple period, it should be noted that this claim is based upon Jewish epitaphs dating from the third to fourth centuries C.E.[186] In view of the arrival in Rome of second and third waves of Jewish slaves in the aftermath of the two Jewish Wars, the use of these inscriptions as evidence for the pre-70 period is highly problematic. Therefore, we must remain content to limit our investigation to the contemporary literary sources cited above, as well as to the one first-century inscription mentioning a *proseucha* (*JIWE* 2.602), which we examined in chapter two.

From this evidence we can infer that a large number of synagogues existed in Rome near the end of our period, with most being located in the Transtiverinum. The synagogues appear to have been organized as a confederacy, with the local congregations administering their own internal affairs. The congregations themselves were classified as *thiasoi*, and, like other *thiasoi*, they were subject to the whims of the emperor. The golden era for the Jews in Rome was during the reigns of Julius

---

[185]The eating of vegetables was to avoid contamination from meat sacrificed to idols. Cf. Dan 1.

[186]For a list of these, see Leon, *The Jews of Ancient Rome*, 135–166; Levinskaya, *The Book of Acts in Its Diaspora Setting*, 182–193. While it is possible that members of the "Synagogue of the Augustesians" (*JIWE* 2.547, 96, 169, 189, 194, 542) and the "Synagogue of the Agrippesians" (*JIWE* 2.130, 170, 549, 562) are descendants of slaves manumitted by Augustus and Marcus Agrippa, it is also possible that the former refers to any of the later emperors while the latter may be a reference to King Agrippa II. In any case, by the third and fourth centuries, the nature of the synagogues had changed dramatically, no longer allowing us to infer anything about their character during the Second Temple period.

Caesar and Augustus, after which they suffered from expulsion orders issued during the reigns of Tiberius and Claudius. In addition, Gaius may have sanctioned attacks against their synagogues, as Philo indicates he did throughout the empire. Some stability seems to have returned to the congregations during Nero's reign, only to be interrupted again with a flood of Jewish captives in 72 C.E.

During our period, the synagogues in Rome functioned as places where Sabbath meetings were held and offerings for the Temple were collected. Envoys regularly traveled to Jerusalem in order to offer sacrifices on behalf of their congregations. The synagogue buildings, known locally as *proseuchai*, were erected primarily by freedmen brought to Rome by Pompey in 61 B.C.E., though some Jews who had lived in Rome even before then may themselves have established such edifices. Whether or not this was the case, many of these Jews initially adhered to the custom of meeting in a corner of the Roman forum, possibly on the Sabbath.

As for the appearance of the synagogues in Rome, evidence suggests that they were patterned after cultic halls, at least to the degree of possessing assembly halls and banquet rooms. Although no synagogues have ever been found in Rome, one originally dating to our period was discovered at nearby Ostia. Since this structure probably typifies the design of the early synagogues in the capital, we now turn to a consideration of this discovery.

Ostia[187]

Situated at the mouth of the Tiber, Ostia was first occupied in the fourth century B.C.E. as a defensive settlement. Later, as Rome's maritime activities increased, it served as the port city for the capital, with the wealth of the empire passing through its harbor. To handle the increasing traffic, larger harbors were built during the reigns of Claudius and Trajan, at which time the city may have boasted a population as high as 60,000. The eventual silting of the harbor led to the town's decline beginning in

---

[187]For a fairly complete account of Ostia's history, see Meiggs, *Roman Ostia*, 16–101, 532–534.

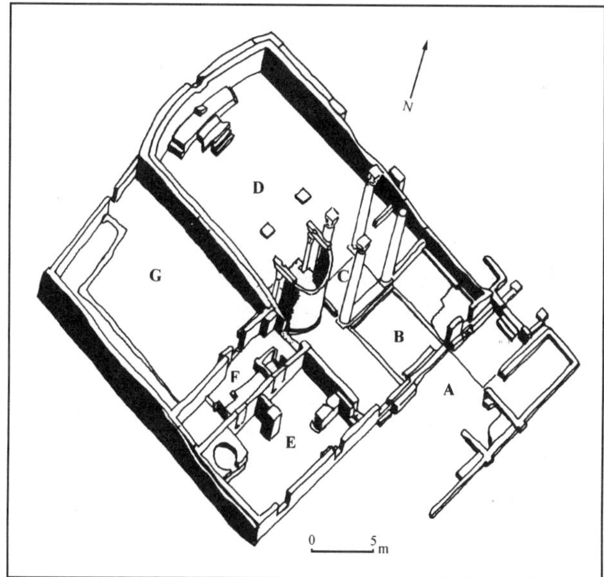

Figure 16. Plan of the Ostia synagogue in its fourth-century C.E. state. Entry into the complex was from the northeast. After walking down some stairs, one came to the vestibule (A). From there, the approach to the main hall (D) was through an entry court (B) and a gateway (C). The synagogue was also equipped with a kitchen (E) and a banquet room (G), the latter accessed through a corridor (F). (Plan: Archivio Fotographico della Soprintendenza Archeologica di Ostia.)

Because the site was quickly covered over and remained undisturbed for centuries, excavations at Ostia have produced many stunning finds, including scores of building-remains and over 4,000 inscriptions. It stands second only to Pompeii in presenting us with a portrait of a Roman city in the early empire.

The Ostia synagogue was discovered in 1961 at the edge of the town, near the ancient coastline (see fig. 16). It was excavated and restored over two seasons (1961–62) by a team led by Maria Squarciapino, then director of the Department of Antiquities of Ancient Ostia. The building was identified as a synagogue on the basis of its monumental size and the presence of Jewish artwork including a relief with a menorah, several lamps with this same motif, and an inscription which makes reference to an ark.[188] In its present state, the synagogue dates to the fourth century C.E. (phase 3), though the excavations revealed two earlier phases of the building (phases 1 and 2), the first of which dates to the middle of the first century C.E. In order to understand the overall layout of the structure, we will begin with a description of the last two phases of the building before broaching the question of whether the earliest phase should also be classified as a synagogue.

The synagogue together with its ancillary rooms occupies a space of 36.60 x 23.50 m. The façade of the building is oriented to the southeast, in the direction of Jerusalem. During the last phases, the synagogue was entered from the northeast through a door flanked by marble pilasters. One then proceeded down two stairs into a long, narrow room that Squarciapino refers to as a vestibule (A). At the foot of the stairs rests a well topped with a marble well-head carved with a wave pattern. The vestibule, though only partially preserved, adjoins a number of small chambers on its southeast side.

Five doors are arranged on the southwest wall of the vestibule. Three of these lead into the synagogue proper, while two others give entry to a kitchen. The main area of the synagogue measures 24.90 x 12.50 m and is divided into three distinctive parts. The first part (B) serves as an entry court connected with the three doors opening from the vestibule. Beginning with the building's second phase (c. II–III C.E.), this area was

[188]The description of the Ostia synagogue is based upon the following sources: Maria Floriani Squarciapino, "La Sinagoga di Ostia: Second campagna di Scavo" in *Atti VI Congresso Internazionale di Archeologia Cristiana* (Rome, 1962), 299–315; idem, "Ebrei a Roma e ad Ostia," *Studi Romani* 11, no. 2 (1963): 129–141; idem, "Die Synagoge von Ostia Antica," *Raggi* 4, no. 1 (1962): 1–8; idem, "The Synagogue at Ostia," *Archaeology* 16 (1963): 194–203; idem, "The Most Ancient Synagogue Known from Monumental Remains: The Newly Discovered Ostia Synagogue in Its First and Fourth Century A.D. Phases." *The Illustrated London News*, September 28 1963, 468–471; "Die Synagoge von Ostia nach der zweiten Ausgrabungskampagne," *Raggi* 5, no. 1 (1963): 13–17. See also A. Thomas Kraabel, "The Diaspora Synagogue: Archaeological and Epigraphic Evidence Since Sukenik" in *ANRW* II.19.1, 497–500; L. Michael White, *Building God's House*, 69–71; idem., *Domus Ecclesiae Domus Dei*, 320–374; idem, "Synagogue and Society in Imperial Ostia: Archaeological and Epigraphic Evidence," *HTR* 90 (1997): 23–58; idem,*The Social Origins of Christian Architecture* (Valley Forge, Pa.: Trinity Press International, 1996–97), 2.379–391; Shanks, *Judaism in Stone*, 162–169; F. Zevi, "La sinagoga di Ostia," *Rassegna mensile di Israel* 38 (1972): 131–145; Wishchnitzer, *The Architecture of the European Synagogue*, 5–7; *JIWE* 1, pp. 23–24; Foerster, *A Survey of Ancient Diaspora Synagogues*, 170; Rutgers, "Diaspora Synagogues," 67–94.

divided into three aisles, first by light walls covered with painted stucco, and later (phase 3) by two balustrades. The floors of each of these aisles were covered with black-and-white mosaics. Of the two preserved patterns in the mosaics, one is a square containing a six-petalled rosette inscribed inside a hexagon, while the other appears to be a chalice and loaf. A shallow water basin was discovered near the doorway of the northeast aisle.

The second part of the main area is an inner gateway formed by four columns (C). Rising to a height of 4.7 m, these columns are made of grey marble and topped with Corinthian capitals. The southwest and northeast aisles running through the gateway were closed off from the main hall by means of screen walls erected between the side walls and the two inner columns up to the height of their capitals. In the screen wall on the northeast aisle was a doorway fitted with metal grating. During the building's last phase, the screen wall of the southwest aisle was removed to make way for an aedicula, which we shall discuss shortly.

After passing through the gateway, one entered the final part of the main area, the assembly hall (D), which measures 15 x 12.5 m and is paved in *opus sectile*. The back wall of this room is slightly curved and directly in front of it is a bema or podium, approached by several steps. It is likely that the Torah was read from a wooden table placed on this bema. Two columns of white marble were placed near the center of the hall, their height and alignment different than the four columns comprising the gateway.

In the building's final phase, the screen wall in the southwest aisle was torn down. Replacing it was an apse-like aedicula made of *opus vittatum* (courses of bricks and tufa blocks), erected on a platform approached by four stairs. Two marble colonettes with composite capitals were placed in front of the aedicula on either side. Eventually, these were incorporated into the platform, as it was at some point extended outward. Two architraves stretch from both sides of the aedicula to the top of the colonettes. The architraves end in corbels incised with various symbols of Jewish art: the right one contains a menorah flanked by shofars (ram's horns), while the left one has a *lulub* (palm branch) and *ethrog* (citron). Deep cuttings in the interior sides of the architraves suggest that they were linked by a transverse section, perhaps a pediment. Clearly the aedicula was erected to contain a wooden ark which housed the Torah scrolls.

During the final phase of the building, the left-hand side of the aisle behind the aedicula was partially blocked by a wall made from *opus vittatum*. A door was left in the southeast side of this wall, allowing access into the kitchen (E). This room contains a stove, two tables and several amphorae (for storage of wine or oil) which were sunk into the floor. In its final state, the floor of the kitchen was paved with a mixture of earth, ash and fragments of marble and terra cotta. Underneath this layer, however, excavators uncovered a black-and-white mosaic floor, patterned with meanders, rosettes and checkerboard squares. The lamps containing the menorahs were also found on this level.

A second door in the aisle behind the aedicula leads into a corridor (F), from which one gains access into a large room on the northwest (G). Against the northwest and southwest walls of this room are wide benches (c. 1.93 m) that clearly served as couches for banquets. A second door in the northwest wall provides entry from the exterior of the structure. The building materials associated with this room and the adjoining corridor suggest that they were constructed during the structure's final phase.

Before turning to Squarciapino's arguments for assigning the erection of the synagogue to the first century C.E., we need to examine White's reasons for maintaining that the building was originally a "house or insula" that was transformed into a synagogue only at the end of the second century.[189] This position was first presented in published form in White's 1990 book, *Building God's House in the Roman World*, but without specific supporting arguments. He merely asserts that the foundation of the synagogue can be correlated with an inscription found on the site. According to White, this inscription states that a certain Mindis Faustus "gave his own rooms for the construction of the building

---

[189]White, *Building God's House in the Roman World*, 69. For similar conclusions, see also idem, *Domus Ecclesiae Domus Dei*, 325; Eric M. Meyers and L. Michael White, "Jews and Christians in a Roman World," *Archaeology* 42, no. 2 (1989): 31–32. We should note that, unlike the situation with the synagogue at Delos, White was the first author to claim that the lower stratum of the Ostia synagogue was a house. So far only Kee and Feldman have joined him in this assessment (Kee, "Defining the First-Century CE Synagogue," 496; Feldman, "Diaspora Synagogues," 587). White's interpretation is challenged in *JIWE* 1, pp. 22–26. For a more recent critique of White's position, see Anders Runesson, "The Oldest Original Synagogue Building in the Diaspora. A Response to L. Michael White," *HTR* 92, no. 4 (1999), forthcoming.

and the Torah ark."[190] The full transcription of the monument reads as follows (*JIWE* 1.13):[191]

pro salute Aug(usti) οἰκοδόμησεν κὲ αἰπο[ί]- ησεν ἐκ τῶν αὐτοῦ δο- μάτων καὶ τὴν κειβωτὸν ἀνέθηκεν νόμῳ ἁγιῳ [[Μίνδις Φαῦστος με]]- [τὰ τῶν ἰ][[διῶ]][ν]	For the safety of the Emperor. Mindius Faustus with his family built and made (it) from his own gifts, and set up the ark for the holy law

Although in his supporting dissertation White presents nearly the same transcription as above (he omits l. 7 and some critical apparatus), his translation differs significantly from the one given in *JIWE*: "For the well-being of the Emperor. Mindis Faustus constructed (the synagogue) and made it from his own rooms, and he set up the 'ark' for the sacred law . . . ."[192] From this translation we can see how White was led to claim that the Ostia synagogue was founded in the second century C.E. from a private house. The difficulty with this proposition, however, is that the word *domatōn*, which White translates "rooms," actually means "gifts."[193] Here, it appears that White has mistaken the word *doma* (omicron) with *dōma* (omega) since in the note attached to this term he writes, "For the use of the word in synagogue dedications compare the Ophel Synagogue inscription."[194] This last, of course, is a reference to the Theodotus inscription (*CIJ* 2.1404) which contains the word *dōma* (omega) in the plural, meaning "rooms." White's initial conclusions about the first phase

---

[190]Ibid., 79. Cf. p. 69. White states that the collection of inscriptions associated with his work (first gathered in his PhD dissertation) was published as L. Michael White, *The Christian Domus Ecclesiae and Its Environment: A Collection of Texts and Monuments* (Harvard Theological Studies 36; Minneapolis, 1990). However, this book never appeared, leading me initially to consult his dissertation. Subsequently, this collection appeared as idem, *The Social Origins of Christian Architecture*, vol. 2 (Harvard Theological Studies 43; Valley Forge, Pa.: Trinity Press International, 1997). On the revised position on the M. Faustus inscription which White presents in this volume, see below.

[191]Translation from *JIWE*. The inscription was found among the discarded materials serving as the flooring of the vestibule. In its initial form, it dates to the late second century C.E.

[192]White, *Domus Ecclesiae Domus Dei*, 326.

[193]See LSJ, BAGD s.v., δόμα.

[194]White, *Domus Ecclesiae Domus Dei*, 326.

of the Ostia synagogue are thus based upon a mistranslation of the above inscription.

More recently, in a volume containing the inscriptions gathered in his dissertation, White alters the translation to read, "Mindus Faustus [. . . DIO . . .] constructed (the synagogue) and made it from his own gifts."[195] Then, however, he goes on to insert the following note (I omit White's references to other works):

> The term δομάτων (line 3) would usually mean "gifts," but it could be read as the derived meaning "funds" (presumably given for the project). Still, the use of this term is unusual, and another option suggests itself. Given the generally poor orthography found in the text, we might well read the omicron for an omega, hence δωμάτων, a variant found in some papyri, and common among Greek epitaphs from Rome. This spelling would seem a natural substitution also in a Latin context, given the regular use of the loan-word *domus* in Greek as δόμος (for δῶμα). Read in this way then, the phrase would refer to the house or rooms from which the synagogue was renovated.[196]

While White's alteration of the translation rather undermines his original position, his revised argument nonetheless merits consideration. In responding to it, we should first of all observe that White is correct in noting that the use of the word *doma* is unusual, since it rarely appears in pagan literature (Plato 2x, Plutarch 2x). However, the one place where it *does* show up with great frequency is in the LXX. There it is used some fifty-four times to translate several Hebrew words, all meaning either "gift" or "offering."[197] Of special interest is the fact that many of these usages are associated with gifts presented to the tabernacle or the Temple. Particularly revealing is a passage from Numbers wherein the Levites are issued the following command: "From all of your gifts you shall offer an offering to the Lord [ἀπὸ πάντων τῶν δομάτων ὑμῶν ἀφελεῖτε ἀφαίρεμα κυρίῳ]" (Num 18:29, LXX; cf 18:11). The close wording of this verse

---

[195]White, *The Social Origins of Christian Architecture*, 2.394. Cf. idem, "Synagogue and Society in Imperial Ostia," 40, n. 49.

[196]Ibid., n. 166.

[197]E.g., תְּנוּפָה ("offering," Lev 7:30), מַתָּנָה ("gift," Num 18:6), נְדָבָה ("freewill offering," Deut 23:24). For other uses of δόμα in the LXX, see: Gen 25:6, 47:22; Exod 28:38; Lev 23:38; Num 3:9, 18:7, 18:11, 18:29, 27:7, 28:2; Deut 12:11, 23:24; 1 Sam 18:25; 2 Sam 19:43; 1 Kgs 13:7; 2 Chr 2:9, 17:11, 21:3, 31:14, 32:23, Jdt 4:14, 16:18; 1 Macc 3:30, 10:24, 10:28, 10:39, 10:54, 10:60, 12:43, 15:5, 16:19; Ps 67:19; Prov 18:16, 19:17; Eccl 3:13, 4:17, 5:18; Sir 7:33, 18:17, 38:2, *Pss. Sol.* 5:14, 18:1; Hos 9:1, 10:6; Mal 1:3; Ezek 20:26, 20:31, 46:5, 46:16, 46:17, Dan 2:6.

with the above inscription suggests that the dedication to the Ostia synagogue (the implied "it" in the inscription) may have been an offering from the Levitical tithes still being collected after the Temple's destruction. Alternatively, the benefaction may have been given by *any* member of the congregation as a general thank-offering for God's benevolence (after Deut 12:11).

In either case, it is likely that the LXX established *doma* as a Jewish term, since its usage is almost exclusively confined to Jewish and Christian writings (e.g., Philo, the New Testament, Patristic writings).[198] The epigraphic evidence supports this view, for a thorough search of Greek inscriptions yielded only one set of monuments containing the term *doma*. Dating from the fourth to fifth century C.E., they come, interestingly enough, from the synagogue at Sardis where they were attached to several appurtenances found within the building (e.g., a mosaic floor). Though as yet unpublished, the relevant portions of the inscriptions have been made available to the author for this study. In each instance, the inscription contains a variant of the phrase "from the gifts of providence" (ἐκ τῶν τῆς προνοίας δομάτων).[199] As for the usage of *doma* in each case, John Kroll, the compiler of the inscriptions states, "No chance at all here that it can pertain to a house or rooms."[200]

While the use of *doma* in the LXX and the Sardis inscriptions argues strongly against White's latest proposal, there is yet a more decisive reason why *domatōn* cannot be translated "rooms" in the above dedication: an examination of the stone itself reveals that the last two lines of the inscription—those containing the name of the original benefactor—have been erased and reinscribed with the name Mindus Faustus. Moreover, it is clear that the erasures were *not* the result of a mistake, since the letter forms differ in the reinscribed lines, dating to about a century *after* the initial inscription (i.e., III C.E.; see fig. 17).[201]

---

[198]See, e.g., Philo, *Mos*. 2.242, *Deus*. 6, *Cher*. 84 (mostly quotes from the LXX); Matt 7:11; Luke 11:13; Eph 4:8; Phil 4:17.

[199]John H Kroll, "The Greek Inscriptions" in *The Synagogue at Sardis* (Cambridge, Mass.: Harvard University Press, forthcoming). Nos. 21 and 22 read ἐκ τῶν τῆς προνοίας δομάτων; no. 20 reads ἐκ τῶν δομάτων τῆς προνοίας; nos. 19 and 20 read ἐκ τῶν τῆς προνοίας (δομάτων implied). For previous allusions to these inscriptions, see *JIWE* 1, pp. 25–26; Trebilco, *Jewish Communities in Asia Minor*, 49–50.

[200]Letter to the author dated 23 August, 1996.

[201]So *JIWE* 1.13; *SEG* 45.916; *NDIEC* 4.112; M. Guarducci, *Epigrafia greca III* (Rome, 1974), 115–117. These erasures were not noted in White's dissertation. More

Figure 17. *JIWE* 1.13: The Mindus Faustus inscription. Note how the last two lines of the dedication have been scratched-out and reinscribed. The different letter forms in the reinscribed section (e.g., M, ll. 2, 4 and 5; μ, l. 6) indicate that the inscription was reused about a century after it was originally inscribed. (Photo: Archivio Fotographico della Soprintendenza Archeologica di Ostia.)

Clearly, the original inscription has been reused. This is significant, for while one might reuse an inscription to dedicate a new piece of furniture or other appurtenance, it is not possible for two different donors living in two different centuries to offer their "rooms" for the foundation of the same synagogue. For this same reason, we must also reject White's view that the monument was a dedication of the synagogue itself, since the building was obviously not founded by different persons in two successive centuries.

---

recently, White has stated that the letters in ll. 6–7 were "corrected in a different hand" and that the last letter in l. 6 (ϵ) was part of the original inscription (White, *The Social Origins of Christian Architecture*, 2.392, n. 163; cf. idem, "Synagogue and Society in Ancient Ostia," 39, n. 43). However, an examination of the inscription reveals not only that the epsilon in question was inscribed over the erasure, but also that it was engraved in a different hand: while the middle bars of the epsilons in ll. 2–5 extend only two-thirds the width of the letter, the one in l. 6 extends the entire width (see fig. 17). Since White also writes that "the inscription has not formally been published" (*The Social Origins of Christian Architecture*, 2.392), he apparently is unaware of the above authorities, which all date the letter-forms of the reinscribed lines to a century after the initial engraving.

Because the inscription mentions the setting up of an ark (l. 4), the monument most likely represents the dedication of a wooden pedestal for this shrine, perhaps one erected near the location of the later aedicula.[202] If so, when the original pedestal became worn or was judged otherwise inadequate, Mindus Faustus built a new pedestal and then had the original donor's name replaced with his own on the inscription. The subsequent erection of the stone aedicula in the fourth century made Mindus Faustus' dedication obsolete, and so the monument was discarded and used as part of the flooring in the vestibule.

Whatever the exact nature of dedications, the preceding arguments are sufficient to demonstrate that White's translation of the Ostia inscription should be rejected. Its removal as a possibility renders White's overall hypothesis problematic, since he nowhere explains how the original form of the Ostia synagogue bore the likeness of a private home or insula. As with his treatment of the synagogue at Delos, White never compares the earliest phase of the Ostia synagogue with local examples of domestic architecture. Had he done this, he would have been hard-pressed to show any similarities between the two types of structures. There simply is no comparison. Ostian houses from this period resemble those encountered in our earlier treatment of Delos: they consist of peristyle courts surrounded by small rooms used for sleeping, eating and other domestic functions.[203] Not only does the first phase of the Ostia synagogue lack all these architectural features, but it also possesses others not characteristic of domestic structures, such as towering marble columns and a hall with an apse measuring 15 x 12.5 m. A comparison of a typical Ostian insula with the earliest phase of the synagogue is even less apt, since the former

---

[202]So *JIWE* 1.13, *SEG* 45.916.

[203]See Meiggs, *Roman Ostia*, 253–262. Very few houses remain in Ostia, since most of these were transformed into insulae to accommodate the population growth in the early years of the empire. The House of Apuleius serves as one example, though this dates to the reign of Trajan. We should note that most recently, White makes reference to a structure west of the synagogue that was excavated after Squarciapino's excavations. It contains an oven and may have been a bakery. Although this structure is separated from the synagogue by an alley, White argues that the buildings may have been connected on a second story, stating, "it is not impossible that the two buildings were originally part of some larger complex and that they remained interrelated even after the renovation" (*The Social Origins of Christian Architecture*, 2.390). This supposition cannot bear the weight of White's claim that the synagogue was a private house in the first century C.E., particularly in view of the architectural features of the actual building (e.g., meeting hall, monumental columns, apse, benches against walls) which point to an opposite conclusion.

is a multistoried structure consisting of rows of small rooms connected by a long corridor. Phase one of the synagogue, on the other hand, reveals absolutely no evidence of this type of arrangement.[204] Thus Squarciapino, who was quite familiar with Ostia's domestic architecture, never even considered the possibility that the Ostia synagogue was originally a private house or insula.

Having demonstrated the implausibility of this view, we turn to Squarciapino's own analysis of the first phase of the synagogue. First of all, Squarciapino dated the erection of the building to the first century C.E. because its original shell (areas B, C, D and E, fig. 16) was built in *opus reticulatum*, a type of wall construction commonly used in this period.[205] More specifically, she held that the erection of the structure coincided with Claudius' construction of a new harbor, which began in 42 C.E. and was completed twenty years later.[206] This view has been confirmed by more recent studies that have correlated the sub-type of *opus reticulatum* used in constructing the first phase of the synagogue (*mixtum a*) with the style of wall construction used elsewhere in Ostia during the reign of Claudius.[207]

---

[204]Meiggs, *Roman Ostia*, 235–252.

[205]Concrete walls set with a facing of tufa blocks arranged in a "fish-net" pattern.

[206]Squarciapino, "Ebrei a Roma e ad Ostia," 140. On the dating of the Claudian harbor, see Meiggs, *Roman Ostia*, 54–56.

[207]See Johannes S. Boersma, *Amoenissima Civitas. Block V.ii at Ostia: Description and Analysis of Its Visible Remains* (Assen, The Netherlands: Van Gorcum, 1985), 15–16 (V.ii.17, Room 14 south); 25–26, fig. 23 (V.ii.1); 160–166, figs. 157, 604, 605 (V.ii.9, Area 5). White incorrectly states that "generally, Boersma dates the *opus reticulatum/mixtum a* masonry in that complex [i.e., Block V.ii] to the Trajanic period" (White, "Synagogue and Society in Imperial Ostia," 29, n. 18; cf. idem, *The Social Origins of Christian Architecture*, 2.382, n. 155). On the contrary, Boersma consistently dates *mixtum a* to the reign of Claudius, as is the case in all the above citations. For example, the east and west parts of the north wall of a row of shops (V.ii.1), which is constructed in *mixtum a*, Boersma dates to the Claudian period, while the center portion of the wall, built in *opus testaceum*, he dates to the reign of Trajan (op. cit., 25–26; fig. 23). For similar dating of this type of wall construction, see Meiggs, *Roman Ostia*, 539, pl. XL a–c (note particularly the nearly identical wall construction of the Horrea of Hortensius, which Meiggs dates to the Julio-Claudian period); Marion Elizabeth Blake and Esther Boise Van Deman, *Ancient Roman Construction in Italy from the Prehistoric Period to Augustus* (Washington: Carnegie Institution of Washington, 1947), 254; Marion Elizabeth Blake, *Roman Construction in Italy from Tiberius through the Flavians* (Washington: Carnegie Institution of Washington, 1959), 161. In order to bolster his view that the synagogue was constructed at the turn of the second century, White also appeals to the more recent

In the first century, then, our building consisted of the main hall, the colonnaded gateway (whose foundations Squarciapino dated to the earliest stage), the entry court and the room later used as a kitchen (see fig. 18). In her reports, Squarciapino argues that the findings from the structure's lowest stratum indicate that the building served as a synagogue from its founding.[208] These findings not only suggest a continuity of function with the later building, but also demonstrate that the earliest phase had some affinities with the Galilean-type synagogues of Palestine. Regarding this last point, after pulling up the *opus sectile* floor in the main hall, Squarciapino discovered the remains of stone benches lining the room's outer walls on the two sides and against the curved back. These benches, of course, are the hallmark of synagogues from our period, as we have seen at Delos and at several sites in Palestine. Their presence alone would be sufficient to identify the first phase of the building as a synagogue. But Squarciapino's other findings are just as suggestive. To begin with, underneath the well with the marble top Squarciapino discovered an earlier well made from *opus reticulatum*. Attached to this well was a wide basin. Since the vestibule was built at a later time, the well and basin were originally erected outside the building. Their location a few meters from the synagogue's main entrance suggests that they were used for ritual washings prior to entry into the building.

Elsewhere, Squarciapino discovered that the entry court and the kitchen were originally one long, continuous room paved in *cocciopesto* (i.e., crushed pottery mixed with concrete). Moreover, benches similar in width to the ones later erected in the banquet room (G, fig. 16) were discovered curving around the sides of the southwest wall, extending out into the first segment of the entry court. Squarciapino argues that the

---

excavations of Pavolini, conducted on the side of the *Via Severiana* opposite the synagogue ("Synagogue and Society in Imperial Ostia," 29, n. 19; idem, *The Social Origins of Christian Architecture*, 2.386, n. 157). However, Pavolini himself adopts Squarciapino's dating of the synagogue to the construction of the Claudian harbor and maintains that the synagogue was one of the earliest structures built in that part of Ostia (Carlo Pavolini, "Ostia [Roma]: Saggi lungo la via Severiana," *Notizie degli Scavi di Antichità* 8, no. 35 [1981]: 141, n. 15). Likewise, Giulia Zappa—who discovered two first-century tile stamps amid the material used in one of the later phases of the synagogue—also accepts Squarciapino's mid-first-century dating of the original synagogue edifice (Giulia Garofalo Zappa, "Nuovi bolli laterizi di Ostia" in *Terza Miscellanea Greca e Romana*, edited by G. Barbieri et al. [Rome, 1971], 283–285).

[208]See Squarciapino, *La Sinagoga di Ostia*, 310–315; idem, "The Synagogue at Ostia," 201–203.

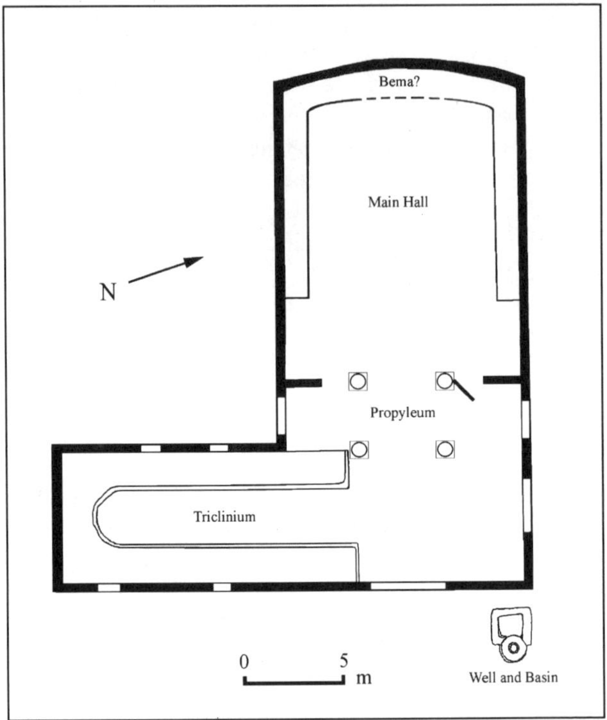

Figure 18. Reconstruction of the first-century synagogue at Ostia. The structure consisted of an entry court with adjoining triclinium, a propyleum and a main hall with benches on three sides. The well and basin outside the main entrance were probably used for ritual cleansings. The façade of the synagogue is oriented toward Jerusalem. (After plan from the Archivio Fotographico della Soprintendenza Archeologica di Ostia.)

banquet room and vestibule of the fourth-century synagogue were built as later replacements for these two areas, which were then refitted to serve other purposes.

Hence we find in the first-century edifice most of the features commonly associated with Second Temple synagogues: a large hall with benches on three sides, a well with an attached basin for ritual washings, and a banquet room for festivals and other occasions.

It should be added that several years after the discovery of the synagogue, the following epitaph was unearthed at Ostia (*JIWE* 1.14):[209]

Plotio Fortunato
archisyn(agogo) fec(erunt) Plotius
Ampliatus Secundinus
Secunda P T N et Ofilia Basilia coiugi b(ene) m(erenti)

For Plotius Fortunatus the *archisynagōgos*. Plotius Ampliatus, Secundinus (and) Secunda made (the monument) . . . , and Ofilia Basilia for her well-deserving husband.

The date of the inscription may be as early as the first century C.E., though its upper terminus runs into the beginning of the second century. It nevertheless provides additional evidence for the existence of an organized Jewish community at Ostia during the first two centuries of our era and further cements the identification of the earliest phase of our building as a synagogue.

Having firmly established this, special attention should be called to the monumental nature of the original edifice, with its handsome marble columns and its triportal gateway, recalling the triple gate of the Jerusalem Temple.[210] We have already noted that the façade of the building is oriented towards Jerusalem, an arrangement that can hardly have been accidental. It is likely that the participants turned toward the entrance at some point during their Sabbath services in order to pray while facing Jerusalem (2 Chr 6:34, 38; Dan 6:10), thus linking the worshipers with the central sanctuary. The sacred nature of the building is suggested by the location of the well and the attached basin near the main entrance, which parallels the placement of water basins known as *perirrantēria* near the entrances of pagan temples and sacred precincts. The general proximity of the structure to the ancient shoreline also implies the importance of ritual bathing before entering the synagogue. This location, moreover, corresponds with that seen with the synagogues at Philippi, Halicarnassus, Delos and Arsinoë.

---

[209]For the report of this find, see Maria Floriani Squarciapino, "Plotius Fortunatus archisynagogus," *La Rassegna Mensile di Israel* 36 (1970): 183–191. As of this writing, White has not discussed this inscription in any of his publications.

[210]Kraabel comments on the "Temple-like" appearance of the four-column entrance in this synagogue ("The Diaspora Synagogue," 499).

We can only speculate upon the exact nature of the meals shared in the dining room. Its fairly small size (it could have fit about thirty persons) suggests that it was preserved for the leadership of the congregation, who may have met there for meals on special days (e.g., the New Moon). If larger communal feasts were held in the synagogue, it is also possible that additional seating may have been added to the rest of the elongated room or even outside the building. The dining room may also have been available for use by individual Jewish families on important occasions such as birthdays, as was frequently the case for dining rooms associated with pagan temples.

Although we have little from Italy with which to compare the Ostia synagogue, it may well be typical of contemporary synagogues once existing in Rome, or for that matter, elsewhere around the diaspora. Indeed, given Ostia's relatively small size, the synagogue there can hardly have been a prototype. It must have been fashioned at least partly in imitation of other synagogues from nearby Rome, which may have been built to an even grander scale. Until one of these is uncovered, we will have to remain content with the Ostia synagogue, which nevertheless offers us a valuable glimpse into the communal life of Jews living in one diaspora city during the period of the Second Temple.

CONCLUSION

In summarizing this chapter, the point needs to be underscored that the evidence surveyed strongly supports the notion that diaspora synagogues served as distant sacred precincts to the main sanctuary in Jerusalem. Indeed, the close relationship between the two institutions has been seen at every turn. Source after source attests to how the synagogues throughout the diaspora served as collection places for the temple tax (e.g., Josephus, *Ant.* 16.164, 168; Philo, *Spec.* 1.76–78). Moreover, the sums sent to Jerusalem each year were substantial: Cicero specifically mentions that a hundred pounds of gold (≈ US $5,400,000) was seized from Jewish offerings in Apamea, while twenty pounds (≈ US $1,080,000) was taken from the collection at Laodicea (Cicero, *pro Flacc.* 68). Other cities such as Antioch and Alexandria, with even larger Jewish populations, were in a position to send even greater sums. Such amounts clearly indicate that the diaspora synagogues were an integral part of a massive economic system that was centered in the Temple cultus in Jerusalem. It should also be noted that the Jews in the diaspora communities were apparently eager to see that their monies reached

Jerusalem: every time their transport was interfered with, the local communities themselves appealed to the highest echelons of imperial government in order to secure their privilege of exporting their funds to Jerusalem (e.g., Josephus, *Ant.* 16.169–170, 172–173). Such an attitude bespeaks a deep commitment among the diaspora synagogues to fulfill their biblically mandated obligations to the national shrine. Conversely, some of the decrees allowing the diaspora synagogues to exercise their "sacred rites" and "native customs" came about as the result of envoys from the Jewish High Priest (e.g., Josephus, *Ant.* 14.223–227, 228–229, 241–243). The head of the Jewish cult thus clearly supported the religious practices of the diaspora synagogues, evidently perceiving them in league with the central shrine.

On a similar note, our sources also indicate that envoys from the diaspora synagogues regularly journeyed to Jerusalem to make sacrifices on behalf of their congregations (Philo, *Legat.* 156, 311). Although prohibited from offering their sacrifices on local altars, the members of the diaspora synagogues were clearly involved in sacrificial worship. This point is further underscored by the various allusions to meetings in the synagogues on days sacred to the cult, such as the Sabbath (e.g., Josephus, *BJ* 2.285–292; *Ant.* 14.256–258, 259–261; Philo, *Mos.* 2.214–216), New Moon (*CJZC* 70–71), Feast of Tabernacles (*CJZC* 71; Philo, *Flacc.* 116–124) and other unspecified festivals (Josephus, *Ant.* 14.257). The mention of prayer and "sacred rites" as activities of the diaspora synagogues likewise suggests that these were coupled with these festivals and sacred days (e.g., Josephus, *Ant.* 14.213–216, 260–261). The orientation of the Ostia synagogue similarly implies that such prayers were offered there while facing Jerusalem, as is suggested in the early literature (1 Kgs 8:30, 44, 48; 2 Chr 6:34, 38; Dan 6:10; 1 Esdr 4:58).

As for the character of the diaspora synagogues, our sources indicate that these were consecrated edifices that bore an affinity to temples or cultic halls. This is seen most clearly in the Egyptian evidence where nearly a dozen inscriptions dedicate the synagogue and/or its appurtenances to the Jewish God.[211] In most cases, these inscriptions are indistinguishable from dedications of pagan temples, except for the substitution of "synagogue" for "temple." In a similar vein, epigraphic and literary evidence also attested such temple-like architectural features as pylons (*JIE* 24), exedras (*JIE* 28) and sacred precincts (*JIE* 9; Philo, *Flacc.* 48). In one case, a land-survey of Arsinoë-Crocodilopolis (*CPJ*

---

[211] *JIE* 9, 13, 22, 27, 28, 117, 24, 25, 105 (?), 126.

1.134, I B.C.E.) located a *proseuchē* on a two-and-a-half acre plot of land, with its congregation leasing out a "sacred garden" (ἱερᾶς παραδείσου) on an adjoining acre. These features suggested that the Egyptian synagogues consisted of a walled precinct with a monumental gate and a cultic hall in the midst of the sacred area. As for the oversight of these complexes, a *neōkoros* or "temple warden" is mentioned as an official of a synagogue in Alexandrou-Nesos (*CPJ* 1.129).

Elsewhere in the diaspora, Josephus could refer to a synagogue at Antioch as a *hieron* (*BJ* 7.44–45), a term also used in reference to the Egyptian synagogues within his writings (*Ant.* 13.65–68; cf. 3 Macc 2:28; Philo, *Spec.* 3.171–172, *Deus.* 7–8). In a letter chastising the Dorans for setting up an idol in the *synagōgē* located in their city, Petronius similarly complained that Caesar's image "was better placed in his own shrine [ἐν τῷ ἰδιῳ ναῷ] than in that of another [ἢ ἐν ἀλλοτρίῳ]" (*Ant.* 19.305). In the Bosporus, slaves were routinely manumitted within the *proseuchē*, a practice that parallels the custom exercised at Delphi where release took place within the temple of Apollo. Votive offerings were discovered among the ruins of the synagogue at Delos, a structure which resembled one of the most prominent cultic halls on the island. Likewise, the Ostia synagogue, with its four-columned gateway, sizable assembly hall and triclinium, also compares favorably with other cultic halls.

These findings tend to support Richardson's recent characterization of the diaspora synagogues as *collegia* with special status, though as indicated at the beginning of this chapter, greater emphasis needs to be placed upon the cultic and national character of these organizations. In addition, the legal distinction between synagogues in Italy and those in the eastern Mediterranean must also be maintained. Thus while the synagogues in Rome were part of a loose confederacy, those in the east were frequently organized within the framework of a politeuma, where civic authority was placed firmly upon the shoulders of the local Jewish authorities. Sources directly attest to such structures in Alexandria, Berenice and Sardis, while the evidence for politeumata at Cyrene, Ephesus, Antioch and Damascus is suggestive. Similar organizations may have existed in other eastern cities, though we presently lack direct attestation. Beyond this, our sources also indicate that in some cases Jewish communities within eastern provinces comprised a regional *koinon*, empowered with emissarial authority. This was clearly the case in Asia, where reference is made to a resolution adopted by the Asian Jews in honor of Augustus (Josephus, *Ant.* 16.165). Such an arrangement may have existed in other provinces, allowing the Jews to deal more effectively with the provincial and imperial governments.

If our investigation has generally supported Richardson's proposal, its findings stand at odds with White's theory that synagogues emerged out of gatherings in domestic residences. While this hypothesis cannot be ruled out, there is no specific evidence to support it, at least for the pre-70 period. Moreover, the existing evidence suggests that if synagogues emerged out of household meetings at all in the diaspora, these cases were probably confined to a few locales, perhaps where persecution was rampant. The more general pattern in our period seems to be that synagogues were formed out of meetings in *public* places, such as those held in a corner of the Roman forum (Cicero, *pro Flacc*. 66). Philo's allusion to a synagogue near an agora in Alexandria (*Spec*. 3.171–172) also suggests that in larger cities, Jewish markets may have sprung up to meet the demand for kosher foods. Sabbath services and other public assemblies may then have been held in these squares prior to the erection of an actual synagogue building in an adjacent area.[212]

Yet another public venue for early Jewish gatherings is suggested by the fact that so many of the synagogues discussed in this chapter were built near bodies of water. Particularly instructive in this regard is a passage where Philo states that, upon receiving news of Flaccus' arrest, the Alexandrian Jews "made their way to the parts of the beach near at hand, since their *proseuchai* had been taken from them" (*Flacc*. 122). There they held an impromptu worship service, giving thanks for their deliverance from the tyrannies of their former prefect. The use of the beach as an alternate worship site in this episode may reflect the practices of the Alexandrian Jews prior to the erection of their synagogues. Such a practice may also be discerned in the Jewish custom of gathering on the Alexandria beach each year in order to celebrate the creation of the Septuagint (Philo, *Mos*. 2.41). Whether or not this was the case, the beach or the riverside would have served as a natural meeting site for Jews, since either provided the means for the ritual washings that appear to have been customary before worship or the explication of scripture (Philo, *Deus*. 8; *Ep. Arist*. 305–306). A spot outside or near the edge of town

---

[212]Levine, extrapolating from his theory about the origin of the synagogue in Palestine, argues that the city gate may have served as the meeting site of diaspora Jews before the erection of synagogues ("Nature and Origin of the Palestinian Synagogue Reconsidered," 443). It should be pointed out, however, that the growth of the diaspora came primarily in the Hellenistic period when the agora (or the forum) served as the primary civic center.

appears to have been preferred in many cases (e.g., Philippi, Arsinoë), perhaps as a way to avoid interference from gawking Gentiles. Philo expresses this last point in his commentary on the *Letter of Aristeas*, wherein he states that the translators of the Septuagint looked for a place to work outside the city walls "for, within the walls, it was full of every kind of living creatures; consequently the prevalence of diseases and deaths, and the impure conduct of the healthy inhabitants made them suspicious of it" (*Mos.* 2.34). For their part, the Gentiles in the diaspora cities may also have restricted Jewish building projects to places removed from the heart of the city. This especially seems to have been the case at Rome, where the synagogues were constructed west of the River Tiber—the place to which the Romans typically restricted the building of temples by the adherents of foreign cults.

The early rise of the synagogues in Egypt can be attributed not only to the large number of Jews living in the country beginning in the third century B.C.E., but also to the amiable relationship the Egyptian Jews seem to have had with the Ptolemaic rulers, who may have served as patrons. The same can be said of the Jewish communities in Cyrenaica, Syria, and parts of Galatia and Asia, which also benefitted from favorable treatment from Alexander's successors, as we have seen. Somewhat later, the emergence of synagogues throughout the rest of the diaspora was similarly facilitated by patronage from the Roman rulers, beginning with Julius Caesar. Augustus, because of his close friendship with Herod the Great, was particularly forceful in protecting the ancestral customs of the Jews throughout the empire, including their right to meet in synagogues. The rest of the Julio-Claudians, while not as accommodating as Augustus, nevertheless tended to gravitate back towards his precedent. Hence, only the Jews in Rome bore the brunt of Tiberius and Claudius' disfavor. Gaius, on the other hand, while hostile toward Jews throughout the empire, was placated by yet another Herodian, Agrippa I, who intervened and persuaded the emperor to abandon his plans to erect a statue of Zeus in the Jerusalem Temple. Because Agrippa also had a hand in seeing Claudius placed on the throne after Gaius' assassination, it is likely that his influence with the new emperor prompted the issue of a decree protecting the rights of the Alexandrian Jews and tolerance for the ancient customs of those living in the eastern provinces. After Claudius' death, up until the outbreak of the Jewish War, Nero likewise seems to have favored the Jews, perhaps because of the influence of his wife, Poppea, who was interested in Jewish customs (Josephus, *Ant.* 20.195).

Hence, by the end of the Second Temple period, synagogues thrived throughout the empire, serving as consecrated houses of worship and community centers for their constituents. Their existence provided a means for diaspora Jews to be connected to the central sanctuary while still remaining located in distant cities throughout the larger Greco-Roman world. This conclusion is in accord with Philo's statement that, while diaspora Jews counted their adopted countries as their "fatherland" (πατρίς), they nevertheless "[held] the Holy City where stands the sacred Temple of the most high God to be their mother city [μητρόπολις]" (*Flacc.* 46).

If the Jewish diaspora so derived its spiritual inspiration from the Holy City, conversely, the Temple cultus benefitted from the constant stream of envoys and pilgrims coming from beyond the borders of Palestine, bringing with them alms and sacrificing burnt offerings on behalf of their people. Thus the Temple drew strength from the diaspora, and the diaspora maintained its Jewish identity through its connection with the Temple. It was a symbiotic relationship, where all parties prospered within this circle of worship that found its center at Jerusalem.

Chapter 5
Synagogue Functionaries

In this chapter, we will attempt to understand the roles of the various synagogue officials. Our review of the evidence will suggest a correspondence between the functionaries of the Temple and the synagogue, one usually unnoted by synagogue scholars. Because there is some overlap in the contrasting terminology, these functionaries will be divided into two major categories: synagogue leaders and synagogue assistants. Omitted from the discussion will be the officials associated with the sectarian synagogues, since they will be considered in the treatment of these groups in chapter seven. We will, however, append to the below discussion a consideration of two groups of interest to contemporary researchers: women and God-fearers. The conclusions drawn from each of these examinations will further suggest the role of the synagogues as sacred precincts linked to a central cultic site.

Synagogue Leaders

Literary and epigraphic sources from the pre-70 period attest to ten separate leadership titles directly associated with the synagogues. These have been summarized in Table 4. The first task in sorting out these titles is to decide whether a term denoted an active functionary or was simply used as an honorific. If the former, then the particular duties of the office need to be discerned. In the case of the latter, the reason for the granting of the honorific must be ascertained. Special attention must also be paid to the context of each usage, since different passages may employ a term in varied ways. As already noted, some overlap exists between several of the titles. The following subsections will arrange the terms according to the most likely concurrences, though additional cross-referencing may be indicated from the ensuing analyses.

Table 4
Terms used in Reference to Synagogue Leaders

	Number of Uses by Source					**Total Uses**
	Literary				**Epigraphic**	
	NT	Philo	Josephus	Papyrus		
Archōn	–	–	2	–	16	18
Archisynagōgos	10	–	–	–	6	16
Archisynagōgos dia Biou	–	–	–	–	1	1
Prostatēs	–	–	–	–	1	1
Archiprostatēs	–	–	–	–	1	1
Hiereus/Cohen	–	1	–	–	3	4
Presbyteros	1	–	–	–	1	2
Gerōn	–	1	–	–	–	1
Dynatos	–	–	2	–	–	2

Archōn

The title *archōn* appears frequently in Greco-Roman literature, where it signifies the magistrate or magistrates of a particular city or region.[1] Consonant with the Greek democratic tradition, these officials were often elected for terms of a year, though reelection was common. Hence in the previous chapter we saw that Julia Severa served as an *archōn* of Acmonia for four years running, between 59 and 63 C.E. Normally, *archontes* tended to the legislative and judicial affairs of the community. They were also called upon to perform liturgies or public works, such as the building or renovation of various public structures. Since these were normally financed out of the *archontes*' own pockets, personal wealth was a prerequisite for election to the office.

Within the LXX *archōn* appears some 598 times, usually as a translation of the Hebrew *naśi'* or *śar*, both meaning "prince" or "ruler."

---

[1]E.g., Josephus, *Ant.* 16.172 mentions the *archontes* of Ephesus, while *Ant.* 14.190 alludes to those of Sidon. See LSJ, BAGD s.v. ἄρχων; Gehrhard Delling, "῎Αρχων" in *TDNT* 1.488–489.

While the word can refer to the officials of various countries, such as Egypt (Gen 12:15) or Philistia (Judg 16:5), most often it designates the rulers of Israel. In particular, the Pentateuch frequently refers to the *archontes* of the twelve tribes of Israel (e.g., Num 1:4, 2:3, 7:10, 11, 12). Corporately, these were known as the *archontes* of the congregation (*synagōgē*) of Israel (e.g., Exod 16:22, 34:31; Num 1:16, 31:13, 26, 32:2; Josh 9:15, 19, 22:30). During the Second Temple period, these *archontes*, along with a somewhat elusive group known as "the elders" (*presbyteroi*; see below), served as subsidiary rulers under the High Priest, forming a *gerousia* or *synedrion*—a legislative and judicial council (1 Macc 12:6; 2 Macc 1:10, 11:27; Josephus, *Ant.* 4.218, 12.143, 14.168–184).[2] Although the composition of this body and the terms of office of its members are still a matter of scholarly debate,[3] it seems safe to say that the membership of the *synedrion*, while not necessarily fixed numerically, numbered about seventy persons (all male) and consisted of a roughly equal mix of priests and laity.[4] Entry into this body was probably by the appointment of the High Priest, though lineage and popularity among the masses were undoubtedly factors as well. Terms appear to have been for life, though changes in political regimes could result in the loss of one's position. The degree of power possessed by the *archontes* varied according to the political strength of the ruler. For example, Josephus

---

[2]The two terms *gerousia* and *synedrion* appear here to be nearly synonymous, with the former perhaps emphasizing the legislative and the latter the judicial role of the official body. Another term used of the Jerusalem leadership is *boulē* or council, which may signify an even larger body of leaders, though this is unclear (Josephus, *BJ* 2.331, 336, 405, 407; 5.532; Mark 15:43; Luke 23:20). See Eduard Lohse, "Συνέδριον" in *TDNT* 7.860–871; *HJP* 2.206–209, 212–214; Smallwood, *The Jews under Roman Rule*, 148–150.

[3]See E. P. Sanders, *Judaism*, 472–488. While Sanders is right to question scholarly assumptions about the Jewish *synedrion*, his position that the *synedrion* was purely an ad hoc body that served as a rubber stamp to the High Priest or monarch's decisions seems to be overstating the matter. Except during the reign of Herod the Great and (perhaps) Archelaus, the *synedrion* probably wielded greater power than Sanders admits, with the High Priest ruling more by consensus than by fiat. Cf. *HJP* 2.199–226 (though this treatment is somewhat tainted by dependence on later rabbinic literature).

[4]Seventy is frequently given as the number of the leaders of Israel in the Hebrew scriptures (e.g., Exod 24:1–9; Num 11:16–25; Ezek 8:11). The roughly equal mix between priests and laity is less certain, being based primarily on Acts' depiction of Paul being pulled apart by the Pharisees (primarily laity) and the Sadducees (primarily priests; Acts 23:6ff). See Smallwood, *The Jews under Roman Rule*, 147–150, 227; E. P. Sanders, *Judaism*, 472–488; Kasher, "Synagogues as 'Houses of Prayer' and 'Holy Places'," 217–218.

mentions that Hyrcanus II—who is called both High Priest and *ethnarch* (*Ant.* 14.148–151)—was not very interested in the affairs of state and consequently left most of the administrative decisions to the *archontes* (*Ant.* 15.182). On the other hand, Herod the Great, upon assuming power, massacred forty-five of Antigonus' party, presumably his appointed *archontes* (*Ant.* 15.1–6). During his rule, moreover, Herod appears to have dispensed with a standing *synedrion*, preferring to convene ad hoc *synedria*, usually consisting of his friends and relatives (*BJ* 1.537, 571–573). When day-to-day control of the country returned to the High Priest after Archelaus' deposal, the *synedrion* seems to have been reconstituted, since it reappears in the New Testament and in Josephus' accounts of this period (e.g., Matt 26:59; Mark 15:1; Luke 22:66; John 11:47; Acts 5:27; Josephus, *Ant.* 2.216–218, 20.200).

While the exact nature of Judea's *synedrion*/*gerousia* will continue to be debated, the point remains that the *archontes* forming the core of this group served as leaders who tended to the legislative and judicial matters of the nation. This same pattern played itself out on a local level in Palestine. Here, Josephus states that Moses proclaimed that seven *archontes* were to administer the affairs of each city (*Ant.* 4.214). Since no number is given in the biblical account (Deut 26.18), the one cited by Josephus likely reflects the customs of his own day. During the Jewish War, Josephus himself created a council of seventy *archontes* to judge over Galilean affairs under his command, stating, "I made them my friends and companions in travel, took them as assessors to cases which I tried, and obtained their approbation of the sentences which I pronounced" (*Vita* 79). Elsewhere he states he appointed to each city under his jurisdiction seven persons to decide petty matters (*BJ* 2.571). These individuals probably also bore the title *archōn*. The Galilean city of Tiberias, on the other hand, was governed by a single *archōn* who, along with ten principal councillors (*prōtoi*), led a *boulē* or city council of 600 (*Vita* 69, 134, 168, 271, 278, 294, 296; *BJ* 2.639).

The situation in the diaspora appears to have largely mirrored that of Palestine, at least in places where politeumata were constituted. This is especially seen in Alexandria, where there was originally a *gerousia* composed of *archontes*, probably numbering seventy or seventy-one.[5] As previously mentioned, the office of ethnarch later replaced the *gerousia*, though Augustus subsequently let the office lapse and reconstituted the

---

[5] *Ep. Arist.* 310, which uses the more general term *hēgoumenoi*, the equivalent of *archontes*.

gerousia in its place.[6] At Antioch, a similar system seems to have been operative, since Josephus mentions an *archōn* (≈*ethnarch*?) of the Jews in that city (*BJ* 7.47).

As stated in the previous chapter, it seems likely that the *archontes* in Alexandria and Antioch made use of the synagogues to conduct their official business since literary and epigraphic sources from elsewhere in the diaspora or from Palestine imply or state as much. The inscriptions from Berenice (*CJCZ* 70–72) are of primary importance in this regard, since they mention that the local *archontes* (seven to ten in number) either conducted business within their synagogue (*amphitheatron*, *CJCZ* 70–71) or contributed to its repair (*CJCZ* 72). The mention of an *archōn* who donated funds for the renovation of the synagogue at Acmonia is similarly suggestive (*DF* 33). Within Palestine, Josephus recounts how during the Jewish War the *archōn* of Tiberias, Jesus son of Sapphias, convened three separate meetings of the Tiberian *boulē* in the synagogue (one on the Sabbath) in order to discuss the removal of Josephus from his command (*Vita* 277–303). At one of these council meetings, Jesus himself was said to have guarded the door of the synagogue to prevent Josephus' supporters from entering (*Vita* 294). At this same convocation, the *archōn* ordered the general populace to leave, but the *boulē* to remain inside the synagogue for continued deliberations (*Vita* 300). Clearly the Tiberian *archōn* had a measure of control over the proceedings within the synagogue. Moreover, his use of the synagogue for official deliberations on three successive days suggests that this was the usual venue for the exercise of his office.[7]

The use of the synagogues by the *archontes* in the above examples supports the view that these buildings served as "distant Temple courts," since in Jerusalem these leaders normally met either within one of the stoas on the Temple mount (Josephus, *BJ* 4.336; Acts 6:14–16) or inside the bouleterion adjoining the complex (*BJ* 5.144, 6.354). It should also be noted that the choice of the Temple as the meeting place for the *synedrion* likely reflects not only Greco-Roman practices, but also the recovery of the pentateuchal custom of having the *archontes* meet before the Tabernacle. In one passage, for instance, Moses is instructed to make two

---

[6]Strabo ap. Josephus, *Ant.* 14.117; Philo, *Flacc.* 74, 80, 117. See Smallwood, *The Jews under Roman Rule*, 226–227; *HJP* 3.1.92–94.

[7]Although it has not been included in Table 4, Luke's mention of Christians being brought "before the synagogues, the *archontes*, and the authorities [ἐπὶ τὰς συναγωγὰς καὶ τὰς ἀρχὰς καὶ τὰς ἐξουσίας]" (Luke 12:11) also suggests that the *archontes* met inside synagogues.

trumpets for use in summoning assemblies: a blast from one trumpet meant that the *archontes* were to gather before the Tent of Meeting, while blasts from both trumpets summoned the entire congregation (*synagōgē*) of Israel (Num 10:1–4, LXX; cf. *Ant.* Josephus, 3.291–292).[8] The existence of the office of *archōn* within both the Temple and the synagogues further suggests that the latter formed in miniature what the Temple precincts served on a larger scale.

Archisynagōgos, *Archisynagōgos dia Biou*

Unlike other titles being examined in this section, *archisynagōgos*, "ruler of the synagogue," is almost exclusively a Jewish term. Gentile employment of the title was confined to a small region of the northern Aegean, as attested in its appearance in six inscriptions connected with pagan cults from that region.[9] Because of this narrow geographical attestation and the fact that the Gentile inscriptions date only from the first through the third centuries C.E., it is improbable that Jewish usage of *archisynagōgos* was borrowed from the Gentiles. This is especially indicated by the Theodotus inscription from Jerusalem (*CIJ* 2.1404) which indicates that the title *archisynagōgos* was used in Palestine for at least three generations prior to the destruction of the Temple. Another inscription from Egypt (*JIE* 18), which we shall examine in another section below, also uses the term *archisynagōgos* and probably dates even earlier than the Theodotus inscription (3 C.E.), further suggesting that Jewish application of the term evolved separately from the Gentile usage in the Aegean.

In view of the inability to establish a Gentile origin for the Jewish usage of *archisynagōgos*, it seems likely that the term was adopted from several references in the LXX to the *archontes tēs synagōgēs* of Israel, as noted in the previous section (e.g., Exod 16:22, 34:31; Num 31:13; Josh 9:15). This proposal is particularly suggested by Luke's treatment of the Marcan account of the healing of Jairus' daughter: while Mark consistently employs the term *archisynagōgos* when referring to Jairus

---

[8]These trumpets, known as *chazozeroth* (חֲצֹצְרֹת), are depicted on the Arch of Titus in Rome.

[9]For transcriptions and translations of these, see Rajak and Noy, "*Archisynagogoi*," 92–93. Of these inscriptions, one is from Perinthus (Thrace, I C.E.), two from Thessalonica (75 C.E., 155 C.E.), one from Olynthus (Chalcidice, I–II C.E.), one from Beroea (Imperial period) and one from Pydna (Macedonia, 250 C.E.). See also *HJP* 2.436 n. 40; *NDIEC* 4.219–220.

(Mark 5:22, 35, 36, 38), Luke, in his opening reference, renders *archisynagōgos* as *archōn tēs synagōgēs* (Luke 8:41 || Mark 5:22)—a usage different from the one employed by his source, but identical to that of the LXX (see above citations). Subsequently, he calls Jairus an *archisynagōgos*, following Mark's rendering (Luke 8:49 || Mark 5:35).[10] Here, it seems clear that Luke is not implying that Jairus was both *archōn* and *archisynagōgos*; rather, he appears to be introducing to his Gentile readers a Jewish term that may not have been familiar to them. In accomplishing this task, he not only breaks the word into its constituent parts, but he draws on the usage of the LXX, as he frequently does throughout his Gospel.[11] Thus while the phrase *archōn tēs synagōgēs* never returns in Luke-Acts, *archisynagōgos* reappears four more times after the Jairus incident (Luke 13:14; Acts 13:15, 18:8, 18:17).[12]

Because the offices of *archisynagōgos* and *archōn* are distinguished in the Acmonia inscription (*DF* 33), scholars have generally held that the function of the former office was neither legislative nor judicial, but entailed leadership of the synagogue's worship services—a proposition which gains some support from two passages from Luke-Acts.[13] In the first, an *archisynagōgos* is portrayed as chastising Jesus for healing on the Sabbath (Luke 13:14).[14] His attempt to silence Jesus implies that Luke believed it was the duty of the *archisynagōgos* to control the flow of the service and the interpretations offered by the speakers. This point is made explicit in the second passage, which depicts Paul and Barnabas' initial visit to the synagogue at Pisidian Antioch. The text states, "After the reading of the law and the prophets, the *archisynagōgoi* sent them a

---

[10]As noted in chapter two, Matthew omits Jairus' name and refers to him with the more generic term *archōn* (Matt 9:18). This, however, should not be understood as meaning that the offices were identical, but should rather be attributed to Matthew's anti-synagogue bias (see discussion in chapter one). This can further be seen from the fact that Matthew never employs the term *archisynagōgos*.

[11]On Luke's frequent use of Septuagintisms, see Fitzmyer, *The Gospel According to Luke*, 1.114–116.

[12]It should be noted that many interpreters have wondered why Luke uses both *archōn tēs synagōgēs* and *archisynagōgos* in reference to Jairus (e.g., Fitzmyer, *The Gospel According to Luke*, 1.745; Rajak and Noy, "*Archisynagogoi*," 79; Schrage, "'Αρχισυνάγωγος" in *TDNT* 7.847). To my knowledge, the above explanation has not hitherto been proposed.

[13]E.g., *HJP*, 2.435; Schrage, "'Αρχισυνάγωγος," 846.

[14]While the passage that contains this saying (Luke 13:10–17) is from Special L, the presence of an Aramaism in v. 11 argues that the saying was not a Lucan composition. See Fitzmyer, *The Gospel According to Luke*, 2.1010–1014.

message, saying, 'Brothers, if you have any word of exhortation for the people, give it'" (Acts 13:15).

While the preceding passages suggest that a primary role of the *archisynagōgos* was to direct the synagogue ritual, this should not be taken to mean this was their *sole* duty.[15] Here, it should be recalled that Acts also depicts Sosthenes, the *archisynagōgos* of the synagogue at Corinth, as leading the Jewish delegation before Gallio, the Roman proconsul (Acts 18:17). Thus, at least in some instances, the *archisynagōgos* appears to have taken on a more political role—a fact that should not be surprising in view of our earlier discussions about the interplay of religion and politics in antiquity.

In addition to serving as a leader of religious ritual and a political representative, the *archisynagōgos* could also function as benefactor.[16] This is apparent from the Theodotus inscription (*CIJ* 2.1404), which states that Theodotus, the *archisynagōgos*, built (οἰκοδομέω) the synagogue.[17] Moreover, the synagogue's foundations had previously been laid (θεμελιόω) by the elders, by a certain Simonides, and by Theodotus' "fathers" (οἱ πατέρες αὐτου), two of whom (his father and grandfather) were also *archisynagōgoi*. Likewise, in the Acmonia inscription (*DF* 33), an *archisynagōgos* is also listed as contributing to the renovations of the building. This same inscription mentions another donor bearing the title *archisynagōgos dia biou* ("*archisynagōgos* for life"). While it is possible that this title was an honorific, in view of the fact that *archisynagōgos* elsewhere designates a functionary, it seems more likely that the title carried the sense of *emeritus*, that is, it refers to a retired

---

[15]This point is forcefully made in Rajak and Noy, "*Archisynagogoi*," 81–84. See also James T. Burtchaell, *From Synagogue to Church: Public Services and Offices in the Earliest Christian Communities* (Cambridge; New York: Cambridge University Press, 1992), 242–243.

[16]On this function more generally, see Rajak and Noy, "*Archisynagogoi*," 87–89; Burtchaell, *From Synagogue to Church*, 242–243.

[17]Richardson, who accepts the pre-70 dating of the Theodotus inscription, nevertheless states, "Though patrons may have been involved in purpose-built Palestinian structures as well, of course, as inscriptions in later buildings attest so clearly, there seems no clear evidence of patronal activity in the early synagogues in the Holy Land. These structures were community buildings, both in the sense of for and by the community" ("Early Synagogues as Collegia," 102). While we would not disagree with the last sentence of this quotation, the Theodotus inscription clearly provides evidence of patronal activity in at least one synagogue from pre-70 Palestine.

archisynagōgos.[18] This interpretation would fit well with the mention made in the Theodotus inscription of the contributions of earlier *archisynagōgoi*. If this view is accepted, then in the Acmonia inscription we have an example of an *archisynagōgos* continuing in his patronal role even after retirement.

The issue of patronage calls to mind the question of whether a person became an *archisynagōgos* as a result of benefactions. As with the office of *archōn*, it seems probable that personal wealth may have been a prerequisite for obtaining the position of *archisynagōgos*, though this cannot be said with certainty in every case. No doubt, however, the *archisynagōgos* also had to have political acumen and a sound knowledge of Torah. That Theodotus' father and grandfather were also *archisynagōgoi* suggests that the office in some cases passed through families, though it probably was not hereditary.[19] This last point is indicated by the fact that the inscription just mentioned specifically states that Theodotus' father and grandfather were *archisynagōgoi* but does not repeat the hereditary title of priest, as this would have been redundant. By the same token, the inscription's recognition of Theodotus' position as priest implies that not all *archisynagōgoi* were priests, though some obviously were.

Our evidence is silent regarding the selection of an *archisynagōgos*. Possibly it involved an election by the congregation or by a college of elders. Alternatively, the outgoing *archisynagōgos* may have chosen his successor. The term of office appears to have been for life (or retirement), though it is not beyond the realm of possibility that more frequent elections or appointments were held, particularly in the diaspora where Greek democratic ideas may have taken hold. As we saw in the passage about the synagogue in Pisidian Antioch, sometimes there was more than one *archisynagōgos* per congregation. This also might have been the case at Corinth, since Crispus and Sosthenes are mentioned as *archisynagōgoi* there (Acts 18:8, 17), though it is also possible that the latter succeeded the former after his conversion to Christianity. In any case, multiple *archisynagōgoi* were probably more common in the diaspora as one *archisynagōgos* per congregation seems to have been the norm in Palestine (*CIJ* 2.1404; Luke 13:14).

---

[18]This suggestion is made in Burtchaell, *From Synagogue to Church*, 242. Cf. Rajak and Noy, "*Archisynagogoi*," 84–87; *NDIEC* 4.218.

[19]See Rajak and Noy, "*Archisynagogoi*," 86; *NDIEC* 4.218.

In summary, during our period the term *archisynagōgos* seems to have denoted a functionary who was responsible for the religious and political leadership of the congregation and who also frequently served as a patron of the synagogue. The term appears to have been derived from the phrase *archontes tēs synagōgēs* found in the LXX, where it refers to the leaders of the various tribes of Israel (e.g., Exod 16:22, 34:31; Num 31:13; Josh 9:15). Presently, only male *archisynagōgoi* are attested for the period prior to 70 C.E. In distinguishing the office of *archisynagōgos* from that of *archōn*, the center of gravity of the former appears to have been fixed on the leadership of the Sabbath services and the maintenance of the synagogue, while the role of the latter was more focused on the legislative and judicial concerns of the community. There seems to have been considerable overlap between the offices, however, particularly in the diaspora. Thus in cities where the Jewish community was not formally constituted as a politeuma, the *archisynagōgos* may have functioned as the de facto political leader of the community, though he would have been limited by the Roman authorities in his power to enact internal judicial decisions and punishments. Conversely, in cities such as Berenice where a politeuma did exist and only *archontes* are mentioned in connection with the synagogue, one of these officers may have been responsible for leading the regular ritual in addition to his legislative and judicial duties.[20]

Prostatēs, Archiprostatēs

The root meaning of the term *prostatēs* is "one who presides." Generally, it could refer to any leader, as is the case, for instance, when Philo uses the word in reference to Moses (*Praem.* 77) or Joseph (*Mutat.* 89). When used as a title, *prostatēs* typically referred to the leader or presiding officer of a corporate body such as a city, association, or military unit.[21] The title was not an honorific, but denoted an active functionary with managerial responsibilities.

Within the LXX, the term occurs infrequently, translating either *śar*, "ruler," *n^e tsîv*, "prefect," or *pāqîd*, "commissioner" in the four instances

---

[20]However, note below the hypothesis that the priest mentioned in one of the Berenice inscriptions (*CJCZ* 72) may have served in this capacity. In further support of the notion that *archontes* could function as teachers of the law in the synagogues is Philo's use of the general term *hēgemōn*, "ruler," to refer to Moses, who is said to have instructed the people on the Sabbath (*Mos.* 2.14–16).

[21]See LSJ s.v. προστάτης; Kasher, *The Jews in Hellenistic and Roman Egypt*, 111–114.

where there is a Hebrew parallel. These usages refer to stewards or military commanders (1 Chr 27:31, 29:6; 2 Chr 8:10, 24:11). In later Jewish writings, *prostatēs* becomes more associated with the Temple hierarchy, as is seen in the title "*prostatēs* of the Temple," assigned to a certain Simeon in 2 Macc 3:4. This office is probably equivalent to the position of Temple *stratēgos* ("captain"), frequently mentioned in Josephus' writings and also in Luke-Acts (e.g., *BJ* 2.409; *Ant.* 10.55, 20.131; Luke 22:4, 52; Acts 4:1, 5:24). The *stratēgos*, who was chosen from among the chief priests, was in charge of Temple security and other administrative matters relating to the Temple complex. He ranked second only to the High Priest himself in authority.

More generally, both the LXX and Josephus could refer to the High Priest as the *prostatēs* of the people (1 Macc 14:47, Sir 45:24, *Ant.* 12.161). This term was also used of another member of the high priestly family, Joseph son of Tobias, in view of his generous payment of the nation's delinquent taxes to Ptolemy Epiphanes (*Ant.* 12.167).

With regard to synagogue leaders, the office of *prostatēs* or *archiprostatēs* ("chief ruler") is attested only twice (once each), both usages occurring in Egypt. The first of these, presented in the previous chapter's discussion of Xenephyris, mentions the donation of a pylon by the Jews of that city during the presidency (προστάντων) of two men, Theodore and Achillion (*JIE* 24, II B.C.E.). The inscription's use of these officials' names to date the dedication corresponds to the more common practice of including the regnal year of the ruling monarch or local leader in public monuments. Because no year is mentioned in the inscription, the term of office may have been confined to a single year, though this is uncertain. In any case, Theodore and Achillion were clearly the primary leaders of the synagogue, though this leadership may have been shared with other lesser officials not mentioned in the monument.

The second attestation mentioned above is found in a dedicatory inscription from Alexandria (*JIE* 18). Though poorly preserved, the monument nevertheless records the year in which the dedication was made, 3 C.E. In addition, the inscription contains the terms *archiprostatēs* (a *hapax legomenon*) and *archisynagōgos* (or *-oi*) alongside each other:[22]

---

[22]The translation is from *JIE*. The Jewishness of this inscription, while questioned by some scholars, seems probable because of its use of *archisynagōgos*, which, as we have seen, is otherwise attested within Gentile associations only in the Aegean. For further discussion, see *JIE* pp. 28–29.

[- - Ἁ]θὺρ ιη´ ἐπὶ τῆς τ[- -]
[- -]ς τῶν ἀπὸ τῆς τ[- -]
[- -]ων ἀρχισυναγω[- -]
[- - ἀρ]χιπροστάτης διο[- -]
[- - ἐπειδὴ β]ρασίδας Ἡρακλε[ίδου - -]
[- -] γλ´ (ἔτους) Καίσαρος [- -]
[- -] ἐν ἅπασι ἀναστ[- -]
[- -]ς καὶ ὑγιῶς ἐπ[- -]
[- -] τὴν δαπάνην π̣[- -]
[- -]ομηνιακὰς ἡμέ[ρας - -]
[- - ἐ]πισκευὰς ἀκολ[- -]
[- -]ου λόγῳ̣ ἐπὶ το[- -]
[- -]οδεξάμενον ι[- -]
[- -] στεφάνῳ ἐπ[- -]
[- -]λοις δυσί [- -]

. . . Hathyr 18, in the . . . of those from the . . . *archisynagōgos* (or *-oi*) . . . *archiprostatēs* . . . Since Brasidas son of Herakleides . . . 33rd year of Caesar . . . in all . . . and soundly, . . . the expense . . . days . . . repair . . . by word in . . . crown . . . with two . . .

Though the fragmentary nature of the monument makes its interpretation difficult, it seems similar to one of the inscriptions from Berenice wherein the *archontes* resolved to present an olive crown to one of the members of their politeuma for plastering the synagogue floor and painting its walls (*CJZC* 70). In the above case, however, the chief officials are the *archisynagōgos* and the *archiprostatēs*. The prefix *archi-* in the latter term indicates that this officer presided over a larger body of *prostatai*, thus suggesting a high degree of institutionalization within this particular synagogue. Further specialization is seen in the distinction made between the *archisynagōgos* and the *archiprostatēs*. This division of offices probably corresponds to the distinction previously drawn between the office of *archōn* and *archisynagōgos*, where the former is primarily responsible for judicial and legislative affairs and the latter for the oversight of religious ritual. The administrative duties normally associated with the term *prostatēs* in its wider usage make this possibility especially likely.

From the preceding it follows that the offices of *prostatēs* and *archiprostatēs* are probably equivalent to that of *archōn*, a conclusion bolstered by the fact that the LXX can render the Hebrew word *śar* as either *archōn* (e.g., Exod 2:14) or *prostatēs* (e.g., 1 Chr 27:31). However, because Philo normally uses the term *archōn* to refer to members of the ruling *gerousia* (e.g., *Flacc.* 117), it is probable that in Egypt the titles *prostatēs* and *archiprostatēs* were reserved for lower-ranking officials associated with the local synagogues both inside and outside of Alexandria. In this case, the Alexandrian *archontes* may have been attached to a central synagogue, perhaps the one Philo mentions as being larger than the others (*Legat.* 134).

Hiereus, Cohen

Synagogue researchers have typically held that a dichotomy existed between the leadership of the Temple and the synagogue, with the former institution being the estate of the priests and the latter the domain of the laity. Such a tendency can perhaps be traced to the belief that the Pharisees dominated the leadership of the synagogues prior to 70 C.E.—a belief, as we have seen, that is based on a dubious reading of later sources.[23] During our period, however, aside from the reigns of Herod the Great and Archelaus, a priestly hegemony dominated the leadership of Palestine (Josephus, *Ant.* 14.91, 20.251). This was true not only on the national stage, but also on the local level. Here we should recall that it was Josephus, a member of the priestly aristocracy, who presided over the council of seventy *archontes* he had appointed to administer the affairs of Galilee during the Jewish War (*Vita* 79). Later, when charges of treason were leveled against Josephus, Ananus the High Priest sent a delegation of four men to investigate. One of the delegation was a member of the high priestly family, another a priest (also a Pharisee), and

---

[23]For the older view, see, e.g., Tcherikover, *Hellenistic Civilization and the Jews*, 124–125; Gutmann, "Synagogue Origins: Theories and Facts," 4; Cohen, "The Temple and the Synagogue," 155. For critiques, see the introductory chapter, above, and also E. P. Sanders, *Judaism*, 170–189. More recently, the older view has been reflected in Burtchaell, *From Synagogue to Church*, 253–256. However, Burtchaell overlooks the significance of the evidence presented below. His claim that priestly leadership vanished in Palestine after 70 C.E., moreover, is contradicted by the presence of coins from the Bar Kokhba revolt inscribed with the name "Eleazar the priest" (e.g., *AJC* 2.7; 2.17; 2.79). Several other coins from this revolt depicting the Temple façade indicate that one of the goals of the revolt was to rebuild the Temple (e.g., *AJC* 2.1; 2.12–13; 2.16; 2.51; 2.53). Kraabel has also expressed a position similar to that of Burtchaell: "[diaspora Jews] dispensed with a priesthood, even while the Jerusalem Temple still stood. Everything we know about Diaspora synagogue organization indicates that it was led by laymen from the outset" (A. T. Kraabel, "Unity and Diversity among Diaspora Synagogues" in *The Synagogue in Late Antiquity*, edited by Lee I. Levine [Philadelphia: American Schools of Oriental Research, 1987], 54). Nowhere does Kraabel produce evidence to support this conclusion.

the last two Pharisees (not priests; *Vita* 197). Thus there was a one-to-one ratio between priests and laity.

While it is unlikely that priests constituted anywhere near fifty percent of the leadership in every city and village in Palestine, they almost certainly assumed a place among the local government simply by virtue of their hereditary office. Josephus states that the priests formed twenty-four courses, each of which rotated into the Temple for a week of sacrificial duty (*Ant.* 7.365–67). Thus the typical priest was only on duty in the Temple for just over two weeks out of the year in addition to the three major festivals. While some priests would have remained in Jerusalem, most of them probably served as scribes, administrators and religious leaders within their cities and villages in the other parts of Palestine. This was clearly the case during the early part of the Second Temple period when Ben Sirach assumed that the priests were the teachers of the nation (e.g., Sir 45:17),[24] and other post-exilic authors took it for granted that they served as local leaders (1 Macc 14:44, 2 Chr 19.5–11; cf. Josephus, *Ant.* 9:4).[25] For example, the priest Mattathias, father of Judas Maccabaeus, is referred to as an *archōn* of the village of

---

[24]See also Rivkin, "Ben Sira and the Non-Existence of the Synagogue," 320–354. Because he held that the synagogues were lay institutions, Rivkin thought they did not exist in Ben Sirach's day since his writings indicate that the priests were invested with so much responsibility. This presupposition kept Rivkin from considering the possibility that the priests might have exercised their duties within the synagogues. Note also the references to the local leadership of the priests and *presbyteroi* in Lam 1:19, 4:16 and Ezek 7:26.

[25]Note that while the passage from 2 Chronicles refers to the time of Jehoshaphat, it probably reflects the situation in the post-exilic period when it was written. See E. P. Sanders, *Judaism*, 171. In addition to the references cited above, the following statement of Hecataeus of Abdera (c. 300 B.C.E.), a Greek author and pupil of Pyrron the Sceptic, is of interest: "[Moses] picked out the men of most refinement and with the greatest ability to head the entire nation, and appointed them priests; and he ordained that they should occupy themselves with the temple and the honours and sacrifices offered to their God. These same men he appointed to be judges in all major disputes, and entrusted to them the guardianship of the laws and customs. For this reason the Jews never have a king, and authority over the people is regularly vested in whichever priest is regarded as superior to his colleagues in wisdom and virtue. They call this man the high priest, and believe that he acts as a messenger to them of God's commandments. It is he, we are told, who in their assemblies and other gatherings announces what is ordained, and the Jews are so docile in such matters that straightway they fall to the ground and do reverence to the high priest when he expounds the commandments to them" (*Aegyptica* 4–6 ap. Diodorus Siculus, *Bibliotheca Historica*, 40.3). For commentary, see *GLAJJ* 1.20–35.

Modein (1 Macc 2:17). That this pattern continued up to the destruction of the Temple can be seen not only in Josephus' activities during the Jewish War, but also in his statement that the duties of the priest included "general supervision, the trial of cases of litigation, and the punishment of condemned persons" (*Ap.* 2.187).[26]

This was the view within the diaspora as well—at least in Egypt, the only major source of diaspora Jewish literature from our period. There, the priests had even more available time, because they did not constitute part of the Temple's priestly rotation. That they formed part of the local leadership can hardly be doubted. Thus 3 Maccabees depicts a certain Eleazar, "famous among the priests of the country," as silencing the elders (πρεσβυτέροι) so that he could pray a long and elaborate prayer for the deliverance of the Egyptian Jews from the wrath of Ptolemy Philopater (3 Macc 6:1). Likewise, yet another Eleazar, "the oldest of the priests," led the prayer prior to the feast thrown by Ptolemy II for the translators of the LXX in the *Letter of Aristeas* (*Ep. Arist.* 184–185; cf. Josephus, *Ant.* 12.97–98). Still elsewhere, a letter from Judas Maccabaeus to a certain Aristobulus "who is of the family of the anointed priests, teacher of King Ptolemy" is contained in 2 Maccabees (1:10–2:18). While the letter is fictitious, it assumes that a priest was the leader of the Jews in Alexandria.[27] Finally, Philo assumed that the priests served as judges (δικασταί) over civil affairs, writing, "who should these [judges] be but the priests, and the head and leader of the priests? For the genuine ministers of God have taken all care to sharpen their understanding and count the slightest error to be no slight error" (*Spec.* 4.191).

Against this backdrop, it should come as no surprise that our evidence indicates that priests served as leaders of the synagogues. In Palestine, Theodotus refers to himself as both priest and *archisynagōgos* of the synagogue in Jerusalem that he constructed and his father and grandfather helped establish (*CIJ* 2.1404). These latter are also listed as *archisynagōgoi* on the inscription. Thus, this particular synagogue had three generations of priests filling this office. Elsewhere, it should be recalled that an ostracon bearing the words "priest's tithe" was found in the Masada synagogue just outside the rear chamber that served as the abode of the building's caretaker.[28] This suggests that the caretaker was

---

[26]Note also that the *Testament of Levi* "predicts" that Levi's descendants will serve as judges (*T. Levi* 8:17).

[27]For commentary on this letter, see Goldstein, *II Maccabees*, 154–188.

[28]See chapter three's treatment of Masada.

a priest, a conclusion bolstered by the fact that other ostraca attest to the presence of priests at Masada during the revolt (including the son of a former High Priest). Several ostraca, for example, come from smashed vessels classified according to their degree of purity, a task normally assigned to the priests.[29] If the caretaker was indeed a priest, then he possibly served as the ad hoc *archisynagōgos* and led the services on the Sabbath and other days.[30]

That priests commonly served in a similar capacity in the synagogues of Egypt is seen in a passage from Philo's writings wherein he briefly outlines a Sabbath service:

> [Moses] required them to assemble in the same place on these seventh days, and sitting together in a respectful and orderly manner hear the laws read so that none should be ignorant of them. And indeed they always assemble and sit together, most of them in silence except when it is the practice to add something to signify approval of what is read. But some priest who is present or one of the elders [τῶν ἱερέων δέ τις ὁ παρὼν ἢ τῶν γερόντων εἷς] reads the holy laws to them and expounds them point by point till about the late afternoon, when they depart having gained both expert knowledge of the holy laws and considerable advance in piety (*Hypoth*. 7.12–13).[31]

While the above description is idealized, the mention of the priest as the reader and expounder of scripture clearly reflects Philo's own experience in the Alexandrian synagogues.[32] Of course this role was shared with the laity, as is clearly attested not only in the above passage, but in several instances in the New Testament where Jesus, Paul or Apollos—all members of the laity—are depicted as reading or preaching in the synagogue (e.g., Mark 1:21; Luke 4:16–28; Acts 13:14–43, 18:26).

---

[29]See Yadin et al., "The Aramaic and Hebrew Ostraca and Jar Inscriptions," 32–39. Cf. Jesus' command to the cleansed leper that he go and show himself to the priest (Mark 1:44).

[30]We should note that the Essenes, who also worshiped in synagogues, likewise had a strong element of priestly leadership. For further discussion of this point, see chapter seven's treatment of this group.

[31]Note that this is the fragment of *Hypothetica* that speaks about Jews in general and not specifically about the Essenes. On the Philonic authorship of *Hypothetica*, see chapter one.

[32]A Jewish priest is also listed as one of the contributors to a dining club on an ostracon from Apollinopolis Magna (Egypt) dating to the first century B.C.E. (*CPJ* 139). Since at least some synagogues had ancillary dining rooms (*CIJ* 2.1404, Ostia), the priest may have been connected to a synagogue there, perhaps as one of the functionaries.

The above passage leads us to recall that a priest was listed as a member of the synagogue in the inscription from Berenice mentioning contributors to the repair of the building (*CJZC* 72).[33] Because the priest's name was placed immediately after the ten *archontes* and because he contributed the same amount as these officials (10 drachmae) in contrast to the varying sums contributed by the rest of the congregation, it seems likely that he was an active functionary of the synagogue, perhaps taking on the role traditionally associated with the office of *archisynagōgos* or *grammateus* (on this latter possibility, see below). That the priest served as a synagogue functionary is further suggested by Cyrenaica's proximity to Egypt, where, as we have seen, this practice was considered normal.

As for the rest of the diaspora, we can only guess the degree of leadership exercised by priestly members of the community. The manumission inscriptions from the synagogues in the Bosporus Kingdom suggest that priests may have been involved in the release ceremony, as this was the custom of the pagan ceremonies after which the Jewish ones seem to have been modeled.[34] Acts 19:14ff recounts the activities of seven sons of a Jewish High Priest in Ephesus, but does not mention whether they functioned as leaders within the synagogue there.[35] In general, priests were probably more involved in the Palestinian synagogues than their diaspora counterparts for the simple reason that the priestly population was more concentrated in the homeland.

Whatever the exact percentage of priestly participation may have been, the sharp dichotomy so frequently drawn between the Temple leadership and that of the synagogues is contradicted by the evidence. On the side of the Temple, while the priests certainly dominated this institution because of the sacrificial role assigned to them by the scriptures, the laity also had a measure of control over the Temple's affairs. This is seen not only during the reigns of the Herodians when the High Priest was appointed by the king (e.g., Josephus, *Ant.* 15.322, 20.15–16), but more broadly in the participation of the laity within the *synedrion* and the scribal class (on this last, see below). The Pharisees, primarily a lay group centered in Jerusalem, also exerted influence in Temple business by virtue of their expertise in the law. Thus just prior to

---

[33]For the list of contributors in this inscription, see the previous chapter's discussion of Berenice.

[34]See chapter four's treatment of the Bosporus Kingdom.

[35]This passage, moreover, contains legendary elements. However, at least the author of Acts believed it plausible that priests could reside in Ephesus. See Conzelmann, *Acts of the Apostles*, 163–164.

the Jewish War when Eleazar, the Temple *stratēgos*, and some of the priests refused to accept sacrifices from Gentiles, the chief priests, the leading citizens (οἱ δυνατοί) and "the most notable of the Pharisees" assembled to attempt to convince the renegade priests that such sacrifices were in accord with their most ancient traditions (*BJ* 2.411ff).

Conversely, our sources have also suggested that priests not infrequently served as leaders within the synagogues. To be sure, nothing scriptural mandated that the priests had to serve in such a capacity, since no animal sacrifice was offered in the synagogues. Hence the laity were free to take on leadership roles there, just as they could inside the Temple complex itself—except, of course, within the Court of Priests. Yet because the priests were not only the leaders of worship within the Temple and knowledgeable in the law, but also in many cases quite wealthy, they possessed most of the qualifications prerequisite for the offices of *archisynagōgos* or village *archōn*. Indeed, recalling Strange's proposal that the Galilean synagogues were modeled after the Court of Israel, the priests probably felt as much at home in the synagogues of Palestine as they did in the Temple, for while they offered animal sacrifices in the latter, in the former they could offer a "sacrifice of the lips."

Presbyteros, *Gerōn*, *Dynatos*

The terms, *presbyteros*, *gerōn* ("elder"), and *dynatos* ("notable") are virtually synonymous within Jewish writings of our period. *Presbyteros* is particularly favored in the LXX, where it is usually found in the plural, translating the Hebrew *z*ᵉ*qēnīm*, "elders." In the Pentateuch, the term typically refers to "the elders of Israel," often numbered as seventy (e.g., Exod 24:1; Num 11:16; Deut 31:9). These leaders represented the people before Mt. Sinai and the tent of meeting (Exod 24:1; Num 11:16). They are also said to have had a measure of God's spirit (Num 11:25) and to have assisted Moses with the judging of civil cases (Num 11:16). In a parallel tradition in Exodus 18:13ff, Jethro advises Moses to choose men to serve as judges over minor disputes. The LXX refers to these leaders as *dynatoi* (= אַנְשֵׁי־חַיִל, "powerful men"). The term *gerōn*, though employed less frequently in the LXX, when used in the plural also translates *z*ᵉ*qēnīm*, as in Proverbs 31:23, which mentions the elders sitting at the city gates. This last usage portrays the usual venue of the elders in the pre-exilic and early post-exilic period, where they posted themselves to judge over local affairs. In Ruth 4:2ff, for example, Boaz sat with ten elders (*presbyteroi*) at the city gate to discuss his potential marriage to Ruth. Likewise, the book of Judith portrays the heroine of that story encountering the city elders (*presbyteroi*) at the village gate (Jdt 10:6, 13:12).

On a national level, the elders formed part of the *gerousia* of the nation. This is particularly apparent in the wording of a decree quoted in 1 Macc 14:27–45 proclaiming Simon Maccabaeus and his progeny as High Priests and ethnarchs in perpetuity. The opening formula of the decree states that the measure was resolved "in the great assembly [ἐπὶ συναγωγῆς μεγάλης] of the priests and the people and the *archontes* of the nation and the *presbyteroi* of the country" (v. 28). Later, Mark's Gospel refers to the chief priests holding council "with the *presbyteroi*, the scribes and the whole *synedrion*" to discuss the fate of Jesus (Mark 15:1). From these and other passages (e.g., Mark 8:31, 11:23; Acts 4:5, 8), it is clear that the elders formed a larger body of councilors surrounding the *archontes* and the High Priest. This arrangement was probably the norm locally, as can be discerned from the composition of the Tiberian *boulē*, which had an *archōn* at its head, ten "leading citizens" (*prōtoi*) and then the remainder of the council of 600 (Josephus, *Vita* 69, 134, 168, 271, 278, 294, 296; *BJ* 2.639). The latter group would thus correspond to a college of elders. Just how the elders on the local and national levels received their offices is unclear. Since the Pentateuch portrays them as the people's representatives, they may have been elected by the populace on the basis of their age, wealth, political influence, and knowledge of the laws and traditions.

Turning now to the synagogue evidence, we find our sources presenting the elders as political functionaries, teachers, and patrons of the synagogues. In the Theodotus inscription, the elders (*presbyteroi*) were said to have laid the foundations of the synagogue along with Theodotus' father, grandfather, and a certain Simonides (*CIJ* 2.1404, ll. 9–10). Luke 7:3–5 similarly depicts elders (*presbyteroi*) being associated with the founding of the synagogue in Capernaum.[36] In this case, however, a Roman centurion is the patron and the elders serve as intermediaries between him and Jesus.

Elsewhere, Josephus records that just prior to the Jewish War twelve elders (*dynatoi*) of the synagogue at Caesarea, led by a tax collector named John, presented a bribe of eight talents of silver to the procurator,

---

[36]For arguments for the inclusion of this segment in Q, see chapter two's discussion of the term *synagōgē*.

Florus, in exchange for an order to the owner of a property adjoining their synagogue (a Greek) to cease construction work. Florus accepted the bribe, but never followed through with the agreement. On the contrary, according to Josephus, he later had the elders arrested for removing their own Torah scrolls from the city following a violent clash with the neighboring Greeks (*BJ* 2.285–292). This passage highlights the role of the elders as political representatives.

The teaching role of the elders is most clearly seen in a passage from Philo's writings, quoted above, which states that either a priest or elder (*gerōn*) read and expounded upon the scriptures on the Sabbath (*Hypoth.* 7.12–13). While this may have been true in Egypt, in Palestine, the role of teacher appears to have been assigned primarily to the scribes (see below), though the elders undoubtedly contributed their own commentary within the services as the phrase "tradition of the elders" in Mark's Gospel implies (Mark 7:3, 5).

Although the elders of the synagogue were probably equivalent to the village elders in smaller communities, in larger urban areas where several synagogues were located, the city elders likely consisted of representatives taken from each of the congregations. Our understanding of this selection process is limited, however, and hence we remain in the dark as to how exactly each synagogue was represented within cities such as Alexandria, Antioch, Rome or Jerusalem.

Synagogue Assistants

As might be expected, the titles of the synagogue assistants are not as well-attested as those of the synagogue leaders. As Table 5 shows, they appear only in literary sources, suggesting that they were not deemed important enough to be listed on dedicatory inscriptions. The one exception to this rule is the scribes who, in Palestine at least, appear to have achieved a special prominence as teachers of the law, almost ranking them with the leaders. Properly understood, however, they belong to a secondary tier, as will be made clear in the ensuing discussion below.

Table 5
Terms used in Reference to Synagogue Assistants

	Number of Uses by Source		Total Uses
	NT	Papyri	
Grammateus	6	2	8
Nakoros (*neōkoros*)	–	1	1
Archypēretēs	–	1	1
Hypēretēs	1	–	1
Eisangeleus	–	1	1
Thyrōros (?)	–	1	1

Grammateus

The term *grammateus*, "scribe," is a common one within ancient Greco-Roman writings, where it denotes a clerk or secretary of an official body.[37] The status of the position varied according to the prestige of the office or institution to which it was attached. On the lower end would have been the village scribe, who did little more than serve as a local notary (Josephus, *BJ* 1.479). On the upper extreme were the scribes connected with the imperial government. They possessed great influence because, while appointed officials came and went, they typically remained in their positions for life. A modern analogy would be the "staffer" in the congressional offices of the United States government. The power of the scribes resulted not only from the longevity of their terms, but also from their knowledge of how official affairs were supposed to be ordered. Hence, in a rare passage wherein he compliments his former prefect Flaccus, Philo states:

> In quite a short time he became thoroughly familiar with Egyptian affairs, intricate and diversified as they are and hardly grasped even by those who have made a business of studying them from their earliest years. His crowd of secretaries [γραμματεῖς] were a superfluity, since nothing small or great was beyond the reach of his experience, so that he not only surpassed them

[37]See LSJ s.v. γραμματεύς; Joachim Jeremias, "Γραμματεύς" in *TDNT*, 1.740–742.

> but thanks to his mastery of detail became the teacher instead of the pupil of his erstwhile instructors (*Flacc.* 3).

As we see, the scribes are portrayed as the educators of appointed officials, particularly knowledgeable about procedural and legal fine-points.

Within the LXX, while *grammateus* (MT, סֹפֵר, "scribe," or שֹׁטֵר, "officer") also designates a public official (e.g., Exod 5:6; 1 Kgs 4:3), in the later books it takes on the additional meaning of "sage." The best known description of this later scribe/sage comes from the writings of Ben Sirach, who contrasts the scribe with the farmer and artisan:

> The wisdom of the scribe depends on the opportunity of leisure; only the one who has little business can become wise. How can one become wise who handles the plow? . . . He sets his heart on plowing furrows . . . So too is every artisan and master artisan . . . So too is the smith, sitting by the anvil . . . So too is the potter sitting at his work and turning the wheel with his feet . . . All these rely on their hands, and all are skillful in their own work. Without them no city can be inhabited, and wherever they live, they will not go hungry. Yet they are not sought out for the council of the people, nor do they attain eminence in the public assembly. They do not sit in the judge's seat, nor do they understand the decisions of the courts; they cannot expound discipline or judgment, and they are not found among the rulers (Sir 38:24–33).

The standard view for most of the twentieth century has been that these scribes should be identified with an emerging leisured class of the laity. According to this position, this scribal class went on to replace the priests and Levites who were withdrawing from teaching and administrative concerns in the later Second Temple period. More recently, scholars such as E. P. Sanders, Anthony Saldarini and Daniel Schwartz have subjected this reconstruction to an extensive critique. Sanders, for example, characterizes the earlier view as a "myth" and demonstrates that its leading proponents (Jeremias, Schürer, Maccoby, Rajak) produce no positive evidence in its favor and, moreover, overlook a great deal of evidence to the contrary.[38] To be sure, there were lay scribes in Palestine

---

[38]See E. P. Sanders, *Judaism*, 173–189; cf. Daniel R. Schwartz, *Studies in the Jewish Background of Christianity* (Tübingen: Mohr, 1992), 89–101; Saldarini, *Pharisees, Scribes and Sadducees*, 241–276. The latter observes that a lay class of ruling scribes "is sociologically unlikely because it puts in power those without wealth, social standing or connection with the Temple" (252). The earlier view is set forth in: Joachim Jeremias, *Jerusalem in the Time of Jesus: An Investigation into Economic and*

during the Second Temple period (e.g., Josephus, *BJ* 1.479). But the evidence strongly suggests that primarily priests and Levites served in this capacity. The model for this was Ezra, whom Ezra 7:11 calls "the priest Ezra, the scribe, a scholar of the text of the commandments of the LORD and his statutes for Israel" (cf. Ezra 7:12, 21; Neh 8:9, 12:26; 1 Esdr 8:8, 9). He, along with the priests and the Levites, are said to have "taught the people" the law (Neh 8:9, 13). Other passages within writings from this period frequently identify the scribes as either priests or Levites. Ben Sirach himself wrote that Moses ordained Aaron not only "to offer sacrifice to the Lord," but also "to teach Jacob the testimonies, and to enlighten Israel with his law" (Sir 45:16–17). For him, the priest represented the sage *par excellence*. Elsewhere, Nehemiah 13:13 mentions that the scribe of the Temple was a certain Zadok, whose name indicates that he was a priest. In 1 Chronicles 23:4, which lists the various job titles assigned to the Levites, the LXX translates the Hebrew *shōterīm*, "officers," as *grammateis*. Later, Josephus follows the rendering of the LXX, suggesting that the Levites served as scribes in his day (*Ant.* 7.364). Similarly, both the MT and the LXX of 2 Chr 34:13 state that the Levites served as scribes (γραμματεῖς/סוֹפְרִים), as well as officials (κριταί/שֹׁטְרִים) and gate-keepers (πυλωροί/שׁוֹעֲרִים) within the Temple. These Levitical scribes are also probably referred to in a letter by Antiochus III to one of his governors, wherein the former exempts officials of the Jerusalem Temple from various taxes:

> And all the members of the nation shall have a form of government in accordance with the laws of their country, and the senate [ἡ γερουσία], the priests, the scribes of the temple [οἱ γραμματεῖς τοῦ ἱεροῦ] and the temple singers shall be relieved from the poll-tax and the crown-tax which they pay (*Ant.* 12.142).[39]

Social Conditions During the New Testament Period (Philadelphia: Fortress Press, 1975), 233–245; *HJP* 2.322–336; Hyam Maccoby, *Revolution in Judea: Jesus and the Jewish Resistance*, 2nd ed. (New York: Taplinger, 1980), 61–62; Rajak, *Josephus*, 19–20.

[39]On the authenticity of this letter, see Elias J. Bickerman, "La charte séleucid de Jerusalem," *REJ* 100 (1935): 4–35. Bickerman's argument in favor of its acceptance are accepted by most researchers (e.g., Rajak, "Was there a Roman Charter for the Jews?" 107–123). The position of the "scribes of the temple" between the priests and the "temple singers" suggests that they were Levites, since the Temple singers certainly were (e.g., Ezra 3:8; Josephus, *Ant.* 11.70, 20.217–218). *Ant.* 11.128 (|| 1 Esdr 8:22, Ezra 7:24), part of a decree from the Persian period, also mentions temple scribes; these too were probably Levites. See E. P. Sanders, *Judaism*, 180–181.

In a somewhat later period, 4 Maccabees, a philosophical discourse dating to the turn of the era, expands on the story of a certain Eleazar, originally told in 2 Macc 6:18–31. In the earlier version, Eleazar, who chose to die rather than eat the pork being forced upon him by the officers of Antiochus Epiphanes, is simply called a scribe (2 Macc 6:18). In 4 Maccabees' retelling, however, Eleazar is referred to as "a man of priestly family, learned in the law [τὸ γένος ἱερεύς τὴν ἐπιστήμην νομικός]" (4 Macc 5:4). The later document thus identifies priests with scribes.[40]

This is the view presented in Josephus' writings when he states that the duties of the priest involved "the training of the entire community" in piety and the dictates of the law (*Ap.* 2.187–188), echoing the position of Ben Sirach. Elsewhere within first-century writings, Mark frequently associates the scribes with the chief priests (Mark 8:31, 10:33, 11:18, 11:27, 14:1, 14:43, 14:53, 15:1, 15:31) or has them coming from Jerusalem to check on the activities of Jesus (Mark 3:22, 7:1).[41] This further suggests that scribes are to be identified with the priests or Levites.

Regarding the latter group, Sanders observes that the Levites must have been literate because they needed to read the hymns they sang in the Temple.[42] Since Josephus' numbers suggest a total of about 20,000 priests and Levites in the first century (*Ap.* 2.108), Sanders argues that most of the latter group (and some of the former) served as local scribes during

---

[40] 4 Maccabees was probably written in Egypt and reflects Platonic and Stoic ideas. The narrative recasts Eleazar as the Jewish philosopher *par excellence*. While the identification of the Jewish priesthood with this ideal is striking, it finds additional attestation in Philo's writings, as we saw in the previous section (e.g., *Spec.* 4.191, *Hypoth.* 7:12–13). For additional discussion, see H. Anderson, "4 Maccabees," in *OTP* 2.531–543. Note also that the *Testament of Levi* lists *grammateus* as an occupation of Levi's descendants (*T. Levi* 8.17).

[41] Of course, elsewhere in Mark the scribes are sometimes associated with the Pharisees (Mark 7:1, 5), though the association is cemented only in the diatribes of Matt 23, which, however, speak to the situation being faced by the Matthean community in the post-70 period. See Saldarini, *Pharisees, Scribes and Sadducees*, 266–268. Interestingly, John 1:19 has the "priests and Levites" being sent from Jerusalem to interrogate John the Baptist. This may be another case in this Gospel where an early tradition is used to frame a passage dealing with a later issue facing the Johannine community (viz., the priority of Jesus over John the Baptist). See Brown, *The Gospel According to John*, 1.42–54

[42] Josephus depicts the Levites as reading the hymns from scrolls up until the time of Agrippa II (*Ant.* 20.217–218).

the majority of the year when they where not on duty in the Temple (*Ant.* 7.367).[43] This view seems likely, as long as we recognize that persons outside of the tribe of Levi may also have served as local scribes. Among these may have been non-priestly members of the Pharisees, a party who is also said to have had scribes (Mark 2:16; Acts 23:9). During the Second Temple period, their influence would not have been as extensive as most scholars have believed, however, since according to Josephus, they numbered only 6,000 and were confined mainly to Jerusalem (*Ant.* 17.42).[44]

From the foregoing, we see that within Jewish tradition, scribes were not only copyists and notaries, but legal experts, whose job it was to educate the masses and assist the principals. Evidence suggests that more often these scribes were Levites or priests, though members of the laity could also serve in this capacity.

With this background, we turn to the passages linking scribes to the synagogues. The bulk of these come from the Gospels, where the scribes are cast as self-serving, ineffective teachers. Mark 1:21–22, for example, states, "[Jesus and his disciples] went to Capernaum; and when the sabbath came, he entered the synagogue and taught. They were astounded at his teaching, for he taught them as one having authority, and not as the scribes." Though the scribes never appear in the scene, they are clearly portrayed as being the usual teachers in the synagogues. How well they functioned in that capacity cannot, of course, be judged from the biased view of the above passage.

The same can be said of the allegation that the scribes sought "the best seats [πρωτοκαθεδρίας] in the synagogues" (Mark 12:29; Matt 23:6 || Luke 20:46, 11:43 = Q).[45] Indeed, if one of the assigned roles of the scribes was to serve as teachers, then it would have been natural for them to sit in the first seats, which probably should be equated with the benches opposite the synagogue's main doorway, as seen at Gamla, Masada and Herodium.

The only other use of *grammateus* in direct connection to the synagogues is in a badly damaged papyrus from Egypt (*CPJ* 1.138; I B.C.E.). While we will examine the contents of the papyrus in the next

---

[43]E. P. Sanders, *Judaism*, 180–181.

[44]See ibid., 380–451; Saldarini, *Pharisees, Scribes and Sadducees*, 277–297.

[45]The statement in Matthew 23:2 that "the scribes and Pharisees sit on Moses' seat" probably points to the appropriation of the *archōn*'s seat (in the synagogues?) by these two groups in the generation following the destruction of the Temple.

chapter, here we note that it appears to be the minutes of a Jewish burial association held inside a *proseuchē*. The term *grammateus* is twice used, probably in reference to the scribe taking the minutes. Although it provides little additional information, the papyrus does highlight the secretarial function of the scribes and how that too was exercised within the synagogues. The thousands of contracts, deeds, wills and bills of sale found within the papyri recovered from Egypt and elsewhere attest to the importance of written documentation in the Hellenistic and Roman periods, even in remote villages. The scribes were responsible for seeing that all this paperwork was done, and that it was done correctly and according to the law.

In summary, the scribes functioned as teachers and legal secretaries within both the Temple and the synagogues. When civil disputes arose, they served as legal advisors to the *archontes* or *archisynagōgoi*. The majority of the scribes in our period were probably Levites or priests, though some members of the laity probably also served in this role. As Saldarini points out, we should not think of them as a unified, political group, but as "typical members of a retainer class and part of the normal structure of society in an agrarian empire."[46]

The Attendants

Our knowledge of other synagogue assistants must be gleaned from two papyri and a single reference in the New Testament. The most interesting of the titles used in these sources is *nakoros*, Doric for *neōkoros*, "temple warden."[47] It will be recalled that this was the title used of an officer of a synagogue in Alexandrou-Nesos in Middle Egypt in a third-century B.C.E. papyrus quoted in the previous chapter (*CPJ* 1.129). As briefly stated there, the title typically referred to temple servants who assisted the priests with their sacrificial duties. An inscription from Pergamum, for example, states that the *neōkoros* in the temple of Athena was to receive a small sum of money for each sacrifice that he helped perform.[48] Similarly, at Delphi the *neōkoros* frequently served as a witness in the manumission ceremonies conducted by the priests.[49]

---

[46]Saldarini, *Pharisees, Scribes and Sadducees*, 266.

[47]See LSJ s.v. νεώκορος.

[48]*AvP* 8.2.255.

[49]E.g., *FD* 3.2, nos. 128, 215, 223.

Elsewhere, the *neōkoroi* functioned as temple guards, custodians and messengers.[50]

Within Jewish writings, both Philo and Josephus use the title exclusively to refer to the Levites.[51] The former, for instance, writes:

> After bestowing these great sources of revenue on the priests, [Moses] did not ignore those of the second rank either, namely the *neōkoroi*. Some of these are stationed at the doors as gate-keepers at the very entrances, some within in front of the sanctuary to prevent any unlawful person from setting foot thereon, either intentionally or unintentionally. Some patrol around it turn by turn in relays by appointment night and day, keeping watch and guard at both seasons. Others sweep the porticoes and the open court, convey away the refuse and ensure cleanliness. All these have the tithes appointed as their wages, this being the portion settled on them as *neōkoroi* (*Spec*. 1.156).

The consistent equation of the title *neōkoros* with the Levites in the writings of these two authors suggests that synagogue officials bearing this same title were normally Levites. While this title appears only once in our sources in connection with the synagogues, because the titles of synagogue servants are not well-attested, the usage may have been more widespread than the single occurrence would normally indicate. Moreover, the remaining terms in our list correspond to the titles held or the functions performed by Levites in the Temple. For instance, *hypēretēs* ("attendant"),[52] used in Luke 4:20 of the synagogue officer who received the scroll from Jesus after his reading from Isaiah, is also used of the Levites by both Philo and Josephus. The latter author, for example, relates that Moses commanded that "two *hypēretai* from the tribe of Levi" were to assist each *archōn* within the cities of Palestine—a set of details missing from the biblical account and hence likely an anachronism

---

[50]See Steven J. Friesen, *Twice Neokoros* (Leiden: E. J. Brill, 1993), 50–53; idem, "Urban Development and Social Change in Imperial Ephesos" in *Ephesos: Metropolis of Asia*, edited by Helmut Koester (Valley Forge, Pennsylvania: Trinity Press International, 1995), 230–231.

[51]In addition to the two usages quoted above, see Josephus *BJ* 1.153; Philo *Fug*. 90, 93, 94; *Mos*. 1.316, 318; 2.72, 159, 174, 276; *Spec*. 2.120; *Praem*. 74. In each case *neōkoros* is synonymous with Levite. *BJ* 5.383 uses the term figuratively, referring to the nation of Israel as the "temple-keeper" of the Jerusalem Temple. This latter usage was becoming common in the first century C.E. (e.g., Acts 19:35).

[52]See K. H. Rengstorf, "'Υπηρέτης" in *TDNT* 8.530–544.

reflecting the practices of Josephus' own period (*Ant.* 4.214; cf. Deut 16:18).[53]

While it is unclear if Luke uses *hypēretēs* generally or as a title in the above passage, the related word *archypēretēs* ("chief attendant"), found in a first-century B.C.E. papyrus from an Egyptian synagogue, is clearly used as a title (*CPJ* 1.138).[54] This official was probably the overseer of the other synagogue servants mentioned in the same papyrus, including the *eisangeleus*, "usher," and the *thyrōros*, "doorkeeper."[55] Although Philo uses neither of these words, his descriptions of the responsibilities of the Levites include the duties normally associated with servants bearing these titles (see passage above; cf. Josephus, *Ant.* 7.364–365; 11.108). Furthermore, in the LXX and in the writings of Josephus, *thyrōros*, though rarely used, almost exclusively refers to the Levites (Ezek 44:11; 1 Esdr 1:15, 5:28, 5:45, 7:9, 8:5, 8:22, 9:25; Josephus, *Ant.* 11.108). While it is true that, unlike *neōkoros*, the other titles just mentioned can designate servants outside of a temple, the overlap of terminology is nevertheless striking.

To summarize: the evidence indicates that the synagogues of our period had one or more servants who assisted the principals with tasks such as guarding the doors, conveying the scriptures to and from readers, and maintaining general oversight of the physical plant. The terminology used of these servants hints that at least some of them were Levites. Because our sources are confined to Egypt and Palestine, however, we cannot be certain whether Levites functioned in such roles throughout the diaspora.

---

[53]For additional uses of *hypēretēs* in reference to the Levites, see Philo, *Spec.* 1.152, *Sacrif.* 132–133; Josephus, *BJ* 2.321.

[54]While the passage in Luke 4:16–28 is Lucan expansion of Mark 6:1–5, some of the narrative trappings may accurately reflect the pre-70 period. See the discussion of interpretive problems in Luke in chapter one, as well as Fitzmyer, *The Gospel According to Luke*, 1.521–539.

[55]This last, however, is a reconstruction.

CONCLUSION

While several recent researchers have proposed that the early synagogue congregations consisted of informal gatherings[56] or of groups that were "democratic" in character,[57] the foregoing discussion has revealed that synagogues in our period were highly institutionalized organizations with several echelons of functionaries. At the top of the hierarchy were *archontes* (or *prostatai* or *archiprostatai*) and *archisynagōgoi*, who served as patrons and as spiritual and political leaders of the synagogues. Although there was a great deal of overlap in their offices, when they were distinguished, the *archōn* seems to have been responsible for the judicial and legislative affairs of the community, while the *archisynagōgos* was in charge of directing the religious services of the community. These principals were surrounded by a college of elders (*presbyteroi*, *gerontes*, *dynatoi*), who served as advisors and representatives of the people's concerns both inside and outside the community. They also appear to have functioned as teachers and patrons. Underneath them were the scribes, who served not only as notaries and legal advisors, but also as teachers. The more prominent of the scribes may have risen to the higher ranks of the synagogal hierarchy. Finally, there were the attendants (*neōkoroi*, *hypēretai*, *archypēretai*, *eisangeleus*, and *thyrōros*), who maintained oversight of the physical plant, provided security, and assisted in the handling of the scriptures.

Our survey has also highlighted the role of the priests and Levites within the synagogues. Here, sources indicate that priests served as *archisynagōgoi* and *archontes*, and suggested that they frequently served as scribes. Similarly, the Levites functioned as scribes and also appear to have filled the role of synagogue attendant. These findings call into question the view that the synagogue was the "people's house" as opposed to the Temple, which belonged to the priests. In fact, the evidence points to the conclusion that the Temple and the synagogue *both* belonged to the priests, Levites and people, with all three groups having a measure of leadership and participation within each institution.

---

[56]E.g., Kee, "New Finds That Illuminate the World and Text of the Bible," 102; R. Horsley, *Galilee*, 224.

[57]Richardson, "Synagogues as Collegia," 102.

EXCURSUS ONE: THE PLACE OF WOMEN IN THE SYNAGOGUES

One of the notable characteristics of Jewish leadership as presented in the writings of the Second Temple period is that it was unabashedly patriarchal. According to these accounts, the chief priests, the priests, the Levites, the *archontes*, the elders, the scribes—even the synagogue attendants—were all males. Occasionally in the historical or literary narratives, we encounter heroines such as Esther, Judith or Alexandra, who provide a welcome relief to the male-dominated story. But these are the exceptions that seem to prove the rule.

From the historian's perspective, part of the problem in interpreting these documents is that men wrote (and preserved) the overwhelming bulk of ancient literature. Consequently, what is left to us in the literary record has been tinted with a male perspective. Fortunately, archaeology has provided a counterpoint to this bias, allowing us to see more of the other half of the picture. Within synagogal studies, the ground-breaking study in this respect was Bernadette Brooten's book, *Women Leaders in the Ancient Synagogue* (1982).[58] In this work, Brooten examined the

---

[58]Bernadette J. Brooten, *Women Leaders in the Ancient Synagogue: Inscriptional Evidence and Background Issues* (Chico, Calif.: Scholars Press, 1982). See also idem, "Inscriptional Evidence for Women as Leaders in the Ancient Synagogue," *Society of Biblical Literature Seminar Papers* 20 (1981): 1–17; Hannah Safrai, "Women and the Ancient Synagogue" in *Daughters of the King: Women and the Synagogue: A Survey of History, Halakhah, and Contemporary Realities*, edited by Susan Grossman and Rivka Haut (Philadelphia: Jewish Publication Society, 1992), 39–49; Matthew S. Collins, "Money, Sex and Power: An Examination of the Role of Women as Patrons of the Ancient Synagogues" in *Recovering the Role of Women: Power and Authority in Rabbinic Jewish Society*, edited by P. Haas (Atlanta, Ga.: Scholars Press, 1992), 7–22; Léonie J. Archer, "The Role of Jewish Women in the Religion, Ritual and Cult of Graeco-Roman Palestine" in *Images of Women in Antiquity*, edited by Averil Cameron and Amélie Kuhrt (Detroit: Wayne State University Press, 1983), 273–287; Susan Grossman, "Women and the Jerusalem Temple" in *Daughters of the King: Women and the Synagogue: A Survey of History, Halakhah, and Contemporary Realities*, edited by Susan Grossman and Rivka Haut (Philadelphia: Jewish Publication Society, 1992), 14–37; Sally Overby Langford, "On Being a Religious Woman: Women Proselytes in the Greco-Roman World" in *Recovering the Role of Women: Power and Authority in Rabbinic Jewish Society*, edited by P. Haas (Atlanta, Ga: Scholars Press, 1992), 61–83; Sharon Lee Mattila, "Where Women Sat in Ancient Synagogues: The Archaeological Evidence in Context" in *Voluntary Associations*, edited by John S. Kloppenborg and Steven G. Wilson (London: Routledge, 1996), 266–286; Peter Richardson and Valerie Heuchan, "Jewish Voluntary Associations in Egypt and the Roles of Women" in *Voluntary Associations*, edited by John S.

epigraphic record and identified several inscriptions referring to individual women with titles such as *archisynagōgos* or *presbytera*. Previously, researchers had postulated that in these particular instances the titles were honorifics or alluded to the husbands of the women mentioned in the inscriptions. Brooten rightly challenged these conclusions, pointing out that there was little to support such interpretations beyond the researchers' assumptions that women could not possibly have served as active functionaries within the synagogues. While questions still remain about the proliferation of honorifics in synagogues of the Late Roman and Byzantine periods,[59] Brooten's interpretation has been accepted by most researchers, and it is now widely recognized that women held leadership positions within synagogues in at least some parts of the Greco-Roman world.[60]

Unfortunately, within the temporal parameters of this study, the issue is not so clear. The inscriptions upon which Brooten bases her conclusions about women holding leadership roles in synagogues nearly all date from the second through sixth centuries C.E. The one exception is an epitaph dating to 28 B.C.E. discovered in a Jewish necropolis near Leontopolis in Egypt (*CIJ* 2.1514). The deceased, a certain Marion

---

Kloppenborg and Steven G. Wilson (London: Routledge, 1996), 226–251.

[59]See Rajak and Noy, "*Archisynagogoi*," 84–87; *NDIEC* 4.219–220. Both of these studies criticize Brooten for her lack of rigor in addressing the possible use of *archisynagōgos* as an honorific in the later period.

[60]E.g., Trebilco, *Jewish Communities in Asia Minor*, 104–126; *NDIEC* 4.219; *HJP* 2.435 n. 39. The recent study of synagogue leaders by Burtchaell, however, rejects Brooten's conclusions: "Brooten . . . in the absence of evidence that these women were not functioning officers, concludes that they must be accepted as such (including female priests). All other interpretations, she writes, are guided by a bias which does not wish to see women as synagogue officers . . . [her] construal of the evidence seems to take little account of the patterned exclusion of women from the public domain in mishnaic culture. Brooten expects that nomenclature referring to females be interpreted similarly to when it refers to males. This ignores much of what we already know about the culture, however. How is it likely in a culture where women were legally forbidden to be counted as members of the worship fellowship, to study Torah, to join in the communal recitation of grace (and by many rabbis, to read Torah in public), that women could have been officers of the community's public affairs?" (*From Synagogue to Church*, 245, n. 98). While Burchaell's warnings about holding an opposite bias must be heeded, his own position relies too heavily on the prescriptive literature of the Mishnah and the Talmuds. Moreover, he does not allow for the possibility of regional variation. As we will note below, all of Brooten's examples of women synagogue leaders come from the diaspora, which was for many centuries outside the influence of the rabbinate in Palestine.

(Μαριν), is referred to with the title *hieris(s)a*, a variant of *hiereia*, meaning "priestess." Although one wants to heed Brooten's call to keep an open mind on the matter, even she admits "that it is impossible to know what *hiereia/hierissa* . . . means" in this and two later Jewish inscriptions bearing this title.[61] While it is just possible that Marion served as a functionary in a synagogue or even in Onias' temple, it should be pointed out that in the one place where Philo uses the term *hiereia* in reference to a Jewish woman, the meaning is clearly "of a priestly lineage" since he mentions it in connection with the restriction placed on the High Priest's choice of a spouse (*Spec*. 1.110; commenting on "a virgin from his own kin [παρθένον ἐκ τοῦ γὲνους αὐτους]" in Lev 21:14, LXX).[62] This usage makes it more probable that *hieres(s)a* in the epitaph refers to Marion's priestly lineage.

We should also note that even in the later period, female synagogue functionaries are attested only in the diaspora, primarily in Asia, Greece and Rome. The absence of similar attestations in Palestine suggests a much more restrictive attitude with regard to women holding leadership positions in the synagogues there—a perspective made amply clear in the rabbinic writings of this period (e.g., *t. Meg* 3.11–12).[63] Prior to 70 C.E., this viewpoint also seems to have prevailed since in *both* literary and epigraphic sources, nearly every leader one encounters—whether in the synagogues or elsewhere—is male. In fact one could go a step further and observe that only a single passage from our period explicitly depicts men and women together in a Palestinian synagogue: Luke 13:10–21, Jesus' healing of the crippled woman. Given this passage's status as an independent tradition and Luke's propensity for pairing incidents about men with incidents about women, one's confidence is hardly inspired.[64]

---

[61]Brooten, *Women Leaders in the Ancient Synagogue*, 98. More recently, the argument that *Marin* was a female priest in Onias' temple is made in Richardson and Heuchan, "Jewish Voluntary Associations in Egypt and the Roles of Women," 234–239. There is currently no outside evidence, however, to support this hypothesis.

[62]Philo's two other uses of *hiereia* are in *Spec*. 1.21 and *Contempl*. 68, both in reference to pagan priestesses. In the latter passage, Philo compares the virginity of some of the women among the Therapeutae with that of Gentile priestesses: "The feast is shared by women also, most of them aged virgins, who have kept their chastity not under compulsion, like some of the Greek priestesses, but of their own free will in their ardent yearning for wisdom."

[63]For a review of the rabbinic literature, see Hannah Safrai, "Women and the Ancient Synagogue," 39–47.

[64]E.g., Luke 1:5–23 (Zechariah)/1:26–38 (Mary); 2:25–35 (Simeon)/ 2:36–38 (Anna). See Fitzmyer, *The Gospel According to Luke*, 2.1009–1014.

Nor is archaeology much help in this regard since one could interpret the absence of women's galleries in the Palestinian synagogues of our period as signifying that only men were allowed in the synagogues or that men and women worshiped at different times.[65]

My purpose in adopting the role of the skeptic in the preceding paragraph is twofold. First of all, it is to highlight the fact that we lack certain knowledge about the customs governing women's participation within the Palestinian synagogues of our period. Secondly, it is to point out that, while it is right to criticize past and present androcentric interpretations of ancient history, we must not fall into the opposite trap of automatically rejecting the view that Palestine in the Second Temple period was highly patriarchal. As distasteful as such a system may be to us, the temptation must be resisted to overlook or minimize evidence pointing to such a reconstruction.[66]

Returning to the question of whether or not men and women worshiped together in the synagogues of Palestine during our period, I am inclined to accept Luke's testimony because supporting evidence exists for his portrayal. First of all, there are several accounts depicting women participating in the assemblies held before the city gates. For example, Nehemiah states that Ezra read from the law at the Water Gate "in the presence of the men and women and those who could understand" (Neh 8:3; cf. 7:73; 1 Esdr 9:41). It is significant that Josephus makes it a point of stating that men *and* women (and children!) were to assemble to hear the High Priest read the law every seven years (*Ant.* 4.209–210). The only difference was that the site had changed from the Water Gate to the Temple courts (*Ant.* 11.154–158). Elsewhere, in two places, Deuteronomy commands that both the father and the mother go before the elders at the city gate to deal with matters concerning their child (Deut. 21:19, 22:15). In yet another passage, either Judith or other women appear before the

---

[65]From chapter three, we should also recall Ma'oz's proposal that the back room of the Gamla synagogue (loc. 1010) served as a seating place for women ("The Synagogue in the Second Temple Period—Architectural and Social Interpretation," 341). Though it is more likely that this area served as a study room (see discussion in chapter three, above), Ma'oz's interpretation cannot be completely ruled out.

[66]For criticism of New Testament scholars on this count, see Antoinette Clark Wire, "Prophecy and Women Prophets in Corinth" in *Gospel Origins & Christian Beginnings: In Honor of James M. Robinson*, edited by James E. Goehring and Helmut Koester (Sonoma, Calif.: Polebridge Press, 1990), 134–150. Wire's caution against the projecting of twentieth-century worldviews upon the past must be heeded.

elders at the city gates at several points in her story (Jdt 7:22, 10:7, 13:12).[67]

On the theory that the synagogues evolved out of assemblies held at the city gates, it seems logical that women would have continued to be active participants in community affairs held within the synagogues, particularly in view of their ongoing participation within the Temple courts. While it is true that there was separation in the Temple between the Court of Women and the Court of Israel, despite this, there was a great deal of mixing between the sexes there (e.g., Jdt 4:11; 4 Macc 4:8; Mark 12:42).[68] Moreover, on the smaller scale of the synagogue, such separation may have been dispensed with as inconvenient. Still, the possibility remains that in at least some synagogues, separation was maintained either through holding different times of service on the Sabbath or by seating men and women on opposite sides of the hall.

As for women serving as synagogue functionaries in Palestine during the Second Temple period, while this possibility should not be altogether ruled out, it seems unlikely given the male dominance within the homeland. If women were allowed greater participation and opportunities for leadership in the synagogues of our period, it is more probable that this occurred outside of Palestine. And even there the evidence is not always uniform.

The situation in Egypt is a case in point. Thus, on the one hand, Philo depicts women as going to the synagogues for individual worship—though he advises that they do this in the late afternoon when the agora is closing (*Spec.* 3.172–173). On the other, he implies that women did not attend corporate Sabbath services when he writes "the [Jewish] husband seems competent to transmit knowledge of the law to his wife" (*Hypoth.* 7.14). Still elsewhere he states that "at each of the yearly seasons [Jews] make their contributions with benediction and thankfulness, men and women alike, and with a zeal and readiness which needs no prompting and an ardour which no words can describe" (*Spec.* 1.144). From these stray references, it is difficult to decide how much participation the Jewish women of Alexandria had in the synagogues.

---

[67]Similarly, if we take the OG of Sus 28 as a reference to a synagogue, then we must further note that Susanna and other women appear at the trial held in this building (vv. 29–30). As observed in chapter two, a Palestinian provenance seems most likely for this document (Collins, *Daniel*, 438).

[68]On a more thorough review of women's participation in the Temple, see Grossman, "Women and the Jerusalem Temple," 15–29. Grossman's discussion is somewhat hindered by her heavy reliance on rabbinic sources.

Given Philo's tendency to sermonize about women, we should probably interpret the second of the above references as a prescriptive statement and conclude that women in Egypt were not usually excluded from the corporate Sabbath services or from other community activities held within the synagogues.

This conclusion gains support from the epigraphic and papyrological evidence from Egypt. As we saw in the previous chapter, an inscription from Athribis (*JIE* 28; II–I B.C.E.) states that "Hermias and his wife Philotera and their children" donated an exedra to the synagogue there. Another inscription of an unknown Egyptian provenance that probably dates to the first century C.E. reads, "Papous built the *proseuchē* on behalf of himself and his wife and children. In the 4th year, Pharmouthi 7."[69] Finally, it should also be recalled from the last chapter that a papyrus dating to third century B.C.E. relates that a certain Gentile woman pursued a thief into the *proseuchē* at Alexandrou-Nesos and had dealings there not only with the thief, but also with the *neōkoros* of the synagogue (*CPJ* 1.129). Taken together, these bits of evidence undermine the notion that the Egyptian synagogues excluded women from participation within the life of the local Jewish community. However, the evidence does not indicate that women served as synagogue functionaries, though they did serve as donors.

This seems to have been the general pattern around the diaspora. At Berenice in Cyrenaica, two women, Isadora and Zosime, are listed among the contributors to the repairs of the synagogue there, each donating five drachmae (*CJCZ* 72).[70] Two of the monuments from the Delos synagogue were offered by women, both in fulfillment of unspecified vows (*CIJ* 1.728, Laodike; 1.730, Marcia). Decrees from Halicarnassus and Sardis specify that both men and women were at liberty to observe their Sabbaths and perform their "sacred rites" in the synagogues (*Ant.* 14.256–258; 14.259–261). Julia Severa, an *archōn* of the city of Acmonia, donated the synagogue to the Jews there (*DF* 33). An inscription from Gorgippia in the Bosporus Kingdom states that a female slave named Chrysa was released in a manumission ceremony held in the synagogue (*CIJ* 1.690). Since the danger of anachronism is slim, we

---

[69]*JIE* 126: Παποῦς οἰκο|δόμηση τὴν|προσευχὴν| ὑπὲρ αὑτοῦ | καὶ τῆς <γ>υν-|αικὸς καὶ τ|ῶν τέκνων·| (ἔτους) δ´ Φαρμοῦθι <ζ>´.

[70]For a larger list of women donors to synagogues, see Brooten, *Women Leaders in the Ancient Synagogues*, 157–165. The above citations all date to our period; some are not included in Brooten's list.

might be forgiven for mentioning that an inscription from nearby Panticapaeum dating to just after our period (81 C.E.) relates that "Chreste, former wife of Drousus" released her slave Heraclas in the synagogue there (*CIJ* 1.683). Similarly, another inscription from Gorgippia (dated 59 C.E.), though badly mutilated, indicates that a Jewish woman manumitted a husband and wife in the synagogue (*CIJ* 1.690b). Finally, Acts refers to the presence of women in synagogues at Philippi (16:13–16), Thessalonica (17:1–9), Beroea (17:10–14), and Ephesus (18:24–26).

While none of these sources specifically mentions the separation of the sexes, Acts' portrayal of Paul's discussion with Lydia and the other women at the synagogue in Philippi suggests that the men and women normally sat together. On the other hand, because only women are depicted as gathering in the synagogue there, it may be that the author of Acts envisioned a Sabbath service scheduled for women only. Against this, however, it could be argued that Luke thought the Jewish population at Philippi so slight that he portrayed the synagogue congregation there as consisting entirely of Jewish women and female God-fearers.[71]

While the first-century phase of the Ostia synagogue displays no firm evidence that men and women were seated in separate rooms, the erection of the dividing wall in the assembly hall of the Delos synagogue suggests the conclusion that one section was reserved for men and the other for women. Despite Brooten's dismissal of this interpretation as arbitrary, it must be considered a serious possibility.[72] In any case, as we have noted, such an arrangement may be more indicative of Samaritan rather than Jewish customs. Our only clear evidence for the division of the sexes in a synagogue comes from Philo's writings about the practices of the Therapeutae. As we saw in chapter two, the women in their synagogue were separated from the men by a six-foot-high wall (*Contempl.* 32). Despite the fact that they were divided on their Sabbath gatherings, Philo depicts the men and women as commingling in the center of the banquet hall during their regular feasts in order to sing hymns of praise

[71]For additional consideration of this passage and the question of women's seating, see Mattila, "Where Women Sat in Ancient Synagogues," 275.

[72]Brooten, *Women Leaders in the Ancient Synagogues*, 123–124. Richardson, who writes that "absent from early synagogues was a separation between men and women" ("Early Synagogues as Collegia," 102) does not consider this possibility.

(*Contempl.* 85–88). We can only guess to what degree these customs reflected those held outside this specialized community.[73]

In summary, while there is no firm evidence for women functionaries in the synagogues of our period, women clearly served as participants within the Sabbath services and at other activities held within the synagogues. In some locales, it is possible that women may have been seated separately from the men or that they may have met at separate times for the weekly services. Epigraphic evidence from the diaspora also portrays women as donors to the synagogues and participants within manumission ceremonies. In general, the climate within the diaspora seems to have been more conducive for allowing women to assume more active roles within the synagogues. Paul Trebilco has suggested that the appearance in Asia of women *archontes*, gymnasiarchs and other public officials within the Gentile population during the first three centuries of our era may have paved the way for the acceptance of women leaders within the synagogues of that region.[74] More liberal inheritance laws for women in this period may also have played a role, permitting Jewish women to accumulate more wealth and independence.[75] This would have allowed them to serve increasingly as patrons of the local synagogues—one of the usual prerequisites for admission to a leadership position. Archaeologists may yet uncover evidence attesting to a woman synagogue functionary in our period. If and when this occurs, it is more likely that the discovery will be made outside of Palestine, since patriarchal attitudes among Jews seem to have been much stronger in the homeland than elsewhere.

---

[73]Again Philo is difficult to interpret. On the one hand, his detailing of the breastwork suggests that such structures were not common in Alexandria. On the other, his statement "for the women too regularly make part of the audience" implies that women did not customarily congregate with the men in the Sabbath services held in Alexandria. In any case, the claim that "among the Therapeutae, women were the virtual equals of men" (Richardson and Heuchan, "Jewish Voluntary Associations in Egypt and the Roles of Women," 236) hardly seems warranted in view of the fact that Philo does not mention that women held offices within the community (as he does for the men; e.g., *Contempl.* 31). See chapter seven's treatment of the Therapeutae, as well as S. G. Wilson, "Voluntary Associations: An Overview" in *Voluntary Associations*, edited by John S. Kloppenborg and Steven G. Wilson (London: Routledge, 1996), 12.

[74]See Trebilco, *Jewish Communities in Asia Minor*, 113–126.

[75]On the expansion of women's legal rights beginning in the late Republic and early Imperial period, see Eva Cantarella, *Pandora's Daughters* (Baltimore, Md.: Johns Hopkins University Press, 1981), 135–170.

EXCURSUS TWO: GOD-FEARERS IN THE SYNAGOGUES

As outlined in the introduction of this study, there has recently been a debate raging over the existence of the God-fearers (φοβούμενοι/σεβόμενοι τὸν θεόν), with scholars such as Thomas Kraabel maintaining that these Gentile sympathizers of Judaism are a Lucan literary invention.[76] Although the storm has now largely subsided and the overwhelming majority of scholars have accepted that Acts' portrayal of the God-fearer reflects historical reality, most recent treatments of this question have relied upon literary and epigraphic evidence from an era well beyond the Second Temple period.[77] In order to guard against anachronism, our consideration of this issue will limit itself to an investigation of sources contemporaneous with the earlier era.

We begin our treatment by observing that the notion of the "pious Gentile" is a very old one within Jewish tradition. Naaman the Syrian (2 Kgs 5) and the widow of Zarephath (1 Kgs 17:8–9) are the two most obvious figures that come to mind (cf. Luke 4:26–27). So is Cyrus the Persian, whom Second Isaiah calls "God's messiah" (Isa 45:1). Within our period, Gentiles are repeatedly portrayed as offering prayers and sacrifices in the Temple. For instance, Josephus claims that Alexander the Great, after his conquest of Palestine "went up to the temple, where he sacrificed to God under the direction of the high priest" (*Ant.* 11.336). Demetrius I of Syria, in a bid to gain support from the Hasmoneans, is said to have doled out 15,000 shekels each year for sacrifices in the Jerusalem Temple (1 Macc 10:40; Josephus, *Ant.* 13.55). Among the

---

[76]Kraabel, "The Disappearance of the 'God-Fearers'," 113–126; idem, "Synagoga Caeca: Systematic Distortion in Gentile Interpretations Of Evidence for Judaism in the Early Christian Period" in *"To See Ourselves as Others See Us": Christians, Jews, "Others" in Late Antiquity*, edited by Jacob Neusner and Ernest S. Frerichs (Chico, Calif.: Scholars Press, 1985), 226–232; idem, "The Roman Diaspora: Six Questionable Assumptions," *JJS* 33 (1982): 445–464; idem, "Afterward" in *Diaspora Jews and Judaism: Essays in Honor of, and in Dialogue with, A. Thomas Kraabel*, edited by J. Overman and R. MacLennan (Atlanta: Scholars Press, 1992), 347–357; MacLennan and Kraabel, "The God-Fearers—A Literary and Theological Invention," 46–53.

[77]E.g., Feldman, "The Omnipresence of the God-Fearers," 58–63; Overman, "The God-Fearers: Some Neglected Features," 145–152; Tannenbaum, "Jews and God-Fearers in the Holy City of Aphrodite," 44–57; Trebilco, *Jewish Communities in Asia Minor*, 145–166; *HJP* 3.1.150–176; Levinskaya, *The Book of Acts in Its Diaspora Setting*, 51–126; Max Wilcox, "The 'God-Fearers' in Acts—A Reconsideration," *JSNT* 13 (1981): 102–122; Gager, "Jews, Gentiles, and Synagogues in the Book of Acts," 91–99; Hemer, *The Book of Acts in the Setting of Hellenistic History*, 444–447.

Romans, Marcus Agrippa offered "ritually proper sacrifices to God and honoured Him with ritually proper prayers" (Josephus, *Ant.* 16.55; cf. 16.14; Philo, *Legat.* 291; 296–97). Likewise, Cestius, Legate of Syria, is said to have prostrated himself (προσκυνέω) before the Temple shrine from the Court of the Gentiles (Josephus, *BJ* 2.341), while one of his predecessors, Vitellius offered sacrifice with Herod Antipas in Jerusalem during one of the festivals (Josephus, *Ant.* 18.123). Finally, it will be recalled from earlier in this chapter that the chief priests, elders and Pharisees assembled just prior to the Jewish War to try to convince the Temple *stratēgos* and other renegade priests that the acceptance of Gentile gifts and sacrifices was established within their most ancient traditions (Josephus, *BJ* 2.411ff).

More broadly, there is an abundance of literary evidence depicting the attraction of Gentiles to Jewish laws and traditions. Josephus, for instance, states, "Many of [the Greeks] have agreed to adopt our laws; of whom some have remained faithful, while others, lacking the necessary endurance, have again seceded" (*Ap.* 2.124).[78] Similarly, Philo writes, "[Jewish customs] attract and win the attention of all, of barbarians, of Greeks, of dwellers on the mainland and islands, of nations of the east and the west, of Europe and Asia, of the whole inhabited world from end to end" (*Mos.* 2.20). To the objection that Josephus and Philo were also inventing the existence of such Gentile sympathizers to further their apologetic purposes, there is the following complaint of Seneca the Younger (4 B.C.E.–65 C.E.): "the customs of this accursed race [the Jews] have gained such influence that they are now received throughout all the world. The vanquished have given their laws to their victors."[79]

Aside from these sweeping statements, our sources also mention specific Gentiles or Gentile populations that had adopted Jewish customs. Thus Philo states that not only Jews "but multitudes of others" joined in the celebration of the Septuagint's composition, held annually on the Alexandria beachfront (*Mos.* 2.41–44). More to the north, the Gentile women of Damascus, according to Josephus, "with few exceptions, had all become converts to the Jewish religion [ἁπάσας πλὴν ὀλίγων

---

[78]For similar remarks by Josephus, see below and *Ant.* 3.217, 318–319; 20.34, 41, 195; *BJ* 2.454, 463; *Ap.* 2.282.

[79]*Cum interim usque eo sceleratissimae gentis consuetudo convaluit, ut per omnes iam terras recepta sit; victi victoribus leges dederunt* (Seneca, *De Superstitione*, ap. Augustine, *De Civitate Dei* 6.11). For a commentary on this text, see *GLAJJ* 1.431–432. If one wanted to go just beyond our period, evidence from pagan writers abounds. The most famous is Juvenal, *Sat.* 14.96–98.

ὑπηγμένας τῇ Ἰουδαϊκῇ θρησκείᾳ]" (*BJ* 2.561). This passage underscores the attraction of Judaism to women, who obviously were not required to undergo circumcision in order to become full proselytes, as most (though not all) Jews believed was necessary for Gentile males.[80] Yet even among women there seems to have been a distinction between God-fearers and proselytes. The latter were probably identified by their commitment to total abandonment of idolatry and adoption of Jewish traditions, perhaps in a formalized ritual. Josephus refers to such a convert as a proselyte, as when he mentions Fulvia, "a woman of high rank who had become a Jewish proselyte [προσεληλυθυῖαν τοῖς Ἰουδαϊκοῖς]" (*Ant.* 18.82). In contrast, he refers to Nero's wife Poppea—who obviously had commitments to other deities—as a *theosebēs*, a "worshiper of God." The women converts of Damascus mentioned above, however many they truly numbered, were probably a combination of God-fearers and proselytes, with the former undoubtedly constituting the majority.

We should further note that Josephus' word *theosebēs* is remarkably similar to one of Luke's expressions for the God-fearers, *sebomenoi ton theon* (Acts 16:14, 18:7). That the two terms should be identified with each other is seen in a passage from Josephus' writings where he employs exactly the same expression. Explaining to his Gentile readers the reason behind the Temple's wealth, Josephus writes, "But no one need wonder that there was so much wealth in our temple, for all the Jews throughout the habitable world, and *sebomenōn ton theon* [God-fearers], even those from Asia and Europe, had been contributing to it for a very long time" (*Ant.* 14.110).[81] From this reference it follows that the appearance of

[80]With respect to this question, Josephus records the interesting case of Izates, King of Adiabene in Mesopotamia, who desired to become a full proselyte by undergoing circumcision, but thought his subjects would object to his practice of this rite. His mother, Queen Helena (herself a convert), along with a certain Jewish merchant named Ananias, tried to convince him that this was not necessary for him. Subsequently, a Jew from Galilee named Eleazar argued against this position, persuading Izates to be circumcised (*Ant.* 20.17–48). Josephus agrees with the latter view.

[81]Θαυμάσῃ δὲ μηδεὶς εἰ τοσοῦτος ἦν πλοῦτος ἐν τῷ ἡμετέρῳ ἱερῷ, πάντων τῶν κατὰ τὴν οἰκουνένην Ἰουδαίων καὶ σεβομένων τὸν θεόν, ἔτι δὲ καὶ τῶν ἀπὸ τῆς Ἀσίας καὶ τῆς Εὐρώπης εἰς αὐτὸ συμφερόντων ἐκ πολλῶν πάνυ χρόνων. The omission of the definite article before "σεβομένων τὸν θεόν" could lead one to argue that the phrase refers to the Ἰουδαίων in the preceding clause. Ralph Marcus, however, notes, "in good Greek when two different classes are associated in some activity or state, the article is omitted before the noun which designates the second of the two classes" (Ralph Marcus, "The Sebomenoi in Josephus," *Jewish Social Studies* 14

sebomenoi ton theon in Acts does not denote a Lucan innovation, but reflects a wider usage.[82]

Josephus also supports Acts' depiction of the God-fearers in the synagogues, for in the sentence immediately following his description of the synagogue at Antioch, he writes, "[the Antiochian Jews] were constantly attracting to their religious ceremonies multitudes of Greeks [ἀεί τε προσαγόμενοι ταῖς θρησκείαις πολὺ πλῆθος Ἑλλήνων], and these they had in some measure incorporated with themselves" (*BJ* 7.45). In other words, while some had become full proselytes, others remained God-fearers. In view of this passage and the others depicting the God-fearers as common throughout the Roman Empire in the first century C.E., Luke can hardly be said to have invented their existence in synagogues at Pisidian Antioch (Acts 13:16, 26, 50), Philippi (Acts 16:14), Thessalonica (Acts 17:4), Athens (Acts 17:17), and Corinth (18:17). Even if one wants to be skeptical and deny the existence of one or more of these individual synagogues, Luke's portrayal of the God-fearers as a class found within the diaspora synagogues clearly reflects the actual circumstances of the period about which he was writing.

Aside from the passages in Acts, Kraabel does not examine or even cite any of the above literary references. In fact, Kraabel hardly mentions texts at all. This lacuna appears to be a consequence of his belief that "enough information has become available to permit fairly detailed reconstructions of Jewish life in the Diaspora which are based *entirely* on archaeological evidence."[83] Yet here it should be observed that even if we wanted, we could not divorce literary from archaeological evidence, since the former provides us with linguistic and historical information that is essential for the interpretation of the latter. Moreover, Kraabel has set up a questionable dichotomy between classes of evidence, pitting one against the other. To be sure, archaeological findings have helped us ameliorate

---

[1952]: 249). See also BDF §276. Trebilco further argues that taking the expression as a reference to the Jews would make the phrase ἔτι δὲ καὶ τῶν ἀπὸ τῆς 'Ασίας καὶ τῆς Εὐρώπης redundant since these would be included among those living κατὰ τὴν οἰκουνένην. Yet understanding ἔτι δὲ καὶ τῶν ἀπὸ τῆς 'Ασίας καὶ τῆς Εὐρώπης to be a reference to the God-fearers would make sense because it would have the meaning of "even those beyond neighboring Egypt and Syria." See Trebilco, *Jewish Communities in Asia Minor*, 147–148.

[82]Kraabel was apparently not aware of this passage, for he writes, "The precise word-combinations in Acts which are usually translated 'God-fearer' do not occur outside the New Testament at all, in Christian or Jewish texts" (*Synagoga Caeca*, 227).

[83]Kraabel, "The Disappearance of the 'God-fearers'," 115. Italics in original.

the biases of ancient authors and fill out the lacunae in their accounts. Yet this does not warrant the methodological strategy of denying the existence of phenomena attested in ancient literary accounts because they have not yet shown up in the archaeological record.

As it turns out, the recent God-fearer debate nicely illustrates this point. Following Kraabel's initial study of this subject, inscriptions attesting to the existence of the God-fearers at Aphrodisias (Asia Minor) and Sardis appeared in print.[84] Yet it should be noted that because the inscriptions date from the second to the fifth centuries C.E., their usefulness in addressing the question of the God-fearers in the Second Temple period is limited. Is there, then, additional epigraphic evidence from the earlier era to support the view presented within the literary record?

Actually, there are several inscriptions which suggest the existence of God-fearers in the synagogues.[85] We encountered one of these in our consideration of the synagogue at Athribis in the last chapter. There, we saw that an inscription from that city reads, "Ptolemy son of Epikydes, chief of police, and the Jews in Athribis (dedicated) the *proseuchē* to the Most High God" (*JIE* 27, II B.C.E.). Although it is possible that Epikydes was a member of the Jewish congregation, the possibility also exists that he was a God-fearer. Of course, even if he were a Gentile, he may simply have been a patron of the Jews in Athribis, like Julia Severa was for the Jewish community of Acmonia (*DF* 33) or Marcus Tittius was for that of Berenice (*CJZC* 71). In these latter instances, there are no obvious indications that the donors adopted Jewish customs. Indeed, Julia Severa's position as a priestess of the Imperial cult essentially rules out such an interpretation. Similar conclusions cannot be made in the case of Epikydes, however, since there was nothing in the office of chief of

---

[84]For the Aphrodisias inscription, see J. M. Reynolds and J. M. Tannenbaum, *Jews and God-fearers at Aphrodisias* (Cambridge: Cambridge Philological Society, 1987), 1–131. Kraabel became aware of this discovery only after writing the main body of his initial article on the subject; he briefly alludes to it in a note ("The Disappearance of the God-Fearers," 125, n. 26). While the catalogue containing the relevant Sardis inscriptions has not yet been published, the inscriptions can be found in Trebilco, *Jewish Communities in Asia Minor*, 158, 252 n. 60.

[85]We will not here review the epigraphic evidence for proselytes, which includes inscriptions from our period, though none directly associated with the synagogues. For a listing of these, see Pau Figueras, "Epigraphic Evidence for Proselytism in Ancient Judaism," *Immanuel* 24/25 (1990): 194–206. For a recent review of the literary evidence, see Levinskaya, *The Book of Acts in Its Diaspora Setting*, 19–49.

police (ἐπιστάτης τῶν πυλακιτῶν) which would have precluded him from adopting at least some Jewish customs.

If the Athribis inscription only suggests the existence of a God-fearer, a first-century C.E. manumission inscription from Panticapaeum provides more decisive evidence (*CIJ* 1.683a = *CIRB* 71):[86]

[- - -]α[- - -]κ̣α[- - -]
κου ἀφίημι ἐπὶ τῆς προσευχῆς Ἐλπία[ν ἐμ]α[υ]τῆς θρεπτ[ὸν]
ὅπως ἐστὶν ἀπαρενόχλητος
καὶ ἀνεπίληπτος ἀπὸ παντὸς
κληρονόμου χωρὶς τοῦ προσ-
καρτερεῖν τῇ προσευχῇ ἐπι-
τροπευούσης τῆς συναγω-
γῆς τῶν Ἰουδαίων καὶ θεὸν
σέβων

I free in the *proseuchē* Elpias, my household slave, so that he will be undisturbed and unassailable by any of my heirs, on condition that he show diligence towards the *proseuchē* under the guardianship of the congregation of the Jews, and reveres God.

The interpretation of this inscription has an interesting history. In the 1960s, H. Bellen and Baruch Lifshitz independently argued that *theon sebōn*, "reverences God," should be emended to read *theo{n}sebōn*, "God-fearers."[87] The reasons given for the emendation are twofold. First of all, Bellen thought that Elpias, a man's name, should be read as Elpis, a woman's name. This would require the emendation since *sebōn* is not in the feminine gender. Secondly, both Bellen and Lifshitz argued that the phrase *theon sebōn*, if read as a condition for the release, was grammatically awkward.

Since these arguments were first presented, most scholars have accepted the emendation and have concluded that the first-century synagogue at Panticapeum consisted of Jews and God-fearers.[88] However, more recently, Irina Levinskaya, who has worked closely with all the Bosporus inscriptions, has presented convincing arguments against the

---

[86]Author's translation. The transcription is from Levinskaya, *The Book of Acts in Its Diaspora Setting*, 74. Kraabel does not discuss this inscription.

[87]H. Bellen, "Die Aussage einer bosporanishen Freilassungsinschrift (*CIRB* 71) zum Problem der 'Gottfürchtigen'," *JAC* 8 (1965): 171–176; Baruch Lifshitz, "Notes d'épigraphie grecque," *RB* 76 (1969): 95–96.

[88]E.g., Trebilco, *Jewish Communities in Asia Minor*, 155–157; *HJP* 3.1.166.

above interpretation.[89] First of all, she points out that reading Elpis for Elpias would require yet another emendation (Ἐλπί<δ>α[ν] for Ἐλπια[ν]). Secondly, Levinskaya notes that the Bosporus inscriptions in general display poor grammar. Hence, the placement of *theon sebōn* at the end of the inscription is not at all unusual in the context of the grammatically loose Bosporan Greek. Thirdly, in other Bosporus inscriptions, two conditions were always given for the release: to be diligent in attending the synagogue (προσκαρτέρησις) *and* to show reverence towards it (θωπεία). If the emendation were accepted, then only one of the conditions normally set forth would be stipulated. On the other hand, the phrase *theon sebōn*, while differing from the usual term *thōpia* ("flatter" or "honor"), has essentially the same sense. Thus *theon sebōn* should be understood as the second condition usually imposed upon the released slave. Finally, Levinskaya points out that the term *theosebēs* has never been found in *any* Bosporus inscription, whether from a synagogue or elsewhere. Consequently, the emendation lacks a local parallel.

While Levinskaya's arguments undermine the interpretation of Bellen and Lifshitz, what is not usually noted is that the conditions of the release clearly indicate that Elpias was a Gentile, since there would have been no need to require Jews or proselytes to reverence God and attend the synagogue services.[90] Essentially, then, the above agreement requires Elpias to become a God-fearer. We should further note that four other inscriptions from Phanagoria and Panticapaeum make similar demands on at least eight more released slaves.[91] Consequently, we are not looking at an isolated case, but what appears to be a larger phenomenon.

While the epigraphic record from our period may not be geographically diverse, it nevertheless undergirds the literary attestations and argues that these latter should be accepted—taking into account, of course, that these probably contain some exaggerations in terms of overall numbers of God-fearers. We should also point out that there is no evidence directly stating that God-fearers were free to frequent the synagogues of Palestine. Nevertheless, because they were not barred from the outer precincts of the Temple and were allowed to offer sacrifices,

---

[89]See Levinskaya, "The Inscription from Aphrodisias and the Problem of God-Fearers," 312–318; idem, *The Book of Acts in Its Diaspora Setting*, 74–76.

[90]See Trebilco, *Jewish Communities in Asia Minor*, 155–157.

[91]*CIJ* 1.683, 684, 691; Levinskaya, *The Book of Acts in its Diaspora Setting*, 237–238, no. 6. The two inscriptions from Panticapaeum date to just after our period (80, 81 C.E.). See the discussion of manumission in the next chapter.

there is little reason to doubt that they were also permitted in the synagogues of Palestine. Josephus in general makes this point clear:

> The consideration given by our legislator [Moses] to the equitable treatment of aliens also merits attention. It will be seen that he took the best of all possible measures at once to secure our own customs from corruption, and to throw them open ungrudgingly to any who elect to share them. To all who desire to come and live under the same laws with us, he gives a gracious welcome, holding that it is not family ties alone which constitute relationship, but agreement in the principles of conduct. On the other hand, it was not his pleasure that casual visitors should be admitted to the intimacies of our daily life (*Ap.* 2.210).

The last sentence is probably a reference to the prohibition against allowing non-proselytes from eating the Passover meal (Exod 12:43). The passage thus implies that God-fearers who had not fully converted, while barred from sharing the Passover, were welcome in the synagogues, whether in Palestine (where Gentiles were the aliens) or the diaspora. As this statement and the other pieces of literary and epigraphic evidence noted above suggest, the God-fearers appear to have been a common fixture of the synagogues of our period, just as they were commonly found within the Temple courts in Jerusalem.

CHAPTER 6
SYNAGOGUE FUNCTIONS

In the ancient Greco-Roman world, religious activity was not confined to a narrow, privatized sphere, but was all-pervasive, touching politics, warfare, family life and just about everything else within the realm of human endeavor. Thus the Roman emperor was not merely the emperor, he was also the *Pontifex Maximus* or high priest of the nation. Likewise, Roman legions as a matter of policy traveled with *augures* or priests who took the auspices before battles or other major events. And, of course, temples were to be found everywhere, both within the city and throughout the countryside.

Consonant with the ancient conception of the interplay between religion and human activity, the temples and sacred areas were not merely for the offering of prayer and sacrifice; rather, they formed the centers around which all civic activities transpired. As we observed in chapter three, forums and agoras were dotted with temple shrines, with the former serving as spatial extensions of the latter, for they too were dedicated to the deities. Indeed, these city squares of various design derived their sanctity from the temples, since the gods were believed to have resided inside the shrines.[1] Such an arrangement was meant to procure the favor of the gods upon the various civic activities conducted within the city squares.[2] Thus, for instance, he Roman Senate customarily met within one of the capital's temples, typically the temple of Apollo Palatinus or the temple of Concordia.[3] In a previous chapter we saw that Augustus convened a council at the former of these sanctuaries to deliberate over the various claims to Herod's throne (Josephus, *BJ* 2.80ff, *Ant.* 17.301). Elsewhere, the temple of Castor in the forum served as the office of the Roman consuls, who erected a podium in front of the building from

---

[1]On the ancient beliefs about the gods residing in the temples, see Burkert, "The Meaning and Function of the Temple in Classical Greece," 29–36.

[2]This, of course, was the dominant view. Certain groups such as the Epicureans held a different view of the gods—at least in philosophical discourse.

[3]See Stambaugh, "The Functions of Roman Temples," 580–581.

whence they conducted official business on a daily basis.[4] Trials were held within the temple of Mars Ultor, and public documents were displayed in the temples of Jupiter and Fides.[5] As for commerce, the forums served as extensions of the various temples, each of which were typically associated with a particular segment of the market. For example, the booksellers plied their trade near the temple of Peace in Rome, while state-sanctioned wine was sold in the porticoes of the temple of Sol.[6] Rome's state treasury was inside the temple of Saturn in the forum, leading bankers to conduct their business in the sacred area of this temple.[7] The temples also served as cultural centers, housing trophies of war, votive statues, and libraries. Augustus' library, for instance, was housed in several rooms adjoining the temple of Apollo Palatinus.[8]

In placing their civic activities in and around temples, the Romans were essentially imitating their Greek counterparts, who had long before adopted such customs. Functionally, the Greek agora with its various temples mirrored the Roman forum in nearly every way: temples and their adjoining stoas served as treasuries, markets, civic meeting places, public archives, and so forth.[9] In the eastern half of the Mediterranean, we see the same pattern emerging following the conquests of Alexander the Great. As argued in chapter three, the Hellenization of Palestine led to the movement of the city civic center away from the city gate and into the agora. In Jerusalem, this meant that the Temple courts became the primary civic center for the city, with the Temple shrine serving as the house of the Jewish Deity (e.g., 1 Kgs 8:17; Ezra 6:3). In this way, the sanctity of the Holy of Holies extended outward into the surrounding areas, consecrating the activities therein.

In the present chapter we will analyze the various functions associated with the synagogues, comparing them to those exercised within the sacred

---

[4]Cicero, *De Har. Resp.* 28; *Pro Sestio* 79. See Stambaugh, "The Functions of Roman Temples," 582.

[5]Suetonius, *Claudius* 33. See Stambaugh, "The Functions of Roman Temples," 581–582.

[6]Ovid, *Fasti* 4.791–792; Aurelianus, 48.4. See Stambaugh, "The Functions of Roman Temples," 585. This last explains why in Rome some Jewish Christians (and Jews, no doubt) refrained from drinking wine (Rom 14:21).

[7]*CIL* 14.153. See Stambaugh, "The Functions of Roman Temples," 586.

[8]See Stambaugh, "The Functions of Roman Temples," 586–587.

[9]See Susan Guettel Cole, "Greek Cults" in *Civilizations of the Ancient Mediterranean: Greece and Rome*, edited by Michael Grant and Rachel Kitzinger (New York: Charles Scribner's Sons, 1988), 2.887–888.

precincts of the Jerusalem Temple. We have, of course, touched on many of these functions in previous chapters. Here, however, we will treat them in greater depth, adding new data to our analysis. The examination will reveal that the synagogues, like the ancient temples, served as centers for a variety of religious and civic activities. In particular, we will see that these functions were strikingly similar to those associated with the courts of the Jerusalem Temple—the chief difference being the substitution of prayer, Torah study and sacrificial giving for animal sacrifice. These similarities will further suggest that the synagogues of the Second Temple period served as distant sacred precincts of the central Jewish shrine.

The discussion will proceed topically, either grouping related functions under one heading or clustering them in proximity to each other. A brief conclusion will summarize the results of the investigation.

PLACES OF RITUAL BATHING

We begin our study at the place where synagogue visits in antiquity appear to have begun: near a river, sea, cistern, well, or immersion pool. The importance of purity laws to Jews is well-known and can hardly be overstated. What is not usually recognized, however, is that many Gentiles also adhered to some form of purity requirements, at least on certain occasions. As early as Homer, mention is made not only of the cleansing of hands before prayer or sacrifice, but of purifying an army after an epidemic in order to turn aside the wrath of Apollo.[10] Thus in the *Iliad* Hector states, "In no way can a man pray to Zeus spattered with blood and filth."[11] Consonant with this sentiment, preparation for entry into Greek temples usually involved dipping the hands into a fountain or special basin (*perirrantērion*) that was placed outside the sacred precinct and sprinkling oneself with water.[12] Sacrificers were typically required to wear clean, white garments and in some instances were further purified by a priest who sprinkled them with a mixture of water and ashes, the latter taken from the altar itself.[13]

As usual, the Romans adopted these same customs from the Greeks, adding to them their own purification festivals, such as the *armilustrium*, a rite held in the temple of Mars each October whereby the sacred armor

---

[10]Homer, *Il.* 1.313–314. See Burkert, *Greek Religion*, 75–84.
[11]Homer, *Il.* 6.267.
[12]E.g., Philo, *Cher.* 94–95. See Burkert, *Greek Religion*, 77.
[13]See Cole, "Greek Cults," 888; Burkert, *Greek Religion*, 77.

and shields of the temple were cleansed and restored in their places until the next year.[14] In both cultures, special purification rites were required for persons and objects that had come into contact with a corpse.[15]

What therefore separated Jews from the larger Greco-Roman milieu in this regard were the particularities of their own laws and the rigor with which some Jews applied them. The Essenes were the extremists, with many of them attempting to live in a state of purity equivalent to that of priests or Levites on duty in the Temple.[16] Though uncertainty exists about the details, the Pharisees also clearly adhered to more rigorous purity requirements than the masses.[17]

The Jewish masses, however, also obeyed purity laws. This is particularly seen in passages referring to the requirements for entry into the Temple's inner courts. For example, Josephus states that during the Jewish War, the Zealot faction had gained control of the Temple's inner and outer courts. When the party of Ananus stormed the Temple mount and dislodged the Zealots from the outer court, they retreated into the Court of Women and barred the gates behind them. Josephus writes that Ananus decided not to press the attack further because "[he] considered it unlawful, even were he victorious, to introduce these crowds without previous purification" (*BJ* 4.205). The Zealots, as usual, are cast as the unscrupulous villains who polluted the Temple's sacred area.

Such was not normally the case, however. All Jews were required to undergo certain purification rites before entry into the Temple's inner courts. Among those excluded were Jews declared lepers (Josephus, *Ant.* 3.261–264), those who had been in recent contact with a corpse (*Ant.* 4.79–81), menstruants (*Ant.* 3.261; *Ap.* 104), and women who had recently given childbirth (*Ant.* 4.79–81). In addition, men who had had a nocturnal emission or intercourse were required to purify themselves "by plunging into cold water" and waiting for sunset before entering the Temple (*Ant.* 3.263). It is likely that total immersion was the norm for

---

[14]See Stambaugh, *The Functions of Roman Temples*, 573; idem, *The Ancient Roman City*, 218, 222; Lesley Adkins and Roy A. Adkins, *Handbook to Life in Ancient Rome* (New York: Facts on File, 1994), 265, 286.

[15]Burkert, *Greek Religion*, 79–80; Stambaugh, *The Ancient Roman City*, 160–161.

[16]See, e.g., *HJP* 2.568–571; E. P. Sanders, *Judaism*, 359–360.

[17]From our period, see e.g., Mark 7:2–5; Matt 23:25–26; Luke 11:38–39. Generally, see Neusner, *From Politics to Piety*, 78–96; E. P. Sanders, *Jewish Law from Jesus to the Mishnah*, 131–254; *HJP* 2.475–478.

everyone prior to entry, as suggested by the large number of pools surrounding the Temple mount.[18]

While it is widely recognized that purity laws were enforced in the Temple, most scholars have failed to make the connection between purification rituals and the synagogues. Joan Branham, for example, states that, in contrast to the Temple, "ritual purity . . . [was] not required in the synagogue."[19] Such an unqualified assertion, however, does not take full account of the literary and archaeological evidence. As we have seen, wherever synagogues from our period have been found in Palestine, either immersion pools or natural bodies of water are located nearby. Likewise, the Theodotus inscription pointedly mentions the construction of "water installations [τὰ χρηστήρια τῶν ὑδάτων]" near the synagogue. These were possibly the *mikvaoth* found adjacent to the discovery site, as suggested in chapter two.

While ritual baths are of various design, the "basic model" consists of stairs descending to the base of a rock-hewn pool deep enough to allow total immersion (c. 2 m).[20] In most cases, the *mikvaoth* uncovered by archaeologists were built to collect undrawn water, often from a channel leading from a spring or from beneath a nearby roof where rainwater collected. This custom appears to have been based on a literal interpretation of Leviticus 11:36 which states that a person could be purified in either a spring (מַעְיָן) or a cistern containing "flowing waters" (בּוֹר מִקְוֵה־מַיִם; cf. Lev 15:13).[21] During the dry season, when rain was not sufficient to fill the pool, sometimes water from a nearby reservoir known as an *otsar* ("treasury") was released through a connecting pipe. Some examples of *mikvaoth* have neither a reservoir nor a channel and thus appear to have been filled with drawn water.[22] Unless there was some sort of plumbing arrangement in these that is no longer extant, then this type

---

[18]For the various water installations on the Temple mount, see Shimon Gibson and David M. Jacobson, *Below the Temple Mount in Jerusalem* (Oxford: Tempvs Reparatvm, 1996). Philo also mentions that worshipers could not enter the Temple area "until they have bathed and purged themselves with purifying water according to the customary rites" (*Spec*. 3.89).

[19]Branham, "Vicarious Sacrality: Temple Space in Ancient Synagogues," 330.

[20]For detailed treatments of the *mikvaoth*, see Reich, "The Synagogue and the *Miqweh* in Eretz-Israel," 289–297; idem, "Ritual Baths" in *OEANE* 4.430–431; E. P. Sanders, *Jewish Law from Jesus to the Mishnah*, 217–219; idem, *Judaism*, 224–229.

[21]See E. P. Sanders, *Jewish Law from Jesus to the Mishnah*, 215.

[22]Ibid., 219. It is also possible in these cases that a pipe that no longer survives led from a rooftop cistern.

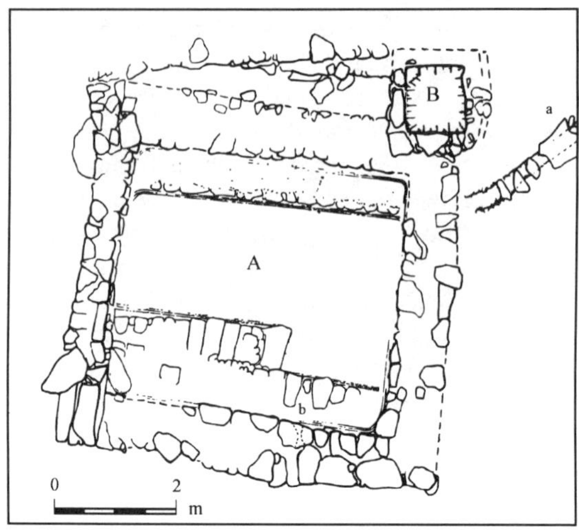

Figure 19. Ritual bath at Gamla. Rainwater was channeled from beneath the synagogue roof by a conduit (a), entering the *mikveh* (A) at point *b*. An *otsar* (B) stored water for use during dry periods. (After plan by Hagit Tahan, Gamla Excavations.)

of *mikveh* is evidence for a diversity of opinion in Palestine about what constituted water acceptable for ritual bathing.

The discovery of *mikvaoth* throughout Palestine presents evidence that many Jews took purity laws seriously not only during festivals in Jerusalem, but also at other times. This particularly seems to have been the case in connection with the synagogues of our period, since *mikvaoth* have been routinely found nearby, suggesting that Jews immersed themselves before entry into the synagogues. Such a conclusion gains further support from a passage in 2 Maccabees which states that upon coming to the city of Adullum, Judas Maccabaeus and his army "[ritually] purified themselves according to the custom, and kept the sabbath there [κατὰ τὸν ἐθισμὸν ἁγνισθέντες αὐτόθι τὸ σάββατον διήγαγον]" (2 Macc 12:38). Because 2 Maccabees was written about a century after the events it describes, the reference may be anachronistic. Yet even in this case, the passage presents literary attestation for the custom of washing in preparation for the Sabbath by the first century B.C.E.[23]

[23]See Goldstein, *II Maccabees*, 447–448.

This custom appears to have been maintained in the diaspora as well. In contrast to Palestinian practices, however, diaspora Jews seem to have made greater use of natural bodies of water for purification rituals, probably for the simple reason that rivers and seas were more often found in or near the cities of the diaspora than those of semi-arid Palestine. As we observed in chapter three, no *mikvaoth* were discovered near the synagogue at Capernaum since none were needed with the Sea of Galilee nearby.

Thus while *mikvaoth* have not yet been found in the diaspora, examples of synagogues from our period are attested near natural bodies of water, including those at Arsinoë-Crocodilopolis, Philippi, Halicarnassus, Delos and Ostia.[24] Indeed, Acts 16:13 states that Paul and his company went to a riverside because that was where they supposed the *proseuchē* was located (παρὰ ποταμὸν οὗ ἐνομίζομεν προσευχὴν εἶναι). Likewise, a decree from Halicarnassus permitted the Jews in that city to build *proseuchai* near the sea "in accordance with their native custom [κατὰ τὸ πάτριον ἔθος]." Most scholars have taken these passages to be allusions to biblical purity requirements.[25] The presence of a well and basin outside the main entrance of the Ostia synagogue similarly suggests that the members of the congregation customarily washed or sprinkled themselves before entering the building, since their placement parallels that of the *perirrantēria* situated near the entry of Gentile sacred areas.[26] The stone water basin just outside the main entrance of the Delos synagogue may have functioned similarly.

This appears to have been the practice in Alexandria, as the following statement from Philo's writings indicates:

> For to whom should we make thank-offering save to God? and wherewithal save by what He has given us? for there is nothing else whereof we can have sufficiency. God needs nothing, yet in the exceeding greatness of His beneficence to our race [πρὸς τὸ γένος ἡμῶν] He bids us bring what is His own. For if we cultivate the spirit of rendering thanks and honour to Him, we shall be pure from wrongdoing and wash away the filthiness which defiles our lives in thought and word and deed. For it is absurd that a man should be forbidden to enter the *hiera* save after bathing and cleansing his body [καὶ

[24]*CPJ* 1.134 (Arsinoë-Crocodilopolis), Acts 16:13–16 (Philippi), Josephus, *Ant.* 14.256–258 (Halicarnassus). It is also possible that cisterns were used for ritual baths, since one was found inside the Delos synagogue. See chapter four, above.

[25]See Sukenik, *Ancient Synagogues in Palestine and Greece*, 49–50; Greeven, "Προσευχή," 808; Levine, "The Second Temple Synagogue," 13.

[26]See Cole, "Greek Cults," 888; Burkert, *Greek Religion*, 77.

> γὰρ εὔηθες εἰς μὲν τὰ ἱερὰ μὴ ἐξεῖναι βαδίζειν, ὃς ἂν μὴ πρότερον λουσάμενος φαιδρύνηται τὸ σῶμα], and yet should attempt to pray and sacrifice [εὔχεσθαι δὲ καὶ θύειν] with a heart still soiled and spotted. The *hiera* are made of stones and timber, that is of soulless matter, and soulless too is the body in itself. And can it be that while it is forbidden to this soulless body to touch the soulless stones, except it have first been subjected to lustral and purificatory consecration, a man will not shrink from approaching with his soul impure the absolute purity of God and that too when there is no thought of repentance in his heart? He who is resolved not only to commit no further sin, but also to wash away the past, may approach with gladness: let him who lacks this resolve keep far away, since hardly shall he be purified. For he shall never escape the eye of Him who sees into the recesses of the mind and treads its inmost shrine (*Deus.* 7–9).

Scholars have typically maintained that Philo is referring to pagan temples in this passage.[27] Yet this is because they are not accustomed to the notion that *hieron*, when used in a Jewish context, can refer to a synagogue. Such is manifestly the case in the above passage, which forms a commentary on Numbers 28:2, "My gifts, My offerings [δόματά μου], My fruits ye shall observe to bring to Me" (*Deus* 6). First of all, Philo's audience is clearly Jewish because he refers to God's beneficence to "our race" (τὸ γένος ἡμῶν). Secondly, he is obviously not alluding to the Jerusalem Temple as *hieron* is in the plural. Thirdly, Philo is not criticizing Gentile behavior since he goes on to bid his Jewish readers to cleanse their hearts and then enter the *hiera*—by which he can scarcely have meant pagan temples.[28] Finally, the use of *thyein*, which normally means "to sacrifice," can also be taken as a reference to any religious ritual—particularly in a Jewish context.[29] In view of the passage from Numbers mentioning various donations, it possibly refers to the presentation of a votive offering.[30] Philo's exhortation to his readers is therefore that they should enter the presence of God not only outwardly cleansed, but also inwardly purified—a notion that is also found in earlier Jewish and Greek writings (e.g., Ps 51:17; Plato, *Phdr.* 224 de). Whereas

---

[27]E.g, E. P. Sanders, *Judaism*, 230.

[28]For Philo's strong words against the worship of idols, see, e.g., *Contempl.* 3–9.

[29]LSJ, s.v., θύω. Note, for example, that the decree from Sardis used similar language, authorizing the Jews there to "offer their ancestral prayers and sacrifices to God [ἐπιτελῶσι τὰς πατρίους εὐχας καὶ θυσίας τῷ θεῷ]" (Josephus, *Ant.* 14.260). Likewise, Philo elsewhere speaks of a woman going to a *hieron* so that she can offer her sacrifices and prayers (θυσίας ἐπιτελοῦσα καὶ ευχάς; *Spec.* 3.171).

[30]It is interesting that the later dedicatory inscription from Ostia (*JIWE* 1.13) uses one of the key words (δόμα) found in the verse upon which Philo is commenting.

the earlier allusions locate the divine presence within temples, Philo, on the other hand, locates it within the synagogues.

A passage from the *Letter of Aristeas*, while not mentioning the synagogues, echoes this same sentiment. The narrator of the tale depicts the translators of the LXX as beginning their workday in the following manner:

> Following the customs of all the Jews, they washed their hands in the sea in the course of their prayers to God, and then proceeded to the reading and explication of each point. I asked this question: "What is their purpose in washing their hands while saying their prayers?" They explained that it is evidence that they have done no evil, for all activity takes place by means of the hands. Thus they nobly and piously refer everything to righteousness and truth (*Ep. Arist.* 305–306).[31]

While it is doubtful that basins of water were set aside for every person in the Alexandrian synagogues to wash their hands as they prayed, the passage may reflect the custom of dipping one's hands in such a basin placed near the gateway of the complexes prior to entry. As we have seen, this was the common practice of Greeks and Romans before entering their sacred areas; Philo's allusion and the presence of the basins outside the entrances of the synagogues at Ostia and Delos suggest that the Jews in Alexandria, Ostia, Delos and elsewhere imitated this custom either in addition to or in lieu of the traditional Jewish immersions.

Beyond the contours of the above evidence, we cannot say in every case how strictly Jews in either Palestine or the diaspora applied the purity laws of the Temple to the synagogues. We do not know if menstruants or women who had recently given childbirth were excluded. Nor do we know in every instance if persons with corpse impurity were admitted to the synagogues. The case of Tiberias suggests that there may have been some laxity on this last point: when Antipas began building the city, he discovered the remains of an ancient cemetery on the site. He nevertheless enticed Jews to live there with grants of land—a policy that earned Josephus' disapproval, as he calls such a settlement "contrary to the law and tradition of the Jews . . . [since] our law declares that such

---

[31]Josephus renders this: "after washing their hands in the sea and purifying themselves [καὶ τῇ θαλάσσῃ τὰς χεῖρας ἀπονιπτόμενοι καὶ καθαίροντες αὑτοὺς], [they] would betake themselves in this state to the translation of the laws" (*Ant.* 12.106). Cf. Homer, *Od.* 2.260, where Telemachus is presented as having "washed his hands in the grey seawater" immediately before praying to Athena.

settlers are unclean for seven days" (*Ant.* 18.38). Hence, the Tiberian Jews clearly did not forbid entry into their synagogue on the basis of corpse impurity, though the other purity laws may have been observed. Josephus' reproach suggests that the situation in Tiberias, however, was atypical for Palestine.

Corpse impurity may also have been tolerated in the diaspora synagogues, since our sources imply that the ashes of the red heifer used in the purification rites were stored in Jerusalem (Num 19:2; Josephus, *Ant.* 4.80; Philo, *Spec.* 1.268).[32] Unless these were sent out to the diaspora for use by the priests there, the diaspora Jews probably adopted other cleansing rites from the surrounding milieu. The book of Tobit (II B.C.E.), for instance, portrays the protagonist—who lived in Nineveh—as washing himself after retrieving the corpse of a fellow Jew who had been strangled in the agora (Tob 2:4). Later, he sleeps in his courtyard in order to prevent his house and everyone in it from being defiled (Tob 2:9; cf. Num 19:14–15).[33] Although Tobit is presented as the model of the pious Jew, such purificatory cleansings were common in the Near East. It is likely that diaspora Jews generally performed some sort of similar ritual, particularly in view of the fact that many of them took great pride in being more pious than their Gentile neighbors. It is also possible that the enormous sums our sources depict being transported to Jerusalem (e.g., Cicero, *pro Flacc.* 68) represented not only the half-shekel tax, but also payments for various purification sacrifices (e.g., Lev 12:6–8; cf. Luke 2:22–24).

In summary, while we must currently remain in the dark about the exercise of specific purity statutes, the literary and material evidence adduced above indicates that some degree of purity was required in the Second Temple synagogues of Palestine and the diaspora. These requirements appear to have been similar to those connected with the entry into both Gentile sacred areas (*hiera*) and the precincts of the Jerusalem Temple. Such parallels further support the hypothesis that the

---

[32]Numbers, Philo and Josephus only specify that the ashes were to be kept outside of the camp or city in a pure place. It is not inconceivable that the ashes could also have been stored in appropriate sites about the diaspora. On the other hand, Acts 21:24–27 depicts Paul purifying himself for seven days after returning from his missionary work in the diaspora. John 11:55 also states that Jews went up from Galilee to Jerusalem ahead of time to purify themselves in preparation for the Passover. These passages imply that one could only be cleansed from corpse impurity in Jerusalem.

[33]For commentary, see Carey A. Moore, *Tobit* (Garden City, N.Y.: Doubleday, 1996), 3–64, 125–136.

pre-70 synagogues served as consecrated edifices connected to the central Jewish shrine.

The Reading and Exposition of Scripture

That the synagogues of our period served as gathering places for the reading and exposition of scripture need hardly be defended: literary, epigraphic and archaeological evidence uniformly support this proposition.[34] In part, we can attribute the frequent appearance of this function in our sources to the distinctiveness of this Jewish custom. To be sure, other religions had their sacred writings. These documents, however, were typically reserved for the priests and were never read in public. As Josephus was quick to point out to his Gentile readers, Jews did not "make a secret of the precepts" to which they adhered, but published them openly among the people (*Ant.* 16.43). Nor can the Jewish scriptures be compared with the various philosophical writings debated by groups such as the Stoics. To the Jews, the Pentateuch contained the very word of God. Most also accepted the divine status of the prophetic books and the Writings. In this shared worldview, an accurate knowledge of the laws and traditions contained in these scriptures was essential for maintaining a right relationship with God.

Such a system demanded a high degree of personal responsibility: ignorance could not be used as an excuse. Therefore sometime early in our period (if not before), the custom arose of using the Sabbath as an assembly time for instruction in the Law. Ezra's reading of the Torah at the rededication of the Temple probably served as the model (Neh 8:9). Thereafter, not only was this practice repeated every Sabbatical year at a grand festival held first at the Water Gate (Neh 8:1) and later in front of the Temple (1 Esdr 9:38; Josephus, *Ant.* 4.209–210), it was also renewed every *seventh day* in local assemblies that eventually met in synagogue buildings. Thus when first-century Jews professed that *Moses* had decreed that the scriptures should be read and studied on the Sabbath (Josephus, *Ap.* 2.175; Philo, *Opif.* 128; Acts 15:21), they probably had in mind the commandment of Deut 31:10–13, which merely prescribes the septennial reading of the Torah. The law was thereby extended both temporally and spatially so that the weekly synagogue assemblies served as microcosms of the larger, national convocation.

---

[34] E.g., *CIJ* 2.1404; Josephus, *Ant.* 16.43–45, *Ap.* 2.175; Philo, *Somn.* 2.123–129; Luke 4:16–30; the scriptures found inside the Masada synagogue (see chapter three).

Another extension of the Torah-reading ceremony was the addition of a reading from the Prophets.[35] Thus in 2 Maccabees (I B.C.E.), we find a passage in which Judas Maccabaeus exhorts his army with words "from the law and the prophets [ἐκ τοῦ νόμου καὶ τῶν προφητῶν]" (2 Macc 15:9).[36] The book of 4 Maccabees presents the same view, as it depicts the protagonist's husband as a teacher "of the law and the prophets" (4 Macc 18:10).[37] The recitation of the prophetic writings in the synagogues is made most explicit in Luke 4:16–21, which portrays Jesus reading from the book of Isaiah in the synagogue at Nazareth:

> When he came to Nazareth, where he had been brought up, he went to the synagogue on the sabbath day, as was his custom. He stood up to read, and the scroll of the prophet Isaiah was given to him. He unrolled the scroll and found the place where it was written: "The Spirit of the Lord is upon me, because he has anointed me to bring good news to the poor. He has sent me to proclaim release to the captives and recovery of sight to the blind, to let the oppressed go free, to proclaim the year of the Lord's favor." And he rolled up the scroll, gave it back to the attendant [ὑπηρέτῃ], and sat down. The eyes of all in the synagogue were fixed on him. Then he began to say to them, "Today this scripture has been fulfilled in your hearing."

Though this scene is a Lucan composition, its portrayal of the Isaiah reading appears to reflect accurately the practice of reading from the prophets in the synagogues of first-century Palestine, as several other New Testament authors—including Paul—make reference to the "law and the prophets" in their arguments (e.g., Rom 3:21, John 1:45, Matt 5:17, 7:12, 11:13 [|| Luke 16:16 = Q], 22:40).[38] The discovery of the Ezekiel scroll in the Masada synagogue further solidifies this claim. Indeed, because scroll fragments of Sirach, *Jubilees* and the *Songs of the Sabbath Sacrifice* were also found at Masada, passages from writings such as these

---

[35]Even the Sadducees appear to have accepted the Prophets as authoritative: the statements of later Christian sources to the contrary (e.g., Origin [*Contra Celsum* 1.49] and Jerome [*In Mat.* 22:29]) find no support from Josephus, who merely states that the Sadducees rejected non-written regulations (*Ant.* 13.297). The Sadducees' denial of the resurrection most likely stemmed not from a rejection of the Prophetic books, but from taking certain passages in them metaphorically rather than literally (e.g., Isa 26:19; Dan 12:2). See *HJP* 2.408–409; E. P. Sanders, *Judaism*, 332–336; Saldarini, *Pharisees, Scribes and Sadducees*, 229–308.

[36]For commentary, see Goldstein, *II Maccabees*, 497.

[37]See Anderson, "4 Maccabees," 531–543.

[38]For a review of the critical issues surrounding the above passage, see Fitzmyer, *The Gospel According to Luke*, 1.525–540.

may also have been read (or sung as hymns) in the Palestinian synagogues.[39]

Despite his accuracy on this point, Luke exercises some artistic freedom in his depiction of the synagogue scene in the above passage. First of all, he omits the reading of the Torah, which almost certainly came before the reading of the Prophets, as all our sources imply (e.g., Josephus, *Ap.* 2.175). Secondly, because Luke was written in Greek, the passage quoted from Isaiah, of course, follows the Septuagint. Still, Luke does not indicate to the reader that the scriptures were read in their original language. While there were undoubtedly some Greek-speaking synagogues in Palestine, they almost certainly would *not* have been located in a village such as Nazareth where Aramaic was commonly spoken. Even so, the reading most likely would have been given in Hebrew rather than Aramaic, since the former was the original language of the texts. The fact that *all* of the scroll fragments of biblical texts uncovered at Masada were written in Hebrew rather than Aramaic supports this conclusion.[40] A final liberty taken in the above segment is that the reading quoted from Isaiah is not a continuous passage, but the splicing together of portions of Isaiah 61:1–2 with a segment from 58:6. Although this combination of verses served Luke's rhetorical purposes

---

[39]See Yadin, "The Excavation of Masada 1963/64," 81–82.

[40]It should also be noted that Hebrew is the language of the overwhelming bulk of the biblical scrolls found in the Qumran excavations. While some scholars have argued for the presence of Aramaic Targums in the synagogues, Perrot rightly points out that we lack early evidence linking the Targums to the recitation of scripture in the synagogues. The statement in Neh 8:8 that Ezra and the Levites "read from the law of God clearly [מְפֹרָשׁ]" need not be understood as the giving of a translation. (The LXX simply states that Ezra read and "taught" [διδάσκω] the people.) It should also be noted that the overwhelming bulk of the Targums are from a later period. The only contemporary examples we have are from Qumran (4Q156, 11QtgJob, 4Q157), and their *Sitz im Leben* is difficult to ascertain. See Charles Perrot, "The Reading of the Bible in the Ancient Synagogue" in *Mikra,* edited by M. Mulder and H. Sysling (Philadelphia: Fortress Press, 1988), 155–156; John Westerdale Bowker, *The Targums and Rabbinic Literature; An Introduction to Jewish Interpretations of Scripture* (Cambridge: University Press, 1969), 14–16; Avigor Shinan, "The Aramaic Targum as a Mirror of Galilean Jewry" in *The Galilee in Late Antiquity*, edited by L. Levine (New York: Jewish Theological Seminary of America, 1992), 241–251; Steven D. Fraade, "Rabbinic Views on the Practice of Targum" in *The Galilee in Late Antiquity*, edited by L. Levine (New York: Jewish Theological Seminary of America, 1992), 253–286. For the older view, see, e.g., *HJP* 1.99.

nicely, it is highly unlikely that the ancient lectors would have jumped around within the scroll from section to section.[41]

Outside of Palestine, a few differences existed in the reading practices of the diaspora synagogues. Chief among these was the use of the Septuagint for the sacred scriptures.[42] Most scholars reject the historicity of the account given in the *Letter of Aristeas*, which maintains that LXX was the product of seventy-two translators sent to Alexandria by the High Priest. Alternative theories for the origins of the LXX have been advanced, the most attractive of which was that it rose to meet the liturgical needs of the Alexandrian Jews within their synagogues.[43] In support of this view is the observation that the *Letter of Aristeas* mentions only the translation of the Pentateuch, which would have been the first thing needed within the synagogues. Indeed, because Philo focuses his treatises solely upon the books of the Pentateuch and merely alludes to the reading of the Law in the synagogues (*Hypoth.* 7.11–14), it may be that *only* the Law was recited in the Egyptian synagogues, even up to the first century.[44] This is somewhat conjectural, however, since Philo also makes use of the Prophets and the Writings within his works.[45] Whether or not the Prophets were recited in the Sabbath services in Egypt, elsewhere in the diaspora both appear to have been read, as Acts 13:15 states that Paul was invited to address the congregation at Pisidian Antioch "after the reading of the Law and the Prophets [μετὰ . . . τὴν ἀνάγνωσιν τοῦ νόμου καὶ τῶν προφητῶν]."[46]

Following the readings, a leader (Philo, *Hypoth.* 7.11–14) or other member of the congregation (Mark 6:1–5; Acts 17:1–9) would begin the

---

[41]For a review of the evidence for lectionaries in our period, see Charles Perrot, *La lecture de la Bible dans la synagogue: les anciennes lectures palestiniennes du Shabbat et des fetes* (Hildesheim: Gerstenberg, 1973); idem, "The Reading of the Bible in the Ancient Synagogue"; idem, "Les lectures de la synagogue," *Foi et Vie* 82 (1983): 16–22.

[42]For a review of the critical issues connected with the LXX, see Emanuel Tov, "The Septuagint" in *Mikra,* edited by M. Mulder and H. Sysling (Philadelphia: Fortress Press, 1988), 161–187.

[43]See e.g., H. St. J. Thackeray, *The Septuagint and Jewish Worship*, 2nd ed. (London: H. Milford, 1923).

[44]See Perrot, "The Reading of the Bible in the Ancient Synagogue," 151–152.

[45]We might also note that by no later than the end of the second century B.C.E., the Prophets and most of the Writings had also been translated, since they were known to the grandson of Ben Sirach (Sir, Greek prologue).

[46]Paul also makes reference to the Law and the Prophets in the arguments he presents to the Roman Christians (Rom 3:21), some of whom were Jewish.

commentary on the scriptures, employing various midrashic techniques.[47] Our sources indicate that the other members of the congregation were not passive participants in this process. On the contrary, the exchanges in the synagogues are presented as being quite animated, often heated. Thus Acts presents Paul as constantly "arguing" (διαλέγομαι) in the synagogues (17:2, 17:17, 18:4, 18:19, 19:8) and states that Apollos "spoke boldly" (παρρησιάζομαι) before the congregation in Ephesus (18:26). Within these accounts, sometimes members of the congregation argued back (Acts 18:6), other times they expressed their approval (Acts 17:11) or disapproval (Mark 6:2–3). Occasionally they became enraged and cast the speaker out (Luke 4:28–29). While stylized, these pericopae nevertheless suggest that the process of interpreting scripture was a community affair, and it was not for the fainthearted. Even the phlegmatic Philo, though trying to paint a serene image of the synagogue proceedings in his descriptions, has to add that the members of the congregation participated in the discussion (*Hypoth.* 7.13, *Somn.* 2.127). Archaeology can contribute to the picture, for the seating arrangement in the synagogues of our period clearly facilitated the exchanges envisioned by the ancient authors. In each case, the placement of the benches cast the focus on the center of the hall, where opinions would meet and dialogue ensue.[48]

While it is commonly recognized that the reading and exposition of scripture took place in the synagogues, not as widely appreciated is the fact that such midrashic discussions also took place within the Temple courts in Jerusalem. This point is nicely illustrated in Paul's statement to Felix (as crafted by Luke) that his accusers "did not find me disputing with anyone in the temple or stirring up a crowd either in the synagogues or throughout the city" (Acts 24:12). Elsewhere in the New Testament, Jesus is depicted as teaching in the Temple (e.g., Mark 12:35, 14:49; John 7:14, 28; 8:2, 20), as are Peter and John (Acts 5:21, 25, 42) and various Jewish leaders (1 Esdr 9:49; Luke 2:46). Josephus even depicts an Essene sage surrounded by his disciples within the Temple (*BJ* 1.78–80; *Ant.* 13.311).

---

[47]For a detailed study of these techniques, see, e.g., Neusner, *What Is Midrash? And, A Midrash Reader*; Gary G. Porton, *Understanding Rabbinic Midrash: Texts and Commentary* (Hoboken, N. J.: Ktav, 1985); Peder Borgen, *Bread from Heaven* (Leiden: E. J. Brill, 1965); William Richard Stegner, "The Ancient Jewish Synagogue Homily" in *Greco-Roman Literature and the New Testament: Selected Forms and Genres*, edited by D. Aune (Atlanta: Scholars Press, 1988), 51–69.

[48]On this point, see Richardson, "Synagogues as Collegia," 102–103.

In addition, the Temple courts were likely the assembly place for many Jerusalemites and pilgrims on the Sabbath, since from there the beginning and the end of the Sabbath were always announced by the blowing of the trumpet (Josephus, *BJ* 4.582–583). Moreover, the Temple also served as the repository for the sacred writings (Josephus, *Ant.* 2.346, 3.28, 303, 5.61). Indeed, Josephus states that "a copy of the Jewish Law" was the last of the Temple spoils to appear in the triumph following the Jewish War, occupying the place of honor (*BJ* 7.150). Doubtless it was given frequent public readings within the Temple courts, though our sources are silent concerning its recitation there on the Sabbath.

It is therefore incorrect to categorize the Temple as "the place of the cult" on the one side, and the synagogue as "the place of the scroll" on the other. As we observed at the beginning of this section, our sources *do* indicate that the septennial Torah reading ceremony took place on the Temple mount at the end of our period, and it was Ezra's first enactment of this custom that probably provided the inspiration for the weekly meetings on the Sabbath to read and discuss scripture. Again, the synagogues formed in miniature what the Temple courts constituted on a grander scale.

PRAYER

While nearly all scholars recognize that the synagogues functioned as assembly places for the reading and explication of scripture, a number of scholars have recently argued or asserted that prayer was not an activity found within the synagogues until after the destruction of the Temple. As we observed in the introduction of this study, Heather McKay is the leading advocate of this position, though it should be pointed out that she confines her studies to the examination of communal prayer as a *Sabbath* activity, concluding that "there is no unequivocal evidence that the sabbath was a day of worship for non-priestly Jews certainly as far as the end of the second century of the common era."[49] Lee Levine is both narrower and more comprehensive in his claims on this subject, for while he concedes that prayer was found within the synagogues of the diaspora, he asserts that aside from the Dead Sea scrolls, "there is no reference in Palestinian sources to the existence of organized communal prayer" in the synagogues prior to 70 C.E. and that "only after the destruction of the Second Temple did the synagogue in Palestine develop and expand as a

---

[49] McKay, *Sabbath and Synagogue*, 251.

place of worship."[50] Meanwhile, Steven Fine and Eric Meyers, in the recently published *Oxford Encyclopedia of Archaeology in the Near East* (1996), state "Communal prayer is not presented as a function of synagogues before 70 CE."[51] In our examination of this topic, we will find reason to question this widely held view, for the early sources clearly attest to the presence of individual and communal prayer as an activity on the Sabbath and on other days within the synagogues of both Palestine and the diaspora.

We begin our discussion by noting the prevalence of prayer and sacrifice within the ancient Near East. A typical pattern is that the king or high priest would pray on behalf of the people and then direct the offering of the sacrifice. Thus on the morning of the triumph following the Jewish War, Vespasian "rose and, covering most of his head with his mantle, recited the customary prayers [εὐχας . . . τὰς νενομισμένας], Titus also praying in like manner" (Josephus, *BJ* 7.128). Immediately after a breakfast with the troops, they "donned their triumphal robes and sacrificed to the gods [θύσαντες θεοῖς]" (*BJ* 7.131). Similarly, at the dedication of the First Temple, Solomon is said to have recited a long prayer after which "fire came down from heaven and consumed the burnt offering and the sacrifices; and the glory of the LORD filled the temple" (2 Chr 7:1). Later, after the lapse of the Davidic monarchy when the High Priest assumed the leadership roles previously held by the king, Philo viewed the ideal High Priest as "a ruler [who] dispenses justice to litigants according to the law, who day by day offers prayers and sacrifices [εὐχας . . . καὶ θυσίας] and asks for blessings" (*Spec.* 3.131).

It was not only the leader who prayed before the sacrifices: all of the people would customarily join in, often prostrating themselves before God. Thus in 1 Chronicles 29:20 when David commanded the people to bless the Lord, "all the assembly blessed the LORD, the God of their ancestors, and bowed their heads and prostrated themselves [προσεκύνησαν/וַיִּשְׁתַּחֲוּו] before the LORD and the king." The same scene repeats itself in nearly every book of the Hebrew Bible. Moses and Aaron bless the people, who fall to the ground as fire consumes their sacrifices (Lev 9:24). Elijah calls down fire from heaven to take up his sacrifice, and the people fall on their faces in worship (1 Kgs 18:39). Ezra opens the scroll of the Law and blesses the multitude and all the people answer "'Amen, Amen,' lifting up their hands" and then bowing their faces to the

[50]Levine, "Synagogues," 1421.

[51]Fine and Meyers, "Synagogues," 118.

ground (Neh 8:6; cf. 1 Esdr 9:47). The scene continues to punctuate the books of the Apocrypha (Jdt 4:11; 1 Macc 4:55; 2 Macc 1:23, 2:10, 3:11; 3 Macc 1:24, 5:50; Sir 50:19) and the writings of Josephus (*Ant.* 7.381, 9.269–270). Moving into the New Testament, according to Luke's portrayal, while Zechariah was offering incense inside the Temple shrine, "the whole assembly of the people was praying outside [πᾶν τὸ πλῆθος ἦν τοῦ λαοῦ προσευχόμενον ἔξω]" in the Court of Israel (Luke 1:10).[52]

Against such a backdrop, even if our sources made no explicit mention of prayer and worship within the synagogues, we would have reason to suspect that prayers were being offered there. If even Gentiles could begin their public assemblies with prayer and sacrifice as automatically as we today sing the national anthem before a sporting event, how much more would Jews have incorporated prayer within their weekly synagogue gatherings?[53]

Fortunately, we need not rest our case on such an *a fortiori* argument, for our sources are not at all silent on this matter. We begin our examination in the diaspora, where we have already encountered evidence for the use of prayer in the synagogues at several junctures in our study. In chapter two we observed how the term *proseuchē*, the most frequent word for synagogues in the diaspora, went from meaning "prayer" to "place of prayer" through the process of metonymy. Thus not only was prayer an element of synagogue gatherings in the diaspora, but it was the *defining element* of the diaspora synagogues, for Jews there took the very name of their buildings from the central activity exercised therein. This activity is made explicit in one of the decrees from Sardis that we encountered in chapter four. The decree stated "that a place [τόπος] be given [the Sardian Jews] in which they may gather together with their wives and children and offer their ancestral prayers and sacrifices to God [ἐπιτελῶσι τὰς πατρίους εὐχὰς καὶ θυσίας τῷ θεῷ]" (Josephus, *Ant.* 14.260). The decree goes on to resolve that "permission shall be given them to come together on stated days to do those things which are in accordance with their laws [συγκεχωρῆσθαι αὐτοῖς συνερχομένοις ἐν ταῖς

---

[52]For additional discussion of the place of prayer in the Temple courts, see Menahem Haran, "Priesthood, Temple, Divine Service: Some Observations on Institutions and Practices of Worship," *HAR* 7 (1983): 121–135; idem, "Temple and Community in Ancient Israel" in *Temple in Society*, edited by Michael V. Fox (Winona Lake: Eisenbrauns, 1988), 17–25. Haran agrees that the prayers offered in the Temple courts were later imitated in the synagogues.

[53]On prayer at the beginning of the sessions of the Athenian *ekklēsia* and *boulē*, see Aeschines, 1.2.3; Thucydides, 8.70; Antiphon, 6.45.

προαποδεδειγμέναις ἡμέραις πράσσειν τὰ κατὰ τοὺς αὐτῶν νόμους], and also that a place [τόπον] shall be set apart by the magistrates for them to build and inhabit, such as they may consider suitable for this purpose" (*Ant.* 14.261).[54] The mention of "stated days" clearly refers to Sabbath assemblies.

While the Sardis decree obviously refers to communal "prayer and sacrifice," it is interesting that Philo uses almost identical language when speaking about *individual* prayer within the synagogues. Thus he refers to the ideal woman discretely making her "sacrifices and prayers [θυσίας ἐπιτελοῦσα καὶ εὐχάς]" in the synagogue (*hieron*) after the agora has closed (*Spec.* 3.171), and to the absurdity of a person cleansing only the exterior before entering a synagogue (*hieron*) to make "prayers and sacrifices [εὔχεσθαι δὲ καὶ θύειν]" (*Deus.* 7–9).[55] The references to "making sacrifice," of course, cannot refer to animal or incense offerings, since these were expressly forbidden outside the Temple, and we have no indications whatsoever that the Jews of Alexandria or Sardis disobeyed these strictures. Therefore, *thyō* must be understood more broadly as "ritual," and may have included prostrations, chanting, and the rendering of votive offerings. This extended sense of "sacrifice" is already seen in Psalm 141:2 (140:2, LXX) which states, "Let my prayer be counted as incense before you, and the lifting up of my hands as an evening sacrifice [κατευθυνθήτω ἡ προσευχή μου ὡς θυμίαμα ἐνώπιόν σου ἔπαρσις τῶν χειρῶν μου θυσία ἑσπερινή/תִּכּוֹן תְּפִלָּתִי קְטֹרֶת לְפָנֶיךָ מַשְׂאַת כַּפַּי מִנְחַת־עָרֶב]." Philo adheres to this view, for while commenting on Temple sacrifices, he makes the following remarks:

> Though the worshippers bring nothing else, in bringing themselves they offer the best of sacrifices, the full and truly perfect oblation of noble living [αὑτοὺς φέροντες πλήρωμα καλοκἀγαθίας τελειότατον τὴν ἀρίστην ἀνάγουσι θυσίαν], as they honour with hymns and thanksgivings [ὕμνοις καὶ εὐχαριστίαις] their Benefactor and Saviour, God, sometimes with the organs of speech, sometimes without tongue or lips, when within the soul alone their minds recite the tale or utter the cry of praise (*Spec.* 1.272; cf. 1.195–197).

It is likely that Philo had the situation of the diaspora synagogues in mind when he wrote the above words: in the synagogues, it was one's noble

---

[54]On the use of *topos* as a word for the synagogue, see chapter two.

[55]For a more detailed examination of *Spec.* 3.171, see the treatment of *hieron* in chapter two. *Deus.* 7–9 is treated more fully in this chapter's examination of ritual bathing, above.

behavior as expressed in hymns of praise and thanksgiving that represented one's sacrifice.

A more vivid example of such expressions of praise is met in Philo's account of the celebration of the Feast of Tabernacles in Alexandria in 38 C.E. While this was normally a joyous occasion, Philo states that in this particular year, none of the customary celebrations were being held on account of Flaccus' measures against the Jewish community. With their *archontes* jailed and their synagogues seized, the people huddled in their homes in a depressed state. In the midst of this despair, news arrived in the middle of the night that Flaccus had been placed under arrest. Still in their homes, families responded "with hands outstretched to heaven," singing hymns and songs of triumph all night long (*Flacc.* 121). Philo goes on to paint the following scene of the activities ensuing at daybreak:

> At dawn pouring out through the gates, they made their way to the parts of the beach near at hand, since their *proseuchai* had been taken from them, and standing in the most open space cried aloud with one accord "Most Mighty King of mortals and immortals, we have come here to call on earth and sea, and air and heaven, into which the universe is partitioned, and on the whole world, to give Thee thanks [εὐχαριστίαν]. They are our only habitation, expelled as we are from all that men have wrought, robbed of our city and the buildings within its walls, public and private, alone of all men under the sun bereft of home and country through the malignancy of a governor. Thou givest also a glimpse of cheering hopes that Thou wilt amend what remains for amendment, in that Thou hast already begun to assent to our prayers [λιταῖς]. For the common enemy of the nation, under whose leadership and by whose instruction these misfortunes have befallen it, who in his pride thought that they would promote him to honour, Thou hast suddenly brought low; and that not when he was afar off, so that they whom he ill-treated would hear it by report and have less keen pleasure, but just here close at hand almost before the eyes of the wronged to give them a clearer picture of the swift and unhoped-for visitation" (*Flacc.* 122–124).

Of interest here is not only the moving expression of corporate thanksgiving so skillfully recreated by Philo, but his comment that the people chose the beach as a gathering place "since their *proseuchai* had been taken from them [τὰς γὰρ προσευχὰς ἀφῄρηντο]." In other words, had the Alexandrian Jews been in possession of their *proseuchai*, these "places of prayer" would have served as the venues for such expressions of praise, as was customary.

Commenting on this passage, McKay, while conceding that its "language of praise and thanks to God is typical of similar thanksgiving hymns in the Psalms," nevertheless goes on to characterize the episode "as a 'one-off' response to a particular perceived intervention of God."[56] In view of Philo's representation of the *proseuchai* as the usual gathering places for such corporate expressions, and of the other evidence adduced above, McKay's subsequent conclusion that "regular sabbath worship is a far cry from an unusual ceremony like this"[57] is unconvincing.[58]

McKay offers a similar interpretation of an episode transpiring within one of the Palestinian synagogues, specifically, the *proseuchē* at Tiberias.[59] The scene takes place during the first year of the Jewish War, when Josephus' leadership was being opposed by some of the Tiberians, including Jesus son of Sapphias, the city *archōn*. Jesus had already convened two council meetings in the synagogue to deal with the matter, one on the Sabbath and one on the following day. Josephus himself was present at the second of these councils and reports that as the meeting was drawing to a close, a certain Ananias proposed that they all return to the synagogue the next day (Monday), unarmed, in order to conduct a public

---

[56]McKay, *Sabbath and Synagogue*, 69–70.

[57]Ibid., 70.

[58]Other data attesting to the place of prayer in the diaspora synagogues include: (1) an inscription from Alexandria may have mentioned that a *proseuchē* was dedicated "for the great God who listens to prayer [θεῷ[ιμε]γάλωι ἐ[πηκό]ωι]" (*JIE* 13, I B.C.E.; the reconstruction presented in *JIE* is based upon parallels with similar pagan dedications); (2) Philo refers to the synagogues as "schools . . . of piety [διδασκαλεῖα . . . εὐσεβείας]"; this last term is typically connected to the exercise of religious ritual (*Mos.* 2.216; also *Hypoth.* 7.13; see the discussion below); (3) a letter quoted by Josephus, purportedly written by Onias IV, refers to the "forms of worship [θρησκείας]" of the Egyptian synagogues (*Ant.* 13.66; the Greek term denotes cultic services typically involving prayer [LSJ s.v. θρησκεία]; see the discussion of the Egyptian synagogues in chapter four); (4) a decree from Halicarnassus refers to the "sacred services to God [αἱ εἰς τόν θεὸν ἱεροποιίαι]" held in the synagogues there and permits the Jews to "observe their Sabbaths and perform their sacred rites [τά τε σάββατα ἄγειν καὶ τὰς τὸ ἱερὰ συντελεῖν] in accordance with the Jewish laws" (Josephus, *Ant.* 14.256–258); the terms employed usually refer to ritual proceedings (LSJ s.v. ἱεροποιία, συντέλεια); (5) likewise, an official letter to Miletus instructs the citizens there to allow the Jews to "observe their Sabbaths [and] perform their native rites [τά τε σάββατα ἄγειν καὶ τὰ ἱερὰ τὰ πάτρια τελεῖν]" (*Ant.* 14.244–246); (6) immediately after describing the synagogue at Antioch, Josephus states that the Jews there "were constantly attracting to their religious ceremonies multitudes of Greeks [ἀεί τε προσαγόμενοι ταῖς θρησκείαις πολὺ πλῆθος Ἑλλήνων]" (*BJ* 7.45; on the language employed, see no. 3 above). While the practices of the Therapeutae will be considered separately in the next chapter, we should mention that they too exercised communal prayer and hymn singing in their synagogue (Philo, *Contempl.* 64–89).

[59]McKay, *Sabbath and Synagogue*, 84.

fast (πανδημεὶ νηστείαν; *Vita* 290). According to Josephus, Ananias said this "not from motives of piety [οὐ δι' εὐσέβειαν], but in order to catch me and my friends in this defenseless condition" (ibid.).[60] This charge was inspired, no doubt, by his later discovery that Jesus had subsequently sent a message to another of Josephus' enemies, John of Gischala, urging him to come with his troops to Tiberias the next morning to seize their opponent. Josephus goes on to describe the next day's assembly in the following terms:

> On the following day I ordered two of my bodyguard, of the most approved valour and staunch loyalty, to accompany me, with daggers concealed under their dress, for self-defense in the event of an assault on the part of our foes. I wore a breastplate myself and, with a sword so girt on so as to be as little conspicuous as possible, entered the *proseuchē*. Orders having been given by Jesus, the chief magistrate, who kept a watch on the door himself, to exclude all my companions, he allowed only me and my [two] friends to enter. We were proceeding with the ordinary service and engaged in prayer [ἤδη δ' ἡμῶν τὰ νόμιμα ποιούντων καὶ πρὸς εὐχὰς τραπομένων], when Jesus rose and began to question me about the furniture and uncoined silver which had been confiscated after the conflagration of the royal palace, asking who had the keeping of them [ἀναστὰς ὁ Ἰησοῦς περὶ τῶν ληφθέντων ἐκ τοῦ ἐμπρησμοῦ τῆς βασιλικῆς αὐλῆς σκευῶν [καὶ] τοῦ ἀσήμου ἀργυρίου ἐπυνθάνετό μου, παρὰ τίνι τυγχάνει κείμενα]. He raised this point merely in order to occupy the time until John's arrival (*Vita* 294–295).

An extended debate ensued, with Josephus' bodyguards hurrying him out of the building when the leaders of the opposition party finally tried to lay hands on him just prior to John of Gischala's arrival.

McKay argues that the above scene does not constitute a true form of ordered, communal prayer since it "could be interrupted for such matters" as those raised by Jesus.[61] E. P. Sanders holds a similar view, writing, "While Josephus was making his morning devotions in the synagogue in Tiberias, someone addressed him."[62] However, the Loeb translation cited above needs revising. The sentence containing the allusion to the prayer service is introduced by a genitive absolute clause containing two participles. While the first of these, *poiountōn* ("proceeding"), is a present participle, the second, *trapomenōn* ("engaging"), is an aorist. Such a

---

[60]On the significance of the term εὐσέβεια, see below.

[61]McKay, *Sabbath and Synagogue*, 81.

[62]E. P. Sanders, *Judaism*, 207. Sanders nevertheless accepts that prayers were customarily offered in the synagogues.

construction requires that the clause be taken in a punctiliar sense in relationship to the main verb of the sentence, in this case *epunthaneto* ("began to question").[63] Thus the first part of the sentence in question should be translated, "When we had performed the customary service and had engaged in prayer, Jesus rose and began to question me." This translation is further indicated by the context, for Jesus would have needed to delay Josephus until John's arrival only if the prayer portion of the assembly had already drawn to a conclusion.

The significance of the term *nomima*, translated "ordinary service" above, must also be recognized. This word carries the sense of "customary," "traditional," even "legal." It appears frequently in the LXX where it usually translates the Hebrew *ḥuqqat*, "statutes" (e.g., Exod 12:14, 27:21; Lev 3:17, 10:9; Num 18:8). Josephus uses the word earlier in *Life* when he refers to the Pharisees as having "the reputation of being unrivalled experts in their country's *nomima*" (*Vita* 191; cf. *Ant.* 8.128, 18.344). By choosing this word in reference to the proceedings inside the Tiberian synagogue, Josephus means to suggest that some well-established order of worship was followed. Unfortunately, we must remain in the dark as to its exact content.

While one might object, as McKay does, that the above episode took place on a Monday and so was therefore in no way indicative of normal *Sabbath* activities,[64] two passages left unexplored by McKay strongly suggest that prayer was as much a Sabbath activity within the synagogues of Palestine as it was within those of the diaspora. The first is a passage from the writings of Agatharchides of Cnidus, a Greek historian of the second century B.C.E. Although we lack complete volumes of

---

[63]See C. F. D. Moule, *A Idiom Book of New Testament Greek*, 2nd ed. (Cambridge: Cambridge University Press, 1959), 100–101; Stanley E. Porter, *Idioms of the Greek New Testament* (Sheffield: JSOT Press, 1992), 184. The closest parallel in the NT is Luke 2:42–43: <u>ἀναβαινόντων</u> <u>αὐτῶν</u> κατὰ τὸ ἔθος τῆς ἑορτῆς <u>καὶ</u> <u>τελειωσάντων</u> τὰς ἡμέρας, ἐν τῷ ὑποστρέφειν αὐτοὺς ὑπέμεινεν Ἰησοῦς ὁ παῖς ἐν Ἰερουσαλήμ, "They went up according to the custom of the feast, and when they had completed the days and began to return, the boy Jesus remained in Jerusalem." Both Moule and Porter delineate the genitive absolute clause here as having a punctiliar relationship to the main verb. Porter, for instance, writes, "The Present participle is used to refer to an action which occurred before the action referred to using the aorist participle" (op. cit., 184). According to Porter, the aorist within the genitive absolute was commonly used as a transitional device in extra-biblical Greek to summarize the event as complete (Stanley E. Porter, *Verbal Aspect in the Greek of the New Testament, with Reference to Tense and Mood* [New York: Peter Lang, 1989], 370).

[64]McKay, *Sabbath and Synagogue*, 84.

Agatharchides' extensive writings, Josephus preserves the following fragment in his *Contra Apion*:

> The people known as Jews, who inhabit the most strongly fortified of cities, called by the natives Jerusalem, have a custom of abstaining from work every seventh day; on those occasions they neither bear arms nor take any agricultural operations in hand, nor engage in any other form of public service, but pray with outstretched hands in the *hiera* until the evening [ἀλλ' ἐν τοῖς ἱεροῖς ἐκτετακότες τὰς χεῖρας εὔχεσθαι μέχρι τῆς ἑσπέρας]. Consequently, because the inhabitants, instead of protecting their city, persevered in their folly, Ptolemy, son of Lagus, was allowed to enter with his army; the country was thus given over to a cruel master, and the defect of a practice enjoined by law was exposed. That experience has taught the whole world, except that nation, the lesson not to resort to dreams and traditional fancies about the law, until its difficulties are such as to baffle human reason (Agatharchides ap. Josephus, *Ap.* 1.209–211).[65]

Agatharchides' mention of the Jerusalem *hiera* is likely a reference to synagogues since the word is in the plural.[66] Because Agatharchides wrote about the events of thc fourth century B.C.E. and from a diaspora perspective (he sojourned in Egypt), we might suspect that his account is tainted by both anachronism and provincialism. However, we should observe that Josephus' subsequent comments imply that *he himself* believed that Agatharchides accurately reflected Jewish customs:

> Agatharcides finds such conduct ridiculous; dispassionate critics will consider it a grand and highly meritorious fact that there are men who consistently care more for the observance of their laws and for their religion than for their own lives and their country's fate [εἰ καὶ σωτηρίας καὶ πατρίδος ἄνθρωποί τινες νόμων φυλακὴν καὶ τὴν πρὸς θεὸν εὐσέβειαν ἀεὶ προτιμῶσιν] (*Ap.* 1.212).

It should be added that the phrase *tēn pros theon eusebeian*, simply translated "religion" above, is better rendered "piety toward God." The

[65]For commentary on this passage and a discussion of Agatharchides, see *GLAJJ* 1.104–109; Whittaker, *Jews and Christians*, 67–68.

[66]Shaye Cohen argues that this was a reference to the synagogues, as do a number of other authors. See Cohen, "Pagan and Christian Evidence on the Ancient Synagogue,"162–163; E. P. Sanders, *Judaism*, 203; Levine, "The Second Temple Synagogue," 13.

key term *eusebeia* ("piety") commonly denoted a reverent attitude expressed in prayers, prostrations, and other ritual acts.[67]

The second passage to be considered comes from *Biblical Antiquities*, which originated in Palestine and was almost certainly written prior to the destruction of the Temple:

> Take care to sanctify the sabbath day. Work for six days, but the seventh day is the sabbath of the Lord. You shall not do any work on it, you and all your help, except to praise the LORD in the assembly of the elders and to glorify the Mighty One in the council of the older men. [*Conserva diem sabbati sanctificare eum. Sex diebus fac opera, septima autem dies sabbatum Domini est. Non facies in eo omne opus, tu et omnis operaio tua, nisi ut in ea laudes Dominum in ecclesia presbiterorum et glorifices Fortem in cathedra seniorum*] (*Bib. Ant.* 11.8).[68]

The rewording is a conflation of the Fourth Commandment (Exod 20:8–11) with Psalm 107:32, "Let them extol him in the congregation of the people, and praise him in the assembly of the elders [וִירֹמְמוּהוּ בִּקְהַל־עָם וּבְמוֹשַׁב זְקֵנִים יְהַלְלוּהוּ]." It thus not only suggests that prayer and worship were normal activities in the Sabbath assemblies of first-century Palestine, but also illustrates how the psalms could be used to illuminate the pentateuchal text.

The above review of the evidence should be sufficient to demonstrate that communal and individual prayer were commonly practiced within the synagogues of both Palestine and the diaspora during the Second Temple period.[69] In view of the larger Near Eastern context, this should come as

---

[67]See LSJ s.v. εὐσέβεια; Werner Foerster, "εὐσέβεια" in *TDNT* 7.175–185; Burkert, *Greek Religion*, 272–275; E. P. Sanders, *Judaism*, 190–195. Note that Josephus uses this term when referring to the public fast held in the Tiberian synagogue (*Vita* 291; see above).

[68]Harrington's translation.

[69]A final piece of evidence attesting to the place of prayer in the synagogues of Syro-Palestine is the following statement in Matthew 6:5: "And whenever you pray, do not be like the hypocrites; for they love to stand and pray in the synagogues and at the street corners, so that they may be seen by others [καὶ ὅταν προσεύχησθε, οὐκ ἔσεσθε ὡς οἱ ὑποκριταί, ὅτι φιλοῦσιν ἐν ταῖς συναγωγαῖς καὶ ἐν ταῖς γωνίαις τῶν πλατειῶν ἑστῶτες προσεύχεσθαι, ὅπως φανῶσιν τοῖς ἀνθρώποις]." While this is an independent Matthean tradition and may therefore be anachronistic, it nevertheless assumes that individual prayer commonly took place in the synagogues no later than c. 85 C.E. McKay does not agree: "This [passage] does not make clear, as has been assumed, that prayer was a commonplace action in synagogues; it may even point to the reverse conclusion, that is, that praying did not normally take place in the

no surprise since the exercise of prayer was universal during our period. As we observed in the first part of this section, Gentile worshipers frequented the temples throughout the Greco-Roman world, offering their prayers and sacrifices to the gods. As we also saw in the passages cited earlier, the Jews formed no exception to this wider phenomenon, for they also had their Temple where they presented their prayers and sacrifices. Within the synagogues, the only difference was that sacrifices were prohibited. Consequently, it would seem that prayers and other unspecified rituals served as the sacrifices of the worshipers within the synagogues (Philo, *Spec.* 1.195–197, 272; see above). This correspondence helps us understand why synagogue assemblies are attested for not only the Sabbath, but also for other days sacred to the cult, such as the New Moon and the Feast of Tabernacles.[70] Since special sacrifices were offered in the Temple on these days, the Jews not able to attend these festivals were still able to offer their prayers within the synagogues at the same time the offerings were being made in the main sanctuary.

In addition to serving as a venue for communal prayers on the Sabbaths, our sources suggest that the synagogues remained available during the rest of the week for individual prayers (Philo, *Spec.* 3.171; Matt 6:5). Such was also the case for the Jerusalem Temple, where both individual worshipers are portrayed as offering prayers and/or prostrations in addition to or in place of sacrifices (Josephus, *BJ* 1.74; 2.341, 2.443; *Ant.* 10.29, 16.55, 20.49; Philo, *Legat.* 291; 296–97). Accordingly, Josephus, embellishing the biblical account of Exodus 25:8ff, represents Moses as saying to the Israelites that the Tabernacle was to be built so that "when we move elsewhere we may take this with us and have no more need to ascend to Sinai, but that He himself,

---

synagogue. For there is something to be criticised about the way the hypocrites pray . . . Something must make synagogues and streetcorners, as locations for prayer, different from *both* the Temple and one's private room—and that can only be the factor of an audience who might marvel and gawp at one's prayers. So, it looks as if praying in a synagogue was just as ostentatious and odd as praying at a street corner, and not at all the normal practice of the true worshipper" (*Sabbath and Synagogue*, 172; emphasis in original). A difficulty with this line of reasoning is that there was also an audience in the *Temple* to gawp at one's prayers (e.g., Luke 18:10–14). While the practices of the Essenes will be examined in the next chapter, we should note that they also clearly engaged in communal prayer (e.g., Josephus, *BJ* 2.128–133).

[70]*CJZC* 70–71. Note here how this even extended into private prayer, as can be seen in Judith's custom of praying at the time of the morning and evening sacrifices in the temple (Jdt 9:1, 12:6).

frequenting the tabernacle, may be present in our prayers [ἀλλ' αὐτὸς ἐπιφοιτῶν τῇ σκηνῇ παρατυγχάνῃ ταῖς ἡμετέραις εὐχαῖς]" (*Ant.* 3.101). Of course, when the Temple later replaced the Tabernacle, the former's fixed location in effect transformed it back into Sinai, so that Jews again, either literally or figuratively, had to ascend the Holy Mountain. As "places of prayer," the synagogues appear to have facilitated this ascent, allowing worshipers throughout the world to enter their sacred precincts and offer their prayers toward the central "house of prayer" (Isa 56:7)—the Temple shrine.

FESTIVALS, HOLY DAYS AND COMMUNAL DINING

In the last section, mention was briefly made of the custom of meeting in the synagogues not only on the Sabbaths, but also on other festivals and holy days. Such traditions underscore the proposition that ancient Jews divided not only space (Philo, *Cher.* 94) but also time into categories of sacred and profane. Just as certain buildings were set aside for the Divine, so were certain days, weeks and months. Philo makes this point most explicit in a segment where he discusses an important set of criteria used by judges in fixing sentences for criminals:

> Unlawful actions differ according as they are committed in a profane or sacred space [βεβήλοις ἢ ἱεροῖς χωρίοις], or at festivals and solemn assemblies and public sacrifices [ἑορταῖς καὶ πανηγύρεσι καὶ δημοτελέσι θυσίαις] as contrasted with days which have no holiday associations or are even quite inauspicious (*Spec.* 3.183).

The division of the year into segments of "sacred" and "profane" time, of course, was not confined to Jewish traditions. During the early empire, Romans observed nearly a hundred separate festivals (*feriae*) each year, during which public sacrifices were offered and no official business could legally be transacted.[71] Around the empire, various local celebrations supplemented the Roman liturgical calendar. At Ephesus, for instance, the entire month of Artemision (March–April) was dedicated to the city's patron goddess Artemis.[72]

---

[71]See Staumbaugh, *The Ancient Roman City*, 221–224; idem, *The Functions of Roman Temples*, 576–579.

[72]See Richard E. Oster, "Ephesus as a Religious Center under the Principate: Paganism before Constantine" in *ANRW* II.18.3.1708.

Wherever they were celebrated, festivals typically involved a sacred procession to a temple during which the participants bore offerings and sacred objects to present before the god or goddess. Prayers and sacrifices were offered, while choruses sang hymns and dancers danced to the accompaniment of musical instruments. Subsequently, the multitudes would feast upon the portions of the sacrificed animals not consumed by the god in the flames.[73]

As we will soon review, the Jews had their own festivals and sacred days, most of which centered on the Temple in Jerusalem. Since these typically involved sacrifice, Jews not able to attend the festivals in Jerusalem—particularly those in the diaspora—could only have limited participation in these sacred days. Nevertheless, there is evidence that Jews gathered locally to observe these days and participated through prayer, fasting, hymn singing and banqueting—this last, albeit not on the returned portions of sacrificed animals. Moreover, the evidence in most cases points to the synagogue as the place where Jews came together to observe these national festivals. Unfortunately, the information from our sources is limited to the synagogal customs of the diaspora, and so we will only be able to offer conjectures for the practices in Palestine. It should be noted, however, that in the homeland, a majority of the Jews appear to have left their cities and villages to celebrate at least the three major feasts/fasts in Jerusalem (Yom Kippur/Sukkoth, Passover, and Pentecost; Josephus, *Ant.* 4.203; Exod 34:23).

In the preceding sections, we observed that the Sabbath was a day set aside for prayer and the reading and study of the scriptures in both the Temple and the synagogues. Within the cycle of the year, the next regular day of observance was the New Moon, commanded in Numbers 28:11–15. In pre-exilic times, the New Moon, like the Sabbath, was a day of rest and rejoicing (Amos 8:5; Hos 2:11). Psalm 81:3–4 commands, "Blow the trumpet at the new moon, at the full moon, on our festal day; for it is a statute for Israel, an ordinance of the God of Jacob" (cf. Num 10:10; Lev 23:24; Isa 1:13). Accordingly, communal dinners were held on the New Moon during this period (1 Sam 20:5). Likewise, special sacrifices are prescribed for this day (Num 28:11–15), and these continued into the Second Temple period (Josephus, *Ant.* 2.238; Philo, *Spec.* 1.177–179). Significantly, after the return of the exiles, Ezra's

[73]See Burkert, *Greek Religion*, 99–107.

reading of the Law before the people took place on the New Moon (Neh 8:2; 1 Esdr 9:40).[74]

This last item suggests that local assemblies gathered on the New Moon to partake of services similar to those held on the Sabbaths. Our evidence for this practice in Palestine, while limited, is nevertheless suggestive. Thus in the story of Judith, the protagonist is said to have "fasted all the days of her widowhood, except the day before the sabbath and the sabbath itself, the day before the new moon and the day of the new moon, and the festivals and days of rejoicing of the house of Israel" (Jdt 8:6; cf. Isa 66:23, Sir 43:7, 50:6). While the author of Judith might have envisioned that the heroine normally went up from Bethulia to Jerusalem for the festivals, it seems doubtful that the same was contemplated for the observance of the New Moon.[75] This hints that there may have been some local observance of the New Moon in Palestine in the second century B.C.E. when Judith was written. At this time, of course, any community gathering would have taken place not in the synagogues, but at the city gates or public square. By the turn of the era, however, these would have moved into the synagogues. In this respect, Paul's statement implying that his Jewish Christian opponents were training the Galatians to observe "months [μῆνας]" (Gal 4:20) suggests that such observances were not only held by Jews in the diaspora, but also by those in Palestine—the most probable origin of the opponents (Gal 2:9).[76]

While we lack evidence specifically attesting to synagogue gatherings of Palestinian Jews on the New Moon, evidence is more forthcoming from the diaspora. As we observed in previous chapters, two inscriptions from Berenice (*CJZC* 70–71) state that the Jews in that city customarily gathered in their synagogue (*amphitheatron*) each New Moon. Though the exact proceedings of these gatherings are not delineated on the monuments, the two benefactors honored in the inscriptions were to be "named [ὀνομάζω]" at each New Moon—probably within the context of communal prayers. Other attestations, while not specifying the synagogues, nevertheless suggest that the practice at Berenice was not unique. We have already mentioned Paul's allusion to the Jewish Christian teachers who believed Gentiles in the diaspora should observe

[74]Notably, this was the New Moon of the Seventh month, Rosh Hashanah. On this, see below.

[75]For commentary, see Carey A. Moore, *Judith* (Garden City, N.Y.: Doubleday, 1985), 31–108, 179–188.

[76]For general discussion of Paul's opponents, see Betz, *Galatians*, 5–9.

"months."[77] Elsewhere, Horace (65–8 B.C.E.) in one of his poems states "Today is the thirtieth day, a Sabbath. Would you affront the circumcised Jews? [*hodie tricensima, sabbata: vin tu curtis Iudaeis oppedere?*]" (*Serm.* 1.9.69–70). Most commentators take this as a reference to the observance of the New Moon.[78] If so, then we have attestation for the observance of this day by the Jews in Rome. Moreover, the equation of the day with the Sabbath suggests that the customs adhered to on both days were similar. Celebrations of the New Moon may also be alluded to in decrees from Sardis and Halicarnassus that simply refer to "stated days [προαποδεδειγμέναις ἡμέραις]" (Josephus, *Ant.* 14.261) or "customary festivals [ἑορταὶ αἱ εἰθισμέναι]" (*Ant.* 14.257).

The earlier tradition of communal dining on the New Moon may also have continued in our period. Noteworthy in this respect is the fact that the Therapeutae, following the liturgical calendar of *Jubilees*, apparently met for a communal feast every fifty days in a dining room adjoining their synagogue (Philo, *Contempl.* 64–89). The difference in their practices may have been limited to the use of another calendar. If so, then the various references to communal dining in conjunction with the diaspora synagogues (Josephus, *Ant.* 14.213–216 [Rome, Delos], 16.162–165 [Asia]) may refer in part to such gatherings on the New Moon. Likewise, the triclinium of the Ostia synagogue and the "rooms" of the synagogue of Theodotus in Jerusalem (*CIJ* 2.1404, l. 6) may also have been used for such communal feasts.

It should be noted that ancillary banquet halls were a common feature of Greco-Roman temples and cultic halls. Worshipers would typically rent them from the officers of the temple and eat their communal meals of sacrificed animals (ἱερόθυτον) inside. This practice was especially associated with public festivals, but private events like birthdays and weddings are also attested.[79] The Jerusalem Temple also had such dining

---

[77]Somewhat later, but perhaps within the parameters of this study, the author of Colossians warns the Christians in that city not to let anyone (probably Jewish Christians) condemn them in matters "of observing festivals, new moons [νεομηνίας], or sabbaths" (Col 2:16).

[78]See *GLAJJ* 1.324–326; *HJP* 3.1.144 n. 26.

[79]See Stambaugh, *The Function of Roman Temples*, 577–578; Burkert, *Greek Religion*, 94, 107; E. Will, "Banquets et salles de banquet dans les cultes la Grèce et de l'Empire romain" in *Mélanges d'histoire des religions offerts à Paul Collart* (Paris: Lausanne, 1976), 353–362; Nancy Bookidis, "Ritual Dining at Corinth" in *Greek Sanctuaries*, edited by Nanno Marinatos and Robin Hägg (London and New York: Routledge, 1993), 45–61; *NDIEC* 1.5–9. Cf. 1 Cor 8:1–13.

rooms, though they were reserved for the exclusive use of the priests (Ezek 42:13). In their incorporation of banquet halls, the synagogues were thus not only meeting the liturgical and communal needs of the local Jewish population, but also imitating the design of both Greco-Roman temples and the Jerusalem Temple.

Special celebrations were possibly held in the synagogues on the New Moon of the seventh month, that is, Rosh Hashanah (1 Tishri, September/October). In Jerusalem, the *shofar* was blown in the Temple on this day, marking the beginning of the "sacred month [ἱερομηνία]" (Philo, *Spec* 2.188, *Dec.* 159). Additional sacrifices were offered in the Temple (Num 29:1–6; Josephus, *Ant.* 3.239; Philo, *Spec.* 1.1.180, 186), as the people recalled the blowing of the trumpets at the time the Law was given to Moses at Sinai (Philo, *Spec*. 2.189; Exod 19:16).[80]

Ten days later came the Day of Atonement, Yom Kippur, a solemn day of fasting and prayer. It was also the only day when the High Priest was allowed to enter the Holy of Holies (Philo, *Legat.* 307), wherein he sprinkled the blood of the sacrificed bullock and kid seven times toward the ceiling and seven times toward the floor (Josephus, *Ant.* 3.242–243). Likewise he sprinkled the outer area of the *naos* and the altar of incense therein, as well as the larger altar at the center of the Court of the Priests (Josephus, *Ant.* 3.243). Ben Sirach presents the following description of the ceremony's conclusion, as enacted by the High Priest Simon II (c. 219–196 B.C.E.):

> Finishing the service at the altars, and arranging the offering to the Most High, the Almighty, [Simon] held out his hand for the cup and poured a drink offering of the blood of the grape; he poured it out at the foot of the altar, a pleasing odor to the Most High, the king of all. Then the sons of Aaron shouted; they blew their trumpets of hammered metal; they sounded a mighty fanfare as a reminder before the Most High. Then all the people together quickly fell to the ground on their faces to worship their Lord, the Almighty, God Most High. Then the singers praised him with their voices in sweet and full-toned melody. And the people of the Lord Most High offered their prayers before the Merciful One, until the order of worship of the Lord was ended, and they completed his ritual. Then Simon came down and raised his hands over the whole congregation of Israelites, to pronounce the blessing of

---

[80]Aside from the evidence attesting to the synagogue assemblies on the New Moon, it should be observed that Philo subsumes the celebration of Rosh Hashana under the fourth commandment (*Dec.* 158–159). Rosh Hashana thus became a "sabbath of months." Note also that this was the day on which Ezra read to the people from the Law (Neh 8:2; 1 Esdr 9:40).

> the Lord with his lips, and to glory in his name; and they bowed down in worship a second time, to receive the blessing from the Most High (Sir 50:14–21).

As previously mentioned, within Palestine, Jews were expected to be in Jerusalem on Yom Kippur (Josephus, *Ant.* 4.203). Whether or not Palestinian Jews who were unable to make the journey met in their local synagogues is open to debate, since our sources are silent on this point. Evidence from the diaspora, however, is more suggestive. To begin with, both the LXX and Philo call Yom Kippur a "Sabbath of Sabbaths [σάββατα σαββάτων]" (Lev 16:31, 23:32, LXX; Philo, *Spec.* 2.194). If diaspora Jews customarily met in the synagogues on the regular Sabbaths, how much more would they have met there on the "Sabbath of Sabbaths"? As Philo puts it, this day was observed "not only by the zealous for piety and holiness [ζῆλος εὐσεβείας καὶ ὁσιότητος] but also by those who never act religiously in the rest of their life. For all stand in awe, overcome by the sanctity of the day, and for the moment the worse vie with the better in self-denial and virtue" (*Spec.* 1.186). In his further treatment of this subject, Philo goes on to delineate the specific contours of the piety exercised on this day:

> [The day] is entirely devoted to prayers and supplications [λιταῖς καὶ ἱκεσίαις], and men [ἀνθρώπων] from morn to eve employ their leisure in nothing else but offering petitions [εὐχάς] of humble entreaty in which they seek earnestly to propitiate God and ask for remission of their sins, voluntary and involuntary, and entertain bright hopes looking not to their own merits but to the gracious nature of Him Who sets pardon before Chastisement (*Spec.* 2.196; cf. *Mos.* 2.23–24).

Yom Kippur appears to have been observed in other places in the diaspora as both Josephus and Philo boasted that in every city of the empire even Gentiles joined in this solemn day (*Ap.* 2.282–284; *Mos.* 2.23–24; cf. Acts 27:9). While exaggerated, the claim presumes that diaspora Jews customarily participated in the prescribed observances.[81]

Within the Jewish liturgical calendar, the Feast of Tabernacles (Sukkoth) came five days after Yom Kippur on 15 Tishri, which was also

---

[81]Scholars have recognized allusions made to the observance of Yom Kippur in a pair of nearly identical epitaphs from Rhenea, the burial island of Delos (*CIJ* 1.725). Since these date to the same period as the Jewish and/or Samaritan synagogues on that island (c. 100 B.C.E.), the observances of this day were possibly held within these structures. See Deissmann, *Light from the Ancient East*, 413–424; *HJP* 3.1.144, n. 26.

the autumnal equinox (Philo, *Spec.* 2.204; Josephus, *Ant.* 3.244; Lev 23:40–43). In Jerusalem, seven days of celebration commenced on this day, followed by a day of rest. The residents and pilgrims constructed tents, placing them either on their roof tops or in the open areas in and around the city, including (at least in Ezra's day) the Temple courts (Neh 8:16; Josephus, *Ant.* 3.244; Philo, *Spec.* 2.206). In the Temple, lavish sacrifices were offered, decreasing in number over the seven days (Josephus, *Ant.* 3.246; Philo, *Spec.* 1.187–188; Num 29:12–34). The people came into the Temple courts each day, bearing their bouquets of myrtle and willow, *lulabs* (palm branches), and *etrogs* (citrons) and "[taking] their part in hymns and prayers and sacrifices" (Philo, *Spec.* 1.193). Lamps were lit within the Temple courts, leading the Johannine Jesus to proclaim "I am the light of the world" in the middle of this festival (John 8:12; cf. Josephus, *Ap.* 2.117–118). The period was further marked by conviviality and communal feasting in places around the city (Philo, *Spec.* 1.192). It was also during this feast that, every seventh year, the High Priest would read the Torah to the assembled multitude from a wooden platform erected inside the Temple courts (Josephus, *Ant.* 4.209–211).

While again, our sources are silent on whether the Palestinian synagogues served as meeting places on these festival days, there is evidence that the Feast of Tabernacles was celebrated in the synagogues of the diaspora. Here, we recall from chapter four that an inscription from Berenice (*CJZC* 71) refers to an assembly in the synagogue (*amphitheatron*) there on this feast day (συλλόγου τῆς σκηνοπηγίας). Unfortunately, the monument only mentions the passage of a resolution to honor a local Roman official and does not delineate the other ritual proceedings that surely took place then. Philo provides evidence to support this view in his description of the Feast of the Tabernacles in Alexandria during the final year of Flaccus' governorship (see above). He remarks:

> The Jews were holding then the national feast of the autumn equinox [ἑορτὴ μὲν γὰρ ἦν πάνδημος τοῖς Ἰουδαίοις], in which it is the custom of the Jews to live in tents. But nothing at all of the festal proceeding was being carried out [οὐδὲν δὲ τῶν ἐν ἑορτῇ συνόλως ἀπετελεῖτο]. The rulers after suffering deadly and intolerable injuries and outrages were still in prison and their misfortunes were regarded by the commoners as shared by the whole nation, while the special sufferings which each of them experienced individually made them extremely depressed. For painful sensations are apt to double themselves most especially at feast time [ἑορτάζειν] in persons who are

> unable to observe the feast, both because they are deprived of the cheerful gaiety which the festal gathering [πανήγυρις] demands and also because they communicate to each other their sorrow—sorrow which in this case laid them prostrate through their powerlessness to find any remedy for their great miseries (*Flacc.* 116–119).

The words or phrases presented above in the original Greek all denote corporate festivities typically involving religious ritual of some sort.[82] We will recall from the previous section that when the Alexandrian Jews received word of Flaccus' arrest during the festival, they assembled at the beach in the morning—because their synagogues had been taken from them—to corporately express thanks to God (*Flacc.* 123–134). Had their synagogues not been seized and their *archontes* jailed, it is highly probable that these festive proceedings would have taken place in their *proseuchai.* We can only surmise what these proceedings might have been, but it should be noted that there was no biblical prohibition against assembling with the traditional bouquets outside of Jerusalem. It is conceivable that these bouquets were brought into the synagogues and waved there in the same way as they were waved in the Temple courts.

In addition to Philo's description of this day, Josephus may allude to the lighting of menorahs in the diaspora synagogues during Sukkoth when he writes, "there is not one city, Greek or barbarian, nor a single nation, to which our custom of abstaining from work on the seventh day has not spread, and where the fasts and the lighting of lamps and many of our prohibitions in the matter of food are not observed [by Gentiles]" (*Ap* 2.282; cf. 2.118). This passage may also be a reference to the festival of Hanukkah, a feast derived from Sukkoth, marking the Maccabean rededication of the Temple. Regarding this feast, 2 Maccabees 1:10–2:18 incorporates a letter, purportedly written by Judas Maccabaeus and the *gerousia* of Jerusalem to the Egyptian Jews, encouraging them to "celebrate the festival of booths and the festival of the fire [i.e., Hanukkah] given when Nehemiah, who built the temple and the altar, offered sacrifices" (1:18). While the letter is a forgery designed to give justification to this "festival of fire," the festival was apparently being observed around the diaspora since Josephus indicates that it was still celebrated in the 90s, when he wrote *Antiquities* (*Ant.* 12.325).[83] Paul's

---

[82]E.g., LSJ s.v. πανήγυρις: "a festal assembly in honour of a national god" (cf. Hos 2:13, 9:5; Amos 5:21; Ezek 46:11, LXX).

[83]For commentary on the passage from 2 Maccabees, see Goldstein, *II Maccabees*, 154–193.

complaint that the Galatians were being induced "to observe . . . seasons [παρατηρεῖσθε . . . καιροὺς]" (Gal 4:10) may likewise point to the expectation that Jews and proselytes in the diaspora adhere to such festivals.[84] Finally, what was written above about the triclinium in the Ostia synagogue and the various general references in decrees to Jewish festivals, communal dining and public banquet halls obviously applies to Sukkoth and Hanukkah (Josephus, *Ant.* 14.261, 14.257). These synagogues likely served as public dining facilities for Jews on these occasions.

The same could have been the case for Passover, though this holiday was the one Jewish feast day that customarily took place within private homes. Biblical strictures prohibited the eating of the Passover lamb outside of "the place that the LORD your God will choose as a dwelling for his name" (Deut 16:6). During our period, "the place" was interpreted by most Jews as Jerusalem (Josephus, *Ant.* 4.200). Consequently, thousands of pilgrims would descend upon the Holy City the week before the feast, which was held on 14 Nisan, near the Spring equinox (March/April). While specified whole-burnt offerings and sin offerings were presented in the Temple by the High Priest during this time, the highlight of the Temple activities was the gathering of the banquet representatives in the Temple courts to participate in sacrificing the Passover lamb. As Philo states, "myriads of victims from noon until eventide are offered by the whole people, old and young alike, raised for that particular day to the dignity of the priesthood" (*Spec.* 2.145; cf. *Dec.* 159; *Mos.* 2.224.).[85] After the traditional Passover meal was eaten in homes and banquet halls around Jerusalem (e.g., the Theodotus synagogue), the Temple gates, normally closed at night, would be thrown open after midnight, allowing the people to pray and mingle in the courts before the morning sacrifices (Josephus, *Ant.* 18.29–30). The following day (15 Nisan) marked the beginning of the Feast of Unleavened Bread, which lasted seven days, during which only unleavened bread was eaten (Josephus, *Ant.* 3.249; Philo, *Spec.* 1.181–182; 2.156–161; Num 28:17–31). The second of these days (16 Nisan) was the ingathering of the barley harvest for the priests (Josephus, *Ant.* 3.250–251; Philo, *Spec.* 2.162–167; Lev 23:11–14).

---

[84]Cf. Betz, *Galatians*, 217–218.

[85]Josephus implies that the people only laid hands on the animals, while the priests actually did the sacrificing (*Ant.* 9.268–69).

Although we have no evidence that diaspora Jews violated the strictures against eating the Passover lamb outside of Jerusalem,[86] there were no such prohibitions against eating meals of unleavened bread outside of the Holy City. Consequently, it is possible that a modified meal was held in the homes and/or banquet halls in the diaspora during these twin feasts.[87] Likewise, the LXX designated the first and seventh days of the Feast of Unleavened Bread as days of rest when there was to be a "holy convocation [ἐπίκλητος ἁγία]" (Num 28:18, 25, LXX). It would seem a logical development that diaspora Jews gathered in their synagogues on these days in addition to the usual Sabbath.

The same can be said of the last of the major Jewish feasts, Pentecost, which came fifty days after the start of the Feast of Unleavened bread on 15 Nisan. This represented the ingathering of the wheat harvest, when two loaves of wheat bread were offered along with animal sacrifices (Josephus, *Ant.* 3.252–254; *Spec.* 1.183–185, 2.179–187; Lev 23:15–22, Num 28:26–31). This also marked the beginning of the period when individuals could bring their first-fruit offerings to the Temple. It was a day of rest, when there was to be a "holy convocation" (Lev 23:21). Because of the numerous attestations for the collection of the Temple tax in the diaspora synagogues—which Philo often refers to as the "first fruits" (ἀπαρχή; e.g., *Legat.* 156–157, 216, 291, 311–316; *Spec.* 1.76–78; cf. *Josephus, Ant.* 16.172)—one wonders whether this day may have been used for the ingathering of these offerings, as well as other gifts.[88]

In addition to the major national feasts, several local festivals were apparently observed in the diaspora. We have already encountered the annual celebration in Alexandria of the Septuagint's translation at several points in our discussion. While this feast was not held in the synagogues but on the Alexandrian beachfront, this venue may harken back to the earliest communal gatherings of the Jews in that city, prior to the construction of their *proseuchai* (see chapter four). Of that celebration, Philo writes:

---

[86]That is, aside from the Jews at Elephantine and Leontopolis. See the treatments of the Leontopolis and Elephantine temples in chapter four. On the question of whether diaspora Jews observed the strictures against eating the Passover lamb outside of Jerusalem, see Sanders, *Judaism*, 133–134; *HJP* 3.1.145.

[87]See *HJP* 3.1.145.

[88]On the use of ἀπαρχή as a term for both tithes and general offerings, see Gerhard Delling, "ἀπαρχή" in *TDNT* 1.484–485. Note also that the Therapeutae held a communal feast on Pentecost, presumably in a banquet hall adjoining their synagogue (Philo, *Contempl.* 65ff). See the treatment of this sect in chapter seven.

> Even to this present day, there is held every year a feast and general assembly [ἑορτὴ καὶ πανήγυρις] in the island of Pharos, whither not only Jews but multitudes of others cross the water, both to do honour to the place in which light of that version first shone out, and also to thank God for the good gift so old yet ever young. But, after the prayers and thanksgivings [τὰς ευχὰς καὶ τὰς εὐχαριστίας], some fixing tents on the seaside and others reclining on the sandy beach in the open air feast with their relations and friends, counting that shore for the time a more magnificent lodging than the fine mansions in the royal precincts (*Mos.* 2.41)

Another feast unique to Egypt was a celebration apparently connected to a conflict between the Jews and one of the Ptolemaic kings. This festival is alluded to in 3 Maccabees' legendary account of the Jews' deliverance from the wrath of Ptolemy Philopater (222–205 B.C.E.). At the end of that tale, the Jews gathered at Ptolemais for a feast, after which they dedicated a synagogue at the site of the festivities (3 Macc 7:20). Curiously, Josephus tells a similar story, but this time the king is Ptolemy Physcon (145–117 B.C.E.). At the end of his account, he writes, "that is the origin of the well-known feast which the Jews of Alexandria keep, with good reason, on this day, because of the deliverance so manifestly vouchsafed to them" (*Ap.* 2.55). While the origin of this feast is shrouded in legend, the resultant festival was apparently real. It may well have had some connections with the story of Esther and the celebration of Purim, a feast which, according to Josephus, "even now all the Jews in the habitable world celebrate . . . by sending portions [of food] to one another" (*Ant.* 11.292).

The foregoing discussion has affirmed the notion that traditional Jewish festivals were celebrated internationally during our period. Moreover, it has suggested a correlation between the liturgical observances of the Temple and the diaspora synagogues. In this respect, it is significant that Josephus states that the High Priest offered the sacrifices only on six special days: the Sabbath, New Moon (including Rosh Hashnah), Passover, Pentecost, Sukkoth and Yom Kippur (*BJ* 5.231; *Ant.* 18.94). Of these days, our sources directly attest to meetings in the synagogues on the Sabbath, New Moon and Sukkoth, and suggest that such gatherings took place on Yom Kippur. While the evidence does not as firmly attest corporate gatherings on Passover and Pentecost, the literary sources *do* allude to the observance of unspecified "customary feasts" (ἑορταὶ αἱ εἰθισμέναι) and to communal dining in the diaspora synagogues (Josephus, *Ant.* 14.257, 14.213–216, 14.261, 16.162–165).

Because Passover and Pentecost were two of the three central festivals prescribed in the Torah (*Ant.* 4.203), and they both involved communal feasting, one wonders to what other feasts these allusions might have been referring. Unless an unattested set of local festivals is posited, a reasonable conclusion is that these feasts included Passover and Pentecost.[89]

The common observance of the traditional feasts points to the intersection of temporal and spatial dimensions, where sacred time and sacred space came together linking the Temple to the synagogues around the world. In this interpretation, the Jews observing Sukkoth in the *proseuchai* of Alexandria, for example, were effectively transported to the inner courts of the Temple as the High Priest offered the customary sacrifices and blessed the assembled multitude. Thus not only Jerusalemites and pilgrims, but also Jews from around the world could join in worship and become the beneficiaries of the divine favor that flowed out from the central shrine. The synagogues thereby provided the means whereby distances were overcome, allowing Jews from abroad to take their place as full citizens of the larger congregation of Israel as they gathered before the Holy One on the sacred days commanded in the sacred law.[90]

TREASURY

Within the Greco-Roman world, temples customarily served as banks and treasuries for both public and private funds. The rationale behind this designation is obvious: monies kept within the temple precincts were believed to have been under the protection of the deity residing therein. Thus Dio Chrysostom wrote concerning the temple of Artemis at Ephesus:

> You know about the Ephesians, of course, and that the large sums of money are in their hands, some of it belonging to private citizens and deposited in the temple of Artemis, not alone money of the Ephesians but also of aliens and of persons from all parts of the world, and in some cases of

---

[89]See also the next chapter for a treatment of Philo's account of the banquet held by the Therapeutae on Pentecost.

[90]The field of Ritual studies has lately underscored the importance of temporal and spatial intersections within the exercise of cultic rites. See, e.g., Richard P. Werbner, *Ritual Passage, Sacred Journey* (Washington: Smithsonian Institution Press, 1989), 187–330.

> commonwealths and kings, money which all deposit there in order that it may be safe, since no one has ever yet dared to violate that place, although countless wars have occurred in the past and the city has often been captured (Dio Chrysostom 31.54–55).[91]

As usual, the Jerusalem Temple differed little from its pagan counterparts in assuming the role of a sacred repository. Private deposits were kept within the Temple treasury (2 Macc 3:10–11; Josephus, *BJ* 4.568), as were sacred monies donated by Jews from around the world (Josephus, *Ant.* 9.163–165, *BJ* 5.200). The "sacred monies" contained within the Temple were considerable: the figure mentioned by Josephus at various places is 2,000 talents (*BJ* 1.152, 179; *Ant.* 14.72). A talent was equivalent to c. 6,000 denarii, each worth about the daily wage of a laborer (Matt 20:2). Assuming the modern figure of $40 for the value of such a day's work in the US, the total sum would have been equivalent to US $480,000,000.

The primary source of this immense sum, as Philo, Josephus, Cicero and imperial decrees make clear, was the annual payment of the two denarii Temple tax by Jews over the age of twenty (e.g., Philo, *Legat.* 156–157, 216, 291, 311–316; *Spec.*1.76–78; Josephus, *Ant.* 16.172; Cicero, *pro Flacc.* 67–69; Exod 30:13). While Jews in the homeland contributed to this fund, the greater portion came from the diaspora, since that was the home of a larger number of Jews. As we noted in chapter four, several imperial decrees and other literary allusions indicate that the diaspora synagogues served as the repositories of this money. A decree of Augustus to Asia, for example, stated, "if anyone is caught stealing their sacred books or their sacred monies from a synagogue [τὰς ἱερὰς βίβλους αὐτῶν ἢ τὰ ἱερὰ χρήματα ἔκ . . . σαββατείου] . . . he shall be regarded as sacrilegious [εἶναι αὐτὸν ἱερόσυλον]" (Josephus, *Ant.* 16.164). Marcus Agrippa likewise wrote to the magistrates at Ephesus, "if any men steal the sacred monies of the Jews and take refuge in places of asylum, it is my will that they be dragged away from them and turned over to the Jews under the same law by which temple-robbers [οἱ ἱερόσυλοι] are dragged away from asylum" (*Ant.* 16.168). Were such culprits to be considered "temple-robbers" because they stole from the Jerusalem Temple or from the synagogues? In legal terms, the decree of Augustus and the letter of Agrippa officially recognized that the Asian synagogues held the status of inviolable precincts. This meant that they

---

[91]See Oster, "Ephesus as a Religious Center under the Principate," 1717–1718.

were protected from the theft of their various possessions, such as their sacred monies and sacred books. Hence we have the basic meaning of the term *asylia*, which literally translated is "prohibition against stealing." Regarding this right, Ulrich Sinn comments:

> One of the basic tenets of Greek religion was that everything inside sacred territory was owned by the god—and the possessions of divinities were of course taboo for human beings. Hence every sanctuary had the status of an inviolable precinct (*asylon hieron*). The inviolability of the sanctuaries guaranteed pilgrims and festival participants security. In the same way it served to protect the often valuable votive offerings. The sanctuaries were predestined to fulfill other functions by virtue of the security afforded by asylia. For example they could perform the function of banks. The sanctuary of Artemis in Ephesus is the most noteworthy example of this.[92]

Sinn's observations lead us to consider a remark by Philo that suggests that synagogues not only in Asia, but throughout the diaspora commonly served as sacred repositories:

> The revenues of the temple are derived not only from landed estates but also from other and far greater sources which time will never destroy. For as long as the human race endures, and it will endure for ever, the revenues of the temple also will remain secure co-eternal with the whole universe. For it is ordained that everyone, beginning at his twentieth year should make an annual contribution of first-fruits [ἀπαρχάς] . . . As the nation is very populous, the offerings of first-fruits are naturally exceedingly abundant. In fact, practically in every city there are banking places [ταμεῖα] for the holy money [ἱερῶν χρημάτων] where people regularly come and give their offerings. And at stated times there are appointed to carry the sacred tribute envoys selected on their merits, from every city those of the highest repute, under whose conduct the hope of each and all will travel safely (*Spec.* 1.76–78).

In Greco-Roman literature, the word *tameia* ("banking places"), when used in connection with *hieros chrēmata* ("sacred monies"), uniformly denotes a temple treasury.[93] When combined with the imperial decrees

---

[92]Ulrich Sinn, "Greek Sanctuaries as Places of Refuge" in *Greek Sanctuaries*, edited by Nanno Marinatos and Robin Hägg (London and New York: Routledge, 1993), 90.

[93]LSJ s.v. ταμιεῖον. See, e.g., Thuc. 1.96 of the treasury on Delos, which was within the sacred precincts of the temple of Apollo.

quoted above, it may be supposed that Philo's reference to such *tameia* is not to pagan temples, but to synagogues.[94]

While the evidence adduced so far may be construed as supporting the view that synagogues in the *diaspora* served as sacred repositories, Josephus' mention of bandits pillaging the synagogues of Judea during the Jewish War (*BJ* 4.406–409) may imply that the synagogues in *Palestine* functioned similarly: clearly these synagogues contained something of value worth pillaging, items exceeding the worth of the sacred scrolls and instruments housed inside. When we add to this the fact that an ostracon with the words "priest's tithe" was found inside the Masada synagogue (see chapter three), it is possible that the synagogues in Palestine, like their diaspora counterparts, served as local repositories for sacred offerings destined for the Temple.

Mention here should also be made of the verse in Matthew referring to almsgiving in the synagogues:

> Whenever you give alms, do not sound a trumpet before you, as the hypocrites do in the synagogues and in the streets, so that they may be praised by others ["Οταν οὖν ποιῇς ἐλεημοσύνην, μὴ σαλπίσῃς ἔμπροσθέν σου, ὥσπερ οἱ ὑποκριταὶ ποιοῦσιν ἐν ταῖς συναγωγαῖς καὶ ἐν ταῖς ῥύμαις, ὅπως δοξασθῶσιν ὑπὸ τῶν ἀνθρώπων] (Matt 6:2).

Despite the fact that the passage is an independent Matthean tradition filled with polemic against the "hypocrites" (=scribes and Pharisees), the allusion to the giving of charity in the synagogues coheres with the ancient Jewish tradition of rendering aid to the poor, the widow, and the orphan (e.g., Exod 22:25, 23:11; Deut 26:12–13; Isa 58:7–10). Although the passage may refer to the simple offering of money to a beggar by the synagogue door, it is also possible that it alludes to the ingathering of the so-called third tithe, which was designated for the sojourner,[95] the widows, and the orphans. According to Deuteronomy 14:28–29, Moses commanded the people to collect this tithe every third year and "store it within your towns [וְהִנַּחְתָּ בִּשְׁעָרֶיךָ]." A more literal rendering of the Hebrew reads, "And deposit it in your gates." If these tithes were actually collected at the city gates in Palestine, later, this function may have been carried over into the synagogues. While in some cases the tithes may have

---

[94]Cf. Josephus, *Ant.* 18.312–313, which refers Jews using *tameia* in the cities of Nearda and Nisibis as depositories for their votive offerings for the Temple.

[95]גֵּר (Deut 14:29, 26:12); later taken as the homeless, the needy or even proselytes (ibid., LXX; Tob 1:8).

been doled out locally (2 Macc 8:28?), they were also to be taken to the Temple to be distributed there to those in need (Josephus, *Ant.* 4.240–241; Tob 1:8). According to 2 Maccabees, widows and orphans had a special fund set aside within the Temple treasury (2 Macc 3:10).

In conclusion, in so far as they may have functioned as local treasuries, the synagogues again assumed one of the primary functions of the Jerusalem Temple, since the central Jewish treasury was located inside the Temple courts (Josephus, *Ant.* 17.264). Because most of the money contributed to the synagogues was transported to the main sanctuary, one might even say that they were "branches" of the central repository. That Augustus and Agrippa both officially recognized the inviolability of the synagogues in Asia further supports the notion that the sacrality of the Jerusalem Temple extended outward to embrace these sacred precincts dispersed throughout the empire.

MUSEUM, ARCHIVE, SCHOOL

The function of the ancient museum was related to that of the treasury, for whereas the latter housed sacred donations in an area restricted to the public, the former displayed these gifts openly for all the world to see. To walk through a Greek or Roman temple was to walk through a museum, for the sacred areas and shrines were covered with every manner of statue, shield, altar, inscription or other type of votive offering.[96] The purpose in displaying these items was one of ostentation, where donors sought to attract the attention not only of human visitors to the temple, but also of the god dwelling within the shrine. It was hoped that, upon seeing the pious offering, the god would look with favor upon the donors and continue to respond to their prayers. Accordingly, as noted in a previous section, one of the Greek words for "votive offering," *euchē*, was also the word for "prayer." The more common term, however, was *anathēma*, a noun derived from the verb *anatithēmi*, "to set up" or "to dedicate."[97] A votive offering was thus "that which is set up and dedicated to a deity."[98] By definition, then, all such offerings were sacred (*hieros*).

Writing in c. 300 B.C.E., the Philosopher Hecataeus of Abdera observed that within the Jerusalem Temple, "there is not a single statue

---

[96]For a list of examples, see Burkert, *Greek Religion*, 92–95; Stambaugh, *The Functions of Roman Temples*, 573–574.

[97]See LSJ s.v. ἀνατίθημι.

[98]See LSJ s.v. ἀνάθημα; Johannes Behm, "'Ανάθεμα" in *TDNT* 1.354–355.

or votive offering [ἀνάθημα], no trace of a plant, in the form of a sacred grove or the like."[99] If this is an accurate depiction, by Hasmonean times the situation had changed dramatically, at least with respect to the votive offerings. Josephus mentions that when Antiochus Epiphanes sacked the Temple, he carried away the many votive offerings (ἀναθημάτα) displayed inside (*BJ* 7.44). Closer to Josephus' own day, the courts of Herod's Temple were said to have contained lavish votive offerings from the Roman emperors and officials (*BJ* 4.181; cf. *BJ* 1.416, 5.562; Philo, *Legat*. 296, 319). Herod himself placed the spoils he had won from his wars "round about the entire temple" as dedications (Josephus, *Ant*. 15.403). The Jews living in the diaspora seem to have been particularly keen on sending votive offerings to the Temple, as Josephus mentions votives arriving from Babylon (*Ant.* 18.313), while archaeologists have uncovered an inscription from a Jew in Rhodes dedicating a pavement in one of the Temple courts.[100] Palestinian Jews must also have contributed such dedications, for Josephus states that even the Essenes, while refraining from rendering sacrifices in Jerusalem, sent votive offerings to the Temple there (*Ant*. 18.19).

As in previous sections, our evidence reveals that the synagogues mirrored this key function of the central sanctuary, for they too served as places where votive offerings were set up. This is made especially clear in the passage where Josephus reports what was later done with the votive offerings taken by Antiochus IV from the Temple. He writes: "[Antiochus'] successors on the throne restored to the Jews of Antioch all such votive offerings as were made of brass [ἀναθημάτων ὅσα χαλκᾶ πεποίητο πάντα], to be laid up in their synagogue [εἰς τὴν συναγωγὴν αὐτῶν ἀναθέντες]" (*BJ* 7.44). The Seleucid rulers later added "richly designed and costly" votive offerings to the ones initially placed there (*BJ* 7.45).

Elsewhere, Philo refers to "the shields and gilded crowns and the slabs and inscriptions" set up inside the Alexandrian synagogues (*Legat.* 133). In our survey of Egyptian synagogues, we encountered nearly a dozen inscriptions of such buildings or their appurtenances dedicated to *Theos Hypsistos* (e.g., *JIE* 9, 13, 22, 24, 25, 28, 117). Also, 3 Maccabees 7:20 refers to a synagogue dedicated in Ptolemais as part of the festivities surrounding the deliverance of the Egyptian Jews. In all these cases we

---

[99]Hecataeus, *De Judaeis* ap. Josephus, *Ap.* 1.199. For commentary, see *GLAJJ* 1.20–44.

[100]See Isaac, "A Donation for Herod's Temple in Jerusalem," 86–92.

should note that the synagogues themselves were votive offerings from either the Jewish community or an individual. They too were the sacred possessions of *Theos Hypsistos*.

In other places around the diaspora, the synagogues likewise served as museums of such inscriptions: at Berenice, inscriptions honoring benefactors were set up in the synagogue (*CJCZ* 70–72); votive offerings were found along with the synagogue at Delos (*CIJ* 1.727–730); a gilded shield with an inscription was erected in the synagogue at Acmonia in order to make known the deeds of the pious contributors (*DF* 33). The dedicatory inscription of the Theodotus synagogue in Jerusalem indicates that the synagogues of Palestine also shared in this function (*CIJ* 2.1404).

If votive offerings sought to attract the attention of the deity or deities, decrees were addressed specifically to human beings. Nevertheless, to give the decrees divine force, temples served as archives for public documents. The more prominent of these were inscribed on stone monuments or bronze pillars and placed on public display in the temple precincts. In Rome, the temples of Jupiter and Fides served as the location of these monuments.[101] Josephus puts this fact to good use in one of his apologetic passages where he writes that "anyone . . . so stupid that he will actually refuse to believe the statements about the friendliness of the Romans" toward the Jews needed only to wander into the temples where the decrees he had reproduced in his writings were still on display (*Ant.* 14.265–267).

For Jews, the Jerusalem Temple served as the central archives for public laws and notifications. As mentioned in a previous section, a copy of the Torah was kept there, though obviously it was not inscribed on stone (Josephus, *BJ* 7.150; *Ant.* 2.346, 3.28, 303, 5.61). Still, ancient Jewish tradition maintained that the Ten Commandments had been given to Moses on two tablets and that these had formerly been placed inside the Ark of the Covenant kept inside the Holy of Holies (Exod 25:16; 2 Chr 5:7–10). Aside from the sacred law, other decrees were posted in the Temple. The book of 1 Maccabees reproduces a decree passed by the Jewish people that Simon I and his progeny should retain the high priesthood in perpetuity "until a trustworthy prophet should arise" (1 Macc 14:27–45). Orders were given "to inscribe this decree on bronze tablets, to put them up in a conspicuous place in the precincts of the

---

[101]See Stambaugh, *The Functions of Roman Temples*, 582–583. For this function in the Artemision, see Oster, "Ephesus as a Religious Center under the Principate," 1720.

sanctuary" (1 Macc 14:48). Elsewhere, this same book indicates that a decree of Demetrius II granting privileges to the Jews was posted in "a conspicuous place" on the Temple mount (1 Macc 11:37; cf. Josephus, *Ant.* 13.128). Also, a list of the succession of High Priests was kept there, as well as genealogies of the priests (Josephus, *Ap.* 1.30–36).

The synagogues replicated the archival function of the Jerusalem Temple in many respects. Obviously, they served as repositories for the Torah scrolls (e.g., Josephus, *BJ* 2.285–292; Luke 4:16–30), which were probably placed in a position of honor such as inside a wooden ark or a niche covered with a veil. Given the association of the scribe with the synagogue (e.g., *CPJ* 1.138; Mark 1:21–29, 12:38–40), other public records may have been kept in the local synagogues as well. We have examples of these in the Bosporus manumission inscriptions, which held the force of legal instruments (e.g., *CIJ* 1.683a, 690, 690a, 691). An inscription from Egypt that we will examine in the next section likewise served as a notification of a certain synagogue's right of asylum (*JIE* 125). It is probable that some of the imperial decrees quoted by Josephus were posted not only in Rome and in the regional imperial temples (*Ant.* 16.165), but also in the local synagogues in order to assert Jewish rights in the face of potential Gentile hostilities.[102]

The open spaces of temple precincts and the availability of reading material naturally led to the adoption of these areas for schools. In Athens, the Stoics derived their very name from their custom of meeting within the Stoa Poikile in the Athenian agora. Likewise in Rome, poets regularly assembled to read and teach their compositions in the temple of Hercules Musarum.[103] We have already reviewed the various passages portraying the courts of the Jerusalem Temple as a site where teaching regularly took place.[104] The synagogues likewise functioned in this

---

[102]Sinn observes that decrees such as the one issued by Augustus making the Asian synagogues inviolate were normally displayed publically at the protected site (*Greek Sanctuaries as Places of Refuge*, 90). Josephus states that priests in the diaspora were required to send copies of their genealogies to Jerusalem (*Ap.* 1.32–36); these records may also have been kept as part of the public record in the local synagogues.

[103]Porphyrio ad Horace, *Serm.* 1.10.38–39; Pliny, *NH* 25.66, 114, 144. See Stambaugh, *The Function of Roman Temples*, 587.

[104]I.e., in the section dealing with the reading and teaching of scripture. See, e.g., Mark 12:35, 14:49; Luke 2:46; John 7:14, 28; 8:2, 20; Acts 5:21, 25, 42; Josephus, *BJ* 1.78–80; *Ant.* 13.311.

Figure 20. Gamla synagogue, loc. 1010. It is likely that this room was used for the study of scripture by small groups. More conjecturally, children may have met here to receive instruction in reading from a local scribe attached to the synagogue. (Drawing by Sissela M. Malmstrom, Gamla Excavations.)

respect on Sabbaths, as we have also seen above. Given the presence of the sacred writings in the synagogues, it is further possible that on other days these buildings were employed for training children to read, since Josephus indicates that this was required of Jewish children by the Mosaic Law (*Ap*. 2.204; cf. Philo, *Legat*. 115, 210, *Spec*. 2.233; Luke 4:16). If this view was shared and enacted by other Jews, it provides a possible interpretation of the small room inside the synagogue at Gamla: one can imagine a scribe sitting there instructing children seated on the rows of benches (see fig. 20).[105] We must also recall that in several places Philo refers to the synagogues as *didaskaleia* or schools. While this designation reflects Philo's own scholarly leanings and his desire to

[105]For a depiction of the young Jesus sitting in the Temple courts discussing the Law with the Jewish experts, see Luke 2:46. On the teaching function of the scribes, see the discussion of this office in the previous chapter.

present Jewish institutions according to Gentile categories, it is nevertheless striking that the only time he employs this term, it is in reference to the synagogues.[106] Keeping in mind that Jews in Alexandria had undergone a fairly high degree of Hellenization, Philo's use of the word *didaskaleion* may not have been inappropriate. Over the centuries it is possible that the Alexandrian synagogues became the venues for Jewish schools in imitation of the Greek philosophical schools meeting in the stoas. Such schools would have served the Jewish intelligentsia, who, like their Greek counterparts, would have met not only on the Sabbath, but on other days as well. Indeed, because some of Philo's treatises are written in question-and-answer format, some scholars have argued that Philo himself served as a catechist.[107] If so, then he may have used the synagogue during the week as a venue for his teaching, either in the main hall or in an exedra similar to the one attested in the *proseuchē* at Athribis (*JIE* 28).

In summary, both the synagogues and the Temple courts functioned as places where dedications, sacred laws and public notifications were kept and displayed. Likewise, both served as venues for the dissemination of knowledge, particularly knowledge pertaining to the Mosaic Laws. While the Sabbath was the school day *par excellence*, it is possible that gatherings in the synagogues (as in the Temple) took place at other times during the week. Yet even if this hypothesis is accepted, such gatherings would likely have been confined to school children and to members of the Jewish aristocracy who had the desire and the leisure to spend weekdays enmeshed in the study of their "ancestral philosophy." With the support of communal monies, sectarians and other Jews zealous for the Law may also have made time for weekday study in the synagogues, as they clearly did within the Temple courts (Josephus, *BJ* 1.78–80, *Ant.* 13.311; Acts 5:42).

---

[106]*Mos.* 2.216, *Dec.* 40, *Spec.* 62, *Praem.* 66, *Legat.* 312. See the treatment of *didaskaleion* in chapter two.

[107]*Quaestiones et solutiones in Genesim*; *Quaestiones et solutiones in Exodum.* Alternatively, it has been suggested that the segments reflect synagogue lections. See Borgen, "Philo of Alexandria," 241–242; *HJP* 3.2.826–830.

PLACES OF REFUGE

In antiquity, refuge was a right associated with temples. The reason for this is analogous to that adduced above for temple treasuries: not only did monies come under the protection of the resident deity, but also human beings. Consequently, the visitor to nearly any ancient temple would encounter every manner of criminal seeking asylum within its sacred precincts. Indeed, the ancient writers would frequently lament this state of affairs. Apollonius of Tyana, for instance, complained that the Artemision in Ephesus had been turned into "a den of robbers."[108]

As might be imagined, political battles would ensue over the extent to which asylum applied. In a previous section, we noted Marcus Agrippa's reference to the law allowing the magistrates at Ephesus to seize asylum suppliants who had stolen Jewish sacred monies (Josephus, *Ant.* 16.168)—the rationale behind the law being that mortals did not want to start a war between the gods. This ruling was possibly connected to Augustus' decree reducing the size of the sacred area of the Artemision; previously Marc Antony had extended it from Mt. Pion into the city, leading Ephesus to become overrun with criminals.[109]

The notion of asylum also formed a part of the Jewish tradition. In pre-exilic times, wrongdoers would apparently flee to the main altar of the Temple and seize its horns. The tactic did not always work, as is seen in the cases of Adonijah and Joab, whom Solomon did not hesitate to slay for their crimes (1 Kgs 1:50–53, 2:28–34). Though it is unclear how they were enforced, biblical laws restricted asylum to those who had accidentally killed another (Exod 21:12–14; Num 35:9–34; Deut 19:1–13). These statutes also created six cities of refuge—all corresponding to priestly or Levitical cities (Deut 4:41–43; Josh 20:7–8; 21:13, 21, 27, 32, 36; 1 Chr 6:63). This fact suggests that at some point these cities contained local cultic sites.

In the post-exilic period, the Temple apparently continued to serve as a place of refuge, at least on a limited basis. The book of 1 Maccabees records a decree from Demetrius II declaring that "all who take refuge at the temple in Jerusalem, or in any of its precincts, because they owe money to the king or are in debt, let them be released and receive back all

---

[108]Apollonius, *Ep.* 65.

[109]Strabo, *Geog.* 14.1.23. See Oster, "Ephesus as a Religious Center under the Principate," 1714–1718. For the ways in which ancient novelists exploited this *topos*, see Thomas, "At Home in the City of Artemis," 98–106.

their property in my kingdom" (1 Macc 10:43; cf. Josephus, *Ant.* 13.56). Later, during the Jewish War, Josephus fled into the Temple's inner courts, seeking refuge from his enemies (*Vita* 20–21). Only certain types of suppliants appear to have been granted asylum, however, since Philo states that "it would be sacrilege for a person responsible for the death of a man, however it was caused, to come within the [Temple's] sacred precincts" (*Spec.* 1.159; cf. 3.88–99).[110] As we shall see shortly, Philo's subsequent remarks may indicate that in his day, those accused of involuntary manslaughter may have been granted asylum in certain *Palestinian* synagogues.

Before examining these statements, however, we need to review the evidence adduced in previous chapters suggesting that the synagogues *in Egypt* possessed the right of asylum. First of all, we observed that the author of a papyrus from the village of Alexandrou-Nesos (*CPJ* 1.129; 218 B.C.E.) accused a Jew of stealing her cloak and then fleeing to the nearby *proseuchē*—this last hinting that the synagogue was a place of asylum. Elsewhere, we suggested that 3 Maccabees contains two allusions to synagogues providing sanctuary to Jews seeking to escape the edicts of Ptolemy Philopater (3 Macc 3:27–29, 4:17–18). The basis for these interpretations is an inscription previously cited, though not reproduced (*JIE* 125 = *CIJ* 2.1449). The inscription reads as follows:

Βασιλίσσης καὶ βασι-
λέως προσταξάντων
ἀντὶ τῆς προανακει-
μένης περὶ τῆς ἀναθέσε-
ως τῆς προσευχῆς πλα-
κὸς ἡ ὑπογεγραμμένη
ἐπιγραφήτω· [*vacat*]
Βασιλεὺς Πτολεμαῖος Εὐ-
εργέτης τὴν προσευχὴν ἄσυλον.
Regina et
rex iusser(un)t

On the orders of the queen and king, in place of the previous plaque about the dedication of the *proseuchē* let what is written below be written up. King Ptolemy Euergetes (proclaimed) the *proseuchē* inviolate. The queen and king gave the order.

---

[110]Elsewhere, Philo alludes to the Temple as possessing the right of *asylon* (*Legat.* 346), suggesting that certain types of suppliants were allowed to seek asylum within the Temple precincts.

While the actual monument dates to the middle of the first century B.C.E., it is a replacement for an earlier inscription probably dating to the reign of Ptolemy Euergetes II (145–116 B.C.E.).[111] The exact provenance of the inscription is unknown, but it clearly grants the right of asylum to the synagogue. J. Gwyn Griffiths notes that the Ptolemies otherwise recognized this right only in *temples* that had been granted special authority.[112] Likewise, Paul Fraser observes that "we know of no other foreign cult similarly respected."[113] Although we currently possess no other inscriptions attesting to this right for other Egyptian synagogues, the allusions in 3 Maccabees and *CPJ* 1.129 suggest that most synagogues in the country enjoyed this privilege.

This returns us to Philo's remarks about the right of asylum vis-à-vis the Jerusalem Temple. Here we must observe that Philo's qualification of this function for the Temple in *Spec.* 1.159 is based upon his exegesis of Numbers 35:2–8, where the Law only prescribes the six cities of refuge as places of asylum for those committing involuntary manslaughter. Of interest to this study is that, after commenting about the Temple, Philo goes on to write the following:

> [Moses] made over to [the Levites] the aforesaid cities [i.e., the cities of refuge] as secondary temples [ἱερὰ δεύτερα], well secured from violation [πολλὴν ἀσυλίαν ἐχούσας] through the privileged and honourable positions of the inhabitants, who, if any stronger power should attempt to use force against the suppliants, would keep them safe, not with warlike preparations, but through the dignities and privileges conferred on them by the laws in virtue of the reverence attached to the priestly office (*Spec.* 1.159).[114]

If taken as an anachronism, Philo's mention of *deutera hiera* possessing the right of invioliability could be read as an allusion to the right of asylum existing in certain Palestinian synagogues during Philo's own

---

[111]So *JIE*. Kasher argues that Euergetes I (247–221 B.C.E.) was the monarch originally granting the right. Fraser, however, notes that asylum was rarely granted in the third century. See Kasher, "Synagogues as 'Houses of Prayer' and 'Holy Places,'" 215; Fraser, *Ptolemaic Egypt*, 2.442, n. 772.

[112]Griffiths, "Egypt and the Rise of the Synagogue," 12. See also Dion, "Synagogues et temples dans l'Égypte hellénistique," 57–59; *NDIEC* 4.201; *HJP* 3.1.47.

[113]Fraser, *Ptolemaic Alexandria*, 1.283.

[114]See also Philo, *Prob.* 148–152; it cannot be decided for certain whether this segment refers to a synagogue or to a pagan temple, though the latter seems more likely given the timbre of the passage.

time.[115] Alternatively, the passage may be a veiled reference to the Jewish situation in Alexandria and its environs, since, as we have seen, the right of asylum was granted to at least some Egyptian synagogues. In either case, it is interesting that Philo is able to speak of "secondary temples" connected with the priestly and Levitical leadership living outside of Jerusalem.

While Philo's remarks in the cited passage remain enigmatic, less ambiguous is the evidence cited above for the synagogues in Egypt. The bestowal of asylum rights upon Egyptian synagogues, seen in an inscription (*JIE* 125) and in literary allusions (*CPJ* 1.129; 3 Macc 3:27–29, 4:17–18), reinforces the view that these structures served as sacred precincts that were officially recognized as falling under the protection of the Jewish Deity residing within the Temple shrine in Jerusalem.

MANUMISSION

Slavery was a pervasive feature of the Near East during our period, with population statistics suggesting that one of every five persons was a slave.[116] Most Greek or Roman families owned at least one slave, while the imperial family possessed some 20,000, each assigned a specific job such as water-carrier, cook or doctor.[117]

While slaves were, of course, bound to their owners for life, there was often the hope for manumission, which could take place in a number of ways. In Rome, slaves were often released upon the owner's death as a public display of the munificence of the deceased. Elsewhere in the empire where this custom was not as prevalent, slaves could obtain their release either by having their freedom purchased by a benefactor or by paying the money themselves from the allowances many of them received. Whatever the course followed, in the eastern half of the empire, it was common for slaves to be released inside the temple precincts with

---

[115]As Moshe Weinfeld has pointed out, in contrast to the Egyptian custom of confining the right of asylum to the sacred precincts of a temple, in Mesopotamia and Syro-Palestine the asylum rights of a temple were frequently extended to the entire city through at least the Hellenistic period (Moshe Weinfeld, "Freedom Proclamations in Egypt and in the Ancient Near East" in *Pharaonic Egypt*, edited by Sarah Israelit Groll [Jerusalem: The Magnes Press, 1985], 317–327).

[116]See K. R. Bradley, *Slavery and Society at Rome* (Cambridge: Cambridge University Press, 1994), 12.

[117]Ibid., 61–64.

priests serving as witnesses. Fortunately, we are well-informed on these proceedings, since more than a thousand manumission inscriptions have been preserved at the temple of Pythian Apollo in Delphi. Because the documents are formulaic, the following inscription exemplifies a large portion of those uncovered there (*SEG* 31.543; I B.C.E.):[118]

[ἄρχοντος N. N. μηνὸς]
[- - - ἀπέδοτο N. N. τῷ 'Απόλλωνι τῷ Πυθίῳ]
[σῶμα ἀνδρεῖον ὧ ὄνομα Θεοφάνης τὸ γένος - - -]
[τιμᾶς ἀργυρίου μνᾶν - - - καὶ]
[τειμὰν ἔχει πᾶσαν, καθῶς ἐπίστευσε Θεοφάν]ῃ̣ς τὰν ὠναν τῷ θε̣[ῷ]
[ἐφ' ῷτε ἐλεύθερος εἶμεν καὶ ἀνέφαπτος ἀπὸ] πάντων τὸν πάντα βίον·
[βεβαιωτὴρ N. N. εἰ δέ τις ἐφέτποιτ]ο Θεοφάνεως ἐπι καταδουλ̣[ισ]μῷ,
[βέβαιον παρεχόντω τῷ Θεῷ τὰν ὠνὰν ὅ τε ἀπ]οδόμενος καὶ ὁ βεβαι-
[ωτὴρ. - - - κύριο]ς ἔστω συλέων Θεο-
[φάνην - - - ἀζάμιος ὢν καὶ ἀνυ]πό[δικο]ος. πάσας δίκας καὶ
[ζαμίας. μάρτυροι οἱ ἱερεῖ]ς τοῦ 'Απ̣[όλλωνος Αἰα]κ̣ί̣δας, *vacat*
['εμμενίδας καὶ Χαλεεῖς Δαμ]ων, Καλλίμ̣[αχος . . . . . .]ς *vacat*

[When N. N. was archon in the month of]
[. . . N. N. gave up to Pythian Apollo]
[a male slave by the name of Theophanes, by race . . .]
[for the price of X silver minae and]
[he has the entire price, just as Theophan]es entrusted the sale to the god
[on condition that he be free and not be seized as a slave by] anyone for the duration of his life.
[Guarantor, N. N. If anyone should seize] Theophanes with a view to enslavement,
[let the sale to the god be confirmed by the one who] gave (him) up and the guarantor.
[. . . Let him be entitled] to rescue Theophanes
[. . . being immune and not liable] to any lawsuit or
[penalty. Witnesses are the priests] of Apollo, Aikidas,
[Emmenidas and Chaleans Dam]on, Kallimachos . . .

As we see, part of the ceremony involved the sale of the slave to the god, with the temple priests receiving the deposited sum. In fact, the sale was fictitious, for various sources make it clear that, after taking their portion of the deposit, the priests would refund the money to the former owner.[119] A stone would be placed in the sanctuary bearing a record of the

---

[118]Translation from *NDIEC* 6.72. The restorations are based upon formulas found in similar inscriptions.

[119]See Westermann, "Parmone as General Service Contract," 9–10.

transaction, which included an authorization for the human guarantor to act on Apollo's behalf in the event that the manumitted slave was ever seized in the future. The freedman was thus placed under the protection of Apollo, with the sanctuary of the temple in effect being extended beyond the sacred precincts.

In about three quarters of the Delphic monuments, including the one quoted above, the released slave is granted unconditional freedom of movement, with no further encumbrances made by the manumitter. The remaining grants contain a so-called *paramonē* clause, requiring the manumitted slaves "to remain" with their master or mistress, providing general, undefined services.[120] This relationship usually continued through the remainder of the former owner's life, though in some cases the *paramonē* was terminated after a number of years, allowing the freedman in effect to become a free agent.[121]

The Jewish manumission inscriptions from the Bosporus follow the general form and phrasing of the Delphic grants, though they dispense with the fictitious sale to the Deity. Accordingly, the ceremony reflected in these inscriptions does not take place in a pagan temple, but in the Jewish synagogue. This latter is also the location where a record of the transaction was placed on public display. Among the Bosporus inscriptions uncovered thus far, both types of manumission grants are attested,[122] though the *paramonē* manumissions differ in terms of the conditions of the release: whereas the pagan examples imply an ongoing economic relationship between the former slave and master, the Jewish manumissions stipulate that the released slave maintain pious behavior with respect to the Deity and to the synagogue. We saw an example of this type of manumission in the previous chapter's discussion of God-fearers (*CIJ* 1.683a). There, the requirement of the release was that the manumitted slave be faithful in attendance in the synagogue and that he "honor God" (θεὸν σέβων; ll. 9, 10). A similar set of conditions was imposed on the three slaves mentioned in the following inscription that was recently discovered in Phanagoria:[123]

---

[120]Ibid., 12–13.

[121]See Westermann, *The Slave Systems of Greek and Roman Antiquity*, 56, n. 75.

[122]For two examples of manumissions from Gorgippia not containing a *paramonē* clause (*CIJ* 1.690, 690a), see the discussion of the Bosporus Kingdom in chapter four.

[123]Author's translation. From D. I. Danshin, "Jewish Community of Phanagoria," *Vestnik Drevnei Istorii* 204, no. 1 (1993): 60 [Russian]; hereafter referred to as Danshin no. 1. See also Levinskya, *The Book of Acts in Its Diaspora Setting*, 237–239; S. R. Tokhtas'en, "The New Jewish Manumission from Phanagoria," *Bulletin of*

[Β]α̣σιλε<ύ>ον[τος] Βα̣-
σι̣λέως Κότυ̣ος
ἔτους <η>μτʹ μηνὸς
Ξ̣ανδικοῦ αʹ. Ψυχα̣-
ρ̣ίων, Σογος, Ἄνος
ο]ἱ τούτο<υ> ὑειοί. Κὰρ-
σάνδανος καὶ Κὰρ-
άγος καὶ Μ̣<η>τ̣ρό-
τ̣ε̣ιμος ἄφετοι τῇ
προσευχῇ, ἀνεπίλ̣<η>-
πτοι, ἀνεπικόλυ-
τοι, χωρὶς εἰς τὴν
προ<σ>ευχὴν προσκαρ-
τ̣ερήσεως καὶ θωπία-
ς καὶ ἔσταν ἄφετ̣[ο]-
ι] συνεπιτροπεο̣ύ̣σ̣-
ης τῆς συναγω̣[γῆ]-
ς] τῶν Ἰουδαί-
ων.

Under the reign of King Cotys, in the year 348 [= 51 C.E.] on the first of the month of Xandikos: Sogos (and) Anos, sons of Psycharios (state that) Karsandanos and Karagos and Metroteimos were released in the *proseuchē*, and are unassailable and cannot be hindered except that they show diligence and devotion toward the *proseuchē*, under the joint guardianship of the congregation of the Jews.

Two of the released slaves (Karsandanos and Karagos) were probably of Scytho-Sarmatian origin bearing Persian or Median names,[124] while the nationality of the third (Metroteimos) is unclear. The wording of the *paramonē* condition in this inscription is identical to that seen in three other inscriptions, one from Phanagoria dating to 16 C.E.,[125] and two

Judaeo-Greek Studies 13 (1993): 27–28.

[124]So Levinskya, *The Book of Acts in Its Diaspora Setting*, 238–239. Danshin had thought that καρ in ll.6–7 indicated that the men were Carian ("Jewish Community of Phanagoria," 60–62). Levinskya, however, points out that ethnic designations were usually placed *after* the name in inscriptions. On Jewish possession of Gentile slaves, see Philo, *Spec.* 2.123; Lev 25:44.

[125]*CIJ* 1.691 = *CIRB* 985: "In the reign of King Aspourgus, friend of the Romans, in the year 313, the seventh day of the month of Daisios, Phodakos, son of Pothon, dedicates his home-bred slave, Dionysios, and Longiona (?) [in the *proseuchē*], . . . devotion and diligence [towards the *proseuchē*]" ([Β]ασιλεύοντος [βα]||[σ]ιλέως Ἀ̣σπούργο[υ] | [φ]ιλορωιμαίου, ἔτους | [γ]ιτʹ, μηνὸς Λαισίου ζʹ | [Φ]όδακος Πόθωνος ἀ||[ν]ατίθησι τὸν ἑαυτοῦ | [θρεπτὸ]ν Διονύσιον | [τ]ὸν καὶ Λ̣ο̣ν[γ]ι(?)ωνα ἐ|[πι] τ[ῆς προσευχῆς] Ἀπόλ|[- - -]ογη̣ || [- - -]ασ | [- - -]τη[- - -] | [- - -] | [- - -] |

from Panticapaeum dating to slightly after our period.[126] What is striking about this formula is that the term *proskartereō* ("to persevere in," "to spend much time in")[127] appears with the word *proseuchē* in several instances in the New Testament.[128] In Romans 12:12, for example, Paul exhorts his readers to "persevere in prayer [τῇ προσευχῇ προσκαρτεροῦντες]." The same formula repeats itself several places in Acts, such as where the disciples are said to have been "constantly devoting themselves to prayer [προσκαρτεροῦντες ὁμοθυμαδὸν τῇ προσευχῇ]" (Acts 1:14; cf. 2:42, 6:4; Col 4:2). When viewed with the Bosporus inscriptions, the recurrent use of this expression in early Christian sources suggests that it was an admonition frequently used by Jews with God-fearers or proselytes. In the case of the manumission inscriptions, however, the prescribed activity is localized so that it occurs within the *proseuchē*, as is indicated by the presence of the preposition *eis* (l. 12). Interestingly enough, the only other use of a preposition with *proskartereō* in the New Testament comes in Acts 2:46 where the early Christian converts are said to have "spent much time together in the temple [προσκαρτεροῦντες ὁμοθυμαδὸν ἐν τῷ ἱερῷ]." This also may have been a widely used formula, reflecting the admonition to be faithful in attending the Temple or the synagogue.

[- - -]αν || [. . . . .]ο[. . . .]ụσ̣[.] | [- - -]ηθε | [- - -]ης θω|π̣ε̣ί[ας ἕνεκα καὶ] προσ|κ̣αρ[τερ]ήσεως). Author's translation.

[126]*CIJ* 1.683 = *CIRB* 70 (81 C.E.): "In the reign of King Tiberius Julius Rescuporis, friend of Caesar and friend of the Romans, pious, in the year 377, the twelfth of the month of Pereitios, I Chreste, former wife of Drusus, release in the *proseuchē*, my home-bred slave Heraclas, free, once and for all, according to my vow, who is to be undisturbed and unharmed by all of my heirs, and who may go wherever he desires, unhindered, as I have vowed, except that he show devotion and diligence toward the *proseuchē* with the agreement both of my heirs Heraclides and Heliconias and also under the joint guardianship of the congregation of the Jews"; *CIJ* 1.684 = *CIRB* 73 (c. 100 C.E.): ". . . in the year . . . in the month of Artemisios . . . , in the *proseuchē*, I have set free [my slaves once and for all], according to a vow I have made . . . , male (?) and Hermas, undisturbed and unharmed by all my heirs . . . during my life . . . according to what is pleasing . . . and until my death all will make. . ., and after my death, it will be permitted them to go to any place they wish, with neither obstacle nor hindrance, according to my vow, except with regards to the *proseuchē*, to which they shall owe devotion and diligence and be under the joint guardianship of the congregation of the Jews." Author's translations.

[127]BAGD s.v. προσκαρτερέω.

[128]I would like to express my gratitude to J. Andrew Overman for pointing out to me the similarity of language between the Bosporus inscriptions and certain passages in the New Testament.

The second of the terms in the *paramonē* clause, *thōpeia*, literally means "flattery."[129] Its use in the Bosporan inscriptions is odd, since it carries the connotation of "bribery" or "coaxing." The word's association with cultic practices, however, can be discerned from Plato's criticism of a segment of the populace who "suppose that in return for small offerings and flatteries [θύματα καὶ θωπείας] the gods lend them aid in committing large robberies, and often set them free from great penalties" (*Laws* 12.948c). Plato's sarcasm aside, his characterization fits the Bosporus manumissions perfectly: whereas normally *paramonē* entailed an ongoing economic relationship with one's former owner, here it entailed a pious attitude and reverent behavior within the synagogue that one was obliged to attend regularly.[130] This interpretation is confirmed by the presence of the parallel phrase *theon sebōn* ("reveres God") in the Bosporus inscription examined in chapter five (*CIJ* 1.683a). The custom of including this clause may reflect an attempt on the part of some Bosporus Jews to fulfill partially the biblical commandment to circumcise their slaves (Gen 17:12, 23–27; Exod 12:44).[131]

While it is unclear if the released Gentile slaves were required to undergo full conversion, the provisions of the manumission clearly sought to encourage reverent behavior. Striking in this respect is the designation of the Jewish community as the "joint guardians" (συνεπιτροπέουσα) of the released slaves. If the congregation was meant to correspond to the "witnesses" (μάρτυροι) or to the "guarantor" (βεβαιωτὴρ) in the Delphic decrees, the language is peculiar. Here, Paul's use of the underlying word *epitropos* ("guardian," "tutor")[132] in reference to the desire of some Galatians to place themselves under the Jewish Law (Gal 4:2) may not be accidental; the term conceivably could have been

---

[129]LSJ s.v. θωπεία.

[130]Cf. Westerman, *The Slave Systems of Greek and Roman Antiquity*, 124–126; *HJP* 3.1.105–106; *NDIEC* 6.72–76; Deissman, *Light from the Ancient East*, 320–330; Levinskya, *The Book of Acts in Its Diaspora Setting*, 110, n. 19; Harrill, *The Manumission of Slaves in Early Christianity*, 174–178. In this vein, Philo's comments regarding the payment of the Temple tax are instructive: "The donors bring them cheerfully and gladly, expecting that the payment will give them release from slavery or healing of diseases and the enjoyment of liberty fully secured and also complete preservation from danger" (*Spec.* 1.77–78).

[131]See Harrill, *The Manumission of Slaves in Early Christianity*, 175–176.

[132]On the connotations of this word, see Betz, *Galatians*, 203–204.

used in the diaspora to designate Jewish catechists.[133] In support of this hypothesis is the fact that Josephus uses the same word when referring to the overseers of the Essene community (*BJ* 2.134).

Whether the members of the synagogue at Phanagoria served as catechists or simply as witnesses to the transaction, it should be noted, finally, that the manumission arrangement need not be understood as a type of coerced proselytism; on the contrary, since the manumitted slaves agreed to the provisions of the release, they may have welcomed the arrangement cheerfully (cf. Gal 4:21). The inscriptions do indicate, however, that an openness existed among the Bosporan congregations toward including Gentiles within their synagogues.

Unfortunately, outside of the Bosporan inscriptions, our sources are silent about Jewish manumission practices during our period. It is not known, for instance, whether slaves were commonly released within the courts of the Jerusalem Temple. Moreover, we do not know if similar release ceremonies took place in synagogues outside the Bosporus Kingdom.[134] Nevertheless, it is revealing that the Bosporan Jews used their synagogues for a function normally associated with temples. This fact, combined with the injunctions that the released slaves were to behave reverently *within the building*, indicates that the Bosporan Jews viewed their synagogues as sacred edifices dedicated to God.

COUNCIL HALLS, COURTS, SOCIETY HOUSES

In the introduction of this chapter, we observed that the precincts of Roman and Greek temples typically served as assembly sites for councils, law courts and popular assemblies. The same was true of the Temple in Jerusalem, as we noted in chapter three. The Sanhedrin normally met in one of the stoas within the courts, or in the bouleterion adjoining the complex (Josephus, *BJ* 4.336, 5.144, 6.354; Acts 6:14–16). Likewise, the high priest or monarch frequently assembled the people in the Temple courts to address matters of public concern (e.g., Josephus, *BJ* 1.122;

---

[133]It is also striking that in Gal 4:1 Paul writes, “the heir, as long as he is a child, is no better than a slave [ὁ κληρονόμος νήπιός ἐστιν, οὐδὲν διαφέρει δούλου].” This sounds rather like a manumitted slave under a revised *paramonē* clause. Paul may be drawing on this imagery rather pointedly in order to convince his Galatian converts not to become disciples of the Jewish Christian teachers.

[134]A badly preserved inscription (*CIJ* 1.731) found with the synagogue at Delos reads “. . . became free [γενόμενος | ἐλεύθερος].” Unfortunately, the fragmentary nature of the monument makes it impossible to draw any firm conclusions from it.

2.1–5, 294–295, 320–324, 411–412; *Ant.* 9.153, 11.168, 12.164, 13.181, 16.132, 17.200–201).

The synagogues of Palestine and the diaspora also functioned as council halls, courtrooms, and public meeting halls. Thus, the *proseuchē* of Tiberias apparently served as the seat of the city *boulē*, as Josephus depicts the council assembling there on three separate occasions (*Vita* 276–303). That this situation was not unique within Palestine can be inferred from a passage in Mark's Gospel where Jesus is depicted warning his disciples that "they will hand you over to councils; and you will be beaten in synagogues [παραδώσουσιν ὑμᾶς εἰς συνέδρια καὶ εἰς συναγωγὰς δαρήσεσθε]" (Mark 13:9 || Matt 10:17 || Luke 21:12; cf. Matt 23:24). Independent attestation of local *archontes* and councils in Palestine during our period (Josephus, *Ant.* 4.214; *Vita* 79) lends support to these depictions.[135]

Moving to the diaspora, two decrees from Sardis make reference to the use of a synagogue (*topos*) for deliberative and judicial assemblies. The first, promulgated by the Sardian *boulē* and *dēmos*, granted the Jews the right to "come together and have a communal life and adjudicate suits among themselves and that a *topos* be given them [πολιτεύωνται καὶ διαδικάζωνται πρὸς αὑτούς, δοθῇ τε καὶ τόπος αὑτους]" (Josephus, *Ant.* 14.260). This right was later reaffirmed in a letter from the proquaestor Lucius Antonius (c. 49 B.C.E.) recognizing that "from the earliest times [the Jews] have had an association of their own in accordance with their native laws and a *topos* of their own, in which they decide their own affairs and controversies with one another [αὑτοὺς σύνοδον ἔχειν ἰδίαν κατὰ τοὺς πατρίους νόμος ἀπ' ἀρχῆς καὶ τόπον ἴδιον, ἐν ᾧ τά τε πράγματα καὶ τὰς πρὸς ἀλλήλους ἀντιλογίας κρίνουσι]" (*Ant.* 14.235). Elsewhere, two inscriptions from Berenice previously quoted (*CJZC* 70–71)[136] refer to assemblies in the local synagogue (*amphitheatron*) where the Jewish politeuma voted to bestow honors upon two benefactors.

---

[135]Of course, the Gospel writers may also have had a diaspora setting in view. We should add that if one accepts that *synagōgē* in the OG version of Sus 28 refers to a building rather than an assembly, as some interpreters maintain, then the passage provides additional evidence that courts convened in synagogues c. 100 B.C.E. in Palestine, the likely date and provenance of this document. See the treatment of *synagōgē* in chapter two.

[136]See chapters two and four.

Within Egypt, the following papyrus, while poorly preserved, nevertheless indicates that a Jewish burial society met in one of the synagogues there (*CPJ* 1.138; I B.C.E., provenance unknown):[137]

] . ἐπὶ τῆς γ[ε]ν̣η̣θ̣ε̣ί̣σης σ̣υ̣ν̣αγωγῆς ἐν τῆι προσευχῆι
Δημητ]ρίωι τῶν [(πρώτων)] φίλων καὶ θ̣[υ(ρωρῶν)]
καὶ εἰσαγγελέων καὶ ἀρχυ̣π̣ηρε(τῶν)
]Κάμακος [. . .] . . [. . . . . . .]ξ[. . . . .] . [. . γραμ]μ̣ατεὺς
. .] . . . . [- - -]κ̣υον εἰς τὴν σ[ύνοδον
.]ου σὺν τοῖ[ς .] . . . . [. . . . . . .] . ρασιος κα̣ὶ̣ συλ̣λ̣ελόχισται
]ρ̣κως το ε . [.] . αλλ εμ̣[. . . .]υ ἐν τοῖς ἐρ̣χο̣[.] . . . . . ντα̣ς
.]μ̣ε̣ δικαι̣ . [. .] . . . . [. . . . . . .]ε̣ιν ἐφ᾽ ὧιτε ἐτεάς [.]ς
σ]υνόδου[- - -] . φ[.] . . [. . .]κ̣αιρ̣οις
.]ωι κ̣α̣τ̣᾽ ἔτ̣ο[ς .]ει επτ̣ . [. . . . .]ιου γ . ι̣λ̣ι̣ . . . ωι με[.]ε̣
.]ινων ε . [.]σ̣ου κ[οινοῦ . . . ταφι]α̣σ̣τ̣ῶν ἐκ τῆς
. .]τ̣ε α̣τ̣ε̣[.] . πον[. . . . .]φαλλισμων κα̣[. . . .]
] . ο τοῦ ἐσομ̣έ̣νου κα̣ι̣[νοῦ . . . . . οὐ]δ [[ι]] ἐ̣ν α̣ὐ̣λ̣ῶ[ι . . . .]
. .]μαι Ευδ[. .] . ι̣[. . . . .]τ̣ο̣υ̣ συνταφιά[στου]
. .]σεται [ο]ἷς προ̣σ̣[ήκει . . . . γ]ρ̣αμματεῖ ἀκολ̣[ούθως]
.]εἰς ἱ̣ερο . [. .] . απ[. . . . .]ια τοῦ δελ . [
το]ῖ̣ς λει[του]ρ̣[γ . . . .]συνόδου τοῦ[
. . .] . . . . . . [. . . . .] . θησεται ξ[
]α̣θ̣ε̣ς̣[

. . . At the session held in the *proseuchē*
To Demetrios of the first friends and the door-keepers (?)
and the ushers and the chief officials
. . . of Kamax . . . secretary . . .
. . . to the association
. . . with . . . and has been incorporated
. . . on the condition that
. . . association . . . the times
. . . every year
. . . the corporation of . . . *taphiastai*
. . . future new
. . . the *syntaphiastes*
. . . whom it concerns . . . to the secretary according
. . . the association

It is unclear whether the association consisted of the entire synagogue congregation or a subgroup. In either case, the association was clearly well-organized, with a group of officers and subordinates forming its bureaucracy. The papyrus further highlights the fact that the synagogue

[137]Translation, *CPJ*.

served as the venue for meetings addressing a variety of community needs.

The evidence concerning the rest of the diaspora, while not conclusive, nevertheless hints that synagogues were used for deliberative and judicial assemblies in other regions outside the homeland. With respect to Alexandria, for example, Strabo wrote that the Jewish ethnarch "governs the people and adjudicates suits and supervises contracts and ordinances, just as if he were the head of a sovereign state [διοικεῖ τε τὸ ἔθνος καὶ διαιτᾷ κρίσεις καὶ συμβολαίων ἐπιμελεῖται καὶ προσταγμάτων, ὡς ἄν πολιτείας ἄρχων αὐτοτελοῦς]"[138] Because the only Jewish public buildings in Alexandria mentioned in our sources are *proseuchai*, it is possible to infer that the ethnarch and the subsequent *gerousia* held court in one or more of these structures.[139] A similar arrangement may have been present in Antioch where Josephus mentions that a Jewish *archōn* ruled in a manner analogous to that of the Alexandrian ethnarch (*BJ* 7.47). Finally, in 2 Corinthians 11:24, Paul mentions that he had received thirty-nine lashes from the Jews on five occasions. The punishment to which Paul alludes is one associated with Jewish courts (Josephus, *Ant.* 4.21; Deut 25:1–3).[140] Unlike a stoning which could be inflicted spontaneously (Josephus, *Vita* 303), its enactment must have followed the rendering of a formal court verdict. Assuming that at least some of the lashings occurred as the result of Paul's missionary activities in the diaspora, the verdicts were possibly delivered in courts held in the synagogues there, with the floggings being inflicted in an adjacent courtyard (cf. Mark 13:9; Matt 10:17, 23:24; Luke 21:12). In support of this view is a letter written by Marcus Agrippa to Ephesus—the city in which Paul wrote 2 Corinthians—ordering those caught stealing the sacred monies of the Ephesian Jews to be handed over *not* to the local magistrates, but to the Jews themselves (Josephus, *Ant.* 16.168). This implies that the Jews of this city were empowered to exercise judicial powers and to inflict punishment on those convicted of certain offenses.

---

[138]Strabo, *Historica Hypomnemata* ap. Josephus, *Ant.* 14.117. For commentary, see *GLAJJ* 1.277–282.

[139]*CPJ* 1.143, ll. 7–8 mentions a "Jewish archive" (Ἰουδαίων ἀρχείου), yet this may have been part of a synagogue complex. See the discussion of archives, above. Regarding the parallels between the Alexandria *gerousia* and the Jerusalem Sanhedrin, see Kasher, "Synagogues as 'Houses of Prayer' and 'Holy Places'," 217–218.

[140]See Furnish, *II Corinthians*, 515–516.

The preceding discussion indicates that at least some synagogues in Palestine and the diaspora served as venues for deliberative proceedings. This is directly attested for the synagogues of Tiberias, Berenice and Sardis. Whether or not the synagogues in other cities functioned in this manner is uncertain, though the evidence pointing in this direction is suggestive, especially for the cities of Ephesus, Alexandria and Antioch. In the places where a deliberative function is directly attested, the leadership consisted of an *archōn* or *archontes* (Josephus, *Vita* 79, *BJ* 2.571; *CJCZ* 70–71). The law code most likely followed would have been the Mosaic Law, as interpreted locally (Josephus, *Ap.* 2.184–187, *Vita* 132–35; Philo, *Legat.* 210). An Egyptian synagogue of unknown provenance also functioned as the meeting place for a burial society. Again, the possibility should not be excluded that other synagogues functioned similarly. One can imagine, for instance, various Jewish trade guilds meeting in the synagogues.

If the Temple courts served as the central civic center for the Jewish nation, the synagogues could thus function in this manner on a local scale. In the cities of Sardis, Berenice, Tiberias, and probably elsewhere, the synagogues mirrored the Temple precincts by serving as venues for courts, councils, and popular assemblies. The former functioned, in essence, as miniature versions of the latter.

CONCLUSION

The investigations of this chapter have revealed that the functions of the synagogues paralleled those of the Temple precincts in many respects. Literary and epigraphic evidence adduced suggested that synagogues in both Palestine and the diaspora functioned as places for prayer, study and the teaching of scripture on the Sabbath.[141] Similar types of evidence attested that at least some synagogues functioned as banks, archives, and museums for votive offerings.[142] An Egyptian inscription revealed that a synagogue there had been invested with the right of asylum (*JIE* 125). Literary evidence implied that this bestowal was not an isolated case in

[141]Prayer: e.g., Josephus, *Ant.* 14.260–261, *Vita* 294–295, *Ap.* 1.209–211; *Bib. Ant.* 11.8; Philo, *Flacc.* 122–124. Scripture study: e.g., *CIJ* 2.1404; Josephus, *Ant.* 16.43–45, *Ap.* 2.175; Philo, *Somn.* 2.123–129; Luke 4:16–30.

[142]Banks: Josephus, *Ant.* 16.164, 168; Philo, *Spec.* 1.76–78. Archives: e.g., *CIJ* 1.683a, 690, 690a, 691; Danshin no. 1; *JIE* 125. Museums: e.g., *JIE* 9, 13, 22, 27, 28, 117, 24, 25, 105,126; *CIJ* 1.727–31, 2.1404; *DF* 33; *CJCZ* 70–72; Josephus, *BJ* 7.44; Philo, *Legat.* 133.

Egypt (*CPJ* 1.129; 3 Macc 3:27–29, 4:17–18). An imperial decree issued by Augustus recognized the inviolability of the Asian synagogues (Josephus, *Ant.* 16.164), thereby securing their places as sacred repositories for the offerings to the Jerusalem Temple. Other decrees, inscriptions and literary accounts indicated that the synagogues of Sardis, Berenice and Tiberias served as venues for deliberative proceedings (Josephus, *Ant.* 14.235, 260; *Vita* 276–303; *CJCZ* 70–71). One of the papyri preserves the minutes of a burial society within an Egyptian synagogue (*CPJ* 1.138). Literary and epigraphic evidence directly attest to synagogal assemblies on Jewish holy days such as the Sabbath (e.g., Josephus, *BJ* 2.285–292, *Ant.* 14.256–258, 259–261; Philo, *Mos.* 2.214–216; Mark 3:1–6), New Moon (*CJZC* 70–71) and Feast of Tabernacles (*CJZC* 71; Philo, *Flacc.* 116–124). Literary and epigraphic sources imply that assemblies took place in the synagogues on Yom Kippur (Philo, *Spec.* 1.186; *CIJ* 1.725). Passover and Pentecost may have been included among the unspecified "customary" feasts celebrated in some synagogues (Josephus, *Ant.* 14.257, 14.213–216, 14.261, 16.162–165). Archaeological and literary evidence suggested that one customarily washed or bathed oneself before entering into a synagogue.[143] That synagogues functioned as "sacred" rather than "profane" buildings is further indicated by the presence of nearly a dozen inscriptions dedicating the building and/or its appurtenances to *Theos Hypsistos*.[144] A function associated with the Bosporus synagogues—that of manumission—while not attested for the Jerusalem Temple, was a common function of pagan temples.[145]

The key function of the Temple *not* shared by any of the synagogues is the one prohibited by the Mosaic Law, namely, the rendering of sacrifices. Yet even here, literary evidence suggests that the offering of prayers and the reading of sacred scriptures served as a form of sacrifice for those worshiping in the synagogues (Philo, *Spec.* 1.195–197, 272). Moreover, Philo calls the synagogues "*didaskaleia* of temperance and justice where men while practicing virtue subscribed the annual first-fruits to pay for the sacrifices which they offer and commissioned sacred envoys to take them to the temple in Jerusalem" (*Legat.* 311; cf. 156). In this way, the synagogue congregations shared in the offering of sacrifices, if only from a distance.

---

[143] *CIJ* 2.1404; *CPJ* 1.134; Acts 16:13–16; Josephus, Ant. 14.256–258; Philo, *Deus* 7–9; *mikvaoth* near the synagogues at Gamla, Herodium and Masada; placement of the synagogues at Ostia, Delos and Capernaum by the sea; the water basins outside the synagogues at Ostia and Delos.

[144] *JIE* 9, 13, 22, 27, 28, 117, 24, 25, 105 (?), 126.

[145] *CIJ* 1.683a, 690, 690a, 691; Danshin no. 1.

CHAPTER 7
SECTARIAN SYNAGOGUES

This chapter is devoted to the study of three groups from our period whose beliefs and practices diverged notably from those of other Jews: the Essenes, the Therapeutae and the Samaritans.

Modern anthropologists define the term *sect* with reference to a specific set of responses a group makes in relationship to the external world. Perhaps the most widely used definition is that of Bryan Wilson, who applies the term *sect* "to all religious movements that emphasize their separateness and distinctiveness of mission, regardless of organizational character."[1] Working from anthropological data obtained from cross-cultural studies, Wilson goes on to enumerate eight general characteristics of sectarian movements:[2] (1) protest, (2) claim to monopoly on religious truth, (3) rigid membership requirements, (4) total commitment to group, (5) self-sacrifice, (6) overarching ideology, (7) lack of centralized leadership, (8) egalitarianism.

On the basis of these criteria, it is possible to classify both the Essenes and the Therapeutae as sects: as we will see in the subsequent sections, many of the items in the above list match the characteristics of these two groups. The same cannot be said of the Samaritans. While our knowledge of this group's origins is obscured by legend and later Jewish polemic, if the Samaritans ever constituted a sect, they very quickly lost many of its defining characteristics. In part this was due to the removal of choice from the equation, since one typically did not choose to become a Samaritan, but was born one. Nevertheless, the protestant nature of the group continued to manifest itself quite clearly.

We should briefly note that three other Jewish groups—the Pharisees, the Sadducees and the Zealots—while having some characteristics of a

---

[1]Bryan Wilson, *Religious Sects* (Wiedenfeld: World University Press, 1970), 16.

[2]See Bryan Wilson, *Religion in Sociological Perspective* (Oxford: Oxford University Press, 1982), 91–92. Wilson further posits seven types of sects, categorized according to their response to the perceived evil of the external world. See Wilson, *Religious Sects*, 38–40. For the more general purposes of this study, these need not be specified here.

sect, also tended to blend in with the larger society, taking the edge off any counter-cultural proclivities.[3] Although these groups may have had their own synagogues during our period, evidence for such structures is not now forthcoming. Our sources do suggest, however, that the Pharisees attended non-sectarian synagogues, mingling with the general populace (e.g., Mark 3:1; Josephus, *Vita* 276–303). As for the Sicarii, while they were clearly involved with the construction of the synagogues at Masada and Herodium, it appears that non-Sicarii were also members of the occupying forces in these fortresses.[4] Since these persons were probably involved in the activities associated with these structures, it would be unwarranted to speak of the synagogues there as sectarian synagogues. Likewise, because arguments for the existence of sects believed to have been connected with the production of certain Jewish documents (e.g., *1 Enoch, Psalms of Solomon*) are of a hypothetical nature, we cannot posit the existence of separatist synagogues for such "groups."[5]

As we observed in the last chapter, the synagogues tended to be unifying institutions, bringing together Jews from different regions and different backgrounds. Indeed, this integrative role is implied by the very meaning of the word *synagōgē*. Since this term and its Hebrew counterparts are used in the scriptures to refer to the legal and cultic congregation of Israel, for a particular group to lay exclusive claim to them was tantamount to declaring independence from the larger Jewish community. The Essenes clearly did this, as did the Samaritans. Whether or not this was the case with the Therapeutae is unclear.

What is striking about each of these groups, however, is that they continued to draw their self-definitions from their central sanctuary. Indeed, some researchers have argued that the settlement at Qumran functioned as a rival temple, replete with altars upon which animal

---

[3]For a discussion of the appropriateness of the sectarian label for the Sadducees, see Saldarini, *Pharisees, Scribes and Sadducees in Palestinian Society*, 298–308. Saldarini sees no direct proof that the Sadducees ever constituted a protest group and suggests the designation "mode of living" would fit better than "sect" (ibid., 305). For the debate over the sectarian status of the Pharisees, see, e.g., ibid., 277–297; Neusner, *From Politics to Piety*, 1–11 and pass.; E. P. Sanders, *Judaism*, 380–451; *HJP* 2.381–403. For a treatment of the Zealots, see *HJP* 2.598–606.

[4]See *HJP* 2.598–606.

[5]For a consideration of such hypothetical groups, see E. P. Sanders, *Judaism*, 452–457.

sacrifices were offered.[6] While such a claim has not been advanced for the Therapeutae, scholars have noted that some of this group's synagogal activities bore an affinity to those exercised in the Temple—particularly with respect to the feasting of priests and Levites within the Temple chambers.[7] The evidence of the Samaritan synagogues, while slight, also implies that the Samaritans viewed their synagogues as sanctuaries closely allied with their rival temple on Mt. Gerizim.[8] Our subsequent investigations will suggest that the synagogues of these three groups, no less than those of their non-sectarian counterparts, served as distant sacred precincts of a central cultic site.

The treatments of the three groups in the following sections will by no means be comprehensive. In particular, the voluminous nature of the material associated with the Essenes makes a full examination of this group impossible. Fortunately, there are currently studies available on nearly every facet of Essene practice and belief; these will be cited at appropriate points in the discussion for the interested reader. While it will be necessary at points to give background information on each group, our focus will remain fixed on the synagogal evidence and the manner in which the synagogues were employed. Following the treatments of the individual groups, a conclusion will briefly summarize the findings of the investigation.

THE ESSENES[9]

Since Philo is the only author to use the term *synagōgē* in connection with the Essenes, we begin our discussion with his description of the Sabbath worship activities of this sect:

> But the ethical part [the Essenes] study very industriously, taking for their trainers the laws of their fathers, which could not possibly have been

---

[6]See F. M. Cross, *The Ancient Library of Qumran* (Minneapolis: Fortress Press, 1995), 101–103; John Strugnell, "Flavius Josephus and the Essenes: Antiquities XVIII.18–22," *JBL* 77 (1958): 144.

[7]See Jean Riaud, "Les Thérapeutes d'Alexandrie et l'ideal Lévitique" in *Mogilany 1989: Papers on the Dead Sea Scrolls Offered in Memory of Jean Carmignac*, edited by Zdzislaw J. Kapara (Krakow: Enigma Press, 1993).

[8]One wonders if this was also the desire of Onias in constructing his temple—i.e., to become the central sanctuary for the Egyptian synagogues. See Josephus, *Ant.* 13.65–68 as well as the discussion of Onias' temple in chapter four.

[9]On the equation of the Essenes with the group that produced the Dead Sea Scrolls, see the treatment of the the Dead Sea Scrolls in chapter one.

> conceived by the human soul without divine inspiration. In these they are instructed at all other times, but particularly on the seventh day. For that day has been set apart to be kept holy and on it they abstain from all other work and proceed to sacred spots [ἱεροὺς . . . τόπους] which they call *synagōgai*. There, arranged in rows according to their ages, the younger below the elder, they sit decorously as befits the occasion with attentive ears. Then one takes the books and reads aloud and another of especial proficiency comes forward and expounds what is not understood (*Prob.* 80–83).

The description matches closely those of non-sectarian Sabbath services we have encountered in this study (e.g., Philo, *Hypoth.* 7.12–13). Even the rows of benches mentioned in the passage correspond to the arrangement seen in the Palestinian synagogues of this period. Particularly noteworthy in this description is the fact that Philo calls the Essene synagogues *hieroi topoi*, "sacred places." By his use of this phrase, Philo implies that the Essene synagogues were communal buildings dedicated to the Deity, separate from "profane" domiciles that remained in human possession.

Also of interest is Philo's statement that the Essenes themselves called their sacred places *synagōgai*. Scholars have typically held that in Palestine, the Aramaic counterpart of the Greek word *synagōgē* was *bēt kᵉnišāh*, "house of the gathering," since this phrase or its Hebrew equivalent appears in the rabbinic literature and in later synagogue inscriptions (e.g., *y. Sanh* 8.2 [20a.43]; *CIJ* 2.1195).[10] While this may have been the case, we currently lack evidence from our period using this term. However, it is interesting to note that in the *War Scroll*, the phrase *bēt mōʿēd*, "house of the meeting" appears:

> On the trumpets of the men of renown, chiefs of the fathers of the congregation [ראשי אבות העדה] when they gather in the house of meeting [בהאספמ לבית מועד], they shall write "Fixed times of God for the holy council" (1QM 3.3–4).[11]

The passage is part of a list of the various trumpets to be blown in each phase of the final war envisioned at the eschaton. Although the reference is therefore future-oriented, *bēt mōʿēd* may reflect one of the terms used by the Essenes to denote their existing synagogue buildings. Here, Hans Kosmala observes that the phrase is rendered naturally by the Greek

---

[10]See Schrage, "Συναγωγή," 808–809; Krauss, *Synagogale Altertümer*, 17–24.

[11]Unless otherwise indicated, all translations of the Dead Sea Scrolls in this chapter are from Charlesworth, *The Dead Sea Scrolls*.

synagōgē, which would explain Philo's use of this word when referring to the name of Essene buildings.[12] It should also be noted that the word *mō'ēd* frequently appears in the Hebrew Bible as part of the phrase used for the tent of meeting (אֹהֶל מוֹעֵד; e.g., Exod 28:43, 29:4ff; Lev 3:3ff).[13] We shall return to this observation below.

Another possible reference to a synagogue building is found in the *Damascus Document*:

> And whoever comes to the house of prostration [בית השתצות], let him not come (when he is still) unclean after washing; and when the trumpets of the assembly sound, let him come before or later, but let them not interrupt the entire service (CD 11.22–23).

In this passage, the words translated "house of prostration" may be a Hebrew counterpart to the Greek word *proseuchē*. In favor of this interpretation is the fact that the reference to washing before entering the place of worship corresponds to one of Philo's statements about the requirement to wash before entering a synagogue (*Deus*. 7–9). Unfortunately, because the above passage could also refer to an area of the Temple courts, we cannot be certain if "house of prostration" denotes a synagogue.[14]

A final set of potential terms for the synagogue within the Essene writings is similarly ambiguous:

> All those who entered the congregation of the men of perfect holiness but recoiled from doing the regulations of the upright . . . have no portion in the house of the Torah [בית התורה]. With the judgment of their neighbors who turned away with the men of mockery they shall be judged, for they spoke deviantly of the statutes of righteousness and despised the covenant and the oath which they had taken in the land of Damascus; that is, the new covenant. And neither they nor their families will have any portion in the house of the Torah [בית התורה] (CD 20.2, 10–13).

---

[12]See Hans Kosmala, *Hebräer-Essener-Christen: Studien zur Vorgeschichte der frühchristlichen Verkündigung* (Leiden: E. J. Brill, 1959), 351–363; Schrage, "Συναγωγή," 809–810. Kosmala further observes that Aquila and Symmachus translate the phrase מוֹעֲדֵי־אֵל in Psalm 74:8 as *synagōgai* (op. cit., 351–352).

[13]Because the Essenes refer to their community with a number of Hebrew words (יחד, עדה, and קהל), all meaning "community" or "congregation," it is possible that they also used one of these terms in conjunction with the word *bēt* to refer to their synagogue buildings. On the various usages, see *HJP* 2.575.

[14]See Kosmala, *Hebräer-Essener-Christen*, 353–354; Schrage, "Συναγωγή," 809–810; E. P. Sanders, *Judaism*, 351.

What is unclear in the above passage is whether the phrase "house of Torah" is to be taken literally as a designation for a synagogue building or metaphorically for the Essene community.[15] In either case, the usage underscores the importance of Torah study to the community, as Philo himself had noted.

Returning to the Philo quotation, the question arises as to whether the philosopher's description of the Essene synagogues refers specifically to those in use by the Qumran community. This seems unlikely, since Philo only mentions the Essenes as living in cities and towns (*Prob.* 76; *Hypoth.* 11.1). Moreover, he also states that the Essenes owned and resided in houses (*Prob.* 85), which was obviously not the case at Khirbet Qumran.[16] Because Philo made at least one pilgrimage to Jerusalem (*Prov.* 64), his knowledge of the sect was probably gleaned from observations he had made there.

This view is supported by several passages from Josephus' writings which imply that an Essene community was located in either Jerusalem or a nearby village. First of all, in two parallel accounts Josephus tells how a certain Essene named Judas, while seated with his disciples in the Temple courts, predicted the assassination of Antigonus I (d. 104 B.C.E.; *BJ* 1.78–80, *Ant.* 13.311–313). Elsewhere, Josephus mentions how an Essene named Manahem stopped Herod the Great on the streets of Jerusalem while he was yet a lad and prophesied that he would be someday rule as the king of the Jews (*Ant.* 15.373–376). Yet a third Essene prophet, Simon, was summoned to the royal court during the reign of Archelaus in order to interpret a dream (*Ant.* 17.347). Finally, Josephus records that at the start of the Jewish War, the Jerusalem council appointed "John the Essene" as commander of the province of Thamna (northwest Judea), which included Lydda, Joppa and Emmaus (*BJ* 2.567). John later died leading an attack against Ascalon (*BJ* 3.9–21).[17]

---

[15]See Schrage, "Συναγωγή," 810.

[16]On the division of the Essenes into those living in villages and cities (reflected in CD) and those living at Qumran (reflected in 1QS), see *HJP* 2.577–578; E. P. Sanders, *Judaism*, 342–366.

[17]Other Essenes apparently took part in the War, for Josephus mentions that the Romans "tried their souls by every variety of test," making them "pass through every instrument of torture, in order to induce them to blaspheme their lawgiver or to eat some forbidden thing" (*BJ* 2.152). While Josephus might here be alluding to the destruction of Khirbet Qumran, it is also possible that some of the tortures took place during the various phases of the battle for Jerusalem.

In a few places, the sectarian writings themselves imply that one or more Essene communities existed in Jerusalem. Thus the *Damascus Document* commands that "no man lie with a woman in the city of the sanctuary" (CD 12.1). Elsewhere, the *War Scroll* states that, after one of the eschatological battles, Essene warriors would "come back to the congregation in Jerusalem [לבוא אל העדה ירושלים]" (1QM 3.22).[18]

Somewhat more problematic is Josephus' mention of an Essene gate (*BJ* 5.145), for it need not be taken as a reference to an "Essene Quarter" in Jerusalem, as some researchers have argued, since gates were often named for the destination to which their streets or paths eventually led. Josephus states that this gate was situated in the southwestern portion of the first wall of Jerusalem below a place called Bethso (βηθσώ; *BJ* 5.145). In 1895, F. J. Bliss argued that the Essene gate should be correlated with one dating to the Early Roman period that he had uncovered in this general location.[19] The gate is unimposing, measuring less than three meters in width. A path leading out of the gate turns toward the southeast into the Hinnom Valley. This is also the general direction of Khirbet Qumran. A second path leads to the northwest, toward the area Josephus had identified as Bethso.

Yigael Yadin later accepted Bliss's identification of the gate and adopted the argument of Joseph Schwartz that the toponym "Bethso," otherwise unknown, should be interpreted as the Hebrew word *bet-ṣoa*, "latrine."[20] Because the *Temple Scroll* indicates that a latrine was to be dug outside the eschatological Holy City on the northwest side (11QT 46.13–16),[21] Yadin argued that the Essene gate received its name because

---

[18]If such communities did exist within the city boundaries, the first passage implies either that only congregations of celibate males lived in Jerusalem or that married members of such a community journeyed to another city or village to engage in sexual relationships. As extreme as this latter possibility might seem, given the generally strict customs of the Essenes, it should by no means be ruled out. Concerning the order of Essenes that married, Josephus writes, "[The Essene men] give their wives, however, a three years' probation, and only marry them after they have by three periods of purification given proof of fecundity. They have no intercourse with them during pregnancy, thus showing that their motive in marrying is not self-indulgence but the procreation of children. In the bath the women wear a dress, the men a loin-cloth. Such are the usages of this order" (*BJ* 2.161).

[19]See Bargil Pixner, "An Essene Quarter on Mount Zion?" in *Studia Hierosolymitana I* (Jerusalem, 1976), 250–254.

[20]Joseph Schwartz, *Crops of the Holy Land* (Jerusalem: Luntz, 1900), 335.

[21]"You are to build them a precinct for latrines [מקום יד] outside the city. They shall go out there, on the northwest of the city; roofed outhouses with pits inside, into

"the ancient inhabitants of Jerusalem would have seen Essenes leaving the walled city through a postern on this flank, in order to 'ease' themselves."[22] More recently, Bargil Pixner has called attention to the discovery of a *mikveh*, similar in type to the ones found at Khirbet Qumran, forty meters northwest of the Essene gate. He argues that after using the latrine the Essenes would have ritually purified themselves before re-entering the city. Other *mikvaoth* have been discovered inside the city walls in an area that Pixner suggests might have served as an Essene Quarter.[23]

While all these arguments are suggestive, the presence of an Essene Quarter in Jerusalem has not yet been archaeologically confirmed. Moreover, the connection between the Essene gate (if we accept Bliss's identification) and the Bethso is highly conjectural. Finally, as observed above, the gate may have been known as the Essene gate simply because one of its paths led in the direction of the Qumran community.

Although we cannot yet conclude that an Essene Quarter existed in Jerusalem, the literary evidence supports the position that non-monastic sectarians had one or more communities in the general vicinity of Jerusalem.[24] According to Philo, these would have consisted of private houses clustered around a synagogue set aside as a "sacred place" (*Prob.* 81–82, 85–87). Because Philo speaks of the Essene *synagōgai* (plural)

---

which the excrement will descend so as not to be visible. The outhouses must be three thousand cubits from any part of the city" (11QT 46.13–16).

[22]Yigael Yadin, "The Gate of the Essenes and the Temple Scroll" in *Jerusalem Revealed: Archaeology in the Holy City, 1968–1974*, edited by Yigael Yadin (Jerusalem: Israel Exploration Society, 1975), 91.

[23]Pixner, "An Essene Quarter on Mount Zion?" 268–275; idem, "Jerusalem's Essene Gateway: Where the Community Lived in Jesus' Time," *BAR* 23, no. 3 (1997): 22–31, 64–66. Pixner further attempts to correlate Bethso with an area called שׂוא in the Copper Scroll (3Q15 8.10, 14; see "An Essene Quarter on Mount Zion?" 259–264). The obscure nature of this document, however, makes this exercise highly problematic. Also problematic is Pixner's attempt to link the Essenes with the nascent Christian church in Jerusalem (ibid., 276–283). While admittedly there are some correspondences between the reported practices of this community and those of the Essenes (e.g., sharing of goods, belief in a non-priestly messiah), this does not establish that there was a connection between the two groups.

[24]The use of the term "monastic" here and throughout this chapter is not intended to invoke a comparison between the Qumran community and later Christian monastics. On the contrary, Philo was the first to employ the underlying Greek term *monatērion*, and this in reference to the Jewish Therapeutae (*Contempl.* 25). The word is simply a convenient term for distinguishing the residents of Khirbet Qumran from the village or city sectarians.

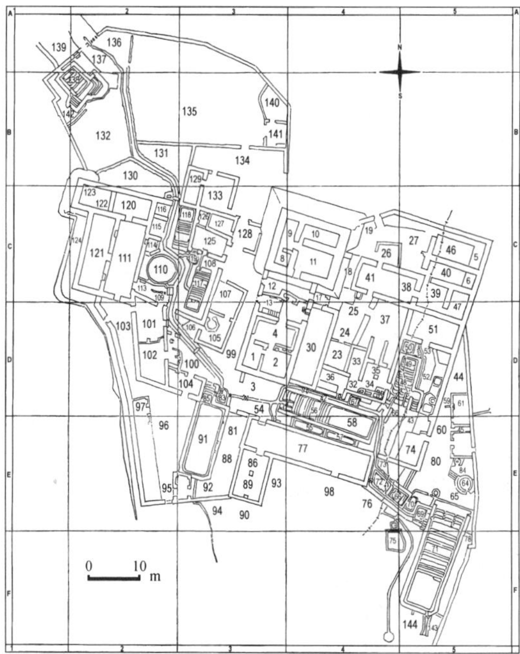

Figure 21. Plan of Khirbet Qumran, periods Ib–II. De Vaux identified locs. 4, 30 and 77 as assembly halls. Loc. 77 also served as a refectory. (From de Vaux, *Archaeology and the Dead Sea Scrolls*, pl. xxxix.)

and elsewhere mentions that Essene communities were scattered throughout the cities and villages of Palestine (*Prob.* 76; *Hypoth.* 11.1, 14; cf. Josephus, *BJ* 2.120, 124; *Ant.* 18.21), this was apparently the arrangement of the non-monastic sectarians throughout Palestine.

Turning now to the synagogal evidence at Khirbet Qumran, we note that Roland de Vaux, the director of the original excavations (1953–56), identified several areas of the site as assembly rooms. The first of these, loc. 4, has plastered benches lining the walls on all four sides of the chamber (see fig. 21).[25] The room measures c. 8 x 4 m and contains two

[25]De Vaux, *Archaeology and the Dead Sea Scrolls*, 7, 10–11, 26, 32–33. The earliest phase of this room dates to period Ib, which de Vaux places during Alexander Jannaeus' rule (103–76 B.C.E.). During Phase II (c. 6 B.C.E.), the entrance way between loc. 4 and loc. 1 was walled-up and additional benches were added to this length of

niches in its southwest wall that may have been used for the storage of sacred writings. An adjoining room (loc. 2) likewise contained a niche, though it lacked benches along the walls. De Vaux hypothesized that this room was used as a library.[26] To the north of loc. 4 is an entry area accessed by stairs from the west (loc. 13), which also must have led upstairs to the scriptorium. A water basin was carved out of a wall of the entry area next to a door that gave access to a long, narrow room (loc. 30). Although it contained no permanent benches, de Vaux thought this room too may have functioned as an assembly hall. Noting that the water basin in the entryway of loc. 4 could be filled with water through a hole in the wall, de Vaux writes, "this feature gives the appearance of having been designed for closed sessions [in loc. 4] in which those taking part did not wish to be disturbed, and thus as a kind of council chamber."[27]

An alternate hypothesis might be advanced from some remarks of Josephus, who states that the Essenes were divided into four grades—these undoubtedly corresponding to the three stages of the novitiate and full membership.[28] The historian writes: "so far are the junior members inferior to the seniors, that a senior if but touched by the junior, must take a bath, as after contact with an alien" (*BJ* 2.150). This remark suggests that the full members may have gathered in loc. 4, while the novices were restricted to the adjoining room (loc. 30) from whence they listened to the exhortations emanating from the inner chamber.[29] Those not in the final year of their novitiate may also have been required to take their meals in this outer room rather than in the main refectory (cf. 1QS 6.16–17).[30]

---

wall in loc. 4, making the benches continuous except for the entry into loc. 2 and the hallway to the north.

[26]De Vaux, *Archaeology and the Dead Sea Scrolls*, 32.

[27]Ibid., 10–11.

[28]I.e., the period between being examined by the Guardian and admitted by the full assembly (grade one), each of the two years of the formal novitiate (grades two and three), and full membership (grade four). See Josephus, *BJ* 2.137–138.

[29]Note also how loc. 12 and 17 run parallel to loc. 13, the former giving access to loc. 30, while the latter giving entry to loc. 4. It is possible that a window was cut on the upper part of the wall dividing loc. 4 and 30, allowing those in loc. 30 to hear better the activities taking place in loc. 4. Cf. the analogous arrangement of the Therapeutae (*Contempl.* 33).

[30]The question of what constituted the "common meal" of the Essenes is complex and currently without a clear answer. For a review of the major points of dispute, see E. P. Sanders, *Judaism*, 352–356.

Although these possible uses of loc. 30 are conjectural, it is reasonable to conclude that loc. 4 functioned as a *synagōgē/bēt mōʿēd* for the Essenes of Qumran, as is suggested by the presence of the benches, water basin and niches. As de Vaux observed, the room's relatively small size further hints that it was reserved for use by the full members of the community or some other special population within the sect.

If loc. 4. served as a synagogue for a segment of the community, another room, loc. 77, appears to have been designed for a larger group. Measuring 22 x 4.5 m, it is the largest room in the complex. De Vaux argued that the room's function as an assembly hall is indicated not only by its size, but also by the presence of a circular paved area at the northwest end of the hall.[31] This paved area clearly served as the base of a wooden podium or lectern that was probably used by the Guardian or one of the priests. In addition to serving as an assembly hall, the room also functioned as a refectory, as the presence of an adjoining crockery indicates (loc. 86, 89). Moreover, a conduit from the main water channel ran through the northeast wall of the room, ending in a spigot. After meals, the spigot could be opened and the room mopped. The floor itself was sloped toward the south, forcing the water to flow toward a door on the opposite end of the hall, where the refuse could be swept outside the complex.

The dual function of this room as a dining room and a synagogue is further indicated by a passage in Josephus' description of the daily routine of the Essenes:

> Their piety towards the Deity takes a peculiar form. Before the sun is up they utter no word on mundane matters, but offer to him certain prayers, which have been handed down from their forefathers, as though entreating him to rise. They are then dismissed by their superiors to the various crafts in which they are severally proficient and are strenuously employed until the fifth hour, when they again assemble in one place [εἰς ἓν συναθροίζονται χωρίον] and, after girding their loins with linen cloths, bathe their bodies in cold water. After this purification, they assemble in a private apartment [ἴδιον οἴκημα] which none of the uninitiated is permitted to enter [ἔνθα μηδενὶ τῶν ἑτεροδόξων ἐπιτέτραπται παρελθεῖν]; pure now themselves, they repair to the

[31]De Vaux, *Archaeology and the Dead Sea Scrolls*, 11; cf. Milik, *Ten Years of Discovery in the Wilderness of Judaea*, 48–49; Ronny Reich, "A Note on the Function of Room 30 (the 'Scriptorium') at Khirbet Qumran," *JJS* 46 (1995): 157, n. 3. Milik further observes that the end of the room with the podium was oriented toward Jerusalem. The room was built during phase Ib and continued in use up until the destruction of the complex during the Jewish War.

> refectory as to some sacred shrine [αὕτοί τε καθαροὶ καθάπερ εἰς ἅγιόν τι τέμενος παραηίνονται τὸ δειπνητήριον]. When they have taken their seats in silence, the baker serves out the loaves to them in order, and the cook sets before each one plate with a single course. Before meal the priest says a grace, and none may partake until after the prayer. When breakfast is ended, he pronounces a further grace; thus at the beginning and at the close they do homage to God as the bountiful giver of life. Then laying aside their raiment, as holy vestments, they again betake themselves to their labours until the evening. On their return they sup in like manner, and any guests who may have arrived sit down with them (*BJ* 2.128–132).

Although Josephus nowhere in his account of the Essenes mentions a monastic center such as the one at Qumran, the above description is consistent with such a setting: the sectarians eat in a common refectory, they are able to assemble at precise times, and they are served by a community cook and baker. Such a routine does not appear to have been envisioned in the *Damascus Document*, where sectarians who live in cities and villages have various types of employment, do not share their goods in common, and contribute only a portion of their wages to the community chest (CD 14.12–16; cf. Philo, *Prob.* 85–87). It therefore seems likely that in the above quotation Josephus is describing the activities of the Qumran Essenes, probably basing his report on his own investigation of the sect as a youth (*Vita* 9–12).[32]

If this is accepted, the passage is still rather cryptic in places. We might ask, for instance, whether the reference to the *idion oikēma* ("private apartment") is a reference to one of the rooms at Qumran (loc. 4?) or to the entire complex? Both interpretations are possible.[33] Likewise, does the word *heterodoxōn* ("uninitiated") refer only to outsiders or to all those who have not completed their novitiate? Again, a clear answer is not forthcoming. Finally, since the above passage outlines the activities of regular workdays, we might wonder whether the refectory was also used as a meeting hall on the Sabbath and other holy

---

[32]In his description, Josephus also states that the Essenes shared all things in common (*BJ* 2.122)—a characteristic of the monastic Essenes. His subsequent statement that such Essenes lived in many towns and cities (*BJ* 2.124) may be a conflation of the village Essenes with the monastic Essenes. Alternatively, it could signify the existence of other monastic communities outside of Khirbet Qumran (Shuafat?). In this later instance, the Qumran community would still be reflected in his description.

[33]Note, for example, Josephus' use of *oikēma* in reference to the synagogue at Tiberias in *Vita* 277.

days. However, since the sectarian writings themselves indicate that Sabbath meetings took place (4Q400–407, 11Q5–6; cf. Philo, *Prob.* 80–83), it seems safe to conclude that either (1) the refectory (loc. 77) was used as a Sabbath meeting place, (2) loc. 4/loc. 30 was used for Sabbath meetings (see above), or (3) loc. 77 and loc. 4/loc. 30 were both used as meeting places for certain portions of the Sabbath.

One function not served by the main complex at Qumran was that of being a residence for the sectarians. On this point, de Vaux himself wrote, "this establishment was not designed as a community residence but rather for the carrying on of certain communal activities."[34] Indeed, since the original excavations, investigators have wondered where the sectarians slept and stored their modest individual belongings. Because the scroll caves showed little evidence of habitation, it was supposed that the sectarians might have lived on a second floor of the complex, though no material remains had been discovered among the roof-fall.[35]

Fortunately, recent excavations of the area surrounding the complex now appear to have solved the puzzle. In the winter of 1995–96, excavations led by Hanan Eshel and Magen Broshi discovered nearly forty caves near Kirbet Qumran that showed signs of habitation. More detailed excavations of three of the caves uncovered dishes, cooking pots and storage jars dating to the Early Roman period. Moreover, north of the sectarian complex, Eshel and Broshi discovered the remains of a tent neighborhood containing vessels matching those uncovered at Khirbet Qumran, along with coins dating to the first century C.E. While the published report is still forthcoming, in a paper presented at the 1996 SBL/AAR/ASOR convention, Eshel concluded that "these discoveries indicate that the members of the [Qumran] community lived in tents and in at least some of the caves around the site."[36] Thus the arrangement of the Qumran settlement is analogous to that adduced above for the sectarians living in the cities and villages of Palestine: domestic residences surrounded a sacred communal site. Here, the sacrality of the central Qumran settlement is implied by the placement of *mikvaoth* near one of the entryways and at other places around the complex.[37]

---

[34]De Vaux, *Archaeology and the Dead Sea Scrolls*, 10. Cf. ibid., 56.

[35]Ibid., 55–56.

[36]Hanan Eshel, "New Data from the Excavations at Qumran" in *1996 AAR/SBL Abstracts*, 270. See also Abraham Rabinovich, "Residential Quarter Found in Qumran Dig," *Jerusalem Post*, 5 January 1996.

[37]Note also Josephus' comparison of the sectarian dining room to a *hagion temenos* (*BJ* 2.128–132; see above) and Philo's reference to the Essene synagogues as

The sectarians' arrangement of houses or tents around a central sacred place leads us to recall *War Scroll*'s use of *bēt mō'ēd*, "house of meeting," a phrase similar to the biblical *'ōhel mō'ēd*, "tent of meeting."[38] When we observe that the sectarians frequently referred to their communities as "camps" (מחנות; e.g., CD 14.3, 9; 1QM 7.1), such an arrangement suggests that the Essenes were attempting to recreate the desert wanderings of the ancient Israelites prior to their coming into the promised land (cf. Num 2:2, 17; 3:38). As their own writings state, the Essenes were literally or figuratively "in the wilderness" in order to "prepare the way of the Lord" (1QS 8.12–16; Isa 40:3).

Such imagery has led scholars to suggest that the Qumran settlement and/or the "sacred places" in the city and village communities functioned as rival temples.[39] However, in his review of this literature, William Grashman has argued these positions find little support from the evidence. First of all, he notes that de Vaux uncovered at Qumran no evidence of an altar or anything else to suggest sacrificial proceedings.[40] Secondly, he reviews the various passages in the Qumran literature and in the writings of Josephus cited as proof texts by these researchers and finds them all problematic.[41] Thirdly, he notes Philo's statement that the Essenes were "devout in the service of God, not by offering sacrifices of animals, but by resolving to sanctify their minds" (*Prob.* 75).[42] Finally, he surveys several passages from the *Temple Scroll* indicating that the sectarians believed that sacrifice could only be offered in the Jerusalem Temple (11QT 52.9, 16; 53.1, 9; 56.5; 60.13). Grashman goes on to

---

"sacred places" (*Prob.* 80–83; see above).

[38]It is noteworthy that בַּיִת and אֹהֶל are nearly synonymous in the Hebrew scriptures: "Thus they shall keep charge of the *tent* of meeting and the sanctuary, and shall attend the descendants of Aaron, their kindred, for the service of the *house* of the LORD [וְאֵת מִשְׁמֶרֶת הַקֹּדֶשׁ וּמִשְׁמֶרֶת בְּנֵי אהֲרֹן אֲחֵיהֶם לַעֲבֹדַת בֵּית יְהוָה וְשָׁמְרוּ אֶת־מִשְׁמֶרֶת אהֶל־מוֹעֵד]" (1 Chron 23:32; cf. Jud 20:8; 2 Sam 7:2, 6; 1Kgs 12:16; 1 Chron 6:23, 9:23, 17:1, 5; Psa 84:10).

[39]See Cross, *The Ancient Library of Qumran*, 101–103; Strugnell, "Flavius Josephus and the Essenes: Antiquities XVIII.18–22," 144.

[40]William Wesley Grashman, "The Priestly Synagogue: A Re-examination of the Cult at Qumran," (Ph.D. diss., University of Aberdeen, 1985), 425–426. Cf. de Vaux, *Archaeology and the Dead Sea Scrolls*, 14.

[41]Grashman, "The Priestly Synagogue," 426–453. The texts examined are Josephus, *Ant.* 18.19; CD 6.11b–15a, 11.17b–20; 1QS 8.4b–10. For a similar critique, see *HJP* 2.570, 582.

[42]Grashman, "The Priestly Synagogue," 434. See also *HJP* 2.570.

suggest that the Essenes established "priestly synagogues" until such time as proper sacrifices could be offered in the central sanctuary:

> The rationale for the existence of the Essene synagogues was not only that they functioned as substitutes for the temple, but they also took the place of the synagogues of normative Judaism . . . the sectarians established a 'new synagogue' in Israel where alone the law was rightly taught and practiced, and where true spiritual sacrifices could be offered up as a sweet smelling savor to the Lord.[43]

Grashman's position that the Essene synagogues were not full substitutes for the Temple is supported by the *Temple Scroll*, which expresses the Essenes' desire to overthrow the existing priestly regime, reconstruct the Temple, and reinstitute a purified sacrificial cultus. Nor was the Temple envisioned in the scroll as a heavenly Temple. As Yadin has pointed out, 11QT 29.8–10 clearly distinguishes between the Temple the Essenes were to build and the eschatological Temple:

> And I [God] will consecrate my Temple by my glory, [the Temple] on which I will settle my glory, until the day of the blessing [or, the day of creation] on which I will create my Temple and establish it for myself for all times, according to the covenant which I have made with Jacob at Bethel.[44]

The *War Scroll* similarly presumes that in an earthly battle, fought in part against the Romans (1QM 1.2), Temple worship would be restored during the seventh year of the forty-year war (1QM 2.6–14). This scenario probably encouraged John the Essene and other sectarians to abandon their otherwise pacifistic ways and fight against the Romans during the Jewish War (Josephus, *BJ* 2.152, 567).

We would therefore agree with Grashman's conclusion and further suggest that the Essene synagogues provided the sectarians a means to obtain partial control of the Temple until it could be reestablished: in their synagogues, they could enact all of the functions of the Temple except for sacrifice. Regarding this last issue, Grashman has observed that the Essene writings indicate that the sect temporarily substituted prayer for animal sacrifices. This last point is made clear in a passage from the *Community Rule* which may be interpreted as a manifesto:

---

[43]Grashman, "The Priestly Synagogue," 455.

[44]Translation Yadin, *The Temple Scroll: The Hidden Law of the Dead Sea Sect*, 113.

> When these exist in Israel in accordance with these rules in order to establish the spirit of holiness in truth eternal, in order to atone for the fault of the transgression and for the guilt of sin and for approval for the earth, without the fats of sacrifice—the offering of the lips [ותרומת שפתים] in compliance with the decree will be like the pleasant aroma of justice and the correctness of behavior will be acceptable like a freewill offering (1QS 9.3–5a).[45]

For the Essenes, an "offering of the lips" (ותרומת שפתים) and purity of behavior substituted for the sacrificial offerings of the cult until the Temple could be purified and the sacrifices offered correctly. The wealth of liturgical texts found among the Dead Sea scrolls, including hymns (1QH, 11Q5, 4Q400–407, 4Q510–511), prayers (1Q34, 4Q507–509, 4Q503) and blessings (1Q28b, 4Q500, 6Q16) attest to the activity of communal prayer among the sectarians. Likewise, scholars have observed that the psalms in the Psalms Scroll (11Q5) are not arranged in canonical order and include sectarian compositions, suggesting the conclusion that the scroll was used as a hymnal. Some of the sectarian hymns were evidently used on the Sabbath, as the discovery of a collection entitled the *Songs of the Sabbath Sacrifice* intimates (4Q400–407, 11Q5–6).[46] Others apparently were sung on feast days, as another sectarian work ascribes to King David psalms "for the offering for the beginning of the month, and for the all the days of the festivals, and for the day of the atonement" (11QPsa 27.7–8)[47]—an ascription probably penned by the sectarians to justify the use of their own "Davidic" compositions within their communal gatherings.

---

[45]Translation, Martinez, *The Dead Sea Scrolls Translated.*

[46]In her treatment of the Essene writings, Heather McKay, while conceding that "on sabbaths there are gatherings of the [Essene] community at which it seems likely that particular songs are sung by the community," goes on to question "whether [the Essenes] can truly be described as non-priestly Jews gathering for worship on the sabbath" (*Sabbath and Synagogue*, 56). Because McKay's own definition of communal prayer requires that *both* clergy and laity be involved, the sectarian practice is disqualified as an example of communal worship on the Sabbath. Aside from questioning the appropriateness of McKay's definition of communal prayer, we must observe that the sectarian writings themselves indicate that laity participated in the plenary gatherings of the community. The Community Rule, for example, states, "This is the rule for the session of the Many: each (member) in his order. The priest shall sit first, the elders second, and the rest of the people shall sit each (member) in his order" (1QS 6.8–9). Likewise, the requirement that a priest be present at all gatherings of ten or more persons presupposes that the sectarian laity out-numbered the clergy (1QS 6.2–5; CD 12:2–3). Thus, even following McKay's restrictive definition, the Essenes can be said to have engaged in communal prayer on the Sabbaths.

[47]Translation, Martinez, *The Dead Sea Scrolls Translated.*

The other synagogal activities of the Essenes resemble those adduced in the previous chapter for non-sectarian synagogues (and the Temple courts), though the Essenes, of course, had their own peculiar customs. Therefore, while it is clear that the Essenes studied scriptures on the Sabbath as did most Jews (Philo, *Prob.* 80–83; see above), their own style of midrash (*pesherim*) differed.[48] Likewise, just as at least some of the festivals were celebrated in some of the non-sectarian synagogues, the Essenes also celebrated feasts in their communal gatherings. The difference here was that the Essenes, while observing nearly identical feasts, followed a liturgical calendar based on a solar rather than a lunar year (11QT 13.10–30.1).[49] Thus whereas the feasts normally brought Jews from around the world together, the Essene observances separated them from the larger congregation of Israel. That the sectarians were very strict about maintaining purity in connection with their synagogues is suggested not only by Josephus (*BJ* 2.129, 150; see above), but also by the numerous ritual baths at Khirbet Qumran.[50] The Essenes thus endeavored to exceed the purity requirements followed in the non-sectarian synagogues.

Other literary evidence alludes to the existence of treasuries in the sectarian communities (CD 14.12–16; Philo, *Prob.* 85–87), as we observed was the case for at least some of the non-sectarian synagogues. According to Josephus, some of the sectarian monies were spent to send votive offerings to the Jerusalem Temple (*Ant.* 18.19). Obviously, sacred writings and other important community documents were produced and stored in the complex at Khirbet Qumran, resembling the archival function attested for the non-sectarian synagogues. Finally, the *Community Rule* and the *Damascus Document* outline deliberative and legislative proceedings that must have transpired within the community meetings held within the Essene synagogues (e.g., 1QS 6.13–15; CD 10.5–10a).

The evidence therefore suggests that, functionally, the difference between the Essene synagogues and their non-sectarian counterparts was more a matter of degree than of kind. Further, the fact that the early

---

[48]For a treatment the Essene *pesherim*, see *HJP* 2.420–456.

[49]For a more detailed treatment of the Essene calendar, see Yadin, *The Temple Scroll: The Hidden Law of the Dead Sea Sect*, 84–111.

[50]A gateway (loc. 139) was built on the northwestern side near a large ritual bath (loc. 138). Several other cisterns and baths were installed throughout the complex (loc. 48–50, 56, 58, 68, 71, 85, 91), all of them fed by channels leading from an aqueduct. On Essene requirements for *mikvaoth*, see CD 10.11–12.

Zadokite leaders of the Essenes chose the synagogue as a venue appropriate to their ritual purposes implies that this institution bore some affinities to the institution from which they had been disenfranchised—the Temple. Their adoption of the synagogues allowed them to preside over a set of precincts more subject to their control. Moreover, as Grashman has argued, in establishing their synagogues, the Essenes were setting up a parallel institution to the non-sectarian synagogues which together formed the larger congregation of Israel. It was within these "sacred places" that the assembled Essene priests, Levites and Israelites were thus able to form the true "congregation of Israel" (1QSa 1.1; CD 1.12) and to offer an acceptable "sacrifice of the lips" (1QS 9.4–5) until such time as God would restore the former Zadokite order to its rightful place in the Holy City.

The Therapeutae

Philo, our only source of knowledge of this group, states that the Therapeutae were dispersed throughout the inhabited world and were particularly numerous in Egypt (*Contempl.* 21–22).[51] Although he does not indicate whether they had separate communities in these scattered locales, Philo does mention that their "fatherland" (πατρίδα) was a community situated along the shores of the Mareotic Lake, which is located to the south of Alexandria. The settlement consisted of a number of private dwellings surrounding a synagogue, which the Therapeutae apparently called a *semneion* (32).[52] Both men and women were members of the community, the latter consisting primarily of elderly virgins (γηραιαὶ παρθένοι; 68). Throughout the week, the Therapeutae would remain confined in their individual dwellings, spending most of their time alone inside a small chamber (μοναστήριον) also called a *semneion* (25).

---

[51]Within this section, all subsequent numbers in parentheses refer to the relevant passages in *De vita contemplativa*. For additional background information on the Therapeutae, see *HJP* 2.593–597; Jean Riaud, "Les Thérapeutes d'Alexandrie dans la tradition et dans la recherche critique jusqu'aux découvertes de Qumran" in *ANRW* 2.20.1189–1295; David M. Hay, "Things Philo Said and Did Not Say about the Therapeutae" in *Society of Biblical Literature: 1992 Seminar Papers*, edited by E. Lovering (Atlanta: Scholars Press, 1992), 673–683; Richardson, "Philo and Eusebius on Monastaries and Monasticism," 334–359; Richardson and Heuchan, "Jewish Voluntary Associations in Egypt and the Roles of Women," 239–251.

[52]For a discussion of this word, see chapter two.

On the Sabbath they gathered in the synagogue wherein the elder (πρεσβύτατος) presented an extended discourse, presumably on a portion of scripture read earlier in the service (31). The men kept separate from the women inside the synagogue by means of a six-foot-high wall (32–33). Unlike the other days of the week, the Therapeutae did not fast until sunset on the Sabbath, but partook of modest meals consisting of bread flavored with salt and hyssop (36–37). They drank only spring water with their meal. Philo does not state whether these Sabbath dinners were eaten in common.

Philo does, however, describe at length the banquets held by the Therapeutae every Pentecost, which was their "chief feast" (μεγίστης ἑορτῆς; 65). Though the text is unclear, Philo seems to indicate that these banquets were held not just annually, but every fifty days. Dressed in white, the Therapeutae assembled on Pentecost eve, evidently in an ancillary room of the synagogue. The men and women feasted together, though at separate tables on the opposite sides of the room (men on the right, women on the left; 67–69). It is not stated whether a screen divided them, though this seems unlikely given the activities of the later part of the banquet.

Prior to the actual banquet, a functionary known as an *ephēmereutē*—a specialized *hypēretēs*[53]—initiated a period of prayer. Following the prayers, all the members reclined on wooden couches covered with papyrus sheets, the elders (πρεσβύτεροι) being placed in the positions of honor (67, 69). Before the tables of food were brought out, the president (πρόεδρος) gave an extended discourse on the scriptures, employing allegory (75–78). When finished, he rose and sang a concluding hymn, either of his own invention or "an old one by poets of an earlier day who [had] left behind them hymns in many measures and melodies, hexameters and iambics, lyrics suitable for processions or in libations and at the altars" (80). After the president finished, they all took turns leading hymns, with the rest of the assembly joining in the antiphons (80).

Following the hymns, another group of servants, the *diakonoi*, brought in the tables of food. Again, the fare consisted of leavened bread seasoned with salt and hyssop "out of reverence for the holy table enshrined in the sacred vestibule of the temple on which lie loaves and salt without condiments, the loaves unleavened and the salt unmixed" (81). Only water was taken with the meal.

---

[53]Philo describes this term as "the name commonly given to those who perform these services [ὑπηρεσίαις]" (66).

The after-dinner symposium—called by Philo a "sacred vigil" (ἱερὰν παννυχίδα)—was a rather lively affair consisting of singing and dancing throughout the remainder of the night. Philo describes it in the following terms:

> They rise up all together and standing in the middle of the refectory form themselves first into two choirs, one of men and one of women, the leader and precentor chosen for each being the most honoured amongst them and also the most musical. Then they sing hymns to God composed of many measures and set to many melodies, sometimes chanting together, sometimes taking up the harmony antiphonally, hands and feet keeping time in accompaniment, and rapt with enthusiasm reproduce sometimes the lyrics of the procession, sometimes of the halt and of the wheeling and counter-wheeling of a choric dance. Then when each choir has separately done its own part in the feast, having drunk as in the Bacchic rites of the strong wine of God's love they mix and both together become a single choir, a copy of the choir set up of old beside the Red Sea in honour of the wonders there wrought. . . . Thus they continue till dawn, drunk with this drunkenness in which there is no shame, then not with heavy heads or drowsy eyes but more alert and wakeful than when they came to the banquet, they stand with their faces and whole body turned to the east and when they see the sun rising they stretch their hands up to heaven and pray for bright days and knowledge of the truth and the power of keen sighted thinking (83–85, 88–89).

From Philo's account it appears that we have in the Therapeutae a group of pious Jews seeking to emulate the behavior of priests and Levites while on duty in the Temple. Thus they did not drink wine, they ate bread that Philo compared to the Bread of the Presence, and they carried on like a Levitical choir. For these reasons, researchers have wondered whether the Therapeutae might have been a branch of the Essenes.[54] While this is not impossible, it is more likely that the two groups independently found meaning in allegorized interpretations of the Temple cultus. Thus the type of oppositional relationship seen between the Temple leadership and the Essenes is absent from Philo's account of the Therapeutae. On the other hand, the mention of the special celebration of Pentecost, as well as of feasts (probably) held every fifty days, suggests that the Therapeutae may have been distantly related to the Essenes, perhaps simply to the extent of being influenced by the alternate liturgical calendar presented in *Jubilees* and *1 Enoch*. Whatever the relationship of

---

[54]For this interpretation, see *HJP* 2.593–597; Vermes, "Essene and Therapeutai," *RevQ* 3 (1962): 494–504; Riaud, "Les Thérapeutes d'Alexandrie dans la tradition et dans la recherche critique jusqu'aux découvertes de Qumran," 1189–1295.

the group to the Temple leadership may have been, it is nevertheless striking that its members drew their inspiration from the Temple cult and employed their synagogue as a center for their ritual activities. A primary difference between the Therapeutae synagogue and the Temple was, of course, that no animals were sacrificed within the former. Here we would suggest that, like the Essenes, the Therapeutae viewed prayer and pure behavior as either a substitute or a supplement to animal sacrifice. We should also note that, if we accept that the meals of the Therapeutae were modeled on those of the priests and Levites while on duty in the Temple, then the participation of the laity and of women in such banquets points to the inclusivist tendencies of this sect.[55]

THE SAMARITANS

While the origin of the Samaritans is obscure,[56] it is clear that sometime in the fourth century B.C.E. this group erected their own temple on Mt. Gerizim. According to Josephus, it was built by a certain Manasses, who had previously shared the high priesthood of the Jerusalem Temple with his brother Jaddus (*Ant.* 11.310). During the persecutions of Antiochus Epiphanes, the Samaritans, claiming a Sidonian heritage, apparently asked to let their temple be dedicated to Zeus Hellenios—a request that was granted by Antiochus. Josephus' claim on this point seems reliable, since he produces two letters—one from the Samaritans and one from Antiochus—that appear to be authentic (*Ant.* 12.257–261). However, 2 Maccabees 6:2 relates a somewhat different version of the story, stating that the Samaritans *unwillingly* submitted to dedicating their temple to Zeus Xenios ("Zeus, protector of strangers").

---

[55]See Richardson and Heuchan, "Jewish Voluntary Associations in Egypt and the Roles of Women," 243–246.

[56]According to Samaritan tradition, the group was a remnant of the tribes of Ephriam and Manasseh left over after the Assyrians deported the population of the Northern Kingdom in 722 B.C.E. In support of this view is the fact that Assyrian archives list only 27,290 deportees, which would have left a significant number of Israelites in the region (*ANET* 284–285). According to the Jewish version, as reported in the Bible and by Josephus (2 Kgs 17; *Ant.* 9.277–291), the Samaritans were descended from Cutheans settled in the area by the Assyrians. It is possible that both positions are correct, with the two groups intermarrying and influencing each other's customs and beliefs. See Robert T. Anderson, "Samaritans" in *ABD* 5.940–947.

In either case, the Samaritan temple only survived until 128 B.C.E. when it was demolished by John Hyrcanus (Josephus, *Ant.* 13.254–256). Though it was never rebuilt, it is possible that worship continued to take place on its ruins, particularly after Pompey's conquest of the region in 63 B.C.E., when the Samaritans were given a reprieve from Jewish persecutions. Recently, archaeologist Itzhak Magen, who has been excavating on Mt. Gerizim since 1983, claims to have uncovered the foundations of the temple beneath the remains of a fifth-century Byzantine church.[57] According to Magen, inscriptions recovered from the site dated to the second century B.C.E. indicate that "the Samaritans adopted everything, from the Jewish prayers to sacrificial ritual."[58]

With this background, we turn now to the synagogue evidence. Here, we will recall from our discussion of the diaspora evidence in chapter four that two Samaritan inscriptions were recently discovered on Delos about 90 m north of the synagogue. The inscriptions read as follows:[59]

[Οἱ ἐν Δήλῳ]
Ἰσραηλῖται οἱ ἀπαρχόμενοι εἰς ἱερὸν ἅγιον Ἀρ-
γαριζείν ἐπίμησαν *vacat* Μένιππον Ἀρτεμιδώρου Ἡρα-
κλειον αὐτὸν καὶ τοὺς ἐγγόνους αὐτοῦ κατασκευάσαντα καὶ ἀναθέντα ἐκ τῶν ἰδίων ἐπὶ προσευχῇ τοῦ
θε̣[οῦ] TON [. . . . .]
ΟΛΟΝΚΑΙΤ̣Ο̣ [. . . . . .καὶ ἐστεφάνωσαν] χρυσῷ στε[φά]-
νῳ καὶ [. . . . .]
KA - -
T - -

---

[57]See "Archaeologists Uncover Replica of Second Temple," *Jerusalem Post*, 4 April 1995. See also Itzhak Magen, "Mount Gerizim" in *NEAEHL* 2.484–492.

[58]"Archaeologists Uncover Replica of Second Temple."

[59]Transcriptions taken from Bruneau, "«Les Israélites de Délos» et la juiverie délienne," 465–504. Author's translations. See also Reinhard Pummer, "Inscriptions" in *The Samaritans*, edited by A Crown (Tübingen: J.C.B. Mohr, 1989), 190–194; Kraabel, "New Evidence of the Samaritan Diaspora has been Found on Delos," 331–334; White, "The Delos Synagogue Revisited," 133–160; idem, *The Social Origins of Christian Architecture*, 2.340–342; McLean, "Voluntary Associations and Churches on Delos," 191–195. For additional background on the Samaritan diaspora, see Alan D. Crown, "The Samaritan Diaspora" in *The Samaritans*, edited by A. Crown (Tübingen: J.C.B. Mohr, 1989), 195–217; Pieter Willem van der Horst, "The Samaritan Diaspora in Antiquity" in *Essays on the Jewish World of Early Christianity*, edited by Pieter Willem van der Horst (Freiburg, Schweiz: Vandenhoeck & Ruprecht, 1990), 136–147.

> [The] Israelites [on Delos] who make first-fruit offerings to the holy temple on Mt. Gerizim honor Menippos, son of Artemidoros, of Herakleion, both himself and his descendants, for constructing and dedicating from his own funds for the *proseuchē* of God the . . . and the walls and the . . ., and crown him with a gold crown and . . . (Bruneau no. 2).

> Ὀι ἐν Δέλῳ Ἰσραελεῖται οἱ ἀ-
> παρχόμενοι εἰς ἵερον Ἀργα-
> ριζεὶν στεφανοῦσιν χρυσῷ
> στεφάνῳ Σαραπίωνα Ἰάσο-
> νις Κνώσιον εὐεργεσίας
> ἕνεκεν τῆς εἰς ἑαυτους

> The Israelites on Delos who make first-fruit offerings to the temple on Mt Gerizim crown with a gold crown Sarapion, son of Jason, of Knossos, for his benefactions toward them (Bruneau no. 1).

The first of the above inscriptions, which dates to 250–175 B.C.E., honors an individual donor, Menippos, who had given all or part of the synagogue as a votive offering.[60] The building thus constituted a sacred edifice. Bruneau dates the second inscription to 150–50 B.C.E. on paleographic grounds, though the reference to the Samaritan temple indicates that it was erected prior to 128 B.C.E. when the temple was destroyed. The monument honors a certain Sarapion for undisclosed benefactions to the synagogue.

While these inscriptions do not supply us with a wealth of information about the Samaritan congregation on Delos, what is striking is how the Samaritans linked their very identity to their temple on Mt. Gerizim. Of course, this is due in part to their desire to distinguish themselves from any Jews on the island. Nevertheless, the mention of the first-fruit offering indicates that the Samaritans sent the half-shekel tax to their temple on Mt. Gerizim, just as Jewish congregations in the diaspora contributed this tax to the Temple in Jerusalem. From this, it is reasonable to infer that the Samaritan synagogue functioned in a manner analogous to that of its Jewish counterparts. Indeed, as was indicated in chapter four, the synagogue-remains discovered on Delos (*GD* 80) may have constituted a Samaritan synagogue.[61] In fact, if we take seriously Josephus' claim that the Samaritans were syncretistic, then the presence

---

[60]Note here the use of the word ἀναθέντα in l. 5.

[61]For this position, see McLean, "Voluntary Associations and Churches on Delos," 191–195.

in the building of lamps with pagan motifs—including one depicting Zeus—would tend to support the position that the synagogue belonged to the Samaritans in one or more phases. Likewise, if there is anything historical about there being a link between the Samaritans and the Sidonians, as Josephus also asserts, then this may help to explain why the synagogue so closely resembles the House of the Poseidoniasts, a cultic house erected by merchants from the region of Sidon.

While it is too early to do more than mull the possibilities regarding the identification of *GD* 80, the inscriptions cited above do suggest a link between a Samaritan synagogue on Delos and the temple on Mt. Gerizim. Just as the Temple in Jerusalem seems to have served as a center around which the Jewish synagogues revolved, so the temple on Mt. Gerizim also appears to have functioned for the Samaritans until it was finally destroyed in the second century B.C.E.

Conclusion

The foregoing analysis has suggested that despite the tendency of sects to "emphasize separateness and distinctiveness of mission," the three groups surveyed in this chapter continued to draw self-definition from institutions located at the center of power. Thus the Essenes appear to have modeled their communities on the desert "camp" of the Israelites, where the ancient Tent of Meeting stood at the center. The difference between their "camps" and the camp of the Israelites was that a synagogue stood at the center of the Essene communities. Accordingly, these synagogues did not have altars as the Tent of Meeting once did, since the Essenes subscribed to the deuteronomic commandments restricting burnt offerings to the Temple in Jerusalem. Nevertheless, with the exception of animal sacrifice, all the functions of the Essene synagogues mirrored those of the Temple precincts from which the sectarian leadership had been disenfranchised. Moreover, the Essene writings plainly state that prayer and righteous behavior were to take the place of burnt offerings (1QS 9.3–5a; see above), while their eschatological writings reveal that the Essenes viewed this arrangement as only an interim solution (11QT 29.8–10; see above). Eventually, they believed, the Temple cultus would again come under the group's control, and sacrifices would once again be correctly offered in Jerusalem.

Though it is not known how the Therapeutae regarded the leadership of the Temple, they too were evidently inspired by the institution itself, as they seem to have behaved in their synagogues as though they were priests or Levites functioning within its courts—not in terms of offering animal sacrifices, of course, but by their feasting on bread that Philo likened to the Bread of the Presence and by their singing of hymns after the manner of a Levitical choir. Their allegorizing of scripture, however, led to inclusivist tendencies. Thus members of the laity and women were able to participate more actively within their synagogue than was allowed within the actual Temple precincts—and to some degree, within non-sectarian synagogues.

Finally, although the Samaritans had a deep dislike of the Jews and their Temple, according to Josephus (*Ant.* 11.310) and the recent findings of archaeology, they nevertheless built their own temple on Mt. Gerizim in imitation of the one in Jerusalem. Moreover, the Samaritan congregation on Delos defined itself according to its relationship with the main sanctuary on Mt. Gerizim. They were "the Israelites who sent their first-fruit offerings to the holy temple on *Mt. Gerizim*." The protestant nature of this group suggests that what primarily distinguished the Samaritan synagogue on Delos from its Jewish counterpart was that the latter defined itself in terms of a relationship with a holy temple *not* on Mt. Gerizim, but on another mountain, namely Mt. Zion.

Conclusion

> How dear to me is your dwelling, O LORD of hosts!
> My soul has a desire and longing for the courts of the LORD
> My heart and my flesh rejoice in the living God (Psa 84:1–2)

In his classic study *The Sacred and the Profane*, anthropologist Mircea Eliade observes the cross-cultural concept of the *axis mundi*, the belief in a sacred vortex, a place where heaven and earth meet. This axis forms a sort of cosmic center around which everything revolves and from which a community takes its existential bearings. Eliade notes that this cosmic axis appears in even the most elementary level of culture, as with the Achilpa, a nomadic people of Australia, whose god, Numbakula, was said to have fashioned their sacred pole (*kauw-auwa*) from the trunk of a gum tree. Anointing it with blood, the god ascended back into heaven, leaving the pole behind for the tribe. The pole became a sacred axis for the Achilpa, a point of reference from which they would base their nomadic movements. Once, when the pole broke, ethnographers observed the "the entire clan were in consternation; they wandered about aimlessly for a time, and finally lay down on the ground together and waited for death to overtake them."[1] Other cultures such as the Celts, the Kwakiutl (British Columbia), and the Nad'a (Indonesia) had analogous sacred pillars that, in their mythologies, "supported the cosmos" and provided a threshold to the heavens.[2]

Within the Near East, Eliade observes, the *axis mundi* was prototypically the temple, which was often built on a mountaintop, the place where the earth came closest to touching the heavens. "The sacred space of the temple," he writes, "makes possible the passage from one level to another; first and foremost, the passage from heaven to earth."[3] One recalls with Eliade the image of Jacob's ladder associated with the

---

[1]Eliade, *The Sacred and the Profane*, 33.

[2]Ibid., 35–36.

[3]Eliade, "Sacred Architecture and Symbolism," 108.

sanctuary at Bethel (Gen 28:11–22), or of Moses' ascent of Mt. Sinai to receive the Ten Commandments (Exod 19:18ff). Of course, within Jewish belief, God did not stay on Sinai, but went on to inhabit his tabernacle and later his Temple in Jerusalem (Exod 40:34, 2 Chr 7:1). Analogously for the Samaritans, God resided within their temple on Mt. Gerizim. For these respective peoples, these sacred places became "an opening towards the beyond, towards the transcendent" where they were able "to communicate with the other world, the world of divine beings."[4] As Josephus put it, God descended into the tabernacle/Temple in order to be "present in our prayers" (*Ant.* 3.101).

Just as one may regard the Temple as the central pillar supporting the sacred canopy, so this study has suggested that the synagogues may be viewed as the surrounding pegs that extended the canopy outward. As Eliade observes, the ancients "sought to live as near as possible to the Center of the World."[5] On the basis of the evidence examined in the preceding chapters, it is reasonable to suggest that the synagogues of the Second Temple period functioned de facto, if not necessarily by design, as vehicles that transported the ancient worshipers closer to the center; that they served in effect as distant courts of the Temple, wherein a congregation had some sense of being near to the *axis mundi*. As we observed in the introduction of this study, within the ancient Near East, the notion of extending the sacrality of a central shrine was widespread. The Greek historians Aelian and Polyainos, for example, both record that when Kroisos was marching toward Ephesus to attack, the ruler Pindaros advised the Ephesians to tie ropes to the temple of Artemis and attach the other ends to the walls and gates of the city. This was suggested in order to transform the entire city into a sacred precinct and thus bring it under the protection of the goddess.[6] Whether or not the tale is true, it illustrates the locative terms in which the ancients viewed sacrality and the way in which that sacrality could be extended outward from a central sanctuary. The same concept is seen in the presence of subsidiary altars in other areas dedicated to the deity such as agoras or city gates. These places were the secondary estates of the god or goddess dwelling in the central shrine.

The suggestion of this study is that the synagogues of the Second Temple period are to be viewed as the Jewish counterparts to the

---

[4]Ibid., 107–108, transposed.

[5]Eliade, *The Sacred and the Profane*, 43.

[6]Aelian *Var. Hist.* 3.26; Polyainos, *Strategemata*, 6.50.

subsidiary altars and sacred areas of the Gentiles. Where they differed primarily was in their omission of animal sacrifice, which the sacred Jewish writings had reserved for the Jerusalem Temple (Deut 12:13–14, 16:5–6). Yet this function was also present in the synagogues, in so far as prayer and study came to be regarded as forms of sacrifice, and collections were taken within the congregations in order that envoys might offer sacrifices on behalf of the congregations at the main sanctuary.

SUMMARY OF FINDINGS AND ARGUMENTS

Within this study we have viewed evidence and have presented arguments supporting the above reconstruction. Our examination proper began in chapter two, where we explored the various terms used of the synagogues. There, the sacred nature of these buildings was seen most clearly in the use of the word *hieron* by Jewish and pagan authors in reference to synagogues in both Palestine and the diaspora.[7] While normally *hieron* referred to a temple (including the Jerusalem Temple),[8] because the basic meaning of *hieron* was "a place dedicated to a god," the use of this term in reference to the synagogues, we argued, was not at all inappropriate. It simply implied that a particular Jewish building had been taken out of profane (*bebelos*), human ownership and given into the possession of the Deity. The building was thus classified as sacred (*hieron*).[9] We observed that the same meaning is denoted by the term *hieros peribolos*, found in an Egyptian synagogue inscription (*JIE* 9) and in a passage wherein Philo alludes to the synagogues scattered throughout the empire (*Flacc.* 48).

While the sacred nature of the synagogues is expressed most overtly in the use of *hieron* and *hieros peribolos*, our investigations further suggested that the employment of the word *topos* for the synagogues derived from the Hebrew use of *māqōm* as a technical term for various cultic sites, including the Jerusalem Temple (e.g., Gen 28:11, 1 Kgs 8:35). Accordingly, in the portion of 3 Maccabees where the narrative action

---

[7]Josephus, *BJ* 4.406–409, 7.139–152, 1.277–278, *Ant.* 14.374; Agatharchides of Cnidus ap. Josephus, *Ap.* 1.209–212 (Palestine). 3 Macc 2:28; Josephus, *BJ* 7.44–45; Onias IV (?) ap. Josephus, *Ant.* 13.65–68; Philo, *Spec.* 3.171–172, *Deus.* 7–8 (2x) (diaspora).

[8]E.g., Josephus, *Ant.* 8.95–97, *BJ* 6.244; Philo, *Legat.* 157; Mark 13:3.

[9]On the division between sacred and profane space in antiquity, see the introduction of this study, as well as Burkert, *Greek Religion*, 269.

takes place in Jerusalem, *topos* refers exclusively to the Temple, seven times by itself (1:9, 23, 29; 2:9, 10, 16) and once in the expression *hagios topos* (2:14). When the action shifts to Egypt, *topos* refers to the synagogues twice (3:29, 4:17). Two decrees from Sardis likewise referred to a *topos* in which the Sardian Jews were allowed to "gather together with their wives and children and offer their ancestral prayers and sacrifices to God" (Josephus, *Ant.* 14.260; cf. 14.235).

This last usage of *topos* suggested that the most common word for a synagogue in the diaspora, *proseuchē*, derived not only from the primary function of the building, but also from the LXX of Isaiah 56:7 which refers to the Temple as a "house of prayer" (οἶκος προσευχῆς). Here, we noted that the LXX uses *oikos* and *topos* interchangeably when referring to the Temple (e.g., 2 Chr 6:20, 7:12; Ps 25:8, LXX).[10] As for the term *synagōgē* itself, our investigations revealed that in Jewish writings this word initially signified the cultic and legal community of Israel that was associated with the tabernacle or the Temple (e.g., Lev 8:3; Deut 5:22; 2 Chr 5:6, LXX). Subsequently, the word was used in the plural to denote the smaller, local congregations of Israel (Sir 24:23, *Pss. Sol.* 17:43). Finally, sometime before the turn of the era, the word came to signify not only the local Jewish community, but also the Jewish community center, the synagogue (e.g., *CIJ* 2.1404; *CJZC* 72; Josephus, *Ant.* 19.300–301, *BJ* 2.285–305, 7.43; Philo, *Prob.* 81). Thus we argued for an implicit connection between the national congregation of Israel that assembled within the Temple courts, and the local congregations that gathered within the synagogues.

In chapter three, we explored the evidence for Palestinian synagogues, testing the hypothesis of several recent researchers that "synagogues" in this region prior to 70 C.E. consisted of gatherings in private homes for study and prayer.[11] The evidence examined did not support this hypothesis. To start with, we observed that Josephus describes a synagogue (*proseuchē*) in Tiberias as "a huge building, capable of accommodating a large crowd [μέγιστον οἴκημα καὶ πολὺν ὄχλον ἐπιδέξασθαι δυνάμενον]" (*Vita* 277). Josephus further reports his attendance in this synagogue at an assembly which consisted of the "entire *boulē*" of the city and "a crowd of the populace" (βουλεὴν πᾶσαν

---

[10]Thus in 1Kgs 8:42, the MT refers to a foreigner who "prays towards this house" (וְהִתְפַּלֵּל אֶל־הַבַּיִת הַזֶּה), i.e., towards the Temple, while the LXX reads "they will pray towards this *place*" (προσεύξονται εἰς τὸν τόπον τοῦτον).

[11]E.g., Kee, "Defining the First-Century CE Synagogue"; R. Horsley, *Galilee*.

. . . καὶ τὸν δημοτικὸν ὄχλον; *Vita* 284). The *boulē* of Tiberias alone consisted of 600 members (*BJ* 2.641). According to Josephus, not only did deliberative proceedings take place in this synagogue, but also a "public fast" (πανδημεὶ νηστείαν; *Vita* 290).

We also noted that Josephus elsewhere alludes to a synagogue "adjoining a plot of ground owned by a Greek" in Caesarea Maritima just prior to the Jewish War (*BJ* 2.285–292). In order to convince the Roman procurator, Florus, to inhibit the Greek from building so close to their synagogue, the "notables" of the synagogue were said to have offered him a bribe of eight talents—equivalent in today's currency rates to US $1,920,000. Even if the figure is exaggerated, the model that seemed to best fit with this account was not that the Caesarea synagogue was a private house (or a meeting inside a private house), but that it was a sacred, monumental building that, unlike a meeting inside a private house, could not be moved because it had been dedicated to the Jewish God and thus transferred into the realm of the sacred. This hypothesis received additional support from the remainder of the account which states that open conflict broke out between the Jewish congregation and the Greeks when some Greeks sacrificed birds near the synagogue entrance. The Jewish reaction implied that the Greeks were committing sacrilege on or near Jewish sacred space.

We went on in the chapter to reiterate the point that *hieron* was used in reference to the Palestinian synagogues. There we observed that Josephus, for instance, alluded to representations of burning *hiera* being paraded in the triumph in Rome following Titus' victory in the Jewish War (*BJ* 7.139–152). In another place he mentioned bandits sacking various *hiera* in unspecified Judean villages (*BJ* 4.406–409). Agarachides of Cnidus likewise referred to Palestinian Jews praying in their *hiera* (Agatharchides ap. Josephus, *Ap.* 1.209–212). In a similar vein, Philo referred to the Essene synagogues as "sacred places" (ἱεροὺς . . . τόπους, οἵ καλοῦνται συναγωγαί; *Prob.* 81).

Epigraphic evidence similarly supported the view that Palestinian synagogues were monumental buildings dedicated to God. A dedicatory inscription from Jerusalem (*CIJ* 2.1404), securely dated to our period, records that a synagogue there was built by Theodotus, "priest and *archisynagōgos*." The inscription further mentions that "water installations [τὰ χρηστήρια τῶν ὑδάτων]" had been built near the synagogue, which recent researchers have suggested might refer to the *mikvaoth* located near the discovery site. Architectural fragments recovered with the dedication were inscribed with rosettes, a design that

Solomon was said to have carved on the walls, doors and door posts of his Temple (1 Kgs 6:29, 32, 35). This motif was also prominent among the remains of Herod's Temple uncovered by excavators.

Our survey of excavations in Palestine identified the remains of four structures as synagogue buildings dating to the Second Temple period. Two of the synagogues (Masada, Herodium) were built out of pre-existing structures during the Jewish War. The other two (Gamla, Capernaum) were originally constructed as synagogues and currently represent the only extant public buildings from our period discovered on their respective sites. Their design conforms to that of the Galilean-type synagogue of which there are numerous examples from the Late Roman and Byzantine periods. Three of the synagogues had ritual baths nearby (Gamla, Masada, Herodium), while the fourth was built near the Sea of Galilee (Capernaum). This suggested that purity requirements were connected with the structures. Likewise, a water basin fed by an outside channel may have served for the washing of hands before the reading of scripture in the Gamla synagogue.

In the back room of the Masada synagogue excavators discovered scroll fragments of Deuteronomy and Ezekiel, suggesting that the chamber was used as a genizah, a repository for sacred writings. An ostracon bearing the words "priest's tithe" discovered outside this room led excavators to propose that it also functioned as the abode of a priest or other attendant who collected tithes for the priests. The rosette motif again appeared on the lintel of the Gamla synagogue. In this case, it was flanked by palm trees, a design that literary references indicate was inscribed on the walls of the Temple's inner courts (Josephus, *Ant.* 8.77–78; Ezek 40–41; 1 Kgs 6–7). This symbol was also found among the ruins of Herod's Temple. We noted that Erwin Goodenough and other scholars have argued that this motif was the precursor of the menorah.[12] Finally, we observed that the façades of one, possibly two of the synagogues (Gamla, Capernaum) were oriented towards Jerusalem, while the remaining two (Masada, Herodium) were oriented towards the east—this last possibly in imitation of the Temple courts, as suggested by contemporary literary evidence (Josephus, *Ap.* 2.10–11).

Our investigation then turned to the question of synagogue origins in Palestine. After noting the inadequacies of earlier models, we adopted a modified version of a hypothesis recently proposed by Lee Levine.[13] This

---

[12]*JSGRP* 4.72–74; Busnick, *Der Tempel von Jerusalem*, 1.272–274.

[13]Levine, "The Nature and Origin of the Palestinian Synagogue Reconsidered."

position maintains that the synagogues emerged out of local gatherings at the city gate, which literary and archaeological evidence indicates functioned as the primary civic center in Near Eastern societies through the Persian period. Our own analysis of the relevant literary and archaeological materials suggested that Levine's proposal did not fully appreciate the sacred character of the city gates. Here, we observed that archaeologist Richard Barnett had pointed to the existence of cultic sites at the gates of several Near Eastern cities.[14] These functioned in annual celebrations where a local god or goddess was invited to enter through the gates and take up habitation in the temple located in the city. Barnett further argued that a similar ceremony could be detected in Solomon's dedication of the Temple. Other researchers suggested that this ceremony was hinted at in the personification of the gates seen in the phrase, "Lift up your heads, O gates . . . that the King of glory may come in" (Ps 24:7). F. M. Cross observed that this passage derived from Ugaritic myths depicting Baʿal surrounded by a heavenly council.[15] The implication was that the gates were lesser sacred precincts surrounding a central cultic site.

Picking up on these observations, our own analysis suggested that Ezra's Torah-reading ceremony, which took place at the Water Gate in Jerusalem at the renewal of Sukkoth, was yet another example of "inviting God into the Temple" (Neh 8–10). This ceremony was subsequently repeated every seven years, first at the Water Gate and then within the Temple courts themselves (1 Esdras 9:38; Josephus, *Ant.* 11.154–158). This shift corresponded to the Hellenization of Palestinian cities, whereby the central civic center moved from the city gates to the agoras. In the case of Jerusalem, the central agora corresponded to the Temple courts. This, we argued, was indicated both architecturally by the addition of stoas to the Temple mount, and functionally by the accrual to the Temple courts of all major civic activities.

It was further argued that a similar shift was seen in the movement of the local congregations from the city gates into synagogue buildings. Here we drew upon the analyses of James Strange, who has recently proposed that the architecture of the Galilean-type synagogue was derived from the Court of Israel. According to Strange, the congregation sat on benches around the walls of the synagogue and viewed the proceedings at the center of the hall between columns just as "one watched the sacred

---

[14]Barnett, "Bringing God into the Temple."

[15]Ibid., 19.

proceedings in the Court of the Priests from the vantage of the Court of Israel."[16] Functionally, the Torah-reading ceremony held every *seventh year* by the national convocation in the Temple courts appears to have been mirrored by the local assemblies meeting every *seventh day* in the synagogues. Thus, we argued, both architecturally and in most respects functionally, the Palestinian synagogues formed in miniature what the Temple courts comprised on a grander scale. These arguments all supported the thesis that the synagogues in Palestine served as subsidiary precincts of the central Temple shrine.

In chapter four we turned to an examination of diaspora synagogues. Here, we tested the recent proposal of Michael White, who maintains that synagogues in the diaspora were private homes gradually transformed into community buildings.[17] Our investigation failed to uncover evidence to undergird this position. On the contrary, our sources repeatedly indicated that the synagogues were consecrated buildings, not houses that remained in private use. Moreover, our survey revealed that these edifices bore an affinity to temples or cultic halls. This was seen most clearly in our examination of the Egyptian evidence where we adduced nearly a dozen inscriptions which dedicate the synagogue and/or its appurtenances to the Jewish God.[18] Indeed, we noted with Paul Fraser that "in most instances the [Jewish] dedication is indistinguishable from a pagan equivalent save for the substitution of the term 'synagogue' for 'the shrine' or 'the temple,' and by the name or names of the dedicating party."[19] Likewise, epigraphic and literary evidence attested such temple-like architectural features as pylons (*JIE* 24), exedras (*JIE* 28) and sacred precincts (*JIE* 9; Philo, *Flacc.* 48). These features suggested that the Egyptian synagogues typically consisted of a walled outer precinct with a monumental gate and a cultic hall in the midst of the sacred area.

In another case, a land-survey of Arsinoë-Crocodilopolis (*CPJ* 1.134, I B.C.E.) located a *proseuchē* on a two-and-a-half acre plot of land, with its congregation leasing out a "sacred garden" (ἱερᾶς παραδείσου) on an adjoining acre. Along with other researchers, we observed that this usage amounted to official recognition of the synagogue as the possession of the Jewish Deity. Such recognition was again evident in a synagogue

[16]Strange, "First Century Galilee from Archaeology and from the Texts," 44.

[17]White, *Building God's House.*

[18]*JIE* 9, 13, 22, 27, 28, 117, 24, 25, 105 (?), 126.

[19]Fraser, *Ptolemaic Alexandria*, 1.283. Cf., e.g., *OGIS* 64, 65, 91, 92; *SB* 429, 1436, 1567, 1570, 4206. See also Dion, "Synagogues et temples dans l'Égypte hellénistique," 55–57.

inscription granting a *proseuchē* the rite of asylum (*JIE* 125, II/I B.C.E.). Literary evidence suggested that this grant was not limited to this single synagogue, but extended to synagogues throughout Egypt during the Hellenistic period (*CPJ* 1.129, 218 B.C.E.; 3 Macc 2:28, 3:29, 4:17).

The sacred nature of the Egyptian synagogues was further seen in some remarks of Philo who states that, during the Greek and Jewish conflicts of 38 C.E., merely the addition of cultic images to the synagogues transformed them into sacred precincts (τεμένη) of the imperial cult (*Legat.* 132–137). Because Philo elsewhere declares that the synagogues were "*hieroi periboloi* where [the Jews] could set forth their thankfulness" for their rulers (*Flacc.* 48), it was argued that the key distinction was between offering prayers "on behalf of" a monarch and praying "to" an idol. The sacred character of the synagogues remained constant; only the divinity being worshiped changed.

A similar picture emerged from our examination of the synagogues found around the rest of the diaspora. Thus we saw that Josephus mentions that votive offerings (ἀναθημάτα) taken by the Seleucids from the Jerusalem Temple were subsequently dedicated within the synagogue at Antioch (εἰς τὴν συναγωγὴν αὐτῶν ἀναθέντες; *BJ* 7.44). Later Syrian monarchs were said to have erected additional votives in the synagogue, leading Josephus to interject that these "formed a splendid ornament to the *hieron* [τῶν ἀναθημάτων τὸ ἱερὸν ἐξελάμπρυναν]" (*BJ* 7.45).

Elsewhere, in a letter chastising the people of Dora for setting up an idol of the emperor inside the *synagōgē* there, Petronius, legate of Syria, complained that Caesar's image "was better placed in his own shrine [ἐν τῷ ἰδιῳ ναῷ] than in that of another [ἢ ἐν ἀλλοτρίῳ]" (Josephus, *Ant.* 19.305). In yet another province, a decree issued by Augustus declared the "sacred writings" and "sacred monies" of the Asian synagogues inviolate; would-be thieves of the synagogues were referred to by Augustus as "temple robbers [ἱερόσυλοι]" (Josephus, *Ant.* 16.162–165; cf. *Ant.* 16.167; Philo, *Legat.* 311–313).

Further afield, we observed that several manumission decrees discovered in Gorgippia, Panticapeum and Phanagoria in the Bosporus Kingdom revealed that release ceremonies took place in the synagogues there (*CIJ* 1.683a, 690, 690a, 691; Danshin no. 1). In a non-Jewish context, such ceremonies normally transpired in a temple under the direction of priests. We also noted that the formula on some of the Bosporan decrees required the released slaves to "show diligence and devotion toward the *proseuchē* [εἰς τὴν προσευχὴν προσκαρτερήσεως καὶ θωπίας]" (Danshin no. 1, cf. *CIJ* 1.683a, 691, 683, 684)—further implying the sanctity of the synagogues.

In the Aegean, we saw that votive offerings were discovered among the ruins of the synagogue at Delos (*CIJ* 1.726, 727, 728, 729, 730). This building (*GD* 80) had a design similar to that of the House of the Poseidoniasts (*GD* 57), one of the most prominent cultic halls on the island. Not only was this latter structure dedicated to the "ancestral gods" of its founders, but it was also referred to as a *temenos* in an inscription recovered at the site (*ID* 1520, ll. 11–12). Our ensuing analysis of *GD* 80 concluded that a Jewish or Samaritan congregation either built the edifice as a synagogue or adapted it following the hall's abandonment by a pagan cultic association.

Finally, our examination revealed that the earliest phase of the Ostia synagogue, far from being a private house or insula, instead featured a four-columned propyleum, spacious assembly hall and triclinium. A well and basin situated near the entryway of this synagogue further suggested a parallel to the *perirrantēria* found outside the entrance to pagan temples or sacred areas. The similar placement of a stone water basin near the main entrance of the building had been observed in the analysis of the synagogue at Delos.

While the findings of chapter four stood at odds with White's theory that synagogues emerged out of gatherings in domestic residences, they tended to support Peter Richardson's recent characterization of the diaspora synagogues as *collegia* with special status.[20] Following Simeon Guterman, however, we drew a legal distinction between synagogues in Italy and those in the eastern Mediterranean, recognizing that the former were *collegia licita* while the latter were "pseudo-national cults" established through the Hellenistic rulers and later ratified by Rome.[21] Thus while the synagogues in Rome were part of an informal confederacy, those in the east were frequently organized within the framework of a politeuma, where civic authority was given to the local Jewish leaders. Such politeumata were directly attested in Alexandria, Berenice and Sardis, while sources suggested their existence in Cyrene, Ephesus, Antioch, Damascus and elsewhere. We also agreed with Mary Smallwood that the legal classification of the synagogues as *collegia* was rather artificial since the synagogues had greater privileges than other *collegia*, a fact that Richardson himself notes. Moreover, the synagogues'

[20]Richardson, "Early Synagogues as Collegia."

[21]Guterman, *Religious Toleration and Persecution in Rome*, 158.

functions were more wide-reaching than those of the *collegia*, their membership was more restricted, and national identity more integral.[22]

Another difference between Richardson's position and the one presented in this study is that whereas Richardson appears to have downplayed or denied the cultic aspect of the diaspora synagogues and their connection to the national cultic site, our survey highlighted both of these elements. We have already reviewed the evidence adduced for the sacred, cultic nature of the diaspora synagogues. It remains to rehearse the findings which suggested their connection to the central cult.

To begin with, we observed that there was an *economic* relationship between the diaspora synagogues and the Temple. Here, our sources attested to how the synagogues throughout the diaspora served as collection places for the temple tax (e.g., Josephus, *Ant.* 16.164, 168; Philo, *Spec.* 1.76–78). The sums sent to Jerusalem each year were considerable: Cicero specifically states that a hundred pounds of gold (≈ US $5,400,000) was seized from Jewish offerings in Apamea, while twenty pounds (≈ US $1,080,000) was taken from the collection at Laodicea (Cicero, *pro Flacc.* 68). The orator further complained that, because of the "the barbaric superstition" (*barbarae supersititioni*) of the Jews, "gold was exported each year in the name of the Jews from Italy and all our provinces to Jerusalem" (*pro Flacc.* 67). Nearly a dozen imperial and local decrees authorizing the transport of such "sacred monies" (ἱερα χρημάτα) to Jerusalem suggested that Cicero's complaint was not exaggerated (Josephus, *Ant.* 14.225–227; 16.28, 45, 160, 164, 166, 167, 170, 172; Philo, *Legat.* 313, 315). Such a widespread pattern of financial disbursement indicated that the diaspora synagogues formed an integral part of a massive economic system that was centered on the Temple cultus in Jerusalem.

The fact that the donated monies were considered "sacred" implied a *spiritual* relationship between the diaspora synagogues and the central cult. Noteworthy in this respect is that every time the transport of these monies was interfered with, the local communities themselves appealed to the highest levels of imperial government in order to assert their privilege of exporting their contributions to Jerusalem (e.g., Josephus, *Ant.* 16.169–170, 172–173). This evinced a moral commitment among the diaspora synagogues to fulfill their biblically mandated obligations to the national shrine. Conversely, we observed that some of the edicts permitting the diaspora synagogues to practice their "sacred rites" and

[22]Smallwood, *The Jews under Roman Rule*, 133–134.

"native customs" came about as the result of envoys from the Jewish High Priest (e.g., Josephus, *Ant.* 14.225–227, 228–229, 241–243). Thus the head of the Jewish cult apparently supported the religious practices of the diaspora synagogues, evidently perceiving them in league with the central shrine. Contemporary authors such as Philo, Josephus and the writer of Acts presented this same view (e.g., Philo, *Legat.* 191; Josephus, *Ant.* 14.223–225, 19.300–301; Acts 9:1–2).

Our examination also indicated that Gentiles viewed the sanctity of the Temple and the synagogues as being intertwined. Thus when Gaius threatened to erect an idol in the Temple, Gentiles around the world rioted against the synagogues, installing statues within them (Philo, *Legat.* 132–137). Philo therefore despaired to make his case before Gaius about the violation of the Alexandrian synagogues, writing, "Shall we be allowed to come near him and open our mouths in defense of the *proseuchai* to the destroyer of the all-holy place [πανιέρου]?" (*Legat.* 191). Philo went on in the passage to characterize the Temple as "that most notable and illustrious shrine [νεών] whose beams like the sun's reach every whither, beheld with awe both by east and west"—imagery suggesting not only the shrine's glory but also its relationship to the synagogues scattered throughout the diaspora.

Another indication of a spiritual relationship between the diaspora synagogues and the Temple was seen in the frequent portrayal of envoys from the diaspora synagogues journeying to Jerusalem to make sacrifices on behalf of their congregations (Josephus, *Ant.* 14.227; Philo, *Legat.* 156, 311, 357). Although barred by biblical mandate from offering sacrifices on local altars, the members of the diaspora synagogues were clearly involved in sacrificial worship. This point was further supported by the various allusions to meetings in the diaspora synagogues on days sacred to the cult, such as the Sabbath (e.g., Josephus, *BJ* 2.285–292; *Ant.* 14.256–258, 259–261; Philo, *Mos.* 2.214–216), New Moon (*CJZC* 70–71), Feast of Tabernacles (*CJZC* 71; Philo, *Flacc.* 116–124) and other unspecified festivals (Josephus, *Ant.* 14.257). We went on to accept the proposal of Areyah Kasher, who argues that the *proseuchai* were created in the diaspora because of the close association between prayer and sacrifice within the Hebrew Scriptures (e.g., Isa 1:11–16; 1 Kgs 8:27–28).[23] Among our ancient sources, Philo made the relationship between prayer and sacrifice most explicit when he wrote, "though the

---

[23]Kasher, "Synagogues as 'Houses of Prayer' and 'Holy Places' in the Jewish Communities of Hellenistic and Roman Egypt," 209–210.

worshippers bring nothing else, in bringing themselves they offer the best of sacrifices, the full and truly perfect oblation of noble living, as they honour with hymns and thanksgivings [ὕμνοις καὶ εὐχαριστίαις] their Benefactor and Saviour" (*Spec.* 1.272). That worshipers in the diaspora offered their prayers while facing Jerusalem was suggested not only by several biblical passages (1 Kgs 8:30, 44, 48; 2 Chr 6:34, 38; Dan 6:10, 1 Esdr 4:58), but also by the orientation of the Ostia synagogue, whose façade was directed towards Jerusalem. We concluded chapter four by proposing that the diaspora synagogues provided a means for Jews to be connected to the central sanctuary while still residing in distant cities throughout the larger Greco-Roman world. This view was in accord with Philo's statement that, while diaspora Jews counted their adopted countries as their "fatherland" (πατρίς), they "[held] the Holy City where stands the sacred Temple of the most high God to be their mother city [μητρόπολις]" (*Flacc.* 46).

In chapter five, we explored synagogue functionaries and noted how these mirrored those existing within the Temple. Thus in the Temple, the High Priest normally ruled as the *ethnarch* and was assisted by a *prostatēs* and *archontes* (Josephus, *Ant.* 14.148–151, 15.182; 2 Macc 3:4). Similarly, officials known variously as *archontes* (*CJCZ* 70–72; *DF* 33; Josephus, *Vita*, 69, 134, 168, 271, 278, 294, 296; *BJ* 2.639), *archisynagōgoi* (*CIJ* 2.1404; *JIE* 18; *DF* 33; Mark 5:22, 35, 36, 38; Luke 8:41, 8:49, 13:14; Acts 13:15, 18:8, 17), and *archiprostatai/prostatai* (*JIE* 18, 24) assumed the principal leadership of the synagogues. Moreover, just as "elders" or "notables" (*presbyteroi*, *gerontes*, *dynatoi*) formed a part of the court of the High Priest in Jerusalem (1 Macc 14:27–45; Mark 8:31, 11:23, 15:1; Acts 4:5, 8), these also constituted a secondary tier of leadership within the synagogues (*CIJ* 2.1404; Josephus, *Vita* 69, *BJ* 2.285–292; Philo *Hypoth.* 7.12–13; Luke 7:3–5). In both the Temple and the synagogue, these principals were further assisted by scribes[24] and by servants variously called *neōkoroi*,[25] *hypēretai/archihypēretai*,[26] and *thyrōroi*.[27] While the priests constituted a higher proportion of the leadership within the Temple, our sources revealed that they also assumed principal leadership positions within the synagogues (*CIJ* 2.1404; *CJCZ*

[24]Temple: Josephus, *Ant.* 12.142; Mark 8:31, 10:33, 11:18, 27, 14:1, 43, 53; 15:1, 31; synagogues: *CPJ* 1.138; Mark 12:29; Matt 23:6 || Luke 20:46, 11:43 = Q.

[25]Temple: *BJ* 1.53; Philo *Fug.* 90–94; synagogue: *CPJ* 1.138.

[26]Temple: Josephus: *BJ* 2.321; Philo, *Spec.* 1.152, *Sacrif.* 132–133; synagogue: *CPJ* 1.138, Luke 4:20.

[27]Temple: 1 Esdr 1:15, 5:28, 45; Josephus, *Ant.* 11.108; synagogue: *CPJ* 1.138.

72; Philo, *Hypoth.* 7.12–13). We also noted that several recent scholars have argued that priests and Levites served as local scribes in the synagogues.[28] In light of the available evidence, we questioned the scholarly characterization of the synagogue as the "people's house," on the one hand, and the Temple as "the house of the priests," on the other. We proposed that the Temple and the synagogues *both* belonged to priests, Levites and people, who nationally and locally constituted the *synagōgē* of Israel. As an appendix to this discussion, we further noted the evidence suggesting the participation of women and God-fearers within both the Temple and the synagogues.[29]

In chapter six we turned our attention to synagogue functions and observed that many of these overlapped with those attested for the Temple precincts. Thus we noted that the placement of *mikvaoth* near the synagogues at Gamla, Masada and Herodium paralleled the placement of similar pools around the Temple. Likewise, the location of the synagogues at Delos, Ostia, Arsinoë-Crocodilopolis (*CPJ* 1.134), Philippi (Acts 16:13) and Halicarnassus (Josephus, *Ant.* 14.256–258) near large bodies of water implied that ritual bathing was required before entering a diaspora synagogue. Literary sources upheld this view, presenting bathing as a requirement for entry into an Alexandrian synagogue (Philo, *Deus.* 7–9). Elsewhere, an edict of Halicarnassus stated that the *proseuchai* in that city were to be built close to the sea because of the "native custom" of the Jews (Josephus, *Ant.* 14.256–258). Similarly, the author of Acts mentioned that Paul and his entourage went to the river outside of Philippi because they expected to find a synagogue there (παρὰ ποταμὸν οὗ ἐνομίζομεν προσευχὴν εἶναι; Acts 16:13). Most scholars, we observed, take these allusions as references to ritual purity requirements.[30]

---

[28]E. P. Sanders, *Judaism*, 173–189; Schwartz, *Studies in the Jewish Background of Christianity*, 89–101; Saldarini, *Pharisees, Scribes and Sadducees*, 241–276.

[29]Women participating in the Temple: e.g., Neh 8:3, 7:73; 1 Esdr 9:41; Josephus: *Ant.* 4.209–210, 11.154–158; 4 Macc 4:8; Mark 12:42; in the synagogues: *JIE* 28, *CJCZ* 72, *CIJ* 1.683, 690, 690b, 728, 730; *CPJ* 1.129; Philo, *Spec.* 1.144, 3.172–173; Josephus, *Ant.* 14.256–258, 259–261; Luke 13:10–21; Acts 16:13–16, 17:1–9, 17:10–14, 18:24–26. Gentiles or God-fearers in the Temple: e.g., 1 Macc 10:40; Josephus, *Ant.* 11.336, 13.55, 16.14, 55; Philo, *Legat.* 291, 296–97; God-fearers in the synagogues: *CIJ* 1.683, 683a, 684, 69; Danshin, no. 1; Josephus, *BJ* 7.45; Acts 13:16, 26, 50; 16:14; 17:4; 17:17; 18:17.

[30]E.g., Sukenik, *Ancient Synagogues in Palestine and Greece*, 49–50; Greeven, "Προσευχή," 808; Levine, "The Second Temple Synagogue," 13.

Teaching and the study of scripture were also portrayed as being functions of both the Temple (e.g., 1 Esdr 9:49; Josephus, *Ant.* 13.311, *BJ* 1.78–80; Mark 12:35 Acts 24:12) and the synagogues (e.g., *CIJ* 2.1404; Josephus, *Ant.* 16.43–45, *Ap.* 2.175; Philo, *Somn.* 2.123–129; Luke 4:16–30). Likewise, corporate prayer was directly attested as taking place within the Temple (e.g., 1 Macc 4:55; 2 Macc 1:23, 2:10, 3:11, 3 Macc 1:24, 5:50, Sir 50:19; Josephus *Ant.* 7.381, 9.269–270; Luke 1:10) and within the synagogues (e.g., Josephus, *Ant.* 14.260–261, *Vita* 294–295, *Ap.* 1.209–211; *Bib. Ant.* 11.8; Philo, *Flacc.* 122–124). Days sacred to the cult such as the Sabbath (e.g., Josephus, *BJ* 2.285–292; *Ant.* 14.256–258, 259–261; Philo, *Mos.* 2.214–216; Mark 3:1–6), New Moon (*CJZC* 70–71), and Sukkoth (*CJZC* 71; Philo, *Flacc.* 116–124) were observed in at least some of the synagogues. Other allusions to unspecified "customary feasts" and communal dining in the synagogues suggested that other special days were also adhered to (Josephus, *Ant.* 14.257, 14.213–216, 14.261, 16.162–165). The triclinium of the Ostia synagogue and a "chamber" in the Theodotus synagogue (*CIJ* 2.1404) may likewise have accommodated such festival proceedings.

We have already alluded to imperial decrees (Josephus, *Ant.* 16.164, 168) and other literary attestations stating that synagogues served as repositories for sacred funds (Philo, *Spec.* 1.76–78)—another function shared with the Temple (e.g., Josephus, *Ant.* 17.264). Like the Temple precincts, at least some synagogues served as museums for votive offerings and dedicatory and honorific inscriptions (*JIE* 9, 13, 22, 27, 28, 117, 24, 25, 105,126; *CIJ* 1.727–31, 2.1404; *DF* 33; *CJCZ* 70–72; Josephus, *BJ* 7.44; Philo, *Legat.* 133). Other synagogues functioned as repositories for sacred writings (e.g., Josephus, *BJ* 2.285–292, the Masada synagogue) or as archives for legal transactions (*CIJ* 1.683a, 690, 690a, 691; Danshin no. 1; *JIE* 125). As we have already mentioned, an inscription recorded the right of asylum for a synagogue in Egypt (*JIE* 125).

Last of all, we noted that at least some synagogues served as places where deliberative proceedings took place—as was also the case in the Temple courts (e.g., Josephus, *BJ* 1.122). Thus, two inscriptions from Berenice preserve resolutions voted upon by the Jewish politeuma meeting in the synagogue there (*CJCZ* 70–71). Similarly, a pair of decrees permitted the Jews of Sardis to "adjudicate suits among themselves [διαδικάζωνται πρὸς αὐτούς]" within their synagogue (Josephus, *Ant.* 14.260; cf. 14.235). Josephus likewise depicted the *boulē* of Tiberias as meeting within the synagogue there on three separate occasions (*Vita* 276–303). Finally, Marcus Agrippa decreed that those caught stealing the Jewish sacred monies at Ephesus were to be handed over for punishment *not* to the local magistrates, but to the Jews themselves, presumably to be tried within their synagogue (Josephus, *Ant.* 16.167; cf. 2 Cor 11:24; Acts 18:9–10, 26:11; Mark 13:9). The overlap of these various functions supported the thesis that the synagogues, in a restrictive sense, may be viewed as counterparts of the Temple courts.

Finally, in chapter seven we explored the synagogues of three groups who diverged from the Jewish mainstream. We began by reiterating that *synagōgai* of the first group, the Essenes, were described by Philo as "sacred places" (ἱεροὺς . . . τόπους; Philo, *Prob.* 80–83). Along with other scholars, we argued that the Essenes modeled their communities on the desert "camp" of the Israelites (מחנות; e.g., CD 14.3, 9; 1QM 7.1), where the synagogue stood at the center of the camp. This was suggested by Philo's description of the Essenes living in Palestinian cities and villages (*Prob.* 81–82, 85–87) and by recent archaeological investigations which indicate that the Essenes dwelt in a tent neighborhood outside the complex at Khirbet Qumran. We also argued that the functions of the Essene synagogues mirrored those of the Temple precincts from which the sectarian leadership had been disenfranchised. The key difference was the omission of animal sacrifice, which Essene writings plainly state had been replaced by prayer and righteous behavior (1QS 9.3–5a) until such time as the sectarians could regain control of the Temple and reinstitute proper sacrifice (11QT 29.8–10).

The synagogue of the second group, the Therapeutae, functioned not only as a gathering place for Sabbath meetings, but also as a banquet hall in which the Feast of Pentecost was celebrated (*Contempl.* 65). It was suggested that the Therapeutae modeled these feasts after those of priests on duty in the Temple because Philo likened their food to the Bread of the Presence and their singing of hymns to a Levitical choir (*Contempl.* 81, 83–89).

The last group studied, the Samaritans, had a synagogue on Delos in the second century B.C.E. We noted that in the two synagogue inscriptions recovered from the island, the Samaritans identified themselves as "the Israelites who send their first-fruit offerings to the holy temple on Mt. Gerizim" (Bruneau no. 2; cf. Bruneau no. 1). Because other evidence suggested that the Samaritans modeled their temple and their cultic rites after that of their Jewish counterparts, we argued that the Samaritans' self-conceptualization paralleled that of Jews living in the diaspora. From this we inferred that the Jewish congregations would also have identified themselves with their central cult—the Jerusalem Temple. That each of these divergent groups could draw self-definition from a centralized cult lent additional support to the view that the synagogues constituted subsidiary sacred precincts.

SUGGESTIONS FOR FURTHER RESEARCH

The task of constructing socio-historical models has recently been addressed by John Elliott, who writes, "Appropriate and adequate models are models that have been constructed on the basis of empirical evidence and that are coherent with both the theory and the material under examination."[31] Consonant with these principles, we have sought in this study to present a model that takes into account the entire range of relevant data. To this end, we have examined the pertinent literary, epigraphic and architectural evidence in order to determine if the model presented at the beginning of this study coheres with these data. The findings and arguments summarized in the previous section suggest that the proposal that the synagogues functioned as distant precincts of a central cultic site finds a broad measure of support from the data. Moreover, this proposal coheres with the cross-cultural examinations of anthropologists as expressed in Eliade's notion of the *axis mundi*, mentioned at the beginning of this chapter. We would therefore like to propose this model as a viable alternative to a number of other models discussed throughout this study. This is done with the caveat that future discoveries may require additional nuancing of this proposal. In the meantime, we believe that the model presented within this study provides a meaningful framework within which to interpret the variety of phenomena associated with both the Temple and the synagogues. As an overture to extending this model's utility, we conclude this study with suggestions for future research in connection with the synagogue's transformation during the Rabbinic period and its relationship to the Christian *ekklēsia*.

Synagogues in the Rabbinic Period

In his book, *Method and Meaning in Ancient Judaism*, Jacob Neusner argues that the worldview presented in the Mishnah represents a shift

---

[31]John Hall Elliott, *What Is Social-Scientific Criticism?* (Minneapolis: Fortress Press, 1993), 45.

from a locative, cosmologically-centered religion to one that is utopian and community-centered. In developing this argument, Neusner states that the impetus for this shift was the destruction of the Temple and the removal of the possibility for its reconstruction:

> When the Temple was destroyed in 70 . . . the center of national life shaped around a cosmic metaphor was in ruins. When Jerusalem became Aelia in 140, with the Temple-site ploughed over, the ruins were made permanent. The problem confronting all Israelites in the ten decades from 70 to 170—the period of the formation of our tractates—is to work out a way of viewing the world, of making sense of a cosmos which, having lost its center, is nonsense.[32]

In view of the reality of the cult's demise, what is striking about the Mishnah, observes Neusner, is that four of its six divisions base their conceptions upon the cult, while the remaining two require the data of the cult. Indeed, the document presents in detail the special rules for the cult such as the layout of the Temple, the manner in which the various offerings were to be carried out, and a description of which animals were acceptable for offerings. In Neusner's words, the Mishnah thus described "a perfect fantasy."[33]

Why the creation of this fantasy? In Neusner's view, by reasserting the biblical cultic requirements, the authors of the Mishnah were being "defiant and triumphant," reconstructing a world "by changing everything while pretending nothing has changed."[34] The change to which Neusner alludes is the replacement of cultic sacrifice with ritual speech acts:

> Mishnah transforms speech into ritual and so creates the surrogate of ritual deed. That which was not present in cult, speech, is all that is present now that the silent cult is gone. And, it follows, it is by the formalization of speech, its limitation to a few patterns, and its perfection through the creation of patterns of relationships in particular, that the old nexus of Heaven and earth, the cult, now is to be replicated in the new and complementary nexus, cultic speech about all things.[35]

---

[32]Jacob Neusner, *Method and Meaning in Ancient Judaism* (Missoula, Mont.: Scholars Press, 1979), 139.

[33]Ibid.

[34]Ibid., 142, 146.

[35]Ibid., 176.

Thus in the study and debate of biblical halakha, as represented in the Mishnah, Jews were able "to experience anywhere and anytime that cosmic center of the world described by Mishnah: *Cosmic center in words is made utopia*."[36]

While we would agree with Neusner's interpretation, we would also point out that after the Temple's destruction, a locus did remain for the performance of "cultic speech"—the synagogue. Indeed, as many researchers have observed, after the Temple's destruction, religious art and iconography became more pronounced in the synagogues, as if to make up for that which had been lost in Jerusalem.[37] Moreover, the Temple ruins, while unapproachable by Jews, still served as a sacred center. As archaeologist A. Oppenheim has observed, in the Near East "the numinous presence of the deity is so precisely located that the sanctuaries cling forever to the same spot."[38] Even today the Western Wall of the Temple mount remains the holiest place within Judaism. Similarly, the synagogues of the Late Roman and Byzantine periods were frequently built with their façades and/or torah shrines oriented toward Jerusalem.[39] Others were oriented toward the east, probably following a divergent halakha which required that synagogue entrances be placed on the east "for we find that in the Temple the entrance faced the east" (*t. Megillah* 3.22).

This study would suggest that these developments were not innovations of the post-70 era, but the accentuation of the existing features of synagogue architecture from the Second Temple period. This is perhaps best exemplified in the addition of a particular style of mosaic in several synagogues during the Byzantine era. The synagogue at Beth Alpha typifies the arrangement of this kind of mosaic in that it has three primary sections (see figure 22). The upper section consists of a large Temple/torah shrine flanked by menorahs. Underneath this section is a large panel containing a zodiac. Finally, at the bottom is a depiction of Abraham's sacrifice of Isaac. The mosaic rests in the center of the synagogue, and worshipers would have sat on benches along the walls

---

[36]Ibid., 152. Italics in original.

[37]See Levine, "Nature and Origin of the Palestinian Synagogue Reconsidered," 445–447; Cohen, "The Temple and the Synagogue," 151–174.

[38]A. L. Oppenheim, *Ancient Mesopotamia* (Chicago: University of Chicago Press, 1965), 131.

[39]Hachlili lists thirty-six examples within Israel alone. See Hachlili, *Ancient Jewish Art and Archaeology in the Land of Israel*, 148–149. The diaspora synagogues at Ostia and Sardis are likewise oriented toward Jerusalem.

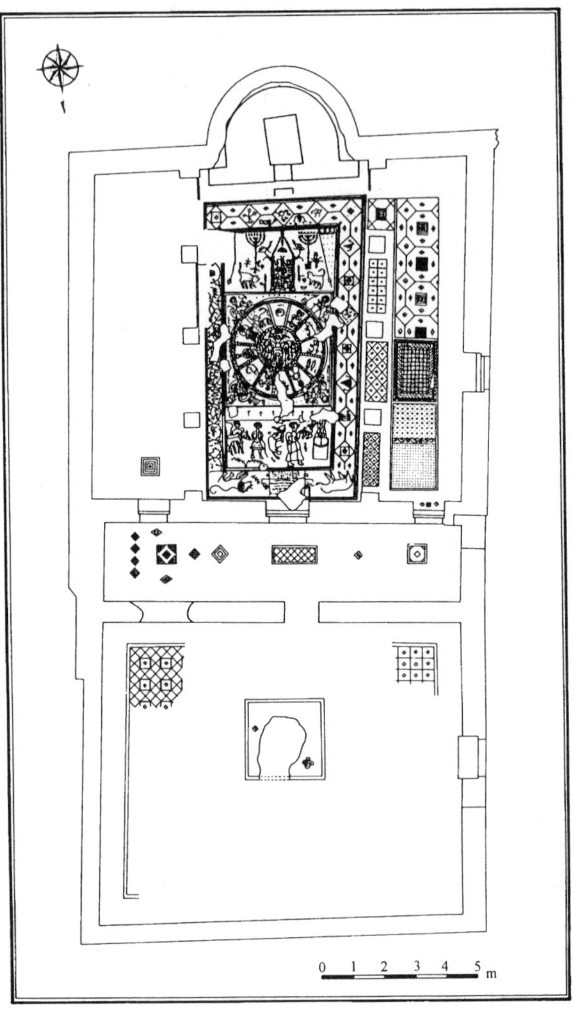

Figure 22. The Beth Alpha synagogue. The interpretation presented in the text suggests that the three panels of the central mosaic correspond to the Temple shrine (shrine), the Temple veil (zodiac) and the Temple altar (Abraham's sacrifice). An ark containing the torah scrolls was placed in the apse, which is oriented towards Jerusalem. Worshipers sat on benches along the walls directing their attention to the center, just as their ancestors had observed sacrifice being offering in the Court of the Priests.

with columns intervening between them and the center of the hall.

Most interpretations of this mosaic have focused on the zodiac panel, suggesting that it served as some sort of festival calendar.[40] In a little-noticed article, however, John Wilkinson has argued that the center panel represents the table of the shewbread, since Philo writes that "the twelve loaves on the Table signified the cycle of the zodiac and the year" (*Her.* 176). Wilkinson goes on to interpret the entire mosaic as follows:

> The overall layout of the Beit Alpha mosaic is yet another reminder of the Temple. The top panel thus occupies the place of the *Devir* or Holy of Holies, the middle panel containing the zodiac and seasons occupies the place of the *Heikhal* where the shewbred was displayed, and the third panel, Abraham's sacrifice, relates to the former two as the altar related to the Temple building. The continuity between the old Temple worship and the new synagogue worship is proclaimed in the layout of the floor design.[41]

While Wilkinson's interpretation seems to point in the right direction, the recent discovery of a mosaic in a synagogue at Sepphoris which depicts the shewbread table separately from the zodiac indicates that his proposal is in need of some modification.[42] Here, we call attention to Josephus' description of the great veil that hung before the main entrance of the Temple shrine:

> Before [the doors of the Temple] hung a veil of equal length, of Babylonian tapestry, with embroidery of blue and fine linen, of scarlet also and purple and fine linen, wrought with marvellous skill. Nor was this mixture of materials without its mystic meaning: it typified the universe. For the scarlet seemed emblematical of fire, the fine linen of the earth, the blue of the air, and the purple of the sea; the comparison in two cases being suggested by their colour, and in that of the fine linen and purple by their origin, as the one is produced by the earth and the other by the sea. On this tapestry was portrayed a panorama of the heavens, *the signs of the Zodiac excepted* (*BJ* 5.212–213).

---

[40] See Hachlili, *Ancient Jewish Art and Archaeology in the Land of Israel*, 308–309.

[41] John Wilkinson, "The Beit Alpha Synagogue Mosaic: Towards an Interpretation," *Journal of Jewish Art* 5 (1978): 26–27.

[42] See Zeev Weiss and Ehud Netzer, "The Synagogue Mosaic" in *Sepphoris in Galilee*, edited by Rebecca Martin Nagy et al. (Winona Lake: Eisenbrauns, 1996), 133–139.

In view of this description, we suggest that the central panel on the Beth Alpha mosaic, and on other mosaics like it, represents the great veil of the Temple, portraying the "panorama of the heavens" with a zodiac, whose depiction was not permitted in Josephus' day because of a stricter interpretation of the Second Commandment.

If this interpretation is accepted, then we have in such synagogues the Court of Priests depicted artistically in the center of the building, with the shrine, veil and sacrificial altar set out before the worshipers seated on the benches behind the columns—just as Strange proposed for the earlier synagogues. We should add that this interpretation is solidified by the fact that both 2 Chronicles and Josephus identify the site where Abraham offered his sacrifice as the Temple mount (2 Chr 3:1, *Ant.* 1.226).

In our view, then, the "cultic speech" to which Neusner refers found a sacred setting within the synagogues of the Late Roman and Byzantine periods. Although the main sanctuary was demolished, these structures nevertheless could continue to function as the distant courts of a Temple whose cult could be perpetuated through the gathering of the congregation of Israel, the reading and study of Torah, and the offering of the prayers.

Synagogue and *Ekklēsia*

If Rabbinic Judaism represented a gradual shift from a locative to a utopian religion, Christianity constituted an earlier and even more abrupt enactment of this shift. Whereas as late as Julian the Apostate, Jews hoped to re-establish the Temple in Jerusalem, Christians interpreted its destruction as a vindication of their belief that the Temple's purpose had been fulfilled in the death and resurrection of Christ. Here, however, it is noteworthy that certain Christian writers did not totally abandon the cult, but reinterpreted it with Christ absorbing the place of the Temple (John 2:21), the high priesthood (Heb 5:5–6), the feasts (John 7:37–38) and the sacrificial victim (Rom 3:24–25; Rev 13:8). The new temple was the one located in the heavens, as so vividly portrayed in the book of Revelation (e.g., Rev 7:15ff.; cf. Heb 8:5, 9:24).

Consonant with their embrace of a utopian worldview, Christians saw fit to hold their assemblies in houses that remained in profane, human use. Thus we have several references in the New Testament to "the *ekklēsia* in so-and-so's house" (Rom 16:5; 1 Cor 16:19; Col 4:15; Philem 1:2). The adoption of the house as a regular meeting place may simply have been an expediency, perhaps one fueled by a belief in the imminence of the Second Coming (1 Thess 4:14–17). It is likewise possible that this move was initially justified in view of the origin of the Lord's Supper in the Passover (Luke 22:1–20; 1 Cor 11:17–34), the one Jewish feast that centered in the home.[43] Concerning this feast, Philo writes, "on this day every dwelling-house is invested with the outward semblance and dignity of a temple [ἑκάστη δὲ οἰκία κατ᾽ ἐκεῖνον τὸν χρόνον σχῆμα ἱεροῦ καὶ σεμνότητα περιβέβληται]" (*Spec*. 2.148).

Although the Christians made use of private homes for their assemblies, the Christian *ekklēsia* was clearly indebted to the Jewish synagogues.[44] Here we should observe that several functions of the *ekklēsia* bore an affinity to those of the synagogues. These include the reading and interpretation of scripture, communal prayer, and the eating of common meals (1 Cor 11:17–34, 14:26). Paul's admonition to the Corinthians to settle their legal affairs within their assembly may likewise be indebted to this practice within the synagogues (1 Cor 6:1–7). Finally, the collection of offerings from the Gentile churches for the mother church at Jerusalem somewhat resembles the sending of envoys bearing the Temple tax from the diaspora synagogues to Jerusalem (1 Cor 16:1–3; Rom 15:25–27; 2 Cor 8, 9).[45]

---

[43]Of course, it is still debated whether the Last Supper took place on Passover (Synoptics) or on the night before Passover (John). (For a recent review of the debate, see John P. Meier, *A Marginal Jew*, 3 vols. [New York: Doubleday, 1991], 1.395–401.) In either case, there is some connection between the two observances.

[44]Researchers have also noted how *synagōgē* and *ekklēsia* are interchangeable in the LXX (Kee, "The Transformation of the Synagogue after 70 CE," 20–24; Burtchaell, *From Synagogue to Church*, 277–284; Karl L. Schmidt, "Ἐκκλησία" in *TDNT* 3.501–536). Normally in the LXX, עֵדָה is translated συναγωγή (e.g., Exod 12:3, Lev 4:13, Num 1:2). In Prov 5:14, however, עֵדָה is rendered ἐκκλησίας καὶ συναγωγῆς. On the other hand, קָהָל is translated in the LXX as either συναγωγή or ἐκκλησία (e.g., Ps 39:10 [LXX], ἐκκλησία; Ps 39:11 [LXX], συναγωγή). Here, it is striking how in Acts 20:28 (Paul's farewell address to the elders of the churches in Asia), an allusion is made to Ps 74:2 (LXX), which uses the word συναγωγή. Luke changes this to ἐκκλησία.

[45]On these similarities, see Wayne A. Meeks, *The First Urban Christians: The Social World of the Apostle Paul* (New Haven: Yale University Press, 1983), 80–81; Burtchaell, *From Synagogue to Church*, 284–288. We should also recall from our discussion of James in chapter one that a passage in this epistle (2:2) possibly uses the word *synagōgē* to refer to *Christian* assemblies or meeting places. On the other hand, the passage may refer to Christians who continued to attend Jewish synagogues. See Schrage, "Συναγωγή," 834–835.

In addition to this overlap in functions, there may have been a connection between church and synagogue officials. Along these lines, James Burtchaell has recently argued that the officers of the *ekklēsia* derived from the synagogue. Hence, he views the *episkopos* (Phil 1:1) as analogous to the *archisynagōgos*, the Christian *presbyteroi* (1 Pet 5:1; James 5:14; Acts 20:17) equivalent to the Jewish *presbyteroi*, and the *diakonos* (Phil 1:1; Rom 16:1) the counterpart of the *hypēretēs*.[46]

Although Christianity emerged as a utopian religion, following the Edict of Milan in 313 C.E., a locative element reasserted itself as churches began to be built upon the remains of places believed to be holy. Foremost among these was the Church of the Holy Sepulcher in Jerusalem, fashioned around the site thought to be the tomb of Christ. What is striking about this and other churches of the Byzantine period are the affinities they bear to synagogues of the same period. Indeed, in not a few cases structures initially believed to have been churches were later identified as synagogues.

In these ancient churches too, one can find architectural traces of the Temple: a reliquary or shrine would rest behind an altar upon which the eucharist was offered. The faithful who frequented the courts of these churches would watch as the priests surrounded the altar and recalled Christ's sacrifice. The true temple may have been removed to the realm of the beyond; but in these sacred buildings, the *axis mundi* had returned, again providing a passageway leading from earth into the courts of the temple in heaven.

---

[46]Burtchaell, *From Synagogue to Church*, 372–338. Burtchaell's study also contains an extensive critique of previous studies of this question, one which documents how conclusions among researchers have tended to correlate with denominational affiliations (i.e., Catholics typically emphasize early church [and synagogue] offices while Protestants downplay them). His own analysis is placed within the context of this debate.

SELECT BIBLIOGRAPHY

"Archaeologists Uncover Replica of Second Temple." *Jerusalem Post*, 4 April 1995.

Adkins, Lesley, and Roy A. Adkins. *Handbook to Life in Ancient Rome*. New York: Facts on File, 1994.

Agua Pérez, Agust n del. "La sinagoga: Origenes, ciclos se lectura y oración: Estado de la cuestión." *Ebib* 41, no. 3–4 (1983): 341–366.

Anderson, H. "3 Maccabees." In *Old Testament Pseudepigrapha* Vol. 2, edited by J. H. Charlesworth, 509–529. New York: Doubleday, 1985.

———. "4 Maccabees." In *Old Testament Pseudepigrapha* Vol. 2, edited by J. H. Charlesworth, 531–543. New York: Doubleday, 1985.

Applebaum, Shimon. *Jews and Greeks in Ancient Cyrene*. Edited by Jacob Neusner. Vol. 28, *Studies in Judaism in Late Antiquity*. Leiden: E. J. Brill, 1979.

———. "The Legal Status of the Jewish Communities in the Diaspora; The Organization of the Jewish Communities in the Diaspora." In *Jewish People in the First Century* Vol. 1, edited by S. Safrai and M. Stern, 420–503. Assen: Van Gorcum, 1974.

Archer, Léonie J. "The Role of Jewish Women in the Religion, Ritual and Cult of Graeco-Roman Palestine." In *Images of Women in Antiquity*, edited by Averil Cameron and Amélie Kuhrt, 273–287. Detroit: Wayne State University Press, 1983.

Atkinson, Kenneth. "On Further Defining the First Century CE Synagogue: Fact or Fiction? A Rejoinder to H. C. Kee." *New Testament Studies* 43 (1997): 491–502.

Attridge, H.W. "Josephus and His Works." In *Jewish Writings of the Second Temple Period*, edited by Michael E. Stone, 185–232. Philadelphia: Fortress Press, 1984.

Aune, David E. *The New Testament in Its Literary Environment*. Philadelphia: Westminster Press, 1987.

Avi-Yonah, M. "Editor's Note." *IEJ* 23 (1973): 43–45.

———. "Maresha." In *The New Encyclopedia of Archaeological Excavations in the Holy Land* Vol. 3., edited by Ephraim Stern, 948–951. Jerusalem: Israel Exploration Society & Carta; New York: Simon & Schuster, 1993.

———. "Mareshah." In *Encyclopedia of Archaeological Excavations in the Holy Land* Vol. 3, edited by Michael Avi-Yonah and Ephriam Stern, 782–790. Jerusalem: The Israel Exploration Society and Massada Press, 1977.

Aviam, Mordechai. "Magdala." In *The Oxford Encyclopedia of Archaeology in the Near East* Vol. 3, edited by Eric M. Meyers, 399–400. Oxford: Oxford University Press, 1996.

Avigad, N. "The 'Galilean' Synagogue and its Predecessors." In *Ancient Synagogues Revealed*, edited by Lee I. Levine, 42–44. Jerusalem: Israel Exploration Society, 1982.

Bacher, W. "Synagogue." In *A Dictionary of the Bible* Vol. 4, edited by James Hastings, 636–643. Edinburgh: Clark, 1902.

Baillet, M., J. T. Milik, and Roland de Vaux. *Les "Petites Grottes" de Qumran, Discoveries in the Judaean Desert of Jordan 3*. Oxford: Clarendon Press, 1962.

Bakker, Jan Theo. *Living and Working with the Gods: Studies of Evidence for Private Religion and its Material Environment in the City of Ostia (100-500 AD), Dutch monographs on ancient history and archaeology; v. 12*. Amsterdam: J. C. Gieben, 1994.

Barag, Dan. "The Table of the Showbread and the Facade of the Temple on Coins of the Bar-Kokhba Revolt." In *Ancient Jerusalem Revealed*, edited by Hillel Geva, 272–276. Jerusalem: Israel Exploration Society, 1994.

Barclay, J. M. C. *Jews in the Mediterranean Diaspora from Alexander to Trajan (323 BCE-117 BCE)* Edinburgh: T. & T. Clark, 1996.

Barghouti, Asem N. "Urbanization of Palestine and Jordan in Hellenistic and Roman Times." In *Studies in the History and Archaeology of Jordan* Vol. 1, edited by Adnan Hadidi, 209–229. Amman, Jordan: Department of Antiquities, 1982.

Barnett, Richard D. "Bringing God into the Temple." In *Temples and High Places in Biblical Times: Proceedings of the Colloquium in Honor of the Centennial of Hebrew Union College-jewish Institute of Religion, Jerusalem, 14–16 March 1977*, edited by Avraham Birah, Inna Pommerantz and Hannah Katzenstein, 10–20. Jerusalem: Nelson Glueck School of Biblical Archaeology of Hebrew Union College-Jewish Institute of Religion, 1981.

Baron, Salo Wittmayer. *A Social and Religious History of the Jews*. 2nd ed. New York: Columbia University Press, 1952.

Baron, Salo Wittmayer, and the Society of America Jewish Publication. *The Jewish Community, The Morris Loeb series*. Philadelphia: Jewish Publication Society of America, 1942.

Barrett, C. K. *Luke the Historian in Recent Study*. New ed. Philadelphia: Fortress Press, 1970.

Bauckham, Richard. *The Book of Acts in Its Palestinian Setting*. Vol. 4, *The Book of Acts in Its First Century Setting*. Grand Rapids, Mich.: William B. Eerdmans Pub. Co., 1995.

Bellen, H. "Die Aussage einer bosporanishen Freilassungsinschrift (*CIRB* 71) zum Problem der 'Gottfürchtigen'." *JAC* 8 (1965): 171–176.

Ben-Dov, Meir. *In the Shadow of the Temple*. Translated by Ina Friedman. New York: Harper & Row, 1985.

Berkovits, Eliezer. "From the Temple to Synagogue and Back." *Judaism* 8 (1959): 303–411.

Betz, Hans Dieter. *Galatians*. Philadelphia: Fortress Press, 1979.

Bickerman, Elias J. "La charte séleucid de Jerusalem." *REJ* 100 (1935): 4–35.

Bilde, Per. *Flavius Josephus between Jerusalem and Rome*. Sheffield, England: JSOT Press, 1988.

Billerbeck, Paul. "Ein Synagogengottesdienst in Jesu Tagen." *ZNW* 55, no. 3-4 (1964): 143–161.

Biran, Avraham. *Biblical Dan*. Jerusalem: Israel Exploration Society, 1994.

———. "'To the God who is in Dan'." In *Temples and High Places in Biblical Times*, edited by Avraham Biran, Inna Pommerantz and Hannah Katzenstein, 142–151. Jerusalem: Nelson Glueck School of Biblical Archaeology of Hebrew Union College-Jewish Institute of Religion, 1981.

Biran, Avraham, Inna Pommerantz, and Hannah Katzenstein, eds. *Temples and High Places in Biblical Times: Proceedings of the Colloquium in Honor of the Centennial of Hebrew Union College-Jewish Institute of Religion, Jerusalem, 14–16 March 1977*. Jerusalem: Nelson Glueck School of Biblical Archaeology of Hebrew Union College-Jewish Institute of Religion, 1981.

Blake, Marion Elizabeth. *Roman Construction in Italy from Tiberius through the Flavians*. Washington: Carnegie Institution of Washington, 1959.

Blake, Marion Elizabeth, and Esther Boise Van Deman. *Ancient Roman Construction in Italy from the Prehistoric Period to Augustus*. Washington: Carnegie Institution of Washington, 1947.

Blue, Bradley. "Acts and the House Church." In *The Book of Acts in Its First Century Setting* Vol. 2, edited by David W. Gill and Conrad Gempf, 119–222. Grand Rapids, Michigan: Wm. B. Eerdmans, 1994.

———. "In Public and In Private: The Role of the House Church in Early Christianity." Ph.D., University of Aberdeen, 1989.

Boersma, Johannes S. *Amoenissima Civitas. Block V.ii at Ostia: Description and Analysis of Its Visible Remains*. Assen, The Netherlands: Van Gorcum, 1985.

Bohak, Gideon. *Joseph and Aseneth and the Jewish Temple in Heliopolis*. Atlanta: Scholars Press, 1996.

Bonani, G., et al. "Radiocarbon Dating of the Dead Sea Scrolls." *Atiqot* 20 (1991): 27–32.

Bonner, Stanley F. *Education in Ancient Rome*. Berkeley: University of California Press, 1977.

Bonz, Marianne P. "The Jewish Community of Ancient Sardis: A Reassessment of its Rise to Prominence." *Harvard Studies in Classical Philology* 93 (1990): 343–359.

Bookidis, Nancy. "Ritual Dining at Corinth." In *Greek Sanctuaries*, edited by Nanno Marinatos and Robin Hägg, 45–61. London and New York: Routledge, 1993.

Borgen, Peder. *Bread from Heaven*. Leiden: E. J. Brill, 1965.

———. "The Early Church and the Hellenistic Synagogue." *ST* 37, no. 1 (1983): 55–78.

———. "Philo of Alexandria." In *Jewish Writings of the Second Temple Period*, edited by Michael E. Stone, 233–282. Philadelphia: Fortress Press, 1984.

Bowker, John Westerdale. *The Targums and Rabbinic Literature; An Introduction to Jewish Interpretations of Scripture*. Cambridge: University Press, 1969.

Bowman, Alan K., and Dominic Rathbone. "Cities and Administration in Roman Egypt." *JRS* 82 (1992): 107–127.

Bradley, K. R. *Slavery and Society at Rome, Key Themes in Ancient History*. Cambridge England; New York, NY, USA: Cambridge University Press, 1994.

Branham, Joan R. "Vicarious Sacrality: Temple Space in Ancient Synagogues." In *Ancient Synagogues: Historical Analysis and Archaeological Discovery* Vol. 2, edited by Dan Urman and Paul Virgil McCracken Flesher, 319–345. New York: E.J. Brill, 1995.

Braude, William G. "Church Fathers and the Synagogue." *Judaism* 9 (1960): 112–119.

Brenk, Beat. "Zu den Grundriestypen der fruehsten Synagogen Palaestinas." In *Atti Del IX Congresso Internazionale Di Archeologia Cristiana: Roma, 21 -27 Settembre 1975* Vol. 1, edited by cristiana Congresso internazionale di archeologia, 539–550. Citta del Vaticano, Roma: Pontificio istituto di archeologia cristiana, 1978.

Bright, John. *A History of Israel, Westminster aids to the study of the Scriptures*. Philadelphia: Westminster Press, 1959.

Brooten, Bernadette J. "Inscriptional Evidence for Women as Leaders in the Ancient Synagogue." *Society of Biblical Literature Seminar Papers* 20 (1981): 1–17.

———. *Inscriptional Evidence for Women as Leaders in the Ancient Synagogue: A Thesis*, 1982.

———. *Women Leaders in the Ancient Synagogue: Inscriptional Evidence and Background Issues*. Vol. 36, *Brown Judaic Studies*. Chico, Calif.: Scholars Press, 1982.

Broshi, Magen. "The Credibility of Josephus." *JJS* 33 (1982): 379–384.

Brown, Raymond Edward. *The Community of the Beloved Disciple*. New York: Paulist Press, 1979.

———. *The Gospel According to John*. 2 vols. Garden City, N.Y.: Doubleday, 1966.

Bruneau, Philippe. "«Les Israélites de Délos» et la juiverie délienne." *BCH* 106 (1982): 465–504.

———. *Recherches sur les cultes de Delos a l'epoque hellenistique et a l'epoque imperiale, Bibliotheque des ecoles francaises d'Athenes et de Rome, fasc. 217*. Paris: E. de Boccard, 1970.

———. *Guide de Delos*. 3rd ed, *Sites et monuments / Ecole francaise d'Athenes; 1*. Paris: Ecole francaise d'Athenes en depot aux Editions E. de Boccard, 1983.

Burkert, Walter. *Ancient Mystery Cults*. Cambridge, Mass.: Harvard University Press, 1987.

———. *Greek Religion*. Cambridge, Mass.: Harvard University Press, 1985.

———. "The Meaning and Function of the Temple in Classical Greece." In *Temple in Society*, edited by Michael V. Fox, 27–47. Winona Lake: Eisenbrauns, 1988.

Burridge, Richard A. *What are the Gospels?* Cambridge: Cambridge University Press, 1992.

Burtchaell, James T. *From Synagogue to Church: Public Services and Offices in the Earliest Christian Communities*. Cambridge; New York: Cambridge University Press, 1992.

Busnick, Th. A. *Der Tempel von Jerusalem*. 2 vols. Leiden: E. J. Brill, 1970.

Campbell, William S. "Did Paul Advocate Separation from the Synagogue?" *SJT* 42, no. 4 (1989): 457–467.

Cantarella, Eva. *Pandora's Daughters*. Baltimore, Md.: Johns Hopkins University Press, 1981.

Charlesworth, James H. *The Dead Sea Scrolls: Hebrew, Aramaic, and Greek Texts with English Translations*. 10 vols, *Princeton Theological Seminary Dead Sea scrolls project*. Tubingen: J.C.B. Mohr (P. Siebeck); Louisville: Westminster/John Knox Press, 1994–.

———. "Jewish Astrology in the Talmud, Pseudepigrapha, the Dead Sea Scrolls, and Early Palestinian Synagogues." *HTR* 70 (1977): 183–200.

———. "A Prolegomenon to a New Study of the Jewish Background of the Hymns and Prayers in the New Testament." *JJS* 33 (1982): 264–285.

Chen, Doron. "Design of the Ancient Synagogues in Galilee." In *Studium Biblicum Franciscanum* Vol. 28, edited by V. Ravanelli and F. Manns, 193–202. Jerusalem: Franciscan Printing Press, 1978.

———. "The Design of the Ancient Synagogues in Galilee." In *Studium Biblicum Franciscanum* Vol. 30, edited by V. Ravanelli and F. Manns, 255–258. Jerusalem: Franciscan Printing Press, 1980.

———. "The Design of the Ancient Synagogues in Judea: Masada and Herodium." *BASOR* 239 (1980): 37–40.

———. "On Planning of Synagogues and Churches in Palaestina: A Comparison with Syria and Illyricum." In *Christian Archaeology in the Holy Land: Essays in Honour of Virgilio C. Corbo, OFM*, edited by G. C. G. Bottini, L. DiSegni and E. Alliata, 523–534. Jerusalem: Franciscan Printing Press, 1990.

Chester, Andrew, and Ralph P. Martin. *The Theology of the Letter of James, Peter and Jude*. Cambridge: Cambridge University Press, 1994.

Chiat, Marilyn J. "First-Century Synagogue Architecture: Methodological Problems." In *Ancient Synagogues: The State of Research*, edited by Joseph Gutmann, 49–60. Chico, California: Scholars Press, 1981.

———. "Synagogue Chronology: A New Hypothesis." *AJA* 88, no. 2 (1984): 240.

———. “A Corpus of Synagogue Art and Architecture in Roman and Byzantine Palestine.” Ph.D., University of Minnesota, 1979.

———. *Handbook of Synagogue Architecture, Brown Judaic studies; no. 29*. Chico, Calif.: Scholars Press, 1982.

———. “Thing or Symbol? Art in the Early Synagogue and Church.” *The Arts in Religious and Theological Studies* 6 (1994): 13–21.

Chiat, Marilyn J. S., and Marchita B. Mauck. “Using Archeological Sources.” In *The Making of Jewish and Christian Worship*, edited by P. Bradshaw, 69–106. Notre Dame: University of Notre Dame Press, 1991.

Clermont-Gannaeu, C. “Découverte à Jérusalem d'une synagogue de l’époque Hérodienne.” In *Syria*, 190–197. Paris, 1920.

Cohen, Shaye J. D. *From the Maccabees to the Mishnah, Library of Early Christianity, 7*. Philadelphia: Westminster Press, 1987.

———. *Josephus in Galilee and Rome: His Vita and Development as a Historian*. Leiden: Brill, 1979.

———. “Masada: Literary Tradition, Archaeological Remains, and the Credibility of Josephus.” *JJS* 33 (1982): 385–405.

———. “Pagan and Christian Evidence on the Ancient Synagogue.” In *The Synagogue in Late Antiquity*, edited by Lee I. Levine, 159–181. Philadelphia: American Schools of Oriental Research, 1987.

———. “Respect for Judaism by Gentiles According to Josephus.” *HTR* 80 (1987): 409–430.

———. “The Temple and the Synagogue.” In *The Temple in Antiquity: Ancient Records and Modern Perspectives*, edited by T. Madsen, 151–174. Provo, Utah: Religious Studies Center, Brigham Young University, 1984.

Cole, Susan Guettel. “Greek Cults.” In *Civilizations of the Ancient Mediterranean: Greece and Rome* Vol. 2, edited by Michael Grant and Rachel Kitzinger, 887–908. New York: Charles Scribner's Sons, 1988.

Collins, Adela Yarbro. *The Beginning of the Gospel.* Minneapolis: Fortress Press, 1992.

———. "Revelation, Book of." In *The Anchor Bible Dictionary* Vol. 5, edited by David Noel Freedman, 694–708. New York: Doubleday, 1992.

Collins, John J. *Daniel: A Commentary on the Book of Daniel.* Minneapolis: Fortress Press, 1993.

Collins, Matthew S. "Money, Sex and Power: An Examination of the Role of Women as Patrons of the Ancient Synagogues." In *Recovering the Role of Women: Power and Authority in Rabbinic Jewish Society* Vol. 59, edited by P. Haas, 7–22. Atlanta, Ga.: Scholars Press, 1992.

Conzelmann, Hans. *Acts of the Apostles: A Commentary on the Acts of the Apostles*. Philadelphia: Fortress Press, 1987.

Cook, Michael J. *Mark's Treatment of the Jewish Leaders*. Leiden: E. J. Brill, 1978.

Corbo, P.V.C. "Scavi Archaelogici a Magdala." *Liber Annuus* 24 (1974): 5–37.

———. "Cafarnao dopo la XIX campagna di scavo." *Liber Annuus* 36 (1986): 297–308.

———. "The Excavation at Herodium." *Qadmoniot* 4 (1968): 132–136.

———. "Gébel Fureidis (Hérodium)." *RB* 75 (1968): 424–428.

———. "L'Herodion de Giabel Fureidis." *Liber Annuus* 13 (1962–63): 219–277.

———. "L'Herodion de Giabel Fureidis." *Liber Annuus* 17 (1967): 65–121.

———. "La Citta romana di Magdala." In *Studia Hierosolymitana* Vol. 1, edited by Michele Piccirillo, Ignazio Mancini, Emmanuele Testa, Bellarmino Bagatti and Giovanni Claudio Bottini, 365–368. Jerusalem: Franciscan Print. Press, 1976.

———. "Capernaum." In *The Anchor Bible Dictionary* Vol. 1, edited by David Noel Freedman, 866–869. New York: Doubleday, 1992.

———. *Herodion: Gli Edifici della Reggia-Fortrezza.* 4 vols. Vol. 1, *Studium Biblicum Franciscanum no. 20.* Jerusalem: Franciscan Printing Press, 1989.

———. "Resti della Sinagoga del Primo Secolo a Cafarnao." In *Studia Hierosolymitana III*, 314–357, 1982.

Cotter, Wendy. "The Collegia and Roman Law: State Restrictions on Voluntary Associations, 64 BCE–200 CE." In *Voluntary Associations*, edited by John S. Kloppenborg and Steven G. Wilson, 74–89. London: Routledge, 1996.

Coulton, J. J. *The Architectural Development of the Greek Stoa.* Oxford: Clarendon Press, 1976.

Cross, F. M. *The Ancient Library of Qumran.* Minneapolis: Fortress Press, 1995.

———. *Canaanite Myth and Hebrew Epic.* Cambridge: Harvard University Press, 1973.

Crown, Alan D. "The Samaritan Diaspora." In *The Samaritans*, edited by A Crown, 195–217. Tübingen: J.C.B. Mohr, 1989.

Danker, Frederick W. *Benefactor: Epigraphic Study of a Graeco-Roman and New Testament Semantic Field.* St. Louis, Mo.: Clayton Pub. House, 1982.

Danshin, D. I. "Jewish Community of Phanagoria." *Vestnik Drevnei Istorii* 204, no. 1 (1993): 59–73.

Davids, Peter H. *The Epistle of James*. Grand Rapids, Mich.: Eerdmans, 1982.

Davies, Philip R. "The Ideology of the Temple in the Damascus Document." *JJS* 33 (1982): 287–301.

de Beor, Martinus C. *Johannine Perspectives on the Death of Jesus*. Kampen, The Netherlands: Kok Pharos, 1996.

de Vaux, Roland. *Archaeology and the Dead Sea Scrolls, The Schweich lectures of the British Academy, 1959*. Oxford: Oxford University Press, 1973.

Deissmann, Gustav Adolf. *Light from the Ancient East: The New Testament Illustrated by Recently Discovered Texts of the Graeco-Roman World*. 4th ed. New York: George H. Doran, 1927.

Delcor, M. "Le Temple d'Onias en Égypte." *RB* 75 (1968): 188–203.

Despland, Michel. *The Education of Desire*. Toronto: University of Toronto Press, 1985.

Dever, William G. "The MB IIC Stratification in the Northwest Gate Area at Shechem." *BASOR* 216 (1974): 31–52.

Dibelius, M., and H. Greeven. *A Commentary on the Epistle of James*. revised ed. Philadelphia: Fortress Press, 1976.

Dion, Paul E. "Synagogues et temples dans l'Égypte hellénistique." *ScEs* 29 (1977): 45–75.

Dodd, C. H. *The Apostolic Preaching and Its Developments*. Chicago: Willett, Clark & Company, 1937.

Dombowski, B . W. W. "Synagôgê in Acts 6:9." In *Intertestamental Essays*, edited by Zdzislaw J. Kapera, 53–65. Krackow: The Enigma Press, 1992.

Downey, Glanville. *A History of Antioch in Syria*. Princeton, NJ: Princeton University Press, 1961.

———. "The Size of the Population of Antioch." *Transactions of the American Philological Association* 89 (1958): 84–91.

Eliade, Mircea. *The Sacred and the Profane*. 1st American ed. New York: Harcourt, 1959.

———. "Sacred Architecture and Symbolism." In *Symbolism, the Sacred, and the Arts*, edited by Mircea Eliade and Diane Apostolos-Cappadona, 105–129. New York: Crossroad, 1985.

Elliott, John Hall. *What Is Social-Scientific Criticism?* Edited by Dan Otto Via, *New Testament Series*. Minneapolis: Fortress Press, 1993.

Esler, Philip Francis. *Community and Gospel in Luke-Acts*. Cambridge: Cambridge University Press, 1987.

Farmer, William F. *The Synoptic Problem, A Critical Analysis*. New York: Macmillan, 1964.

Feldman, Louis H. "Diaspora Synagogues: New Light from Inscriptions and Papyri." In *Studies in Hellenistic Judaism*, 577–602. London: E. J. Brill, 1996.

———. "The Omnipresence of the God-Fearers." *BAR* 12, no. 5 (1986): 58–63.

Figueras, Pau. "Epigraphic Evidence for Proselytism in Ancient Judaism." *Immanuel* 24/25 (1990): 194–206.

Filson, Floyd V. "Ancient Greek Synagogue Inscriptions." *BA* 32, no. 1 (1969): 41–46.

Fine, Steven. "Gamla." In *The Oxford Encyclopedia of Archaeology in the Near East* Vol. 2, edited by Eric M. Meyers, 382. Oxford: Oxford University Press, 1996.

———. *This Holy Place. On the Sanctity of the Synagogue during the Greco-Roman Period.* Edited by Gregory E. Sterling. Vol. 11, *Christianity and Judaism in Antiquity Series*. Notre Dame, Indiana: University of Notre Dame Press, 1998.

———. "Synagogue Inscriptions." In *The Oxford Encyclopedia of Archaeology in the Near East* Vol. 5, edited by Eric M. Meyers, 114–118. Oxford: Oxford University Press, 1996.

Fine, Steven, and Eric M. Meyers. "Synagogues." In *The Oxford Encyclopedia of Archaeology in the Near East* Vol. 5, edited by Eric M. Meyers, 118–123. Oxford: Oxford University Press, 1996.

Fine, Steven, ed. *Sacred Realm: The Emergence of the Synagogue in the Ancient World*. New York: Oxford University Press and Yeshiva University Museum, 1996.

Finkel, Asher. "Jesus' Preaching in the Synagogue on the Sabbath (Luke 4:16–28)." In *The Gospels and the Scriptures of Israel*, edited by Craig A. Evans and W. Richard Stegner, 325–341. Sheffield, England: Sheffield Academic Press, 1994.

Finkelstein, Louis. "The Origin of the Synagogue." In *The Synagogue: Studies in Origins, Archaeology, and Architecture*, edited by Joseph Gutmann, 3–59. New York: Ktav Pub. House, 1975.

———. *The Pharisees*. 3rd ed, *The Morris Loeb series*. Philadelphia: Jewish Publication Society of America, 1962.

Fiorenza, Elisabeth Schüssler. *The Book of Revelation: Justice and Judgment*. Philadelphia: Fortress Press, 1985.

Fisher, Nicholas R. E. "Greek Associations, Symposia, and Clubs." In *Civilizations of the Ancient Mediterranean: Greece and Rome* Vol. 2, edited by Michael Grant and Rachel Kitzinger, 1167–1195. New York: Charles Scribner's Sons, 1988.

———. "Roman Associations, Dinner Parties, and Clubs." In *Civilizations of the Ancient Meditteranean: Greece and Rome* Vol. 2, edited by Michael Grant and Rachel Kitzinger, 1199–1225. New York: Charles Scribner's Sons, 1988.

Fitzmyer, Joseph A. *The Gospel According to Luke*. 2 vols. Garden City, N.Y.: Doubleday, 1981.

Flesher, Paul Virgil McCracken. "Palestinian Synagogues before 70 C.E.: A Review of the Evidence." In *Ancient Synagogues: Historical Analysis and Archaeological Discovery* Vol. 1, edited by Dan Urman and Paul Virgil McCracken Flesher, 27–39. New York: E.J. Brill, 1995.

———. "Palestinian Synagogues Before 70 CE: A Review of the Evidence." In *Approaches to Ancient Judaism*, Vol. 6, *Studies in the Ethnology and Literature of Judaism*, edited by J. Neusner and Ernest S. Frerichs, 67–81. Atlanta: Scholars Press, 1989.

Foerster, Gideon. "The Ancient Synagogues of the Galilee." In *The Galilee in Late Antiquity*, edited by L. Levine, 289–319. New York: Jewish Theological Seminary of America, 1992.

———. "Architectural Models of the Greco-Roman Period and the Origin of The 'Galilean' Synagogue." In *Ancient Synagogues Revealed*, edited by Lee I. Levine, 45–48. Jerusalem: Israel Exploration Society, 1982.

———. "Dor." In *Encyclopedia of Archaeological Excavations in the Holy Land* Vol. 1, edited by Michael Avi-Yonah and Ephriam Stern, 334–337. Jerusalem: The Israel Exploration Society and Massada Press, 1977.

———. "Herodium." In *The New Encyclopedia of Archaeological Excavations in the Holy Land* Vol. 2, edited by Ephraim Stern, 618–621. Jerusalem: Israel Exploration Society & Carta; New York: Simon & Schuster, 1993.

———. "A Survey of Ancient Diaspora Synagogues." In *Ancient Synagogues Revealed*, edited by Lee I. Levine, 164–171. Jerusalem: Israel Exploration Society, 1982.

———. "The Synagogues at Masada and Herodion." *Journal of Jewish Art* 3–4 (1977): 6–11.

———. "The Synagogues at Masada and Herodium." In *Ancient Synagogues Revealed*, edited by Lee I. Levine, 24–29. Jerusalem: Israel Exploration Society, 1982.

———. "The Synagogues at Masada and Herodium." In *Eretz-Israel* Vol. 11, edited by J. Aviram, 224–228. Jerusalem: Israel Exploration Society, 1973.

Foerster, Werner. "Σεμνός, Σεμνότης." In *Theological Dictionary of the New Testament* Vol. 7, edited by Gerhard Kittel, Geoffrey William Bromiley and Gerhard Friedrich, 191–196. Grand Rapids, Michigan: Wm. B. Eerdmans Publishing Company, 1964–1976.

Ford, J. Massyngberde. *Revelation*. Edited by David Noel Freedman, *The Anchor Bible, vol. 38*. New York: Doubleday, 1975.

Fraser, Paul M. *Ptolemaic Alexandria*. 3 vols. Oxford: Clarendon Press, 1972.

Frey, Jean Baptiste. *Corpus Inscriptionum Iudaicarum*. 2 vols. Rome: Poniticio Instituto di Archeologia Christiana, 1936–52.

———. *Corpus of Jewish Inscriptions: Jewish Inscriptions from the Third Century* B.C. *to the Seventh Century* A.D., *The Library of Biblical Studies*. New York: Ktav Pub. House, 1975.

Friesen, Steven J. *Twice Neokoros*. Leiden: E. J. Brill, 1993.

———. "Urban Development and Social Change in Imperial Ephesos." In *Ephesos: Metropolis of Asia*, edited by Helmut Koester, 229–250. Valley Forge, Pennsylvania: Trinity Press International, 1995.

Fritz, Volkmar. *The City in Ancient Israel*. Sheffield, England: Sheffield Academic Press, 1995.

Furnish, Victor Paul. *II Corinthians*. Vol. 32A, *The Anchor Bible*. Garden City, N.Y.: Doubleday, 1984.

Gager, John G. "Jews, Gentiles, and Synagogues in the Book of Acts." *HTR* 79, no. 1–3 (1986): 91–99.

———. "Jews, Gentiles, and Synagogues in the Book of Acts: Essays in Honor of Krister Stendahl on His Sixty-fifth Birthday." In *Christians among Jews & Gentiles*, edited by G. Nicklesburg and G. Macrae, 91–99. Philadelphia: Fortress Press, 1986.

Gallo, Italo. *Greek and Latin Papyrology*. London: Institute of Classical Studies, 1986.

Geva, H. "Jerusalem: The Roman Period." In *The New Encyclopedia of Archaeological Excavations in the Holy Land* Vol. 2, edited by Ephraim Stern, 758–767. Jerusalem: Israel Exploration Society & Carta; New York: Simon & Schuster, 1993.

Gibson, Shimon, and David M. Jacobson. *Below the Temple Mount in Jerusalem*. Oxford: Tempvs Reparatvm, 1996.

Gill, David W.J. "Macedonia." In *The Book of Acts in Its Palestinian Setting*, edited by Richard Bauckham, 397–431. Grand Rapids, Mich.: William B. Eerdmans Pub. Co., 1994.

Glueck, Nelson. "Ostraca from Elath." *BASOR* 82 (1941): 7–11.

Goldman, Bernard. *The Sacred Portal: A Primary Symbol in Judaic Art*. Lanham, Md: University Press of America, Inc., 1986.

Goodenough, Erwin R. "The Bosporus Inscriptions to the Most High God." *JQR* 47 (1956): 221–244.

———. *Jewish Symbols in the Greco-Roman Period*. 13 vols. New York: Pantheon Books, 1953–68.

Goodman, Martin. "Jewish Proselytizing in the First Century." In *The Jews among Pagans and Christians: In the Roman Empire*, edited by Judith Lieu, John A. North and Tessa Rajak, 53–78. New York: Routledge, 1992.

———. "A Note on the Qumran Sectarians, the Essenes and Josephus." *JJS* 46 (1995): 161–166.

Gordon, Arthur Ernest. *Illustrated Introduction to Latin Epigraphy*. Berkeley: University of California Press, 1983.

Gordon, Evelyn. "News In Brief." *Jerusalem Post*, 21 November 1995.

Grabbe, Lester L. "Synagogues in Pre-70 Palestine: A Re-assessment." *JTS* 39 (1988): 401–410.

———. "Synagogues in Pre-70 Palestine: A Re-assessment." In *Ancient Synagogues: Historical Analysis and Archaeological Discovery* Vol. 1, edited by Dan Urman and Paul Virgil McCracken Flesher, 17–26. New York: E.J. Brill, 1995.

Grashman, William Wesley. "The Priestly Synagogue: A Re-examination of the Cult at Qumran." Ph.D., University of Aberdeen, 1985.

Greeven, H. Προσεύχομαι, Προσευχή." In *Theological Dictionary of the New Testament* Vol. 2, edited by Gerhard Kittel, Geoffrey William Bromiley and Gerhard Friedrich, 807–808. Grand Rapids, Michigan: Wm. B. Eerdmans Publishing Company, 1964–1976.

Griffiths, J. Gwyn. "Egypt and the Rise of the Synagogue." *JTS* 38 (1987): 1–15.

———. "Egypt and the Rise of the Synagogue." In *Ancient Synagogues: Historical Analysis and Archaeological Discovery* Vol. 1, edited by Dan Urman and Paul Virgil McCracken Flesher, 3–16. New York: E.J. Brill, 1995.

Groh, Dennis E. "Jews and Christians in Late Roman Palestine: Towards a New Chronology." *BA* 51 (1988): 80–96.

———. "The Stratigraphic Chronology of the Galilean Synagogue from the Early Roman Period Through the Early Byzantine Period (ca. 420 C.E.)." In *Ancient Synagogues: Historical Analysis and Archaeological Discovery* Vol. 1, edited by Dan Urman and Paul Virgil McCracken Flesher, 51–69. New York: E.J. Brill, 1995.

Grossman, Susan. "Women and the Jerusalem Temple." In *Daughters of the King: Women and the Synagogue: A Survey of History, Halakhah, and Contemporary Realities*, edited by Susan Grossman and Rivka Haut, 14–37. Philadelphia: Jewish Publication Society, 1992.

Grossman, Susan, and Rivka Haut, eds. *Daughters of the King: Women and the Synagogue: A Survey of History, Halakhah, and Contemporary Realities*. Philadelphia: Jewish Publication Society, 1992.

Guarducci, M. *Epigrafia greca III*. Rome, 1974.

Guterman, Simeon L. *Religious Toleration and Persecution in Ancient Rome*. London: Aiglon, 1951.

Gutman, Shmaryahu. "Gamala." In *The New Encyclopedia of Archaeological Excavations in the Holy Land* Vol. 2, edited by Ephraim Stern, 459–463. Jerusalem: Israel Exploration Society & Carta; New York: Simon & Schuster, 1993.

———. "Gamla-1983." *ESI* 3 (1984): 26–27.

———. *Gamla: Historical Setting: The First Season of Excavations*. Tel Aviv: Department of Information, 1977.

———. *Gamla: The First Eight Seasons of Excavations*. Tel Aviv: Kibbutz Meuhad, 1981.

———. "The Synagogue at Gamla." In *Ancient Synagogues Revealed*, edited by Lee I. Levine, 30–34. Jerusalem: Israel Exploration Society, 1982.

Gutman, Shmaryah, and Yoel Rapel. *Gamla—A City in Rebellion*. Israel: The Ministry of Defense, 1994.

Gutman, S., A. Segal, Y. Patrich, et al. "Gamla-1987/1988." *ESI* 9 (1989–1990): 9–15.

Gutman, S., and D. Wagner. "Gamla-1984/1985/1986." *ESI* 5 (1986): 38–41.

Gutmann, Joseph. "The Origin of the Synagogue: The Current State of the Research." In *The Synagogue: Studies in Origins, Archaeology, and Architecture*, edited by Joseph Gutmann, 72–76. New York: Ktav Pub. House, 1975.

———. "Prolegomenon." In *The Synagogue: Studies in Origins, Archaeology, and Architecture*, edited by Joseph Gutmann, ix–xxxi. New York: Ktav Pub. House, 1975.

———. "Sherira Gaon and the Babylonian Origin of the Synagogue." In *Occident and Orient: A Tribute to the Memory of Alexander Scheiber*, edited by Robert Dan, 209–212. Leiden: E.J. Brill, 1988.

———. "Synagogue Origins: Theories and Facts." In *Ancient Synagogues: The State of the Research* Vol. 22, edited by Joseph Gutmann, 1–6. Chico, California: Scholars Press, 1981.

———., ed. *Ancient Synagogues: The State of Research.* Edited by Jacob Neusner, Wendell S. Dietrich, Ernest S. Frerichs, Sumner B. Twiss and Alan Zuckerman. Vol. 22, *Brown Judaic studies*. Chico, Calif.: Scholars Press, 1981.

———., ed. *The Synagogue: Studies in Origins, Archaeology, and Architecture, The Library of Biblical Studies*. New York: Ktav Pub. House, 1975.

Hachlili, Rachel. *Ancient Jewish Art and Archaeology in the Land of Israel*. Vol. 7, *Handbuch der Orientalistik*. New York: E.J. Brill, 1988.

———. "Characteristic Features of Synagogue Architecture in the Land of Israel." In *Studies in the Archaeology and History of Ancient Israel*, edited by Moshe Dothan, Michael Heltzer, Arthur Segal and Daniel Kaufman, 157–194. Haifa: University of Haifa, 1993.

———. "Diaspora Synagogues." In *The Anchor Bible Dictionary* Vol. 6, edited by David Noel Freedman, 260–263. New York: Doubleday, 1992.

———. "The Niche and the Ark in Ancient Synagogues." *Bulletin of the American Schools of Oriental Research* 223 (1976): 43–53.

———. "The State of Ancient Synagogues Research." In *Ancient Synagogues in Israel: Third-Seventh Century* CE, edited by R. Hachlili, 1–6. Oxford, England: B.A.R., 1989.

———., ed. *Ancient Synagogues in Israel: Third-Seventh Century* CE. Oxford, England: B.A.R., 1989.

Hadras, M. *The Third and Fourth Book of Maccabees*. New York: Harper, 1953.

Haenchen, E. "The Book of Acts as Source Material for the History of Early Christianity." In *Studies in Luke-Acts*, edited by Leander E. Keck, Paul Schubert and J. Louis Martyn. Nashville: Abingdon Press, 1966.

———. *The Book of Acts: A Commentary*. Philadelphia: Westminister, 1971.

Hansen, G. Walter. "Galatia." In *The Book of Acts in Its Palestinian Setting*, edited by Richard Bauckham, 377–395. Grand Rapids, Mich.: William B. Eerdmans Pub. Co., 1994.

Haran, Menahem. "Priesthood, Temple, Divine Service: Some Observations on Institutions and Practices of Worship." *HAR* 7 (1983): 121–135.

———. "Temple and Community in Ancient Israel." In *Temple in Society*, edited by Michael V. Fox, 17–25. Winona Lake: Eisenbrauns, 1988.

———. "Temples and Cultic Open Areas as Reflected in the Bible." In *Temples and High Places in Biblical Times: Proceedings of the Colloquium in Honor of the Centennial of Hebrew Union College-Jewish Institute of Religion, Jerusalem, 14–16 March 1977*, edited by Avraham Birah, Inna Pommerantz and Hannah Katzenstein, 31–46. Jerusalem: Nelson Glueck School of Biblical Archaeology of Hebrew Union College-Jewish Institute of Religion, 1981.

Hare, Douglas R. A. "Ancient Anti-Semitism, Review Article." *RelSRev* 2, no. 3 (1976): 15–22.

Harrill, J. Albert. *The Manumission of Slaves in Early Christianity*. Tübingen: J.C.B. Mohr (Paul Siebeck), 1995.

Harrington, D. J. "Pseudo-Philo." In *Old Testament Pseudepigrapha* Vol. 2, edited by J. H. Charlesworth, 297–377. New York: Doubleday, 1985.

Hay, David M. "Things Philo Said and Did Not Say about the Therapeutae." In *Society of Biblical Literature: 1992 Seminar Papers*, edited by E. Lovering, 673–683. Atlanta: Scholar's Press, 1992.

Hayward, Robert. "The Jewish Temple at Leontopolis: A Reconsideration." *JJS* 33 (1982): 429–443.

Heinemann, I. "Philo von Alexandrien." In *Paulys real-encyclopadie der classischen Altertumswissenschaft. Supplement.* Vol. 20.1, col. 3. Stuttgart: J.B. Metzler, 1941.

Hemer, Colin J., and Conrad H. Gempf. *The Book of Acts in the Setting of Hellenistic History*. Tübingen: J.C.B. Mohr, 1989.

Hendlin, David. *Guide to Biblical Coins*. New York: Amphora Books, 1987.

Hengel, Martin. "Der Jakobusbrief als antipaulinische Polemik." In *Tradition and Interpretation in the New Testament*, edited by G. F. Hawthorn and O. Betz. Grand Rapids: Wm. B. Eerdmans, 1987.

———. "The Geography of Palestine in Acts." In *The Book of Acts in Its Palestinian Setting*, edited by Richard Bauckham, 27–78. Grand Rapids, Mich.: William B. Eerdmans Pub. Co., 1995.

———. *Judaism and Hellenism: Studies in Their Encounter in Palestine During The Early Hellenistic Period*. Philadelphia: Fortress Press, 1981.

———. "The Pre-Christian Paul." In *The Jews among Pagans and Christians: In the Roman Empire*, edited by Judith Lieu, John A. North and Tessa Rajak, 29–51. New York: Routledge, 1992.

———. "Proseuche und Synagoge: jüdische Gemeinde, Gotteshaus und Gottesdienst in der Diaspora und in Palästina." In *Tradition und Glaube: Das fruehe Christentum in seiner Umwelt*, edited by Gert

Jeremias, Karl G. Kuhn, Heinz-Wolfgang Kuhn and Hartmut Stegemann, 157–184. Gottingen: Vandenhoeck & Ruprecht, 1971.

Hirschberg, J. W. "The Remains of an Ancient Synagogue on Mount Zion." In *Jerusalem Revealed: Archaeology in the Holy City, 1968–1974*, edited by Yigael Yadin, 116–117. Jerusalem: Israel Exploration Society, 1975.

Hirschfeld, Yizhar. *The Palestinian Dwelling in the Roman-Byzantine Period, Studium Fransciscanum Collectio Minor* no. 34. Jerusalem: Franciscan Printing Press; Israel Exploration Society, 1995.

Hoenig, Sidney B. "The Ancient City-Square: The Forerunner of the Synagogue." In *ANRW* Vol. II.19.1, edited by W. Haase, 448–476. New York: W. de Gruyter, 1979.

———. "Supposititious Temple-Synagogue." *JQR* 54 (1963): 115–131.

Holladay, Carl R. *Fragments from Hellenistic Jewish Authors*. Chico, Calif.: Scholars Press, 1983.

Hoppe, Leslie J. *The Synagogues and Churches of Ancient Palestine*. Collegeville, Minn.: Liturgical Press, 1994.

Horbury, William. "Jewish Inscriptions and Jewish Literature in Egypt, with Special Reference to Ecclesiasticus." In *Studies in Early Jewish Epigraphy*, edited by Jan Willem Van Henten and Pieter Willem Van der Horst, 9–43. New York: E. J. Brill, 1994.

Horbury, William, and David Noy. *Jewish Inscriptions of Graeco-Roman Egypt: With an Index of the Jewish Inscriptions of Egypt and Cyrenaica*. Cambridge: Cambridge University Press, 1992.

Horowitz, G. "Town Planning of Hellenistic Marisa: A Reappraisal of the Excavations after Eighty Years." *PEQ* 112 (1980): 93–111.

Horsley, G. H. R. "The Inscriptions of Ephesos and the New Testament." *NovT* 2 (1992): 105–168.

———. *New Documents Illustrating Early Christianity: A Review of the Greek Inscriptions and Papyri Published in 1976*. North Ryde, N.S.W.: The Ancient History Documentary Research Centre, 1981.

———. *New Documents Illustrating Early Christianity: A Review of the Greek Inscriptions and Papyri Published in 1977*. North Ryde, N.S.W.: Ancient History Documentary Research Centre, 1982.

———. *New Documents Illustrating Early Christianity: A Review of the Greek Inscriptions and Papyri Published in 1978*. North Ryde, N.S.W.: Ancient History Documentary Research Centre, 1983.

———. *New Documents Illustrating Early Christianity: A Review of the Greek Inscriptions and Papyri Published in 1979*. North Ryde, N.S.W.: Ancient History Documentary Research Centre, 1987.

———. "The Politarchs." In *The Book of Acts in Its Palestinian Setting*, edited by Richard Bauckham, 419–431. Grand Rapids, Mich.: William B. Eerdmans Pub. Co., 1994.

———. "Towards a New *Corpus Inscriptionum Iudaicarum*?" *Jewish Studies Quarterly* 2 (1995): 77–101.

Horsley, Richard A. *Archaeology History and Society in Galilee*. Valley Forge, Pa: Trinity Press International, 1996.

———. *Galilee*. Valley Forge, Pa: Trinity Press International, 1995.

Horst, Pieter Willem van der. *Ancient Jewish Epitaphs*. Kampen, The Netherlands: Kok Pharos Publishing House, 1991.

———. "Jews and Christians in Aprodisias in the Light of Their Relations in Other Cities of Asia Minor." In *Essays on the Jewish World of Early Christianity* Vol. 14, edited by Pieter Willem van der Horst, 166–181. Freiburg, Schweiz: Vandenhoeck & Ruprecht, 1990.

———. "The Samaritan Diaspora in Antiquity." In *Essays on the Jewish World of Early Christianity* Vol. 14, edited by Pieter Willem van der Horst, 136–147. Freiburg, Schweiz: Vandenhoeck & Ruprecht, 1990.

Hruby, Kurt. *Die Synagoge. Geschichtliche Entwicklung einer Institution*. Vol. 3, *Schriften zur Judentumskunde*. Zürich: Theologisher Verlag, 1971.

Hüttenmeister, Frowald G. "'Synagoge' und 'Proseuche' bei Josephus und in anderen antiken Quellen." In *Begegnungen zwischen Christentum und Judentum in Antike und Mittelalter: Festschrift fur Heinz Schreckenberg*, edited by Dietrich-Alex Koch and Hermann Lichtenberger, 163–181. Gottingen: Vandenhoeck & Ruprecht, 1993.

———. "Synagogues et écoles en Palestine, Iue-VIIue siècles." In *Art et archéologie des Juifs en France* Vol. 9, edited by Bernhard Blumenkranz, 143–156. Toulouse: Privat, 1980.

Hüttenmeister, Frowald, and Gottfried Reeg. *Die antiken Synagogen in Israel*. 2 vols. Vol. 12, *Beihefte zum Tubinger Atlas des Vorderen Orients. Reihe B, Geisteswissenschaften*. Wiesbaden: Reichert, 1977.

Isaac, Benjamin. "A Donation for Herod's Temple in Jerusalem." *IEJ* 33 (1983): 86–92.

Jacobson, Howard. *A Commentary of Pseudo-Philo's Liber Antiquitatum Biblicarum*. 2 vols. Leiden; New York: E.J. Brill, 1996.

Jacoby, Ruth, and Rina Talgam. *Ancient Jewish Synagogues: Architectural Glossary*. Jerusalem: Israel Exploration Society, 1988.

Jeremias, Joachim. *Jerusalem in the Time of Jesus: An Investigation into Economic and Social Conditions During the New Testament Period*. Philadelphia: Fortress Press, 1975.

Jobst, Werner. "Zur Lokalisierung des Sebastion-Augusteum in Ephesos." *Istanbuler Mitteilungen* 30 (1980): 241–260.

Johnson, Luke Timothy. *The Acts of the Apostles*. Collegeville, Minn.: Liturgical Press, 1992.

———. *The Letter of James*. New York: Doubleday, 1995.

Juster, Jean. *Les Jeufs dans l'Empire Romain: leur condition juridique, économique et sociale*. 2 vols. Paris: Paul Geuthner, 1914.

Kant, Laurence H. "Jewish Inscriptions in Greek and Latin." In *ANRW* Vol. II.20.2, edited by W. Haase, 671–713. New York: W. de Gruyter, 1987.

Karageorghis, Vassos. "The Sacred Area of Kition." In *Temples and High Places in Biblical Times*, edited by Avraham Biran, Inna Pommerantz and Hannah Katzenstein, 82–90. Jerusalem: Nelson Glueck School of Biblical Archaeology of Hebrew Union College-Jewish Institute of Religion, 1981.

Kasher, Aryeh. *Jews and Hellenistic cities in Eretz-Israel: Relations of the Jews in Eretz-Israel with the Hellenistic Cities during the Second Temple Period (332 BCE-70 CE), Texte und Studien zum antiken Judentum, 21*. Tübingen: J.C.B. Mohr, 1990.

———. *The Jews in Hellenistic and Roman Egypt: The Struggle for Equal Rights*. Rev. English ed. Vol. 7, *Texte und Studien zum antiken Judentum*. Tübingen: J.C.B. Mohr (Paul Siebeck), 1985.

———. "Synagogues as 'Houses of Prayer' and 'Holy Places' in the Jewish Communities of Hellenistic and Roman Egypt." In *Ancient Synagogues: Historical Analysis and Archaeological Discovery* Vol. 1, edited by Dan Urman and Paul Virgil McCracken Flesher, 205–220. New York: E.J. Brill, 1995.

———. "Synagogues in Ptolemaic and Roman Egypt as Community Centers." In *Synagogues in Antiquity*, edited by Aryeh Kasher, Aharon Oppenheimer and Uriel Rappaport, 119–132. Jerusalem: Yad Izhak Ben Zvi, 1987.

Kasher, Aryeh, Aharon Oppenheimer, and Uriel Rappaport, eds. *Synagogues in Antiquity*. Jerusalem: Yad Izhak Ben Zvi, 1987.

Kähler, Martin. *The So-called Historical Jesus and the Historic, Biblical Christ*. Philadelphia: Fortress Press, 1964.

Kee, Howard Clark. "The Changing Meaning of Synagogue: A Response to Richard Oster." *NTS* 40 (1994): 281–283.

———. "Defining the First-Century CE Synagogue." *NTS* 41 (1995): 481–500.

———. "Early Christianity in the Galilee: Reassessing the Evidence from the Gospels." In *The Galilee in Late Antiquity*, edited by Lee I. Levine, 3–22. New York: The Jewish Theological Seminary of America, 1992.

———. "New Finds That Illuminate the World and Text of the Bible: The Greco-Roman Era." In *The Bible in the Twenty-First Century*, edited by Howard Clarke Kee, 89–108. Philadelphia: Trinity Press International, 1993.

———. *The New Testament in Context: Sources and Documents*. Englewood Cliffs, N.J.: Prentice-Hall, 1984.

———. "The Transformation of the Synagogue after 70 CE: Its Import for Early Christianity." *NTS* 36 (1990): 1–24.

———. *Understanding the New Testament*. 4th ed. Englewood Cliffs, N.J.: Prentice-Hall, 1983.

Kelber, Werner H. *The Kingdom in Mark: A New Place and a New Time*. Philadelphia: Fortress Press, 1974.

———. *Mark's Story of Jesus*. Philadelphia: Fortress Press, 1979.

Kennett, Robert Hatch. *Old Testament Essays*. Cambridge: Cambridge University Press, 1928.

Kenyon, Kathleen M. *Digging Up Jerusalem*. New York: Praeger, 1974.

Klauck, Hans J. "Gemeinde ohne Amt: Erfahrungen mit der Kirche in den johanneischen Schriften." *BZ* 29, no. 2 (1985): 193–220.

Kloner, A. "Ancient Synagogues in Israel: An Archeological Survey." In *Ancient Synagogues Revealed*, edited by Lee I. Levine, 11–18. Jerusalem: Israel Exploration Society, 1982.

Kloppenborg, John S. "Collegia and *Thiasoi:* Issues in Function, Taxonomy and Membership." In *Voluntary Associations*, edited by John S. Kloppenborg and Steven G. Wilson, 16–30. London: Routledge, 1996.

———. *Q Parallels: Synopsis, Critical Notes, and Concordance.* Sonoma, Calif.: Polebridge Press, 1988.

Knipe, David M. "The Temple in Image and Reality." In *Temple in Society*, edited by Michael V. Fox, 105–138. Winona Lake: Eisenbrauns, 1988.

Koenig, Jean. "L'origine exilique de la synagogue." In *Mélanges d'historie des religions*, edited by A. Bareau, 33–55, 1974.

Koester, Helmut. *Ancient Christian Gospels: Their History and Development.* London: SCM Press; Philadelphia: Trinity Press International, 1990.

———. "Ephesos in Early Christian Literature." In *Ephesos: Metropolis of Asia*, edited by Helmut Koester, 119–140. Valley Forge, Pennsylvania: Trinity Press International, 1995.

———. *Introduction to the New Testament.* Vol. 1. New York: Fortress Press, 1995.

Kohl, Heinrich, and Carl Watzinger. *Antike Synagogen in Galiläa.* Leipzig: O. Zeller, 1916.

Kosmala, Hans. *Hebräer-Essener-Christen: Studien zur Vorgeschichte der fr ühchristlichen Verkündigung.* Leiden: E. J. Brill, 1959.

Köster, Helmut. "Tόπος" In *Theological Dictionary of the New Testament* Vol. 8, edited by Gerhard Kittel, Geoffrey William Bromiley and Gerhard Friedrich, 187–208. Grand Rapids, Michigan: Wm. B. Eerdmans Publishing Company, 1964–1976.

Kraabel, A. Thomas. "Afterward." In *Diaspora Jews and Judaism: Essays in Honor of, and in Dialogue with, A. Thomas Kraabel*, edited by J. Overman and R. MacLennan, 347–357. Atlanta: Scholars Press, 1992.

———. "The Diaspora Synagogue: Archaelogical and Epigraphic Evidence Since Sukenik." In *ANRW* Vol. II.19.1, edited by W. Haase, 477–510. New York: W. de Gruyter, 1979.

———. "The Disappearance of the 'God-Fearers'." *Numen* 28 (1981): 113–126.

———. "Impact of the Discovery of the Sardis Synagogue." In *Diaspora Jews and Judaism: Essays in Honor of, and in Dialogue with, A. Thomas Kraabel*, edited by J. Overman and R. MacLennan, 269–291. Atlanta: Scholars Press, 1992.

———. "Melito the Bishop and the Synagogue at Sardis: Text and Context." In *Studies Presented to George M.A. Hanfmann* Vol. 2, edited by David Gordon Mitten, John Griffiths Pedley and Jane Ayer Scott, 77–85. Mainz, W. Germany: Verlag P. von Zabern, 1971.

———. "Melito the Bishop and the Synagogue at Sardis: Text and Context." In *Diaspora Jews and Judaism: Essays in Honor of, and in Dialogue with, A. Thomas Kraabel*, edited by J. Overman and R. MacLennan, 197–207. Atlanta: Scholars Press, 1992.

———. "New Evidence of the Samaritan Diaspora has been Found on Delos." In *Diaspora Jews and Judaism: Essays in Honor of, and in Dialogue with, A. Thomas Kraabel*, edited by J. Overman and R. MacLennan, 331–334. Atlanta: Scholars Press, 1992.

———. "New Evidence of the Samaritan Diaspora has been Found on Delos." *BA* 47 (1984): 44–46.

———. "Paganism and Judaism: The Sardis Evidence." In *Paganisme, Judaïsme, Christianisme: Influences et affrontements dans le monde antique*, edited by André Benoit, Marc Philonenko and Cyrille Vogel, 13–33. Paris: Éditions E. De Boccard, 1978.

———. "The Roman Diaspora: Six Questionable Assumptions." In *Diaspora Jews and Judaism: Essays in Honor of, and in Dialogue with, A. Thomas Kraabel*, edited by J. Overman and R. MacLennan, 1–20. Atlanta: Scholars Press, 1992.

———. "The Roman Diaspora: Six Questionable Assumptions." *JJS* 33 (1982): 445–464.

———. "Social Systems of Six Diaspora Synagogues." In *Diaspora Jews and Judaism: Essays in Honor of, and in Dialogue with, A. Thomas Kraabel*, edited by J. Overman and R. MacLennan, 257–267. Atlanta: Scholars Press, 1992.

———. "Social Systems of Six Diaspora Synagogues." In *Ancient Synagogues: The State of Research* Vol. 22, edited by Joseph Gutmann, 79–91. Chico, California: Scholars Press, 1981.

———. "Synagoga Caeca: Systematic Distortion in Gentile Interpretations Of Evidence for Judaism in the Early Christian Period." In "To See Ourselves as Others See Us": Christians, Jews, "Others" in Late Antiquity, edited by Jacob Neusner and Ernest S. Frerichs, 219–246. Chico, Calif.: Scholars Press, 1985.

———. "The Synagogue at Sardis: Jews and Christians." In *Diaspora Jews and Judaism: Essays in Honor of, and in Dialogue with, A. Thomas Kraabel*, edited by J. Overman and R. MacLennan, 225–236. Atlanta: Scholars Press, 1992.

———. "Unity and Diversity among Diaspora Synagogues." In *The Synagogue in Late Antiquity*, edited by Lee I. Levine, 49–60. Philadelphia: American Schools of Oriental Research, 1987.

———. "Unity and Diversity among Diaspora Synagogues." In *Diaspora Jews and Judaism: Essays in Honor of, and in Dialogue with, A. Thomas Kraabel*, edited by J. Overman and R. MacLennan, 21–33. Atlanta: Scholars Press, 1992.

Kraemer, Ross S. "A New Inscription from Malta and the Question of Women Elders in The Diaspora Jewish Communities." *HTR* 78, no. 3–4 (1985): 431–438.

Kramer, Samuel Noah. “The Temple in Sumerian Literature.” In *Temple in Society*, edited by Michael V. Fox, 1–16. Winona Lake: Eisenbrauns, 1988.

Krauss, Samuel. *Synagogale Altertümer*. Berlin: Hildesheim, 1922.

Kunin, Seth. “Judaism.” In *Sacred Place*, edited by J. Holm, 115–148. New York: Pinter Publishers, 1994.

Kurz, William S. “Hellenistic Rhetoric in the Christological Proof of Luke-Acts.” *CBQ* 42 (1980): 171–195.

Kümmel, Werner George. *Introduction to the New Testament*. Translated by Kee, Howard Clark. revised ed. Nashville: Abingdon Press, 1975.

Künzl, Hannelore. “Das Judentum.” In *Orientalischen Religionen im Römerreich*, edited by M. Vermaseren, 459–484. Leiden: Brill, 1981.

Künzl, Hannelore. “Die archäologischen Funde aus der Zeit des Frühjudentums und ihre religionsgeschichtliche Bedeutung.” In *Literatur und Religion des Frühjudentums: Eine Einfuhrung*, edited by J. Maier, 414–437. Wurzburg: Echter Verlag, 1973.

Kvarme, Ole C. M. “Torah and Christ: on the Use of the Old Testament in the Early Synagogue and in the Early Church.” *Evangelical Review of Theology* 8, no. 2 (1984): 183–201.

Landman, Leo. “The Origin of the Synagogue.” In *Essays on the Occasion of the Seventieth Anniversary of the Dropsie University, 1909–1979*, edited by Abraham I. Katsh and Leon Nemoy, 317–325. Philadelphia: Dropsie University, 1979.

Landsberger, Franz. “The House of the People.” *HUCA* 22 (1949): 149–155.

———. “The Sacred Direction in Synagogue and Church.” *HUCA* 28 (1957): 181–203.

La Piana, G. “Foreign Groups in Rome During the First Centuries of the Empire.” *HTR* 20 (1927): 183–403.

Langford, Sally Overby. "On Being a Religious Woman: Women Proselytes in the Greco-Roman World." In *Recovering the Role of Women: Power and Authority in Rabbinic Jewish Society* Vol. 59, edited by P. Haas, 61–83. Atlanta, Ga.: Scholars Press, 1992.

Laperrousaz, Ernest Marie. "A propos des deux plus anciennes synagogues actuellement connues de Palestine, et dernières nouvelles archéologiques de Jèrusalem." *REJ* 144, no. 1–3 (1985): 297–304.

Lawrence, A. W. *Greek Architecture*. 5th ed. New Haven: Yale University Press, 1996.

Leon, Harry J., and Carolyn Osiek. *The Jews of Ancient Rome*. Updated ed. Peabody, Mass.: Hendrickson Publishers, 1995.

Levenson, Jon D. "From Temple to Synagogue: 1 Kings 8." In *Traditions in Transformation: Turning Points in Biblical Faith*, edited by Baruch Halpern and Jon D. Levenson, 143–166. Winona Lake, IN: Eisenbrauns, 1981.

Levick, Barbara. *Roman Colonies in Southern Asia Minor*. Oxford: The Clarendon Press, 1967.

Levine, Lee I. "Ancient Synagogues: A Historical Introduction." In *Ancient Synagogues Revealed*, edited by Lee I. Levine, 1–10. Jerusalem: Israel Exploration Society, 1982.

———. "Caesarea's Synagogues and Some Historical Implications." In *Biblical Archaeology Today, 1990: Proceedings of the Second International Congress on Biblical Archaeology, Jerusalem, June-July 1990*, edited by Avraham Biran and Joseph Aviram, 666–678. Jerusalem: Israel Exploration Society, 1993.

———. "The Form and Content of the Synagogue in the Second Temple Period." In *Synagogues in Antiquity*, edited by Aryeh Kasher, Aharon Oppenheimer and Uriel Rappaport, 11–30. Jerusalem: Yad Izhak Ben Zvi, 1987.

———. "The Nature and Origin of the Palestinian Synagogue Reconsidered." *JBL* 115 (1996): 425–448.

———. "The Sages and the Synagogue in Late Antiquity: The Evidence of The Galilee." In *The Galilee in Late Antiquity*, edited by L. Levine, 201–222. New York: Jewish Theological Seminary of America, 1992.

———. "The Second Temple Synagogue: The Formative Years." In *Ancient Synagogues Revealed*, edited by Lee I. Levine, 20–21. Jerusalem: Israel Exploration Society, 1982.

———. "The Second Temple Synagogue: The Formative Years." In *The Synagogue in Late Antiquity*, edited by Lee I. Levine, 7–31. Philadelphia: American Schools of Oriental Research, 1987.

———. "Synagogues." In *The New Encyclopedia of Archaeological Excavations in the Holy Land* Vol. 4, edited by Ephraim Stern, 1421–1424. Jerusalem: Israel Exploration Society & Carta; New York: Simon & Schuster, 1993.

———., ed. *Ancient Synagogues Revealed.* Jerusalem: Israel Exploration Society, 1982.

———., ed. *The Synagogue in Late Antiquity*. Philadelphia: American Schools of Oriental Research, 1987.

Levinskaya, Irina. *The Book of Acts in Its Diaspora Setting*. Grand Rapids, Mich.: Wm. B. Eerdmans Publishing Company, 1996.

———. "The Inscription from Aphrodisias and the Problem of God-Fearers." *TynBul* 41 (1990): 312–318.

———. "A Jewish or Gentile Prayer House? The Meaning of *Proseuche*." *TynBul* 41 (1990): 154–159.

Liebreich, Leon J. "The Impact of Nehemiah 9:5–37 on the Liturgy of the Synagogue." *HUCA* 32 (1961): 227–237.

Lifshitz, B. *Donateurs et fondateurs dans les synagogues Juives*. Paris: J. Gabalda et Cie, 1967.

———. "Notes d'épigraphie grecque." *RB* 76 (1969): 95–96.

Llewelyn, S. R. *New Documents Illustrating Early Christianity: A Review of the Greek Inscriptions and Papyri Published in 1980–81*. North Ryde, N.S.W.: Ancient History Documentary Research Centre, 1992.

Lloyd, John. *Excavations at Sidi Khrebish Benghazi (Berenice)*. Vol. 5, *Supplements to Libya Antiqua*. Tripoli: Department of Antiquities, 1979.

Lods, Adolph. *The Prophets and the Rise of Judaism*. Translated by Hooke, S. H. London: Kegan Paul, Trench, Trubner & Co., 1937.

Loffreda, Stanislo. "Alcune osservazioni sulla ceramica di Magdala." In *Studia Hierosolymitana* Vol. 1, edited by Michele Piccirillo, Ignazio Mancini, Emmanuele Testa, Bellarmino Bagatti and Giovanni Claudio Bottini, 338–354. Jerusalem: Franciscan Print. Press, 1974.

———. "Capernaum." In *The New Encyclopedia of Archaeological Excavations in the Holy Land* Vol. 1, edited by Ephraim Stern, –. Jerusalem: Israel Exploration Society & Carta; New York: Simon & Schuster, 1993.

———. "Capernaum." In *The Oxford Encyclopedia of Archaeology in the Near East* Vol. 1, edited by Eric M. Meyers, 416–419. Oxford: Oxford University Press, 1996.

———. "Ceramica Ellenistico-Romana nel Sottosuolo della Sinagoga di Cafarnao." In *Studia Hierosolymitana III*, 273–313, 1982.

———. "The Late Chronology of the Synagogue of Capernaum." In *Ancient Synagogues Revealed*, edited by Lee I. Levine, 52–56. Jerusalem: Israel Exploration Society, 1982.

———. *Recovering Capharnaum*. Jerusalem: Franciscan Printing Press, 1993.

———. "A Reply to the Editor." *IEJ*, no. 23 (1973): 184.

Lohse, Eduard. "Σάββατον, Σαββατισμός, Παρασκευή." In *Theological Dictionary of the New Testament* Vol. 7, edited by Gerhard Kittel, Geoffrey William Bromiley and Gerhard Friedrich, 1–34. Grand

Rapids, Michigan: Wm. B. Eerdmans Publishing Company, 1964–1976.

———. "Temple and Synagogue." In *Jesus in His Time*, edited by H. Schultz, 75–83, 1971.

Lund, Nils. *Chiasmus in the New Testament*. Chapel Hill: The University of North Carolina Press, 1942.

Luschan, Felix von. *Ausgrabungen in Sendschirli*. Vol. 2–3. Berlin: W. Spemann, 1902.

Lüderitz, Gert. "What is the Politeuma?" In *Studies in Early Jewish Epigraphy*, edited by Jan Willem Van Henten and Pieter Willem Van der Horst, 183–225. New York: E. J. Brill, 1994.

Lüderitz, Gert, and Joyce Maire Reynolds. *Corpus jüdischer Zeugnisse aus der Cyrenaika*. Wiesbaden: Ludwig Reichert, 1983.

Ma'oz, Z. "The Art and Architecture of the Synagogues of the Golan." In *Ancient Synagogues Revealed*, edited by Lee I. Levine, 98–115. Jerusalem: Israel Exploration Society, 1982.

———. "The Synagogue of Gamla and the Typology of Second-Temple Synagogues." In *Ancient Synagogues Revealed*, edited by Lee I. Levine, 35–41. Jerusalem: Israel Exploration Society, 1982.

———. "Ancient Synagogues of the Golan." *BA* 51 (1988): 116–128.

———. "The Synagogue in the Second Temple Period—Architectural and Social Interpretation." In *Eretz-Israel* Vol. 23, edited by J. Aviram, 224–228. Jerusalem: Israel Exploration Society, 1992.

Mack, Burton L. "Imitatio Mosis: Patterns of Cosmology and Soteriology in the Hellenistic Synagogue." *Studia Philonica* 1 (1972): 27–55.

MacLennan, Robert S. "In Search of the Jewish Diaspora." *BAR* 22, no. 2 (1996): 44–51.

MacLennan, Robert S., and A. Thomas Kraabel. "The God-Fearers—A Literary and Theological Invention." *BAR* 12, no. 5 (1986): 46–53.

MacMullen, Ramsay. *Roman Social Relations, 50 B.C. to A.D. 284*. New Haven: Yale University Press, 1974.

Macrae, George. "The Temple as a House of Revelation in the Nag Hammadi Texts." In *The Temple in Antiquity: Ancient Records and Modern Perspectives*, edited by T. Madsen, 175–190. Provo, Utah: Religious Studies Center, Brigham Young University, 1984.

Madden, Frederic William. *History of Jewish Coinage*. New York: Ktav Pub. House, 1967.

Magen, Itzhak. "Samaritan Synagogues." In *The New Encyclopedia of Archaeological Excavations in the Holy Land* Vol. 4, edited by Ephraim Stern, 1424–1427. Jerusalem: Israel Exploration Society & Carta; New York: Simon & Schuster, 1993.

Maier, Johann. "Zur Verwendung der Psalmen in der synagogalen Liturgie (Wochentag und Sabbat)." In *Liturgie und Dichtung: Ein interdisziplinares Kompendium* Vol. 1, edited by H. Becker and R. Kaczynski, 55–90. St. Ottilien: EOS Verlag Erzabtei St. Ottilien, 1983.

Mantel, Hugo. "Nature of the Great Synagogue." *HTR* 60 (1967): 69–91.

Marcus, Ralph. "The Sebomenoi in Josephus." *Jewish Social Studies* 14 (1952): 247–250.

Martinez, Florentino Garcia. *The Dead Sea Scrolls Translated*. Leiden: Brill, 1994.

Martyn, J. Louis. *History and Theology in the Fourth Gospel*. 2nd ed. Nashville: Abingdon, 1979.

———. "A Law-Observant Mission to the Gentiles: The Background of Galatians." *SJT* 38 (1985): 307–324.

Maser, Peter. “Synagoge und Ecclesia—Erwägungen zur Frühgeschichte des Kirchenbaus und ser christlichen Bildkunst.” *Kairos* 32-33 (1990): 9–26.

Mason, Steve N. *Philosophiai:* Graeco-Roman, Judean and Christian.” In *Voluntary Associations*, edited by John S. Kloppenborg and Steven G. Wilson, 31–58. London: Routledge, 1996.

Mattila, Sharon Lee. “Where Women Sat in Ancient Synagogues: The Archaeological Evidence in Context.” In *Voluntary Associations*, edited by John S. Kloppenborg and Steven G. Wilson, 266–286. London: Routledge, 1996.

Mazar, B. “The Archaeological Excavations near the Temple Mount.” In *Jerusalem Revealed: Archaeology in the Holy City, 1968–1974*, edited by Yigael Yadin, 25–51. Jerusalem: Israel Exploration Society, 1975.

———. “The Royal Stoa in the Southern Part of the Temple Mount.” In *American Academy for Jewish Research Jubilee Volume* Vol. 2, edited by Salo W. Baron and Isaac E. Barzilay, 381–387. Jerusalem: American Academy for Jewish Research, 1980.

Mazar, Eilat. “The Royal Quarter of Biblical Jerusalem: The Ophel.” In *Ancient Jerusalem Revealed*, edited by Hillel Geva, 64–72. Jerusalem: Israel Exploration Society, 1994.

Mazur, Belle D. *Studies on Jewry in Greece*. Athens: Printing Office Hestia, 1935.

McCready, Wayne O. “Johannine Self-Understanding and the Synagogue Episode of John 9.” In *Self-Definition and Self-Discovery Early Christianity: A Study in Changing Horizons: Essays in Appreciation of Ben F. Meyer from Former Students* Vol. 26, edited by David J. Hawkin and Tom Robinson, 147–166. Lewiston: E. Mellen Press, 1990.

McKay, Heather A. “New Moon or Sabbath?” In *The Sabbath in Jewish and Christian Traditions*, edited by Tamara C. Eskenazi, Daniel J.

Harrington and William H. Shea, 12–27. New York: The Crossroads Publishing Company, 1991.

———. *Sabbath and Synagogue: The Question of Sabbath Worship in Ancient Judaism, Religions in the Graeco-Roman World, vol. 122.* Leiden; New York: E.J. Brill, 1994.

McLean, B. Hudson. "The Place of Cult in Voluntary Associations and Christian Churches on Delos." In *Voluntary Associations*, edited by John S. Kloppenborg and Steven G. Wilson, 186–225. London: Routledge, 1996.

———., ed. *Origins and Method: Towards a New Understanding of Judaism and Christianity: Essays in Honour of John C Hurd.* Sheffield, Eng: JSOT Press, 1993.

McRay, John. *Archaeology and the New Testament*. Grand Rapids, Mich.: Baker Book House, 1991.

Meeks, Wayne A. *The First Urban Christians: The Social World of the Apostle Paul*. New Haven: Yale University Press, 1983.

Meeks, Wayne A. , and Robert L. Wilken. *Jews and Christians in Antioch in the First Four Centuries of the Common Era*. Missoula, Mont.: Scholars Press, 1978.

Meiggs, Russell. *Roman Ostia*. 2nd ed. Oxford: Clarendon Press, 1973.

Meshorer, Y. *Ancient Jewish Coinage*. 2 vols. New York: Amphora Books, 1982.

———. "The Coins of Masada." In *Masada: The Yigael Yadin Excavations, 1963-1965: Final Reports* Vol. 1, edited by Ehud Netzer, 71–132. Jerusalem: Israel Exploration Society: Hebrew University of Jerusalem, 1989.

Meyers, Eric. "Ancient Synagogues: An Archaeological Introduction." In *Sacred Realm: The Emergence of the Synagogue in the Ancient World*, edited by Steven Fine, 3–20. New York: Oxford University Press, 1996.

———. "The Current State of Galilean Synagogue Studies." In *The Synagogue in Late Antiquity*, edited by Lee I. Levine, 127–137. Philadelphia: American Schools of Oriental Research, 1987.

———. "Early Judaism and Christianity in the Light of Archaeology." *BA* 51 (1988): 69–79.

———. "Synagogue." In *The Anchor Bible Dictionary* Vol. 6, edited by David Noel Freedman, 251–260. New York: Doubleday, 1992.

———. "Synagogue, Architecture." In *The Interpreter's Dictionary of the Bible: Supplementary Volume*, edited by Keith R. Crim, 842–844. Nashville: Abingdon, 1976.

Meyers, Eric M., and A. Thomas Kraabel. "Archaeology, Iconography, and Nonliterary Written Remains." In *Early Judaism & its Modern Interpreters;* Vol. 2, edited by R. Kraft and G. Nickelsburg, 175–210. Philadelphia: Fortress Press, 1986.

Meyers, Eric M., and James F. Strange. *Archaeology, the Rabbis, & Early Christianity*. Nashville: Abingdon, 1981.

Meyers, Eric M., and L. Michael White. "Jews and Christians in a Roman World." *Archaeology* 42, no. 2 (1989): 26–33.

Michel, Otto. "Οἶκος." In *Theological Dictionary of the New Testament* Vol. 5, edited by Gerhard Kittel, Geoffrey William Bromiley and Gerhard Friedrich, 119–131. Grand Rapids, Michigan: Wm. B. Eerdmans Publishing Company, 1964–1976.

Milik, J. T. *Ten Years of Discovery in the Wilderness of Judaea*. Translated by Strugnell, J. First English ed. Naperville, Il.: Alec R. Allenson, 1959.

Millar, Fergus. "Epigraphy." In *Ancient Greece and Rome: The Sources of History*, edited by Michael Crawford, 80–136. Cambridge: Cambridge University Press, 1983.

Mimouni, Simon C. "La synagogue 'judéo-chrétienne' se Jérusalem au Mont Sion: Texte et contexte." *Proche Orient Chrétien* 40, no. 3-4 (1990): 215–234.

Mitten, David Gordon. "New Look at Ancient Sardis." *BA* 29 (1966): 38–68.

Momigliano, Arnaldo. "Religion in Athens, Rome, and Jerusalem in the First Century BC." In *Approaches to Ancient Judaism: Theory and Practice* Vol. 5, edited by W. Green, 1–18. Missoula, Mont.: Scholars Press, 1985.

Monshouwer, Dirk. "The Reading of the Bible in the Synagogue in the First Century." *Bijdragen* 51 (1990): 68–84.

Monshouwer, Dirk. "The Reading of the Prophet in the Synagogue at Nazareth." *Bib* 70, no. 1 (1991): 90–99.

Moore, Carey A. *Judith*, *AB*. Garden City, N.Y.: Doubleday, 1985.

———. *Tobit*, *AB*. Garden City, N.Y.: Doubleday, 1996.

Moore, George Foot. *Judaism in the First Centuries of the Christian Era: The Age of the Tannaim*. Cambridge: Harvard University Press, 1927.

Morgenstern, Julian. *Studi Orientalistici in onore di Giorgio Levi Della Vida*. 2 vols. Vol. 2. Rome: Istituto per l'Oriente, 1956.

Morris, Leon. "The Gospels and the Jewish Lectionaries." In *Studies in Midrash and historiography* Vol. 3, edited by R. France and D. Wenham, 129–156. Sheffield, England: JSOT Press, 1983.

Morris, Leon. "The Saints and the Synagogue." In *Worship, Theology and Ministry in the Early Church: Essays in Honor of Ralph P. Martin* Vol. 87, edited by Ralph P. Martin, Michael J. Wilkins and Terence Paige, 39–52. Sheffield: JSOT Press, 1992.

Moule, C. F. D. *A Idiom Book of New Testament Greek*. 2nd ed. Cambridge: Cambridge University Press, 1959.

Myers, Jacob M. *I and II Esdras*. Garden City, N.Y.: Doubleday, 1974.

Nagy, Rebecca Martin, Carol L. Meyers, Eric M. Meyers, et al., eds. *Sepphoris in Galilee*. Winona Lake: Eisenbrauns, 1996.

Narkiss, Bezalel. "Pagan, Christian, and Jewish Elements in the Art of Ancient Synagogues." In *The Synagogue in Late Antiquity*, edited by Lee I. Levine, 183–188. Philadelphia: American Schools of Oriental Research, 1987.

Naveh, Joseph. "Ancient Synagogue Inscriptions." In *Ancient Synagogues Revealed*, edited by Lee I. Levine, 133–139. Jerusalem: Israel Exploration Society, 1982.

———. "Did Ancient Samaritan Inscriptions Belong to Synagogues?" In *Ancient Synagogues in Israel: Third-Seventh Century* CE, edited by R. Hachlili, 61–63. Oxford, England: B.A.R., 1989.

———. "Some Considerations on the Ancient Samaritan Inscriptions." In *Studia Semitica Necnon Iranica: Rudolpho Macuch septuagenario ab amicis et discipulis dedicata*, edited by Maria Macuch, Christa Muller-Kessler and Bert G. Fragner, 179–185. Wiesbaden: O. Harrassowitz, 1989.

Neal, Randall Stranton. *Synagogue and Church: The Model of the Jewish Synagogue in the Formation of First Century Christianity*. Ann Arbor: University Microfilms International, 1989.

Negev, Avraham. *Nabatean Archaeology Today, Hagop Kevorkian series on Near Eastern art and civilization*. New York: New York University Press, 1986.

Neil, William. *The Acts of the Apostles*. London: Oliphants, 1973.

Netzer, Ehud. "Did the Magdala Springhouse Serve As a Synagogue?" In *Synagogues in Antiquity*, edited by Aryeh Kasher, Aharon Oppenheimer and Uriel Rappaport, 165–172. Jerusalem: Yad Izhak Ben Zvi, 1987.

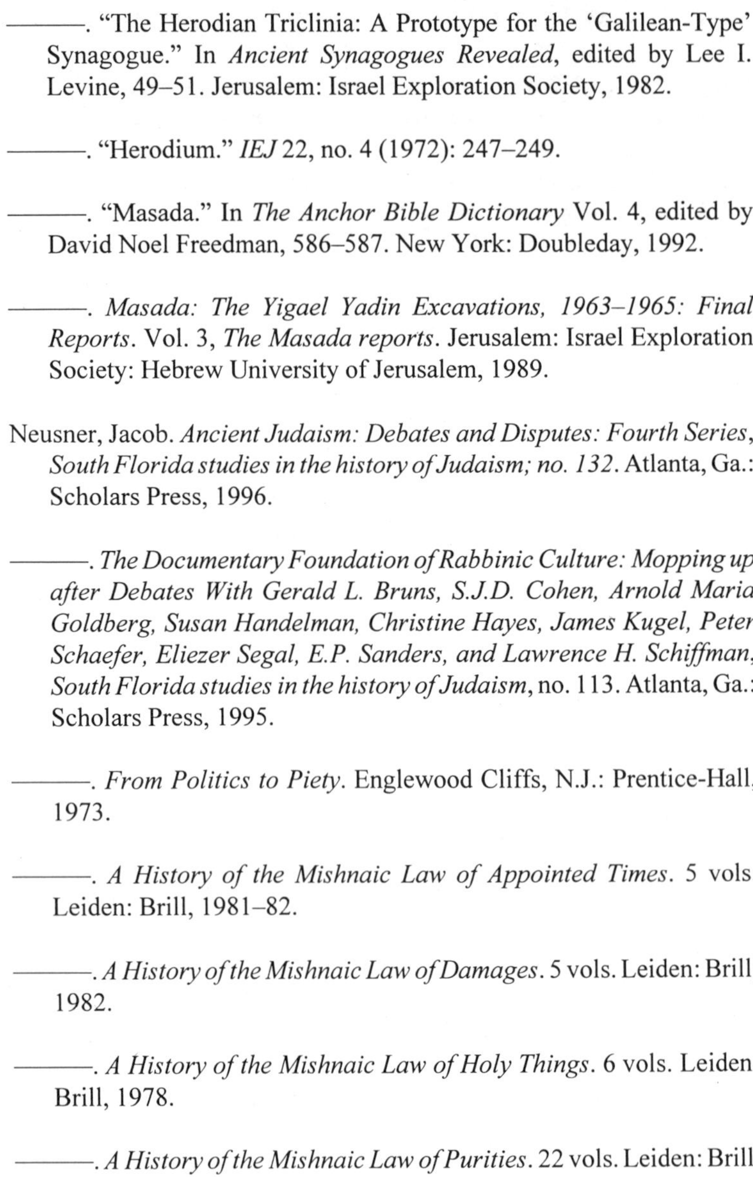

———. "The Herodian Triclinia: A Prototype for the 'Galilean-Type' Synagogue." In *Ancient Synagogues Revealed*, edited by Lee I. Levine, 49–51. Jerusalem: Israel Exploration Society, 1982.

———. "Herodium." *IEJ* 22, no. 4 (1972): 247–249.

———. "Masada." In *The Anchor Bible Dictionary* Vol. 4, edited by David Noel Freedman, 586–587. New York: Doubleday, 1992.

———. *Masada: The Yigael Yadin Excavations, 1963–1965: Final Reports*. Vol. 3, *The Masada reports*. Jerusalem: Israel Exploration Society: Hebrew University of Jerusalem, 1989.

Neusner, Jacob. *Ancient Judaism: Debates and Disputes: Fourth Series, South Florida studies in the history of Judaism; no. 132*. Atlanta, Ga.: Scholars Press, 1996.

———. *The Documentary Foundation of Rabbinic Culture: Mopping up after Debates With Gerald L. Bruns, S.J.D. Cohen, Arnold Maria Goldberg, Susan Handelman, Christine Hayes, James Kugel, Peter Schaefer, Eliezer Segal, E.P. Sanders, and Lawrence H. Schiffman, South Florida studies in the history of Judaism*, no. 113. Atlanta, Ga.: Scholars Press, 1995.

———. *From Politics to Piety*. Englewood Cliffs, N.J.: Prentice-Hall, 1973.

———. *A History of the Mishnaic Law of Appointed Times*. 5 vols. Leiden: Brill, 1981–82.

———. *A History of the Mishnaic Law of Damages*. 5 vols. Leiden: Brill, 1982.

———. *A History of the Mishnaic Law of Holy Things*. 6 vols. Leiden: Brill, 1978.

———. *A History of the Mishnaic Law of Purities*. 22 vols. Leiden: Brill, 1974–77.

———. *A History of the Mishnaic Law of Women*. 5 vols. Leiden: Brill, 1979–80.

———. *Judaism, the Evidence of the Mishnah*. Chicago: University of Chicago Press, 1981.

———. *Method and Meaning in Ancient Judaism*. Missoula, Mont.: Scholars Press, 1979.

———. *The Rabbinic Traditions about the Pharisees before 70*. 3 vols. Leiden: E. J. Brill, 1971.

———. "The Symbolism of Ancient Judaism: The Evidence of the Synagogues." In *Ancient Synagogues: The State of Research* Vol. 22, edited by Joseph Gutmann, 7–17. Chico, California: Scholars Press, 1981.

———. *Uppsala Addresses: And Other Recent Essays and Reviews on Judaism Then and Now*. Atlanta, Ga.: Scholars Press, 1996.

———. *What Is Midrash? And, a Midrash Reader*. Atlanta: Scholars Press, 1994.

———., ed. *Judaism in Late Antiquity*. 2 vols. Leiden; New York: E.J. Brill, 1995.

Newsom, C. A., and Y. Yadin. "The Masada Fragment of the Qumran *Songs of the Sabbath Sacrifice*." *IEJ* 34 (1984): 77–88.

Niehoff, Maren R. "Two Examples of Josephus' Narrative Technique in His 'Rewritten Bible'." : 31–45.

Nikiprowetzky, Valentin. "Le De Vita Contemplativa revisité." In *Sagesse et religion*. Paris: Presses universitaires de France, 1979.

Nobbs, Alanna. "Cyprus." In *The Book of Acts in Its Palestinian Setting*, edited by Richard Bauckham, 279–289. Grand Rapids, Mich.: William B. Eerdmans Pub. Co., 1994.

Nock, Arthur Darby. *Conversion: The Old and the New in Religion from Alexander the Great to Augustine*. London: Oxford University Press, 1933.

———. "The Gild of Zeus Hypsisto." *HTR* 29 (1936): 39–87.

Noth, Martin. *The History of Israel*. New York: Harper, 1958.

Noy, David. "The Jewish Communities of Leontopolis and Venosa." In *Studies in Early Jewish Epigraphy*, edited by Jan Willem Van Henten and Pieter Willem Van der Horst, 162–182. New York: E. J. Brill, 1994.

———. *Jewish Inscriptions of Western Europe*. 2 vols. Cambridge; New York: Cambridge University Press, 1993–95.

———. "A Jewish Place of Prayer in Roman Egypt." *JTS* 43 (1992): 118–122.

O'Connor, Michael Patrick, and David Noel Freedman, eds. *Backgrounds for the Bible*. Winona Lake, Ind: Eisenbrauns, 1987.

Oded, Bustanay, ed. *Studies in the History of the Jewish People and the Land of Israel*. Vol. 3. Haifa, Israel: Univ of Haifa, 1974.

Oppenheim, A. L. *Ancient Mesopotamia*. Chicago: University of Chicago Press, 1965.

Oppenheimer, Aharon. "Benevolent Societies in Jerusalem at the End of the Second Temple Period." In *Intertestamental Essays in Honor of Jozef Tadeusz Milik* Vol. 6, edited by Z. Kapera, 149–165. Krakow, Poland: Enigma Press, 1992.

Oster, Richard E. "Ephesus as a Religious Center under the Principate: Paganism before Constantine." In *ANRW* Vol. II.18.3, edited by W. Haase, 1661–1728. New York: W. de Gruyter, 1987.

———. "Supposed Anachronism in Luke-Acts' Use of ΣΥΝΑΓΩΓΗ: A Rejoinder to H C Kee." *NTS* 39 (1993): 178–208.

Ovadiah, Asher, and Talila Michaeli. "Observations on the Origin of the Architectural Plan of Ancient Synagogues." *JJS* 38 (1987): 234–241.

Overman, J. Andrew. "The Diaspora in the Modern Study of Ancient Judaism." In *Diaspora Jews and Judaism: Essays in Honor of, and in Dialogue with, A. Thomas Kraabel*, edited by J. Overman and R. MacLennan, 63–78. Atlanta: Scholars Press, 1992.

———. "The God-Fearers: Some Neglected Features." In *Diaspora Jews and Judaism: Essays in Honor of, and in Dialogue with, A. Thomas Kraabel*, edited by J. Overman and R. MacLennan, 145–152. Atlanta: Scholars Press, 1992.

Owens, E. J. *The City in the Greek and Roman World*. London and New York: Routledge, 1991.

Palmer, Randall. "Israelis Find What May Be 2,000-year-old Synagogue." *Reuters*, 20 November 1995.

Patrich, Joseph. "Corbo's Excavations at Herodium: A Review Article." *IEJ* 42 (1992): 241–245.

Pavolini, Carlo. *Ostia*, *Guide archeologiche Laterza, no. 8*. Bari: G. Laterza, 1983.

———. "Ostia (Roma): Saggi lungo la via Severiana." *Notizie degli Scavi di Antichità* 8, no. 35 (1981): 115–143.

Pelletier, A. "La philantropia de tous les jour chez les écrivains juifs hellénisés." In *Paganisme, Judaïsme, Christianisme: Influences et affrontements dans le monde antique*, edited by André Benoit, Marc Philonenko and Cyrille Vogel, 35–44. Paris: Éditions E. De Boccard, 1978.

Pelser, Hans Otto. "Synagoga." *Kairos* 3, no. 1 (1961): 37–39.

Perrin, Norman, and Dennis C. Duling. *The New Testament: An Introduction*. 2nd ed. New York: Harcourt Brace Jovanovich, 1982.

Perrot, Charles. “La lecture de la Bible dans la diaspora hellénistique.” In *Etudes sur le Judaïsme Hellénistique: Congrés des Strasbourg (1983)*, edited by R. Arnaldez, R. Kuntzmann and J. Schlosser, 109–132. Paris: Editions du Cerf, 1984.

———. *La lecture de la Bible dans la synagogue: les anciennes lectures palestiniennes du Shabbat et des fetes*. Hildesheim: Gerstenberg, 1973.

———. “Les lectures de la synagogue.” *Foi et Vie* 82 (1983): 16–22.

———. “Luc 4:16–30 et la lecture biblique de l’ancienne synagogue.” *RevScRel* 47 (1973): 324–340.

———. “The Reading of the Bible in the Ancient Synagogue.” In *Mikra*, edited by M. Mulder and H. Sysling, 137–159. Philadelphia: Fortress Press, 1988.

Petrie, W. M. Flinders. *Egypt and Israel*. London: Society for Promoting Christian Knowledge, 1911.

———. *Hyksos and Israelite Cities*. London: School of Archaeology, 1906.

Petuchowski, Jakob J. “Liturgy of the Synagogue.” In *The Lord’s Prayer and Jewish Liturgy*, edited by J. J. Petuchowski and M. Brocke, 45–57. New York: Seabury Press, 1978.

———. “The Liturgy of the Synagogue: History, Structure, and Contents.” In *Approaches to Ancient Judaism: Theory and Practice* Vol. 4, edited by W. Green, 1–64. Missoula, Mont.: Scholars Press, 1983.

———. “Zur Geschichte der jüdischen Liturgie.” In *Jüdische Liturgie: Geschichte, Struktur, Wesen*, edited by Johann Maier and Hans Hermann Henrix, 13–32. Freiburg: Herder, 1979.

Picard, Ch. *L’Établissement des Poseidoniastes de Bérytos*. Paris: E. de Boccard, 1921.

Pixner, Bargil. "An Essene Quarter on Mount Zion?" In *Studia Hierosolymitana I*, 245–285. Jerusalem, 1976.

———. "The Jerusalem Essenes, Barnabas and the Letter to the Hebrews." In *Intertestamental Essays in Honor of Jozef Tadeusz Milik* Vol. 6, edited by Z. Kapera, 167–178. Krakow, Poland: Enigma Press, 1992.

———. "Jerusalem's Essene Gateway: Where the Community Lived in Jesus' Time." *BAR* 23, no. 3 (1997): 22–31, 64–66.

Plassart, André. "La synagogue juive de Délos." In *Mélanges Holleaux, recueil de mémoirs concernant l'antiquité grecque*, 201–215. Paris: Picard, 1913.

———. "La synagogue juive de Délos." *RB* 23 (1914): 523–534.

Porter, Stanley E. *Verbal Aspect in the Greek of the New Testament, with Reference to Tense and Mood.* New York: Peter Lang, 1989.

———. *Idioms of the Greek New Testament.* Sheffield: JSOT Press, 1992.

———. "The 'We' Passages." In *The Book of Acts in Its Graeco-Roman Setting*, edited by Richard Bauckham, 545–574. Grand Rapids, Mich.: William B. Eerdmans Pub. Co., 1994.

Porton, Gary G. "Defining Midrash." In *The Study of Ancient Judaism* Vol. 1, edited by Jacob Neusner, 55–92. New York: Ktav, 1981.

———. *Understanding Rabbinic Midrash: Texts and Commentary.* Hoboken, N. J.: Ktav, 1985.

Pritchard, James B., ed. *Ancient Near Eastern Texts*. 3rd ed. Princeton, NJ: Princeton University Press, 1969.

Pritsak, Omeljan. "The Role of the Bosporus Kingdom and Late Hellenism as the Basis for the Medieval Cultures of the Territories North of the Black Sea." In *Mutual Effects of the Islamic and Judeo-*

Christian Worlds: The East European Pattern, edited by A. Ascher, 3–21. New York: Columbia University Press, 1979.

Pummer, Reinhard. “Inscriptions.” In *The Samaritans*, edited by A Crown, 190–194. Tübingen: J.C.B. Mohr, 1989.

———. “Samaritan Material Remains and Archaeology.” In *The Samaritans*, edited by A. Crown, 135–177. Tübingen: J.C.B. Mohr, 1989.

Rabello, A. M. “Ostia.” In *Encyclopedia Judaica* Vol. 12, 1506–1509, 1971.

———. “The Legal Condition of the Jews in the Roman Empire.” In *ANRW* Vol. II.13, edited by W. Haase, 662–762. New York: W. de Gruyter, 1980.

Rabinovich, Abraham. “Oldest Jewish Prayer Room Discovered on Shuafat Ridge.” *Jerusalem Post*, 8 April 1991.

———. “Residential Quarter Found in Qumran Dig.” *Jerusalem Post*, 5 January 1996.

Rahmani, L. Y. “Stone Synagogue Chairs: Their Identification, Use and Significance.” *IEJ* 40, no. 2-3 (1990): 192–214.

Rajak, Tessa. “The Jewish Community and its Boundaries.” In *The Jews among Pagans and Christians: In the Roman Empire*, edited by Judith Lieu, John A. North and Tessa Rajak, 9–28. New York: Routledge, 1992.

———. “Jewish Rights in the Greek Cities under Roman Rule.” In *Approaches to Ancient Judaism: Theory and Practice* Vol. 5, edited by W. Green, 19–35. Missoula, Mont.: Scholars Press, 1985.

———. “Jews and Christians as Groups in a Pagan World.” In *“To See Ourselves as Others See Us”: Christians, Jews, “Others” in Late Antiquity*, edited by Jacob Neusner and Ernest S. Frerichs, 247–262. Chico, Calif.: Scholars Press, 1985.

———. *Josephus*. Philadelphia: Fortress Press, 1983.

———. "Josephus and the 'Archaeology' of the Jews." *JJS* 33 (1982): 465–477.

———. "Was there a Roman Charter for the Jews?" *JRS* 74 (1984): 107–123.

Rajak, Tessa, and David Noy. *Archisynagogoi:* Office, Title and Social Status in the Greco-Jewish Synagogue." *JRS* 83 (1993): 75–93.

Ramsay, William M. *Cities and Bishoprics of Phrygia*. 2 vols. Oxford: Clarendon Press, 1897.

Rankin, O. S. "The Extent of the Influence of the Synagogue Service upon Christian Worship." *JJS* 1 (1949): 27–32.

Reich, Ronny. "Ritual Baths." In *The Oxford Encyclopedia of Archaeology in the Near East* Vol. 5, edited by Eric M. Meyers, 430–431. Oxford: Oxford University Press, 1996.

———. "A Note on the Function of Room 30 (the 'Scriptorium') at Khirbet Qumran." *JJS* 46 (1995): 155–160.

———. "Synagogue and Ritual Bath During the Second Temple and the Period of the Mishna and Talmud." In *Synagogues in Antiquity*, edited by Aryeh Kasher, Aharon Oppenheimer and Uriel Rappaport, 205–212. Jerusalem: Yad Izhak Ben Zvi, 1987.

———. "The Synagogue and the *Miqweh* in Eretz-Israel in the Second-Temple, Mishnaic, and Talmudic Periods." In *Ancient Synagogues: Historical Analysis and Archaeological Discovery* Vol. 1, edited by Dan Urman and Paul Virgil McCracken Flesher, 289–297. New York: E.J. Brill, 1995.

Reif, Stefan C. "The Early History of Jewish Worship." In *The Making of Jewish and Christian Worship*, edited by P. Bradshaw, 109–136. Notre Dame: University of Notre Dame Press, 1991.

Renfrew, Colin. "The Archaeology of Religion." In *The Ancient Mind: Elements of Cognitive Archaeology*, edited by Colin Renfrew and Ezra B. W. Zubrow, 47–54. Cambridge: Cambridge University Press, 1994.

Renov, I. "The Seat of Moses." In *The Synagogue: Studies in Origins, Archaeology, and Architecture*, edited by Joseph Gutmann, 223–238. New York: Ktav Pub. House, 1975.

Reumann, John. "History of Lectionaries: From the Synagogue at Nazareth to Post-vatican II." *Int* 31 (1977): 116–130.

Reynolds, J. M. "Inscriptions." In *Excavations at Sidi Khrebish Benghazi (Berenice)* Vol. 1, edited by J. A. Lloyd, 233–254. Hertford: Stephen Austin and Sons, 1977.

Reynolds, Joyce Maire, and Robert Tannenbaum. *Jews and God-Fearers at Aphrodisias: Greek Inscriptions with Commentary: Texts from the Excavations at Aphrodisias Conducted by Kenan T. Erim*. Vol. 12, *Supplementary Volume*. Cambridge: Cambridge Philological Society, 1987.

Riaud, Jean. "Les Thérapeutes d'Alexandrie dans la tradition et dans la recherche critique jusqu'aux découvertes de Qumran." In *ANRW* Vol. II.20.2, 1189–1295. New York: W. de Gruyter, 1987.

———. "Les Thérapeutes d'Alexandrie et l'ideal Lévitique." In *Mogilany 1989: Papers on the Dead Sea Scrolls Offered in Memory of Jean Carmignac* Vol. 2, edited by Zdzislaw Kapara, J. Krakow: Enigma Press, 1993.

Richardson, Peter. "Early Synagogues as Collegia in the Diaspora and Palestine." In *Voluntary Associations*, edited by John S. Kloppenborg and Steven G. Wilson, 90–109. London: Routledge, 1996.

———. "Law and Piety in Herod's Architecture." *SR* 15, no. 3 (1986): 347–360.

———. "Philo and Eusebius on Monasteries and Monasticism: The Therapeutae and Kellia." In *Origins and Method*, edited by Bradley H McLean. Sheffield: JSOT Press, 1993.

———. "Religion, Architecture and Ethics: Some First Century Case Studies." *HBT* 10 (1988): 19–49.

Richardson, Peter, and Valerie Heuchan. "Jewish Voluntary Associations in Egypt and the Roles of Women." In *Voluntary Associations*, edited by John S. Kloppenborg and Steven G. Wilson, 226–251. London: Routledge, 1996.

Riesner, Rainer. "Das jerusalemer Essenerviertel Antwort auf einige Einwände." In *Intertestamental Essays*, edited by Zdzislaw J. Kapera, 179–186. Krackow: The Enigma Press, 1992.

———. "Die bisher ältest Synagoge gefunden." *Idea Spekrum*, 28 August 1991 1991, 17.

———. "Neue Funde in Israel." *BK* 46 (1991): 181–183.

———. "Synagogues in Jerusalem." In *The Book of Acts in Its Palestinian Setting*, edited by Richard Bauckham, 179–211. Grand Rapids, Mich.: William B. Eerdmans Pub. Co., 1995.

Ritmeyer, Kathleen, and Leen Ritmeyer. *Reconstructing Herod's Temple Mount in Jerusalem*. Englewood Cliffs, N.J.: Prentice-Hall, 1990.

Ritmeyer, Leen. "Locating the Original Temple Mount." *BAR* 18, no. 2 (1992): 24–45.

Rivkin, Ellis. "Ben Sira and the Non Existence of the Synagogue: A Study in Historical Method." In *In the Time of Harvest, Essays in Honor of Abba Hillel Silver on the Occasion of his 70th Birthday*, edited by Daniel Jeremy Silver, 320–354. New York: Macmillan, 1963.

Robert, L. "Un corpus des inscription juives." *REJ* 101 (1937): 73–86.

Robertson, D.S. *Greek and Roman Architecture*. 2nd ed. Cambridge: Cambridge University Press, 1969.

Rostovtzeff, M. *Iranians and Greeks in South Russia*. New York: Russell and Russel, 1969.

Roth, Cecil. "The 'Chair of Moses' and its Survivals." *PEQ* 81 (1949): 100–111.

———. "Ecclesiasticus in the Synagogue Service." *JBL* 71, no. 3 (1952): 171–178.

———. "Problem of Jewish Art." *Judaism* 6 (1957): 118–125.

Roth-Gerson, Lea. "Similarities and Differences in Greek Synagogue Inscriptions of Eretz-Israel and the Diaspora." In *Synagogues in Antiquity*, edited by Aryeh Kasher, Aharon Oppenheimer and Uriel Rappaport, 133–146. Jerusalem: Yad Izhak Ben Zvi, 1987.

Rowley, H. H. *Worship in Ancient Israel: Its Forms and Meaning*. London: S. P. C. K., 1967.

Runesson, Anders. "The Oldest Original Synagogue Building in the Diaspora. A Response to L. Michael White." *HTR* 92, no. 4 (1999): forthcoming.

———. "The Synagogue at Ancient Ostia. The Building and its History From the First to the Fifth Century." In *The Synagogue of Ancient Ostia and the Jews of Rome: Interdisciplinary Studies*, edited by J. Blomqvist, O. W. Brandt, B., Olsson, forthcoming. Stockholm: Swedish Institute in Rome, 1999.

———. "Water and Worship. Ostia and the Ritual Bath in the Diaspora Synagogue." In *The Synagogue of Ancient Ostia and the Jews of Rome: Interdisciplinary Studies*, edited by J. Blomqvist, O. W. Brandt, B., Olsson, forthcoming. Stockholm: Swedish Institute in Rome, 1999.

Rutgers, Leonard Victor. "Diaspora Synagogues: Synagogue Archaeology in the Greco-Roman World." In *Sacred Realm: The*

Emergence of the Synagogue in the Ancient World, edited by Steven Fine, 67–94. New York: Oxford University Press, 1996.

Safrai, Hannah. "Women and the Ancient Synagogue." In *Daughters of the King: Women and the Synagogue: A Survey of History, Halakhah, and Contemporary Realities*, edited by Susan Grossman and Rivka Haut, 39–49. Philadelphia: Jewish Publication Society, 1992.

Safrai, Shmuel. "Gathering in the Synagogues on Festivals, Sabbaths and Weekdays." In *Ancient Synagogues in Israel: Third-Seventh Century CE*, edited by R. Hachlili, 7–15. Oxford, England: B.A.R., 1989.

———. "The Synagogue and Its Worship." In *Society and Religion in the Second Temple Period*, edited by Michael Avi-Yonah and Zvi Baras, 65–98. Jerusalem: Jewish History Publications Ltd., 1977.

———. "Temple." In *Jewish People in the First Century. Historical Geography, Political History, Social, Cultural and Religious Life and Institutions* Vol. 2, edited by S. Safrai and M. Stern, 865–970. Assen: Van Gorcum, 1976.

Safrai, Zeev. "Dukhan, Aron and Teva: How Was the Ancient Synagogue Furnished?" In *Ancient Synagogues in Israel: Third-Seventh Century CE*, edited by R. Hachlili, 69–84. Oxford, England: B.A.R., 1989.

———. "From the Synagogue to 'Little Temple'." In *Proceedings, 10th World Cong of Jewish St, B, II: History*, edited by D. Assaf, 23–28, 1990.

———. "The Origins of Reading the Aramaic Targum in Synagogue." *Immanuel* 24-25 (1990): 187–193.

———. "The Temple and the Synagogue." In *Synagogues in Antiquity*, edited by Aryeh Kasher, Aharon Oppenheimer and Uriel Rappaport, 77–96. Jerusalem: Yad Izhak Ben Zvi, 1987.

Saldarini, Anthony J. *Matthew's Christian-Jewish Community*. Chicago: The University of Chicago Press, 1994.

———. *Pharisees, Scribes and Sadducees in Palestinian Society: A Sociological Approach*. Wilmington, DE: M. Glazier, 1988.

Saller, Sylvester J. *Second Revised Catalogue of the Ancient Synagogues of the Holy Land*. Jerusalem: Fransiscan Printing Press, 1972.

Samain, Etienne. "Le discours-programme de Jésus a la synagogue de Nazareth: Lc 4:16–30." *Foi et Vie* 70, no. 5 (1971): 25–43.

Sanders, E. P. *Jewish Law from Jesus to the Mishnah*. Philadelphia: Trinity Press International, 1990.

———. *Judaism: Practice and Belief, 63 BCE–66 CE*. London: Trinity Press International, 1992.

———. *Paul and Palestinian Judaism: A Comparison of Patterns of Religion*. Philadelphia: Fortress Press, 1977.

Sanders, Jack T. *The Jews in Luke-Acts*. Philadelphia: Fortress Press, 1987.

———. *Schismatics, Sectarians, Dissidents, Deviants: The First One Hundred Years of Jewish-Christian Relations*. London: SCM Press, 1993.

Sarfatti, Gad B. "The Tablets of the Law as a Symbol of Judaism." In *Ten Commandments in History and Tradition*, edited by Ben-Zion Segal and Gershon Levi, 383–418. Jerusalem: Magnes Press, 1990.

Saunders, Ernest W. "Christian Synagogues and Jewish-Christianity in Galilee." *Explor* 3, no. 1 (1977): 70–77.

Scharlemann, Martin H. "Theology of Synagogue Architecture as Reflected in the Excavation Reports." *CTM* 30 (1959): 902–914.

Scherrer, Peter. "The City of Ephesos." In *Ephesos: Metropolis of Asia*, edited by Helmut Koester, 1–25. Valley Forge, Pennsylvania: Trinity Press International, 1995.

Schiffman, Lawrence H. *Reclaiming the Dead Sea Scrolls: The History of Judaism, the Background Of Christianity, the Lost Library of Qumran*. Philadelphia: Jewish Publication Society, 1994.

Schmithals, Walter. "Der Konflikt zwischen Kirche und Synagoge in neutestamentlicher Zeit." In *Altes Testament und christliche Verkundigung: Festschrift fur Antonius A.H. Gunneweg zum 65. Geburtstag*, edited by Manfred Oeming and Axel Graupner, 366–384. Stuttgart: W. Kohlhammer, 1987.

Schönfeld, Hans Gottfried. "Zum Begriff 'Therapeutai' bei Philo von Alexandrien." *RevQ* 3 (1961): 219–240.

Schrage, Wolfgang. "Συναγωγή." In *Theological Dictionary of the New Testament* Vol. 7, edited by Gerhard Kittel, Geoffrey William Bromiley and Gerhard Friedrich, 798–852. Grand Rapids, Michigan: Wm. B. Eerdmans Publishing Company, 1964–1976.

Schrenk, Gottlob. "Ἱερός, Ἱερόν." In *Theological Dictionary of the New Testament* Vol. 3, edited by Gerhard Kittel, Geoffrey William Bromiley and Gerhard Friedrich, 221–247. Grand Rapids, Michigan: Wm. B. Eerdmans Publishing Company, 1964–1976.

Schürer, Emil. "Die Juden im bosporanischen Reiche und die Genossenschaften der σεβόμενοι θεὸν ὕψιστον ebendaselbst." In *Sitzungsberichte der Königlich Preussischen Akademie der Wissenschaften zu Berlin*, 1.200–225. Berlin, 1897.

Schürer, Emil , Geza Vermes, and Fergus Millar. *A History of the Jewish People in the Time of Jesus Christ*. Revised English ed. 3 vols. Edinburgh: T. & T. Clark, 1973–86.

Schwabe, Moshe, and Baruch Lifshitz. *Beth She'arim II*. Jerusalem: Massada Press, 1974.

Schwartz, Daniel R. "Philo's Priestly Descent." In *Nourished with Peace: Studies in Hellenistic Judaism in Memory of Samuel Sandmel*, edited by Burton L. Mack, Earle Hilgert, Samuel Sandmel and Frederick E. Greenspahn, 155–171. Chico, Calif.: Scholars Press, 1984.

———. *Studies in the Jewish Background of Christianity*. Tübingen: Mohr, 1992.

———. "Temple or City: What did Hellenistic Jews See in Jerusalem?" In *The Centrality of Jerusalem*, edited by M. Poorthuis and Chana Safrai, 115–127. Kampen, the Netherlands: Pharos, 1996.

Schwartz, Joseph. *Crops of the Holy Land*. Jerusalem: Luntz, 1900.

Schwartz, Joshua. "Sinai in Jewish Thought and Tradition." *Immanuel* 13 (1981): 7–14.

Schwartzman, Sylvan D. "How Well Did the Synoptic Evangelists Know the Synagogue?" *HUCA* 24 (1953): 115–132.

Scrinari, Valnea Santa Maria, Angelo Pellegrino, and Giuseppina Lauro. *Ostia e porto: Le zone archeologiche, i musei, Guide pratiche; 16.* Milano: F. Garolla, 1989.

Seager, Andrew. "The Recent Historiography of Ancient Synagogue Architecture." In *Ancient Synagogues in Israel: Third–Seventh Century CE*, edited by R. Hachlili, 85–92. Oxford, England: B.A.R., 1989.

———. "Ancient Synagogue Architecture: An Overview." In *Ancient Synagogues: The State of Research* Vol. 22, edited by Joseph Gutmann, 39–47. Chico, California: Scholars Press, 1981.

———. "Herodium." *IEJ* 23, no. 1 (1973): 27–29.

Segal, Judah Benzion. *The Hebrew Passover*. London: Oxford University Press, 1963.

Seland, Torrey. "Philo and the Clubs and Associations of Alexandria." In *Voluntary Associations*, edited by John S. Kloppenborg and Steven G. Wilson, 110–127. London: Routledge, 1996.

Shanks, Hershel. "Gamla: The Masada of the North." *BAR* 5, no. 1 (1971): 12–19.

———. *Judaism in Stone: The Archaeology of Ancient Synagogues*. New York: Harper & Row, 1979.

Shinan, Avigdor. "Sermons, Targums, and the Reading from Scriptures in the Ancient Synagogue." In *The Synagogue in Late Antiquity*, edited by Lee I. Levine, 97–110. Philadelphia: American Schools of Oriental Research, 1987.

Silber, Mendel. *The Origin of the Synagogue*. New Orleans: Steeg, 1915.

Simon, Marcel. "L'ascétisme dans les sectes juives." In *La tradizione dell'enkrateia*, edited by U. Bianchi. Roma: Edizioni dell'Ateneo, 1985.

Sinn, Ulrich. "Greek Sanctuaries as Places of Refuge." In *Greek Sanctuaries*, edited by Nanno Marinatos and Robin Hägg, 88–109. London and New York: Routledge, 1993.

Smallwood, E. Mary. *The Jews under Roman Rule: From Pompey to Diocletian*. Vol. 20, *Studies in Judaism in Late Antiquity*. Leiden: Brill, 1976.

Sonne, Isaiah. "Synagogue." In *The Interpreter's Dictionary of the Bible* Vol. 4, edited by George Arthur Buttrick, 476–491. Nashville: Abingdon Press, 1962.

Squarciapino, Maria Floriani. "Die Synagoge von Ostia Antica." *Raggi* 4, no. 1 (1962): 1–8.

———. "Die Synagoge von Ostia nach der zweiten Ausgrabungskampagne." *Raggi* 5, no. 1 (1963): 13–17.

———. "Ebrei a Roma e ad Ostia." *Studi Romani* 11, no. 2 (1963): 129–141.

———. "La Sinagoga di Ostia: Second campagna di Scavo." In *Atti VI Congresso Internazionale di Archeologia Cristiana*, 299–315. Rome, 1962.

———. "The Most Ancient Synagogue Known from Monumental Remains: The Newly Discovered Ostia Synagogue in Its First and Fourth Century A.D. Phases." *The Illustrated London News*, September 28 1963, 468–471.

———. "Plotius Fortunatus archisynagogus." *La Rassegna Mensile di Israel* 36 (1970): 183–191.

———. "The Synagogue at Ostia." *Archaeology* 16 (1963): 194–203.

Stahli, Hans-Peter. *Antike Synagogenkunst*. Stuttgart: Calwer Verlag, 1988.

Stallman, Robert C. "Levi and the Levites in the Dead Sea Scrolls." *Journal for the Study of the Pseudepigrapha* 10 (1992): 163–189.

Stambaugh, John E. *The Ancient Roman City*. Baltimore, Md.: The Johns Hopkins University Press, 1988.

———. "The Functions of Roman Temples." In *ANRW* Vol. II.16.1, edited by W. Haase, 554–608. New York: W. de Gruyter, 1978.

Stegner, William Richard. "The Ancient Jewish Synagogue Homily." In *Greco-Roman Literature and the New Testament: Selected Forms and Genres* Vol. 21, edited by D. Aune, 51–69. Atlanta: Scholars Press, 1988.

Stern, Ephriam. "Dor." In *The New Encyclopedia of Archaeological Excavations in the Holy Land* Vol. 1, edited by Ephraim Stern, 357–368. Jerusalem: Israel Exploration Society & Carta; New York: Simon & Schuster, 1993.

Stern, Menahem. *Greek and Latin Authors on Jews and Judaism*. 3 vols, *Fontes ad res Judaicas spectantes*. Jerusalem: Israel Academy of Sciences and Humanities, 1974–84.

Stewart, Roy A. "The Synagogue." *EvQ* 43 (1971): 36–46.

Strange, James F. "Archaeology and the Religion of Judaism in Palestine." In *ANRW* Vol. II.19.1, edited by W. Haase, 646–685. New York: W. de Gruyter, 1979.

———. "The Art and Archaeology of Ancient Judaism." In *Judaism in Late Antiquity* Vol. 1, edited by Jacob Neusner, 64–114. Leiden; New York: E.J. Brill, 1995.

———. "The Eastern Basilical Building." In *Sepphoris in Galilee*, edited by Rebecca Martin Nagy, Carol L. Meyers, Eric M. Meyers and Zeev Weiss, 116–121. Winona Lake: Eisenbrauns, 1996.

———. "First Century Galilee from Archaeology and from the Texts." In *Archaeology and the Galilee: Texts and Contexts in Graeco-Roman and Byzantine Periods*, edited by Douglas R. Edwards and C. Thomas McCollough, 39–48. Atlanta: Scholars Press, 1997.

———. "Magdala." In *The Anchor Bible Dictionary* Vol. 4, edited by David Noel Freedman, 463–464. New York: Doubleday, 1992.

Strange, James F., and Hershel Shanks. "Synagogue Where Jesus Preached Found at Capernaum." *BAR* 9, no. 6 (1983): 25–31.

Strugnell, John. "Flavius Josephus and the Essenes: Antiquities XVIII.18–22." *JBL* 77 (1958): 144.

Struve, I. *Corpus Inscriptionum Regni Bosporani*. Leningrad: Academia Scientiarum URSS, 1965.

Sukenik, Eleazar Lipa. *Ancient Synagogues in Palestine and Greece, The Schweich lectures of the British Academy*. London: Oxford University Press, 1934.

———. "The Present State of Ancient Synagogue Studies." *Bulletin of the Lewis M. Rabinowitz Fund* 1 (1949): 21–23.

Syon, Danny. "Gamla: Portrait of a Rebellion." *BAR* 18, no. 1 (1992): 21–37.

Talbert, Charles H. *The Apocalypse*. Louisville, Kentucky: Westminster John Knox Press, 1994.

Tannenbaum, Robert F. "Jews and God-Fearers in the Holy City of Aphrodite." *BAR* 12, no. 5 (1986): 44–57.

Tcherikover, Avigdor. *Hellenistic Civilization and the Jews*. Philadelphia: Jewish Publication Society of America, 1959.

———. "Prolegomena." In *Corpus Papyrorum Judaicarum* Vol. 1, edited by Avigdor Tcherikover, Alexander Fuks and Menahem Stern, 1–47. Cambridge, Mass.: Harvard University Press, 1957.

Tcherikover, Avigdor, Alexander Fuks, and Menahem Stern. *Corpus Papyrorum Judaicarum*. 3 vols. Cambridge, Mass.: Harvard University Press, 1957-64.

Thackeray, H. St. J. *The Septuagint and Jewish Worship*. 2nd ed. London: H. Milford, 1923.

Thomas, Christine M. "At Home in the City of Artemis." In *Ephesos: Metropolis of Asia*, edited by Helmut Koester, 81–117. Valley Forge, Pennsylvania: Trinity Press International, 1995.

Thompson, Homer A. *The Agora of Athens: The History, Shape, and Uses of an Ancient City Center*. Princeton: American School of Classical Studies at Athens, 1972.

Thompson, Leonard. *The Book of Revelation: Apocalypse and Empire*. New York: Oxford University Press, 1990.

Tippy, Worth Marion. "The Synagogues of the Dispersion and Early Christianity." *Methodist Review* 82 (1900): 446–460.

Tokhtas'en, S. R. "The New Jewish Manumission from Phanagoria." *Bulletin of Judaeo-Greek Studies* 13 (1993): 27–28.

Tov, Emanuel. "The Septuagint." In *Mikra*, edited by M. Mulder and H. Sysling, 161–187. Philadelphia: Fortress Press, 1988.

Tracey, Robyn. "Syria." In *The Book of Acts in Its Palestinian Setting*, edited by Richard Bauckham, 223–278. Grand Rapids, Mich.: William B. Eerdmans Pub. Co., 1994.

Trebilco, Paul R. "Asia." In *The Book of Acts in its First Century Setting, Vol 2*, edited by D. Gill and et al., 291–362, 1994.

———. *Jewish Communities in Asia Minor, Monograph series / Society for New Testament Studies; 69*. Cambridge England; New York: Cambridge University Press, 1991.

Treister, Michail J., and Yuri G. Vinogradov. "Archaeology on the Northern Coast of the Black Sea." *Archaeology* 97 (1993): 521–563.

Tyson, Joseph B. *The New Testament and Early Christianity*. New York: Macmillan, 1984.

Tzapheres, Vasileios. *Excavations at Capernaum*. Winona Lake, Ind.: Eisenbrauns in association with Pepperdine University, 1989.

Urman, Dan, and Paul Virgil McCracken Flesher, eds. *Ancient Synagogues: Historical Analysis and Archaeological Discovery*. 2 vols. Vol. 47, *Studia Post-Biblica*. New York: E.J. Brill, 1995.

Urman, Dan, and Paul Virgil McCracken Flesher. "Ancient Synagogues—A Reader's Guide." In *Ancient Synagogues: Historical Analysis and Archaeological Discovery* Vol. 1, edited by Dan Urman and Paul Virgil McCracken Flesher, xvii–xxxvii. New York: E.J. Brill, 1995.

VanderKam, James C. *The Dead Sea Scrolls Today*. Grand Rapids, Mich.: Eerdmans, 1994.

Vardaman, E. Jerry. "History of Herodium." In *The Teacher's Yoke: Studies in Memory of Henry Trantham*, edited by E. Jerry Vardaman and James Leo Garrett, Jr. Waco, Tx.: Baylor University Press, 1964.

Vermes, G. "Essene and Therapeutai." *RevQ* 3 (1962): 494–504.

Vincent, L. H. "Dècouverte de la «synagogue des affranchis» a Jérusalem." *RB* 30 (1921): 247–277.

Waldow, H. Eberhard von. "The Origin of the Synagogue Reconsidered." In *From Faith to Faith: Essays to Honor of Donald G. Miller on his Seventieth Birthday* Vol. 31, edited by Dikran Y. Hadidian, 269–284. Pittsburgh: Pickwick Press, 1979.

Ward-Perkins, J. B. *Cities of Ancient Greece and Italy: Planning in Classical Antiquity*. New York: George Braziller, 1974.

———. *Roman Architecture*. New York: Electa/Rizzoli, 1988.

———. *Roman Imperial Architecture*. 2nd ed. New York: Penguin Books, 1989.

Wardy, Bilhah. "Jewish Religion in Pagan Literature during the Late Republic and Early Empire." In *ANRW* Vol. II.19.1, edited by W. Haase, 592–644. New York: W. de Gruyter, 1979.

Weill, Raymond. *La cité de David. Compte rendu des fouilles executeés à Jérusalem, sur le site de la ville primitive, campagne de 1913–1914*. Paris: P. Geuthner, 1920.

Weinfeld, Moshe. "Freedom Proclamations in Egypt and in the Ancient Near East." In *Pharaonic Egypt*, edited by Sarah Israelit Groll, 317–327. Jerusalem: The Magnes Press, 1985.

Weingreen, J. "The Origin of the Synagogue." *Hermathena* 98 (1964): 68–84.

Weiss, Zeev, and Ehud Netzer. "The Synagogue Mosaic." In *Sepphoris in Galilee*, edited by Rebecca Martin Nagy, Carol L. Meyers, Eric M. Meyers and Zeev Weiss, 133–139. Winona Lake: Eisenbrauns, 1996.

Wellhausen, Julius. *Israelitische und Jüdische Geschichte*. Berline: Georg Reimer, 1897.

Werbner, Richard P. *Ritual Passage, Sacred Journey*. Washington: Smithsonian Institution Press, 1989.

Westermann, William L. “Parmone as General Service Contract.” *The Journal of Juristic Paprology* 2 (1947): 9–50.

———. *The Slave Systems of Greek and Roman Antiquity*. Vol. 40, *Memoirs of the American Philosophical Society*. Philadelphia: American Philosophical Society, 1955.

White, L. Michael. *Building God’s House in the Roman World: Architectural Adaptation among Pagans, Jews, and Christians*, *ASOR Library of Biblical and Near Eastern Archaeology*. Baltimore, Md.: Published for the American Schools of Oriental Research by Johns Hopkins University Press, 1990.

———. “The Delos Synagogue Revisited: Recent Fieldwork in the Graeco-Roman Diaspora.” *HTR* 80 (1987): 133–160.

———. *Domus Ecclesiae Domus Dei: Adaptation and Development in the Setting For Early Christian Assembly*. Ann Arbor, Mich.: University Microfilms International, 1990.

———. *The Social Origins of Christian Architecture*. 2 vols, *Harvard theological studies 42–43*. Valley Forge, Pa.: Trinity Press International, 1996–97.

———. “Synagogue and Society in Imperial Ostia: Archaeological and Epigraphic Evidence.” *HTR* 90 (1997): 23–58.

———. “Urban Development and Social Change in Imperial Ephesos.” In *Ephesos: Metropolis of Asia*, edited by Helmut Koester, 27–79. Valley Forge, Pennsylvania: Trinity Press International, 1995.

Whittaker, Molly. *Jews and Christians: Graeco-Roman Views*. Cambridge: Cambridge University Press, 1984.

Wilcox, Max. “The ‘God-Fearers’ in Acts—A Reconsideration.” *JSNT* 13 (1981): 102–122.

Wilkinson, John. “The Beit Alpha Synagogue Mosaic: Towards an Interpretation.” *Journal of Jewish Art* 5 (1978): 16–28.

Wilkinson, John. "Orientation, Jewish and Christian." *PEQ* 116 (1984): 16–30.

Will, E. "Banquets et salles de banquet dans les cultes la Grèce et de l'Empire romain." In *Mélanges d'histoire des religions offerts à Paul Collart*, 353–362. Paris: Lausanne, 1976.

Williams, David S. *3 Maccabees*: A Defense of Diapsora Judaism?" *Journal for the Study of the Pseudepigrapha* 13 (1995): 17–29.

Wilson, S. G. *Related Strangers: Jews and Christians, 70-170 C.E.* Minneapolis, MN: Fortress Press, 1995.

———. "Voluntary Associations: An Overview." In *Voluntary Associations*, edited by John S. Kloppenborg and Steven G. Wilson, 1–15. London: Routledge, 1996.

Wire, Antoinette Clark. "Prophecy and Women Prophets in Corinth." In *Gospel Origins & Christian Beginnings: In Honor of James M. Robinson*, edited by James E. Goehring, James McConkey Robinson and Helmut Q. Koester, 134–150. Sonoma, Calif.: Polebridge Press, 1990.

Wirgin, Wolf. "The Menorah as Symbol of Judaism." *IEJ* 12, no. 2 (1962): 140–142.

Wiseman, James R. "Corinth and Rome I: 228 B.C.–A.D. 267." In *ANRW* Vol. II.17.1, edited by W. Haase, 438–548. New York: W. de Gruyter, 1979.

Wishchnitzer, R. *The Architecture of the European Synagogue*. Philadelphia: The Jewish Publication Society of America, 1974.

Woodhead, A. G. *The Study of Greek Inscriptions*. 2nd ed. Cambridge; New York: Cambridge University Press, 1981.

Woolley, C. L. *Carchemish II*. London: The British Museum, 1921.

Woolley, C. L., and Richard D. Barnett. *Carchemish III*. London: The British Museum, 1952.

Yadin, Yigael. "Beer-sheba: The High Place Destroyed by King Josiah." *Bulletin of the American Schools of Oriental Research* 222 (1976): 5–17.

———. "The Excavation of Masada 1963/64: Preliminary Report." *IEJ* 15 (1965): 1–120.

———. "The Gate of the Essenes and the Temple Scroll." In *Jerusalem Revealed: Archaeology in the Holy City, 1968–1974*, edited by Yigael Yadin, 90–91. Jerusalem: Israel Exploration Society, 1975.

———. "Masada." In *Encyclopedia of Archaeological Excavations in the Holy Land* Vol. 3, edited by Michael Avi-Yonah and Ephriam Stern, 793–816. Jerusalem: The Israel Exploration Society and Massada Press, 1977.

———. *Masada*. New York: Random House, 1966.

———. "The Synagogue at Masada." In *Ancient Synagogues Revealed*, edited by Lee I. Levine, 19–23. Jerusalem: Israel Exploration Society, 1982.

———. *The Temple Scroll*. 3 vols. Jerusalem: Israel Exploration Society, 1983.

———. *The Temple Scroll: The Hidden Law of the Dead Sea Sect*. London: Weidenfeld and Nicolson, 1985.

———., ed. *Jerusalem Revealed: Archaeology in the Holy City 1968–1974*. New Haven: Yale Univ Press, 1976.

Yadin, Yigael, and Joseph Naveh. "The Aramaic and Hebrew Ostraca and Jar Inscriptions." In *Masada: The Yigael Yadin Excavations, 1963–1965: Final Reports* Vol. 1, edited by Ehud Netzer, 1–68. Jerusalem: Israel Exploration Society: Hebrew University of Jerusalem, 1989.

Yarden, Leon. *The Spoils of Jerusalem on the Arch of Titus: A Re-Investigation, Skrifter utgivna av Svenska institutet i Rom. 8o; 16*. Stockholm: Svenska Institutet i Rom, 1991.

Yegul, F. “The Bath-Gymnasium Complex in Asia Minor during the Imperial Roman Age.” Ph.D., Harvard University, 1975.

Zahavy, Tzvee. “The Politics of Piety: Social Conflict and the Emergence of Rabbinic Liturgy.” In *The Making of Jewish and Christian Worship*, edited by P. Bradshaw, 42–68. Notre Dame: University of Notre Dame Press, 1991.

Zappa, Giulia Garofalo. “Nuovi bolli laterizi di Ostia.” In *Terza Miscellanea Greca e Romana*, edited by G. Barbieri, P. Cavuoto, G. Garofalo Zappa, L. Gasperini, V. La Bua and A. Russi, 257–289. Rome, 1971.

Zeitlin, Solomon. “The Origin of the Synagogue.” In *The Synagogue: Studies in Origins, Archaeology, and Architecture*, edited by Joseph Gutmann, 14–26. New York: Ktav Pub. House, 1975.

———. “There Was No Synagogue in the Temple.” *JQR* 53 (1962): 168–169.

Zevi, F. “La sinagoga di Ostia.” *Rassegna mensile di Israel* 38 (1972): 131–145.